The Battle over

The Battle over Patents

History and Politics of Innovation

Edited by

STEPHEN H. HABER AND NAOMI R. LAMOREAUX

OXFORD UNIVERSITY PRESS

Oxford University Press is a department of the University of Oxford. It furthers the University's objective of excellence in research, scholarship, and education by publishing worldwide. Oxford is a registered trade mark of Oxford University Press in the UK and certain other countries.

Published in the United States of America by Oxford University Press
198 Madison Avenue, New York, NY 10016, United States of America.

Library of Congress Cataloging-in-Publication Data
Names: Haber, Stephen H., 1957– editor. | Lamoreaux, Naomi R., editor.
Title: The battle over patents : history and the politics of innovation /
edited by Stephen Haber and Naomi R. Lamoreaux.
Description: New York, NY, United States of America : Oxford University Press, [2021] |
Includes bibliographical references and index.
Identifiers: LCCN 2021021172 (print) | LCCN 2021021173 (ebook) |
ISBN 9780197576151 (hardback) | ISBN 9780197576168 (paperback) |
ISBN 9780197576182 (epub) | ISBN 9780197576199
Subjects: LCSH: Patents—History. | Patents—Economic aspects. |
Intellectual property—Political aspects. | Patent laws and legislation.
Classification: LCC T333 B38 2021 (print) | LCC T333 (ebook) |
DDC 608—dc23
LC record available at https://lccn.loc.gov/2021021172
LC ebook record available at https://lccn.loc.gov/2021021173

DOI: 10.1093/oso/9780197576151.001.0001

1 3 5 7 9 8 6 4 2

Paperback printed by Marquis, Canada
Hardback printed by Bridgeport National Bindery, Inc., United States of America

Table of Contents

Preface

Volumes such as this one have the names of the editors on the cover and the names of the chapter authors in the table of contents, but there are many other individuals and organizations who worked together for several years to make this book a reality. The idea for this volume grew out of our participation in Stanford University's Hoover Institution Working Group on Intellectual Property, Innovation, and Prosperity (Hoover IP2), which was founded in 2013 to support academic research on the impact of laws, regulations, government agencies, and international organizations on innovation and economic growth. The central purpose of Hoover IP2 was to extend the debate about whether patent systems frustrate or facilitate innovation from the dominion of legal scholars and government officials to include economists, political scientists, and historians, as well as the practicing attorneys and business professionals who actually work with the patent system on a day-to-day basis. Over a series of roughly ten conferences designed to improve the quality of academic research on patent systems the group came to the view that many of the claims being made about the effect of patents on innovation drew on the historical record, but did so in an ad hoc—indeed, often misleading—manner. The result was the idea for this book, whose goal is to get the history right.

The authors of this book worked together over a period that spanned several years, periodically coming together for conferences designed not only to get the facts right but to develop a common conceptual language so that the chapters would add up to more than the sum of their parts. That process of research, writing, critique, and revision led us to realize that complaints about the patent system are nothing new. Virtually all the sources of market friction that critics seize upon today as pretexts for patent reform ("patent thickets," "patent trolls," "patent holdup," "excessive litigation," and so on) were raised as matters of concern in the nineteenth century.

We also came to understand that the reason why those complaints resurface again and again is because the firms in any production chain are engaged in a battle over the producer surplus generated by their combined efforts to meet a consumer demand. Firms at the end of a production chain—that is, those that sell the final good or service to consumers—want to retain as much of the producer surplus as they can. Firms further up the chain, from the producers of raw materials to those that develop the patented technologies that make the product function, also want to maximize their share of the surplus by getting the best possible price for their inputs from the firms at the end of the chain. Every firm—up and down the production chain—fights with every arrow in its quiver, including lobbying to change the laws governing patents. As a general rule, firms that specialize in technology development tend to lobby for stronger patent laws, because that improves their negotiating position vis à vis the firms in the rest of the production chain. The other firms in the production chain, by contrast, tend to lobby for weaker patent laws in order to improve their negotiating position. In short, any coherent understanding of the history of the patent system requires scholars to examine critically the claims about the patent system made by actors in the past by situating them relative to the actors' places in the production chain.

Precisely because human beings are guided by self-interest in the battle over economic surplus, we also came to understand that patent systems are necessarily riven with imperfections. Nirvana cannot be on the menu of possible outcomes when it is in people's interest to exploit any source of friction and to shape any market, including the markets for law, regulation, and politics, to achieve their goals. This is not just true about patent systems; the same could be said about any system of property rights, laws, and regulations whose purpose is the generation and apportionment of economic surplus. The regulation of banking institutions and securities markets are obvious examples; like the patent system those regulations are designed, not by robots programmed to maximize social welfare, but by human beings driven by self-interest.

The meaningful question, therefore, is not how patent systems are imperfect, but why historically they have come to dominate all other methods of encouraging inventive activity. The chapters in this book pursue that question at length. Because this is a work of social science, not a mystery novel, permit us to outline a brief version of the answer that we came to as a group. Patents dominate because they create a property right that facilitates a productive division of labor, because they allow firms to transfer technological knowledge to one another, even across countries, and because they allow for incremental improvements to existing technologies. In short, patent systems foster the kind of decentralized, cumulative improvement that extends the frontiers of what is economically possible.

Once the book began to take shape, we invited a group of economists, historians, political scientists, and legal academics, as well as practicing IP attorneys, venture capitalists, and tech entrepreneurs, to critique the chapters at a conference that stretched over two days in May 2018. We wish to thank the participants in that conference for their tough—indeed, sometimes withering—criticisms of chapter drafts. We hope that the resulting volume does justice to the close reading and sharp critiques offered by Michael Andrews, Richard Epstein, Catherine Fisk, Andrew Hall, Wesley Hartmann, Philip Hoffman, John Howells, Ron Katznelson, Benjamin Kwitek, Ron Laurie, Ross Levine, Scott Masten, Damon Matteo, Douglas Melamed, Natasha Nayak, Roger Noll, Lisa Larrimore

Ouellette, Nicolas Petit, Paul Rhode, George Schultz, Henry Smith, Richard Sousa, and Lew Zaretzki.

A research project that stretches over several years, and that ultimately involves several dozen people, does not happen all by itself; it requires dedicated people who do organizational, logistical, and financial planning, and then execute the plan so perfectly that it looks as though no planning was needed at all. We are deeply in debt to Richard Sousa, who co-directed Hoover IP2 with one of us (Haber) from its inception in 2013 until he retired in 2019, and Isabel Lopez, who served as program manager and research administrator of Hoover IP2 from 2015 to 2019. They made all good things happen.

A multi-year research project involving dozens of academics and practitioners was a costly undertaking. We therefore wish to extend our gratitude to the individuals and corporations—most particularly InterDigital, Pfizer, and Qualcomm—who generously supported Hoover IP2 through unrestricted gifts to Stanford's Hoover Institution. Their willingness to make unrestricted gifts to support independent scholarly research and an open (and sometimes acrimonious) debate about the evidence, empirical methods, and theories that underpinned that research, was, to say the least, unusual. This book could not have been brought to fruition without their support.

Contributors

Jonathan M. Barnett is Torrey H. Webb Professor of Law at the Gould School of Law, University of Southern California.

Christopher Beauchamp is Professor of Law at Brooklyn Law School.

Sean Bottomley is VC Senior Fellow at the Newcastle Business School, Northumbria University.

Gerardo Con Díaz is Associate Professor of Science and Technology Studies at the University of California, Davis; National Fellow, Hoover Institution, Stanford, California.

Alexander Galetovic is Senior Fellow, Universidad Adolfo Ibáñez, Santiago, Chile; Research Fellow, Hoover Institution, Stanford, California; and Research Associate, CRIEP (Centro di Ricerca Interuniversitario sull'Economia Pubblica), Padua, Italy.

Stephen H. Haber is A. A. and Jeanne Welch Milligan Professor of Humanities and Sciences and Peter and Helen Bing Senior Fellow of the Hoover Institution, Stanford University.

B. Zorina Khan is Professor of Economics at Bowdoin College and a Research Associate at the National Bureau of Economic Research.

Naomi R. Lamoreaux is Stanley B. Resor Professor of Economics and History at Yale University, Senior Research Scholar at the University of Michigan Law School, and a Research Associate at the National Bureau of Economic Research.

Victor Menaldo is Professor of Political Science at the University of Washington.

Steven W. Usselman is H. Bruce McEver Professor of Engineering and the Liberal Arts at the School of History and Sociology, Georgia Institute of Technology.

Introduction: The Battle over the Surplus from Innovation

Stephen H. Haber and Naomi R. Lamoreaux

> There are a considerable number of patents issued annually from the Patent Office which are of no force or value except for black-mailing and for interfering with the business of parties competing with their owners.
>
> [These patents] do not cover practical machines, but contain principles upon which other more practical inventors have buil[t], and which are infringed by the other patent devices, and are good for nothing except to be bought and speculated upon by those who are justly called patent sharks.
>
> —J. H. Raymond, Secretary and Treasurer of the Western Railroad Association

Were it not for his use of the word "shark" instead of our more familiar term "troll," J. H. Raymond might be taken for someone complaining about the patent system in the present day. The quotations, however, come from testimony he gave before the Committee on Patents of the US Congress in the 1870s (US Senate 1878, pp. 123, 230). Raymond was lobbying (unsuccessfully, it turned out) for a bill to reform the patent system and cure it of the evils inflicted on the public by the "curse" of worthless patents. Whatever problems Raymond attributed to the granting by the Patent Office of "about fifteen times as many patents as ought to issue," the failure of the reform effort did not prevent the United States from embarking on the half century of rapid technological progress known as the Second Industrial Revolution. Nor did it prevent the US from rising to world leadership in such new technologically advanced industries as electricity, steel, telecommunications, and automobiles.[1]

[1] The patent reform bill proposed, among other things, to institute renewal fees for patents, impose a statute of limitations on infringement suits, and limit the damages that could be claimed for

Stephen H. Haber and Naomi R. Lamoreaux, *Introduction: The Battle over the Surplus from Innovation* In: *The Battle over Patents*. Edited by: Stephen H. Haber and Naomi R. Lamoreaux, Oxford University Press. © Oxford University Press 2021. DOI: 10.1093/oso/9780197576151.003.0001

As Raymond's testimony suggests, complaints about the patent system—and about how it could be abused to the detriment of legitimate businesses—are nothing new. Indeed, virtually all the sources of market friction that critics seize upon today as pretexts for patent reform ("patent thickets," "patent trolls," "patent holdup," "excessive patenting," and so on) were raised as matters of concern in the nineteenth century. These complaints have resurfaced again and again for the simple reason that the issues that underpin them have enormous consequences for the distribution of the producer surplus from innovation. Basically stated, producer surplus is the sum total of all the profits earned by the firms that make up the production chain for a good or service.[2] Innovators create surplus by developing new products that consumers want to buy or by devising new ways to make existing products more cheaply, but ultimately the total amount of surplus available to producers is determined by consumers' demand for the final good or service. Regardless of whether or not they are innovators, firms at the end of the production chain—that is, those that sell the final good or service to consumers—want to retain as much of the producer surplus as they can. Firms further up the chain, from the producers of raw materials to those that make intermediate inputs, also want as much of the surplus as they can get, regardless of whether they are innovators. Every firm in the production chain battles over the surplus, and they fight with all the arrows in their quivers, including lobbying to change the laws governing patents. As a general rule, firms that develop the innovations that create surplus tend to lobby for stronger patent laws, because stronger property rights improve their negotiating position vis à vis businesses in the rest of the production chain. The other firms in the production chain, by contrast, tend to lobby for weaker patent laws in order to improve their negotiating position.

J. H. Raymond's gripes about worthless patents illustrate this point. Raymond was secretary and treasurer of the Western Railroad Association—the organization that coordinated the railroads' legal defense against patent suits, served as a clearing house for information about patents of interest, and (with its sister organization for eastern railroads) lobbied for patent reform (Usselman 1991). He certainly had cause for his complaints; railroads across the country were facing

infringement. See US Senate (1878, pp. 1–9). The additional quotations from Raymond's testimony are from pp. 110 and 123. On the failure of the legislation in Congress, see Usselman (1991). On the Second Industrial Revolution in the United States, see Mowery and Rosenberg (1989).

[2] Economic surplus emerges from the purchase by consumers of a good or service that they value. It is divided into producer surplus and consumer surplus. Consumer surplus is the difference between the maximum price a consumer is willing to pay and the price that the consumer actually pays. Aggregate consumer surplus is the sum of the consumer surplus for all individual consumers. Producer surplus is the amount that producers benefit by selling a good or service at a market price that is higher than the lowest price that they would accept.

expensive lawsuits from people who bought up patents with the aim of forcing deep-pocketed businesses to pay licensing fees. The lawsuits filed by these "sharks" generated outrage in the late nineteenth century for much the same reason as those brought by "patent trolls" today, and Raymond's protests about the sharks' exploitation of worthless patents allowed him to build support for the railroads' proposed reforms.[3]

Ultimately, however, Raymond was after bigger game—namely, the firms and entrepreneurs whose valuable patents gave them a claim on the railroads' revenues—and he used the House and Senate hearings to take swipes at them. Belittling George Pullman's achievements, for example, Raymond asked rhetorically, "Why should Mr. Pullman, by reason of having a patent on the triangular space in the roof for the upper berth, which is his most important patent, the validity of which is least questioned, prevent the railroad companies from using any kind of sleeping cars that the public accept?" He went on to imply that George Westinghouse's patents were a crime against humanity. "[W]hy should we be obliged to buy any power-brake of Westinghouse or Lockridge or Eames or Smith, and, in order to be able to protect the lives and property of the people, pay them $150 for what it costs them $10 or $12 to make in the first instance?" (US Senate 1878, p. 115).

Many business people, of course, were on the other side of this debate. They benefited from patent protection and objected that the proposed legislation would drastically limit their ability to enforce their intellectual property. Patentees who testified at the hearings complained that the "inventors of this country have not been represented" in the drafting of the bill. As W. Wheeler Hubbell, an inventor and lawyer, charged, "This whole thing is got up to facilitate the infringement of patents, and it is got up by infringers" (US Senate 1878, pp. 158, 162). *Scientific American*, whose editors considered themselves spokespersons for inventors, came out against the bill, decrying it as an attempt by the railroads to establish a legal process for confiscating intellectual property. Under the guise of declaring inventions that had an obvious utility to be "worthless," the railroads sought to use for free technology that they would otherwise have had to pay to license.[4]

[3] The most notorious example of lawsuits targeting railroads involved a series of overlapping brake patents. Railroads that bought licenses for one or another of the patents found themselves sued for infringement on the others, all of which were for a time owned by one Thomas Sayles. See Usselman (1991, pp. 1062–64; 2002, pp. 108–17). Sharks also generated outrage by targeting farmers and other end users of patented items. See Hayter (1942; 1947) and Magliocca (2007). For an example of current hostility toward "trolls," listen to the podcast "When Patents Attack!" from the series *This American Life*, https://www.thisamericanlife.org/441/transcript.

[4] "Wanted: A Legal Process for Confiscating Inventions," *Scientific American*, 16 March 1878, p. 16. See also, "The Proposed Emasculation of the Patent Law," *Scientific American*, 13 April 1878, p. 224; "Arguments for Section 11," *Scientific American*, 11 May 1878, p. 288; "A Raid on Inventors' Rights," *Scientific American*, 18 May 1878, p. 304; "The Discouragement of Invention," *Scientific*

The witnesses who testified at the Patent Committee's hearings in the late 1870s were exclusively parties with practical experience with patents: inventors, representatives of the railroads and other patent users, attorneys who handled infringement cases, and officials from the Patent Office (US Senate 1878, p. 13). In recent years, however, another group has figured prominently in the list of experts that policymakers consult about problems with the patent system: academics. For example, the hearings conducted in 2008 and 2009 by the Federal Trade Commission (FTC) on reforming the patent system included more than 30 witnesses with academic appointments, about a quarter of the total, and the hearings themselves were hosted by the University of California, Berkeley (US FTC 2011, pp. 280–91). Scholars are sought today as witnesses precisely because they are not practitioners. Because they are not directly involved in the contest over the surplus, the hope is they can provide more objective advice about how to improve the workings of the patent system.[5]

Most of the academics who have participated in recent debates about the patent system are economists and legal scholars whose work is either highly theoretical or based on the analysis of very recent experience. Despite the contemporary focus of their research, they often attempt to validate their claims about problems with the patent system by invoking historical experience. And when they do, they just as often fall into errors—accepting uncritically claims made by interested parties, repeating older allegations in the secondary literature that historians have discounted or outright rejected, and/or proclaiming that some source of market friction in the patent system today is unprecedented when in fact it has a long history and may even have taken a more extreme form in the past.[6]

It is important, of course, to correct such basic errors, but getting the history right involves much more than that. It requires scholars to examine critically the claims about the patent system made by actors in the past, situate those claims relative to the disputants' places in the production chain, and understand the political environment in which claims were made and adjudicated. The essays in this volume take up this challenge and thus enable us to see the patent system as a very human creation, the product of contending interests battling over surplus in specific economic and political contexts that varied over time and across different locations.

American, 17 August 1878, p. 97; "An Amendment to Discourage Invention," *Scientific American*, 28 December 1878, p. 401.

[5] Of course, there is still always the worry that scholars are not truly disinterested but are working for participants.

[6] Examples include Boldrin and Levine (2008), Jaffe and Lerner (2007), and Kramer (1998). For critiques of these works, see Bottomley (2014), Beauchamp (2016), and Khan (2015).

Like all human creations, patent systems are necessarily riven with imperfections. As Adam Smith (1776) noted, it is a natural human tendency to barter, truck, and trade. As he also made clear, however, bartering, trucking, and trading arise not from the goodness of human hearts but from self-interest. That same self-interest means that human beings will use markets for law and politics, as well as the economic marketplace, to achieve their goals. They will search out, generate, and exploit any and all sources of friction as they battle over economic surplus, and the larger the potential surplus, the more extreme will be their efforts. Imperfections, in short, are an inherent feature of *any* system that is designed to generate and apportion economic surplus. Nirvana is not on the menu of available options.

What Is the Question to Which Patents Are the Answer?

The most interesting intellectual issue, therefore, is not how patent systems are imperfect, but why historically they have come to dominate all other methods of encouraging inventive activity. To answer that question one must first ask how patents work to stimulate technological discovery. The answer most commonly given—that they reward inventors by granting them a temporary monopoly for the technologies they develop—is, to say the least, misleading. A patent is a right to exclude others from using a particular technology, but the extent to which that right also confers market power depends on the existence of potential substitutes. At one extreme, if there are no substitutes for the technology and if it cannot be reverse engineered, there is no incentive for an inventor to patent. To secure a patent, an inventor has to reveal information about how the technology works that others can use against her after the term of the patent expires. The inventor would be better off if she kept the discovery as a trade secret and used her proprietary knowledge to dominate the market. The result would be a monopoly, but one that had nothing to do with patents. If the technology can be reverse engineered, however, then the breadth of the right to exclude conferred by the patent can affect the availability of substitutes. Historically, patents for inventions that examiners considered to be path breaking might receive the designation "pioneer" invention and thus obtain property rights that were broader scope than most other patents. In addition, under the legal doctrine of "equivalents," a producer whose technology did not literally infringe on a pioneer patentee's claims might nonetheless be found guilty of infringement if the technology performed "substantially the same function in substantially the same way to obtain the same result."[7] Not surprisingly, securing the designation pioneer patent was an important way in which inventors sought to increase their share of the producer

[7] *Sanitary Refrigerator Co. v. Winters*, 280 U.S. 30 (1929) at 42, quoted in Love (2012; p. 388). However, according to Love (p. 388, n. 27), suits brought for literal infringement of the claims were more likely to be successful.

surplus. The value of the label should not be overstated, however, as pioneer patents still often faced substitutes from competing technologies. To give an obvious example, holders of the basic aluminum smelting patents might have been able initially to exclude others from producing the same metal, but they still had to compete for business with producers of steel (Smith 1988).

Patents are valuable to inventors for two reasons. First, the right to exclude protects them against competitors seeking to free-ride on their ideas. Second, the right to exclude takes the form of a temporary property right that can be sold, licensed, and traded. Most technologically creative people are eager to profit from their discoveries (Sokoloff 1988; Khan and Sokoloff 1993); even those who just enjoy inventing for its own sake need to earn revenues in order to keep doing what they love. Inventors are not always good at running businesses, however, so they often prefer to transfer the task of commercialization to others whose abilities are better suited to that activity. This transfer can occur within a firm, as, for example, when inventors in an R&D department develop technologies used in products that are manufactured and marketed by other units in the same firm. Or inventors can set up their own R&D firms, as Thomas Edison did with Menlo Park, with the aim of selling or licensing their patents to other enterprises better placed to exploit them.[8] Either way, inventors need assurances that their discoveries will not be appropriated without compensation: those inside a manufacturing firm need their accomplishments to be legally recognized to ensure they feed into salary negotiations; those outside a manufacturing firm need to be able to reveal enough information about their discoveries to close a licensing deal or a sale without fearing that their ideas will be stolen. The temporary property right that comes with a patent grant provides the requisite assurance, facilitating a division of labor in which inventors can specialize in what they do best.[9]

The same temporary property right that enables inventors to specialize in invention also makes it possible to assemble the numerous technologies needed to produce complex products (Kieff 2006). Most products are not themselves patented; what are patented are the technologies that make the products possible. Many people reading these words are doing so on a laptop computer, a tablet, or (eyesight permitting) a smartphone. There is no patent for a laptop, tablet, or smartphone. Rather, there are tens of thousands of patented technologies that are embedded in these devices and allow readers to download this book, display the words on a screen, make notes in the margins, share their thoughts with other

[8] Edison set up companies to exploit some of his patents, but he was a poor businessman and typically ended up fighting with his financial backers, most notably J. P. Morgan. He was most productive at patenting when he was not involved in business. The great inventor Elmer Sperry had a similar experience. See Israel (1998) and Hughes (1971).

[9] This point about the gains from specialization goes back as far as Smith (1776), while its specific application to invention goes back at least to Arrow (1962). For a historical application, see also Lamoreaux and Sokoloff (1999; 2007) and Lamoreaux, Sokoloff, and Sutthhiphisal (2013).

readers—and do all of these things regardless of the type and brand of device they own. Most of these patented technologies were not developed by the firm whose brand name appears on the device. They were developed by specialized firms, many of which do not manufacture any part of the device but instead focus on developing the technologies that permit the parts and the whole to function.

Basic economic logic suggests that the patents held by these specialized firms do not confer monopolies. A monopoly allows a firm to restrain output and raise the market price. If you have ever purchased a hot dog at a baseball game or a bag of popcorn at a movie theater, you have had firsthand experience with monopoly pricing, and you know that the stadium or theater can maintain its monopoly because there are no substitutes. You cannot grill your own hotdogs in the stands or pop your own popcorn at the multiplex. Nor can you turn to competing suppliers. A direct test for the existence of a monopoly, therefore, is to look at the prices charged. If any of the firms that owns the patented technologies in your laptop, tablet, or smartphone is a monopolist, the royalty paid by the manufacturer to the patent owner would reflect that monopoly, and the manufacturer would pass it along to you. Simply put, laptops, tablets, and smartphones would be priced in much the same way as movie theater popcorn. That prediction does not square, of course, with the fact that the prices for these devices have been falling like stones for years and are now so low that parents give them as toys to children (Galetovic, Haber, and Levine 2015). To be sure, you can pay over a $1,000 for a top of the line Apple iPhone. But for Christmas 2020 you can also buy a low-end iPhone on Amazon for around $250 and you can get perfectly serviceable smartphones from reputable companies like Nokia and Samsung for substantially under $100.[10] For purposes of comparison, $100 is roughly one-hundredth the inflation-adjusted cost of the mobile phone introduced by Motorola in 1983—a 1G phone that had no data or texting capabilities, was the size of a brick, weighed a kilo, and had a battery that lasted for half an hour (Galetovic, Haber, and Zaretzki 2017).

The patents as monopolies hypothesis would also predict that the owners of the patents in the smartphone production chain would capture a huge portion of the revenues generated by smartphone sales. In order to test that prediction against evidence, Alexander Galetovic, Stephen Haber, and Lew Zaretzi (2018) compiled data on total licensing revenues for the main holders of patents used in smartphones in 2016 and compared them to the value of all smartphones shipped that year. They calculated that royalties on patents accounted on average for 3.4 percent of the value of these phones. Even adding in generous estimates of royalties paid to less important patent holders not included in the

[10] See https://www.t3.com/us/news/best-cheap-smartphone; https://www.amazon.com/s?k=inexpensive+smart+phone&ref=nb_sb_noss_2.

data and taking into account the possibility that some firms were able to evade paying royalties on the phones they shipped, the estimate rises only to 5.6 percent. Galetovic, Haber, and Zaretzi (2017) also parameterize a model, based on actual smartphone prices and number of units sold and estimate that a single patent holder acting as a monopolist would have charged a royalty equal to roughly two-thirds of the value of the average smartphone and that, had all of the patent holders in the smartphone production chain acted as independent monopolists, they would have charged a royalty equal to roughly 80 percent of the value of the average smartphone. In short, the actual royalties paid to patent holders in the smartphone industry are an order of magnitude lower than the royalties predicted by the hypothesis that patents confer monopolies. Moreover, because the higher royalties would have been passed on to consumers, the price of phones would have been much higher.[11]

The falling price of electronic equipment has often been attributed to what is known as Moore's law, the observation made by Intel co-founder Gordon Moore that the number of transistors on a chip doubles every two years while the costs per transistor are halved. The implication is that the falling prices of high-tech products, such as smartphones, occurred for technological reasons having nothing to do with the patent system. However, as Galetovic notes in his chapter in this volume, "Patents in the History of the Semiconductor Industry: The Ricardian Hypothesis," Moore's Law is not a law of nature, like the speed of light, but is a rule of thumb about an empirical regularity that has been observed in a particular institutional context. The validity of Moore's Law depends on certain physical properties of silicon, the material out of which chips are made, but those properties alone are not sufficient to explain the relentless improvement in quality and decline in price. What enabled the semiconductor industry to accomplish this feat was the emergence of a productive division of labor between chip manufacturers and the myriad of small design firms that developed integrated circuits for specialized uses.

Galetovic details how this vertically disintegrated structure emerged in the early 1980s as a consequence of fundamental technological advances and how patents played a key role in making the division of labor possible. As the industry became increasingly decentralized, the number of patents soared from about 400 semiconductor patents per year in the 1960s to 10,000 per year in the 2000s to more than 20,000 per year today. Chip designs are simple to reverse engineer, so firms can easily free ride on other firms' investments in technology,

[11] Galetovic, Haber, and Zaretzki (2017) estimate that a single patent holder acting as a monopolist would have driven up the average price of a smartphone from $281 to $816. If all patent holders had acted as monopolists, the price of a smartphone would have been higher still, $1,320—almost five times the actual average market price. For further evidence on this point, see Galetovic and Haber (2017; 2021).

copying their designs without incurring the R&D costs. However, if the means of achieving electronic functionality in a chip is patented, other firms cannot use it for free; they must bear the R&D costs of inventing around the patent or alternatively, purchase or license it. Design firms derive their revenues mainly from the licensing royalties they charge users of their designs, but the rich abundance of capable design firms that this property-rights environment supports means that substitutes are always at hand, keeping royalty rates relatively low. Because patents allowed semiconductor firms to behave as if free riding did not exist, the industry was able efficiently to adjust its horizontal and vertical structure to fit its developing technology.

One implication of Galetovic's analysis is that patents do more than give inventors a claim to a share of the economic surplus generated by a consumer good that makes use of their invention. They also facilitate the transfer to others of the non-patented knowledge necessary to produce that good. The owner of the patent cannot earn royalties if the end user is unable to make the technology work, but the patentee will be reluctant to supply the necessary knowledge in the absence of a secure property right (Arrow 1962). This point is explored by Victor Menaldo in his chapter, "Do Patents Foster International Technology Transfer? Evidence from Spanish Steelmaking, 1850–1930." Menaldo's central point is that not all of the information necessary to turn a patented technology into a commercially viable product can be imparted in a patent's written description; much of it remains tacit. Unless the firm or individual that initially developed the technology, and thus holds the patent, cooperates by providing drawings, blueprints, machinery, tutorials, and training, the patented technology cannot be used effectively by a firm further down the production chain. Patents thus allow firms at different points in the chain to align one another's incentives. A patent allows Firm A to show Firm B exactly how to produce a good or service, using both Firm A's patented technology and its vast store of unpatented knowledge; but that tacit knowledge is made available to Firm B only if it pays for the patented technology.[12]

It follows, therefore, that patents are also an important part of the answer to the question of how a technologically laggard country can catch up with the rest of the world. A patent system gives firms in, say, Country X a claim on the use of their technologies by firms in Country Y—provided that Country Y has a patent system that allows foreign firms to patent the technologies they developed (and patented) in their home country. Because the use of those technologies by firms in Country Y produces a flow of licensing royalties to the firms in Country X,

[12] The importance of tacit knowledge for the diffusion of technology has long been recognized in the literature, but most scholars have used this point to emphasize the insufficiency of patent disclosures and have failed to consider the importance of patents for facilitating other forms of communication. For a recent example, see Lee (2012).

the firms in Country X have an incentive to transfer their tacit knowledge to the firms in Country Y. Without a patent system in Country Y, however, there will be no incentive for Country X firms to transfer any of that knowledge. Firms in Country Y will have to operate with antiquated technologies.

Menaldo illustrates this general principle through a detailed examination of the role of patents in the transfer of technology to the Spanish steel industry over the course of nearly a century. Steel making is the quintessential example of an industry in which a substrate of tacit knowledge was (and is) a necessary input to production: turning hunks of rock into steel shapes requires an intricate ballet of ores, fuels, furnaces, rolling mills, and human beings. Most of the knowledge about how to perform this ballet could not be conveyed in a written description. Like an actual ballet, its performance requires practice under the tutelage of experienced teachers. Without knowledge about how small differences in temperature, timing, or the chemical composition of ore affect steel qualities, rails would fracture under the stresses imposed by heavy trains, girders would sag under the weight of buildings, and ships would leak because hull laminates would not align properly. Tacit knowledge was also necessary to economize on fuel costs and prevent damage to equipment from repeated heating and cooling. Thus, the central theme of Menaldo's essay is that Spanish patent law facilitated the necessary transfer of knowledge as the technology of steel production changed over time, from the Chenot process to the Bessemer Converter to the Siemens Martin open hearth furnace. Patent licensing agreements not only gave Spanish manufacturers access to cutting-edge technologies developed by innovators elsewhere but also, by giving those innovators access to improvements made in the course of adapting their technologies to the ores and other special conditions of Spanish manufacture, increased knowledge about steel production in ways that furthered the transfer of steel technology to new settings.

Menaldo's chapter covers one industry in one country, but other scholars have come to similar conclusions for other locales. For example, Alexander Donges and Felix Selgert (2019) found that patents played an important role in the transfer of technology to Germany in the late nineteenth century. For the recent period, Shih-tse Lo (2011) has demonstrated the positive effect of an exogenously imposed set of patent reforms on R&D spending and patenting activity in Taiwan. Countries will of course vary in their capacity to innovate, depending on the extent of prior investments in the requisite types of human capital. The competitive structure of the global industry also affects the extent to which local firms can effectively exploit particular technologies. Thus scholars have obtained somewhat different results for different countries and industries at different points in time (see, for example, Qian 2007). However, the available cross-country quantitative evidence generally supports Menaldo's generalization about the importance of patent protection for the transfer of technology to developing countries (Chen and Puttitanun 2005; Branstetter, Fisman, and Foley 2006; Kim et al 2012).

"Excessive Litigation" as Compared to What?

In contrast to Galetovic's argument about the importance of patents for spurring technological change, or Menaldo's about the role of patents in facilitating the diffusion of technology internationally, critics of the patent system point to cases where (at least so they claim) patent holders were able to block technological progress for considerable periods of time by suing competing inventors for infringement. An example is Michele Boldrin and David Levine's argument that steam engine inventor James Watt and his partner Matthew Boulton aggressively used patents to suppress the supposedly better steam engine developed by Jonathan Hornblower. Because Hornblower's engine built on Watt's early work, "Boulton and Watt were able to block him in court and effectively put an end to steam engine development." Boldrin and Levine go so far as to assert that "[b]y keeping prices high and preventing others from producing cheaper or better steam engines, Boulton and Watt hampered capital accumulation and slowed economic growth" (Boldrin and Levine 2008, p. 4).

In his chapter in this volume, "Did James Watt's Patent(s) Really Delay the Industrial Revolution?," Sean Bottomley uses new archival research to demolish Boldrin and Levine's claim. Hornblower patented his steam engine in 1781 and actively marketed it to the same client base as Boulton and Watt. Yet Boulton and Watt did not take legal action against Hornblower until 1799, the year before their steam engine patent expired. The delay was partly because Boulton and Watt were able for a while to collect royalty payments from many purchasers of Hornblower engines that used their technology. But it was also because Boulton and Watt were reluctant to risk enforcing a patent they thought was legally vulnerable until forced to do so by engine users' growing reluctance to pay them royalties. Regardless, the important point is that Hornblower was able to develop his steam engine unmolested for nearly two decades, and when Boulton and Watt finally moved against him and won, he had only to wait for one more year before their patent expired.

Bottomley's analysis of the market for steam engines provides additional evidence against Boldrin and Levine's argument. In the late eighteenth century, engine manufacturers' most important customers were mine owners, who used the machines to pump water out of their shafts. Boulton and Watt convinced mine owners to substitute their engine for the more primitive Newcomen model then in use by setting their royalty rate at an amount equivalent to one-third of the fuel savings that resulted from using their new technology. They understood that they could not extract all or even most of the surplus generated by their engine and still get mine owners to buy it. Many of their competitors adopted essentially the same pricing strategy. Hornblower sought, however, to go them one better by pegging his royalties at one-third of his engines' fuel savings over the Boulton and Watt engine. Hornblower thus had every incentive to improve the efficiency of his engines, and every opportunity to do so during the nearly two decades in which Boulton and Watt left him alone. If, as Boldrin and Levine assert, he failed to produce an improvement over the Boulton and Watt engine, that failure was chargeable to either his own ineptitude, the inherent difficulties of the task, or both—not to legal harassment by Boulton and Watt.

Even though Boulton and Watt held back from suing Hornblower for a long time, other patent holders in similar situations were not so restrained. By now, however, it should be obvious that litigation, or the threat of it, has strategic value in the battle over the producer surplus. To return to the examples of laptops, tablets, and smartphones, the owners of the patents that permit these devices to be compatible and interoperable often sue manufacturers for infringement, while manufacturers often sue the owners of those standard essential patents for breach of contract (for instance, for charging a royalty that is not FRAND—Fair, Reasonable, and Non-Discriminatory). Litigation is simply one negotiating tool among many others.

Critics of the patent system acknowledge this basic fact, but then frequently claim that the rate of patent litigation has recently become "excessive" (Bessen and Meurer 2008, ch. 6; Jaffe and Lerner 2007, pp. 13–16). Any statement about something being too high or too low necessarily implies a comparison: excessive as compared to what? This question is taken up in Christopher Beauchamp's essay in this volume, "Dousing the Fires of Patent Litigation." Using a unique dataset of nineteenth-century patent lawsuits that he laboriously collected, Beauchamp shows that present-day patent litigation rates were dwarfed by the levels reached during the 1840s to 1880s. This fact holds true regardless of whether one scales the number of suits by the number of patents in force, the size of the economy, or the total caseload of the federal courts (Beauchamp 2016).

Although patent litigation rates were sky-high in the middle part of the nineteenth century, they fell dramatically during the final decades and remained at low levels from roughly 1900 to the 1980s. This drop occurred despite the failure of patent reforms (advocated, as we have seen, by the railroads) that would have made it more difficult to enforce patents against infringers. Legal changes were nonetheless an important part of the story. Patent systems must balance the incentive to invent that derives from the grant of a temporary property right against the possible discouragements to technological progress that the right to exclude might entail if patents are too broad or long-lived. Beauchamp shows that a large fraction of the litigated patents had been extended beyond their original term by Congress or the Patent Office and that a great deal of the decline in litigation rates can be explained by statutory changes that phased out such extensions. Another large fraction involved patents that had been reissued after the original grant. Patentees were increasingly using the reissue process to broaden the scope of their patents ex post and, in that way, transform competitors into infringers with the stroke of a pen. During the 1870s the Supreme Court reined in this practice. Patentees then had to be satisfied with their initial claims and take care to specify them with greater clarity.

Changes in the legal rules governing the patent system thus helped lower litigation rates during the late nineteenth century, but they were by no means the whole story. Beauchamp finds that changes in the organization of the economy contributed to the decline as well. Large horizontally and vertically integrated firms came to dominate many lines of manufacturing that previously had been the domain of small and midsized enterprises. As the number of firms in the production chain fell, there were fewer firms to sue, and the large firms that remained had the wherewithal to tie up potential litigants in the courts for years, making lawsuits a less attractive proposition. The change in the number and size distribution of firms also helped by reducing the collective action problems involved in achieving a negotiated settlement. Moreover, as R&D moved out of small, specialized firms and into the research departments of the new giant enterprises, independent inventors became employees, transforming the battle over the surplus from conflicts among firms into salary negotiations within large-scale enterprises.

In recent years, litigation rates have been increasing again (though not to anywhere near the levels Beauchamp observed for the mid-nineteenth century), and the large firms that are frequent targets of infringement suits have been lobbying for legislation to reduce the enforceability of patents, just as the railroads did in the late nineteenth century. One implication of Beauchamp's study is that policymakers should, before taking such a radical step, consider other ways in which changes in the law or legal doctrine may have increased the number of lawsuits. For example, much of the recent growth in litigation is an artifact of the 2011 America Invents Act (AIA), which altered the rules regarding "joinder" (the practice of including multiple defendants in a single lawsuit). By raising the standards for joinder, the AIA increased the number of lawsuits filed: if different defendants with different products could no longer be joined to the same suit, plaintiffs simply filed more suits, one for each defendant. Other recent changes, such as the reorganization of the courts to create a centralized Court of Appeals for the Federal Circuit (CAFC) to hear patent cases, may also have contributed to the number of lawsuits (Jaffe and Lerner 2007). Bessen and Meurer's list of potential causes for the recent growth in litigation includes an increase in the practice of filing what are called "continuing applications." Like nineteenth-century reissues, this practice allows patentees to alter their claims after the initial application, making it more difficult for competitors to know what constitutes infringement (Bessen and Meurer 2008, pp. 62–63, 150–151).

Another implication of Beauchamp's study for the current debate over excessive litigation is that changes in the structure of the economy can affect the amount of litigation. Just as the late nineteenth-century rise of large firms with in-house R&D laboratories reduced the number of patent lawsuits, the declining power of these kinds of enterprises in the late twentieth century may have reversed that trend (Lamoreaux, Raff, and Temin 2003). As large firms began to cut their research budgets and acquire more of their technology from outside, their share of non-federal R&D expenditures dropped from about two-thirds in 1980 to only about one-third in 2005, while the share of small- and medium-sized firms (SMEs) increased commensurately (Arora and Gambardella 2010).[13] The mid-nineteenth century litigation explosion took place during a period when American manufacturing was characterized by large numbers of highly specialized SMEs engaged in the development of new second-industrial-revolution technologies. The parallel to the present day is striking. Most of the patent lawsuits filed today involve high-tech firms, and as Galetovic shows for the semiconductor industry, the tech sector is characterized by some very large firms but also large numbers of highly specialized SMEs.

Finally, Beauchamp's work reminds us that there is no relationship between litigation rates, innovation, and economic growth. The mid-nineteenth century period of high litigation was a period of extraordinarily rapid innovation and industrial expansion. The equilibrium outcome that is of interest to the public is not the number of lawsuits but rather the standard of living. If the creation of new products that continually improve in quality and fall in price is generated by a system in which small and midsized firms at the front end of a production chain bargain with larger firms further down that chain through patent litigation, it is naïve to think that one could eliminate the lawsuits without altering the production chain. One likely outcome would be the integration of R&D and commercialization into a much smaller number of very large firms, as occurred in the early twentieth century. That is, the reduction of lawsuits might come at the expense of an increase in vertical and horizontal concentration.

[13] Federal R&D expenditures (which disproportionately went to large firms with R&D labs) were also dropping in relative terms, from a peak of about two-thirds in the mid-1960s to about 30 percent in 2005 (Dworin 2015).

The Political Reshaping of the Patent System

Congress created the CAFC in 1982 in an attempt to put an end to forum shopping by patent holders and foster the development of a uniform set of legal rules for patent suits across the country. Prior to 1982, appeals involving patent cases were heard by each of the regional federal circuit courts of appeal. That system had been set up by the Judiciary Act of 1891 in order to reduce the burden of cases of all types on the US Supreme Court.[14] In the area of patents the act accomplished its purpose very well; after 1891 the Supreme Court only rarely heard appeals involving patents. But the resulting lack of judicial oversight meant that the regional appeals courts had considerable leeway to interpret patent law as they saw fit, with some demonstrating a greater propensity than others to enforce patent rights. According to Adam Jaffe and Josh Lerner (2007, p. 100), for example, during the third quarter of the twentieth century judges in the Tenth Circuit (based in Denver) found against infringers nearly 60 percent of the time, whereas in the Eighth Circuit (based in St. Louis) the equivalent figure was less than 10 percent.

Steven Usselman's chapter, "Ninth Circuit Nursery: Patent Litigation and Industrial Development on the Pacific Coast, 1891–1925," analyzes the uses to which appeals-court justices put their autonomy in the third of a century following the Judiciary Act. Focusing on the Ninth Circuit, which included the rapidly growing economy of California, Usselman exploits a treasure trove of nearly 1,500 volumes of appeal documents, including trial transcripts, briefs, and exhibits. These documents allow him to reconstruct all 148 patent cases for which the Ninth Circuit issued a formal ruling during this period. They also allow him to track whether the US Supreme Court considered the case on appeal, and if so, what the justices decided.

A superficial count of decisions of the type offered by Jaffe and Lerner would suggest that the Ninth Circuit was aggressively anti-patent, because the justices found in favor of infringers most of the time. On closer examination, however, a more nuanced picture emerges. Many of the cases involving charges of infringement were brought by large national enterprises against small Western producers. Usselman finds that the court exhibited a strong regional bias in its decisions, ruling in ways that protected local firms from outsiders' claims of infringement at the same time as it strengthened local inventors' patent rights vis à vis the rest of the country. In this way, Usselman shows, the justices of the Ninth Circuit nurtured the growing California economy, allowing firms at the

[14] The Judiciary Act of 1891 limited the categories of cases that could be appealed directly to the Supreme Court and at the same time created a system of regional circuit courts to hear cases on appeal from trial courts. It also eliminated the requirement of "circuit riding" by Supreme Court justices, under which the justices sat as trial judges on cases heard by federal district courts.

beginning of production chains to get a foothold in new technologies such as oil drilling and fruit processing, while protecting fruit growers, contractors, and other local firms at the end of production chains from claims of patent infringement by large, established firms in the East and Midwest. Within the region, the court pursued similar principles, bolstering technology firms in northern California while protecting end users of patented equipment in the southern part of the state from infringement suits.

There were, of course, limits to the Ninth Circuit's autonomy. The favoritism that it displayed toward firms within the region sometimes attracted the scrutiny of the US Supreme Court, particularly in cases where the judges had rather brusquely ruled against prominent national companies. Nonetheless, under the leadership of Chief Justice William Howard Taft in the 1920s, the general trend toward reducing the burden on the Supreme Court continued, and thus so did the regional decentralization of the patent system. Over time, moreover, the Ninth Circuit's bias in favor of small local producers received significant reinforcement as jurists' antipathy to large-scale enterprises grew under the influence of the antitrust movement.

That antipathy, as Jonathan Barnett shows in his chapter, "The Great Patent Grab," would eventually allow Justice Department officials to attack the use of patents by large-scale enterprises. Concerns about the problem of monopoly surged during the late 1930s when the economy, which by 1936 had seemed to be recovering from the Great Depression, collapsed for a second time (Hawley 1966). The most visible manifestation of the revival of interest in trust busting was a three-year investigation into the "Concentration of Economic Power," launched in 1938 by a specially created commission, the Temporary National Economic Committee (TNEC). The committee began its hearings by examining large firms' use of patents to acquire market power and then held a second set of hearings to solicit ideas about how the patent system could be reformed (Hintz 2017). Thurmond Arnold, assistant attorney general in charge of the Justice Department's antitrust division, played a leading role in the hearings and the remedy he proposed was compulsory licensing—requiring firms to license their technology to anyone who wanted to use it. Although this recommendation made its way into the TNEC's final report, it did not go anywhere in Congress (Waller 2004). Yet, as Barnett shows, Arnold had already begun implementing it at the Justice Department. As early as 1938, for example, he put pressure on Alcoa to settle an antitrust suit by, among other things, opening up licenses on a particular set of patents. By the time Alcoa agreed to the arrangement in a 1942 consent decree, Arnold had already secured five other compulsory licensing orders. Many more were to come. Barnett has compiled a list of such orders from 1938 to 1975 and found as many as 133 of them. Although most of the decrees allowed firms to recoup some of their investment in the form of "reasonable" royalties, a third did not allow them to charge anything at all for the use of their intellectual property.

These compulsory licensing orders came at an unusual time in US history, when the federal government was playing a larger role in the economy than ever before and was financing an enormous amount of industrial R&D spending—fully two-thirds of the US total by the mid-1960s (Usselman 2014). Most of this funding went to large firms. In a sense, the government was giving with one hand and taking with the other—making decisions about the allocation of R&D funds in ways that encouraged economic concentration while pursuing novel antitrust policies to limit the monopolistic consequences of that spending. The result was as close to a managed economy as the United States has ever had, and it involved the entire policy apparatus, including the courts. Thus compulsory licensing became a tool to manage market power even if there was no evidence that patents were being abused. In justifying the imposition of a licensing order on the United Shoe Machinery Company in 1953, for example, the Supreme Court admitted, "Defendant is not being punished for abusive practices respecting patents, for it engaged in none, except possibly two decades ago in connection with the wood heel business. It is being required to reduce the monopoly power it has, not as a result of patents, but as a result of business practices."[15]

One of the implications of Barnett's "The Great Patent Grab" is that public officials and judges are not robots programmed to maximize social welfare, but political actors responding to the environment in which they operate. As the conviction that government planning was superior to market coordination waxed during the late New Deal, support for the patent system waned. Antitrust officials were confident they could manage the extent of concentration in the economy. By weakening the patent system, they thought they could encourage the entry of small firms, generate a more competitive market, and benefit consumers. As Barnett shows, however, this policy did not have the intended consequences. There was no decline in concentration. Large firms continued to dominate their respective product lines, relying on secrecy to protect their discoveries, enjoying access to abundant funding through defense procurement programs, and capturing the returns from innovation by integrating vertically rather than contracting in the market with smaller enterprises. Investment in R&D grew as long as government provided the funding, but when federal agencies cut spending during the late 1960s, companies scaled back their R&D efforts commensurately. Not surprisingly, as faith in government's ability to manage the economy plummeted during the stagflation of the 1970s, compulsory licensing agreements fell into disfavor.

[15] *United Shoe Machinery v. U.S.*, 110 F.Supp. 295 (1953).

Stretching the Interpretation of the Rules

The creation and distribution of economic surplus necessarily entails a strategic interaction among firms—a game as it were—with the prize being a share of the producer surplus generated by a new product or an improvement to an already existing product. The laws that govern the patent system, as well as the courts and government agencies tasked with enforcing and interpreting the laws, set the rules of play. Companies can try to influence the formation of the rules, but as Barnett's chapter shows, there is an important level at which they have to take the rules as given and adjust their business strategies accordingly, shifting for example from patenting to secrecy and moving more activities out of the market and into the firm to prevent compulsory licensing from eroding their competitive advantage. Even in such a setting, however, it is in the interest of all the players battling over the surplus to try to stretch the interpretation of the rules in their favor.

Gerardo Con Diaz's chapter, "The Long History of Software Patenting in the United States," provides a case study of successful rule stretching. The targeted rule in this case was the so-called "mental steps doctrine," which held that any sequence of steps (for example, adding a column of numbers) that a human being with proper training could perform in his or her mind was ineligible for patent protection. As a practical matter, the mental steps doctrine meant that to be patent eligible a process had to be implemented by a tangible machine or cause a transformation in something tangible. How, then, did it come to pass that something as intangible and inherently mathematical as computer code could be interpreted as patentable?

Con Diaz points out that when computers were first developed in the 1940s there was less of a distinction between the machine and the programs that controlled it than exists today. Programming, in fact, was a physical task that required operators to manually rewire circuits into new arrangements. The act of programming, therefore, did cause a transformation in something tangible. The great insight of the Bell Labs lawyers, who in 1948 wrote the first patent for a computer program, an error correction routine, was that they should not focus their claims on the novelty of the code itself, but on the specific way it enabled a machine made up of physical circuits to detect its own errors. The resulting patent, issued in 1951, was effectively granted for the computerization of a mathematical algorithm. Nonetheless, as Con Diaz shows, the decision to grant the patent was not at all controversial. It took two years for the lawyers to write the application but only one year for the Patent Office to approve it, and the examiners expressed no concerns whatsoever about the substance of the invention.

Once Bell Labs had performed this crucial stretching of what was patent eligible, other firms, such as the British Tabulating Machine Company (BTM), the International Business Machines Company (IBM), the Radio Corporation of America (RCA), and Texas Instruments adopted Bell's patenting strategy. Success with the patent office required patent lawyers to highlight the way a program controlled a physical machine made up of electrical circuits rather than the algorithm itself. Even after the emergence in the 1960s of general purpose computers that were designed to run a variety of programs, the key to getting a patent for operating code approved remained the same: focus on the physicality of the apparatus. In 1963, for example, IBM submitted a patent for automatic text recognition that was rejected. As Con Diaz shows, IBM then resubmitted the application, but changed the wording of the claims so that "a method of generating an unambiguous output in a system" became "an apparatus for generating an unambiguous outcome in a system." The patent was approved.

One of the ironies of Con Diaz's account is that throughout the 1960s and 1970s IBM was a vocal opponent of software patenting. What may at first glance seem incongruous makes sense once it is understood that IBM had negotiated a consent decree in an antitrust suit with the Justice Department in 1956 that compelled it to license its programs to almost anyone who asked, at a rate to be determined by the District Court for the Southern District of New York. IBM was not, therefore, seeking to earn licensing revenues. In fact, until 1969 IBM did not sell its software programs separately from its hardware: it bundled them together, leasing its hardware to businesses and then throwing in the software, training, and other services free of charge. The whole point of IBM's strategy—aggressive patenting of its own programs, aggressive lobbying against software patenting, and the bundling of hardware and software—was to reduce the incentives of would-be competitors to enter the computer industry. The strategy worked extraordinarily well until 1969, when a new rival, Advanced Data Research (ADR), sued IBM for constraining the growth of the computer industry through its bundling practices. That same year, the Department of Justice initiated an antitrust suit against IBM. IBM responded by abandoning its bundling strategy, and the ADR suit was settled out of court. The antitrust action nonetheless ground on for thirteen years, until it was ultimately dropped by the government (Usselman 2009).

In what might be considered a double irony, ADR secured a patent in 1968 for a computer program called "Sorting System." The literature has conventionally designated "Sorting System" as the first software patent and has credited ADR with initiating an unprecedented expansion in the categories of inventions eligible for patent protection. As Con Diaz demonstrates, however, ADR's lawyers used precisely the same drafting strategy that IBM, Bell Labs, and other hardware manufacturers had pioneered to secure their patents for their programs. Given the prior success of this strategy, it was but a small step for the Patent Office to recognize that computer apparatuses are built out of programs in the same way that they are built out of patent-eligible components such as tape drives and transistors. ADR and other software development firms did not actually have to manufacture any hardware to invent something patentable; their software transformed a bunch of parts into a patent-eligible "special electrical circuit." The result was the emergence in the late twentieth century of one of America's most vibrant industries, and also of an entirely new group of producers to contend over the surplus generated by sales of computers.

Nirvana is Never on the Menu

Lawsuits over software patents have been important drivers both of the recent rise in patent litigation and of academic criticism of the patent system (Bessen and Meurer 2008; Allison, Lemley, and Walker 2009). Undoubtedly, there are useful ways to reform the process of obtaining software patents—for example, tightening up on continuing applications and on drafting standards for claims—that might reduce the number of lawsuits, just as limitations on reissues did in the late nineteenth century. But much of the recent rise in litigation is simply the inevitable result of the contest over surplus that arises with especial vehemence in new dynamic, competitive industries. Some critics have taken the imperfections of the patent system that we have highlighted in this essay—the politics, the lobbying, the litigation, the attempts to stretch the legal rules—as evidence that there must be a better way to promote inventive activity. But any critique of what actually exists necessarily implies a comparison: imperfect as compared to what? The statement that patents are a flawed and inefficient way of incentivizing innovation implies that there are other, more effective methods of encouraging technological development.

As B. Zorina Khan shows in "History Matters: National Innovation Systems and Innovation Policies in Nations," countries have experimented over the last several centuries with a number of different ways of encouraging inventive activity. Patent systems were not created out of whole cloth, but instead took form over time as nations tried out a variety of incentive systems in an environment characterized by intense international competition. The British patent system, for example, was not purposefully created to promote technological progress, but rather grew out of the early seventeenth-century struggles between the king and Parliament that eventuated in the English Civil War. The primary purpose of the Statute of Monopolies that Parliament enacted in 1624 was to prevent the king from raising revenue by selling economically valuable privileges to wealthy supporters, but the act left open the possibility of granting temporary property rights to originators of inventions.[16] Over the next century or so, this possibility

[16] See Mossoff (2001) for a discussion of the intellectual history of emergence of patents as property rights in England, focusing in particular on the importance of natural-law conceptions of the social contract and the moral significance of labor.

gradually took on the contours of a patent system—more through the gradual articulation of bureaucratic procedures by fee-seeking officials than through any legislative act or design. As a result, by the middle of the eighteenth century, inventors could secure patents for their inventions through a relatively standard—albeit cumbersome and expensive—process involving payments to multiple offices (Khan 2005; MacLeod 1988). During this same period, however, the British government was consciously and actively using more top-down methods to promote the development of new technologies, particularly those of military importance (Khan 2015; Satia 2018).

One of the methods the government used during this period was to offer prizes for the solution of difficult technological problems. Technology prizes are much favored currently by critics of the patent system, and advocates have put forward a number of historical examples in support of their views (Stiglitz 2006; Brunt, Lerner, and Nicholas 2012; Burton and Nicholas 2017). The most famous example, the prize offered by Parliament in 1714 for a precise way of measuring longitude at sea, illustrates the main drawbacks of the method. In the first place, prizes must be awarded by human beings whose judgments may be clouded by prior beliefs about the way problems are most likely to be solved and about the kinds of people who are most likely to come up with solutions. The longitude problem was solved by John Harrison, a craftsman without formal education, who ran into both types of biases in his effort to collect his reward. Prominent members of the committee that Parliament created to administer the prize believed that the solution would be based on principles of celestial navigation, whereas Harrison instead produced a new type of clock capable of keeping time to an extraordinary degree of accuracy for long periods under adverse conditions. Harrison also faced skepticism because the committee, all of whose members came from the elite, expected the problem to be solved by a gentleman scientist of their own class. After decades of lobbying, including direct appeals to the king, Harrison was able in his old age to secure substantial remuneration from the British government, but the committee was never willing to declare he had won the prize (Sobel 1995; Khan 2015; Burton and Nicholas 2017).

The longitude example illustrates a second major problem with prizes. Harrison succeeded in making a clock with the necessary precision, but his chronometer was not commercially practicable. Indeed, chronometers remained so expensive that, despite the hazards of navigating without them, most ships continued to use less accurate celestial methods (Sobel 1995). What ultimately reduced the cost of the device sufficiently to spur mass adoption was the large number of follow-on inventions that materialized in the second half of the nineteenth century. In 1852, Parliament reformed the patent system so that it more resembled that of the United States. As the number of patents soared, so did patents for chronometers (Khan and Sokoloff 1997; Burton and Nicholas 2017).

Another drawback of prizes like the one for longitude is that the problems for which they invite solutions are well known. Many technological breakthroughs occur, however, when inventors discover solutions to problems that no one had ever thought to pose before. In order to encourage these kinds of unanticipated breakthroughs, both governments and private organizations have staged open competitions and fairs to reward outstanding developments in broad technological categories. Khan has studied a number of such competitions and found them to be infected by the same kinds of social and intellectual biases that confounded Harrison's attempts to secure the longitude prize. For example, the prizes awarded by Britain's Royal Society for the Encouragement of Arts, Manufactures, and Commerce during the century following its formation in 1754 went disproportionately to members of the elite. The practice was so blatant that contemporaries groused openly about it (see also Khan 2015). The case of the Royal Society is particularly telling because the organization prohibited prize winners from patenting their inventions. Khan found that inventors, including prominent members of the society, voted with their feet and patented their most valuable inventions, submitting their less significant (or non-patentable) ideas to the competitions. In the end, the society abandoned its system of prizes and devoted its resources instead to lobbying for reforms to strengthen the patent system.

Khan shows that other top-down methods of encouraging technological change, such as government buyouts of important inventions or direct efforts to promote specific types of technological change, were rife with similar problems and, on top of that, attracted hordes of rent seekers.[17] Governments have never definitively rejected these methods—perhaps because in some circumstances like war they have had useful outcomes—but over time they have gravitated toward patent systems through a trial-and-error process in which they learned from one another's successes and failures. The US patent system, for example, was a deliberate attempt to improve on the workings of the British patent system by simplifying the process of securing a patent and dramatically lowering the cost, so that every member of society could potentially contribute to technological progress. The Patent Act of 1793 put in place a registration system under which the Patent Office conducted only the most cursory checks for patentability, but mounting complaints by inventors seeking more certainty about the

[17] Kremer (1998, p. 1138) credits the French government's buyout of Louis-Jacque-Mandé Daguerre's patent for photography with the rapid worldwide adoption and improvement of the technology, but the actual story is very different. Daguerre never obtained a French patent for the government to buy out, and the main inventor was actually his deceased business partner. With the patronage of an important member of the Académie des Sciences, he successfully lobbied the French government for a lifetime pension of 10,000 francs a year in exchange for making the technology available to the world. At the same time, however, he and a British patent agent were applying for a British patent for the same invention under the agent's name, and once they obtained the patent, they made a similar buyout offer (this time unsuccessfully) to the British government. See Khan (2015, pp. 637–38).

validity of their temporary property rights led to the creation of an examination system in 1836 (Khan 2005). After the American display at London's Crystal Palace exhibition in 1851 prompted worries about Britain's loss of technological leadership, the United Kingdom moved closer to the US model, lowering fees and simplifying the process of obtaining patents.[18] The US system also became the basis for Germany's patent law of 1877, as well as the Japanese patent law in 1888. The German patent system, in turn, influenced the patent systems of Argentina, Austria, Brazil, Denmark, Finland, Holland, Norway, Poland, Russia, and Sweden (Khan 2008).

Because patent systems are everywhere dominant, their imperfections are readily observable and open to criticism. But it is naïve to believe that any system devised by human beings to apportion economic surplus is going to be frictionless. For all their imperfections, US-style patent systems spread because they had multiple advantages. By creating property rights that could be traded in a market, they facilitated the development of a productive division of labor, either within the firm or through the market, that enabled inventors to specialize in technological discovery and leave the task of developing and commercializing their ideas to others. They also, as we have seen, made it possible for firms to transfer technological knowledge to other firms, even to firms in other countries. Moreover, patents are available not just to inventors of breakthrough technologies but also to those who improve existing technologies incrementally or find novel ways to use them in other applications. This "democratization of invention" is a strength, not a weakness (Khan 2005). The vast majority of inventions have always had this follow-on character (Mokyr 1990). Precisely because the value of a patent does not inhere in the award itself but rather in the market value of the resulting property right, patent systems foster the kind of decentralized, cumulative improvement that extends the frontiers of what is economically possible. Moore's Law takes a specific form in the case of computer chips, but the underlying principle is more general.

References

Allison, John R., Mark A. Lemley, and Joshua Walker. "Extreme Value or Trolls on Top? The Characteristics of the Most-Litigated Patents." *University of Pennsylvania Law Review* 158, no. 1 (2009): 1–37.

Arora, Ashish, and Alfonso Gambardella. "The Market for Technology." In *Handbook of the Economics of Innovation*, edited by Bronwyn H. Hall and Nathan Rosenberg, Vol. 1, pp. 641–78. Amsterdam: Elsevier, 2010.

[18] Britain finally moved toward an examination system in stages in 1883 and 1902 (Khan 2008).

Arrow, Kenneth. "Economic Welfare and the Allocation of Resources." In *The Rate and Direction of Inventive Activity: Economic and Social Factors*, edited by Universities-National Bureau Committee for Economic Research, Committee on Economic Growth of the Social Science Research Council, pp. 609–26. Princeton, NJ: Princeton University Press, 1962.

Beauchamp, Christopher. "The First Patent Litigation Explosion." *Yale Law Journal* 125, no. 4 (2016): 848–944.

Bessen, James, and Michael J. Meurer. *Patent Failure: How Judges, Bureaucrats, and Lawyers Put Innovation at Risk*. Princeton, NJ: Princeton University Press, 2008.

Boldrin, Michele, and David K. Levin. *Against Intellectual Monopoly*. New York: Cambridge University Press, 2008.

Bottomley, Sean. *The British Patent System during the Industrial Revolution, 1700–1852: From Privilege to Property*. Cambridge, UK: Cambridge University Press, 2014.

Branstetter, Lee G., Raymond Fisman, and C. Fritz Foley. "Do Stronger Intellectual Property Rights Increase International Technology Transfer? Empirical Evidence from U.S. Firm-Level Panel Data." *Quarterly Journal of Economics* 121, no. 1 (2006): 321–49.

Brunt, Liam, Josh Lerner, and Tom Nicholas. "Inducement Prizes and Innovation." *Journal of Industrial Economics* 60, no. 4 (2012): 657–96.

Burton, M. Diane, and Tom Nicholas. "Prizes, Patents and the Search for Longitude." *Explorations in Economic History* 64, no. 2 (2017): 21–36.

Chen, Yongmin, and Thitima Puttitanun. "Intellectual Property Rights and Innovation in Developing Countries." *Journal of Development Economics* 78, no. 2 (2005): 474–93.

Donges, Alexander, and Felix Selgert. "Technology Transfer via Foreign Patents in Germany, 1843–77." *Economic History Review* 72, no. 1 (2019): 182–208.

Dworin, Jonathan. "The Changing Nature of U.S. Basic Research: Trends in Funding Sources." State Science and Technology Institute (SSTI), 2015. http://ssti.org/blog/changing-nature-us-basic-research-trends-funding-sources.

Galetovic, Alexander, and Stephen Haber. "The Fallacies of Patent-Holdup Theory." *Journal of Competition Law & Economics* 13, no. 1 (2017): 1–44.

_____. "SEP Royalties: What Theory of Value and Distribution Should Courts Apply?" *Ohio State Technology Law Journal* 17 (2021), forthcoming.

Galetovic, Alexander, Stephen Haber, and Ross Levine. "An Empirical Examination of Patent Holdup." *Journal of Competition Law & Economics* 11, no. 3 (2015): 549–78.

Galetovic, Alexander, Stephen Haber, and Lew Zaretzki. "An Estimate of the Average Cumulative Royalty Yield in the World Mobile Phone Industry: Theory, Measurement and Results." *Telecommunications Policy* 42, no. 3 (2018): 263–76.

_____. "Is There an Anticommons Tragedy in the World Smartphone Industry?" *Berkeley Technology Law Journal* 32, no. 4 (2017): 1527–57.

Hawley, Ellis W. *The New Deal and the Problem of Monopoly: A Study in Economic Ambivalence*. Princeton, NJ: Princeton University Press, 1966.

Hayter, Earl W. "The Western Farmers and the Drivewell Patent Controversy." *Agricultural History* 16, no. 1 (1942): 16–28.

_____. "The Patent System and Agrarian Discontent, 1875-1888." *Mississippi Valley Historical Review* 34, no. 1 (1947): 59–82.

Hintz, Eric S. "The 'Monopoly' Hearings, Their Critics, and the Limits of Patent Reform in the New Deal." In *Capital Gains: Business and Politics in Twentieth-Century America*, edited by Richard R. John and Kim Phillips-Fein, pp. 61–79. Philadelphia: University of Pennsylvania Press, 2017.

Hughes, Thomas Parke. *Elmer Sperry: Inventor and Engineer*. Baltimore, MD: Johns Hopkins Press, 1971.

Israel, Paul. *Edison: A Life of Invention*. New York: John Wiley, 1998.

Jaffe, Adam B., and Josh Lerner. *Innovation and Its Discontents: How Our Broken Patent System Is Endangering Innovation and Progress and What To Do About It*. Princeton, NJ: Princeton University Press, 2007.

Khan, B. Zorina. *The Democratization of Invention: Patents and Copyrights in American Economic Development, 1790–1920*. New York: Cambridge University Press, 2005.

_____. "An Economic History of Patent Institutions." In *EH.Net Encyclopedia*, edited by Robert Whaples, 2008, http://eh.net/encyclopedia/an-economic-history-of-patent-institutions/.

_____. "Inventing Prizes: A Historical Perspective on Innovation Awards and Technology Policy." *Business History Review* 89, no. 4 (2015): 631–60.

Khan, B. Zorina, and Kenneth L. Sokoloff. "'Schemes of Practical Utility': Entrepreneurship and Innovation Among 'Great Inventors' in the United States, 1790–1865." *Journal of Economic History* 53, no. 2 (1993): 289–307.

_____. "Patent Institutions, Industrial Organization and Early Technological Change: Britain and the United States, 1790–1850." In *Technological Revolutions in Europe: Historical Perspectives*, edited by Maxine Berg and Kristine Bruland, pp. 292–313. Cheltenham, UK: Edward Elgar, 1997.

Kieff, F. Scott. "Coordination, Property, and Intellectual Property: An Unconventional Approach to Anticompetitive Effects and Downstream Access." *Emory Law Journal* 56, no. 2 (2006): 327–438.

Kim, Yee Kyoung, Keun Lee, Walter G. Park, and Kineung Choo. "Appropriate Intellectual Property Protection and Economic Growth in Countries at Different Levels of Development." *Research Policy* 41, no. 2 (2012): 358–75.

Kremer, Michael. "Patent Buyouts: A Mechanism for Encouraging Innovation." *Quarterly Journal of Economics* 113, no. 4 (1998): 1137–67.

Lamoreaux, Naomi R., Daniel M. G. Raff, and Peter Temin. "Beyond Markets and Hierarchies: Towards a New Synthesis of American Business History." *American Historical Review* 108, no. 2 (2003): 404–33.

Lamoreaux, Naomi R., and Kenneth L. Sokoloff. "Inventors, Firms, and the Market for Technology in the Late Nineteenth and Early Twentieth Centuries." In *Learning by Doing in Firms, Markets, and Countries*, edited by Naomi R. Lamoreaux, Daniel M. G. Raff, and Peter Temin, pp. 19–57. Chicago, IL: University of Chicago Press, 1999.

_____. "The Market for Technology and the Organization of Invention in U.S. History." In *Entrepreneurship, Innovation, and the Growth Mechanism of the Free-Enterprise Economies*, edited by Eytan Sheshinski, Robert J. Strom, and William J. Baumol, pp. 213–43. Princeton, NJ: Princeton University Press, 2007.

Lamoreaux, Naomi R., Kenneth L. Sokoloff, and Dhanoos Sutthipisal. "Patent Alchemy: The Market for Technology in US History." *Business History Review* 87, no. 1 (2013): 3–38.

Lee, Peter. "Transcending the Tacit Dimension: Patents, Relationships, and Organizational Integration in Technology Transfer." *California Law Review* 100, no. 6 (2012): 1503–72.

Lo, Shih-tse. "Strengthening Intellectual Property Rights: Experience from the 1986 Taiwanese Patent Reforms." *International Journal of Industrial Organization* 29, no. 5 (2011): 524–36.

Love, Brian J. "Interring the Pioneer Invention Doctrine." *North Carolina Law Review* 90, no. 1 (2011): 379–459.

Magliocca, Gerard N. "Blackberries and Barnyards: Patent Trolls and the Perils of Innovation." *Notre Dame Law Review* 82, no. 5 (2007): 1809–38.

MacLeod, Christine. *Inventing the Industrial Revolution: The English Patent System, 1660–1800*. Cambridge, UK: Cambridge University Press, 1988.

Mokyr, Joel. *The Lever of Riches: Technological Creativity and Economic Progress*. New York: Oxford University Press, 1990.

Mossoff, Adam. "Rethinking the Development of Patents: An Intellectual History, 1550–1800." *Hastings Law Journal* 55, no. 6 (2001): 1255–1322.

Mowery, David C., and Nathan Rosenberg. *Technology and the Pursuit of Economic Growth*. New York: Cambridge University Press, 1989.

Qian, Yi. "Do National Patent Laws Stimulate Domestic Innovation in a Global Patenting Environment? A Cross-Country Analysis of Pharmaceutical Patent Protection, 1978–2002." *Review of Economic and Statistics* 89, no. 3 (2007): 436–53.

Satia, Priya. *Empire of Guns: The Violent Making of the Industrial Revolution*. New York: Penguin, 2018.

Smith, Adam. *An Inquiry into the Nature and Causes of the Wealth of Nations*. London: W. Strahan and T. Cadell, 1776.

Smith, George David. *From Monopoly to Competition: The Transformations of Alcoa, 1888–1986*. New York: Cambridge University Press, 1988.

Sobel, Dava. *Longitude: The True Story of a Lone Genius Who Solved the Greatest Scientific Problem of his Time*. New York: Walker, 1995.

Sokoloff, Kenneth L. "Inventive Activity in Early Industrial America: Evidence from Patent Records, 1790–1846." *Journal of Economic History* 48, no. 4 (1988): 813–50.

Stiglitz, Joseph. "Give Prizes not Patents." *New Scientist*, 16 September 2006, 21.

US FTC (United States Federal Trade Commission). "The Evolving IP Marketplace: Aligning Patent Notice and Remedies with Competition," March 2011, https://www.ftc.gov/sites/default/files/documents/reports/evolving-ip-marketplace-aligning-patent-notice-and-remedies-competition-report-federal-trade/110307patentreport.pdf.

US Senate. *Arguments before the Committee on Patents of the Senate and House of Representatives*. Misc. Doc. No. 50, 45th Cong., 2d Sess. Washington, DC: Government Printing Office, 1878.

Usselman, Steven W. "Patents Purloined: Railroads, Inventors, and the Diffusion of Innovation in 19th-Century America." *Technology and Culture* 32, no. 4 (1991): 1047–75.

Usselman, Steven W. *Regulating Railroad Innovation: Business, Technology, and Politics in America, 1840–1920*. New York: Cambridge University Press, 2002.

Usselman, Steven W. "Unbundling IBM: Antitrust and the Incentives to Innovation in American Computing." In *The Challenge of Remaining Innovative: Insights from Twentieth-Century American Business*, edited by Sally H. Clarke, Naomi R. Lamoreaux, and Steven W. Usselman, pp. 249–79. Stanford, CA: Stanford University Press, 2009.

Usselman, Steven W. "Research and Development (R&D)." In *Oxford Encyclopedia of the History of American Science, Medicine, and Technology*, edited by Hugh Richard Slotten, Vol. 2, pp. 369–87. New York: Oxford University Press, 2014.

Waller, Spencer Weber. "The Antitrust Legacy of Thurman Arnold." *St. John's Law Review* 78, no. 3 (2004): 569–613.

1

Patents in the History of the Semiconductor Industry

The Ricardian Hypothesis

Alexander Galetovic

With suitable legal measures, information may become an appropriable commodity. Then the monopoly power can indeed be exerted.

—Kenneth Arrow, 1962

The key to high-value intellectual property is finding a need, finding a cost-effective solution, and protecting it so other suppliers cannot copy it. Because a high number of ASIC suppliers all offer comparable products, unique intellectual property is mandatory for commanding respectable profit margins.

—Bryan Lewis, 1993

Introduction: The Patent Paradox in Semiconductors

Ever since Arrow's (1962) classic paper, economists have viewed patents as an incentive mechanism. According to Arrow's hypothesis, innovation creates information, a non-rival good, which can be easily copied. A patent grants a right to exclude, which prevents competitors from copying and creates a monopoly. The monopoly rent remunerates the investments in R&D that firms make in the expectation of profit. Thus, patents incentivize innovation by creating the monopoly necessary to appropriate the returns generated by investments in R&D—or so the argument goes.

While Arrow (1962) is the theory that most economists use to think about patents, empirical research has been rather unsupportive. Two influential surveys by Levin et al. (1987, the Yale survey, taken in 1983) and Cohen, Nelson, and Walsh (2000, the Carnegie-Mellon survey, taken in 1994) showed that firms in many industries did not consider patents as revenue generators that remunerate investments in R&D. Firms used a variety of strategies—secrecy, first

Alexander Galetovic, *Patents in the History of the Semiconductor Industry In: The Battle over Patents.* Edited by: Stephen H. Haber and Naomi R. Lamoreaux, Oxford University Press. © Oxford University Press 2021.
DOI: 10.1093/oso/9780197576151.003.0002

mover advantages, manufacturing or design capabilities, distribution networks and other complementary assets—which, with the exception of a few industries, outranked patents in importance.[1] Surveys therefore suggest a paradox: if firms do not use patents to generate revenues and profit from their investments in R&D, why do they patent so much? The purpose of this chapter is to resolve that paradox.

I focus in the semiconductor industry because it is a canonical case of the patent paradox: semiconductor firms reported in the Yale and the Carnegie Mellon surveys that they did not rely primarily on patents to generate revenues; but at the same time, they have been prolific patentees since the industry's inception in the early 1950s.[2] Moreover, since the early 2000s, semiconductor firms account for roughly 7 percent of all US utility patents every year.

The patent paradox in semiconductors is compounded by several facts. One is that, according to Hall and Ziedonis (2001), the propensity of semiconductor firms to patent, measured by the number of patents per dollar of R&D spending, rose in the 1980s after the creation of the Court of Appeals for the Federal Circuit (CAFC) in 1982, which strengthened patent rights.[3] If patents were unnecessary to profit from R&D, then why did semiconductor firms patent more after patent rights were strengthened? And if firms do not use patents to appropriate the returns of R&D, why do we observe so little free riding in this industry? Semiconductor devices are easy to copy, because they can be reverse engineered; chip designs are coded, transferred electronically, and can be copied like software; and the production of semiconductor devices is routinely subcontracted to specialist manufacturers, which requires full disclosure of the design.[4] Moreover, skilled individuals routinely spin off from established firms to form their own

[1] See Williams (2017) for a recent review of the theory and evidence of Arrow's hypothesis. Sometimes, Arrow's hypothesis is called the incentive thesis for patents. See Barnett (2011a, b).

[2] Semiconductor devices are usually classified as discrete, memory, logic, and optical. Discrete semiconductors are one-component devices. Memory and logic are the main integrated circuits (or chips). Memory is used to store information; logic semiconductors process digital data to control electronic systems such as microprocessors, microcontrollers, graphic-processing units, and chip sets; these run computers, phones, and electronic systems. Optical semiconductors comprise light-emitting diodes and laser diodes, which transform an electric signal into light.

Semiconductors are embedded in almost all the electronic devices we use. Memory and microprocessors are in all laptops and personal computers, and in servers (29.5 percent of world semiconductor sales in 2016 according to the Semiconductor Industry Association [2017]). Semiconductors also make smartphones run and all the equipment that is necessary to transmit voice and data (cellular towers, radios, switching and routing equipment, and so on) run, which by now are as important as computers (31.5 percent of world semiconductor sales). The automobile industry accounts for more than one-tenth of semiconductor sales (11.6 percent), almost the same as all manufacturers of electronic consumer goods (13.5 percent) or the entire industrial sector (12.9 percent).

[3] On CAFC see Adelman (1987).

[4] Reverse engineering of semiconductor devices is legal. The Semiconductor Chip Protection Act allows reverse engineering for teaching, analyzing, or evaluating the concepts or techniques embodied in the mask work or circuitry.

startups, taking with them the information they acquired from their former employer. Last, semiconductor firms routinely announce their breakthroughs in trade shows and reveal technical information to their potential customers as part of their marketing efforts, even before products are introduced to market.[5]

To resolve the paradox many authors have argued that patents are "defensive," a description widely used by industry participants until the early 1980s.[6] The argument is that a chip manufacturer is vulnerable to lawsuits and may be held up and even shut down with an injunction unless it owns patents and threatens to countersue.[7] Patenting buys protection against lawsuits and gains freedom to operate through cross licenses.[8] In this sense, semiconductor patents are like the French Maginot line: had there not been a German threat, France would not have invested in costly fortifications. So, had there been no threat of lawsuits, no semiconductor firm would have bothered to patent.

An additional implication of the defensive hypothesis is that patenting and cross licensing are socially costly means to share technologies with no differential benefit over an open source regime. On the contrary, an open source regime would have prevented a lot of costly patenting and zero-sum cross licensing among firms.[9] Moreover, wasteful patenting implies that the rate of technological progress in semiconductors would have been largely the same, or even faster, without patents. Indeed, one view is that technological progress in semiconductors was the outcome of Moore's Law and was largely preordained after the invention of the transistor in 1947.[10]

The defensive hypothesis does not provide a compelling resolution to the patent paradox, however. As a matter of logic, if patenting is defensive, a firm patents only if another firm does. But assume, for example, that Firm A produces a valuable technology, which is also useful for Firm B. If Firm B does not patent, A is better off patenting and charging royalties to Firm B. Alternatively, if Firm B patents, Firm A is better off patenting and cross licensing, instead of paying a

[5] As Arrow (1962, p. 615) explains: "there is a fundamental paradox in the determination of demand for information; its value for the purchaser is not known until he has the information, but then he has in effect acquired it without cost." Semiconductor firms routinely ignore Arrow's information paradox.

[6] See Levin (1982), von Hippel (1982), Grindley and Teece (1997), Hall and Ziedonis (2001), and Ziedonis and Hall (2001).

[7] See von Hippel (1982, footnote 9).

[8] See Levin (1982, p. 81) and Grindley and Teece (1997). Levin et al. (1987, pp. 79–82) argue that the cumulative nature of semiconductor innovation guaranteed wide cross licensing—firms who patent the original technology will cross licence with firms that patent improvements. See also von Hippel (1982, footnote 9).

[9] At the extreme, some claim that patents in semiconductors have been mostly about known, obvious, or useless information. See, for example, Taylor and Silberston (1973), who cite experts claiming that up to 90 percent of semiconductor patents are not truly novel and therefore invalid (cited by Bessen and Maskin 2009).

[10] Moore's Law states that the number of electrical components and transistors in a chip of roughly fixed size and cost doubles every two years. See Moore (1965; 2005) and Hutchenson (2003).

royalty. It follows that patenting is a dominant strategy for Firm A, whose best response does not depend on Firm B's decision. Thus, as a matter of logic, Firm A's patenting strategy cannot be defensive. Moreover, it can be shown that patenting and cross licencing are wasteful only if there are no free riders that copy and erode Firm A and Firm B's Ricardian rents.[11]

As a matter of empirics, the predictions of the defensive hypothesis are inconsistent with the facts of the semiconductor industry. One is that Moore's Law is the endogenous outcome of investments in R&D made in the expectation of profit.[12] Also, the defensive hypothesis cannot explain how semiconductor firms prevent free riding or whether it matters at all. Last, the defensive hypothesis cannot explain why, since the beginning of the industry, many semiconductor firms with strong patent portfolios generate considerable royalty revenue from licensing and trade in intellectual property. If patenting in semiconductors is defensive, then who are firms that license defending against, and why are other firms quite willing to license from them?

One might save the defensive hypothesis by arguing that firms find ways other than patents to appropriate the returns wrought by R&D, such as trade secrets, first mover advantages, or design and manufacturing capabilities. But this argument is difficult to sustain in light of three facts. As said, semiconductor firms actively diffuse technical information about their devices, a marketing strategy inconsistent with secrecy; semiconductors are notoriously easy to copy through reverse engineering, a fact that limits the first-mover advantages that might be enjoyed by superior design capabilities; and there are numerous specialist manufacturers of semiconductors, which vitiates the advantage that might accrue to a firm's manufacturing capabilities.

There is an alternative way to resolve the patent paradox, which I call the Ricardian hypothesis. It builds on the fact that semiconductor devices are easy to copy. As Sutton (2001, p. 329) notes, whether patents are necessary to preserve the incentives to invest in R&D depend, inter alia, on the intensity of spillovers across firms, the extent to which knowledge can be transferred via designs, blueprints, or formulas, and the time lag required by imitating firms to develop related knowhow. Thus, when copying an innovation is easy, cheap, and fast, as it is in semiconductors, a free riding business model—a business model based on copying the ideas of others—is feasible, unless patent protection is effective. This is the main role of patents in the semiconductor industry.

While both the Ricardian and Arrow's hypothesis maintain that patents prevent free riding, only Arrow's conflates exclusion and monopoly—the ability to

[11] See the Appendix.

[12] See Moore and Davis (2004). Rhines (2019, ch. 2) shows that for more than 35 years the industry has invested roughly 14 percent of sales per year in R&D.

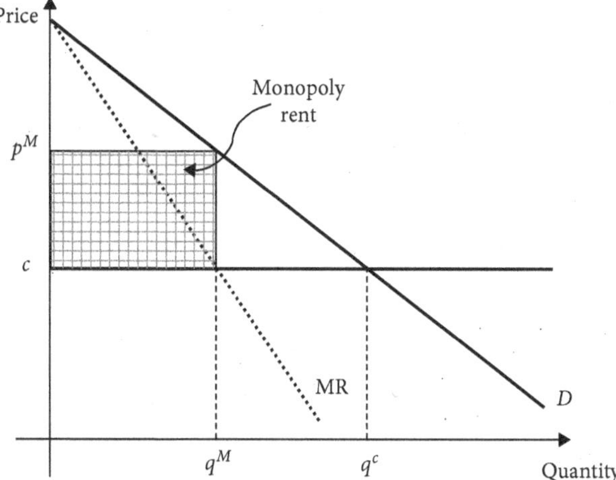

Figure 1.1 A monopoly that exploits market power by constraining quantity from q^c to q^M to increase price to p^M and earn a monopoly rent, which equals the shaded area; the patent creates and protects the monopoly and is the direct generator of revenues.

drive up prices by constraining output. Nevertheless, semiconductor devices seldom enjoy a monopoly because there are many different ways of achieving the same electronic functionality.[13] Thus, most semiconductor innovations must compete with alternatives, and are threatened by subsequent innovations.[14] Rather than conferring monopolies, therefore, semiconductor patents protect Ricardian rents.

The difference between a monopoly rent and a Ricardian rent cannot be overstated. Consider first a monopoly rent. As is well known and Figure 1.1 shows, a monopolist constrains output from q^c to q^M until marginal revenue is equal to marginal cost and raises price from c (long-run marginal cost) to p^M. The monopoly rent, the difference between total revenue and total long-run cost, remunerates investments in R&D. Under Arrow's hypothesis, therefore, patents create a market structure to remunerate the investment in R&D.

[13] The electronic functionality of a semiconductor device is the output it achieves in an electronic product. For example, a chip can make a dishwasher run.

[14] Indeed, the so-called clean room technique is used to copy the functionality of a chip without infringing on its patents. Team A reverse engineers a chip and describes its functionalities to team B, but not the means whereby the chip achieves them. Team B, which does not know how the chip works and achieves the functionalities, then designs a new chip from scratch that achieves the same functionalities by independent means.

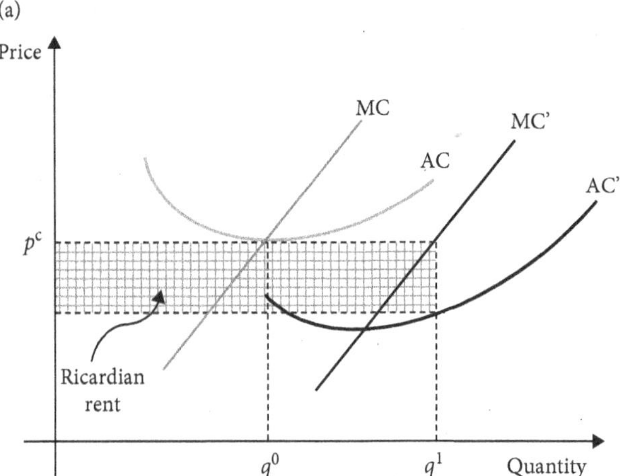

Figure 1.2a The Ricardian rent obtained by a firm that owns a proprietary production process that reduces average and marginal costs. The firm increases production from q^0 to q^1 and obtains a Ricardian rent equal to the shaded rectangle—the difference between price p^c and average cost. The patent protects Firm A's Ricardian rent, but the rent is generated by A's ability to produce more output per unit of input, not by constraining output to raise price. R&D is remunerated in a competitive market.

A Ricardian rent, by contrast, emerges when a firm produces more output or higher quality per unit of input than its competitors.[15] Consider Figure 1.2(a), which shows Firm *A* before and after implementing a cost saving innovation. Firm *A*'s marginal and average costs fall, and production increases from q_0 to q_1 . Because Firm *A* is more efficient, it earns a Ricardian rent equal to the shaded rectangle when selling at the market price p .

Similarly, Figure 1.2(b) shows Firm *B* before and after implementing an innovation that increases quality and consumers' willingness to pay by a factor $\lambda > 1$ over the next best alternative. *B*'s product now commands a market premium equal to $(\lambda - 1)p$. Thus, Firm *B* increases production from to , and earns a Ricardian rent equal to the shaded rectangle.

In both cases, patents protect the Ricardian rent from competition by free riders, but do not confer monopoly power. On the contrary, Figure 1.2 assumes that *A* and *B* sell into a competitive market. Thus, the figure emphasizes that market power is not necessary to remunerate investments in R&D. The cash

15 A Ricardian rent arises from differential productivity or costs per unit among factors of production (see Noll, 2005). In the business literature this is usually called a competitive advantage or a differential firm capability. See Sutton (2012) for a rigorous definition of differential firm capability.

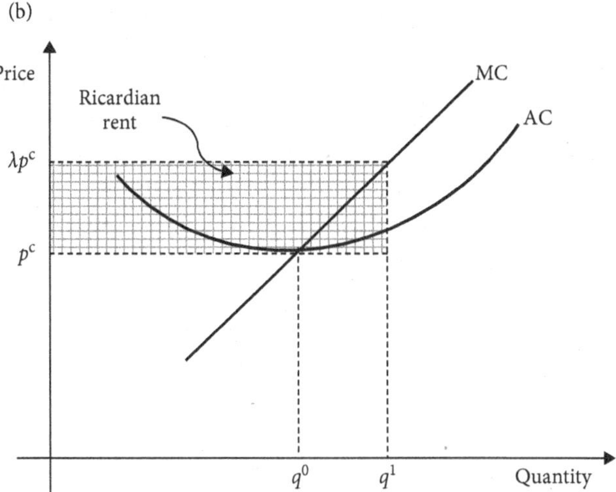

Figure 1.2b The Ricardian rent earned by Firm B, which sells a better product than the rest of the market. After introducing the improved product, Firm B expands production from q^0 to q^1 and obtains a Ricardian rent equal to the shaded rectangle. While the patent protects Firm B's Ricardian rent from being eroded by competitors, revenue is generated by B's ability to produce more value per unit of input, not by constraining output to raise price. R&D is remunerated in a competitive market.

flows wrought by Ricardian rents stem from selling a better product or using a more efficient production process, not from constraining output to raise price. The patent just prevents free riders from copying the source of the firm's competitive advantage and does not alter market structure in any meaningful way.

The Ricardian hypothesis explains why free riding is seldom observed, despite the fact that semiconductor devices can be easily copied and employees routinely start their own firms with knowledge acquired while working for their former employer. It also resolves Arrow's information paradox: semiconductor firms engage in technical marketing and reveal how their devices work, because their intellectual property is protected by patents.[16] And it explains why firms with strong patent portfolios engage in widespread licensing. Indeed, since the 1990s, entire subindustries within semiconductors have been created and driven by the entry of so-called chipless firms, specialized design and technology firms that do not produce and that rely mainly or exclusively on licensing and royalties to appropriate the returns from their R&D investments.[17]

[16] See Barnett (2011a).
[17] See Barnett (2011a).

The Ricardian hypothesis also explains the evolution of horizontal and vertical specialization in the semiconductor industry. As Barnett (2011a) observes, patents allow firms to act as if free riding did not exist and enlarge the set of business models, strategies, and contracts that they can use to create and exploit competitive advantage. Since the 1950s semiconductor firms have specialized horizontally, giving rise over time to an increasing array of subindustries, most created by spinoffs; patents sustain horizontal specialization by resolving the tension between spinoffs and free riding. At the same time, semiconductor firms seldom integrate into the production of electronic products; patents sustain vertical separation by resolving Arrow's information paradox. Last, since the 1980s, semiconductor firms increasingly contract out manufacturing to foundries, chip manufacturers who neither design nor sell chips; patents allow foundries to commit not to free ride, despite the fact that the same technological breakthroughs that made specialization in manufacturing feasible also made it much easier to copy chip designs.

Finally, the Ricardian hypothesis explains how exceptionally fast rates of total factor productivity (TFP) growth in semiconductors, an economic free lunch, coexisted with protracted investments in R&D made in the expectation of profit. By preventing free riding, patents protect the Ricardian rents that remunerate investments in R&D. Then they facilitate practices that diffuse knowledge fast and for free and allow a large group of firms to access a common pool of knowledge.

An ideal test of the Ricardian hypothesis and the role of patents would be to estimate a structural equilibrium model of the semiconductor industry that replicates its entire history. The researcher would then take away patents (or weaken or strengthen them as desired), compute again the industry's equilibrium, and quantify the impact of that change on the outcome variables of interest, such as the rate of change of the capacity, speed, and quality-adjusted prices of chips. The problem is that computing a structural model that captures change over time is so difficult that it is almost never done. As Sutton (1991, 2001) pointed out, the equilibrium of an industry depends on subtle details of its game tree and firms' strategies, which many times are difficult to observe, let alone measure with the precision that structural models require. Perhaps more fundamentally, firms' strategies, business models and contracts, industry structure, and the rate of innovation coevolve over time; they are the emergent outcome of a complex system characterized by exogenous variables that are non-additive, and endogenous variables that feed back on one another.[18] A researcher cannot fully specify such a model.

[18] A phenomenon is emergent relative to an explanation if the explanation is not sufficient. See Gordon (2010, p. 20).

Another test of the Ricardian hypothesis would exploit an exogenous shock to patent strength. The researcher would then estimate the marginal effect of this shock on the outcome variables across subindustries. This approach requires, however, a model in which the strength of patents and the outcome variable are separable from the rest of the system that generates fast and inexpensive semiconductors. The problem is that firm strategies, business models, technological opportunities, and industry structure are affected by many exogenous variables other than patent strength, and they interact with one another and the strengths of patents over time. Satisfying the ceteris paribus condition in the semiconductor industry is very difficult.

The test I employ in this chapter is an historical study that exploits the quasi-experiments created by exogenous technology shocks. In the early days of an industry that emerges to exploit a significant technological opportunity, or right after a breakthrough that creates a new subindustry, firms spend some time out of equilibrium.[19] Then, firms' actions are out-of-equilibrium best responses, and one can test whether these actions are those predicted by the theory. The Ricardian hypothesis predicts that in the early days of a subindustry, firms will patent and then pick actions as if free riding did not threaten their competitive advantage. Later, I will repeatedly use this method to test the Ricardian hypothesis. Before doing that, I briefly review the data on patenting in the semiconductor industry.

Patenting in the Semiconductor Industry

The semiconductor industry emerged after the invention of the transistor in 1947. The number of patents granted every year by the United States Patent and Trademark Office (USPTO) grew from 60 in 1952, to about 300 during early 1960s, and about 1,500 during the early 1970s.[20] Then, according to Figure 1.3, which shows three-year moving averages of the number of semiconductor patents granted since 1976, around 1,000 patents were granted every year until the mid-1980s. Since the 1980s the number grew fast, reaching roughly 10,000 patents per year in 2000, and roughly 20,000 patents per year in 2017. Thus, in

[19] Industries and subindustries are defined by the range of products that a given group of firms manufacture (for example the semiconductor industry). A market, on the other hand, is defined by a break in the chain of substitution. For example, memory chips cannot substitute for processors—they are in different submarkets. Similarly, firms that specialize in memory tend not to produce processors—memory and processors are different subindustries. See Sutton (2001, especially pp. 14 and 15; Klepper and Thomson 2006).

[20] See Tilton (1971, table 4.2) and Levin (1982, table 2.9). Data on patenting in the semiconductor industry in the 1950s and 1960s is not fully comparable with data since 1976 because classifications changed over time.

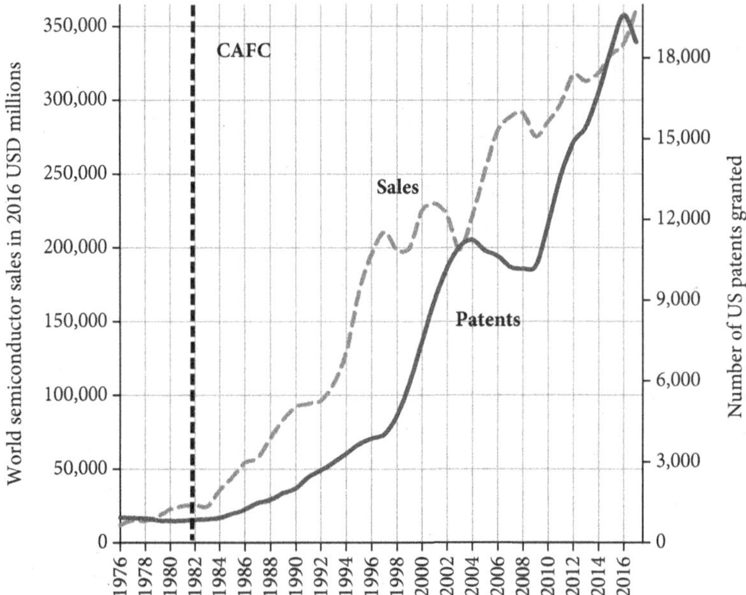

Figure 1.3 Three-year moving averages of the number of patents granted each year in the United States in the WIPO semiconductor category; worldwide semiconductor sales, in 2016 dollars; and the date of CAFC's inception, 1982.
Sources: Patents: USPTO, PatentsView database. WIPO classification, Electrical Engineering, Semiconductors (id 8). Downloaded from https://www.patentsview.org/download/.
Sales: Semiconductor Industry Association, *Historical Billing Reports, 1976–2017*. Downloaded from https://www.semiconductors.org/resources/.

the four decades between 1976 and 2017 the number of semiconductor patents granted grew on average by 7 percent per year and multiplied 20 times.[21]

Without attempting a causal explanation, I note two associations. One appears in Figure 1.3, which also shows the size of the industry, as measured by worldwide semiconductor sales. It can be seen that the number of granted patents follows sales growth with a lag.[22] Thus, the larger the industry, the more semiconductor firms patent.[23] Next, Figure 1.4 shows the share of electronics patenting in utility patenting. The share of semiconductor patents grew from slightly less than 1 percent in the 1960s to 6–7 percent in the 1990s

[21] I made the calculations with USTPO data with WIPO classification. The NBER classification, which the USPTO discontinued in 2015, gives very similar results. For additional analysis, see Tamme et al. (2013).

[22] As Barnett (2020b) notes, Even though patents issued by the USPTO do not have extraterritorial force, owners of US patents can seek "exclusion orders" from the International Trade Commission to block the importation of infringing goods that are made outside the United States.

[23] I measure the size of the market with world sales because most semiconductor firms sell into the world market. Measuring activity with world sales is the practice of the industry.

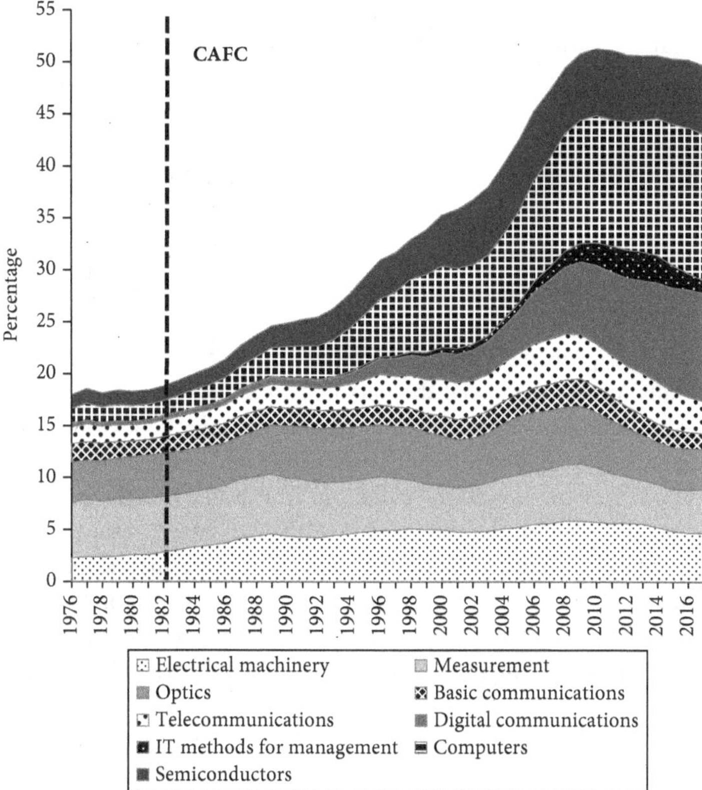

Figure 1.4 Three-year moving averages of the share of electronic patents in all utility patents granted; and the date of CAFC's inception, 1982.

Sources: USPTO, PatentsView database. WIPO classification, Electrical engineering: Electrical machinery (id 1); Telecommunications (id 3); Digital communications (id 4); Basic communications (id 5); Computers (id 6); IT methods for management (id 7); Semiconductors (id 8); Instruments: Optics (id 9); Measurement (id 10). Downloaded from https://www.patentsview.org/download/

and remained steady since then. Moreover, Figure 1.3 shows that the growth of semiconductor patenting coincided with the growth of patenting in digital electronic products.

The surge in patenting since the 1980s is part of the patent paradox. In two influential papers, Bronwyn Hall and Rosemarie Ziedonis reported that capital intensive firms increased their propensity to patent after the creation of the CAFC in 1982, which strengthened patent rights.[24] They argued

[24] See Hall and Ziedonis (2001) and Ziedonis and Hall (2001). They also noted that part of the surge in patenting came from design firms that entered the industry after 1982. On patenting in semiconductors and capital intensity se also Galasso (2012).

that capital intensive firms patented more after CAFC to defend themselves against lawsuits whose aim was to hold them up by threatening to shut down production with injunctions. According to their interviews with industry participants, these lawsuits seemed to be more likely after the creation of the CAFC in 1982.[25] A firm with a large patent portfolio could countersue, thus making lawsuits less likely.[26] Defensive patenting would therefore explain the timing and the magnitude of the surge in patenting in the 1980s which is apparent in Figures 1.1 and 1.2.

Nevertheless, the association between patenting and market size revealed by Figure 1.3 suggests that the surge in patenting may be also be the consequence of a growing market for electronic devices. For example, in the early 1980s Apple introduced the personal computer and IBM established a standard that led to its mass diffusion. Moreover, semiconductors began to be used in many new applications like automobiles and embedded systems. Also, according to Katznelson (2007), patenting accelerated because protracted innovation shortened product life cycles. And, as Figure 1.4 shows, patenting in all digital electronics surged after 1980. Thus, the increase in patenting in semiconductors is also a consequence of the spread of consumer and industrial electronics. While it is tempting to see the creation of the CAFC as a quasi-natural experiment, in the 1980s and after everything else was not constant.

Patents in the Semiconductor Industry

Patents and Free Riding

A claim of this chapter is that the most important function of patents in the semiconductor industry is to weaken business models based on copying and implementing the ideas and products created by the investments of others.

Figure 1.5, adapted from Mead (1979, Figure 5), is useful to see why copying and free riding are relevant threats to semiconductor firms. The horizontal axis graphs the stages of the production of an integrated circuit—product conception, circuit design, layout, photomask generation, and wafer fabrication.[27] The

[25] See Ziedonis and Hall (2001, pp. 142, 146). From their interviews with semiconductor firms they concluded that attitudes towards patenting were changed by Texas Instrument's aggressive enforcement of its patents in the 1980s, and by the injunction that Polaroid won over Eastman Kodak in 1986, which forced Kodak to exit the instant camera market. For a description of these cases see Warshofsky (1994).

[26] See Hall and Ziedonis (2001, p. 104) and Ziedonis and Hall (2001, pp. 137, 142, 146).

[27] A photomask is a negative that allows light to shine through and chemically print the integrated circuit on the wafer. A wafer is a slice of silicon on which many integrated circuits are printed.

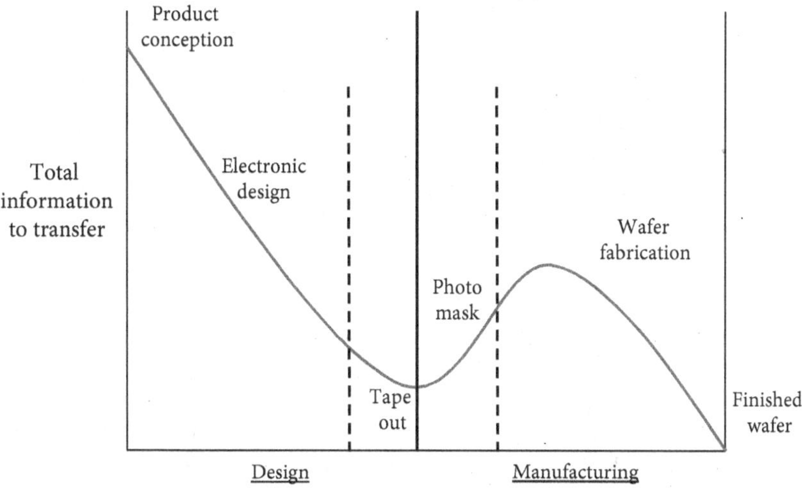

Figure 1.5 Production stages of a semiconductor device from product conception to manufacture of the final chip. The horizontal axis shows the progression overtime. The vertical axis shows the amount of information and knowledge that must be transferred from one group of individuals to the next group of individuals in charge of the next step, at each stage of the process.
Source: Author, adapted from Mead (1979)

vertical axis graphs the amount of information possessed by the group of individuals in charge of that part of the process.

A product's life begins when skilled individuals conceive it within the semiconductor firm. At this stage the information about the future product and integrated circuit resides in these individuals and, as Mead (1979) points out, transferring it to another group of individuals is difficult, because it requires knowledge of the customer base, the economics of the business, the skills of the personnel in the company, cost constraints, timing constraints, and so on.

As design proceeds, the integrated circuit is still a sketch, which lacks information about a myriad of special requirements.[28] Thus, considerable information still resides in the group of individuals working on the project. The firm can protect part of the information with confidentiality agreements and trade secrets. But the firm is vulnerable to individuals leaving to join another firm or a startup, in part because there is a lot of information that is difficult to transfer. At this stage patent protection is of little use—the invention is not easy to describe.

[28] Mead (1979, p. 23).

At some point, however, the design coalesces into a circuit layout that implements the electronic functions that the integrated circuit must perform and defines the product that the firm will sell. A hardware description language (HDL) turns the layout into a program stored in a file—the so-called tape out—which can be transferred to a manufacturing plant.[29] The manufacturing plant then uses the tape out to produce the photomask of the integrated circuit. At this point, it would be easy for the manufacturer to copy the design and layout of the integrated circuit, unless patents protect its functionality.

To produce the integrated circuit, the manufacturing plant must generate the photomask and then use it to print the circuit on the wafer. Both the photomask and manufacturing require information that depends upon the details of the wafer fabrication process. Some of that information resides in the group of individuals working in the manufacturing plant. Indeed, historically, manufacturing of semiconductors has relied on trade secrets, while the equipment and materials are protected by patents. At the end of the process, however, after the integrated circuit is manufactured and in the market, others can reverse engineer and copy, but patents protect the particular way of achieving the device's electronic functionality.[30]

Figure 1.5, in short, shows that a semiconductor firm is vulnerable to free riding at several parts of the design and production process. It follows that the free riding business model—the systematic exploitation of other people's ideas and products for commercial gain—is technically feasible. The challenge facing semiconductor firms was to reduce the returns to this business model.

Patents in the Early Decades of the Industry

I will now examine the first out-of-equilibrium episode, the creation of the industry after the invention of the transistor, which was followed a decade later with the emergence of subindustries after the invention of the integrated circuit and the planar printing process. I make two points. First, very soon the horizontal structure of the industry coalesced into what seems to be its efficient configuration, largely ignoring free riding. Second, without patents, it would not have been possible to prevent free riding and industry structure would have been different and less efficient.

[29] In the early 1980s the layout was saved on a magnetic tape; hence the term tape out. Before electronic design, circuits were drawn by hand.

[30] On reverse engineering see Torrance and James (2011). Specialists in reverse engineering like Chipworks and Semiconductor Insights sell reverse engineering services. One of the uses of reverse engineering is to detect patent infringement.

More than thirty years after the invention of the transistor, famed Caltech engineering professor Carver Mead (1979, p. 22) described the way in which the structure of the semiconductor industry had evolved:

> Historically, innovation in the [semiconductor] industry has been spearheaded by small start-up firms and later taken up by large existing organizations. It is significant that the major suppliers of vacuum tubes did not become the major suppliers of transistors. The major suppliers of discrete transistors did not give us semiconductor memories. More recently, companies dominant in the semiconductor memory business did not bring us the multiplexed address random access memory. The microprocessor did not come from mainframe or minicomputer firms. Each of these innovations was brought to market fruition by a small start-up firm which rapidly gained market share by virtue of its innovation.

The pattern described by Mead has not changed. Thus, all through the industry's history, semiconductor firms have specialized horizontally, giving rise to an increasing array of subindustries, most created by a technological breakthrough. The observed outcome at the industry level is the proliferation of horizontally differentiated, and largely independent, subindustries, each populated by a handful of firms. At the same time, until recently semiconductor firms seldom integrated into the production of electronic products or systems.[31]

Patents and Horizontal Specialization

The initial technological shock in the semiconductor industry was the invention of the germanium point-contact transistor at AT&T's Bell Labs.[32] While the potential applications of semiconductor technology were unknown at the time, the first transistor patent was broad. As Golding (1972, p. 286) points out, it covered both the transistor effect in general (thus any transistor, however made) and the use of any transistor in a circuit (thus any electrical circuit containing a transistor). So any manufacturer of transistors, and any user of transistors in any device, infringed AT&T's patent and was compelled to ask for a license.[33] Yet, as it had done with other inventions, Bell Labs diffused transistor technology through publication, symposia, visits to Bell Labs, and the granting licenses to all who requested one with the payment of a 2 percent royalty on sales.[34]

[31] This may be changing as large users of AI chips like Google and Amazon design them, tailor made for their business needs.

[32] See Golding (1972), Tilton (1971), and Braun and Macdonald (1982).

[33] During the 1950s and 1960s Bell Labs continued to develop key semiconductor technologies. See Tilton (1971) and Braun and Macdonald (1982).

[34] Western Electric, a subsidiary of AT&T which was in charge of licensing, set the royalty at 5 percent in 1950, and reduced it to 2 percent in 1953. Nobody ever paid the 5 percent royalty, however, because the first commercially viable transistor became available only in 1954, manufactured by

Some argue that AT&T granted non-exclusive licenses to appease the Department of Justice. In 1956, after nearly eight years of litigation, the Department of Justice compelled AT&T to grant royalty-free, non-discriminatory licenses to all its existing patents to any interested US firm and to license all future patents at reasonable rates. AT&Ts licensing policy is thus sometimes explained as an attempt to preempt the regulator (Gertner 2012, p. 111), or to avoid calling attention to the monopoly granted by the transistor patent (Mowery 2011).[35] A second explanation is that AT&T realized early on that replacing vacuum valves in telephone networks would require protracted and substantial investments in R&D that no single organization could manage. Langlois and Steinmueller (1999) argue that AT&T bet that the spillover benefits to telephony from others' innovations would outweigh the forgone revenues of proprietary development.[36] Indeed, Grindley and Teece (1997, p. 5) argue that the 1956 consent decree did little more than put AT&T's de facto policy in writing.

Whatever the explanation, the fast diffusion of AT&T's knowledge accelerated the development of semiconductor technology.[37] Commercial production of transistors began in 1951. By 1953, 13 firms were manufacturing transistors in the United States, and the number of manufacturers in developed economies had risen to 74 by the end of the 1950s.[38] Entrants were not just users of AT&Ts technology. On the contrary, their innovations made semiconductors viable commercial products. For example, in 1954 Texas Instruments, a new manufacturer of electronic components, produced the first silicon transistor and opened the military market.[39] In 1959 Texas Instruments and Fairchild independently invented the integrated circuit, and in 1960 Fairchild introduced the planar process, which allowed integrated circuits to be chemically printed instead of manually assembled.

Established manufacturers of vacuum tubes, such as Sylvania, Philco, and General Electric, also entered the semiconductor business, but none succeeded

Texas Instruments. Golding (1972, section. 9.3.4) describes Western Electric's licensing policy in the 1950s and 1960s. See also Barnett (2011a, pp. 1870–72).

[35] See also Watzinger et al. (2020) and Barnett's chapter in this volume.

[36] See Sparks (1972), Braun and Macdonald (1982, p. 54) and Levin (1982, pp. 76–77).

[37] Many years later Gordon Moore would designate a symposium organized by Bell Labs, which took place in September 1951 and was attended by 426 individuals from government agencies, educational institutions, and industrial organizations the true birth of the industry, because many of the attendees would later be founders of the main semiconductor companies (see Moore and Davis, 2004). In April 1952 a symposium for industry was attended by 25 US and 10 foreign companies; and in January 1956, yet another symposium was attended by 41 US and 31 foreign companies (see Golding 1972, table 9.3).

[38] These were: 32 in the United States, 16 in Great Britain, 9 in France, 6 in Germany and 11 in Japan. See Tilton (1971).

[39] The silicon transistor, which Texas Instrument invented, extended the semiconductor market to military applications because it raised the temperature that semiconductor devices could bear and made them viable in missiles.

in becoming a leading semiconductor manufacturer, and most exited the industry in the 1960s. On the contrary, successful firms were small entrants, each specialized a in a narrow set of devices designed to perform a particular function, often for a particular electronic product.

In part, this pattern reflected the structure of the demand for semiconductors. As Sutton (2001, p. 358) pointed out, semiconductor devices are differentiated on the demand side by the function they perform (for example memory, storage, processing, amplification), and by the end product that uses them (for example personal computers, servers, smartphones, embedded control systems). Thus, semiconductor devices split into submarkets, and some are further fragmented into an array of specialized products.[40] But more important, on the supply side, semiconductor firms became focused specialists, not multiproduct firms. Indeed, since the 1950s technological progress in semiconductors has been driven by innovations introduced by specialized startups, many spinning off from existing firms.

The constant flow of new specialized firms reflects the fact that developing each technological opportunity into a product requires organizational focus. According to Gordon Moore:

> Ultimately, both the advantage and the challenge of a start-up company is the ability to focus all energies on realizing the commercial possibilities of whatever product the company sees as important. Any established company has other things to maintain and can only devote a small portion of total available energy to a particular new enterprise. This lack of focus does not usually exist in a start-up. There are no distractions from existing product lines. Often, a start-up will have a much more powerfully capable team focused in an area than a big company can muster, as a larger company has many other positions in which it will want to employ its better people. Start-ups can also take more risk than can an established firm. There is no reputation to protect. This can speed products to market without all the precautions taken by the bigger, better-established firm. Running with the ideas that big companies can only lope along with has come to be the acknowledged role of the spin-off or start-up.[41]

An implication is that diseconomies of scope hamper horizontally integrated firms. By contrast, a specialized firm can focus and is more efficient and effective at exploiting technological and business opportunities.[42]

[40] See also Mead (1979).

[41] Moore and Davis (2004).

[42] A regularity in the semiconductor industry is that specialized and focused firms tend to do better. See Rhines (2019, ch. 8).

A second characteristic of the semiconductor industry, which also emerged during its first decade, is that the skilled individuals who create specialized firms—electrical engineers, physicists, chemists and, since the 1980s, computer scientists—usually get their ideas while working for an employer and then leave to pursue them. This is a natural consequence of the fact that semiconductor firms exploit a colossal technological opportunity opened by the invention of the transistor, but it creates a tension. On the one hand, these skilled individuals tend to come up with more ideas than a single organization can handle, and it is efficient for them to leave and start their own specialized firms.[43] On the other hand, startups may copy the ideas and products of their former employer, which would make R&D investments not viable.

Patents resolve this tension. The employer can enforce them when individuals free ride but let them go when startups develop a different market opportunity. Patents, therefore, allow firms discretion to decide when to enforce intellectual property rights and when to let employees go, thus sustaining the mechanics of horizontal specialization in the semiconductor industry. Note that preventing free riding, while important, does not generate revenues directly, and it is unsurprising that such a role of patents appeared neither in the Yale survey nor in the Carnegie Mellon survey.

Second Sourcing

Integrated circuits followed Moore's Law and improved quickly during the 1960s and 1970s, but system developers (firms that develop electronic products) adopted them at a slow pace. During the 1950s and 1960s and even into the 1970s, most system developers made their own proprietary circuits by buying vacuum tubes and transistors and wiring them.[44] To convince a system developer to switch to an integrated circuit, the semiconductor firm had to provide better and reliable electronic performance at lower prices. Nevertheless, the understanding of semiconductor materials and manufacturing processes was imperfect. Low and variable yields were a problem, and that made supply unreliable.[45] System developers increased reliability by forcing semiconductor manufacturers to licence their patents and transfer know-how and trade secrets to a second manufacturer, which would be able to produce the same product. This practice became known as second-sourcing.

[43] Moore and Davis (2004). See also Saxenian (1996) and Golman and Klepper (2016).

[44] Technical progress in vacuum tubes continued, and semiconductor devices overtook them in sales only in the late 1960s.

[45] "Yield" is the fraction of integrated circuits printed in a wafer that does not have defects and can perform reliably. In the 1960s yields were around 20 percent—80 percent of all printed integrated circuits were discarded. It took decades and protracted technical progress in manufacturing equipment and materials to increase yields to the current 90 percent.

Firms that specialized in second sourcing emerged as early as the 1960s.[46] Second sourcing became a means for smaller firms to get a toe-hold in the industry: they would grant a second source license to a major semiconductor manufacturer to prove that they had a workable product. Sometimes second sourcers just copied the original device, without asking for a license. Nevertheless, patents limited copying, because the firms that owned the designs filed lawsuits against the free-riders (Swann 1987).[47] Patents thus resolved the tension between reliability of supply and free riding, allowed the industry to provide reliability more efficiently, and fostered horizontal specialization.

It is clear that second sourcing did not generate revenues directly. Moreover, while patent protection was important for the licensor, it was not important for the licensee. Thus, surely semiconductor firms that specialized in second sourcing did not deem patents important revenue generators, nor did the firms that granted second sourcing licenses. Again, it is unsurprising that this role of patents appeared neither in the Yale nor in the Carnegie Mellon surveys.

Technical Marketing and Arrow's Information Paradox

Firms and consumers do not demand semiconductor devices but products that deliver something they care about—music, information to run a business, or the control of an industrial process. Different applications require different designs. For example, the design of a microprocessor that powers a laptop is different from the design of a microprocessor that makes a phone work. Thus, there is a tight link between chip design and the consumer electronics industry. Yet with few exceptions, semiconductor firms do not integrate into the manufacturing of electronic products. Indeed, over time many notorious attempts to do so ended in commercial disaster, suggesting that vertical integration into the manufacture of electronic devices is an unsustainable business model. Many anecdotes suggest that designing, producing, and delivering semiconductor devices is very different from divining consumer tastes.

This poses a challenge: on the one hand, a semiconductor firm must produce a device suitable for the electronic product it powers. At the same time, the semiconductor firm cannot learn from consumers directly. The solution is technical marketing. Since the industry's inception semiconductor firms have announced their innovations in trade conferences and explained to system firms how their devices work and the functionalities they can expect. Nevertheless, technical marketing is vulnerable to Arrow's information paradox. By patenting their devices, however, semiconductor firms avoid the paradox. Thus, as Barnett

[46] See Webbink (1977), Swann (1985; 1987), and Sutton (2001).

[47] A few semiconductor firms even tolerated some unauthorized second sourcing as a means of providing insurance against supply shortages.

(2011a) argues, patents support commercialization and, moreover, facilitate vertical specialization.[48]

Like spinoffs and second sourcing, technical marketing emerged while the industry was out of equilibrium and firms could have chosen to vertically integrate into producing electronic products to prevent free riding. Instead, they acted as if Arrow's information paradox did not exist. Like spinoffs and second sourcing, overcoming free riding in technical marketing does not generate revenues directly. Such roles of patents will likely be overlooked in surveys like Yale's or Carnegie Mellon's.

Patents and the Vertical Organization of the Semiconductor Industry

For more than 70 years the vertical structure of the semiconductor industry has protractedly evolved toward vertical specialization. Initially, semiconductor firms were integrated from product conception, design, and equipment manufacturing to manufacturing, marketing, and sales. Specialized equipment and materials manufacturers emerged in the 1960s, but during the first three decades of the industry, and until the early 1980, semiconductor firms remained vertically integrated, each designing, manufacturing, and selling its devices.[49]

Today few vertically integrated semiconductor firms remain.[50] They were substituted by three types of firms. First, specialized chip manufacturers called foundries manufacture most semiconductor devices under contract. They own fabrication plants but neither design nor sell chips,[51] Second, chipless firms, which do not sell chips, specialize in designing specialized IP blocks or design modules, which they licence for royalty revenue.[52] Third, fabless semiconductor firms, which do not own fabrication plants, license IP blocks to design chips, outsource manufacturing to foundries, and then sell.[53] For example, more than 90 percent of the smartphones sold each year run a processor that uses ARM's RISC architecture. ARM, a chipless firm, only licenses for a modest royalty the designs that embed the technology; it neither manufactures processors, nor sells them.

48 The point has also been made by Kitch (1977), and Kieff (2001; 2005).

49 On the vertical separation of equipment manufacturers see Pillai (2017).

50 They are called IDMs, for integrated device manufacturers.

51 Most plants are located in Taiwan and Singapore. See Macher, Mowery, and Di Minin (2007) and Barnett (2011a).

52 An IP block is a design that can be inserted into a larger chip. It saves time and expense when designing chops. See Dibiaggio (2007). On IP blocks see Nenni and McLellan (2014). On design firms see Macher, Mowery, and Hodges (1998; 1999) and Macher, Mowery, and Simcoe (2002).

53 Firms that design and sell semiconductor devices but do not manufacture them are called fabless, because they do not own a fabrication plant. See Barnett (2011a), Kumar (2008), Monteverde (1995), Macher and Mowery (2004), Nenni and McLellan (2014), Linden and Somaya (2003).

Next, I show that protracted vertical separation and specialization in the semiconductor industry emerged in the early 1980s to conciliate two different technological and economic trends that pulled scale in opposite directions. On the one hand, the electronic design of chips (called EDA, for electronic design automation), which appeared in the late 1970s, reduced the efficient scale of design and allowed for the electronic transfer of chip designs. On the other hand, continual improvements in speed and miniaturization increased the efficient size of fabrication plants.[54] I will argue that patents allowed these trends to foster vertical specialization by sustaining trade in technology, enabling specialized manufacturers to credibly commit to not copying the semiconductor devices they manufactured. Had there not been patents, semiconductor firms would have remained vertically integrated, and horizontal structure would have been determined by the efficient scale of manufacturing.

Technological Change and Efficient Scale

In 1979 Carver Mead and Lynn Conway published *Introduction to VLSI Systems*, which systematized hardware-description languages (HDLs).[55] An HDL is a specialized language to formally describe electronic circuits and their behavior. A chip described with an HDL can be analyzed and simulated before it is manufactured, and the circuit's description and specifications are written into a data file. When HDLs were introduced in the late 1970s, they made design rules less dependent on the specifics of the manufacturing process and enabled designers to transmit the design to the fabrication plant electronically.[56] Shortly thereafter, Mead and David Johannsen designed the first compiler, which took the designer's specifications and automatically generated the layout of the integrated circuit. This made the widespread diffusion of EDA possible.[57] Designs no longer had to be drawn by hand; from then on, they would be coded.

EDA spread very fast.[58] In 1981, Mead, Johannsen, Edmund K. Cheng and others formed Silicon Compilers. Then, three startups—Daisy, Valid Logic Systems, and Mentor Graphics—spun off from manufacturers like Intel and Hewlett Packard and specialized in developing and commercializing EDA hardware and software. Soon there were several differentiated specialists selling EDA tools. In parallel, specialized design firms emerged and used EDA tools, among

[54] See also Arora, Fosfuri, and Gambardella (2004, ch. 3, section 5).

[55] VLSI means very large-scale integration, a rather imprecise way of describing the complexity of an integrated circuit. It is the continuation of SSI (small), MSI (medium), LSI (large), but comes before ULSI (ultra large).

[56] For a short history, see Casalle-Rossi (2014).

[57] IBM pioneered EADs (also called computer-aided design or CAD) in the late 1950s, but these techniques were not commercially viable until around 1980 because the cost of computing time was too high.

[58] On the evolution of the EDA subindustry, see Rhines (2019, ch. 7).

them, VLSI Technology (founded in 1979) and LSI Logic (founded in 1981).[59] According to Macher, Mowery, and Hodges (1998), by the mid-1990s there were about 500 design firms around the world, around 300 of them located in the United States.

A direct consequence of HDLs and EDA was the emergence of fabless semiconductor firms. As Mead (1979) explained, before HDLs and EDA the transfer from design to manufacturing required the active participation of the design team, who needed a thorough understanding of manufacturing. By contrast, as can be seen in Figure 1.5, the transfer between layout and pattern generation now became the point of minimum information—that point at which direct communication between two teams became almost redundant. Mead (1979) explains why:

> The minimum in information required to transfer between layout and pattern generation is no accident. This is a very special point in the evolution of a product. It is the end of the design process and the beginning of a pattern replication process. Everything to the left of that point has been involved with the specifics of a given product. Every action to the right of that line does not depend upon the specific product, but only upon the process by which the product will be replicated.

Fabless firms emerged because of their economics. While HDLs and EDA reduced the efficient scale of design, increasing miniaturization of chips required larger fabrication plants.[60] Mead (1979) anticipated the change in vertical structure that the new design techniques would cause:

> If innovation by a myriad of small groups and individuals is to carry us into the VLSI revolution, we must not expect these groups and individuals to provide their own fabrication facilities. The level of innovation required can be achieved only if fabrication is provided as a service by a few well capitalized firms. . . . What is needed is a clean, standard interface between a multitude

[59] Hall and Ziedonis (2001) reported significant entry of specialized design firms after 1982. Nevertheless, a special report in *Businessweek* shows that by the end of 1981 there had been already significant entry (see, The '80s Look in Chips: Custom, not Standard, January 18, 1982). See also Dorfman (1987, p. 211).

[60] The regularity became known as Rock's Law: the investment cost of a state-of-the-art fabrication plant doubles every four years. Nevertheless, this formulation is a bit misleading because it suggests that chips became more expensive to manufacture over time. Indeed, the relevant trend is the protracted increase of the throughput produced by an efficient fabrication plant over its useful life, which requires ever increasing production volumes per plant and investment outlies. The cost of a square inch of silicon, by contrast, remained roughly constant for almost 70 years. Thus the cost per transistor fell, because every two years the number of transistors per square inch of silicon doubled.

of small diverse VLSI design groups and a few state-of-the-art fabrication suppliers.

During the first half of the 1980s there were no specialized chip manufacturing firms. Instead, vertically integrated manufacturers sold manufacturing services to design firms as a side business, mainly to occupy spare capacity. But in 1987 the Taiwanese government and Phillips created the Taiwan Semiconductor Manufacturing Co. (TSMC). TSMC was followed in 1994 by United Microelectronics Corp (UMC), also a Taiwanese company, which focused on contract manufacturing.[61]

The specialized design firm, which neither manufactures nor sells semiconductor devices, also emerged with HDLs and EDA. These "chipless" firms make economic sense because as speed and miniaturization increased, chips became so complex that nobody could design them from scratch.[62] Chipless firms specialize in designing blocks or modules (the so-called IP cores) that are put together by fabless semiconductor firms to create a single integrated circuit, or system-on-a-chip (SoC), which embed an entire system in one chip. Chipless firms allowed some manufacturers of electronic products to design their own devices. These firms designed their chips with IP cores they licensed from chipless firms and then contracted out the production of the chips to foundries.

Over time the industry became characterized by even deeper specialization driven by the growth of mobile telephony. SoCs became even more complex, as manufacturers of electronic devices demanded complete functional blocks—for example processors, radios, and so on—and firms that specialize in entire blocks became important. For example, one IP-core designer, ARM, developed the architecture that is now used to manufacture the microprocessors that power most smartphones and tablets. Each microprocessor that uses ARM's design pays a royalty.

The Challenges that Patents Overcame: Credibility and Compensation

The vertically separated business model must overcome two challenges. One is preventing specialized fabrication plants from copying and reselling designs and semiconductor devices. Because HDLs and EDA made electronic transfers of designs possible, they potentially worsened the free riding problem. Patents protect the proprietary designs of fabless and chipless firms, thus allowing the industry to efficiently separate manufacturing from design. Vertical separation would have been harder had there been no patents, because specialization in manufacturing would have been less credible.

[61] See Lammers (2015).

[62] See Linden and Somaya (2003) and Arora, Fosfuri, and Gambardella (2004).

The second challenge is to ensure that chipless design firms get paid. The link between patents and revenue generation is direct, because royalties have been the main compensation of chipless firms since the 1980s.[63] For example, the empirical results reported in Hall and Ziedonis (2001) suggest that design firms relied on patents from the very beginning of HDLs and EDA. Indeed, the design firms that they interviewed explained that they protected themselves from copiers by patenting. When asked what would be the effect of abolishing the patent system, they answered that it would chill innovation and entry. Design firms were five times more likely to patent than the rest of the semiconductor firms, ceteris paribus.

Hall and Ziedonis (2001) also argue that the entry of specialized design firms since the 1980s may have been the consequence of the creation of CAFC in 1982. An empirical test of this claim would have difficulty in disentangling its effect from the impact of Carver Mead and Lynn Conway's textbook and the development of HDLs and EDA, which happened at the same time. It is likely that both developments were complements: specialization and entry into design wrought by HDLs, and EDA were supported by stronger patents rights—perhaps a happy coincidence. It is not likely, however, that CAFC was pivotal for the emergence of specialized design firms; as seen, patents had been used in the industry since the 1950s. And it is implausible that CAFC "caused" the emergence of design firms in any meaningful sense. Such an hypothesis would ignore the fundamental technological advances ushered by HDLs and EDA.

Whatever the impact of CAFC, patents allowed firms to pick the lowest-cost organizational form to deliver semiconductor devices.[64] Had there been no patents, vertical specialization would not have been sustainable, and the efficient scale of manufacturing would have driven the size and scope of semiconductor firms.[65]

Both the Yale and the Carnegie Mellon survey missed the emergence of fabless and chipless semiconductor firms and the role that patents played in their business models. As a matter of timing, the Yale survey, taken in 1983, would at best have captured the initial steps of fledging subindustries. As a matter of survey

[63] See Anand and Galetovic (2000a) who model how strong patent rights enable small firms to overcome holdup, specialize in R&D, and receive venture capital financing.

[64] See Barnett (2011a).

[65] Sometimes the Semiconductor Chip Protection Act of 1984 is credited with protecting proprietary designs from copy. Before 1984, it was not necessarily illegal to copy a design and produce a competing product (though the function of the design may have been protected by a patent). In the early eighties Intel, along with the newly formed Semiconductor Industry Association (SIA), lobbied for legislation whose aim was to prevent copying by foreign manufacturers.

Nevertheless, this new type of intellectual property seems to have been of little consequence, perhaps because soon after the act was passed integrated circuits became too complex for a blunt copy to be useful. In the 33 years since enactment, there have only been a handful of cases that even mentioned the Act (Robert Taylor, personal communication).

design, both concentrated on large firms and excluded small design firms. And as a matter of content, both surveys excluded too many roles that patents play. It is unlikely, for example, that a foundry, which patents mainly processes, would have given patents a prominent role in revenue generation.

Patents as Revenue Generators

The patent paradox stems from semiconductor firms claiming that patents were not important revenue generators. This section shows that contrary to the belief that sustains the paradox, semiconductor firms have used patents to generate revenues.

Licensing, Royalties, and the Market for Technology

The defensive hypothesis cannot explain why several semiconductor firms with strong patent portfolios have generated considerable royalty revenues through licensing since the beginning of the industry.

Fairchild, for example, who owned patents on the planar process and the integrated circuit, had about 50 licensees in 1973. It charged a royalty in the 4–6 percent range of final sales and through Nippon Electric, licensed its patents to Japanese firms for a royalty equal to 4.5 percent of sales.[66] Similarly, in 1974 AT&T, through its subsidiary Western Electric, maintained 179 semiconductor licenses charging a maximum royalty of 2.5 percent of sales. Texas Instruments began seeking licensees in 1968, reportedly asking for a 4 percent royalty, and used its patents on the integrated circuit to force MITI to allow its entry into the Japanese market.[67] Altogether during the 1970s Japanese firms paid about 10 percent of their semiconductor sales in royalties to American firms.[68]

Until the 1980s only those firms with the largest patent portfolios found it worthwhile to incur the expenses necessary to seek licensees and charge royalties. Figure 1.3 suggests that the constraint was a small semiconductor market, which limited potential royalties. It is probably no coincidence that firms with large patent portfolios like Texas Instruments, IBM, and Motorola expanded the breadth of their licensing programs as sales of semiconductors began to grow quickly during the 1980s.[69]

[66] See Finan (1975, ch. 4) and Tilton (1971). Note that 50 licensors is a significant number: according to Braun and Macdonald (1982, p. 150) in 1978 there were some 160 semiconductor companies worldwide.

[67] See Golding (1972, p. 299), and Warshofsky (1994).

[68] "IC makers Shaken at the Dawn of IC Liberalization: Request for 7 Billion Yen Subsidy and the Rush to Establish Their Own Technology for Mass Production," *Nihon Keizai Shimbun*, 18 April 1973, cited by Flamm (1996, pp. 71–72).

[69] See Warshofsky (1994), and Ziedonis (2003).

With the emergence of chipless firms and fabless semiconductor companies in the 1990s, licensing for royalties became a key part of many firms' business models. For example, this was the case as mobile telephony spread.[70] In 1988 Qualcomm developed code-division-multiplexing (CDMA), a technology that significantly increases bandwidth capacity, and eventually made the smartphone possible. CDMA is embedded in the baseband processor, the chip that manages the radio functions of a smartphone. Importantly, Qualcomm specialized in R&D, chip design, and licensing. Its processors and SoCs are manufactured by foundries under contract. Except for a short while, and then only to demonstrate that CDMA worked, Qualcomm did not manufacture phones or equipment.[71] Qualcomm was not an outlier. Rather, it became a model. Companies like Ericsson, Nokia, and Motorola initially focused both on technology development and phone manufacturing. These companies eventually abandoned the manufacture of phones, concentrating instead in technology development and licensing.[72]

The fact that many semiconductor firms rely on royalties and attain large shares in their submarket may lead one to think that their patents confer monopolies, as Arrow's hypothesis would suggest. It is possible to directly test this hypothesis. As has been well known since Spengler (1950), when manufacturers use an input in fixed proportions to produce a final good, any provider of an essential input with no substitutes can fully exploit monopoly power.[73] Therefore, a direct test of the Arrow hypothesis is to compare the observed royalties charged by specialists in an industry with those predicted by monopoly theory. Galetovic, Haber, and Zaretzki (2017) did just that in the smartphone value chain, which is a canonical case of an industry dependent on semiconductors. They show that in the 2016 world smartphone market the royalties paid to a single monopolist patent holder would have been roughly two-thirds of the average smartphone wholesale price, and the cumulative royalty paid to all patent holders, each acting as a monopolist, would have been roughly 80 percent of the average smartphone wholesale price. By contrast, the actual cumulative royalty in 2016 (not just to the firms that hold the relevant patents for semiconductors but to every patent holder in the industry) was only 3.4 percent.[74] This confirms that these chipless and fabless firms do not have monopoly power and that their profits are Ricardian rents.

[70] On licensing practices in semiconductors see Tamme et al. (2013).

[71] Qualcomm manufactured handsets and towers at the very beginning, but its aim was to show that CDMA technology worked. After many operators adopted CDMA, it withdrew from manufacturing.

[72] On patent licensing in the mobile phone industry see Blecker, Sánchez, and Stasik (2016) and Galetovic, Haber, and Zaretzki (2018).

[73] See also Tirole (1988, p. 174).

[74] See Galetovic, Haber, and Zaretzki (2018).

The Ricardian hypothesis, therefore, is consistent with the evidence about the smartphone industry. Without a property right, it would be much more difficult, perhaps impossible, to force downstream manufacturers to pay royalties.

Intel and Arrow's Hypothesis

A new subindustry emerged in the early 1980s as the personal computer spread, and it followed a different trajectory from the rest of the industry. Very soon, Intel's x86 family of CISC processors (central processing units or CPUs) became the de facto standard.[75] Intel, a vertically integrated firm, then used patents to prevent entry of competitors. Intel thus followed a strategy predicted by Arrow's hypothesis.

At the beginning of the subindustry, Intel was not the only designer and manufacturer of microprocessors. Circa 1981, five companies produced most designs: Intel, Motorola, Texas Instruments, Zilog, and Mostek. The organization of the industry changed when IBM chose Intel's 8086 processor for its personal computer in 1982. IBM's platform became the industry standard because, with the exception of Apple, all other PCs were manufactured to be compatible with it. By default, therefore, Intel's x86 instruction set (the set of instructions that software uses to command the CPU) also became the standard. Programmers wrote software that worked with Intel's instruction set, because that is what powered the industry standard PC platform. Users demanded Intel-powered computers because they ran software applications that had been designed to that standard. Thus, soon Intel dominated the market for PC CPUs. That process would be repeated in the 1990s, when Intel's x86 instruction set became the standard in server processors, and yet again in the early 2000s when Intel's x86 instruction set became the standard in in high-performance computers.

A standard need not concentrate production in a single firm, however. The owner of the technology can license it in exchange for a royalty, as, for example, ARM or Qualcomm chose to do. Or the standard may be open and royalty free, in which case nobody charges for using it. Intel, however, chose neither to license nor to allow competitors to freely use its instruction set. Rather, Intel decided to use the roughly 1,600 patents on its instruction set in order to prevent entry into CPU manufacturing.[76] As Intel explains it and Arrow's hypothesis would predict:

[75] There are two families of processors, CISC (complex instruction set computer) and RISC (reduced instruction set computer). CISC works with complex, more general instructions, which require more power to be processed. CISC CPUs are used in personal computers, laptops, and data centers. RISC instructions, by contrast, are simpler and use less power, and are used in portable devices, due to their power efficiency.

[76] See Rodgers and Uhlig (2017). At the time of writing, Rodgers was Intel's chief counsel.

> Intel carefully protects its x86 innovations, and we do not widely license others to use them. Over the past 30 years, Intel has vigilantly enforced its intellectual property rights against infringement by third-party microprocessors. One of the earliest examples, was Intel's enforcement of its seminal Crawford '338 Patent. In the early days of our microprocessor business, Intel needed to enforce its patent rights against various companies including United Microelectronics Corporation, Advanced Micro Devices, Cyrix Corporation, Chips and Technologies, Via Technologies, and, most recently, Transmeta Corporation. Enforcement actions have been unnecessary in recent years because other companies have respected Intel's intellectual property rights.[77]

The only challenge to Intel came, ironically, from a second source provider of x86 CPUs, Advanced Micro Devices (AMD). Recall that in the early years of the industry, the users of semiconductors required that there be a second source provider of chips in order to mitigate the supply problems caused by low yields. Thus, as part of their agreement in 1982, IBM required a second source provider, a request that Intel accommodated with a second source agreement with AMD, which has bound Intel ever since. The two firms have been engaged in contentious litigation almost continually since 1987, when Intel tried (unsuccessfully) to claim that its licensing agreement with AMD did not extend to newer iterations of the 8086 chip. No other successful entrant emerged. Whether Intel exercises market power has been a subject of debate, but it is safe to say that its profit margins have not been inconsistent with the predictions of the Arrow hypothesis. As Goettler and Gordon's (2011) dynamic oligopoly model suggests, market outcomes in Intel's submarket under duopoly are not far from those under monopoly.[78]

Even if one were to call Intel a monopoly, however, something more than its patents would have been necessary to sustain its market power rents. As Gawer and Henderson (2007) show, without the efforts to stimulate the development of new applications that used faster processor speed, it would not have been possible for Intel to find and develop applications at the rate necessary to sustain continual improvements in speed and miniaturization, thereby earning rents on the basis of continually faster processors. Intel's strategy, therefore, confirms that technical marketing and patents are important.

[77] See Rodgers and Uhlig (2017). On Intel's litigation of the Crawford '338 patent see Kulver (2012).

[78] Because CPUs and computers are durable goods, and Intel and AMD compete both by selling CPUs and investing in R&D, the static model is an incomplete tool to analyze competition in the x86 CPU market.

In any case, Intel's use of patents to appropriate the returns of its R&D is a significant counterexample to the logic of defensive patenting and further evidence that there is no patent paradox in semiconductors. Moreover, it is a bit ironic that both surveys missed that the world's largest semiconductor company at the time based its strategy on enforcing its intellectual property to exclude competitors.

Unintended Consequences

One of the striking facts of the semiconductor industry is the unusually fast rate of growth of multi factor productivity (MFP), which equals the rate of change of the quality-adjusted relative price.[79] For example, Grimm's (1998) study reports that the price index for memory chips fell on average 37 percent per year between 1975 and 1985, and 20 percent per year between 1985 and 1996; Grimm's price index for microprocessors fell on average 35 percent per year between 1985 and 1996. Aizcorbe, Oliner, and Sichel (2008) report that a price index that combines memory and processors fell on average 23 percent per year between 1975 and 1994, 41 percent per year between 1994 and 2001, and 28 percent between 2001 and 2004. Recent work by Byrne, Oliner, and Sichel (2018) suggests that between 2000 and 2013 the quality-adjusted price of Intel's desktop microprocessors fell nearly 50 percent per year on average. Last, Byrne, Kovak, and Michaels (2017) found that the quality-adjusted price index of chips manufactured by foundries fell on average 11 percent per year between 2004 and 2010.[80] MFP growth in semiconductors has been so fast that in some periods it has accounted for most of the growth of MFP in the United States and the world economy.[81,82]

The fast growth of MFP creates a different paradox. On the one hand, the semiconductor industry invests about 14 percent of sales in R&D at least since the early 1980s, and maybe before that as well.[83] Indeed, as Galasso and Ziedonis (2019) point out, it invests the highest share of revenues in R&D of any industry. On the other hand, MFP growth is a free lunch—the residual growth of real product not accounted for by the growth of real factor input.[84] The fast rate of

[79] See Galetovic, Haber, and Levine (2015). Price decreases wrought by changes in demand and competitive conditions can be mistakenly attributed to changes in the rate of technological progress. Pillai (2013) shows, however, that engineering measures of technological progress like the increase in processing speed account for most of the fall of quality-adjusted prices.

[80] Further studies on memory are Flamm (1993), Aizcorbe (2002), Victor and Ausubel (2002), and Aizcorbe, Oliner, and Sichel (2008). On microprocessors see Dulberger (1993), Aizcorbe, Corrado, and Doms (2003), Holdway (2001), Jorgenson (2001), Flamm (2004; 2007), Aizcorbe, Oliner, and Sichel (2008), and Pillai (2010; 2013).

[81] MFP growth in semiconductors affects the economy-wide TFP through the industries that use semiconductors as an input. See Jorgenson and Stiroh (2000).

[82] See Jorgenson and Stiroh (2000), and Jorgenson and Vu (2016) on the effect of MFP growth in semiconductors on US TFP growth. See Jorgenson, Ho, and Samuels (2016) on the effect on the rate of growth of the world economy.

[83] See Rhines (2019, ch. 2)

[84] See, for example, Hulten (2001).

price decline benefits mainly consumers of semiconductors, who pay less for an input of consumer and capital goods.[85] Why do semiconductor firms invest in R&D, if most gains accrue to consumers?

The Ricardian hypothesis reconciles investment in R&D and fast MFP growth. Ricardian rents wrought by R&D investments coexist with the flow of free information that sustains fast MFP growth, because patents prevent free riding. This free lunch works through the channels that I have already described: individuals that move from one firm to another, technical marketing, trade shows, and reverse engineering. Patents also allowed firms to pool their inventions via cross licensing, a point made by Robert Noyce (1982), one of the founders of Fairchild and, later, Intel:

> The industry has broadly cross-licensed competition on patents. Without so doing, no firm could be using the latest technology in all areas. One might be using epitaxy without diffusion, another oxide masking but not planar techniques, yet another making MOS transistors without the possibility of making integrated circuits. Clearly such pooling of inventions on devices and processes has been absolutely essential to the growth of our industry.

In a way, cross licensing is the legal expression of the free lunch. Depending on the point of view, therefore, Moore's Law is the outcome or the cause of Ricardian rents and fast MFP growth. Doubling the number of transistors crammed in the same silicon area every two years is the outcome of protracted investments in R&D by the entire industry, which are made in the expectation of appropriating Ricardian rents. On the other hand, protracted investments in R&D are driven by the cost declines anticipated by Moore's Law.

A Counterfactual

The history of an industry is largely the outcome of a dynamic Nash equilibrium. Thus, researchers can use out-of-equilibrium episodes to test a theory, by checking whether firms' predicted profitable out-of-equilibrium best responses match their observed actions. One can then use the same insight about the behavior of an industry being the outcome of a dynamic Nash equilibrium to posit a counterfactual. That is, one can ask: what would have happened had there been no patents? What strategy combination would have been a dynamic Nash

[85] For example, Triplett (1996) shows that a substantial portion of the price declines in computer output are due to price declines in semiconductors.

equilibrium, and what actions would have been observed along the equilibrium path?

According to the Ricardian hypothesis, without patents firms would have been forced to cope with free riding without recourse to property rights. Therefore, spinoffs to free ride would have been more profitable and more difficult to prevent. At the same time, semiconductor firms would have been affected by Arrow's information paradox, and vertical separation with system developers would have been more difficult.[86] The endogenous response by existing firms, therefore, would have been horizontal integration in semiconductors and vertical integration into electronic product manufacturing. Free riding would still have been a possibility, but it is easier for an oligopoly to sustain an equilibrium where firms do not poach each other's human capital.[87] More generally, as Barnett (2021a) points out, when intellectual property rights are weak, firms appropriate the returns of R&D through production and distribution, economies of scale, and other assets that small firms cannot replicate.

Similarly, vertical separation between design and chipless firms and manufacturing would have been more difficult, because the point of minimum information would have made both chipless and fabless semiconductor firms vulnerable to free riding by foundries. For the same reason, trade in IP cores between chipless firms and fabless semiconductor firms or manufacturers would have been much harder: why would firms pay for IP if they could free ride? The endogenous response would have been to vertically integrate. Firm size would have been dictated by the efficient scale of manufacturing, which is to say that the industry would be characterized by a few very large firms.

It would be an exaggeration to claim that, had there been no intellectual property rights (or had they been much weaker), semiconductor technology would not have developed at all. In point of fact, a regulated, vertically integrated monopoly (AT&T) discovered several of the fundamental technologies that made semiconductors possible and kept introducing path breaking innovations for at least a quarter century. Another vertically integrated firm, IBM, was one of the main contributors to semiconductor and computing technology.

Nevertheless, as Gordon Moore pointed out, large, vertically integrated firms are subject to diseconomies of scope. Startups and specialized firms can focus, compete, and cooperate nimbly; large firms must be managed by a bureaucracy. Coping with the increasing complexity of designs would have been difficult in a bureaucratized environment. Large and bureaucratized firms would also have likely yielded slower learning by individuals within firms and limited

[86] One may argue that confidentiality agreements could have substituted for patents. Barnett (2011a) explains why confidentiality agreements are not effective to overcome Arrow's information paradox.

[87] See Anand and Galetovic (2000b; 2006).

knowledge flows across firms. There would have been little free riding, but the business models and industry structure that allowed specialization in innovation to emerge, coevolve, and develop during almost 70 years would not have been possible. Therefore, the pace of exploration of the large technological opportunity opened by the invention of the transistor would have been slower and less intense, and innovation in the semiconductor industry would have been slower.

Conclusion: There is No Patent Paradox in the Semiconductor Industry

How can it be that patents permeate nearly every nook and cranny in the semiconductor industry—so much so that one can sustain the argument that they were crucial to the emergence and rapid growth of the industry—but respondents to the Yale and Carnegie Mellon surveys reported that patents were not the most important way that they appropriated the returns to R&D—so much so that scholars generated the hypothesis that patents in semiconductors were purely defensive?

We would suggest, in the first place, that the patent paradox originated in studies that surveyed the semiconductor industry right before or in the middle of a large technological transformation that led to the massive spread of personal computers, embedded systems, and electronics in general. The Yale and Carnegie Mellon surveys largely missed key developments in which patents were key, such as Intel becoming the standard in microprocessors for PCs, laptops, and servers (which allowed Intel to behave much as predicted by the Arrow hypothesis) and the emergence of specialist foundries, fabless firms, and chipless firms made possible by HDLs and EDAs, whose business models could not have been sustained without patent licensing.

We would also suggest that scholars ignored important concurrent facts. For example, the Yale survey only included large firms; it thus probably picked many firms specialized in second sourcing, whose business models did not require intense R&D investment.[88] For these firms patents were not important—they did not own the intellectual property. Both surveys also ignored the many small design firms that were entering new subindustries in the early 1980s, with business models sustained by patenting. The surveys, and the defensive patenting hypothesis that followed, also largely ignored the active patent licensing market in semiconductors—a market that emerged in the 1950s. If patents were defensive, what explains firms that do not produce chips at all, but earn royalties with designs that are easy to copy?

[88] See Sutton (2001, ch. 14).

Scholars also ignored several technological trends that should have cast doubts on the defensive hypothesis as a resolution of the patent paradox. Between the 1980s and 2000, the number of semiconductor patents awarded each year grew much faster than utility patents in general. Moreover, the number of semiconductor patents awarded each year grew pari passu with semiconductor sales. Rather than being paradoxical, patenting trends reflected fast technological progress in semiconductors and the fast rate of growth of the markets for digital electronic products that relied upon semiconductors. Indeed, the rapid growth in patenting in semiconductors was matched by the rapid growth in patenting in all fields of digital electronic products. At root, scholars came to believe that there was a patent paradox because Arrow's famous 1962 paper led them to believe that patents matter because they generate monopoly rents.

The Ricardian hypothesis explains why semiconductor firms patent. Patents need not directly generate revenues to incentivize innovation, because they allow firms to act as if free riding did not exist, thus enlarging the set of available business models, strategies, and contracts. The Ricardian hypothesis is also consistent with patents being instrumental in generating revenues, as they are necessary to sustain specialization and trade in technology as well as to sustain business models based on royalty revenues. There is, in short, no patent paradox in semiconductors. Rather, there is an industry that has emerged, that is organized in a particular way, and whose leading firms are located in a particular place, in part because it is underpinned by patents and intellectual property rights.

Appendix: The Logic of the Defensive Hypothesis

In the introduction I claim that: (i) patenting is a dominant strategy—there are neither aggressors nor defenders; (ii) if free riding is possible and patents prevent it, then patenting is not socially wasteful; (iii) patenting and cross licensing are socially wasteful if and only free riding does not exist. In this appendix I develop a simple game that proves these propositions.

Timeline of the game. The game is as follows. There are two symmetric firms, A and B. In stage 1 of the game A and B choose simultaneously whether to invest $I > 0$ in R&D to create a new product. A firm that does not invest exits the game. In the second stage, and conditional on having invested, A and B choose simultaneously whether to patent, which costs $\pi > 0$.

Innovation. The outcome of R&D is an innovation that creates surplus V_L. In addition, if Firm A uses B's intellectual property, it can create value $V_H > V_L > I$, with $\Delta V \equiv V_H - V_L$. If A does not patent, then B can improve its innovation for free using A's intellectual property. Symmetrically, the same holds for B.

Free riding. If A does not patent, it will be victim of free riding, which will reduce its surplus by f_L if the value of *its* innovation is V_L; and by f_H if the value of its innovation is V_H. Symmetrically, the same holds for B.

Patents and intellectual property. If A owns a patent it can ask B for a license. Nash bargaining ensues and each firm keeps $\frac{1}{2}\Delta V$ of the surplus created by A's intellectual property; A's revenue is B's royalty payment. Also, the patent protects A against free riding. Symmetrically, the same holds if B patents. Last, if both patent, they can cross licence their intellectual property and compensate each other's royalty payment $\frac{1}{2}\Delta V$.

Defensive patenting. It is useful to define "defensive patenting."

Definition: Let Σ_j be the set of strategies available to player j, $j \in \{A, B\}$; let $S_j \in \Sigma_j$ be a strategy; and let $\Sigma_A^{BR}(S_B)$ be the set of best responses of A to strategy S_B. A's patenting is defensive if for all $S_B \in \Sigma_B$, the outcome of the game when A plays any best response $S_A \in \Sigma_A^{BR}(S_B)$ is such that A patents if and only if B patents.

The intuitive meaning of defensive patenting is that along the outcome path induced by any best response $S_A \in \Sigma_A^{BR}(S_B)$, A patents if and only if B does. If B does not patent, then A does not patent either. This formalizes the notion that the only reason why A patents is to defend from B's patenting. For the same reason, patenting is not defensive if there exists a best response $S_A \in \Sigma_A^{BR}(S_B)$ such that along the outcome path induced by (S_A, S_B), A patents but B does not. For if A would patent but B does not, then A would not be defending against B's patenting

I will now show that if there is free riding, then patenting cannot be defensive.

Proposition 1: Assume that (i)$V_i - f_i < V_i - \pi$, $i \in \{L, H\}$(it is better to patent than to be victim of free riding); (ii)$V_i - f_i < I$, $i \in \{L, H\}$ (a victim of free riding does not invest). Then patenting cannot be defensive.

Proof. To show that patenting cannot be defensive it suffices to find a strategy S_B and a best response $S_A \in \Sigma_A^{BR}(S_B)$ such that along the outcome path B does not patent and A's best response is to patent. So, assume that B's strategy is such that B does not invest. Then A's best response S_A is such that A invests and then patents to obtain payoff $V_L - \pi - I > 0$. ▪

Essentially, when free riding is a concern then firms patent to defend against free riders, not to "defend" against other firms with a patent portfolio.

Next, I show that with no free riding, patenting cannot be defensive either.

Proposition 2: Assume that (i)$f_H - f_L = 0$ (there is no free riding).Then patenting cannot be defensive.

Proof. Assume that B's strategy is such that B invests but does not patent. Then A's best response S_A is such that A invests and patents. To see why, note that by investing and patenting A's payoff is $V_H + \frac{1}{2}\Delta V - \pi - I > 0$. This is better than not investing. Consider next the subgame that starts after both A and B invested. If B does not patent then A's payoff is $V_H + \frac{1}{2}\Delta V - \pi - I$ if it patents and $V_H - I$

if does not; thus, *A*'s best response is to patent. Hence there is a best response such that along the outcome path induced by $(S_A, S_B) A$ patents and *B* does not. ▪

Equilibrium and wasteful patenting. Next, I characterize the set of subgame perfect equilibria of the game to examine whether patenting can be wasteful. Proposition 3 assumes that free riding is a concern.

Proposition 3: Assume that (i)$V_i - f_i < V_i - \pi$, $i \in \{L,H\}$(it is better to patent than to be victim of free riding); (ii)$V_i - f_i < I$, $i \in \{L,H\}$(a victim of free riding does not invest) (iii) $\frac{1}{2}\Delta V - \pi > 0$ (patenting costs less than the incremental royalty revenue). Then(a) the outcome of any subgame perfect equilibrium is that *A* and *B* invest, and patent;(b) patenting sustains investment in R&D in equilibrium, and is not wasteful.

Proof. Consider first the subgame that starts after both *A* and *B* invested. If *B* does not patent then *A*'s payoff is $V_H + \frac{1}{2}\Delta V - \pi - I$ if it patents and $V_H - f_H - I$ if does not; thus, *A*'s best response is to patent. If, on the other hand, *B* patents, then *A*'s payoff is $V_H - \pi - I$ if it patents and $V_H - \frac{1}{2}\Delta V - f_H - I$ if does not; thus, *A*'s best response is to patent. It follows that patenting is a dominant strategy in the subgame. Consider next the subgame where only *A* invests. If *A* patents, then its payoff is $V_L - \pi - I$; if it does not, its payoff is $V_L - f_L - I$. So, *A*'s best response is to patent.

Now given that *A* always patents if it invests and that $V_L - \pi - I > 0$, it follows that *A* is better off by patenting. Thus, in any subgame perfect equilibrium *A* invests and patents. Moreover, because the game is symmetric, in any subgame perfect equilibrium *B* invests and patents. It follows that in any subgame perfect equilibrium *A* and *B* invest and patent. This proves (a).

To prove (b) note that if patents were not available, then *A* and *B* would rather not invest than invest and be a victim of free riding. Therefore, patenting is not wasteful; on the contrary, it sustains investment. This completes the proof. ▪

Proposition 3 implies that when patents prevent free riding, it is a dominant strategy to patent—it is always worth to protect against free riding. Thus, if free riding is a concern, then patenting sustains investment and cannot be, as a matter of logic, wasteful.

The next proposition shows that patenting is wasteful only if free riding is not a concern.

Proposition 4: Assume that (i)$f_H = f_L = 0$ (there is no free riding); (ii) $\frac{1}{2}\Delta V - \pi > 0$ (patenting costs less than the incremental royalty revenue). Then:(a) the outcome of the only subgame perfect equilibrium is that *A* and *B* invest and patent;(b) patenting does not sustain investment in R&D and is wasteful.

Proof. If both A and *B* invest, then it is a dominant strategy in that subgame for *A* and *B* to patent. Next, in the subgame where only *A* invests, if *A* patents, then its payoff is $V_L - \pi - I$; if it does not patent, its payoff is $V_L - I$. So, *A*'s best response is not to patent. Now if B invests, A obtains 0 if it does not invest, and $V_H - \pi - I$ if it invests. So, A's best response is to invest. By contrast, if B does not invest, A obtains 0 if it does not invest, and $V_L - I$ if it does; hence A's best response is to invest. Because the game is symmetric, it follows that both A and B invest and patent, which proves part (a). Last, note that both would be better off investing and not patenting—their payoff would be equal to $V_H - I > V_H - \pi - I$. Hence patenting is wasteful and is not needed to sustain investment in R&D. This completes the proof. ▪

Thus as a matter of logic, when there is cross licensing patenting may be wasteful, but only if free riding is not a concern.

Acknowledgments

I gratefully acknowledge the research support provided by the Working Group on Intellectual Property, Innovation, and Prosperity (IP2) of the Hoover Institution at Stanford University and the comments and conversations with Pilar Alcalde, Jonathan Barnett, Steve Haber, Wes Hartman, Dana Hayter, John Howells, Zorina Kahn, Ron Katznelson, Naomi Lamoreaux, Keith Mallinson, Scott Masten, Damon Matteo, Noel Maurer, Victor Menaldo, Nicolas Petit, James Pooley, Robert Taylor, Steve Usselman, Lew Zaretzki, Rosemarie Ziedonis, an anonymous referee, seminar participants at Universidad de los Andes and participants the IP2 workshop on the history of patenting in October 2017 in Washington DC and the IP2 conference at Hoover in May 2018. I am very grateful to Claudio Montenegro for help in processing the USPTO patent database.

References

Adelman, Martin J. "The New World of Patents Created by the Court of Appeals for the Federal Circuit." *University of Michigan Journal of Law Reform* 20, no 4 (1987): 979–1007.

Aizcorbe, Ana M. "Price Measures for Semiconductor Devices." Board of Governors of the Federal Reserve System (U.S.), Finance and Economics Discussion Series No. 2002-13, Washington, DC, 2002.

Aizcorbe, Ana M., Carol A. Corrado, and Mark E. Doms, (2003), "When Do Matched-Model and Hedonic Techniques Yield Similar Measures?" Federal Reserve Bank of San Francisco, Working Papers in Applied Economic Theory 2003-14, San Francisco, CA, 2003.

Aizcorbe, Ana M., Stephen D. Oliner, and Daniel E. Sichel. "Shifting Trends in Semiconductor Prices and the Pace of Technological Progress." *Business Economics* 43, no. 3 (2008): 23–39.

Arora, Ashish, Andrea Fosfuri, and Alfonso Gambardella. *Markets for Technology: The Economics of Innovation and Corporate Strategy.* Cambridge, MA: MIT Press, 2004.

Anand, Bharat, and Alexander Galetovic. "Weak Property Rights and Hold Up in R&D." *Journal of Economics and Management Strategy* 9, no. 4 (2000a): 615–62.

———. "Information, Non-Excludability and Financial Market Structure," *Journal of Business* 73, no. 3 (2000b): 357–402.

———. "Relationships, Competition, and the Structure of Investment Banking Markets." *Journal of Industrial Economics* 54, no. 2 (2006): 151–99.

Arrow, Kenneth. "Economic Welfare and the Allocation of Resources for Invention." In *The Rate and Direction of Inventive Activity*, edited by Richard R. Nelson, pp. 609–26. Princeton, NJ: Princeton University Press, 1962.

Barnett, Jonathan. "Intellectual Property as a Law of Organization," *Southern California Law Review* 84, no. 3 (2011a): 785–858.

———. "Do Patents Matter? Empirical Evidence on the Incentive Thesis." In *Handbook on Law, Innovation and Growth*, edited by Robert E. Litan, pp. 178–99. Cheltenham: Edward Elgar, 2011b.

———. "The Great Patent Grab." This volume, 2021a.

———. *Innovators, Firms, and Markets: The Organizational Logic of Intellectual Property.* New York: Oxford University Press, 2021b.

Bessen, James, and Erik Maskin. "Sequential Innovation, Patents, and Imitation." *Rand Journal of Economics* 40, no. 4 (2009): 611–35.

Blecker, Marvin, Tom Sánchez, and Eric Stasik. "An Experience-Based Look at the Licensing Practices that Drive The Cellular Communications Industry: Whole Portfolio/Whole Devise Licensing." *Les Nouvelles* 51, no. 4 (2016): 221–33.

Braun, Ernest, and Stuart Macdonald. *Revolution in Miniature.* 2nd ed. Cambridge, UK: Cambridge University Press, 1982.

Byrne, David, Brian K. Kovak, and Ryan Michaels. "Quality-Adjusted Price Measurement: A New Approach with Evidence from Semiconductors." *Review of Economics and Statistics* 99, no. 2 (2017): 330–42.

Byrne, David, Stephen D. Oliner, and Daniel E. Sichel. "How Fast are Semiconductor Prices Falling?" *Review of Income and Wealth* 64, no. 3 (2018): 679–702.

Casalle-Rossi, Marco. "The Heritage of Mead & Conway: What Has Remained the Same, What Has Changed, What Was Missed, and What Lies Ahead." *Proceedings of the IEEE* 102, no. 2 (2014): 114–19.

Cohen, Wesley M., Richard R. Nelson, and John P. Walsh. "Protecting Their Intellectual Assets: Appropriability Conditions and Why U.S. Manufacturing Firms Patent (or Not)." NBER Working Paper No. 7552, Cambridge, MA, 2000.

Dibiaggio, Ludovic, "Design Complexity, Vertical Disintegration and Knowledge Organization in the Semiconductor Industry." *Industrial and Corporate Change* 16, no. 2 (2007): 239–67.

Dorfman, Nancy S. *Innovation and Market Structure.* Boston: Ballinger, 1987.

Dulberger, Ellen R. "Sources of Price Decline in Computer Processors: Selected Electronic Components." In *Price Measurements and their Uses*, edited by Murray F. Foss, Marilyn E. Manser, and Allan H. Young. Chicago, IL: University of Chicago Press, 1993.

Finan, William F. "The International Transfer of Semiconductor Technology Through U.S.-Based Firms." National Bureau of Economic Research Working Paper No. 118, New York, 1975.

Flamm, Kenneth S., "Measurement of DRAM Prices: Technology and Market Structure." In *Price Measurements and their Uses*, edited by Murray F. Foss, Marilyn E. Manser, and Allan H. Young, pp. 157–206. Chicago, IL: University of Chicago Press, 1993.

———. *Mismanaged Trade? Strategic Policy and the Semiconductor Industry*. Washington, DC: Brookings, 1996.

———. "Moore's Law and the Economics of Semiconductor Price Trends." In *Productivity and Cyclicality in Semiconductors: Trends, Implications, and Questions*, edited by Dale W. Jorgenson and Charles W. Wessner, pp. 151–70. Washington, DC: National Academy Press, 2004.

———. "The Microeconomics of Microprocessor Innovation." Unpublished manuscript, 2007.

Galasso, Alberto. "Broad Cross-License Negotiations." *Journal of Economics and Management Strategy* 21, no. 4 (2012): 873–911.

Galasso, Alberto, and Rosemary Ziedonis. "Patent Rights and Innovation: Evidence from the Semiconductor Industry." In *Research Handbook on the Economics of Intellectual Property Law*, edited by Ben Depoorter, Peter Menell, and David Schwartz, Vol. 2, pp. 423–44. Cheltenham, UK: Edward Elgar, 2019.

Galetovic, Alexander, Stephen Haber, and Ross Levine. "An Empirical Examination of Patent Holdup." *Journal of Competition Law and Economics* 11, no. 3 (2015): 549–78.

Galetovic, Alexander, Stephen Haber, and Lew Zaretzki. "Is There an Anti-commons Tragedy in the Smartphone Industry?" *Berkeley Technology Law Journal* 32, no. 4 (2017): 1527–58.

———. "An Estimate of the Average Cumulative Royalty Yield in the World Mobile Phone Industry Theory, Measurement and Results." *Telecommunications Policy* 42, no. 3 (2018): 263–76.

Gawer, Annabelle, and Rebecca Henderson. "Platform Owner Entry and Innovation in Complementary Markets: Evidence from Intel." *Journal of Economics and Management Strategy* 16, no.1 (2007): 1–34.

Gertner, Jon. *The Idea Factory: Bell Labs and the Great Age of American Innovation*. New York: Penguin, 2012.

Goettler, Ronald L., and Brett R. Gordon. "Does AMD Spur Intel to Innovate More?" *Journal of Political Economy* 119, no. 6 (2011): 1141–200.

Golding, Anthony M. "The Semiconductor Industry in the United States and Great Britain: A Case Study of Innovation, Growth, and the Diffusion of Technology." PhD diss. University of Sussex, 1972.

Golman, Russel, and Stephen Klepper. "Spinoffs and Clustering." *Rand Journal of Economics* 47, no. 2 (2016): 341–65.

Gordon, Deborah. *Ant Encounters: Interaction Networks and Colony Behavior*. Princeton, NJ: Princeton University Press, 2010.

Grimm, Bruce. "Price Indexes for Selected Semiconductors, 1974–96." *Survey of Current Business* 78, no. 2 (1998): 8–24.

Grindley, Peter C., and David Teece. "Managing Intellectual Capital: Licensing and Cross-Licensing in Semiconductors and Electronics." *California Management Review* 39, no. 1 (1997): 1–34.

Hall, Bronwyn H., and Rosemarie Ziedonis. "The Patent Paradox Revisited: An Empirical Study of Patenting in the U.S. Semiconductor Industry, 1979–1995." *Rand Journal of Economics* 32, no. 1 (2001): 101–28.

Hippel von, Ernest. "Appropriability of Innovation Benefit as a Predictor of the Source of Innovation." *Research Policy* 11, no. 2 (1982): 95–115.

Holdway, M. "Quality-Adjusting Computer Prices in the Producer Price Index: An Overview." Unpublished Manuscript, Bureau of Labor Statistics, Washington, DC, 2001.

Hulten, Charles R. "Total Factor Productivity: A Short Biography." In *New Developments in Productivity Analysis*, edited by Charles R. Hulten, Edwin R. Dean, and Michael J. Harper, pp. 1–54. Chicago, IL: University of Chicago Press, 2001.

Hutcheson, G. (2003), "The Economic Implications of Moore's Law." In *Into the Nano Era: Moore's Law Beyond Planar Silicon CMOS*, edited by Howard R. Huff, pp. 11–38. Springer: Berlin and Heidelberg, 2003.

Jorgenson, Dale W. "Information Technology and the U.S. Economy." *American Economic Review* 91, no. 1 (2001): 1–32.

Jorgenson, Dale W., and Kevin J. Stiroh, "Raising the Speed Limit: U.S. Economic Growth in the Information Age." *Brookings Papers on Economic Activity* no. 1 (2000): 125–235.

Jorgenson, Dale W., and Kuhong Vu. "The ICT Revolution, World Economic Growth, and Policy Issues." *Telecommunications Policy* 40, no. 5 (2016): 383–97.

Jorgenson, Dale, Mun S. Ho, and Jon D. Samuels. "The Impact of Information Technology on Postwar US Economic Growth." *Telecommunications Policy* 40, no. 5 (2016): 398–411.

Katznelson, Ron. "Patent Continuations, Product Life Cycle Contraction, and Patent Scope Erosion: A New Insight Into Patenting Trends." Unpublished Manuscript, 2007.

Kieff, Scott. "Property Rights and Property Rules for Commercializing Inventions." *Minnesota Law Review* 85, no. 3 (2001): 697–754.

———. "IP Transactions: On the Theory & (and) Practice of Commercializing Innovation." *Houston Law Review* 42, no. 3 (2005): 727–58.

Kitch, Edmund W. "The Nature and Function of the Patent System." *Journal of Law and Economics* 20, no. 2 (1977): 265–90.

Klepper, Stephen, and Peter Thompson. "Submarkets and the Evolution of Market Structure." *Rand Journal of Economics* 37, no. 4 (2006): 861–86.

Kulver, John. "Intel vs. The World—The Infamous '338 Patent." *The CPU Shack*, 2012. http://www.cpushack.com/2012/09/06/intel-vs-the-world-the-338-patent/.

Kumar, Rakesh. *Fabless Semiconductor Implementation*. New York: McGraw Hill, 2008.

Langlois, Richard N., and W. Edward Steinmueller. "The Evolution of Competitive Advantage in the Worldwide Semiconductor Industry, 1947–1996." In *Sources of Industrial Leadership: Studies of Seven Industries*, edited by David C. Mowery and Richard R. Nelson, pp. 19–78. New York: Cambridge University Press, 1999.

Lammers, David. "Moore's Law Milestones." *IEEE Spectrum*, 2015. https://spectrum.ieee.org/tech-history/silicon-revolution/moores-law-milestones.

Linden, Greg, and Deepak Somaya. "System-on-a-Chip Integration in the Semiconductor Industry: Industry Structure and Firm Strategies." *Industrial and Corporate Change* 12, no. 3 (2003): 545–76.

Levin, Richard C. "The Semiconductor Industry." In *Government and Technical Progress: A Cross Industry Analysis*, edited by Richard R. Nelson, pp. 9–100. New York, NY: Pergamon Press, 1982.

Levin, Richard C., Alvin K. Klevorick, Richard R. Nelson, and Sidney R. Winter. "Appropriating the Returns from Industrial Research and Development." *Brookings Papers on Economic Activity* no. 3 (1987): 783–820.

Lewis, Bryan. "Japanese ASIC Suppliers Hit Hard Times in 1992." *Dataquest Perspective*, February 22, 1993. https://manualzz.com/doc/21099145/dataquest.

Macher, Jeffrey T., and David C. Mowery, "Vertical Specialization and Industry Structure in High Technology Industries." *Advances in Strategic Management* 21 (2004): 317–56.

Macher, Jeffrey T., David C. Mowery, and David Hodges, "Reversal of Fortune? The Recovery of the U.S. Semiconductor Industry." *California Management Review* 41, no.1 (1998): 107–36.

———. "Semiconductors." In "*U.S. Industry in 2000: Studies in Competitive Performance*, edited by David C. Mowery, pp. 245–86. Washington, DC: National Academy Press, 1999.

Macher, Jeffrey T., David C. Mowery, and Alberto Di Minin. "The 'Non-Globalization' of Innovation in the Semiconductor Industry." *California Management Review* 50, no.1 (2007): 217–42.

Macher, Jeffrey T., David C. Mowery, and Timothy Simcoe. "e-Business and the Disintegration of the Semiconductor Industry Value Chain." *Industry and Innovation* 9, no.3 (2002): 155–81.

Mead, Carver. "VLSI and Technological Innovation." *Proceedings of the Caltech Conference on VLSI*. Los Angeles, CA, 15–28, 1979. https://authors.library.caltech.edu/54831/.

Mead, Carver, and Lynn Conway. *Introduction to VLSI Systems*. Boston: Addison Wesley, 1979.

Monteverde, Keith. "Technical Dialog as an Incentive for Vertical Integration in the Semiconductor Industry." *Management Science* 41, no. 10 (1995): 1624–38.

Moore, Gordon. "Cramming More Components onto Integrated Circuits." *Electronics Magazine* 38, no. 8 (1965): 114–17.

———. "Moore's Law at 40." In *Understanding Moore's Law: Four Decades of Innovation*, edited by David C. Brock, pp. 67–84. Philadelphia, PA: Chemical Heritage Press, 2005.

Moore, Gordon, and Kevin Davis. "Learning the Silicon Valley Way." In *Building High Tech Clusters: Silicon Valley and Beyond*, edited by Timothy Bresnahan and Alfonso Gambardella, pp. 7–39. New York: Cambridge University Press, 2004.

Mowery, David C. "Federal Policy and the Development of Semiconductors, Computer Hardware, and Computer Software: A Policy Model for Climate Change R&D?" In *Accelerating Energy Innovation: Insights from Multiple Sectors*, edited by Rebecca M. Henderson and Richard G. Newell, pp. 159–88. Chicago, IL: University of Chicago Press, 2011.

Nenni, Daniel, and Paul McLellan. "Fabless: The Transformation of the Semiconductor Industry." Semiwiki.com, 2014.

Noll, Roger G. "Buyer Power and Economic Policy." *Antitrust Law Journal* 72, no. 2 (2005): 589–624.

Noyce, Robert. "Competition and Cooperation—A Prescription for the Eighties." *Research Management* 25, no. 2 (1982): 13–17.

Pillai, Unni. "Technological Progress in the Microprocessor Industry." *Survey of Current Business* 90, no. 2 (2010): 14–16.

———. "A Model of Technological Progress in the Microprocessor Industry." *Journal of Industrial Economics*, 61, no. 4 (2013): 877–912.

———. "The Emergence of Tools Suppliers in the Semiconductor Industry." Unpublished Manuscript, SUNY Polytechnic Institute, Albany, NY, 2017.

Rhines, Wally. *History of the Semiconductor Industry*. 2019. https://semiwiki.com/author/wally-rhines/.

Rodgers, S., and R. Uhlig, "X86: Approaching 40 and Still Going Strong: Nearly Four Decades of Consistent Investment and Improvement." Intel Newsroom, 2017. https://newsroom.intel.com/editorials/x86-approaching-40-still-going-strong/#gs.7dudkk.

Saxenian, Anna Lee. *Regional Advantage*. Cambridge, MA: Harvard University Press, 1996.

Semiconductor Industry Association. *Annual Databook: Review of Global and U.S. Semiconductor Competitive Trends, 1996–2016*. Washington, DC: Semiconductor Industry Association, 2017.

Sparks, Morgan. "25 Years of Transistors." *Bell Laboratories Record* 50, no. 11 (1972): 342–46.

Spengler, Joseph J. "Vertical Integration and Antitrust Policy." *Journal of Political Economy* 58, no. 4 (1950): 347–52.

Sutton, John. *Sunk Costs and Market Structure*. Cambridge, MA: MIT Press, 1991.

———. *Technology and Market Structure*. Cambridge, MA: MIT Press, 2001.

———. *Competing in Capabilities*. Oxford: Oxford University Press, 2012.

Swann, G. M. P. "Product Competition in Microprocessors," *Journal of Industrial Economics* 34, no. 1 (1985): 33–53.

———. "A Decade of Microprocessor Innovation: An Economist's Perspective." *Microprocessors and Microsystems* 11, no. 1 (1987): 49–59.

Tamme, Stefan, Stephen Schott, Dogan Gunes, Jeffrey Wallace, Richard Boadway, Frank Razavi, and Marc Pépin. "Trends And Opportunities in Semiconductor Licensing." *Les Nouvelles* 48, no. 4 (2013): 226–28.

Taylor, C. T., and Aubrey Z. Silberston. *The Economic Impact of the Patent System: A Study of the British Experience*. Cambridge, UK: Cambridge University Press, 1973.

Tilton, John E. *International Diffusion of Technology: The Case of Semiconductors*. Washington, DC: Brookings, 1971.

Tirole, Jean. *The Theory of Industrial Organization*. Cambridge, MA: MIT Press, 1988.

Torrance, Randy, and Dick James. "The State-of-the-Art in IC Reverse Engineering." Proceedings of the 48th Design Automation Conference, DAC 2011. San Diego, CA, 2011.

Triplett, Jack E. "Performance Measures for Computers." In *Deconstructing the Computer: Report of a Symposium*, edited by Dale W. Jorgenson and Charles W. Wessner, pp. 99–139. Washington, DC: National Academy Press, 1996.

Victor, Nadejda M., and Jesse H. Ausubel. "DRAMs as Model Organisms for Study of Technological Evolution." *Technological Forecasting and Social Change* 69, no. 3 (2002): 243–72.

Warshofsky, Fred. *The Patent Wars*. New York: John Wiley & Sons, 1994.

Watzinger, Martin, Thomas A. Fackler, Markus Nagler and Monika Schnitzer. "How Antitrust Enforcement Can Spur Innovation: Bell Labs and the 1956 Consent Decree." *American Economic Journal: Economic Policy* 12, no. 4 (2020): 328–59.

Webbink, Douglas W. *The Semiconductor Industry: A Survey of Structure, Conduct, and Performance*. Staff Report to the FTC. Washington DC: US Government Printing Office, 1977.

Williams, Heidi. "How Do Patents Affect Research Investments?" *Annual Review of Economics* 9, no. 1 (2017): 441–69.

Ziedonis, Rosemarie. "Patent Litigation in the U.S. Semiconductor Industry." In *Patents in the Knowledge-Based Economy*, edited by Wesley Cohen and Stephen Merrill, pp. 180–215. Washington, DC: National Academy Press, 2003.

Ziedonis, Rosemarie, and Bronwyn H. Hall. "The Effects of Strengthening Patent Rights on Firms Engaged in Cumulative Innovation: Insights From the Semiconductor Industry." In *Entrepreneurial Inputs and Outcomes: New Studies of Entrepreneurship in the United States*, edited by Gary Libecap, pp. 133–87. New York: Elsevier Science Publishers, 2001.

2

Do Patents Foster International Technology Transfer?

Evidence from Spanish Steelmaking, 1850–1930

Victor Menaldo

International technology transfer is the conveyance of processes, goods, and new ways of organizing production from one country to another. Throughout history, late industrializing countries have relied on sundry methods to acquire technology from the industrial frontier. Among the most time-honored measures practiced by governments and firms in developing nations, some of which date to the seventeenth century, are: conducting industrial espionage; enticing skilled technicians to immigrate to their shores; sending their best and brightest students abroad to identify, study, and absorb the latest innovations; importing machinery; and courting foreign direct investment (FDI). A more recent conduit of international technology transfer, dating to around the Second Industrial Revolution, is individuals and firms in developing countries signing licensing agreements with foreign patent holders in exchange for royalties and other perks.

When and why do late industrializers opt for protecting the intellectual property rights (IPR) of foreign inventors in order to facilitate technology transfer from the industrial frontier? Are patents a substitute for industrial espionage, skilled labor from abroad, imported machinery, and joint ventures? Or do they complement those measures?

This chapter addresses these questions by telling the story of when and how technology was transferred via patent licensing from the industrial frontier to Spanish iron and steelmakers. It focuses on the period between 1850 and 1929, during which foreigners' IPR were relatively well protected, as reforms to the Spanish patent system in late 1929 strengthened introduction patents at the expense of original inventors. Not coincidentally, the most important transfer of iron and steel technology to Spanish firms occurred between 1850 and 1929.[1]

[1] As I will discuss later in the chapter, the Spanish system was reformed once again in 1986 to again strongly protect foreign investors. By then, however, most of the major innovations that drove the modernization of iron and steel had already taken place and transferred to Spain. Therefore, it makes sense for me to narrow attention to the earlier period.

Victor Menaldo, *Do Patents Foster International Technology Transfer? In: The Battle over Patents.* Edited by: Stephen H. Haber and Naomi R. Lamoreaux, Oxford University Press. © Oxford University Press 2021. DOI: 10.1093/oso/9780197576151.003.0003

Modern steelmaking was a quantum leap over previous techniques vis-à-vis scale and sophistication. In turn, this required a revolution in technology, knowledge, and skills. However, the transition to modern steelmaking was marked by a challenging process that has gone largely unrecognized by researchers: inventors had to find ways to transfer tacit knowledge to adopters that was inordinately difficult to codify, as it was arrived at via intuition and learning by doing.

The technical, managerial, and marketing know-how that complements inventions cannot be disclosed in a patent itself. Provided that there is an IPR regime that protects foreigners, however, it will be willingly shared by original inventors in the industrializing frontier with licensees in the developing world. Licensing agreements outline an ongoing relationship between these parties that enables them to work together and adjust inventions to differences in raw materials and other inputs, industrial organization, and consumer tastes.

In conjunction with importing machinery, procuring technical assistance from foreign firms, and hiring skilled labor from abroad, Spanish firms used IPR to acquire, learn, and improve new iron and steelmaking technologies from France, Belgium, England, and Germany. Patents played a key role in broadcasting new steelmaking techniques to Spaniards working in that industry. Similar to the story told by Lamoreaux and Sokoloff (2003) about the United States, Spanish entrepreneurs, managers, engineers, and metalworkers scoured the patent record to learn about and acquire new inventions. Patents also helped Spaniards connect with original, foreign inventors and establish enduring relationships with them. The latter shared their know-how and expertise with the former under the aegis of licensing agreements and brought them into their networks of suppliers and technicians. Moreover, when disruptive steelmaking innovations were patented in Spain, this spurred second generation foreign inventors to patent improvements. It also induced Spanish inventors to come out of the woodwork and contribute their own add on innovations to iron and steelmaking—inventions they themselves patented.

To tell the story, this chapter does several things. It first outlines the history of the Spanish patent system, which experienced four major changes that affected the ability of foreigners to protect their intellectual property and thus affected international technology transfer. It then elucidates the basic political economy behind each IPR system and identifies and explains the major process inventions around modern iron and steelmaking elaborated in industrialized countries. Next, it explores when the inventors behind these innovations obtained Spanish patents and the details behind those patents. Finally, the chapter investigates how inventors transferred their know-how to Spanish firms via patent licenses and identifies follow-up innovations patented in Spain by both foreigners and Spaniards.

While I exploit here a seemingly esoteric episode of economic history to shine light on key questions about international technology transfer, this is not just an academic exercise. Technology transfer can complement, or even substitute for, indigenous technological development. Indeed, it may be the most important development driver in the industrializing world (Abramovitz 1993; Robertson and Patel 2007). On the one hand, it can improve efficiency and help firms achieve economies of scale. On the other hand, it can undergird the incremental innovation that is typical of the smaller, low technology intensive firms that dominate the developing world (Santamaría 2009).

Moreover, this issue increasingly weighs on US policymakers and is splashed across the headlines. China has increasingly attracted outsized attention from US politicians, if not average citizens, for its aggressive efforts to acquire cutting edge American technology. China stands accused by the Trump Administration of several transgressions around intellectual property: engaging in widespread industrial espionage; compelling US firms to enter into joint ventures that divulge trade secrets in exchange for access to the Chinese market; and conducting onerous security reviews and testing requirements, as well as deploying billions of dollars to acquire US companies operating in high-tech industries, to achieve similar ends.[2]

This animated an unusually strong response by the US government between 2017 and 2019; it introduced stiff tariffs on Chinese imports, threatened additional ones, imposed stringent restrictions on FDI from China, and curtailed semiconductor exports to China. In turn, this spurred Chinese retaliation and a full-blown trade war.[3]

What has garnered less attention from interested publics, however, is that Chinese companies have also acquired foreign technology through copious patent licensing. Chinese companies operating in sectors such as transportation, energy, and robotics have paid top dollar to foreign patent holders to gain access to technology from the industrial frontier: Japanese and American firms have received billions of dollars in royalties in exchange for these licenses (Taplin 2018). China's royalty payments to the US grew dramatically faster than its GDP over the last two decades: IPR payments to US entities increased 25-fold while GDP

[2] On all of these points see Navarro (2018). Chinese firms also attempted to secure American technology by recruiting computer engineers and data scientists in Silicon Valley. According to the FBI and US Joint Chiefs of Staff, the Chinese government is behind the theft of billions of dollars of US companies' trade secrets across a wide swath of sectors, including aviation, pharmaceuticals, and extractive industries.

[3] Beijing imposed tit-for-tat tariffs on US exports and increased regulation of US firms doing business in China; for example, Chinese antitrust authorities' decision to nix the attempt by Qualcomm to merge with Dutch chipmaker NXP. See Brown and Davis (2018). US politicians have, in turn, complained about Chinese tariffs on US imports, China's supposed currency manipulation, its subsidies of state-owned enterprises, and its flooding of the international market with cheap industrial goods such as steel.

(measured in constant 2017 international dollars and adjusted for Purchasing Power Parity) increased roughly 5-fold. In 2019, alone, China paid over $34 billion to rest of world for legal use of Intellectual Property (IP). The US accounted for 23 percent of this amount (on all these points see Menaldo and Wittstock forthcoming).[4]

Spain, a late industrializing country that only really began to converge economically with the rest of Europe during the second half of the twentieth century, is reminiscent of contemporary China in many respects. During the eighteen and nineteen centuries, the Spanish Crown orchestrated and bankrolled wide-scale industrial espionage and spirited away trade secrets from the industrial frontier by, among other measures, encouraging British and French engineers and machinists to move to Madrid, Barcelona, and Bilbao. Indeed, as late as the Franco regime, industrial espionage continued. Yet, by the middle of the nineteenth century, Spanish companies began to strongly rely on licensing patents from foreign inventors to obtain technology from abroad, a practice that continued into Franco's tenure and remains true today. As I will argue later, Spanish steelmakers are perhaps the quintessential example of this phenomenon.

This chapter continues as follows. The first section summarizes the debate around patents and international technology transfer. The second section outlines a theoretical justification for why patents should foster international technology transfer between the industrial frontier and late industrializing countries. The third section outlines the history of the Spanish patent system, which experienced four major changes that affected the ability of foreigners to protect their intellectual property and thus affected international technology transfer. Within that section, I also discuss the basic political economy behind each IPR system. The fourth section provides a general overview of modern steelmaking and the Spanish steelmaking industry between 1850 and 1929. The fifth section discusses several major iron and steelmaking innovations that occurred during this period, the first being the so-called direct Chenot Sponge Iron System, the second the Bessemer Steel Process, and next the Siemens-Martin Steel System. I discuss how these were transferred by original foreign inventors to Spanish firms and identify the patents obtained by foreign inventors and their Spanish partners before their initial introduction to Spain, and also the patents associated with subsequent adjustments, improvements, and offshoots.

[4] This reflects China's manifold improvements in protecting IPRs. Beijing has joined all major international IP conventions and ramped up its enforcement capacity. Between 2006 and 2011, foreign companies brought 10 percent of patent infringement cases in China and won over 70 percent of those. In 2018, injunction rates averaged around 98 percent (see Menaldo and Wittstock forthcoming).

The Debate around Patents and Technology Transfer

Researchers have suggested a variety of methods for transferring technology from developed to developing countries. These include cooptation and imitation—including industrial espionage—courting skilled labor from abroad, importing machinery, and conducting joint ventures under the aegis of FDI (see Odagiri et al. 2010, p. 11). Some researchers contend that, by underpinning the web of contracts that foster the commercialization of innovation, strong IPR should also help industrializing countries close the technology gap with industrialized countries (Haber 2016) and may catalyze cumulative innovation in developing nations (see Scotchmer 1991). Focusing attention on the transfer of technology from US firms to developing countries between 1982 and 1999, Branstetter, Fisman, and Foley (2006) adduce evidence for these notions.

Some scholars who study Spain's industrialization experience also corroborate this idea. Sáiz (2006) examines the 32,000 patent applications that were filed in Spain during the nineteenth century and breaks them down by industry, Spanish region, and the nationality of the patentee. He argues that the Spanish patent system was explicitly designed to encourage technology transfer and demonstrates that, by patenting widely in Spain, foreigners made a noteworthy contribution to industrialization in that country.[5] Cebrián and López (2004) argue that patent licensing between firms in the industrialized world and Spanish firms helped drive the so-called Spanish miracle: the rapid, unprecedented growth acceleration that Spain experienced between 1960 and 1973.[6]

Others arrive at similar conclusions by focusing attention on particular Spanish industries. Frax et al. (1996) explore the role of patents in facilitating technology transfer around ports. Cayón et al. (1999) do the same for railroads. Sáiz (2016) does so for steam boilers and steam generators.

Quite apposite to us is Quijada (1998), who indirectly blames the lack of strong patenting and licensing around steam engines for retarding the introduction of these machines to Spain, as well as their dissemination. He recounts how the Spanish Crown was complicit in infringing upon the Boulton and Watt steam engine patent when it condoned the purchase of several pirated versions by Tomás Pérez—a mining expert hired by the state to pump water from mercury mines in Almadén—from John Wilkinson. Quijada argues that this greatly delayed getting the steam engines up and running, because it meant that Boulton and Watt were not available to offer the Spanish authorities technical assistance

[5] Others reach similar conclusions. They include Ortiz-Villajos (2004) and (2006); Sáiz (2013) and (2016); Sáiz and Pretel (2013); Sáiz and Castro (2017).

[6] They argue that, despite Spain's relatively weak IPR during this time, patents helped technology transfer take place in combination with increased imports of foreign machinery on the heels of trade liberalization circa 1960.

installing and mounting the machines, which is what they would have done had the Spaniards instead purchased patented versions from them.

However, there is another, increasingly popular, literature that is skeptical that patents encourage international technology transfer (Boldrin and Levine 2008; 2013; Lerner 2002).[7] Some researchers argue that late industrializers did not rely on strong patenting to catch up to industrialized countries; instead, they simply copied existing ideas, especially process inventions (for example, Kelly 2009; Richter and Streb 2011). The so-called Asian Tigers—for example, South Korea—adopted "export-oriented industrialization models" in which they borrowed freely from industrialized countries and relied on importing machinery (Asian Development Bank 2015).

In this vein, there are also works that are skeptical that patents made that much of a difference to transferring technology to Spain. Ortiz-Villajos (2014) argues that patents did not really impact the introduction and dissemination of gas engines and internal combustion engines during the late nineteenth and early twentieth centuries. Anduaga (2009) intimates the same regarding the oil industry.

Most apposite to us, Houpt and Rojo (2006) examine technology transfer in Spanish steelmaking and shipbuilding. They focus primarily on non-patent methods. Indeed, they are reluctant to admit that IPR helped Spanish steelmaking firms to acquire and improve novel methods. Similarly, Anduaga (2011) argues that Basque engineers trained in Europe were much more important than patents for transferring technology to Spain's steel industry. Later in the chapter, I strongly challenge these claims.

Finally, other researchers who look outside of the Spanish case make a more nuanced argument. Some argue that patents complement other channels and are rarely sufficient on their own. For example, host countries with robust IPR regimes may attract greater FDI inflows and have an easier time securing imports from firms at the technological frontier; in combination, these forces drive international technology transfer (Maskus 1998).[8] Other researchers aver that patents can sometimes substitute for alternative channels, but that depends: IPR may foster technology transfer from developed to developing countries only in some industries (for example, Lee and Mansfield 1996), or under specific conditions (see Braga and Fink 1998).

[7] Moser (2013) is bearish about patents fostering innovation; yet, she is oddly bullish about their ability to fuel technological diffusion and, by implication, technology transfer across borders.

[8] Although see Hall and Helmers (2018), who analyze the effects of accession to Europe's regional patent office, which afforded joining countries membership in the European Patent Convention. They find that FDI did not materially increase in joining countries during the post accession era, despite investors' access to a seemingly stronger IPR regime.

Why Patents Encourage International Technology Transfer

New processes and products cannot simply be transferred in a simple and frictionless process. Technologies cannot be fully codified as important elements remain tacit. The technical, managerial, and marketing know-how that complements inventions cannot be disclosed in a patent itself. Moreover, know-how is costly to transfer (Arora 1995). And processes and products have to be adapted by inventors and entrepreneurs to new markets. This takes time and learning.

Even the most highly skilled and accomplished entrepreneurs in the developing world cannot rely on the information available in the patent alone to put the idea it describes into service. They do not have access to the same technological, managerial, and financial resources as developed world patent holders and licensees. They simply lack the knowledge and experience accumulated by original inventors during "learning by doing." This knowledge may go beyond their command of ancillary machinery not enumerated in the patent and include logistical and management innovations as well.[9]

Fortunately, when original, foreign inventors secure enforceable patents in developing countries, they may enjoy the right incentives and opportunities to help entrepreneurs implement and commercialize innovations. Patent licenses may outline how this critical know-how will be conveyed from licensors to licensees (see Arora 1995). A licensing contract can specify how a licensee will gain access to the plans, goods, services, and human capital needed to put the idea codified in the patent into practice. This may include the provision of drawings, blueprints, and machinery by the original inventor, as well as bespoke tutorials and training conducted by inventors or their envoys.

A patent licensing contract may also enjoin the licensor to take on the role of intermediary. It may obligate the licensee to connect to a coterie of suppliers, technicians, and even customers. A patent license may thus serve as a passport into a network of upstream firms that manufacture inputs to the novel processes, and potentially downstream firms and entities too.

In light of increasing technological and managerial complexity, this has been true at least as early as the Second Industrial Revolution. No amount of industrial espionage conducted by late industrializing countries could hope to deliver the sophisticated know-how required to introduce new processes and products tied to advances in physics, chemistry, electromagnetism, and organizational

[9] On these points, see Arora (1995). And see Moser (2013, p. 39), who offers the instructive example of the chemical industry; she recounts how, after the outbreak of World War I, US Winthrop Chemical Company struggled to apply Bayer patents for drugs it acquired from the US government. The latter expropriated these from the original patentee, but in doing so deprived the American firm from accessing critical, uncodified knowledge from Bayer.

dynamics. Nor has it been enough for later adopters to lean solely on their experiences studying and working abroad, knowledge of basic science, exposure to technical literature, membership in international technical societies, and travel to industrial exhibitions.

Instead, since the mid-nineteenth century, original inventors who license their patents in host countries, as well as entrepreneurs and laborers acting at their behest, have travelled to distant lands to help their licensees introduce inventions to new markets, adapt them to those markets, and help with their upkeep.[10] Examples include the transfer of process innovations associated with the manufacturing of textiles, glass, pulp and paper, machinery, chemicals, electricity, the telegraph, and railroads (see Moser 2011). They also include, as we shall see shortly, steelmaking.[11]

IPR in late industrializing countries also help undergird transnational networks that further stimulate innovation. When inventors try to introduce a process to a new country they encounter differences in raw materials and other inputs, industrial organization, and consumer tastes. To confront these types of challenges, foreign patentees, their licensees, and other entrepreneurs must adapt these processes to unique circumstances. Patents and licenses help them do that.

Consider that a patent represents a focal point around which inventors, entrepreneurs, financiers and manufacturers can coordinate, learn from each other, and build upon one another (see Kieff 2006). In this vein, it is often the case that a flurry of additional patenting accompanies the attempt by inventors to adjust their idea to new markets in the developing world—and quite often, this is undertaken by new, previously unknown inventors who use the information in the patent to piggyback on the original invention. Moreover, these improvements may eventually make their way back to the home country.[12] Therefore, international feedback loops centered on patents that undergird knowledge sharing and collaboration may foster incremental innovation.

[10] Of course, the international transfer of technology can be non-linear and complicated by a host of factors. For example, younger workers may choose to make specific human capital investments in older technologies—such as training to operate dated machinery—if a critical mass of older workers have also made those investments; in turn, this may slow down the diffusion of new technology across borders (see Chari and Hopenhayn 1991). Moreover, the diffusion of new processes may depend on the degree to which an industry is competitive, the capital costs of initial investments, and managerial incentives to take risks (see Mansfield 1961).

[11] For an account of how technology was transferred to Scandinavia by foreigners patenting and disseminating their inventions across these sectors see Bruland and Smith (2010).

[12] For example, during the latter part of the nineteenth century, German and French inventors who improved upon English steelmaking inventions after acquiring licenses for them then turned around and obtained patents in England to protect their follow-up innovations.

Spain's Efforts at Acquiring Technology

Spain has always been a technology laggard. Throughout its history, it has exhibited an all-of-the-above strategy for acquiring technology from the industrial frontier. Patents are the most recent among several methods that Spanish governments have used to try to catch up.

Throughout the latter half of the eighteenth century, King Carlos III opted for a diversified approach to acquiring technology from countries such as Britain and France. He hired several foreign scientists, encouraged skilled European machinists to migrate to Spain, pushed for the importation of new machinery, and sent Spanish scientists, engineers, and technicians to study abroad in a bid to improve their knowledge and skills (see Sáiz 1995, p. 49; 1999, p. 78). He also oversaw the creation of royal laboratories and scientific academies (Sáiz 1999, p. 107). Finally, he encouraged and bankrolled industrial espionage (Helguera 2011; Sáiz 1999, pp. 78, 109). These efforts continued, albeit with less enthusiasm, under his son's reign (see Sáiz 1995, p. 40).[13]

Under both Carlos III and Carlos IV, the Spanish government also experimented with unorthodox intellectual property tools. It sponsored prizes to stimulate new inventions, mostly around efforts to boost agricultural production (Sáiz 1999, p. 108). The crown also awarded royal privileges, a precursor to patents, to inventors. While these privileges endowed inventors with exclusive rights, Spanish monarchs only granted these sparingly, capriciously, and at a high cost. They also required that inventors first prove that their innovations worked (Sáiz 1999, p. 81).

Beginning in the early nineteenth century, however, the Spanish government followed up these desultory policies with more deliberate, formal attempts to attract foreign technology. These were embodied in a series of evolving laws governing industrial policy and intellectual property; important reforms extended into the late twentieth century. In what follows, I describe Spain's numerous patent regimes and flesh out their underlying political economy.[14]

[13] These measures paralleled what was done in other countries to acquire advanced machinery and knowledge from Britain, the leading technological power at the time. Other measures experimented with across European capitals included bestowing private firms with imported machinery and setting up model factories, as well as giving them financial incentives to use more advanced technology: rebates and exemptions on import duties (see Landes 1969, pp. 150–151). Ironically, long before the industrial revolution, Henry VII tried to lure skilled wool weavers from the Netherlands and Venice to England to acquire new technologies (see Reinert 1995).

[14] Before going into details, it behooves us to put Spain's relative technological backwardness in perspective, however. During the 1880s, the number of invention patents awarded in Spain was somewhere north of 2,000; over the same time period, this number was closer to 30,000 in the United Kingdom. Also, the patenting gap between Spain and the United Kingdom, as well as between Spain and other developed countries, widened over time. See Ortiz-Villajos (2004).

Spain's First Patent System

Spain's first (modern) patent law was decreed by Joseph Bonaparte in 1811, under French occupation. The system introduced by the French was then adopted by Spain's sovereign government in 1820, after the restoration of the Spanish Crown, and ratified with few changes in 1826 by Fernando VII through a royal decree. Spain's patent system was originally vested in the language of natural rights: intellectual property was declared to be private property.[15]

Despite these classical liberal underpinnings, however, the actual elements of Spain's nineteenth century patent system betray a hybrid approach. Products could not be patented, only novel processes. The system included both "invention" and "introduction" patents—legal monopolies granted to Spaniards for putting into practice processes and products that had already been invented abroad.[16] Internationally speaking, this made Spain somewhat exceptional.[17] Also, Spanish patents had a working requirement: patentees were compelled to put their invention into practice within one year, lest their property right expire.[18]

Most patent requests were granted without much fanfare or delay by the Spanish patent office (see Sáiz 1999, p. 104). It did not administer technical examinations prior to granting a patent. Also, while patent seekers were required to explain their inventions in writing and affix drawings, or even models, it was sometimes difficult for patent officers to ascertain whether the person filing the patent was actually the original inventor. Moreover, original inventors were not treated with priority. Spanish nationals could beat foreign inventors to the punch and obtain introduction patents for the latter's inventions. Indeed, foreign inventors were not explicitly allowed to "repatent" inventions they had already patented elsewhere.[19]

In terms of duration and cost, Spain's IPR was not particularly strong during this era. Inventors could obtain invention patents for 5, 10, or 15 years (five-year patents could be extended another five years). Introduction patents were

[15] Terms such as "property" and "rights" were dropped in 1826, and replaced with language denoting royal "prerogatives" and "privileges." Despite these semantic changes, Spain's patent system remained centered on protecting temporary property rights to ideas (see Sáiz 1995, p. 95).

[16] Readers should note that if an introduction patent was granted by the government to an entrepreneur to manufacture a new invention in Spain, this did not bar others from importing it into Spain. In practice, however, this happened on a de facto basis if import tariffs were high.

[17] While Spain granted introduction patents until 1985 (more on that later in the chapter), the United Kingdom abolished them by 1852. Moreover, the United States never had any; nor did France or Germany. Other countries with introduction patents were the Netherlands (before they abolished patents) and Austria.

[18] Spanish authorities stringently enforced this stricture between 1849 and 1877 (see Sáiz 2013).

[19] Foreign inventors found ways around this restriction and patented their original inventions in Spain after patenting them elsewhere; indeed, as we shall soon see, this was the case for French and British inventors working in the steel industry during the mid-nineteenth century.

granted for only five years. The fees associated with either invention or introduction patents had to be paid by patentees in full and upfront. Invention patent fees were a function of their duration, and were significantly more expensive than introduction patents. In terms of the ratio of patent costs to (yearly) unskilled wages, the cost of invention patents was always over 100 percent during Spain's first patent regime, and the cost of an introduction patent was only over 100 percent of (yearly) unskilled wages during the early 1800s, and well below that afterward.[20]

Despite its heterodoxies, many features made Spain's first patent system somewhat strong. Patent owners were allowed to transfer or sell their patent rights to assignees, as well as license them. There were no restrictions associated with inventions related to chemicals, plants, or animals. And, as just outlined, invention patents were granted for a longer duration than introduction patents. Moreover, both inventors and the introducers of foreign inventions were instructed to focus on narrow novelty claims so that others could work around these innovations.

The Spanish patent office adopted a multipronged approach to disseminating information about patents and inventions.[21] Patents were registered, archived, and publicized to anybody who sought them, free of charge. The patent office also provided access to technical support to understand how to use machines or put new production methods into practice. Eventually, it doubled as a degree granting engineering school, stored a huge library detailing international and Spanish inventions, and boasted a museum populated with mechanical models. Moreover, several sources widely disclosed patents throughout the kingdom.[22]

In terms of enforcement, patentees had multiple, complementary ways to redress infringements.[23] They could receive injunctive relief, in the form of an embargo placed by the courts on competing processes or products that violated their patents. They could also win monetary relief, in which infringers paid patentees a steep fine in addition to "treble" damages. Finally, in 1868 the possibility of criminal action against patent infringement was introduced by the Spanish government, a feature that lasted until 1985.

The Political Economy of Spain's First Patent Regime

Spain's 1826–1877 patent system was largely a response to three factors. First, by the turn of the eighteenth century, it became increasingly hard for the kingdom

[20] To calculate these figures I used data on patent fees from Sáiz (1995). I deflated them using the producer price index available in Taylor (2016). The wages data are from Williamson (1995).

[21] On all of the points contained in this paragraph, see Sáiz (1995; 1996; 2013).

[22] In 1886, the patent office began to print a journal that disclosed and publicized patents called *Boletín Oficial de la Propiedad Intelectual e Industrial*. Before that, other magazines and periodicals regularly broadcast new patents.

[23] On all of these points, see Sáiz (1995, p. 95).

to gain access to cutting-edge technology through industrial espionage, encouraging skilled workers to migrate to Spain, and importing machinery. Second, during French occupation (1808–1814), Napoleonic forces had experimented with modernizing reforms, including the introduction of a patent system. Third, after it secured its independence from France, Spain faced an unprecedented economic, fiscal, and political catastrophe. Liberal reformers sought to remedy several crises by promoting economic development; a patent system was only one of several measures they undertook.

In 1719, Britain imposed a ban on the outmigration of skilled labor in response to attempts by French and Russian firms to recruit skilled British labor.[24] Over the course of the eighteenth century, the English Crown honed its countermeasures and tightened their enforcement. Englishmen who emigrated abroad to work incurred stiff fines, lost their rights to land and other assets, had their citizenship revoked, and were imprisoned. This ban was in place until 1825.

Similarly, throughout the eighteenth century, Britain increasingly banned the export of machines. In 1750, this included the "tools and utensils" used in its wool and silk industries. In 1774, a ban on machine exports in the cotton and linen industries was imposed by the crown. By 1781, most tools and industrial machines, including engines, were covered by the ban. This was followed with another update introduced by British authorities in 1785, which included any machinery overlooked by the previous two bans. These restrictions lasted until 1842.

In first reforming its patent system in 1811, Spain therefore followed a new regional trend that sought to circumvent British imposed barriers to technology transfer. For example, France adopted a modern patent system in 1791, with a 15-year protection tenure for novel inventions. Other nations besides Spain that followed suit include the United States (1793), Austria (1810), Russia (1812), Prussia (1815), Belgium and the Netherlands (1817), Sweden (1819), Bavaria (1825), Sardinia (1826), Sweden (1834), Württemberg (1836), Portugal (1837), and Saxony (1843).[25] In short, IPR were widely used by European governments to coax British inventors to willingly introduce and commercialize their inventions.

In the Spanish case, it took the French to do the dirty work: introduce a patent system on the back of a host of liberalizing reforms that had been resisted hitherto by the ruling elite. Joseph Bonaparte, who ruled Spain from 1808 to 1813, promulgated decrees to end semi-feudalism and modernize commercial codes,

[24] This and the next paragraph builds on Chang (2003) and Harris (1996).

[25] See Penrose (1951, p. 13). Holland had a very weak patent system—with no disclosure of inventions, introduction patents, the nullification of foreign patents in favor of domestic ones, and with wide latitude for infringement—and abandoned it in 1869. Switzerland did not adopt a patent system until 1888, and it was a rather weak one until reformed in 1907 (Chang 2003).

including rights to conduct free trade within Spanish territory and standardizing customs, and complemented these measures with a modern IPR regime.

What did this mean for Spain's exiled government in Cádiz? On the one hand, it had to compete with the Napoleonic reformers in Madrid for hearts and minds, and modernization was part of a broader propaganda war aimed at the Spanish public. On the other hand, Bonaparte's reform efforts were a welcome opportunity: for the most part, Cádiz insurgents were frustrated liberals whose reform agenda had been repeatedly blocked by the crown before Bonaparte arrived. Thanks to French occupation, a coalition of lawyers, intellectuals, bureaucrats, merchants, and modernizing army officers (see Ringrose 1996, p. 326) now had a chance to make a difference.[26]

The Cádiz Court imbued Spain's 1812 Constitution with Enlightenment principles. The charter called for a constitutional monarchy vested in the separation of church and state. It abolished the Inquisition and eliminated noble prerogatives. It codified equality before the law, free speech, private property, and the freedom to contract. It also introduced universal suffrage.

Spain's reformers sought to end the ancien régime's absolute monarchy, feudalism, and mercantilism. They believed a radical break from the past was necessary because Spain had become a peripheral, backward, and vulnerable country. On the eve of Napoleon's invasion, Carlos IV's kingdom found itself in a death spiral.

Consider the country's dire fiscal situation.[27] Spain had accumulated a huge debt load associated with the kingdom's participation in countless wars; yearly deficits were common. By 1808, Spain's sovereign debt had risen to over 150 percent of GDP (Tedde de la Lorca 1994, p. 530). Not that the crown found it easy to borrow, however: it had defaulted on its debt several times and endlessly debased the currency, which stoked inflation and invited repeated bankruptcies.

The Spanish kingdom was fiscally vulnerable. It had come to rely excessively on volatile revenues from its Latin American colonies that were no longer available after the collapse of the Spanish Empire.[28] What remained of the country's own fiscal base was taxed by Spanish authorities in a grossly inefficient manner. Several time-honored sources of revenue had run dry.[29] By 1814, government revenues were reduced by more than a third (Ringrose 1996, p. 324).

[26] Fernando VII had quickly abdicated in the face of France's 1808 invasion and occupation and, in a sense, had countenanced Spain's takeover by a foreign empire. The Cádiz Court soon filled the political void, as did provisional regional Juntas, and was able to gain popular support.

[27] This paragraph builds on Tortella and Comín (2001).

[28] To be sure, the crown liberalized trade between the mainland and its colonies and among the colonies in the late 1700s; this contributed to a short-lived boost in revenues. However, rising military expenditures largely offset these new revenues; besides, trade liberalization was rendered moot when Latin American countries won their independence.

[29] Consider, for example, tax receipts associated with the Mesta: the French army had laid waste to the once-valuable sheep trade, therefore killing what was once a government fiscal cow.

It did not help matters that Spain had fallen behind the rest of Europe economically (Harrison 1985, p. 15). Its largely informal economy was overwhelmingly agricultural. It produced commodities and food inefficiently and could barely feed its people. Moreover, the country was quite sparsely populated, predominantly rural, and economically Balkanized.

Political problems also abounded. As political factions turned to violence to settle their differences, unrest beset both the cities and countryside. The military services were riven with internal strife. The navy was rendered a shell of its former self, and the military was depleted and demoralized. Popular resistance to conscription was growing.

These problems were themselves symptoms of deeper institutional and cultural deficiencies. Spain failed to liberalize and modernize its government and economy before 1800. There was never a Magna Carta–type moment or Glorious Revolution in which the monarchy was tamed by a bill of rights, let alone an independent judiciary or representative legislature. Therefore, Spain's monarchs did not seek to protect individual liberties and were not prevented from indulging in overzealous spending and inflationary finance.

In many ways, the Enlightenment passed Spain by. The church continued to have an outsized political influence. Spain largely missed out on the scientific revolution. It lacked great universities. Nor did it produce great scientists. Therefore, unlike in the Netherlands, Britain, Belgium, or even France and Germany, Spain did not cultivate the seeds of a commercial revolution, let alone an industrial one (see Mokyr 2016).

Finally, a host of new issues that arose during the bloody and protracted guerilla war to dislodge the French army compounded the problems just outlined. Large stocks of physical capital were destroyed, including workshops, factories, and laboratories. Also, skilled laborers fled the scene, and undisciplined French troops indulged in plunder and shakedowns (Esdaile 2002).

After the Peninsular War, the liberal coalition that was holed up in Cádiz emerged to reform the country. They sought to foster a more stable and prosperous Spain that could produce greater tax revenues. They believed that economic development and a stronger military could serve as a bulwark against the country's European adversaries. The humiliating Napoleonic era was seared deep into the nation's consciousness.[30]

Reformers wanted to stimulate economic development by increasing economic exchange, modernizing agriculture, and nourishing domestic manufacturing. Beyond the patent system, these goals would be achieved by "dismantling the legal basis of a society of estates" (Ringrose 1996, p. 327), which would in

[30] On the struggle faced by Spanish authorities to finance both external defense and internal security after the Peninsular War, see Tortella and Comín (2001, p. 164).

turn create and lubricate markets for tradable goods. Reformers therefore began by bolstering secure and tradable property rights to land.

This meant putting an end to Spain's peculiar rural political economy. They abolished the Mesta in 1836, quasi-feudal (seigneurial) land rights in 1836–1841, and the tithe in 1841.[31] Reformers also passed new mining laws (in 1849 and 1859) that abrogated the crown's ownership over Spain's subsoil and sold off scores of mines to private actors (Berend and Ránki 1982, p. 38).

To stimulate commercial exchange, reformers pursued a multipronged approach. They sought to integrate the kingdom's fragmented market by eliminating internal tariffs and local restrictions on domestic trade. They also sought to create a modern labor market and thus eased restrictions on labor mobility. A cognate agenda was to establish a competitive and more liquid financial system, with private banks organized as limited liability corporations and endowed with the ability to issue notes, discount bills, make loans, and undertake investments.[32] This included judicial reforms that improved contracting and reforms to public finance intended to increase and improve tax collection and provide public goods.[33] Finally, and despite strong pushback and many false starts, reformers liberalized cross border trade (Tortella 2000, p. 196).

In short, Spain's first patent system was a creature of the times. It drew inspiration from a larger liberal movement and from patent systems introduced in other European countries during that era. IPR complemented a bid by reformers to strengthen property rights.

Spain's Second Patent System

Both before and after Napoleon's invasion, the Spanish Crown's oligarchic supporters included municipal government officials, high placed church officers, and seaport merchants involved in the Spanish Empire's Atlantic trade routes (see Ringrose 1996). They also included a motley crew of provincial, landholding aristocrats with special property rights; for example, loosely organized Castilian cereal producers, the Barcelona association of cotton producers (see Tortella 2000, pp. 196–97), and shepherds who were members of the Mesta.

[31] At the end of the eighteenth century, most Spanish land could not be sold, even if its owner wanted to sell it, because it was tied up in "special" holdings that faced strong sale and use restrictions. This was true for land that belonged to the Catholic Church and municipal governments or land that was held by the nobility in entail. Moreover, many tracts were held in common by villagers. Finally, the crown bestowed privileges to the Mesta—a powerful sheep owners' organization—which monopolized pasturing rights over huge swaths of land in exchange for taxes levied on the lucrative wool trade (see Simpson 1995, p. 64; Tedde de la Lorca 1994, p. 531).

[32] On paper, distinctions were made between savings banks, mortgage banks, and investment banks; in practice, these distinctions were not always respected (see Tortella 2000, Chapter 6).

[33] On Spain's fiscal and budgetary reforms, see Tortella and Comín (2001, pp. 161–73).

What these groups shared in common is that they depended on the state for privileges and rents. These were centered on barriers to entry and arbitrage opportunities: high import tariffs, archaic mercantilist practices such as a flag tax on merchandise delivered by foreign vessels, and the outright banning of goods such as cotton cloth, wool, and cereals (see Tortella 2000, pp. 195–96).

Because these special interest groups never truly disappeared after the Peninsular War, Spain's Liberal Revolution was a one step forward and two steps back process. To be sure, the crown and its economic allies seemed to agree that technology could play an instrumental role in driving industrialization and growth; thus, they did not threaten the patent system. Yet, whenever the so-called absolutists returned to power on the back of armed interventions or subterfuge, they watered down or abandoned other liberal reforms. And they were challenged at every step by reformers with their own supporters within the military and greater society.

To put this political-economic tug of war in perspective, consider Spain's numerous nineteenth-century revolutions and counterrevolutions. Upon returning to the throne in 1814, Fernando VII abolished the 1812 Constitution. However, the charter was revived between 1820 and 1823 after a military revolt. Its recrudescence was accompanied by radical reforms such as abolishing the guilds and confiscating monastic lands (Berend and Ránki 1982, p. 35). Between 1824 and 1835, however, reactionary forces were again able to beat back liberal reformers.[34]

While a reinvigorated Fernando VII again brushed aside the 1812 Constitution, as did his daughter Isabela II after she succeeded him in 1833, this time around the crown largely tolerated the modernization efforts spearheaded by reformers. Indeed, the liberal charter was again restored in 1834, after yet another revolution. And a revolt spearheaded by absolutists and fanatical Catholic bishops (the Carlist War) was snuffed out in 1839, further buoying reformers.

Yet, in another twist, the 1850s saw another reactionary backlash by the church and landed oligarchs. The pendulum thus swung toward neo-feudalism and rent-seeking once again.[35]

But this was not to last either. In 1873, Spain's "First Republic" came into existence on the heels of the abdication of King Amadeo I, who was affiliated with the

[34] Ironically, this time around they had the support of the French, who (once again) occupied Spain to help Fernando VII cling to power.

[35] While absolutists were, for the most part, aligned with landed interests who sought trade protection, their alliance was complicated by the fact that some agriculturalists sought protection from imported foodstuffs and commodities while seeking duty free fertilizers and machinery. And nascent Spanish industries often sought protection from imports, even though their economic interests coincided with those of liberal reformers over matters such as access to a free, mobile labor force, credit, and cheap energy (Tortella 2000, pp. 193–94). As we shall see later, this was the case for the steel industry.

House of Savoy. This Italian carpetbagger had replaced Isabela II in 1870, after she was deposed in a military coup in the wake of a revolution, which broke out in 1868. The revolt was spearheaded by reformers—both within the armed forces and outside of them—upset with the country's direction: Isabela, like her father before her, had not fully committed herself to the country's liberal agenda.

Spain's republican experiment proved stillborn, however. The monarchy was quickly restored in 1875. That year, Isabela's son, Alfonso XII, ascended to the throne. This marked the second restoration of the Bourbon monarchy in less than a century.

Yet, Alfonso accepted the strictures of parliamentary government, including a new constitution that echoed the 1812 charter. The charter called for a bicameral legislature whose seats would be contested by competitive political parties. It also codified free speech and free assembly, jury trials, and universal suffrage. Citizens were now equal under the law and had the ability to have a say over taxes and public spending (see Tedde de la Lorca 1994).

During the ensuing era, known as the Restoration, conservatives and liberals struck a political pact to share power in the legislative branch; they therefore took turns controlling the cabinet under parliamentary monarchy. Many economic changes were promulgated by reformers. They included the Bank of Spain obtaining the sole right to emit currency.[36] They also included a national system for regulating railroads and a new commercial code. By the second half of the nineteenth century, the Spanish labor market was fully integrated on the back of further liberalizing measures (Rosés 2003, p. 1000). More tax reforms also followed. Finally, so did trade liberalization: the government appreciably reduced tariffs and Spain signed commercial treaties with Europe's major powers, including England (Tortella 2000, p. 199).

Patent Changes Mirror the Consolidation of Liberal Reforms

It should therefore be unsurprising to readers that IPR were also strengthened during this period. Specifically, in 1878 an important series of reforms were made by lawmakers to Spanish patent law.[37] This included reducing the costs of patenting, strengthening invention patents, and bolstering foreigners' patent

[36] In 1874, the Banco de España was made the sole issuer of legal tender; in 1885, it established the first nationwide network of bank branches. The bank acted as a lender of last resort, but mandated no capital requirements from banks and demanded only minimal disclosure requirements. There was free entry for non-issue commercial banks until 1920. See Martín-Aceña, Pons, and Betrán (2014). I should note, however, that the central bank had an outsized influence on the economy, focusing much of its energy on financing the country's explosive sovereign debt; also, the Spanish financial system remained quite underdeveloped in comparison to the rest of Europe (Tortella 2000).

[37] Rather than a decree, it came in the form of legislation proposed and authored by reformers in the Spanish Parliament. Specifically, it was crafted by a joint committee of the country's two legislative chambers (see Sáiz 1995, p. 125). I should also note that Spain introduced a system of trademark registration and enforcement in 1850.

rights.[38] While invention patents were extended to twenty years, the law explicitly recognized that original, foreign inventors had the right to patent their inventions in Spain for ten years, even if they had already obtained a patent in their home country and/or other countries.[39] The working requirement was also extended to two years, thus allowing inventors/entrepreneurs more time to put processes and products into place.[40] Perhaps more importantly, the government weakened the verification process employed by authorities to evaluate that patents had been put into practice and sanction non-compliers (see Sáiz 2013). Finally, inventors/entrepreneurs acquired the right to patent products, not only processes.[41]

Spain's Third Patent System

In 1929, Spain's patent system again experienced reform under a new law governing industrial property.[42] This time around, however, policymakers' main goal was to strengthen introduction patents; this was coupled with efforts aimed at speeding up industrialization at the expense of invention patents. Needless to say, this was a rebuke of the previous patent regime.

Several changes highlight the new patent system's "mercantile" DNA. The cost of acquiring an invention patent increased significantly. While the same was true

[38] While the total price tag for an invention patent increased, patent fees were now due in installments, rather than upfront in one lump sum. The amount owed by a patentee increased progressively over time. This meant that a greater number of inventors/entrepreneurs could afford a patent and smooth out the amortization of their IPR.

[39] This implied that, for the first time, foreign inventors had a priority over the Spanish nationals who might have sought to introduce these previously existing inventions to Spain. Foreigners had up to two years after first obtaining a patent abroad to patent their invention in Spain. Moreover, in 1884 Spain joined the International Union for the Protection of Industrial Property (IUPIP) as a founding member. Signatories obliged themselves to respect a priority right: the filing of an application for a patent in one country gave the applicant the right to obtain a recognition of that claim in all other IUPIP member countries. However, readers should keep in mind that the IUPIP was vested in a non-reciprocity approach: foreign citizens were entitled to receive the same treatment as nationals, but signatories were not required to reciprocate by furnishing foreign citizens the full scope of rights they enjoyed in their own countries.

[40] I should note that, as a share of total patents, corporations began to patent in Spain at increasing rates around this time, paralleling a trend seen throughout the industrialized world. The majority of these companies were foreign multinationals (Ortiz-Villajos 2004; Sáiz 2016).

[41] Spanish patent law now explicitly barred the patenting of "naturally occurring" things, as well as pharmaceuticals, and gave original inventors priority when patenting further additions to their inventions. And further patent reforms were made by Spanish lawmakers in 1902. Foreigners were afforded the same twenty-year protection for their invention patents as Spaniards, even if they had previously patented their inventions in their home country or elsewhere; the working requirement was extended to three years; temporary patents were given, at no cost, to inventors who debuted their innovations at international expositions; the patent office was required to keep inventions with national security implications secret; and the state could use eminent domain to "expropriate" patents if doing so advanced the national interest (see Sáiz 1995, pp. 144–47).

[42] See Sáiz (1995, pp. 152–162; 1999, pp. 95–96) on all of the following points.

for introduction patents,[43] their duration was extended from five to ten years. Patentees now had only one year to put inventions into practice. Also, inventions not associated with industrial applications faced restrictions: products could not be patented—only processes. The 1929 law also introduced "utility model patents" for minor inventions: a 20-year protection for products manufactured in Spain for the first time. It also introduced "exploitation patents," which granted monopoly rights to entrepreneurs who sought to introduce a whole new industry to Spain rather than a particular invention; these were to be granted by the government for ten years.[44] Finally, policymakers restored the strict system used to verify whether patents had been put into practice (Sáiz 2013).

In short, a new IPR regime centered on rewarding domestic entrepreneurs who sought rents, if not monopoly profits, emerged. Original inventors, especially foreign ones, were hurt.

The Political Economy of Spain's Third Patent Regime

What explains this sharp turn away from relatively strong IPR? It was years in the making. Cartels of nascent manufacturers, most prominently textile producers, were able to capture successive Spanish governments during the last decade of the nineteenth century. They secured a slew of protectionist measures that ramped up import substitution industrialization. The Spanish government levied tariffs on imports in 1891, 1906, and 1922.[45] They also passed non-tariff laws that subsidized domestic manufacturing in 1907, 1909, 1917, 1918, and 1922 (Rosés 2003, p. 999).

A political takeover by Miguel Primo de Rivera consolidated the new normal. He ruled as a dictator and used the rhetoric of nationalism and self-sufficiency as a smokescreen to erect further barriers to entry and to pick winners and losers.[46]

Francisco Franco later put this "development model" on steroids during the 1940s. With the support of the so-called Falingists, he adopted a cascading tariff structure, quantitative import restrictions via licenses, and foreign exchange controls with multiple exchange rates. Franco also nationalized several private enterprises under the auspices of the Institute of National Industry, a state

[43] These increased fees were introduced by the government in 1924 (see Sáiz 1995, p. 153).

[44] Exploitation patents were abrogated in 1930, however (see Sáiz 1999, p. 96). There were other, less important, changes made by the Spanish government to the patent system under the 1929 law; this included a host of regulations governing "addition patents" (see Sáiz 1995, p. 165).

[45] Some researchers argue that these tariffs were not protectionist per se, and that they instead served as revenue generating measures (Berend and Ránki 1982, p. 106; Tortella 2000, p. 201; Tortella and Comín 2001, p. 179).

[46] De Rivera was a military general who had the support of King Alfonso XIII. He lasted in office six years; after he gave up power, Spain's Second Republic was ushered in.

holding company. This served to promote rapid industrialization and employment growth.

What remained of the private economy was heavily regulated to achieve national investment and employment goals, as well as to boost the earnings of industrial sector wage earners.[47] Tax breaks and subsidies were doled out by the Spanish government to a host of manufacturing industries, including textiles, domestic appliances, and vehicles.[48] The state also encouraged mergers to "help firms reach economies of scale" (de la Torre and García-Zúñiga 2014, p. 169). FDI was part of this process, albeit under the umbrella of stringent local content requirements: the Franco government was bent on achieving the domestic production of intermediate inputs (de la Torre and García-Zúñiga 2014, pp. 167–169).[49]

Spain's Fourth Patent System

Spain democratized in 1977 and joined the European Union (EU) in 1986. These political developments set off a cascade of economic reforms. They included (further) reductions in barriers to trade and foreign investment and reforms to the financial system intended to make it more competitive. By 1991, Spain's capital account was fully open.[50]

It is no surprise, therefore, that in 1986 the Spanish patent system saw reform again.[51] The government sought to harmonize the system with international best practices. Lawmakers therefore strengthened invention patents by introducing a technical examination process and eliminated introduction patents. They allowed products to be patented once more.[52] They retained protections for utility models, however (their duration set at ten years), as well as working

[47] There were two reasons for this. First, Franco included important labor unions in his coalition. Second, the regime feared political instability associated with labor militancy.

[48] On all of these points, see Pons (2002).

[49] This crony capitalist system relied on financial repression and concomitant economic distortions. The government restricted entry into the banking system and capped interest rates, so credit was artificially rationed. The upshot was a highly concentrated, inefficient financial system centered on five big banks. In exchange for barriers to entry and associated market power rents, these banks held controlling stakes in important industries, many of them state-run enterprises, to which they directed subsidized credit. These oligopolistic banks also held the government's debt at below market rates, which helped the latter fund large budget deficits.

[50] Trade liberalization began in 1959 a part of a stabilization plan. The government reduced quantitative restrictions on external trade and tariffs reductions (see Tortella 2000, pp. 431–33).

[51] On all of the following points, see Sáiz (1999, pp. 97–98).

[52] The government barred scientific discoveries from being patented, along with software or innovations centered on plants, animals, medicine, and food. In 1992, Spain allowed chemical substances to be patentable once again, however (see Chang 2001, p. 306).

requirements—inventors now had four years to put their innovations into practice.

These changes were foreshadowed by international agreements. Since 1973, inventors can receive a patent from the European Patent Office, which is valid across as many EU countries as they care to designate, including Spain after 1986, the year it signed the Munich Convention. In 1989, Spain became a signatory of the Patent Cooperation Treaty; since then, inventors can include Spain within the group of countries for which they may obtain a "universal" patent from the World Intellectual Property Organization.

Spanish Iron and Steelmaking: Technology Transfer via Patenting

Steel is pure iron that contains carbon, which hardens it, but less carbon than cast iron, however, which makes it both more malleable and stronger. Steel is produced by skilled laborers from iron ore, which is a compound of iron, oxygen, and earthy material. Steel comes in several varieties that depend on the mixture of pig iron (blocks of crude iron from the smelting furnace) and different alloys and metals.

During the Second Industrial Revolution, the mushrooming demand for new products that employed cast iron and steel drove several innovations in metallurgy and stimulated an increased production scale. What ultimately emerged was a vertically integrated system of steel production that used heavy machinery, new technologies, and an assembly line technique in which skilled laborers choreographed a ballet of seamless motion: from smelting iron ore to creating finished products such as laminated steel or steel bars and ingots.

It is useful for readers to consider all of the steps involved. First, hot blast furnaces powered by charcoal or coke (converted coal) convert iron ore to molten pig iron with the help of limestone. These furnaces reduce the iron ore as it comes into contact with carbonic oxide and separate out the earthy matter. After this smelting process, Bessemer converters or Siemens open hearth furnaces convert pig iron into purified iron. Next, metalworkers soak, roll, cool, and cut the metal in rolling mills, where they give it its final shape. Across these processes, they employ equipment of various kinds to cool, manipulate, reheat, and polish the metal.

Modern steel mills are characterized by much greater efficiency vis-à-vis the traditional ironworks they replaced. Steelmakers obtain cost savings in several ways. First, by reducing the use of heat. Second, by increasing coordination across each step in the chain. Third, by reaching economies of scale that eliminate duplicate efforts.

It should therefore not surprise readers to learn that the fabrication of steel in large amounts and for different uses under one roof requires sophisticated human capital. On the one hand, the adoption by steelmakers of sophisticated technologies calls upon skilled laborers to acquire and hone knowledge of material sciences, chemistry, and engineering. On the other hand, it entails organizational innovations and thus skilled and nimble managers.

Spanish Steelmaking: Historical Overview

Modern steelmaking in Spain had its roots in Bilbao, a port city off the Bay of Biscay, in Basque country (northcentral Spain).[53] Ironworkers, and later steelmakers, located there because there were substantial iron ore deposits in the vicinity. Indeed, many of the companies that first produced Basque steel were capitalized by their founders with revenues from iron ore exports.

During the second half of the nineteenth century, and into the beginning of the twentieth century, Spain experienced a mining boom. This was catalyzed by the elimination of export tariffs by the crown in 1849, which coincided with a huge inflow of FDI and new technologies. The Biscayan iron ore industry consequently took off during the mid-1800s. Its life and success were due largely to FDI from Britain (see Maluquer de Motes 1988, pp. 18–20). The Spanish mining code was liberalized by the government in 1868, encouraging an even greater amount of FDI.

This accompanied the introduction of new mining technologies by foreigners who obtained numerous Spanish patents. For example, English inventors acquired several patents to protect methods for extracting low quality ores buried deep underground, including the so-called flotation system (Madrid Correspondence 1919). Foreign mining firms also imported sophisticated machinery, which also aided technology transfer (Fernández de Pinedo 1983, p. 19).

Biscayan mining thus experienced a period of modernization followed by exponential growth. Because the area's hematite lacked phosphorous, it was exported to England in massive quantities to feed Bessemer steelmaking.[54]

[53] While the rest of this chapter focuses on post-1850 steelmaking in that region of Spain, there was considerable "pre-modern" iron and steelmaking in other parts of Spain: Andalusia, on the southern, Mediterranean coast, and Asturias, in northwest Spain, where there were abundant coal reserves; there were two additional, albeit tiny, enclaves in Barcelona and Toledo. See Nadal (1970) for the etiology of iron and steelmaking in these regions, as well as their relative contribution to overall Spanish steelmaking until 1868. There were also failed modern steelmaking experiments undertaken by firms and the Spanish state in Andalusia.

[54] The first generation of the process required phosphorous free iron ore. In 1878, Sidney Gilchrist Thomas and Percy Gilchrist innovated a way to remove phosphorous from the iron during Bessemer steelmaking, however: they added limestone to the converter and then removed the resulting slag. This significantly reduced the selling power of Biscayan iron ore.

Figure 2.1 Spain's income from iron ore (1830–1929)

Notes: This variable measures income from iron ore expressed in 2007 dollars. Historically, Spain's commercial mineral production has also included metals such as lead, copper, manganese, zinc, silver, and gold. Natural log of income from iron ore subtracted from 1830 log value and multiplied by 100.

Sources: Haber and Menaldo (2011) and Carreras (2005).

Between 1880 and 1913, 91 percent of Basque iron ore was exported—the vast majority to England (see Riera i Tuebols 1993, p. 150). Figure 2.1 graphs Spain's (real) Iron Ore Income between 1830 and 1929 and recounts the story just told: first a piecemeal, steady ascent, followed by a palpable boom that begins to peter out around 1908.

Transition to Ironmaking and Steelmaking

During the 1850s, Biscayan iron ore began to be used by Basques to fabricate sweet iron and steel in Bilbao. Besides the presence of copious amounts of high-quality iron ore, agglomeration effects had a positive impact on the emergence and consolidation of steelmaking in and around Bilbao. The colocation of several firms dedicated to iron ore mining and metallurgy meant that a relatively deep pool of engineers and skilled laborers could be drawn on by employers. This fostered a relatively rapid spread of knowledge, technology, and innovations.

Basque steel production surged between 1879 and 1889 (see Figure 2.2). This is because, by the 1880s, large, integrated steel mills in and around Bilbao were producing plentiful amounts of steel. These included San Francisco de Mudela, Altos Hornos de Bilbao (Baracaldo), and La Vizcaya (Sestao). The latter two firms merged in 1901, creating Altos Hornos de Vizcaya. This hegemon began its life with a capital stock that exceeded 32 million pesetas; it eventually produced over 60 percent of Spanish steel (Gárate 2000, p. 160).

In terms of its commercial success, Spanish steelmaking falls into roughly two eras during the period under study. The first era was when a respectable portion of Basque steel was exported to European countries. The second was when it was produced mostly for the Spanish market.

The "export oriented" period corresponds roughly to between the early 1860s and late 1880s (see Fernández de Pinedo 1983, p. 16). In the face of tough competition from imported steel and insufficient domestic demand, Basque steelmakers sought foreign outlets for their product. The most important export markets included England, France, the Netherlands, Belgium, Italy, and Germany. Between 1881 and 1890, 30 percent of Biscayan steel was exported (Escudero 1999), a feat that required Bilbaoan firms to import substantial amounts of coal and coke from Britain, as it was relatively cheap to ferry this fuel from Cardiff on the same

Figure 2.2 Spanish steel production (1842–1929)

Notes: Natural log of steel production subtracted from 1842 log value and multiplied by 100.

Source: Carreras (2005)

vessels that shuttled iron ore from Biscay to that English city (see Fernández de Pinedo 1983, p. 13).[55]

The second era of Spanish steel's commercial success was when Basque steelmakers revved up production to satisfy new sources of internal demand between 1888 and 1914. This phenomenon was mainly driven by trade protectionism (see Tena-Junguito 2006); without it, Biscayan steel could simply not compete. For example, in the wake of the 1855 law that ushered in the construction of Spain's rail network, the French companies involved in building railways and railroads found that it was cheaper and more practical to employ French steel during the production process.

And this protectionism was in large part propelled by Spain's major steelmakers, which had formed the Asociación de la Industria Siderúrgica (which was later replaced by the Liga Vizcaína de Productores in 1894) to lobby for tariffs, both for steel and for the products manufactured by Spanish firms that were composed of steel.[56] Due in part to their alliance with cereal producers and Catalan textile producers, they achieved several victories (see Sáez-García 2017, p. 166). In 1889, Spain imposed stiff tariffs on imported machinery of all kinds and slapped tariffs across most imported inputs and products, including iron and steel, in 1891 and 1896. Also, in 1896 the government rescinded the tariff exemption that railway firms had secured in 1855. Even more tariffs were adopted by Spanish authorities in 1906 to stoke import substitution.

Moreover, the Spanish armed forces' procurement policies were intended to benefit the domestic steel sector and machinery industries. As early as 1883, the Spanish Navy invited Biscayan firms to supply 1,200 tons of laminated steel for the construction of cruisers (Fernández de Pinedo 1983, p. 17). This was followed by the navy's requisition in 1887 that Spanish companies supply the materials for the construction of six warships. Another round of tenders by the navy to manufacture warships followed in 1907, again benefiting the domestic steel industry (Sáez-García 2017, p. 166).

Tariffs on imports and "nationalistic" procurement policies by the Spanish army and navy continued into the twentieth century and were complemented by increased spending by the government on public works during the late 1920s (Sáez-García 2017, p. 167). These policies represented a reliable source of demand for Biscayan steel that lasted decades. In turn, a host of domestic firms

[55] To be sure, there were substantial coal deposits to Bilbao's west, in Sama de Langreo, Asturias. Yet, the lack of infrastructure linking these two regions made transportation costs, and thus the costs of shipping that coal east, prohibitive (see Riera i Tuebols 1993, p. 150).

[56] Escudero (1999, p. 199) offers several reasons why Spanish steelmakers were uncompetitive vis-à-vis European ones and thus sought protection: the advent of the Thomas Gilchrist adjustment to Bessemer steelmaking—which allowed convertors to use pig iron with phosphorous—meant that Biscayan iron ore lost its competitive edge; Bilbaoan steelmakers were unable to achieve economies of scale; and countries such as Italy and Germany adopted tariffs on imported steel.

sprang up to manufacture agricultural and industrial machines and tools; they used iron and steel produced in Bilbaoan mills to do so (Fernández de Pinedo 1983, pp. 18–19).

These metals were also used to fabricate steel pipes, railway bars, bridges, ship boilers, cranes, sundry metal structures, including warehouses and ports, and ships, arms, and tanks. The upshot is that Altos Hornos de Vizcaya, Spain's leading steelmaker at the turn of the twentieth century, clocked impressive growth: "the production of coke increased between 1913 and 1929 by 60 percent; that of cast iron by 46 percent; that of steel by 71 percent and that of rolled steels by 56 percent" (Sáez-García 2017, p. 167).

Figure 2.2 graphs raw steel production between 1842 and 1929. While it traces a trajectory that corresponds to the events discussed here—a steady ascent that really booms in the 1880s—there are other interesting patterns to note. Spanish steelmaking experienced another boom during World War I; on the back of its neutrality, Spain was able to step in and export steel to countries that were formerly supplied by Britain, Germany, and France (see Aldcroft 2016, p. 129). Yet, by 1920, with the war related boom at an end, and the onset of an international recession, Bilbaoan steel experienced a crash. This was followed by a healthy recovery and yet another crash due to the Great Depression that is not shown in the figure.[57]

Biscayan Steel: A Story of Technology Transfer from Europe

In cursory ways, the technological innovations that shaped the Biscayan steel industry paralleled those taking place in the rest of the world; more fundamentally, however, technology transfer occurred with an appreciable lag. For example, it took until 1848 for a charcoal blast furnace to be fired for the first time, let alone a blast furnace powered by coke. And while pig iron was smelted in a furnace using coke for the first time in 1856, it took several years for this practice to spread. Spanish firms instead extended their reliance on the direct processing of iron ore, which in any event only really began to bear fruit as late as 1859, and puddling techniques, which made their belated arrival in 1860.[58]

[57] It is important to note that, internationally speaking, the Spanish steel industry never achieved the size one would want to write home about; nor was it ever really all that competitive on world markets (Aldcroft 2016, p. 128). Between 1882 and 1922, Spain only produced 0.69 percent of world iron and steel output (Houpt and Rojo, p. 329). Several hypotheses have been put forth by economic historians to explain this. They include lackluster internal demand, high levels of protectionism that stifled competitiveness, and rent-seeking. Also, a civil war that raged between 1873 and 1876 deterred investors from building and expanding Biscayan mills (Nadal 1970).

[58] For the onset of each of these techniques see Fernández de Pinedo (1983) and Houpt and Rojo (2006, pp. 324–25). See Nadal (1970, pp. 220–21, table 4.3) for a list of Spanish iron and steelmaking establishments in 1865 and the technologies possessed by each of these.

However, modern steelmaking did eventually arrive in Basque country. And its rise paralleled that of iron-ore mining, with several technology transfer measures complementing each other. Both industries employed a large stock of imported machinery. Both relied on Spanish engineers who had studied abroad. Both also employed the services of foreign-born engineers, chemists, smelters, machinists, and boiler stokers.[59] Indeed,

> technical transfer in (Spain's) steel processing plants is not much different from the previous mechanisms of transfer of iron techniques. Foreign trained engineers and foreign consultants determined the items to be transferred, they chose among various machine factories or designing engineers from abroad and the process or installation was brought to Spain with technical supervision from the constructing or designing firm. Foreign staff was hired during a training period or contracted if their specific diagnostic skills were required over longer periods. (Houpt and Rojo 2006, p. 340)

And, as with iron-ore mining before it, patenting by foreign inventors was also a key vehicle for transferring technology and know-how about modern steelmaking to Spanish firms. On the one hand, there was widespread patenting by foreign steelmakers in Spain. On the other hand, Basque and foreign-born engineers and skilled laborers employed by San Francisco de Mudela, Altos Hornos de Bilbao, and La Vizcaya, as well as smaller firms, took a lead role in identifying patents that would increase steel production or cut costs. They then secured patent licenses and drew up contracts with foreign inventors that guaranteed technical assistance. Biscayan firms also adapted new technologies to the conditions on the ground, and sometimes engineers and steelworkers made noteworthy innovations themselves during the learning by doing process—many of which were subsequently patented in Spain.[60]

Before going into details, we should note that, at least in regards to steelmaking, the evidence points to the fact that it may not have mattered much that Spain's 1826 patent law did not explicitly allow foreign inventors to patent their inventions after already acquiring a patent in their home country. Sáiz (1995, p. 126) argues that foreign inventors found ways to circumvent this restriction before 1878 and obtained numerous invention patents in Spain. In terms of iron and steelmaking, I corroborate this claim here across several process innovations.

[59] See Anduaga (2011) and Houpt and Rojo (2006). Unlike in the iron ore industry, however, the nascent steel industry had a low level of FDI, so this did not play much of a role, if any, in facilitating the transfer of technology.

[60] I exploited electronic access to the actual patents through the Spanish Patent and Trademark Office (OEPM); they were put into a searchable database by Patricio Sáiz and his collaborators. See Sáiz n.d.

The Chenot Process

Direct steelmaking refers to several distinct methods in which iron or steel is oxidized by applying carbon and other alloys. This calls on heating iron ore to extremely high temperatures below its melting point. Cementation involves packing wrought iron in charcoal and heating the resultant slab inside stone boxes, removing and breaking up the iron bars, and repacking and reheating them again. This removes impurities such as manganese and silicon. The crucible steel process involves melting the "blister steel" produced after heating and oxidizing wrought iron via cementation, while also adding a flux that further removes slag.

The Chenot process is a refinement of the crucible steel process. It was developed by Adrian Chenot, a French engineer, during the 1830s and 1840s. He designed it to produce sponge iron in a modified, rectangular blast furnace that contains only the upper, "reducing" region.

The steps are as follows. Ironmakers vertically array pieces of iron ore by size within a twenty-five-foot-high retort (reduction chamber) and follow this step by adding a reducing agent composed mostly of charcoal. They then heat the retort's brick interior until its walls are red hot using a coal-fired oven that runs parallel to the retort and that communicates with it through horizontal and vertical channels. Ironmakers next wait for the sponge iron to cool inside a hermetically sealed cylinder directly below the retort—to prevent over-oxidation—and blast it with cold air. They then remove the sponge iron and use magnets to separate it from the earthy matter.

The result is a process that, between the reduction of iron ore and the removal of the sponge iron after cooling, takes six days. Four tons of fuel translate into one ton of iron for a loss of about 45 percent of the iron. Steelmakers can then convert the sponge iron into steel by carburizing it through cementation with charcoal (and sometimes magnesium), compressing it into cakes, and fusing it in a crucible.

Bilbao was the first place on earth where Chenot steel was produced in commercial quantities; patents played an instrumental role in introducing the process to Spain, perfecting it, and spreading it to other countries.[61] Chenot first acquired an invention patent in France in 1846 for his direct sponge iron technique. He then acquired a five-year introduction patent in Spain that same year (#310: Método para el tratamiento de los óxidos metálicos o de sus compuestos llevados a tal estado, etc.). Chenot followed this with another Spanish introduction patent in 1850 for an improvement he had previously patented in France (#522: Método para el tratamiento de los óxidos metálicos o de sus compuestos).

[61] Chenot steelmaking then spread to Belgium, France, Italy, and Russia (see Uriarte 1998).

But these initial patents were merely false starts: the Spanish patents he actually commercialized were invention patents of longer duration. In 1854, Chenot acquired two separate 15-year invention patents in Spain for his now almost 10-year old process (#1199: Sistema para la fabricación de acero, hierro, fundidos, soldados y moldeados; #1200: Sistema de normalización, enriquecimiento, generación y empleo general de los gases en los usos metalúrgicos).[62] These later patents caught the eye of the Baracaldo steel mill, which was owned and operated by a family of Biscayan mine owners and iron ore traders, the Ybarras. Along with their business partner, José de Vilallonga, a French-trained engineer who had previously traveled throughout Europe to acquire knowledge about new advances in iron and steel making, they were on the constant lookout for new techniques (see Anduaga 2011).

The Chenot direct steelmaking process was the first of many they experimented with and adopted in their mills. The Ybarras and Vilallonga acquired these patents from Chenot and tailored their Baracaldo plant to the inventor's process, which had achieved international attention after Chenot won a gold medal in 1851 at London's Universal Exposition. In exchange, the French inventor was entitled to 25 percent of the profits associated with the steel produced by his invention. In the same contract, Chenot committed himself to providing the Spaniards with technical assistance, including setting up a laboratory to test the quality of the iron and steel produced by his method (see Morlán 2002, p. 88; Uriarte 1998, p. 21).

Despite his help, the technology transfer experience vis-à-vis Chenot's process was protracted. While experiments with Chenot ovens were carried out in the Ybarras's Guriezo plant as early as 1855 under the French inventor's guidance, Chenot furnaces were only fully installed and actually running at the Baracaldo factory in 1859.[63] In the run up to the factory's completion, Vilallonga, Juan Maria Ybarra, and Jose Antonio Ybarra toured Belgium and France to gain exposure to steelmaking developments that could inform them about how they should best set up production. They also went there to hire engineers and skilled laborers to staff the new plant.

Other inventors then went on to make numerous improvements to the Chenot process. They also patented these additions in Spain and took an active role in putting them into practice there.

Consider Ernesto Tourangin. Between 1859 and 1865, he obtained three 15-year invention patents that eliminated or simplified many of the steps enumerated

[62] Later that year, Chenot followed this with a five-year introduction patent for steps that complemented his steelmaking process (#1212: Procedimiento para el tratamiento de los óxidos metálicos o sus compuestos llevados a tal estado).

[63] The plant eventually boasted eight Chenot ovens, several blast furnaces, and several puddling furnaces (see Fernández de Pinedo 1983, p. 13; Morlán 2002, p. 88).

earlier, including reducing the amount of total fuel needed for the process by switching the source of fuel to wood charcoal.[64] These patented inventions also improved the design of the retorts and parallel heating ovens. Tourangin's innovations were: #1999: Horno para la desoxidación de los minerales de hierro; #2271: Procedimiento para convertir la esponja de hierro en hierro de comercio; #4028: Procedimiento para la fabricación directa del hierro. The Frenchman then disseminated his process throughout Biscay and undertook adjustments centered on the idiosyncrasies he encountered in each ironwork along the way.[65]

Another notable improvement to the Chenot process was contributed by Chenot's son, Alfred, who registered it in Spain as a 15-year invention patent in 1865 (#3063: Procedimiento para obtener el hierro dulce y el acero directamente del horno alto). He then licensed it to the Ybarras and provided them with technical assistance to implement it in Baracaldo.

The Bessemer Process

During the first half of the 1850s, Henry Bessemer invented a steelmaking process centered on a converter—a tiltable, pear-shaped receptacle. Here is how it works: A steelmaker pours molten pig iron into the converter, which allows for control and shaping of the flowing mass. The iron is then purified by blowing cold, compressed air into the convertor, thus reducing its carbon content and stripping out any silicon: the air combines with the carbon and induces the iron to boil and burn until the carbon is reduced. After this oxidation process is completed, a steelmaker pours the converter's contents out and prepares them for rolling. This only takes about 20 minutes.

The Bessemer process was revolutionary. It obviated the need for steelmakers to mix liquid cast iron and carbon, a much more onerous and energy laden process. This meant that no outside fuel was needed by steelmakers to make steel, which considerably reduced costs and preparation time. Basically, the Bessemer process could create 30 tons of high quality (strong) steel in 30 minutes; it was widely adopted by industrialists for machine-making railway bars, bridges and shipbuilding.

During the second half of the 1850s, Henry Bessemer & Company, a firm founded by Bessemer in London, acquired patents associated with his steelmaking process in the United Kingdom and several European countries.[66] It

[64] Tourangin first obtained a French invention patent in 1853, followed by a Spanish introduction patent in 1855 (#1275: Procedimiento de fabricación del hierro por el método catalán haciéndolo mas rápido, económico, y lucrativo).

[65] For a description of these inventions and how Tourangin spread them around, see Uriarte (1998).

[66] Bessemer's basic steelmaking patent was granted in 1856. Over the years, he also patented improvements upon his original process. In the United States, William Kelley obtained a patent for the same technique in 1857: a US court ruled he discovered the process independently.

then widely licensed this patent to metalworkers and other manufacturers who had access to blast furnaces.[67] But selling a license to foreign steelmakers was only the beginning of the relationship between the company and its licensees.

Mastering the Bessemer technique is no small task. It requires workers to obtain considerable knowledge and skills centered on controlling temperatures, movements, and sequences. When pouring the molten pig iron into the converter, manipulating it through tilting and blowing, and pouring it out of the converter, it is paramount that steelmakers exercise the right technique and judgment, lest the oxidation process fail or the pig iron lose its malleability.

While much of this can be learned through experience, the accumulation of knowledge around Bessemer steelmaking involved considerable trial and error. Over time, the diagnostic and calibration skills honed by Bessemer steelmakers grew increasingly sophisticated. This led to vast improvements in efficiency as well as cost reductions.

Consider the following example. As a first step, Bessemer steelmakers melt iron ore in a blast furnace powered by coke. To ascertain that the pig iron they used had obtained the right consistency before introducing it into the converters, the first generation of Bessemer steelmakers cooled it after removing it from the blast furnace and then re-melted it in cupola furnaces. Over time, however, steelmakers learned how to manipulate the iron ore during the melting process itself, allowing them to pour the resulting pig iron straight into preheated converters. Finally, the Bessemer process involves rolling and shaping the cooled metal with utmost precision and care; a skill that takes steelmakers considerable time to learn and perfect.[68]

To help his licensees learn this elaborate and delicate process, which was constantly evolving, Bessemer deployed engineers and other skilled laborers abroad; sometimes, he himself was directly involved.[69] They took an active role in calibrating the disparate processes outlined here with whatever raw materials they found in situ. Bessemer and his envoys taught their licensees the analytic and diagnostic tools associated with each step in the process. This included not only the oxidation process, but also blast furnacing and rolling and shaping—how to manipulate the malleable metal to make it the right size, shape, and strength.[70]

[67] Within the first year of acquiring his patent, Bessemer collected £107,000 in royalties (Morlán 2002, p. 91). Bessemer collected royalties from three sources. First, he sometimes transferred his patent to a foreign agent outright. Second, he sometimes charged a fee for its general use. Third, he sometimes earned royalties on each unit of steel that was produced by a licensee.

[68] On all of these points, see Nuwer (1988).

[69] Patenting and licensing complemented other methods by which foreign steelmakers became aware of, and acquired knowledge about, the new process. The latter included Bessemer's attendance at international exhibitions, conferences about iron and steel, and seminars organized by the Institution of Mechanical Engineers. There, he and other metallurgists discussed their experiments, inventions, patents, and products.

[70] This paragraph builds upon Houpt and Rojo (2006).

They often shared insights with their licensees that they had acquired through learning by doing.

The introduction of the Bessemer steelmaking process to Spain was precocious. In September 1856, a mere months after acquiring his British patent, Henry Bessemer acquired a 15-year invention patent for his steelmaking technique in Spain (#1510: Procedimiento para mejorar la fabricación del hierro y el acero). He then demonstrated his process in London to José de Vilallonga and Jose Maria Ybarra. Bessemer sold his Spanish patent to the Ybarras in 1857 for £5,000, which was supposed to be paid in four installments: the first upfront and the next three spread over the subsequent three years.

Importantly, Bessemer and the Ybarras signed a contract that committed the English inventor to providing the Spaniards with technical assistance in exchange for his Spanish patent rights. This included sharing plans and know-how not included in the patent itself (Morlán 2002, p. 93). Consequently, between 1857 and 1858, Bessemer oversaw the installation of a converter in the Ybarras's ironworks facility in Guriezo (see Pretel and Sáiz 2012, pp. 102, 112, n. 14; Morlán 2002, p. 95). Moreover, while the storied inventor committed himself to sharing any improvements to his process with the Ybarras, they were obligated to reciprocity: they were to report to Bessemer any advances they innovated while making steel using his process.[71]

In this way, Bessemer was implementing a playbook he used in other countries. The Swedish example should prove instructive to readers.[72] Similar to the Spanish case, Bessemer was granted a patent in Sweden only months after filing his original British patent, and he immediately granted a license to a Swedish metalworking firm. This was accompanied by the migration of skilled workers who were familiar with the Bessemer process from Yorkshire, England, to Stockholm and other Swedish cities. While the Englishmen began to help their Swedish counterparts implement the new process as early as 1857, it took them about a year of challenges and experimentation to achieve success. Along with having to teach their Swedish licensees how to heat, tilt, mix, and cool the molten pig iron and other additives, the British were also tasked with installing and operating a sophisticated hydraulic system and other supporting machinery.

Unlike in the Swedish case, however, the Spaniards decided to delay putting Bessemer's process into widespread use. This despite the fact that Bessemer steel had been produced in Basque country a mere 16 months after the English inventor had introduced his revolutionary process to the world, and despite the

[71] This was similar to the patent licensing agreements that were often made between multinationals and Spanish subsidiaries (see Sáiz 2016 for the case of Babcock and Wilcox).

[72] This paragraph draws strongly on Bruland and Smith (2010, p. 87).

fact that the Ybarras had already paid £2,000 of the £5,000 they owed Bessemer & Company for the patent rights (Houpt and Rojo 2006, p. 326).

Instead, the Ybarras decided to double down on the Chenot process, the centerpiece of their new ironworks plant in Baracaldo, where they had already spent five million reales and put in over three years of construction under the guidance of French engineers (Houpt and Rojo 2006, p. 327; Morlán 2002, p. 96). The Chenot process as applied to the Baracaldo steel mill ultimately proved uneconomical, however (see Fernández de Pinedo 1983, p. 14). It was abandoned in 1871.

It was not until the late 1880s, therefore, and well after the Bessemer invention patent had expired, that Bessemer steel was produced in Spain in commercial quantities—and despite additional trials outside of Bilbao in Trubia (1861) and El Pedroso (1865).[73] This first occurred in San Francisco de Mudela in 1885, a mill that was, originally, a subsidiary of a British firm, John Brown Company, and was able to exploit four coke-fired blast furnaces previously imported into Spain by its parent company.[74] Then two new firms, La Vizcaya and Altos Hornos de Bilbao (AHB), followed suit in 1886.

La Vizcaya was founded in 1882 as a limited liability company by three Basque engineers trained in Belgium and England: Víctor Chávarri, his brother Benigno, and José A. de Olano. The new firm was capitalized with 12.5 million pesetas.[75] Their plan was to manufacture steel using modern, indirect techniques to service the construction of railways and steel hulls for shipbuilding (see Harvey and Taylor 1987). La Vizcaya invested in blast furnaces fueled by coke and the infrastructure required to fabricate Bessemer steel, including five lamination trains. To procure the technology and expertise it needed to produce steel at a large scale, La Vizcaya contracted with a Belgian firm named Cockerill. Federico de Echevarría was named manager of the Sestao plant and charged by the firm with overseeing its launch. He received help from several Belgian engineers, foremost

[73] Several theories have been put forth to explain this delay, in particular, and the overall reluctance of Basque firms to adopt blast furnaces powered by coke, despite their eagerness to learn about and even acquire these technologies early on (see Fernández de Pinedo 1983; Morlán 2002; Houpt and Rojo 2006, p. 328; Uriarte 1998). One popular theory is that Basque iron ore was of such high quality that Spanish ironworkers could "afford" to continue to rely on direct methods that yield sponge iron. Another is that internal demand was too low to achieve the necessary cost efficiencies associated with economies of scale. Still another reason is the relatively low quality and reliability of Bessemer steel before the advent of add-on innovations such as the Mushet system, which helped prevent over-oxidation by reintroducing some carbon.

[74] It was purchased by a Spaniard, Francisco de las Rivas, in 1879. I have not been able to ascertain whether this firm continued to produce steel after 1886 using Bessemer convertors. If it did, it was infringing on the patent rights that were locked up by AHB that year (as is shown later in the chapter).

[75] Major shareholders included miners and merchants from Bilbao, Barcelona, and London. For a complete list, see Portilla (1985, p. 41).

among them A. Greiner, and sent workers to Cockerill headquarters, in Seraing (Liege), to gain the necessary technical knowhow (Portilla 1985, p. 42).

However, because AHB had already secured a patent for Bessemer steelmaking—as we shall discuss later—La Vizcaya turned to an alternative, Bessemer-like process known as Robert invented by a Frenchman named Gustave Louis Robert (see Houpt 2003, p. 362; Portilla 1985, pp. 63–64). He obtained a 20-year invention patent in Spain in 1888 (#8321: Un procedimiento para la fabricación de hierros finos y aceros fundidos mediante el aparato destinado a este efecto) and licensed it to La Vizcaya in 1891.[76] Echevarría erected five Robert converters in Sestao under Robert's tutelage, and steel production using his process began in 1892 (see Houpt 2003, p. 363).

Finally, we come to the last of the big three: in 1882, the Ybarras helped to create—and control—AHB, a limited liability company. The new firm combined their assets in Guriezo and Baracaldo and was capitalized with 12.5 million pesetas.[77] Its purpose was to adopt Bessemer steelmaking techniques in a refurbished Baracaldo mill, and they budgeted 1.75 million pesetas (203,000 pounds sterling) toward that goal (Portilla 1985, p. 78). The new firm also hired specialized human capital from Germany, France, Belgium, and England to do so. AHB installed the new process with the help of a French engineer, Alexandre Pourcel, who had worked at the Terre Noire ironworks in France; the mill was then put under the direction of Edward Windsor Richards, a famed English engineer and expert in Bessemer steelmaking who had been the manager of the Eston ironworks in England (owned by Bolckow, Vaughan & Company).

AHB saw fit to patent several modifications to the Bessemer system that were especially suited to the Baracaldo factory's specifications. This included a five-year invention patent in 1884 that improved blast furnace heating through the use of so-called Cowper stoves (#3732: Uso de las estufas Cowper, destinadas a calentar el viento que se inyecta en los altos hornos con aprovechamiento de sus gases). It also included another five-year invention patent obtained in 1886 that allowed AHB to monopolize the Bessemer technique within Spain according to the modifications they made to it (#5837: Procedimiento "Bessemer" para convertir el hierro colado en acero o hierro dúctil haciendo uso de los convertidores giratorios de su sistema). While the Ybarras could no longer lean on the licensing agreement they had made with Henry Bessemer decades earlier, they sent some of their most trusted employees to train with Bessemer

[76] I should also note that La Vizcaya obtained a 5 year invention patent in 1887 (#7479, Hornos para acero en solera, "Sistema Bech") that codified some of the modifications that its engineers made to the Sestao blast furnaces in order to accommodate indirect steelmaking techniques.

[77] For a list of original investors, shareholders, and the capital each invested, see Morlán (2002, pp. 122–24).

steelmakers at Eston to get the system up and running (Houpt and Rojo 2006, p. 336).

The result was Spain's most impressive integrated steel mill to date. The Baracaldo facility eventually boasted coke making ovens, two coke-fueled blast furnaces, two Bessemer converters, three reheating furnaces, two large cupolas, three small cupolas, and rolling mills.

The Siemens Brothers Open-Hearth Process

The invention of the open-hearth steelmaking process in 1863 by William Siemens, a German-born inventor living in England who was helped by his brother Friedrich, represented another revolution in the fabrication of cheap and reliable steel at a large scale. This process calls for steelmakers to slowly boil a mixture of iron ore or scrap metal into molten pig iron, thus reducing the latter's carbon content via oxidation. Steelmakers melt these materials in a dish-like open bath heated by a regenerative gas furnace fueled by either coal or natural gas.

The open-hearth conversion process differs from Bessemer's in four key ways. First, it uses the gases generated during the coke making process (which fuels the blast furnace that melts iron ore into pig iron) to fire the furnace and reuses the hot waste gases emitted during the steelmaking to preheat the incoming fuel and air used to melt the steel and its additives. Second, the process spans hours, therefore allowing the steelmaker to repeatedly evaluate the metal's chemical and physical features along the way, and make any needed modifications. Third, it enables the production of greater amounts of steel, albeit over a longer period of time. Fourth, it allows for the possibility of using recycled scrap metal. Taken together, these advantages translate into much cheaper, higher quality steel.

Like the Bessemer process before it, the Siemens-Martin system was both sophisticated and supremely delicate. For the steelmaking process to operate smoothly,

> it was necessary to take into consideration the proper charging of the furnace, and the proper distribution of the materials in it; also, whether it was a furnace which under all circumstances had every part of it exactly adapted in the best possible manner to the work that had to be done, whether the hearths were the proper size, whether the boshes were right, whether too steep or too flat, and many other points, any of which would interfere with perfect results. (Iron and Steel Institute 1874, p. 51)

As in the case of Bessemer steelmaking, patenting and licensing was a critical pathway by which William Siemens disseminated his open-hearth process.[78] He

[78] In 1864, under Siemens's guidance, a French licensee named Pierre-Émile Martin was able to find a way to add scrap metal and wrought iron to the furnace in order to complement pig iron, thus

first patented his invention in the United Kingdom and immediately licensed it to several manufacturers there. Siemens also licensed his patent across the European continent and the United States

The terms that appear throughout the licensing contracts entered into by Siemens and his licensees adduce the technology transfer mechanisms that this chapter has stressed.[79] They prominently discuss how Siemens will convey his licensor with the know-how needed to operate the open-hearth furnace. These contracts also spell out a long-term relationship between Siemens and his licensors. Specifically, they compel Siemens to transfer knowledge of any new innovations that may arise over time to his licensors.

Let us now consider how the open-hearth process was introduced to Spain. As early as 1863, William and Friedrich acquired a ten-year invention patent that codified the regenerative furnace used in the open-hearth process (#2669: Perfeccionamientos introducidos en la disposición y calentamiento de los hornos). William then registered, in 1872, a ten-year invention patent for the Siemens steelmaking process itself (#4902: Procedimientos de tratamiento de minerales de hierro, en la fabricación del acero fundido, y en sus aparatos).

After the open-hearth process was introduced to Spain by the Siemens brothers, they and others conveyed know-how on the back of patent licenses that proved critical to consolidating and disseminating the invention. Specifically, Friedrich was instrumental in helping La Vizcaya implement the open-hearth process in its Sestao ironworks, which took several years to finalize. Under the aegis of his Spanish patents, Friedrich helped the Spaniards install and learn to use the Siemens steelmaking process in exchange for royalties.[80] By 1889, La Vizcaya finished construction on three Siemens-Martin ovens—setting aside 350,000 pesetas that year to install those ovens (Portilla 1985, p. 63)—and added another in 1890 (Houpt 2003, p. 361), for which it spent another 82,823 pesetas (Portilla, 1985, p. 63).[81]

reducing costs to an appreciable degree. It is for this reason that the open-hearth process came to be referred to the world over as Siemens-Martin steelmaking.

[79] For an example of one of these contracts in English that can be accessed online see House of Commons (1872).

[80] William died in 1883, but not before bequeathing his patents and the royalties associated with the open-hearth inventions to Friedrich. Niebel (2009, p. 60) recounts how Friedrich offered critical technical assistance to Federico Echevarría during the implementation of the Martin-Siemens process in Sestao. As discussed earlier, Echevarría was La Vizcaya's manager; he went on to own and operate his own metallurgical firm and later became a senator in the Spanish parliament. Several biographies of Echevarría's life echo this account about his relationship with Siemens.

[81] Fernández de Pinedo and Uriarte (2013, p. 225) report that AHB erected a Martin-Siemens oven in 1887. However, I could not find any records of a license granted by Friedrich to AHB or his involvement in transferring know-how to that firm. This does not mean that AHB infringed on his patents, however, as Friedrich's brother, William, had only obtained a ten-year invention patent in 1872. Similarly, I could not ascertain exactly what patent was connected to the licenses he granted to La Vizcaya; by implication, I could not identify whether Friedrich transferred know-how under

Between 1884 and 1907, Friedrich obtained ten additional invention patents in Spain. These codified follow-up improvements to either his regenerative heating process or the Siemens steelmaking process.[82] These patents were put into practice in Sestao and other Bilbaoan steel mills. By 1919, the Sestao mill boasted 10 Siemens-Martin ovens that could produce 20 tons of steel (Houpt 2003, p. 362).[83]

Moreover, between 1895 and 1929, inventors from Belgium, Germany, Italy, France, and the United States also patented close to 20 follow-up inventions to the Siemens steelmaking process in Spain.[84] After 1901, they were adopted by Altos Hornos de Vizcaya in Sestao and Baracaldo.

Conclusion

This chapter shows that, between 1850 and 1930, foreign inventors who made major innovations in the iron and steelmaking industry patented their inventions in Spain, licensed these to Spanish firms, and helped the latter acquire the know-how to put these inventions into practice. This helped new processes from abroad transfer to Spain. It also fostered further adjustments and improvements by both foreigners and Spaniards. These were tailored to the challenges and idiosyncrasies they encountered on the ground and were themselves patented in Spain.

Cutting edge inventions associated with steelmaking in modern, integrated mills probably could not have been appropriated by Spanish entrepreneurs through espionage or copying. Instead, because they were complemented by a deep substrate of tacit knowledge, original inventors' willing consent and ongoing cooperation were required. Since Spanish authorities granted foreign inventors and their representatives patents that were enforceable, this underpinned the

the auspices of a contract connected to any patent(s). Instead, as noted in endnote 80, I am relying on overlapping accounts about this phenomenon that include Niebel (2009) and other Federico Echevarría biographers.

[82] These were registered in 1884 (#4562: Un nuevo método de operar con hornos de hogar abierto para la producción de lingotes de hierro y acero), 1885 (#5518; Perfeccionamientos introducidos en la construcción y funcionamiento de los hornos, gasógenos y hogares de calderas calentadas por el gas), 1889 (#9922: Un procedimiento para utilizar los gases perdidos y demás productos gaseosos de la combustión por la mera construcción de un horno para el calor regenerado que permite alcanzar dicho objeto y cuya construcción puede emplearse también de la manera usual), 1890 (#10441: Perfeccionamientos introducidos en los hornos para gas de calor regenerado), 1897 (#20422: Mejoras en hornos regeneradores de gas), 1898 (#23383: Perfeccionamientos en los hornos de gas de calor regenerado), 1902 (#30583: Mejoras en los hornos regeneradores de gas), 1903 (#32035: Mejoras en los hornos de gas recuperadores para recalentado), 1904 (#33194: Mejoras en hornos regeneradores de gas), 1906 (#38973: Mejoras en los hornos de gas recuperadores para recalentado).

[83] By this time, La Vizcaya and AHB had merged to form Altos Hornos de Vizcaya.

[84] Details can be obtained through the Spanish Patent and Trademark Office.

licenses that spelled out mechanisms by which technology would be transferred. In turn, this gave them the incentives and opportunities to introduce their steelmaking innovations to Spain.

These insights should encourage policymakers interested in promoting economic development. Developing countries that register low levels of spending on R&D and low levels of human capital may nonetheless grow their economies if they can acquire state-of-the-art international technology (Abramovitz 1993). That is, if they can enforce patent regimes that incentivize, and create opportunities for, the transfer of innovative processes from the technology frontier. This may also stimulate cumulative innovation associated with learning by doing. And some of these innovations may even make their way back to the developed world.

Acknowledgments

I thank participants at three Hoover Institution IP2 symposiums on the history of patents organized by Stephen Haber and Naomi Lamoreaux. The first two were held in Washington, DC, in October 2016 and October 2017. The third was held at Stanford University in May 2018. I am especially indebted to the organizers for their comments and suggestions, as well as Ross Levine. I also thank participants at the University of Washington's Wesley Forum on Politics and Economics (March 2017), Princeton University's Comparative Politics Seminar (May 2017), and a seminar held at Dartmouth University (May 2018) for their helpful feedback on earlier drafts of this paper. I am especially indebted to Carles Boix. Finally, I benefited from conversations, both in person and electronically, with Scott Kieff, Alexander Galetovic, Zorina Khan, Jonathan Barnett, Lisa Oulette, and Patricio Sáiz.

References

Abramovitz, Moses. "The Search for the Sources of Growth: Areas of Ignorance, Old and New." Journal of Economic History 53, no. 2 (1993): 217–43.

Aldcroft, Derek. *Europe's Third World: The European Periphery in the Interwar Period*. New York: Routledge and Taylor, 2016.

Anduaga, Aitor. "Autarchy, Ideology, and Technology Transfer in the Spanish Oil Industry, 1939–1960." *Comparative Technology Transfer and Society* 7, no. 2 (2009): 172–200.

———. "The Engineer as a 'Linking Agent' in International Technology Transfer: The Case of Basque Engineers Trained in Liège." *Engineering Studies* 3, no. 1 (2011): 45–70.

Arora, Ashish. "Licensing Tacit Knowledge: Intellectual Property Rights and the Market for Know-how." *Economics of Innovation and New Technology* 4, no. 1 (1995): 41–60.

Asian Development Bank. *Thailand: Industrialization and Economic Catch-Up*. Manila: Asian Development Bank, 2015.

Berend, Ivan, and Gyorgy Ránki. *The European Periphery and Industrialization 1780–1914*. Cambridge, UK: Cambridge University Press, 1982.

Boldrin, Michele, and David Levine. *Against Intellectual Monopoly*. New York: Cambridge University Press, 2008.

———. "The Case Against Patents." *Journal of Economic Perspectives* 27, no. 1 (2013): 3–22.

Braga, Carlos, and Casten Fink. "The Relationship Between Intellectual Property Rights and Foreign Direct Investment." *Duke Journal Of Comparative & International Law* 9, no. 163 (1998): 163–87.

Branstetter, Lee, Raymond Fisman, and C. Fritz Foley. "Do Stronger Intellectual Property Rights Increase International Technology Transfer? Empirical Evidence from US Firm-Level Panel Data." *The Quarterly Journal of Economics* 121, no. 1 (2006): 321–49.

Brown, Eliott, and Bob Davis. "Qualcomm Abandons NXP Deal Amid U.S.-China Tensions. *Wall Street Journal*, 26 July 2018. https://www.wsj.com/articles/qualcomm-plans-to-abandon-nxp-deal-1532549728?mod=searchresults&page=1&pos=4.

Bruland, Kristine, and Keith Smith. "Knowledge Flows and Catching Up Industrialization in the Nordic Countries: the Roles of Patent Systems." In *Intellectual Property Rights, Development, and Catch-up*, edited by Hiroyuki Odagiri, Akira Goto, Atsushi Sunami, and Richard Nelson, 63–94. Oxford: Oxford University Press, 2010.

Carreras, Albert. "Industria." In *Estadísticas Históricas de España, Siglos XIX–XX. Volumen 1*, edited by Albert Carreras and Xavier Tafunell, 357–454. Madrid: BBVA, 2005.

Cayón, Francisco, Esperanza Frax, María Jesús Matilla, Miguel Muñoz, and Patricio Sáiz. "Patentes y Evolución Tecnológica del Ferrocarril Español: 1826–1936." In *Siglo y Medio del Ferrocarril en España, 1848–1998: Economía, Industria y Sociedad*, edited by Miguel Muñoz, Jesús Sanz, and Javier Vidal, 739–60. Madrid: FFE, 1999.

Cebrián, Mar, and Santiago López. "Economic Growth, Technology Transfer and Convergence in Spain, 1960–73." In *Technology and Human Capital in Historical Perspective*, edited by Jonas Ljungberg and Jan-Pieter Smits, 120–44. New York: Palgrave Macmillan, 2004.

Chang, Ha-Joon. "Who benefits from the New International Intellectual Property rights regime? And what should Africa do?" Technopolicy Brief Series No. 1, Nairobi, Kenya: African Technology Policy Studies Network, 2001.

Chang, Ha-Joon. *Kicking Away the Ladder: Development Strategy in Historical Perspective*. London: Anthem Press, 2003.

Chari, V. V., and Hugo Hopenhayn. "Vintage Human Capital, Growth, and the Diffusion of New Technology." *Journal of Political Economy* 99, no. 6 (1991): 1142–65.

de la Torre, Joseba, and Mario García-Zúñiga. "Was it a Spanish Miracle? Development Plans and Regional Industrialization, 1950–1975." In *Industrial Policy in Europe after 1945*, edited by Christian Grabas and Alexander Nutzenadel, 162–86. London: Palgrave Macmillan, 2014.

Escudero, Antonio. "Dos Puntualizaciones sobre la Historia de la Siderurgia Española entre 1880 y 1930." *Revista de Historia Industrial* 15 (1999): 191–200.

Esdaile, Charles. *The Peninsular War: A New History*. London: Allen Lane, 2002.

Fernández de Pinedo, Emiliano. "Nacimiento y Consolidación de la Moderna Siderurgia Vasca (1849-1913): el Caso de Vizcaya." *Información Comercial Española, ICE: Revista de Economía* 598 (1983): 9–20.

Fernández de Pinedo, Emiliano, and Rafael Uriarte. "La Siderurgia: Cambio Técnico y Geografía Industrial." In *Técnica e Ingenieria en España. Volume VII. El Ochocientos. De Las Profundidades a las Alturas*, edited by Manuel, Silvia, and Inmaculada Aguilar, 189–234. Zaragoza: Real Academia de Ingenieria, 2013.

Frax, Esperanza, María Jesús Matilla, Miguel Muñoz, and Patricio Sáiz. "La Innovación Tecnológica en los Puertos Españoles en el Siglo XIX a Través del Sistema de Patentes." In *Puertos y Sistemas Portuarios (Siglos XVI-XX)*, edited by Agustín Guimerá and Dolores Romero, 275–92. Madrid: Ministerio de Fomento-CEDEX-CEHOPU-CSIC, 1996.

Gárate, Montserrat. "The Economic Background to the Basque Question in Spain." In *Economic Change and the National Question in Twentieth-Century Europe*, edited by Alice Teichova, Herbert Matis, and Pátek Jaroslav, 150–72. Cambridge, UK: Cambridge University Press, 2000.

Haber, Stephen. "Patents and the Wealth of Nations." *George Mason Law Review* 23, no. 4 (2016): 811–35.

Haber, Stephen, and Victor Menaldo. "Do Natural Resources Fuel Authoritarianism? A Reappraisal of the Resource Curse." *American Political Science Review* 105, no. 1 (2011): 1–26.

Hall, Bronwyn, and Christian Helmers. "The Impact of International Patent Systems: Evidence from Accession to the European Patent Convention." Working Paper, Max Planck Institute for Innovation & Competition Research Paper No. 18-03, Nijmegen, Germany, 2018.

Harris, John. "Law, Espionage and Transfer of Technology from Eighteenth-Century Britain." In *Technological Change: Methods and Themes in the History of Technology*, edited by Robert Fox, 123–36. Amsterdam: Harwood Academic Publishers, 1996.

Harrison, Joseph. *The Spanish Economy in the Twentieth Century*. London: Croom Helm, 1985.

Harvey, Charles, and Peter Taylor. "Mineral Wealth and Economic Development: Foreign Direct Investment in Spain, 1851-1913." *The Economic History Review* 40, no. 2 (1987): 185–207.

Helguera, Juan. "The Beginnings of Industrial Espionage in Spain (1748–1760)." In *History of Technology Volume 30, European Technologies in Spanish History*, edited by Ian Inkster, 21–32. London: Bloomsbury, 2011.

Houpt, Stefan. "Competir en los Mercados Internacionales: Altos Hornos de Vizcaya, 1882-1936." *Revista de Historia Económica* 21, no. 2 (2003): 335–371.

Houpt, Stefan, and Juan Carlos Rojo. "Technology Transfer in the Northern Spain's Heavy and Metalworking Industries, 1856–1936." In *Les Transferts de Technologie en Mediterranee*, edited by Michele Merger, 321–43. Paris: Presses de la Sorbonne, 2006.

House of Commons. *Reports from Committees*, Vol. 11. London: House of Commons, 1872.

Iron and Steel Institute. *Journal of the Iron and Steel Institute*, Vol. 1. London: M&M.W. Lambert, 1874.

Kelly, Morgan. "Technological Progress under Learning by Imitation." *International Economic Review* 50, no. 2 (2009): 397–414.

Kieff, Scott. 2006. "Coordination, Property, and Intellectual Property: An Unconventional Approach to Anticompetitive Effects and Downstream Access." *Emory Law Journal* 56 (2006): 327–438.

Lamoreaux, Naomi, and Kenneth Sokoloff. 2003 "Intermediaries in the US Market for Technology." In *Finance, Intermediaries, and Economic Development*, edited by Stanley

Engerman, Phillip Hoffman, Jean-Laurent Rosenthal, and Kenneth Sokoloff, 209–46. New York: Cambridge University Press, 2003.

Landes, David. *Unbound Prometheus: Technological Change and Industrial Development in Western Europe from 1750 to the Present.* New York: Cambridge University Press, 1969.

Lee, Jeong-Yeon, and Edwin Mansfield. 1996. "Intellectual Property Protection and U.S. Foreign Direct Investment." *Review of Economics and Statistics* 78, no. 2 (1996): 181–86.

Lerner, Josh. 2002. "150 Years of Patent Protection." *American Economic Review* 92, no. 2 (2002): 221–25.

Madrid Correspondence. "Status of Flotation in Spain." *Engineering and Mining Journal* 106, no. 8 (1919): 316–17.

Maluquer de Motes, Jordi. 1988. "Factores y Condicionamientos del Proceso de Industrialización en el Siglo XIX: El Caso Español." In *La Industrialización Del Norte De España: Estado De La Cuestión Crîtica/Historia*, edited by Emiliano Fernández de Pinedo and Marco Hernández, 13–36. Barcelona: Universidad del Paîs Vasco Editorial Crîtica, 1988.Mansfield, Edwin. "Technical Change and the Rate of Imitation." *Econometrica* 29, no. 4 (1961): 741–66.

Martín-Aceña, Pablo, Maria Pons, and Concepción Betrán. "150 Years of Financial Regulation in Spain: What Can We Learn?" *Journal of European Economic History* 43, no. 1/2 (2014): 35–81.

Maskus, Keith. 1998. "The Role of Intellectual Property Rights in Encouraging Foreign Direct Investment and Technology Transfer." *Duke Journal of Comparative & International Law* 9, no. 1 (1998): 109–161.

Menaldo, Victor, and Nicolas Wittstock. "Does Technology Transfer from the US to China Harm American Firms, Workers, and Consumers? A Historical and Analytic Investigation." *Economic and Political Studies*, (forthcoming).

Mokyr, Joel. *A Culture of Growth: The Origins of the Modern Economy.* Princeton, NJ: Princeton University Press, 2016.

Morlán, Pablo Díaz. *Los Ybarra: una Dinastía de Empresarios, 1801–2001.* Madrid: Marcial Pons Historia, 2002.

Moser, Petra. "Do Patents Weaken the Localization of Innovations? Evidence from World's Fairs." *Journal of Economic History* 71, no. 2 (2011): 363–82.

———. "Patents and Innovation: Evidence from Economic History," *Journal of Economic Perspectives* 27, no. 1 (2013): 23–44.

Nadal, Jordi. "Los Comienzos de la Industrialización Española (1832–1868): La Industria Siderúrgica." In *Ensayos sobre la Economîa Española a mediados del siglo XIX realizados en el Servicio de Estudios del Banco de España*, edited by Pedro Giron, 203–34. Madrid: Banco de España, 1970.

Navarro, Peter. "Trump's Tariffs are a Defense Against China's Aggression." *Wall Street Journal*, 20 June 2018. https://www.wsj.com/articles/trumps-tariffs-are-a-defense-against-chinas-aggression-1529533046.

Niebel, Ingo. *Al infierno o a la Gloria: Vida y Muerte del Cónsul y Espía Wilhelm Wakonigg en Bilboa 1900–1936.* Ixtaropena: Alberdania, 2009.

Nuwer, Michael. "From Batch to Flow: Production Technology and Work-Force Skills in the Steel Industry, 1880–1920." *Technology and Culture* 29, no. 4 (1988): 808–38.

Odagiri, Hiroyuki, Akira Goto, Atsushi Sunami, and Richard Nelson. "Introduction." In *Intellectual Property Rights, Development, and Catch-up*, edited by Hiroyuki Odagiri, Akira Goto, Atsushi Sunami, and Richard Nelson, 1–30. Oxford: Oxford University Press, 2010.

Ortiz-Villajos, José. "Spain's Low Technological Level: an Explanation." In *Technology and Human Capital in Historical Perspective*, edited by Jonas Ljungberg, and Jan-Pieter Smits, 182–204. New York: Palgrave Macmillan, 2004.

———. "Patentes y Desarollo Económico en la España Contemporánea. In *Les Transferts de Technologie en Mediterranee*, edited by Michele Merger, 53–68. Paris: Presses de la Sorbonne, 2006.

———. "Patents, What For? the Case of Crossley Brothers and the Introduction of the Gas Engine into Spain, c. 1870–1914." *Business History* 56, no. 4 (2014): 650–76.

Penrose, Edith. *The Economics of the International Patent System*. Baltimore, MD: Johns Hopkins Press, 1951.

Pons, Maria. *Regulating Spanish Banking, 1939–1975*. Burlington: Ashgate, 2002.

Pretel, David, and Patricio Sáiz. "Patent Agents in the European Periphery: Spain (1826–1902)." *History of Technology* 31 (2012): 103–25.

Portilla, Manuel. *La Siderurgia Vasca, 1880–1901: Nuevas Tecnologías, Empresarios y Política Económica*. Bilbao: Servicio Editorial Universidad del Paîs Vasco, 1985.

Quijada, Juan. "Tomas Pérez Estala y la Introducción de las Primeras Máquinas de Vapor en las Minas de Almadén a Finales del Siglo XVIII. In *La Industrialización y el Desarrollo Económico de España*, edited by Albert Carreras, Pere Pascual, David Reher, and Carles Sudria, 827–45. Barcelona: Biblioteca de la Universitat de Barcelona, 1998.

Reinert, Erik. "Competitiveness and its Predecessors—a 500-year Cross-national Perspective." *Structural Change and Economic Dynamics* 6, no. 1 (1995): 23–42.

Riera i Tuebols, Santiago. "Industrialization and Technical Education in Spain, 1850–1914." In *Education, Technology and Industrial Performance, 1850–1939*, edited by Robert Fox and Anna Guagnini, 141–70. Cambridge: Cambridge University Press, 1993.

Richter, Ralf, and Jochen Streb. "Catching-up and Falling Behind: Knowledge Spillover from American to German Machine Toolmakers." *Journal of Economic History* 71, no, 4 (2011): 1006–31.

Ringrose, David. *Spain, Europe, and the "Spanish Miracle," 1700–1900*. Cambridge, UK: Cambridge University Press, 1996.

Robertson, Paul, and Parimal Patel. "New Wine in Old Bottles: Technological Diffusion in Developed Economies." *Research Policy* 36, no. 5 (2007): 708–21.

Rosés, Joan Ramón. "Why Isn't the Whole of Spain Industrialized? New Economic Geography and Early Industrialization, 1797–1910." *Journal of Economic History* 63, no. 4 (2003): 995–1022.

Sáez-García, Miguel. "Business and State in the Development of the Steel Industry in Spain and Italy (c. 1880–1929)." *Business History* 59, no. 2 (2017): 159–78.

Sáiz, Patricio. *Propiedad Industrial y Revolución Liberal: Historia del Sistema Español de Patentes, 1759–1929*. Madrid: OEPM, 1995.

———. *Legislación Histórica sobre Propiedad Industrial. España (1759–1929)*. Madrid: OEPM, 1996.

———. *Invención, Patentes e Innovación en la España Contemporánea*. Madrid: OEPM, 1999.

———. "The Spanish Patent System (1770-1907)." *History of Technology* 24, no. 1: 45–80, 2002.

———. "Transferencia Tecnológica Internacional Hacia España a Través del Sistema de Patentes (1759-1900)." In *Les Transferts de Technologie en Mediterranee*, edited by Michele Merger, 29–52. Paris: Presses de la Sorbonne, 2006.

———. "Did Patents of Introduction Encourage Technology Transfer? Long-term Evidence from the Spanish Innovation System." *Cliometrica* 8, no. 1 (2013): 49–78.

———. "Patents as Corporate Tools: Babcock & Wilcox's Business and Innovation Strategies in Spain." *Enterpises et Histoire* 82, no. 4 (2016): 64–88.

———"Cataloguing and Studying of Patent, Trademark, and Industrial Design Historical Files at the OEPM."

https://www.ibcnetwork.org/project.php?id=18

Sáiz, Patricio, and Rafael Castro. "Foreign Direct Investment and Intellectual Property Rights: International Intangible Assets in Spain over the Long Term." *Enterprise & Society* 18, no. 4 (2017): 846–92.

Sáiz, Patricio, and David Pretel. "Why did Multinationals Patent in Spain: Several Historical Inquiries." In *Organizing Global Technology Flows: Institutions, Actors, and Processes*, edited by Pierre-Yves Donzé and Shigehiro Nishimura, 39–59. New York: Routledge, 2013.Santamaría Sánchez, Luis. "Beyond Formal R&D: Taking Advantage of Other Sources of Innovation in Low and Medium-technology Industries." *Research Policy* 38, no. 3 (2009): 507–18.

Scotchmer, Suzanne. "Standing on the Shoulders of Giants: Cumulative Research and the Patent Law." *Journal of Economic Perspectives* 5, no. 1 (1991): 29–41.

Simpson, James. *Spanish Agriculture: The Long Siesta, 1765–1965*. New York: Cambridge University Press, 1995.

Spanish Patent and Trademark Office (OEPM). Spanish Patents Historical Archive. http://historico.oepm.es/buscador.php.

Taplin, Nathaniel. "Chinese Innovation Won't Come Easily Without U.S. Tech." Wall Street Journal, 14 May 2018. https://www.wsj.com/articles/can-chinas-red-capital-really-innovate-1526299173.

Taylor, Bryan. "Guide to the Global Financial Database." Alhambra, CA: Global Financial Data, 2016.

Tedde de la Lorca, Pedro. "Cambio Institucional y Cambio Económico en la España del Siglo XIX." *Revista de Historia Económica*. 12, no. 3 (1994): 525–38.

Tena-Junguito, Antonio. "Spanish Protectionism during the Restauracion, 1875-1930." In *Classical Trade Protectionism 1815-1914*, edited by Jean-Pierre Dormos and Pedro Lains, 265–97. New York: Routledge Press, 2006.

Tortella, Gabriel. *The Development of Modern Spain: An Economic History of the Nineteenth and Twentieth Centuries*. Cambridge, UK: Harvard University Press, 2000.

Tortella, Gabriel, and Francisco Comín. "Fiscal and Monetary Institutions in Spain." In *Transferring Wealth and Power from the Old to the New World: Monetary and Fiscal Institutions in the 17th through the 19th Centuries*, edited by Michael Bordo and Roberto Cortés-Conde, 140–86. Cambridge, UK: Cambridge University Press, 2001.

Uriarte, Rafael. "Desarrollo Científico y Cambio Técnico en la Siderurgia Vasca del Siglo XIX: las Experiencias Chenot, Tourangin y Gurlt." *Llull* 21 (1998): 779–800.

Williamson, Jeffrey. "The Evolution of Global Labor Markets since 1830: Background Evidence and Hypotheses." *Explorations in Economic History* 32, no. 2 (1995): 141–96.

3

Did James Watt's Patent(s) Really Delay the Industrial Revolution?

Sean Bottomley

> I have been branded with folly and madness for attempting what the world calls impossibilities, and even from the great engineer, the late James Watt, who said . . . I deserved hanging for bringing into use the high-pressure engine.
>
> —Richard Trevithick to Davies Gilbert, *c.* 1832–1833.

Introduction

A patent constitutes the (temporary) right to exclude others from employing a particular technology or invention, and since the time when the world's first patent law was promulgated in Venice in 1474, they have been awarded in the expectation that offering inventors this right would incentivize their efforts.[1] Later, at the beginning of the Industrial Revolution, political economists were agreed that offering patents was a preferable policy choice compared with alternatives such as offering rewards or prizes. Adam Smith, for example, observed in 1767 that "the inventor of a new machine . . . has the exclusive privilege of making and vending that invention for the space of 14 years by the law of this country, as a reward for his ingenuity, and it is probable that this is as equal a one as could be fallen upon."[2] Abroad, Britain's burgeoning industrial prowess was attributed in

[1] "There are men in this city . . . who have most clever minds, capable of devising and inventing all kinds of ingenious contrivances. And should it be legislated that the works and contrivances invented by them could not be copied and made by others so that they are deprived of their honour, men of such kind would exert their minds, invent and make things that would be of no small utility and benefit to our State." (L. Bently and M. Kretschmer, Venetian Statute on Industrial Brevets, http://copy.law.cam.ac.uk/cam/tools/request/showRepresentation?id=representation_i_1474).

[2] Continuing: "For if the legislature should appoint pecuniary rewards for the inventors of new machines, etc., they would hardly ever be so precisely proportioned to the merit of the invention as this is. For here, if the invention be good and such as is profitable to mankind, he will probably make a fortune by it; but if it be of no value he also will reap no benefit" (Meek and Stein 1982, p. 116). Later, in 1795, Jeremy Bentham expressed himself in similar terms: "[A] patent considered as a recompense

Sean Bottomley, *Did James Watt's Patent(s) Really Delay the Industrial Revolution? In: The Battle over Patents.* Edited by: Stephen H. Haber and Naomi R. Lamoreaux, Oxford University Press. © Oxford University Press 2021. DOI: 10.1093/oso/9780197576151.003.0004

part to its development of the world's first recognizably modern patent system. In 1823, Goethe observed "that [the] clever Englishman transforms [invention] by a patent into real possession . . . one may well ask why they are in every respect in advance of us" (quoted in Klemm, 1964, 173).

Over the course of the nineteenth century, though, with the growing ascendancy of the free trade movement, attention came to fall less on the rewards that accrued to the inventor and more on the exclusion that patents supposedly foisted on other parties. The classical liberal publication *The Economist*, for example, decried patents: "On all inventors it is especially a prohibition to exercise their faculties; and in proportion as they are more numerous than one, it is an impediment to the general advancement" (*The Economist* 1851, p. 113).

In essence, the debate concerning the utility of patents has changed little over the intervening period, although criticisms of patenting have become more variegated and sophisticated. Broadly speaking, there are four main lines of attack deployed by critics of patenting:

(i) That the exclusion operated by patents prevents or "blocks" follow-on innovations that could have been developed if the patented technology was freely available. Of course, a patentee can choose to forgo this right in return for payment (licensing) but they are not usually compelled to do so. This problem is exacerbated if patents are vaguely worded, allowing a patentee to subsequently expand the scope of their patent beyond what they have invented.

(ii) This exclusion might be justifiable if patents incentivized the development of inventions that would not have appeared otherwise within a reasonable timeframe. However, inventions are less the product of an individual inventive mind and more the inevitable outcome of collaborative, socially embedded processes—that inventors are really "conduits filled by an invention that just had to happen" (Kelly 2011, p. 133). This is evidenced by the alleged ubiquity of Simultaneous Innovation, the phenomenon whereby multiple inventors hit upon precisely the same idea at virtually the same moment—most famously Alexander Graham Bell and Elisha Gray both patenting the telephone on the same day. As such, patents are needless and represent an "extraordinary" and monopolistic imposition on the natural order of things (Boldrin and Levine 2008, p. 128).

for the increase given to the general stock of wealth by an invention, as a recompense for industry and genius and ingenuity, is proportionate and essentially just. No other mode of recompense can merit either the one or the other epithet."

(iii) That inventors themselves rarely use patents. Notoriously, for example, very few of the exhibits displayed at the world's first great fair in 1851 (the Great Exhibition in London) had been patented, and it has been inferred that inventors must have preferred alternative means of protection such as trade secrecy (Moser 2013). This inference, though, relies on the flawed assumption that each exhibit represented a patentable invention.

(iv) Patents embroil inventors in legal disputes and commercial engagements, distracting them from what they are best at—inventing.

Many apparent examples of these processes have been adduced from recent technological and economic history,[3] and this chapter is concerned with examining the plausibility of each of these four arguments in the context of one of the most frequently invoked examples of a monopolistic, innovation blocking patent—James Watt's patent for the sperate condenser, obtained in 1769 at the outset of the British industrial revolution. The industrial revolution was an event of undoubted first-order importance, marking the beginning of modern economic growth. Previously, all global economies had been fundamentally constrained by their reliance on the annual cycle of plant growth as virtually their sole energy input. This ostensibly immutable constraint on production could only be overcome with the adoption of inorganic sources of energy—fossil fuels, in particular coal. By 1700, the transition from organic to inorganic energy sources was already underway in England where coal was being used as a source of heat in a wide variety of industries such as brewing, glassmaking, metal works, and brick making. However, "without a parallel breakthrough in the provision of mechanical energy to solve the problem associated with dependence on human or animal muscle to supply motive power in industry and transport, energy problems would have continued to frustrate efforts to raise manpower productivity." (Wrigley 2010, p. 45). This problem was only solved by the development of the steam engine, which transformed the heat energy produced by burning coal into mechanical energy. Consequently, Tony Wrigley posits that "the steam engine was arguably the single most important technical advance of the whole industrial revolution period."[4]

[3] To give but one other example, it is commonly supposed that by 1917—just as the United States was entering the First World War—endemic patent litigation "had brought the US production of planes to a halt." The impasse was only resolved by the forcible intervention of the government, imposing a patent pool whereby the major US plane companies could share one another's technology (Moser 2013, p. 33). The myth of patent hold-up has now been debunked in Katznelson and Howells (2014).

[4] Wrigley (2010, p. 44). Quantitative contributions to the literature usually suggest that the impact of steam engines was in fact very limited. Von Tunzelmann (1978, p. 157), notably, estimated that the cost savings involved with using steam-power as opposed to alternative power sources such as water was, in 1800, equivalent to only 0.2 percent of National Income. This social savings methodology, though, has been much criticized. See, for example, Leunig (2010).

Watt's condenser, described later in this chapter, represented a sudden and dramatic improvement in the fuel efficiency of steam engines, enabling their application to a plethora of industrial activities such as cotton spinning, iron smelting, and pumping water out of mines. As such, the condenser can certainly be regarded as one of the single most important inventions of the industrial revolution. However, Watt's acquisition and enforcement of his patent is supposed to be illustrative of each of the anti-patent arguments outlined earlier. In brief:

(i) Watt and his business partner Matthew Boulton are alleged to have enforced a much broader interpretation of their patent than they were fairly entitled to and used this to obstruct new developments in steam engineering which might have threatened their monopoly—especially high-pressure steam engines, to which Watt was inveterately opposed. However, high-pressure engines would predominate during the nineteenth century and their delayed appearance prompts Michele Boldrin and David Levine to suggest that Watt's patent "most likely delayed the industrial revolution by a couple of decades" (2013, 38).

(ii) Mark Lemley (2012, p. 716) asserts that Watt has been lionized as the inventor of the steam engine when really, he was just one of many engineers engaged in an unconsciously collaborative effort. This is a strawman. No one has seriously suggested that Watt invented the steam engine. Another version of this argument is that he was one of many steam engineers working during this period and that he was lucky to get just "one step ahead of the pack" when patenting his condenser (Boldrin and Levine 2008, 2). This is distortionary. It is true that there were many steam engineers working in England in the 1760s (around 500 engines had been erected by this point; Kanefsky and Robey 1980, p. 169) but there is no credible evidence of anyone else developing a working condenser. This was Watt's invention.

(iii) Scherer (1965) speculates that Watt may have been relatively unconcerned with obtaining patent protection while developing his condenser. Watt's personal correspondence, though, makes clear that his development of the condenser was motivated by the allure of a patent—or rather the profits he hoped that would ensue therefrom. The same goes for his business partner Matthew Boulton, who went to the trouble of petitioning Parliament for an extension to the patent term in 1775. Similarly, many of the most important developments in steam engineering during this period were patented.

(iv) It has been suggested that once Watt finished developing his condenser, he refrained from further developments, instead concentrating on profiting from the condenser and enforcing his patent.[5] This ignores his

[5] For example, Merges and Nelson (1990, p. 872, n. 141); Lemley (2012, pp. 740–41).

enormous inventive and scientific output during the last quarter of the eighteenth century, detailed later. Watt was the pre-eminent steam engineer of the time.

(v) A slight variation of this argument is that as an enterprise, Boulton & Watt only cared about "extracting hefty monopolistic royalties through licensing" (Boldrin and Levine, 2008, p. 2). We will see instead how the firm endeavored to manufacture as many of the components for its engines as possible; they were the world's first firm to offer entire steam engines for sale.

The rest of this chapter is divided into two halves. The first provides an analytical narrative of the development of the condenser and the foundation of the business partnership that commercialized it, Boulton & Watt (hereafter, the firm is shortened to "B&W," the two individuals as Boulton and Watt). It deals with the last three of the four points discussed earlier. In brief, it will argue that patents were an essential motivating factor in the development and commercialization of the separate condenser. It will also serve as an introduction to the second half of the paper, which is concerned with the first of the four points. It will demonstrate that B&W's patent(s) did not act as an insuperable obstacle to the development of high-pressure steam engines, or indeed other potential developments in steam engines.

The Newcomen and Watt Engines

The world's first commercially viable steam engine had been developed by Thomas Newcomen at the beginning of the eighteenth century. Used mainly to pump water at coal mines, Newcomen's engine was worked by pumping steam into a cylinder which was open at the top and where a piston was positioned. When the cylinder was filled with steam, a spout of cold water was discharged inside the cylinder, reducing its temperature and condensing the steam into water. The condensation of the steam created a partial vacuum underneath the piston, which was now driven down by the (higher) pressure of the atmosphere acting on it from above. The piston was attached via a rocking beam to the pumping gear, so that as the piston was driven downward, the pumping gear moved upward. Steam would then be readmitted to the cylinder, forcing the condensed water out, while equalizing the pressure inside the cylinder with that of the atmosphere outside, whereon the piston would revert to its starting position at the top of the cylinder (Bottomley, 2014, p. 236–37).

Newcomen's engine, though, was extremely inefficient and attention focused on reducing its coal consumption. Especially noteworthy was the work of John

Smeaton, commonly regarded as "the father of English civil engineering," who over the course of two years of experiments was able to determine the optimal configuration and dimensions of the Newcomen engine according to the desired power output.[6] The essential design, however, was unchanged and even after half a century, its use was still largely confined to pumping water out of coal mines where fuel was effectively free.[7] It was during the course of his work as an instrument maker, repairing a model of Newcomen's engine for Glasgow university, that Watt realized that the alternate cooling and heating of the cylinder in each operating cycle of the Newcomen engine was inefficient. His solution was to introduce a second vessel where steam condensation could occur outside the cylinder (hence "separate condenser"), allowing the cylinder to retain its temperature. In addition, whereas previously condensation had occurred in the cylinder, which could never be cooled quickly enough to create anything but a partial vacuum underneath the piston, a more complete vacuum could be achieved by condensing in the much colder separate condenser. Watt's insight formed quickly, and he would later recall that during the spring of 1765 "all . . . improvements followed as corollaries in quick succession, so that in the course of one or two days the invention was thus far complete in my mind, and I immediately set about an experiment to verify it practically." (Muirhead 1854, p. lxxvi).

As elegant as Watt's new design was, it is worth emphasizing that in the previous sixty years since the Newcomen engine had been first introduced, there is no solid evidence that the same idea had occurred to any other engineer. In particular, over the course of nearly ten years of legal battles concerning the validity of Watt's patent for the condenser (patent no. 913), his opponents were unable to adduce any convincing evidence that his invention was not new. If they had, Watt's patent would have been annulled. It can also be asked, if Watt's idea had been the inevitable outcome of his contemporary social/scientific milieu, why it had not occurred to as eminent an engineer as John Smeaton, who had also started experimenting with steam engines in 1765 (Hills 1989, p. 29).

There remained, however, a significant amount of work required to transform Watt's idea into a working engine, and from there into a viable commercial proposition. For example, for the engine to work, the fit between the piston and cylinder had to be as air tight as possible (to maintain the vacuum), but without causing too much friction in the movement of the piston. The solution Newcomen had adopted was to place a flexible leather disk on top of the piston

[6] It was the historian of industrial technology and engineering, B. F. Duckham (1965), who first described Smeaton as "the father of English civil engineering."

[7] Of the 453 steam engines erected to 1769 where a commercial usage is recorded, 338 were used for pumping water out of coal mines, 75 percent of the total; derived from Kanefsky (1979, pp. 448–55). Coal mines could use the cheapest grades of coal for their engines, which often could not be sold commercially and would otherwise have had to be disposed of (von Tunzelmann, 1978, p. 62).

and then a quantity of water above the disk to act as a seal. This method, though, was less suitable for Watt's engine, as he wanted to keep the cylinder as hot as possible, and he knew that water seeping into the cylinder would absorb heat from the working steam. It was only in 1774, after countless experiments, that Watt was able to report cylinders that were being adequately machined.[8] Soon thereafter, an even better solution presented itself, when John Wilkinson patented his new technique for boring iron cannon (partly achieved by the simple expedient of rotating the gun barrel, rather than the boring-bar). It also proved eminently suitable for boring Watt's cylinders and Wilkinson would supply the cylinders for all but a handful of B&W's engines until 1796.

Problems such as these occurred repeatedly in manufacturing a working engine and in total, from when Watt first conceived his idea in April 1765, it took ten years until the first engines constructed according to his design were erected for paying customers. Sums expended on experimentation and development are more difficult to gauge, partly because it occurred under three separate business arrangements. Initially, Watt attempted to finance this himself (spending £1,200), but to do so required he undertake surveying work which inevitably consumed time he wanted to spend on his condenser (Scherer 1965, p. 168). Consequently, in 1768, he entered into a partnership with John Roebuck, an English ironmaster working in Scotland. Roebuck took on Watt's debts and agreed to pay the costs of developing and patenting the condenser, in return for a two-thirds share of the patent. Roebuck, though, was unable to sustain the expenses (his other business ventures were failing and would bankrupt him in 1770), and Watt was forced into undertaking more surveying jobs. Roebuck estimated that the costs of experiments at this stage were £3,000, although some were borne by Matthew Boulton, who would step in to replace Roebuck (albeit, only when he was able to acquire Roebuck's share of the patent from his trustees in 1773; Tann 2013). Finally, once Boulton had become Watt's long-term business partner, J. E. Cule (1940, p. 320) suggests that it took a further £3,370 to render the condenser a marketable proposition, not including set-up costs for manufacturing components and erecting engines.

This was a long-term research and development project, costing at the very least £7,500 and taking ten years to finish. Watt and his partners did not invest so much time and money out of their own beneficence. In 1769, for example, a few months after he had obtained his patent for the condenser Watt wrote to his friend William Small: "It was four years ago when I invented the fire engine and foresaw even before I made a model every circumstance that has since occurred.

[8] An experimental process described in Scherer (1965, pp. 177–78). Watt tinkered with different shaped cylinders, different materials for the piston, and mercury, oil, graphite, tallow, horse dung, and vegetable oil as potential sealants.

I was at that time spurred on by the alluring hope of placing myself above want."[9] Writing to Watt in February 1769, Boulton was similarly forthright:

> I was excited by two motives to offer you my assistance, which were, love of you, and *love of a money-getting, ingenious project* . . . [To] produce the most profit, my idea was to settle a manufactory near to my own, by the side of our canal, where I would erect all the conveniences necessary for the completion of engines, and from which manufactory we would serve all the world with engines of all sizes . . . It would not be worth my while to make for three counties only; but I find it very well worth my while to make for all the world.[10]

Two other important points emerge from the letter besides Boulton's monetary imperative. First, the envisaged scale of the enterprise. Boulton had no interest in a small localized business venture ("three counties only"), as was the case with previous engine builders.[11] This would not have enabled them to recoup the costs of developing the condenser. Instead, he understood that it would be necessary "to make for all the world." This scale of enterprise, though, would never have been possible without patent protection: it would have been nigh-on impossible for B&W to control access to the condenser once their engines had been sold to customers and the workings of the condenser would have been deducible to any reasonably competent engineer.[12] Trade secrecy was never an option and any advantage from "lead-time" fleeting.

Consequently, at around the time when Watt's condenser was becoming a patentable proposition, friends started to press him to acquire his patent. One correspondent, the scientist John Robison, was particularly insistent, writing to Watt in July 1768: "you see my dear Sir how many reasons in a manner force you to bestir yourself in getting your property secured. I have fulfilled my promise to Mr Boulton and Dr Small by pressing the thing upon you in the strongest manner."[13] Watt's apparent reluctance to obtain the patent in mid-1768 may be because he was uncertain whether the invention was yet ready to be adequately specified, but he yielded, and worked incessantly to finish the specification in time (which was eventually quite a short document, as we will see in the following section). Watt,

[9] James Watt to William Small, 28 July 1769, (*The Industrial Revolution* 1993, Reel 1, Item 8).

[10] The letter appears in Rolt (1962, pp. 47–48).

[11] At this moment, the largest engineer by engines erected was probably William Brown, who between 1752 and 1778 was responsible for 32 engines. Similarly, Smeaton was responsible for erecting 26 engines between 1755 and 1786. By contrast, B&W would erect 478 between 1774 and 1800 (Kanefsky and Robey 1980, p. 175). Moreover, previous steam engine erectors did not manufacture the components of the engine themselves, but usually sub-contracted this task to local tradesmen.

[12] The legal mechanisms by which B&W could have prevented customers from reverse-engineering the condenser almost certainly did not exist. For a general discussion of the history of British trade secrecy law, see Bottomley (2017).

[13] John Robison to James Watt, 8 July 1768 (Robinson and McKie 1970, p. 14).

though, was probably right to worry about obtaining the patent prematurely, which was awarded to him in January 1769. The standard patent term was fourteen years and so Watt's patent was due to expire in January 1783. With the time lost in further development, B&W would only have enjoyed an effective ten-year patent term. Consequently, once he had acquired Roebuck's share of the patent in 1773, Boulton used his extensive political contacts to petition Parliament for a 17-year extension to the patent term, so that it would end in 1800. It is revealing of the importance of the patent, that the business partnership between Boulton and Watt was only formalized once this extension was granted in 1775, and arranged to formally end with the patent term on 5 January 1800: the existence of B&W had been entirely contingent on not only the patent but also the extension to its term. It is also worth stressing that without the financial capital and manufacturing plant Boulton provided, it is extremely doubtful that Watt would have been able to turn the condenser into a marketable proposition with his own resources; as he himself acknowledged "without [Boulton] the invention could never have been carried by me to the length it has been."[14]

Returning to Boulton's 1769 letter, the second point to emerge is his determination, years before the partnership had been formalized, to manufacture the components for the steam engines themselves. Previously, it had been usual to obtain engine components from local tradesmen and for the engineer to "only" erect the engine. B&W, though, faced a novel situation. They needed to convince potential customers that their new engine design offered a superior fuel efficiency to the old-style Newcomen engines. The solution they arrived at was to supply the engine parts at or near cost, but to charge a royalty for their engines, calculated as a third of the value of the coal saved. They would thereby incur the risk involved with fuel savings, not the customer. Boldrin and Levine criticize this royalty structure as monopolistic and price discriminatory, although once the principle was established, B&W's customers *asked* to be charged in this manner.[15] Subsequent steam engineers attempting to introduce their own engines designs such as Jonathan Hornblower and Arthur Woolf also adopted this pricing strategy (Hills 1989, p. 107).

Calculating the license fee in this manner, though, tied the financial fortunes of the partnership directly to the performance of their engines. A poorly erected or maintained engine would consume more coal, reducing the fuel differential between Watt's engine and a Newcomen engine. Consequently, there was a pressing

[14] Quoted in Dickinson (1936, p. 200). Dickinson adds his own opinion that without Boulton, Watt "would never have brought his engine into general use, nor derived any reward for his invention, nor followed it up by those equally brilliant inventions connected with the rotative engine."

[15] One customer sought "leave to recommend you to settle the premium per savings [of coal] it appearing to me the most equitable," (Robert Wild to Boulton and Watt, 28 November 1789 [Tann 1981, p. 294]). Later, the partnership offered customers a fixed license fee, although this was ultimately based on the estimated fuel savings as well (Bottomley 2014, p. 255).

commercial reason for the partnership to ensure that engine components were durable and of the highest possible quality. Of course, as Boulton appreciated in his 1769 letter, the best guarantor of quality was to manufacture all the engine components himself at his Soho manufactory near Birmingham, although the logistical and organizational challenges inherent to establishing their new type of business meant that initially the partnership only made the smaller precision parts themselves, relying on subcontractors for the rest. This, though, brought its own set of problems, especially guaranteeing that the parts would arrive on time to where an engine was being erected. Also, at least one major subcontractor, John Wilkinson, exploited their dependence on him as the only provider of cylinders for their steam engines to infringe the patent on a massive scale. In a 1795 letter written to the partnership's lawyer, Watt listed 35 engines (!) erected by Wilkinson without their permission.[16] The matter was only resolved to the partnership's satisfaction once they were able to establish their own iron foundry in 1795, freeing them from their reliance on Wilkinson and enabling them to apply much greater legal pressure on him. Wilkinson eventually relented, and agreed to pay license fees (Bottomley 2014, p. 254).

Consequently, there were pressing reasons for B&W to expand their own manufacturing base and to end their reliance on subcontractors—they could never have been content to simply let the royalty payments come in, as alleged by Boldrin and Levine. This can be clearly seen in their manufacturing accounts (see Table 3.1). Table 3.1 covers the period from 1779 (from when the manufacturing accounts survive) to the end of the patent in 1800. The first column provides the number of engine sales recorded for that year. The second column shows the value of goods manufactured at Soho. The third column divides the value of the goods manufactured by engine sales, to give an indication of how B&W sought to increase the proportion of engine components they were supplying. This though, is only a very rough indication, as some of these components would have been made to replace worn out ones on older engines. For example, by 1797, the account of manufactured goods distinguishes between "whole engines" (£12,770 for 1796–1797) and "extra and other articles" (£2,394).

The accounts clearly demonstrate that B&W grew rapidly to become a major manufacturing concern long before their patent expired in 1800. By 1791, they were making goods valued at almost £10,000 p.a. By 1800, this figure stood at £28,617 (for comparison, nominal GDP per capita in 1801 was around £25). Also, the partnership were contributing a significant proportion of the components for their engines by the late 1780s. For comparison with the figures in the third column, B&W's price list for new engines from 1798 shows that a 4 hp engine cost £262 to construct (and sold at £350, with manufacturing profit of 5 percent

[16] James Watt to Ambrose Weston, 10 September 1795 (Tann 1981, p. 131–36).

Table 3.1 Boulton & Watt, manufactured goods, 1779–1800.

Year	Engines sales[a]	Goods manufactured[b]	Goods manufactured per engine
1779	10	£923	£92
1780	10	£480	£48
1781	4	£92	£23
1782	2	£582	£291
1783	10	£344	£34
1784	15	£806	£54
1785	19	£1,515	£80
1786	21	£2,348	£112
1787	11	£3,639	£331
1788	14	£4,200	£300
1789	20	£3,594	£180
1790	21	£3,800	£181
1791	25	£9,858	£394
1792	18	£9,866	£548
1793	17	£11,831	£696
1794	13	£9,879	£760
1795	26	£5,821	£224
1796	31	£15,295	£493
1797	21	£15,168	£722
1798	23	£17,847	£776
1799	47	£23,139	£492
1800	47	£28,617	£609

a Tann (1977) produces a slightly reduced number of B&W engines manufactured for the period from Kanefsky and Robey (1980), although her figures have been used here as they are annualized.

b Accounts and balance sheets 1783 to 1797 (*The Industrial Revolution* 1993, Reel 75). Value of goods manufactured was not recorded over a calendar year, but from October to September. So the first figure in this column actually relates to the period October 1778 to September 1779.

and royalty charge). A 32 hp engine would have cost around £850 to manufacture and sold for £1156.[17]

[17] J. Watt junior to Boulton junior, 11 September 1798 (*The Industrial Revolution* 1993, Reel 6, Item 61).

The partnership's determination to ensure that engines built to their design were of the highest quality, also meant that they were loath to license the use of their technology to other engineers. They were conscious that a poorly erected engine would damage their reputation as well as limit their royalty payments. This had important repercussions for their relations with other engineers, as we will explore in the following section. In the interim, what this signifies is that the portrayal of B&W as idle parasites, succored by their patents and uninterested in manufacturing could not be a grosser misrepresentation. As we have seen, they had pressing commercial reasons for manufacturing their own engines. Indeed, together, they created an enterprise the likes of which had never been seen before, a factory that could manufacture steam engines in their entirety and then erect them for a customer. They even introduced a rudimentary form of after-sales service. They could not have achieved this scale of production without their patent for the condenser.

Finally, it has been claimed that once Watt finished developing his condenser and the partnership's legal position was secured by an extension to their patent term, he was uninterested in pursuing further developments in steam engineering: he "simply decide[d] to make money from [his] existing invention rather than keep working to improve it" (Lemley 2012, pp. 740–41).[18] This claim is usually attributed to a letter Watt wrote to Boulton:

> On the whole, I find it now full time to cease attempting to invent new things, or to attempt anything which is attended with any risk of not succeeding or creating trouble in the execution. Let us go on executing the things we understand, and leave the rest to younger men, who have neither money nor character to lose. (first quoted in Scherer 1965, p. 174)

The letter, though, reveals more about Watt's personality and his neuroticism than about his inventive output: he was the most innovative steam engineer of the last quarter of the eighteenth century. Among other things, Watt invented sun and planet gearing (patent no. 1306), so that steam engines could produce rotative motion (a competing and ultimately more successful crank may have been stolen from Watt; patent no. 1263; Tann 2013), double acting cylinders (where steam acted on both sides of the piston in a cylinder; no. 1321), parallel motion (allowing a pumping rod to move up and down in a directly straight line; no. 1432), the poppet valve (an improved valve for controlling steam flow into the engine; no. 1432). Watt also developed the concept of "horsepower" (hp) as a means of measuring the power output of engines.

[18] See also Merges and Nelson (1990, p. 872).

Admittedly, Watt wrote his letter at the end of 1785 (it is usually cited as if indicative of the whole patent term), but after this date, he still developed the centrifugal governor for steam engines in 1788 (adopted from windmills and used to regulate the operating speed of the engine). As a firm, also, B&W remained innovative. One employee, John Southern, developed the indicator, used to measure the pressure inside the engine at each stage of the operating cycle (useful for maximizing power output and fuel efficiency). B&W were also probably the first firm to use elliptical cast iron beams in 1797, improving the durability of their engines and their flexural strength.[19] Finally, while it has been suggested that engines capable of producing 100 hp only appeared in the nineteenth century, it appears that the largest B&W engines were capable of this power output before the end of the eighteenth century (Tann 2014).

Boulton & Watt and High-Pressure Steam Engineering

Over the course of the nineteenth century, the greatest gains in fuel economy and power output would be achieved by using steam at ever greater pressures to actively "push" against the piston, rather than using atmospheric pressure to "pull" the piston down. This would also allow for the development of the steam locomotive, which would revolutionize world transport. Watt had conceived of this possibility when working on his separate condenser and included it as the fourth article of his 1769 specification, where he stated his intention "to employ the expansive Force of Steam to press on the pistons."[20] Watt, though, was not the first to have had this idea. In Europe, for example, Jacob Leupold had described a high-pressure engine in *Theatrum Machinarum Generale* in 1720 (Selgin and Turner 2011, p. 848). Similarly, in 1698, Thomas Savery had patented an engine which used steam at high pressures—although it did not use pistons and encountered too many technical problems to ever be considered a success (in particular, the engine's soldered joints could not withstand the high pressures required). At this time, British patent law did not recognize the rights of the first inventor per se, but those of the first domestic "publisher." Use abroad, or domestic use that had been in secret and/or fallen into abeyance, would not invalidate a subsequent patent, at least, not for want of novelty (Bottomley 2014, pp. 165–67).

[19] Nuvolari (2004, pp. 30–31). Cardwell (1994, p. 208) suggests that the company Aydon & Elwell were the first to use these beams in 1795.

[20] In full: "Fourthly, I intend in many cases to employ the expansive Force of Steam to press on the Pistons, or whatever may be used instead of them, in the same Manner as the Pressure of the Atmosphere is now employed in common Fire Engines: In Cases where cold Water cannot be had in Plenty, the Engines may be wrought by this Force of Steam only, by discharging the Steam into the open Air after it has done it's Office." Watt, James. 1769. "Method of lessening the consumption of steam and fuel in fire-engines." England Patent 913, awarded Jan. 5, 1769.

Consequently, although the idea had been previously expressed, if Watt had invented an engine worked by high-pressure steam, then it probably would have been patentable. It is doubtful, however, that at the time when Watt submitted his specification, he had indeed accomplished a finished machine and/or model using the expansive force of steam; the fourth article refers only to an intention and in its 78 words, offers no specific indication of how Watt intended to use the expansive force in practice. It was this vague and elusive article that would be the major source of Watt's legal difficulties over the coming years: specifications were adjudged by stringent criteria at this time. Watt well knew this, but he seems to have believed that concision was the best strategy when preparing his 1769 specification.[21] He was also poorly advised to omit technical drawings from his specification.

This vulnerability in Watt's patent gradually became apparent as others sought to pursue the same technological opportunities; the first British engineer after Watt to experiment with the expansive power of steam was Jonathan Hornblower who patented a compound engine design in 1781. In Hornblower's compound engine, higher pressure steam was used to drive a piston in a smaller, closed top cylinder. The steam then passed to a second cylinder where it expanded further, driving a second piston. High pressure compound engines of this type became the predominant design during the course of the nineteenth century, due to their fuel economy and the smoothness of action that could be achieved by using two working cylinders instead of one. Hornblower, though, never came close to realizing the full potential of his design. Firstly, Hornblower never used the engine at pressures high enough to realize anything like the fuel economy that might have been achieved, and this despite the urging of friends such as Davies Gilbert (later elected as president of the Royal Society, 1827–1830), to do so. Criticism on this point, though, ought to be tempered by acknowledging that metal working techniques at the end of the eighteenth century were not yet reliable enough to ensure that boilers could always contain the steam at the requisite pressures.[22] Secondly, there were technical faults with his engines (as shown in drawings of his ten Cornish engines erected from 1791 to 1794), which also undermined their efficacy. For example, Hornblower's engines used a separate condenser to improve their fuel efficiency, although this had to be limited in size "probably to try and avoid Watt's patent" (Hills 1989, p. 147).[23] Thirdly, Hornblower was

[21] Boulton and Watt (1993, Part I, 1:4).

[22] Matters improved in the nineteenth century, although between 1800 and 1866, 4,067 people were killed in more than 1,000 recorded boiler explosions (Selgin and Turner p. 855).

[23] Hornblower referred obliquely to his use of the condenser in his 1781 patent specification: "Sixthly, that the condensed vapour shall not remain in *the steam-vessel in which the steam is condensed*, I collect it into another vessel." Hornblower, Jonathan. 1781. "Machine or engine for raising water and other liquids by means of fire and steam, and for other purposes." England Patent 1298, awarded July 13. 1781.

determined to pursue an unworkable scheme to develop his engine so that it could pump water out of mines *and* grind corn simultaneously, requiring that the engine work in both horizontal and vertical directions (Todd 1959, pp. 4–6). One wonders what might have been possible if Hornblower had had Watt's good fortune and entered into partnership with a more acute business mind.

Not only was Hornblower infringing the sperate condenser, but also, B&W believed, their sole right to use steam expansively. In 1792, for example, in their published opposition to Jonathan Hornblower's application to Parliament for an extension to his own 1781 patent, they asserted that one of their principle contributions had been to develop "the piston [which] is pressed down by the expansive power of steam; *and not* (as in Newcomen's) *by the weight of the atmosphere*" (original italics).[24] Such, likewise, was the view of informed contemporaries as well. In an undated note, John Smeaton observed that one of the "prohibitions concerning the structure of fire engines injoined by the specification in Mr Watt's Act of Parliament" was "not to employ the expansive force of steam to press on pistons or whatever else may be used instead of them in the same manner as the pressure of the atmosphere is now employed in common fire engines."[25] There can be no doubt that the partnership believed that Hornblower was working in contravention of their patent rights. Interestingly, it appears from a letter Hornblower wrote to his uncle in 1789 that he acknowledged that in his engine "the mechanism is similar to Watt's in most respects," one of which was that "steam is convey'd thither in a state stronger than the atmosphere and acts upwards with a force" (Torrens 1982, pp.191–92). However, despite these infringements, Boulton and Watt failed to take legal action against Hornblower until the very end of their patent term in 1799. This obviously begs the question why they waited for so long. In roughly chronological order, there were three reasons.

(1) In the 1780s, Hornblower's engines performed poorly. In 1782, for example, John Southern, one of B&W's most accomplished agents, inspected Hornblower's engine erected at Radstock. Although he confirmed it was an infringement of the partnership's patents, it made "so wretched a performance as not to equal an Old Usual Engine" (Tann 1981, p. 96). Indeed, it ran so badly that by 1785, Hornblower's engine man at Radstock had started to pass information on to James Watt in the hope of gaining employment with him instead, warning in particular about visitors arriving to inspect the engine from Cornwall.[26]

[24] Boulton and Watt Collection, Library of Birmingham (LB), MS 3147.2.51, Item 22.

[25] LB, MS 3147.2.23, undated.

[26] LB, MS 3147.2.35, Item 5, letter from Shore, dated 12 June 1787. Hornblower's engine man (Thomas Shore) also discussed the failure of his recently erected engine at a coal mine in Timsbury. Here, there were three six-inch pumps working at the mine, but only one pump could be worked "with his engine, he have not got power enough that do work the other 2 pumps with horses" (sic) (LB, MS 3147.2.35, Item 3, letter from Shore, dated 21 February 1785).

Although initially alarmed by the threat posed by Hornblower, the partnership decided against intervening until his engines posed a direct commercial threat: as Watt wrote to Boulton in 1786, "to the trumpeting [Hornblower] if anybody is wicked enough to erect one of their Engines let them, and when we can do no better lett [sic] us try the law."[27] Moreover, Hornblower's first engines ran at coal mines (Radstock and Timsbury), where, of course, fuel prices were extremely low. As such, because the royalty payments to B&W were calculated according to fuel savings, engines at these mines would have paid little to them in any case. Consequently, while Hornblower's engine was in its developmental stage during the 1780s, the partnership refrained from legal action to enjoin his activities: so long as he remained uncompetitive, there was, from a financial perspective, no pressing reason to do so. It also means that Boldrin and Levine's casual "decade or two" can be narrowed down to a certain decade.

Beginning in the 1790s, however, Hornblower started to reach parity with Watt's engines in terms of fuel efficiency, as measured by duty (incidentally, a measurement introduced by Watt). Appropriately, as most engines were used to pump water out of mines, duty was expressed in terms of how many pounds of weight could be raised one foot, by consuming one bushel of coals (standard weight being 86lbs).[28] The Newcomen engines averaged around 4–5 million lbs of duty, although the best could achieve 10 million (Hills 1989, p. 37). The best Watt engine, by contrast, had attained 27.5 million by 1798, although they tended to work at around 18–20 million (Hills 1989, p. 103). Trials of Hornblower's engines indicate that he was only ever able to achieve parity with B&W's engines, at least in respect of duty. Richard Trevithick, for example, measured the duty of one Hornblower engine at Tin Croft mine at 16.6 million lbs; another trial reached 19.8 million lbs. One trial by Hornblower himself (presumably under ideal conditions and with a view to maximizing the result) yielded a figure of 28.5 million lbs.[29]

Hornblower had also started to erect steam engines at mines in Cornwall—by far the most lucrative area of B&W's operation—where he offered terms which were also far more advantageous to mine owners. As has already been discussed, B&W charged their license premium at one-third of the value of the coal savings

[27] James Watt to Matthew Boulton, 23 September 1786 (*The Industrial Revolution*, Reel 4, Item 71).

[28] The weight of a bushel of coals did vary from place to place, though. The standard bushel was 86lbs, but in London, it was 82½lbs and in Cornwall, 94lbs. Jim Andrew, "Old weights and measures," mimeo, 2008, see http://www.museumsassociation.org/download?id=77607. Moreover, it varies from source to source—Hills (1989, p. 36) gives the weight of a London bushel as 88lbs (!).

[29] LB, MS 3147.2.52, Item 4 "History of Jonathan Hornblower's Engine. Thomas Wilson, 22 July 1799." This was a document prepared by Thomas Wilson, B&W's agent in Cornwall, so it might be expected that he would be tempted to underreport the figures for Hornblower's engine. However, the document was prepared with a view to calculating the license payments to be demanded of those using Hornblower engines. This was premised on the work achieved by the engines, and so here, if anything, the temptation would have been to overstate the work achieved by Hornblower's engines.

achieved by using their steam engine, compared with an old Newcomen engine; this saving was considerable. Hornblower offered the identical terms—charging one-third of the coal savings incurred by using his steam engine, but in comparison with a Watt engine.[30] Even though this saving was modest, if indeed there was a saving at all, there was now a considerable incentive for the Cornish mine owners to use Hornblower engines instead of Boulton &Watt's, especially if they discounted the enforceability of the latter's patent. For an illustration using roughly representative figures, let us say a Newcomen engine at a mine consumed £4,000 in coal p.a. If the coal usage was halved by replacing it with a B&W engine, then the mine owner was now only spending £2,666 p.a.—£2,000 on fuel and a royalty of £666 to B&W, as a third of their fuel savings. Now let us say they then replace their B&W engine with a Hornblower engine, which yields an additional £300 p.a. fuel saving. The owner is now only spending £1,800 p.a.—£1,700 in fuel and a £100 royalty to Hornblower.[31] After the first Hornblower engine was erected in Cornwall, at Tincroft in 1791, nine more were erected to 1794, as well as eight other pirate engines by Edward Bull (Tann 1979, pp. 104–05). Unlike his earlier engines at coal mines, this posed a serious threat to the finances of B&W. Worse still, mines with Watt's engines started to withhold royalty payments, in the hope that the separate condenser patent would prove to be unenforceable.

(2) Still, however, Boulton and Watt refrained from enjoining the use of the Hornblower engine. The second reason why they waited so long before prosecuting Hornblower was because they appreciated that their patent was poorly specified and "weak." In 1791, for example, when they were beginning to prepare for legal action, they sought the private opinion of Sir John Scott, then the solicitor-general, and Thomas Plumer, another prominent lawyer, on the sufficiency of their specification. Both were of the decided opinion that the specification was inadequate, Plumer observing that "in what manner the [invention] is to be performed," the specification "seems to be entirely silent."[32] By the terms of English patent law at this time, this should have been sufficient to invalidate their entire patent.

[30] Inevitably, some of the Cornish mine owners who erected Hornblower engines, decided to challenge their license payments on the basis that the savings achieved were not what Hornblower claimed. See, for example, the correspondence between Hornblower and Wheal Wherry mine. LB, MS 3147.2.51, Item 36.

[31] These figures are intended to be representative. Firstly, the fuel savings are broadly in line with the gains in duty seen between different types of engine discussed in the main text. Indeed, it probably understates the savings involved with using a B&W engine compared with a Newcomen engine, and overstates the savings involved with using a Hornblower engine compared with a B&W engine. On the monetary savings involved with adopting a B&W engine (see Matthew Boulton to James Watt, 6 September 1777 [Tann 1981, 173]).

[32] He therefore sought to "impress Messrs Boulton and Watt with such a degree of hesitation and doubt on this subject, as to prevent their hazarding a litigation, which in one event might be so injurious to them, without consulting the advice of their other counsel." (LB, MS 3147.2.34, Item 1, copy of Mr Plumer's opinion, 20 September 1791, covering note).

The partnership also feared that the patent might be revoked by writ of *scire facias*. This was a writ obtainable by third parties who could represent to the attorney-general that the patent in question was invalid and request that a case be brought in the name of the Crown to have the validity of the patent properly tried at common law. The writ was not demandable as a matter of right, and the burden of evidence concerning the (in)validity of the patent sought by the law officer prior to issuing the writ was probably high: while it was not so great that issuance of the writ was unusual, once it was issued and pursued to trial, patentees very seldom won (the first reported instance of success occurring in 1850).[33] Whatever the threshold, B&W's patent certainly flirted with it. In June 1795, for example, their lawyer Ambrose Weston wrote to the pair, "I shall continue to use every exertion in my power to ward off the *scire facias*, which I dread as much as you" and intriguingly, a draft of a writ to annul their patent survives in the National Archives in London.[34]

For whatever reason, though, the writ was never issued and in the final analysis, no attorney-general at the time thought B&W's patent so demonstrably invalid that a writ of *scire facias* ought to issue. Still, vulnerabilities in their patent persuaded the partnership to proceed cautiously, moving in successive steps. First, of all they moved to prosecute only the most blatant infringers, especially Edward Bull who was also working in Cornwall. Bull's engine was in almost every respect the same as Watt's, although he had ingeniously inverted the cylinder directly over the mine shaft, removing the need for the rocking beam that usually connected the pumping rod with the steam engine. His use of the separate condenser, though, was certainly an infringement. Initially, Bull had sought a license from the partnership for the use of their technology when erecting his engines, although this had been refused for the reasons mentioned earlier.[35] Bull, however, chose to press on without their license, and between 1791 and 1794, erected at least eight engines according to his design in Cornwall (Tann 1979, p. 104).

[33] The first reported *scire facias* case relating to patents of invention occurred in 1782 (K.B.: 1 Oldham 1992, p. 767), and there were six more reported cases before the end of the century: *Rex* v. *Else* (1785, K.B.): Bull. N.P. (6th ed.) 76; Davies 144; 1 Carp. P.C. 103; 1 Web. P.C. 64; 11 East 109 n.(*c*); *Times*, Dec. 24, 1785, p. 3; *Rex* v. *Arkwright* (1785, K.B.): 1 Web. P.C. 64; 1 Carp. P.C. 53; Davies 61; *The Trial of a Cause Instituted by Richard Pepper Arden* &c (1785) *Rex* v. *Argand* (1786, K.B.): *Times*, Dec. 6, 1786, p. 3; *Manchester Mercury*, Dec. 12, 1786, p. 2; *Rex* v. *Eley* (1790, K.B.): *Times*, Dec. 9, 1790, p. 3; *World*, Dec. 9, 1790, p. 3; *Rex* v. *Miles* (1797, K.B.): 7 T.R. 367; *Times*, Feb. 21, 1797, p. 3; *Oracle*, Feb. 21; *Rex* v. *Boileau* (1799, K.B.): Farey Report, p. 191.

[34] Ambrose Weston to Boulton & Watt 4 June 1795, (*The Industrial Revolution* 1993, Reel 108, Item 11). National Archives (NA), C217/152.

[35] In October 1791, James Watt wrote to Thomas Wilson, his agent in Cornwall, on the matter of Bull's application: "In respect to Bull, the less we have to do with him the better, if he applies to you on our terms & brings respectable persons as principles you will fix the premium with him & take his order for the size of the Engine but we will not be directed how to make it. Had we agreed to have let him made one of our Engines in such a manner he pleased, he would have made a bad thing & we should have had our share of the disgrace as it now stands" (quoted in Stewart [2017, pp. 137–38]; original at Cornwall Record Office (CRO), AD 1583/4/91).

Once B&W obtained a favorable verdict at common law against Edward Bull in 1795, and then again against Jethro Hornblower (brother of Jonathan) and Stephen Maberley in 1799, they were in a much stronger position to enforce their patent against other engineers who were infringing their rights to the separate condenser. However, two of the judges who had supported the validity of the patent in *Boulton & Watt* v *Bull* (1795) expressed doubts concerning the enforceability of the fourth article of Watt's specification regarding the use of the expansive force of steam. Justice Rooke, for example, noted that Watt "could [not] maintain an action for breach of these articles."[36] This raises a second important point—it is doubtful, at the conclusion of the B&W cases, that they could have enforced this specific clause of the specification. The corollary of this is that Boulton and Watt would not have been able to enjoin the development and use of single cylinder, high pressure engines that did not use a separate condenser—a type of engine that would subsequently be developed by Richard Trevithick in the early part of the nineteenth century (the "puffer")—had such an engine appeared during their patent term. Put another way, their patent would have done nothing to prevent the development and commercialization of this type of engine at the end of the eighteenth century.

Nonetheless, the partnership's overall legal position had been strengthened by their success at common law, and over the course of the 1790s, they obtained *at least* fifteen separate injunctions. There is no record of a single injunction beforehand. But in another important respect, they adopted a more accommodating attitude to their rivals than had previously been the case. It will be remembered that in 1791, the partnership had been unwilling to license Edward Bull, a dispute that ultimately led them to try their right at law. Later, though, they were willing to license Bull's engines, "provided our dues are paid," which admittedly was not always the case and injunctions had to be obtained to prevent Bull from erecting more engines (quoted in Stewart 2017, p.142). Thus, once they strengthened their legal position, by virtue of favorable verdicts at common law supporting the validity of their patent, they moved to collect royalty payments from less egregious infringers, especially those using Jonathan Hornblower's engines (whose efforts to avoid infringing B&W's patent by minimizing the size of his condenser have already been mentioned), alleging that they made use of the technology that they had patented.

(3) Herein lies the third reason why the partnership refrained from legal action against Hornblower for much of the 1790s. Ultimately, they had always

[36] Hayward (1987, 1:383–84). Similarly, Chief Justice Eyre noted that "some weighty observations have been made upon parts of this specification, but those parts appear to me not properly to relate to the method described in the patent; they are rather intimations of new projects of improvement in fire-engines, and some of them, I am very ready to confess either very loosely described or not very accurately conceived . . . they are the fourth and fifth articles" (Hayward 1987, 1:393).

hoped that their financial losses would be minimized by claiming royalties from those mines that used Hornblower engines. The partnership had monitored the use of the Hornblower engines very closely with a view to handing in demands for license fees owed when the time was opportune. The partnership had also made periodic requests for such royalties throughout the 1790s, but they were not backed up with the credible threat of legal action—as contemporaries were well aware. In 1795, for example, after legal action had already commenced against him, Edward Bull observed that B&W had "never attempted to interrupt the working of [Hornblower's engines] except by threats only."[37] Although Bull's engine may have offered certain advantages over Boulton and Watt's engine, it was a clear infringement of their patent. Interestingly, Hornblower seems to have been pleased that Bull lost his case: "I must say I rejoice at it . . . Bull's was a palpable infringement without any improvement whatever' (Torrens 1982, p. 196). Speculatively, Hornblower may have hoped that with this avenue of evading B&W's patent closed off, mine owners would now be minded to adopt his own engine instead.

After the final contest at common law against Jonathan's brother Jethro and his business partner Stephen Maberley had been resolved to the partnership's satisfaction in 1799, they moved quickly, presenting royalty demands to every mine using a Hornblower engine. These were calculated precisely, according to the length of time the engine had been working and the size of the engine's cylinders, as a proxy measure for the coal savings which formed the usual basis of B&W's royalties. For example, Trescavean mine was assessed at £1435 11s. 6d. for a Hornblower engine with 30 and 36-inch cylinders, which had been at work for 80 months and 6 days.[38] In total, B&W calculated that they were due £10,560 from mines working Hornblower engines.[39]

Subsequent events can be traced in the voluminous legal bill B&W accrued over the entire period from 1794 to 1801. Initially, the mines refused to pay, and injunctions were obtained to prevent the working of Hornblower engines. Hornblower himself was served on 21 October 1799.[40] Initially, it did not appear that Hornblower would back down (it was reported to B&W that when served, Hornblower "only said that he thought it was foolish in you to give him any trouble") and Boulton and Watt made serious preparations for the case to proceed to common law, meeting with their counsel in London several times in February 1800 to discuss the subject.[41] Matters proceeded all the way to Hornblower being

[37] NA, C12/204/15, fol. 1. The partnership had made periodic requests to users of these mines throughout the 1790s, but with the favorable verdict in Bull, it seems that the threat of legal action became far more menacing.

[38] LB, MS 3147.2.52, Item 1.

[39] LB, MS 3147.2.52, Item 1.

[40] LB, MS 3147.2.52, Item 20, dated 21 October 1799.

[41] LB, MS 3147.2.52, Item 20, dated 21 October 1799.

served with notice of the trial, when presumably, to judge from B&W's bill, Hornblower surrendered. It is not clear what prompted Hornblower to concede at the last minute. It may simply be that he had been bluffing in the hope that B&W would blink first. In any case the first mine to pay up was Wheal Unity, which paid £2,100 in satisfaction of royalties that had originally been assessed at £3011 5s. 0d in September 1800.[42] A few weeks later, Tincroft, the first mine to erect a Hornblower engine and with the largest assessed royalty (initially at £3,684), paid £2,569 in satisfaction thereof.[43]

Thus, although the story is a detailed and complex one, the outcome is relatively straightforward. Use of a Hornblower engine was possible, free from legal interference from Boulton and Watt, so long as royalties were paid to the partnership for their savings. This was not just the case with those using Hornblower engines. In the middle of the legal action against Edward Bull, for example, mines using his engine could obtain an accommodation with B&W. In 1795, for example, B&W obtained an injunction, preventing the working of the engine at Ding Dong mine which, although based on Bull's design, had been erected and altered by Richard Trevithick.[44] In particular, Trevithick was responsible for increasing the pressure at which the engine worked to achieve better fuel economy, the resultant success of which led to his appointment as chief engineer at the mine (Trevithick 1872). The *Life of Richard Trevithick*, written by his son Francis, records Trevithick's apparent intransigence in the face of this legal action, altering the engine to avoid the patent (by opening up the top of cylinder, thus reverting to the use of atmospheric pressure) and by supplementing its power with a windmill. A more prosaic document survives in the B&W archives in Birmingham—a copy of the licensing agreement Trevithick reached with B&W later in 1796, when he agreed to pay £162 18s. 8d. "as the premium for the using of a certain Steam Engine of twenty-eight inches diameter in the cylinder that is now working on a mine called Ding Dong Mine, for so long time as the said engine shall continue to work single, or by steam pressed on one side of the piston only."[45] Similarly, after B&W had successfully obtained an injunction against Bateman & Sherratt in 1796 (their largest competitor in terms of engines erected), they were also licensed and continued to erect engines using B&W's technology during the patent term (Kanefsky 1979, p. 478).[46]

Herein lies the crucial point. B&W's patent(s) did not act as an insuperable obstacle to the development of high-pressure steam engines, or indeed

[42] LB, MS 3147.2.52, Item 26.

[43] LB, MS 3147.2.52, Item 30.

[44] NA, C12/213/16, f. 3.

[45] LB, M3 3147.2.17, Item 6.

[46] Although they were a very distant second. Between 1782 and 1800, Bateman & Sherratt made 45 steam engines, whereas B&W made 451 (Kanefsky and Robey 1980, p. 175).

other potential developments in steam engines. As the experience of Jonathan Hornblower, Richard Trevithick, and Bateman & Sherratt shows, they were eventually able to obtain licenses to use James Watt's patented technology. Neither was the expiration of B&Ws patent term in 1800 marked by any sudden change in behavior: it did not mark the opening of a new opportunity. Hornblower did not suddenly start using higher pressures in his steam engines; not a single engine was erected according to his design after 1800 (Farey 1827, p. 390). Instead, the opportunities of using Hornblower's engine at higher pressures were left to Arthur Woolf, who patented his design in 1810 (Carlyle 2004). Trevithick continued his work on high-pressure engines, but was hampered by safety issues (seized upon in publicity by B&W) and the dissipation of his energy over multiple ventures, which eventually bankrupted him in 1811 (Hills 1989, pp. 102–03). As with Hornblower, one wonders whether Trevithick would have enjoyed greater success if he had had the same good fortune as Watt in finding a business partner with the foresight and nous of Matthew Boulton.

Conclusion

The story of Watt's patent is an almost ideal illustration of patents working to stimulate the development and commercialization of new technology. It incentivized Watt's costly development of the condenser, a project which took ten years and at least £7,500 to complete. Without the prospect of patent protection, it is unclear why he would have made this investment. Neither would he have been able to join in a partnership with Matthew Boulton, one of the largest and most ambitious manufacturers of the day, and commercialize the condenser. Put another way, without patenting, industry would have been waiting for the condenser to appear "organically" for a very long time. The protection afforded by the patent also allowed the partnership to invest in the establishment of a business the likes of which had never been seen before—a manufactory that constructed steam engines in their entirety, provided for the installation, and then also a rudimentary form of after-sales service.

Neither do the supposed downsides of awarding patents appear in the instance of Watt. He continued to develop improvements, and work on the underlying theory of steam engineering, throughout the lifetime of the patent. Finally, the claim that Watt was able to use his patent to stymie the development of high-pressure steam engineering can be discarded. The partnership had refrained from interfering with Hornblower's engine when it was in its developmental phase and only resorted to legal action at the very end of the patent term in an effort to collect royalty payments from mines using his engine.

Reference List

Boulton and Watt Collection, MS 3147. Birmingham Archives and Heritage. Library of Birmingham.

Boulton, Matthew, and James Watt, *Industrial Revolution: Series 1, The Boulton and Watt Archive and the Matthew Boulton Papers from the Birmingham Central Library*. Marlborough: Adam Matthew, 1993.

Boldrin, Michele, and David Levine. *Against Intellectual Monopoly*. Cambridge: Cambridge University Press, 2008.

———. "What's Intellectual Property Good for?" *Revue économique* 64, no. 1 (2013): 29–53.

Bottomley, Sean. *The British Patent System during the Industrial Revolution, 1700–1852*. Cambridge: Cambridge University Press, 2014.

———. "The Origins of Trade Secrecy Law in England, 1600–1851." *Journal of Legal History* 38, no. 3 (2017): 254–81.

Cardwell, D. S. L., *The Fontana History of Technology*. London: Harper, 1994.

Carlyle, E. I. "Woolf, Arthur (bap. 1766, d.1837)." Rev. Philip Payton. In Oxford Dictionary of National Biography, edited by Brian Harrison and Colin Matthew. Oxford: Oxford University Press, 2004. Also available online at https://doi-org.ezp.lib.cam.ac.uk/10.1093/ref:odnb/29953.

Cornwall Record Office. Matthew Boulton (1728–1809) and James Watt (1736–1819), Engineers, AD 1583. Redruth.

Cule, J. E. "Finance and Industry in the Eighteenth Century: The Firm of Boulton and Watt." *Economic Journal* 50, no. 1 (1940): 319–25.

Dickinson, H. W. *James Watt: Craftsman & Engineer*. Cambridge: Cambridge University Press, 1936.

Duckham, B. F. "John Smeaton; the Father of English Civil Engineering." *History Today* 15, (1965), 200–06.

Farey, John. *A Treatise on the Steam Engine, Historical, Practical and Descriptive*, London: Longman, 1827.

Hayward, Peter. *Haywards Patent Cases: 1600 1883*. 13 vols. Abingdon: Professional Books Ltd., 1987.

Hills, Richard. *Power from Steam. A History of the Stationary Steam Engine*. Cambridge: Cambridge University Press, 1989.

The Industrial Revolution: A Documentary History. The Boulton and Watt Archive and the Matthew Boulton Papers from the Birmingham Central Library. Marlborough: Adam Matthew Publications, 1993.

Kanefsky, John. "The Diffusion of Power Technology in British Industry, 1760–1870." PhD diss. University of Exeter, 1979.

Kanefsky, John, and John Robey. "Steam Engines in 18th-Century Britain: A Quantitative Assessment." *Technology and Culture* 21, no. 2 (1980): 161–86.

Katznelson, Ron D., and John Howells. "The Myth of the Early Aviation Patent Hold-Up—How a US Government Monopsony Commandeered Pioneer Airplane Patents." *Industrial and Corporate Change* 24, no. 1 (2014): 1–64.

Kelly, Kevin. *What Technology Wants*. London: Penguin Books, 2011.

Klemm, Friedrich. *A History of Western Technology*. Cambridge, MA: MIT Press, 1964.

Lemley, Mark. "The Myth of the Sole Inventor." *Michigan Law Review* 110 no. 5 (2012): 710–60.

Leunig, Tim. "Social Savings." *Journal of Economic Surveys* 24 no.5 (2010): 775–800.

Meek, R., D. Raphael, and P. Stein. *Lectures on Jurisprudence: The Glasgow Edition of the Works and Correspondence of Adam Smith*. Indianapolis: Liberty Fund, 1982.

Merges, Robert P., and Richard R. Nelson. "On the Complex Economics of Patent Scope." *Columbia Law Review* 90, no. 4 (1990): 839–916.

Moser, Petra. "Patents and Innovation: Evidence from Economic History." *Journal of Economic Perspectives* 27, no.1 (2013): 23–44.

Muirhead, J. P. *The Origins and Progress of the Mechanical Inventions of James Watt*. London: J. Murray, 1854.

National Archives. Chancery Records, C 12 & C 217. London.

Nuvolari, Alessandro, "The Making of Steam Power Technology: A Study of Technical Change during the Industrial Revolution." PhD diss. Eindhoven University of Technology, 2004.

Oldham, James, *The Mansfield Manuscripts and the Growth of English Law in the Eighteenth Century*. 2 vols. Chapel Hill: University of North Carolina Press, 1992.

Robinson, Eric, and Douglas McKie, eds. *Partners in Science, Letters of James Watt and Joseph Black*. London: Constable, 1970.

Rolt, L. T. C. *James Watt*. London: Batsford, 1962.

Scherer, F. M., "Invention and Innovation in the Watt-Boulton Steam-Engine Venture." *Technology and Culture* 6, no. 2 (1965): 165–87.

Selgin, George, and John L. Turner, "Strong Steam, Weak Patents, or the Myth of Watt's Innovation-Blocking Monopoly, Exploded." *The Journal of Law and Economics* 54, no. 4 (2011): 841–61.

Stewart, R. J., *Mine Pumping Engines in Eighteenth Century Cornwall*. Exeter, UK: The Trevithick Society, 2017.

Tann, Jennifer "Boulton and Watt's Organisation of Steam Engine Production before the opening of Soho Foundry." *Transactions of the Newcomen Society* 49, 1 (1977): 41–56.

Tann, Jennifer "Mr Hornblower and His Crew: Watt Engine Pirates at the End of the 18th Century." *Transactions of the Newcomen Society* 51, no.1 (1979): 95–109.

Tann, Jennifer. *The Selected Papers of Boulton and Watt, 1775–1825*. London: Diploma Press, 1981.

Tann, Jennifer "Boulton, Matthew (1728-1809)" In *Oxford Dictionary of National Biography*, edited by Brian Harrison and Colin Matthew. Oxford: Oxford University Press, 2004. Also available online at https://doi-org.ezp.lib.cam.ac.uk/10.1093/ref:odnb/2983.

T

Todd, A. C. "Davies Gilbert-Patron of Engineers (1767–1839) and Jonathan Hornblower (1753–1815)." *Transactions of the Newcomen Society* 32, no. 1 (1959): 1–13.

Torrens, H. S., "Some Newly Discovered Letters from Jonathan Hornblower (1753–1815)." *Transactions of the Newcomen Society* 54, no. 1 (1982): 189–200.

Trevithick, Francis. *Life of Richard Trevithick*. 2 vols. London: E. & F. N. Spon, 1872.

von Tunzelmann, G. N. *Steam-Power and British Industrialization to 1860*. Oxford: Clarendon Press, 1978.

Wilson, James, ed., "The right of property in inventions," *The Economist*, 1 February 1851.

Wrigley, Tony. *Energy and the English Industrial Revolution*. Cambridge: Cambridge University Press, 2010.

4

Dousing the Fires of Patent Litigation

Christopher Beauchamp

To anyone impressed with the twenty-first-century patent "crisis," history offers some sharp retorts. For example, the US patent system in the mid-to-late nineteenth century was extremely litigious—even more so than during the reputed "patent litigation explosion" of recent times. The rate of patent litigation in that era reached historic highs relative to the number of patents in force, the size of the economy, and the caseload of the federal courts (Beauchamp 2016). The scale of patent litigation was dramatic, even by modern standards: New York City in 1880 saw more patent suits filed than any US district court as late as 2010, and would still have ranked second on the list of districts with the most patent cases filed in 2019.[1] In this climate, patent assertion was no less controversial than it is today. Leading voices in Congress and the courts denounced the patent laws as "instruments of great injustice and oppression" that permitted "legalized blackmailing and robbery" on a grand scale.[2]

By 1900, however, the rate of patent contests had slowed considerably, and for most of the twentieth century it remained relatively low, especially compared to the evergrowing number of issued patents. The number of suits filed each year rarely cracked 1,000 nationwide between the 1920s and the 1980s (Katznelson 2014). The wildfire of nineteenth-century litigation had given way to a field of law "reputed to be dull, tedious, undramatic" (Rifkind 1955).

So what changed? This chapter describes the shifting nature and composition of patent litigation in the late nineteenth and early twentieth centuries. For all that we know about the history of patent law's various rules and doctrines, the actual working of the enforcement system on the ground is far less understood.[3] Even some basic facts are unclear: for example, there are no national-level data on the number of patent suits before the 1920s.[4] Fortunately, the archival records

[1] In all, 381 suits were filed in the Southern District of New York in 1880 (Beauchamp 2016). District data for 2010 and 2019 are available from Lex Machina, https://lexmachina.com/.

[2] *Mfg. Co. v. Ladd*, 102 U.S. 408, 411 (1880); *Cong. Rec.* 1878, 8:303.

[3] There are valuable studies of litigation through the lens of adjudicated and reported cases, and of patent contests within specific industries. But these perspectives are necessarily limited, either to the subset of cases that are judicially reported or to the particular industry involved. See, for example, Usselman (2002), Khan (2005), Beauchamp (2015), and Henry and Turner (2016).

[4] The earliest national-level reporting is captured by Katznelson (2014).

Christopher Beauchamp, *Dousing the Fires of Patent Litigation In: The Battle over Patents.* Edited by: Stephen H. Haber and Naomi R. Lamoreaux, Oxford University Press. © Oxford University Press 2021. DOI: 10.1093/oso/9780197576151.003.0005

of earlier patent cases still exist and can offer up rich data on the parties and patents involved.

This is, to be sure, a vantage point with limits. Most patents are never litigated; most patent owners never sue. Looking at the patent system through the courts is like squinting through a narrow keyhole: only a sliver of the whole is visible. Still, litigation matters. It is the means by which patents are enforced and disputed, thereby shaping—at least at the contested margin—the scope and strength of protection that patents afford. Participants in the patent system who never enter court must still account for what happens there, since they must "bargain in the shadow of the law" based on their expectations about the ultimate enforceability of the right. Litigation also has a disproportionate influence on the politics of the patent system, shaping public perceptions of a regime of rights that otherwise operates mostly unseen.

For all these reasons, the decline in litigation at the end of the nineteenth century matters to the history of the US patent system. This episode is of potential current interest too. Both the scale and the significance of the twenty-first century's own "patent litigation explosion" are subjects of intense debate, but there is no question that burgeoning patent enforcement in the last two decades has contributed to the narrative of dysfunction in the patent system (Burk and Lemley 2009a; Chien 2009; Mossoff 2012; Cotropia, Kesan, and Schwartz 2014). Both Congress and the courts have responded to calls to limit the quantity, venue, defendant population, remedies, and subject matter of patent suits (Yeh and Lanza 2015; Grinvald 2015; Gugliuzza 2015).[5] The nineteenth-century forebear of today's supposed "patent crisis" is by no means a perfect parallel or precedent for modern patent reform. But against this recent background, it is worth taking a longer view, both of changes in the litigiousness of the patent system and of the role of public policy in changing it.

The First Patent Litigation Explosion

The first patent litigation explosion covered a period lasting roughly from the mid-1840s to the mid-1880s. Especially in its early stages, it was characterized by the appearance of large-scale enforcement campaigns. A relatively small number of patent grants accounted for what was, by the standards of the time, an enormous quantity of litigation.

[5] Responses by the Supreme Court include *TC Heartland LLC v. Kraft Foods Group Brands LLC*, 137 S. Ct. 1514 (2017) (venue); *Alice Corp. v. CLS Bank Int'l*, 134 S. Ct. 2347 (2014) (subject-matter eligibility); *Octane Fitness, L.L.C. v. ICON Health and Fitness, Inc.*, 134 S. Ct. 1749 (2014) (attorney's fees); *Highmark Inc. v. Allcare Health Mgmt. Sys., Inc.*, 134 S. Ct. 1744 (2014) (same); *eBay Inc. v. MercExchange, L.L.C.*, 547 U.S. 388, 396 (2006) (Kennedy, J., concurring) (injunctions).

The details of these efforts varied. Some of the most notable early examples involved older technologies from the first wave of American industrialization, including woodworking machinery and water power. Others involved new technologies of the 1840s: inventions such as the mechanical harvester, telegraph, and rubber goods. Among the leading litigants of the antebellum period were Charles Goodyear, who brought more than two hundred suits under his vulcanized rubber patent; the brothers Austin and Zebulon Parker, who filed hundreds more cases for infringement of their patent for reaction water wheels; and the owners of the Woodworth wood-planing machine patent, who created an empire of licensing and assignment that generated litigation from New England to the Carolinas (Beauchamp 2016, pp. 861–65).

Patent assertion only expanded in range and scale after the Civil War. In 1866, the Goodyear Dental Vulcanite Company began a nationwide legal campaign under its patents to extract license payments from every dentist who provided rubber dentures. More than 2,000 cases were reportedly filed in the federal courts. In Pennsylvania oil country, the holder of a patent for well-blasting "torpedos" filed more than 2,000 suits during the 1870s. Neither of these was the most expansive or controversial enforcement effort taking place after the Civil War. That honor went to a campaign asserting the "driven well" patent, issued in 1868 to Nelson W. Green. Driven wells were a low-cost technique for drawing groundwater, widely used by farmers. The driven-well patent interests and their licensees began a vast campaign of patent assertion stretching from Long Island to Oregon. The precise amount of litigation that resulted is not clear, but the number of suits filed ran into the thousands (Beauchamp 2016, pp. 867–70).

These mass-enforcement events were only the most visible part of the patent litigation phenomenon. They were not alone: other campaigns involving hundreds of suits included the "Sewing Machine War" of the 1840s and 1850s, struggles over barbed wire in the Midwest, battles within the early electric lighting industry, and the more than 600 cases filed to enforce the American Bell Telephone Company's monopoly of telephone technology. All of these episodes are well documented, and for good reason: while they only accounted for a small proportion of patentees and litigants, they generated enough suits to have a substantial impact on the patent litigation system as a whole. Even so, they give only a partial picture of the litigation landscape.

To construct a fuller description of the underlying patent litigation system, we must turn to other sources. There are no national-level data about the number of patent suits filed before the 1920s. But the archives of the federal courts contain rich, if somewhat inaccessible, details of cases that were filed in this period. By searching dockets and case files it is possible to count patent suits over time and to obtain information about the parties, patents, and technologies at issue.

This chapter uses data from two very active courts: the US Circuit Courts for the Southern District of New York (SDNY), in New York City, and the Eastern District of Pennsylvania (EDPA), in Philadelphia. The sample from those courts includes just over 2,000 total cases filed in eight sample years: 1840, 1850, 1860, 1870, 1880, 1890, 1900, and 1910. The two jurisdictions were chosen for their economic and legal prominence and for the completeness of their records; the aim being to capture as rich a view as possible of the workings of patent litigation rather than to obtain a representative sample. New York and Pennsylvania were generally the top two states in terms of patents issued, and together accounted for a large share—between a fifth and a third—of all US patents issued annually.[6] Their metropolitan centers, New York City and Philadelphia, were two of the four largest cities in the United States throughout this period (Carter et al. 2006, 1:1-28 to 1-29 table Aa6-8; Gibson 1998, tables 7–14). Their economies may have been the most diverse in the country: New York was the leading urban center in both manufacturing and services, preeminent in industries from garment manufacture to publishing, while the economy of Philadelphia and eastern Pennsylvania was just as varied, including heavy-industrial sectors such as steelmaking and locomotive building as well as machine tools, textiles, brewing, furniture, chemicals, and farming.[7]

The Southern District of New York/Eastern District of Pennsylvania (SDNY/EDPA) sample provides an opportunity to measure directly the quantity of patent litigation in the nineteenth-century courts. Figure 4.1 describes the number of suits filed in each of the sample years and the number of patents at issue in those suits. Table 4.1 compares these numbers to the total number of US patents in force in each year. This summary data offers three perspectives on the quantity of patent litigation during the period.

First, the absolute number of suits in the two districts suggests an expansion of patent litigation that began before the Civil War and peaked in the post-war years. Figure 4.1 shows more than 200 patent suits filed in the two courts in each of 1850 and 1860, rising to more than 300 in 1870 and peaking in 1880 with 469 suits brought under 313 patents. The number of suits then fell back to prewar levels in 1890 and 1900 (though on a much larger number of patents) before climbing over 300 again in 1910.

[6] US Patent Office, *Annual Report of the Commissioner of Patents for the Year 1910* (1911); S. Doc. No. 56-138 (1901); S. Misc. Doc. No. 51-58 (1891); US Patent Office, *Report of the Commissioner of Patents* (1880); H.R. Exec. Doc. 41-89 (1871); S. Exec. Doc. No. 36-7 (1861); H.R. Exec. Doc. No. 31-32 (1851).

[7] In 1909, Philadelphia reported manufacturing establishments in 211 of the Census Bureau's 264 industry classifications, second only to New York City's 217 and well ahead of Boston's 175 and Chicago's 131. US Bureau of the Census, 9 Thirteenth Census of the United States, Taken in the Year 1910: Manufactures, 1909: Reports by States, with Statistics for Principal Cities, 265, 500, 815, 1052 (1912).

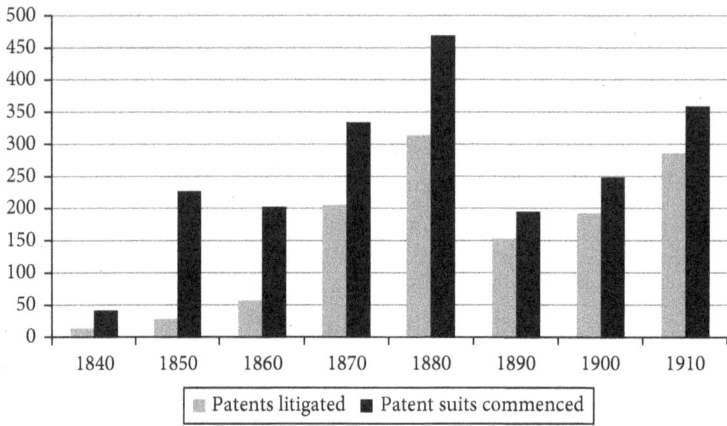

Figure 4.1 Patent litigation in SDNY and EDPA, sample years 1840–1910.
Sources: Decadal sample of patent cases from National Archives at New York City, law and equity dockets and case files, US Circuit Court for the Southern District of New York, 1840–1910 and National Archives at Philadelphia, law and equity dockets and case files, US Circuit Court for the Eastern District of Pennsylvania, 1840–1910 [hereafter Decadal sample of patent cases, SDNY/EDPA].

Changes in the absolute quantity of litigation were influential in their own right, notably in fostering the development of the patent bar and shaping judicial attitudes to patent law and procedure (Beauchamp 2016, pp. 908–33). But propensity to litigate is better measured by a second metric: litigation relative to the size of the patent system (Table 4.1). By that measure, the patent explosion was at its height in mid-century, the wave of lawsuits having begun in the 1840s before patent grants started to accelerate. During the second half of the century, patenting expanded faster than litigation—perhaps unsurprisingly, since the third quarter of the nineteenth century saw the highest year-on-year growth rates in patenting in US history (Marco et al. 2015, pp. 16–17). Whereas New York City and Philadelphia saw 30 lawsuits filed per 1,000 US patents in force in 1850, by the end of the century the number was less than 1 per 1,000. The proportion of total US patents that were involved in litigation in those districts slid less dramatically, from 3.8 per 1,000 patents in force to around 0.5 per thousand.

Even so, from a long-run perspective, litigation intensity was historically high in the mid-to-late nineteenth century: far greater than the twentieth-century norm and comparable (at least) to the early twenty-first century peak. According to data compiled by Ron Katznelson from Patent Office reporting, an average of just under 1,000 patent suits were filed each year across the entire United

Table 4.1 Patent litigation in the SDNY and EDPA, sample years 1840–1910, relative to the total number of US patents in force.

Year	Estimated total US utility patents in force[a]	Suits filed in SDNY and EDPA per 1,000 US patents in force	Patents litigated in SDNY and EDPA per 1,000 US patents in force
1840	7,074	5.9	2.1
1850	7,571	30.0	3.8
1860	22,294	9.0	2.6
1870	84,828	4.0	2.4
1880	186,235	2.5	1.7
1890	283,800	0.7	0.5
1900	369,887	0.7	0.5
1910	455,701	0.8	0.6

Sources: US Patent Office, *Annual Reports of the Commissioner of Patents*, 1836–1910; Carter et al. Historical Statistics of the United States, 3:3-426 to 3-427 table Cg27-37; Decadal sample of patent cases, SDNY/EDPA.

[a] Estimated totals for 1840–1910 assume that all patents remained in force for the standard statutory fourteen- or seventeen-year term, adding where relevant the number of patents remaining in force under seven-year administrative extensions. The number of patents in force is given as of January 1 each year.

States in the 1920s and 1930s.[8] Between the 1952 Patent Act and the creation of the Federal Circuit in 1982, only around 800 suits were filed on average each year. Throughout this period, the annual number of suits remained below 2 per 1,000 US patents in force. Even at their peak in 2013, the then-record number of cases filed nationwide (6,092) represented 2.7 suits per 1,000 US patents in force (Byrd and Howard 2014, p. i; World Intellectual Property Organization 2013, p. 83). That rate of litigation was exceeded in 1840, 1850, 1860, 1870, and nearly matched in 1880 by suits filed in New York City and Philadelphia alone. In 1890, 1900, and 1910, by contrast, the rate in these two courts had fallen below 1 suit per 1,000 patents in force. If one looks at patents litigated rather than lawsuits: the 4,917 patents on which suit was filed nationwide in 2013 represented 2.2 litigated patents per 1,000 patents in force (Byrd and Howard 2014, pp. ii, 9; World Intellectual Property Organization 2013, p. 83). Filings in New York City and Philadelphia alone outstripped that pace in 1850, 1860, and 1870. The figures

[8] These figures are derived from the underlying data used in Katznelson (2014). I am grateful to Mr. Katznelson for sharing this information.

from these two districts again suggest that the national number would have comfortably cleared modern levels in 1880 and perhaps would have done so in 1890, 1900, and 1910 as well, if the volume of litigation in other industrial centers around the country was in any way comparable.[9] The nineteenth-century patent litigation explosion was not just a matter of mass enforcement on a few patents; a historically high proportion of grants were litigated as well.

What Causes Patent Litigation?

A patent suit is the result of both circumstance and choice. The number and quality of patents; the size and organization of the economy; the business strategies of plaintiffs and defendants; and the costs, benefits, and uncertainties of enforcement in the courts all play a part in how many disputes arise and whether parties choose to go to court rather than resolve them privately. Nineteenth-century sources may not be sufficient to capture many of the variables (especially fine-grained details of business activity) that would affect the volume of litigation. But some important factors can be discerned from the historical record.

One set of inputs affects the number of potential patent disputes. At the most basic level, the number of patents in force constitutes the population of rights that might be infringed, while the size of the economy and the number of enterprises affect the extent to which a patented technology may be used. In the aggregate, these broad measures are not the moving forces of our story: as described earlier, rates of litigation per patent changed wildly during the rise and fall of the nineteenth-century litigation boom and declined in the face of rapid growth in patenting and the economy toward the end of the period.

The incidence of actionable infringement depends on more than just the use of patented inventions, though. Two related contextual variables are crucial to the number of disputes. One is the timing of enforcement. While a patented invention is in the early stages of commercialization, the pool of adopters who might infringe is likely to be low. Conversely, an older invention may be widely diffused, creating more opportunities for liability. This effect is certainly visible in the nineteenth century's most litigated cases: the peak of the driven well litigation, for example, occurred when the technology had spread across the country and was reputedly used by half a million farmers.[10] Instances like these could be the result of technologies diffusing more rapidly than patentees' enforcement

[9] As long as the Southern District of New York and Eastern District of Pennsylvania made up no more than a quarter of all patent suits filed nationwide in 1890–1910, the national rate of suits relative to patents in force would have exceeded 2013 levels. There were approximately 70–80 federal judicial districts nationwide in those years.

[10] *Eames v. Andrews*, 122 U.S. 40, 48 (1887).

could keep up with. But as we shall see, they could also arise from strategic behavior aimed at asserting patents over mature technologies.

The other key contextual variable is information. Information—on both sides—was fundamental to the timing and number of disputes. Patent owners can only sue if they can detect infringement. Depending on the technology and the type of user, this can be a daunting informational challenge even today; in the nineteenth century, information costs were generally much higher. A striking feature of the large patent enforcement campaigns was the intelligence-gathering that enabled them. In the Goodyear Dental Vulcanite Company's legal efforts, for example, "servants of dentists were bribed, next-door neighbors were questioned, and intimidation was often resorted to" (*New York Times*, 24 April 1879, p. 5). The Roberts oil torpedo interests employed a "legion of spies" to detect uses of their invention (unlicensed operators learned to blast by night, earning the name "moonlighters") (McLaurin 1898, p. 386). The incidence of realized patent disputes depended, in large part, on patentees' monitoring capabilities.

For users too, information mattered. Knowing when a technology is covered by a patent is a challenge that we have hardly mastered today (Mulligan and Lee 2012). In the nineteenth century, patent specifications were officially published and widely circulated in technical journals, and patentees had a duty to mark their own products as patented (Lamoreaux and Sokoloff 2003, pp. 209, 213–14; *Patent Act of 1842*). But one might reasonably be skeptical of how far such information would reach, and indeed, liability of "innocent infringers" was an often-raised complaint about the patent laws (Usselman 2002 pp. 148–49).

This last issue goes to the heart of how we understand patent infringement. James Bessen and Michael Meurer have distinguished between a "cheating" account of infringement, in which the accused parties have deliberately imitated a patented technology, and an "exposure" story, in which the infringers have developed their own technology in ignorance of the patentee's version, or acquired it from others who did so, but are nonetheless liable under the strict-liability principle of patent infringement (Bessen and Meurer 2013, pp. 403–04). It is hard to know how many patent suits in the nineteenth century arose from copying and how many from unwitting exposure. But the answer makes a difference to one's normative view of large-scale litigation. If the litigation explosion resulted from patentees struggling to enforce their rights in the face of mass copying, then it might reflect the lamentable weakness of protection. If mass enforcement reflected patent claims emerging, with vague scope and/or little public notice, to extract rents from the investments made by unwitting technology adopters, then that raises a different set of concerns about the costs imposed by patent rights.

All of the variables mentioned so far bear on the population of potential patent disputes. But the fact of a known infringement by itself does not automatically lead to a lawsuit. Litigation exists on a spectrum of patent assertion, which more often (though not always) begins with the patent-holder demanding that the accused infringer cease their activity or take a license (Lemley, Richardson, and Oliver 2019; Risch 2019). Given that legal process is costly, both sides generally have some incentive to reach a negotiated solution before turning to the courts. For a lawsuit to occur, then, implies some kind of bargaining failure or strategic choice on the part of the parties.

There are a number of reasons why parties in patent disputes might not resort to litigation. One is uncertainty. Where entitlements are clear, parties can predict legal outcomes and more readily agree on negotiated settlements. Unfortunately, patents are rife with uncertainties, including the famously unclear scope of patent claims, the possible invalidity of the patent over as-yet-undiscovered prior art, vagueness in the law itself, even uncertainty about how a new technology works (or will be understood to work by a court) (Lemley and Shapiro 2005). Subsequent sections of this chapter will suggest that sources of uncertainty were both present in exaggerated form during the nineteenth century and subject to discernible changes over time.

The decision to litigate also depends on the parties' objectives. Patent enforcement and infringement litigation have always served a variety of distinct goals. Some plaintiffs sought a direct monetary return in the form of damages or a settlement for a license: large scale, nonpracticing plaintiffs such as the Goodyear Dental Vulcanite Company fell into that category. Others used patents to gain competitive advantage against a rival business. Litigation could be called on to manage business relationships with licensees, either in a coercive fashion (enforcing the terms of a patent license against a recalcitrant licensee) or a cooperative one (supporting licensee operating companies against their competitors) (Vaughan 1925, pp. 36–43; Carlson 1991, pp. 9–10; Beauchamp 2015, pp. 173–74). Or it could be personal and idiosyncratic: many suits historically were brought by individual inventors, who had their own reasons of reputation or pride for wanting to be vindicated as the first inventor. Finally, litigation could be opportunistic, taking advantage of the high cost of defending a suit to extract nuisance-value settlements from its targets. Farmers' representatives in the nineteenth century strongly suggested that rural patent enforcement campaigns had this character: patentees could compel farmers "to travel hundreds of miles to defend against your claim, or, as more frequently occurs, to pay an unjust demand as the cheapest way of meeting it" (*Congressional Record* 1878, 8:303).

Likewise, on the defendant side, the reasons not to acquiesce in a license varied. Many accused infringers surely doubted the validity or scope of the patent and believed that they would win in court. But others may have simply wished to impose costs on the patentee, either to improve their bargaining position or to exhaust a less well-resourced plaintiff. In some of the most heated mass-enforcement campaigns of the nineteenth century, resistance was a collective and political act: dentists organized to resist the Goodyear dental vulcanite patents; farmers formed associations to defy the driven well and barbed wire patents (Beauchamp 2016, p. 875).

The heterogeneity of motivations in patent litigation makes it hard to generalize about, let alone measure over time, the private benefits of going to court. Parties litigating for competitive advantage or other business reasons had their own idiosyncratic calculus of whether to sue. Even where parties sought money, the historical record of their experience is opaque. Direct financial awards, such damages payments, are the most obvious metric of returns to patent litigation. But they are less useful than one might think. Most filed cases settled, in the nineteenth century as today—at least 70 percent of the sampled SDNY/EDPA suits were discontinued or terminated by consent of the parties, with the monetary or other terms of those resolutions unknown.[11] And in any case, the major form of judicial remedy for patent infringement at that time was an injunction. Injunctive relief entitled the patentee to block the infringing activity, but often just set the stage for further negotiation over what the infringer was willing to pay to continue. Meanwhile money recoveries were difficult to obtain. Obtaining an award of damages or profits generally required additional expert testimony and hearings before a court-appointed special master, yet another unpredictable phase that made the returns to litigation unclear ex ante (Edelman 1915, p. 174; Risch 2016b, pp. 200–01).

Patent litigation arises from complexity built upon complexity. As Michael Risch (2016a) has noted, it is a system constructed in "layers," with changes in patenting, in legal conditions, in business strategies, and in technology and the economy all overlaying and interacting with each other. The remainder of the chapter unpacks these layers to gauge how each changed in the late nineteenth and early twentieth centuries.

Changing Patents

What if patents themselves changed? A patent is, after all, a malleable legal instrument, governed by shifting law and consisting of claims strategically drafted by the patentee (Biagioli, Jaszi, and Woodmansee 2011). Throughout the period considered here, most of the basic features of the patent were stable. After 1836, all patents were examined prior to issue by the Patent Office and protected the same set of exclusive rights to make, use, and sell the claimed invention. But

[11] Decadal year sample of law and equity dockets and case files, US Circuit Court for the Southern District of New York (National Archives at New York City) and US Circuit Court for the Eastern District of Pennsylvania (National Archives at Philadelphia), 1840–1910 [hereafter decadal year sample, SDNY/EDPA].

other aspects of the grant changed over time. Three in particular stand out: term extension, reissues, and claiming.

The rise and fall of extensions and reissues coincided strikingly with the arc of the litigation explosion (Beauchamp 2016, pp. 883–94). Both were practices that expanded a patent right beyond its dimensions as originally granted. Each was supposed to ensure that patentees received a properly tailored reward for their inventions, but both ended up becoming associated with aggressive patent assertion and were eventually reformed by Congress or the courts.

Term extensions were meant to reward inventors who had not received their due. In the words of the 1836 Patent Act, these 7-year additions to the usual 14-year term sought to relieve a deserving patentee who had "without neglect or fault on his part . . . failed to obtain, from the use and sale of his invention, a reasonable remuneration for the time, ingenuity, and expense bestowed upon the same" (*Patent Act of 1836*, 125). Extensions could be granted legislatively, by congressional private act, or administratively, by the Commissioner of Patents.[12] In practice, energetic lobbying secured extensions for several of the most lucrative patents of their day, including such widely enforced patents as the Parker water wheel, Goodyear's rubber, and Isaac Howe's sewing-machine grant.

As Figure 4.2 shows, more than two-thirds of suits in the 1850 sample involved a patent that had received at least one seven-year term extension. More than a third of the suits in 1860 and 1870 involved patents that had similarly been extended. The Patent Office during this period granted extensions readily: between 1857 and 1877, around 80 percent of applications for extension were approved. Typically around 5–8 percent and sometimes as high as 11 percent of the patents expiring each year received an additional term (US Patent Office, 1857–1877). To be sure, extended patents were always a minority, even among litigated grants: in no year sampled here did they exceed 15 percent of the unique patents in suit. However, they were predictable litigation magnets because of the rents they could extract from more mature technologies, which in turn motivated users of the technology to resist them.

The phenomenon of extended patents was itself time limited, though. After a series of bitterly controversial fights over legislative term extensions, Congress in 1861 prospectively abolished extensions for all patents issued after that date, instead lengthening the standard patent term from 14 to 17 years (*Patent Act of 1861*, 249). The Commissioner of Patents granted the last extension in 1877. After 1880 no suits on extended patents appear in the SDNY/EDPA sample.

[12] *Bloomer v. McQuewan*, 55 U.S. (14 How.) 539, 543–44 (1852) (listing 25 patent extensions by private act between 1808 and 1847). Under the 1836 Patent Act, reissues were approved by a board of senior federal officeholders consisting of the Secretary of State, the Solicitor of the Treasury, and the Commissioner of Patents. *Patent Act of 1836*, 124. From 1848, the power to grant extensions was vested in the Commissioner of Patents alone. *Patent Act of 1848*, 231.

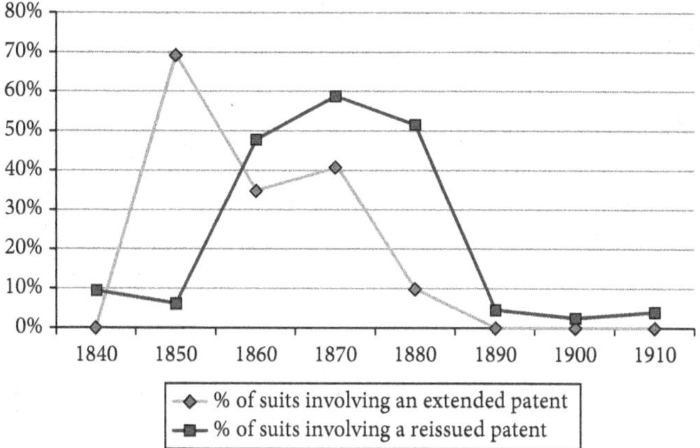

Figure 4.2 Percentage of suits involving extended and reissued patents, SDNY and EDPA, sample years 1840–1910.
Source: Decadal sample of patent cases, SDNY/EDPA.

Reissued patents traced a similar rise and fall. Around half of the suits filed in 1860, 1870, and 1880 included at least one reissued patent (Figure 4.2). Reissue was an administrative process by which patentees were allowed to amend their specifications and claims, even years after the original grant. In theory, it was available where a patent had, by the applicant's mistake, been issued with invalidating flaws or covering less than the inventor could lawfully have claimed. In practice, reissue allowed patentees to adapt their claims to stretch their scope or otherwise cover later developments in the technology. Some of the most famous broad patents gained their expansive scope from a reissue, including Charles Goodyear's patent for vulcanized rubber and Samuel Morse's (ultimately invalidated) claim to telegraphic transmission (Beauchamp 2016, pp. 889–90). The Patent Office long took the position that reissues existed for the benefit of the inventor and were "intended to provide for the correction of whatever stood in the way of the broadest equity" (Cox 1881, p. 731). Reissues were much more common than extensions: more than a third of the unique patents in those three sample years had been reissued at some point before litigation,[13] and the Patent Office approved hundreds of reissues each year during the relevant decades.[14] Seeking a reissue during that period appears to have been a fairly standard tactic for patentees preparing for litigation.

[13] Decadal year sample, SDNY/EDPA.

[14] Reissue grants rose from a few dozen a year before 1857 to an average of over 500 annually in the 1870s, before falling dramatically in the 1880s. US Patent Office, *Annual Reports of the Commissioner of Patents*, 1850–1890.

During the 1870s and early 1880s, the courts began to apply greater scrutiny to the validity of reissues. (Cox 1881, pp. 732–36; Dood 1991, pp. 1015–16). By 1880, the Supreme Court's disfavor was clear. A unanimous Court in that year described reissue abuse in scathing terms:

> [A] monopoly of the business is very desirable . . . . The usual remedy in such cases is resorted to. A reissue of the patent is sought, with expanded claims, sufficiently general and comprehensive to embrace a wide monopoly of structure, and to shut up competing establishments. In this way the patent laws have been made the instruments of great injustice and oppression. The real object and design of a reissue of a patent have been abused and subverted.[15]

Two years later, the Court held that any broadening reissue obtained after an unreasonable delay "may justly be declared illegal and void."[16] Patentees evidently got the message: the number of applications for reissue received by the Patent Office fell from over 600 per year in the late 1870s to under 200 by 1884 and under 100 by 1887.[17] By the end of the decade, patent owners appeared reluctant to bring reissued grants into court: only 4 percent of litigated patents in the 1890 SDNY/EDPA sample had been reissued, accounting for only 5 percent of suits in that year.[18]

Overall, the prevalence of extensions and reissues seems to fit the "exposure" rather than the "cheating" account of patent liability during the litigation explosion. Older patents were revived—and frequently redrafted—to extract rents from users of inventions that had already diffused widely. As one leading patent attorney put it in 1878, "speculators . . . club together to buy up a patent or patents relating to something in general use in different parts of the country, subject their purchases to the reissuing process, establish headquarters, and, with a great flourish, proceed to levy on manufacturers who were ignorant of the existence of the patent" (Howson 1878, pp. 117–18). One such speculator, a former Commissioner of Patents, noted privately of a pending reissue that "I think we shall be so able to shape the patent and the claims as to subordinate most of the harvesting machines that are made in the United States."[19]

Perhaps the simplest gauge of these strategies is the age of patents in litigation. The median suit by age in the 1850 sample involved a patent that was over 20 years old (Figure 4.3), at a time when the nominal term of a patent was just

[15] *Mfg. Co. v. Ladd*, 102 U.S. 408, 411 (1880).

[16] *Miller v. Bridgeport Brass Co.*, 104 U.S. 350, 355 (1882).

[17] US Patent Office, *Annual Reports of the Commissioner of Patents*, 1887, p. xiv; 1884, p. iv; 1879, p. iii.

[18] Decadal year sample, SDNY/EDPA.

[19] Diary of Charles Mason, April 20, 1876, Charles Mason Remey Family Papers, Box 17, Manuscript Division, Library of Congress.

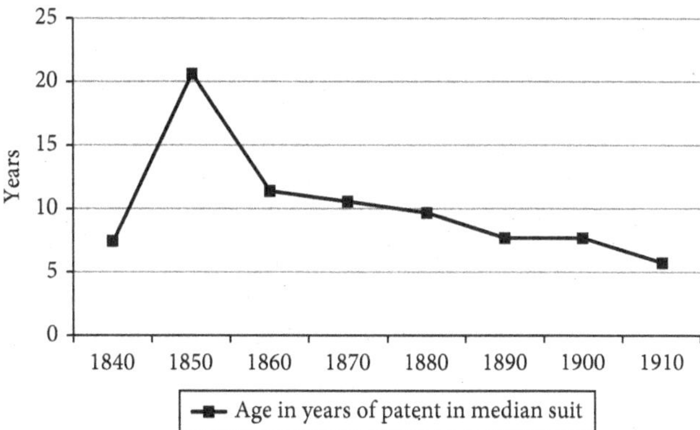

Figure 4.3 Age of patent in the median suit, SDNY and EDPA, sample years 1840–1910.
Source: Decadal sample of patent cases, SDNY/EDPA.

14 years.[20] With the demise of extensions and reissues after 1880, the pattern of old patents deployed against established technologies faded. By 1910, the median suit involved a patent that was little over five years old.

Extension and reissue were aspects of the patent system that conspicuously lent themselves to rent-seeking and were eventually wound down by Congress and the courts. Cleaning up these practices of patent stretching seemingly played a part in dousing the litigation explosion. As these practices ended, though, another shift began: this one a quieter transformation in the boundaries of patent rights.

Of all the dimensions of patent protection, scope is notoriously the hardest to fix. The boundaries of the exclusive right are rife with uncertainty, thanks to the inherent difficulties of claim drafting, the unpredictability of judicial interpretation, and the presence of doctrines that blur the scope of claims. The greater the fluidity of patent scope, the more litigation one would expect, and the more opportunities are available to patent owners to assert broad rights over a technology, including coverage of inventions and improvements far from the inventor's original conception. These aspects of patent law have been repeatedly and persuasively identified as engines of litigation from the mid nineteenth century to the software patents of the present day.[21]

Conventional chronology suggests a possible shift in patent scope in the late nineteenth century: a move toward greater precision that one would expect to

[20] This result was due to the large number of suits filed in the Eastern District of Pennsylvania on the extended Parker water wheel patent.

[21] See, for example, *Winans v. Denmead*, 56 U.S. (15 How.) 330, 347 (1853) (Campbell, J., dissenting); Bessen and Meurer 2009, pp. 8–11.

reduce disputes. This period is often seen as the birth of modern claim practice. Nineteenth century claiming looked very little like today's patent law, which requires stand-alone claims that carefully delineate the scope of the invention—an approach sometimes known as "peripheral claiming" for its work in marking the outer limits of the right (Burk and Lemley 2009b, p. 1744). Instead, nineteenth-century practice was characterized by a "central claiming" method. In this regime, the claims by themselves did not explicitly define the boundaries of the exclusive right, but were meant to be read together with the description of the invention to indicate the content of the invention and hence the scope of the patent (Woodward 1948, p. 760; Burk and Lemley 2009b, pp. 1766–70). Many claims did little more than refer to the specification and lay claim to any device substantially similar to what was disclosed. An 1862 patent for a pencil, for example, had as its sole claim "the combined sleeve and eraser, constructed to operate substantially in the manner and for the purposes specified."[22]

This holistic approach to defining the invention began to change only later in the century, especially from the 1870s onward, as the courts and the Patent Office began to place more emphasis on the role of the claim in interpreting patent scope (Lutz 1938, pp. 487–88; Fromer 2009, pp. 731–35). The 1870 Patent Act added statutory language requiring a patentee to claim "distinctly"—apparently not a congressional innovation, but an attempt to ratify court decisions pushing for more precise claiming (Lutz 1938, p. 470). Shortly afterward, the Supreme Court reinforced the role of claims in *Merrill v. Yeomans*. The "variety and magnitude of the interests involved" in the patent system, observed Justice Miller in that case, "require accuracy, precision, and care in the preparation of all the papers on which the patent is founded. . . . The developed and improved condition of the patent law and of the principles which govern the exclusive rights conferred by it leave no excuse for ambiguous language or vague descriptions."[23]

Evidence from the SDNY/EDPA sample bears out the idea that claim practice was changing. Three metrics are available: the length of claims, the number of claims in each patent, and the style of those claims. Tables 4.2 and 4.3 report these three metrics for all the SDNY/EDPA patents litigated in 1870, 1890, and 1910.

All other things being equal, the longer a claim, the narrower its scope. Each additional word or phrase adds specificity: "a flexible and detachable blade for safety-razors" is broader and covers more devices than "a flexible and detachable razor-blade made from sheet-steel of uniform thickness and provided with two opposite cutting edges."[24] As Table 4.2 shows, the average word count of each

[22] U.S. Patent no. 35,467, "Combination of Pencil Sleeve and Eraser," issued to F. E. Oliver, June 3, 1862.

[23] *Merrill v. Yeomans*, 94 U.S. 568, 573 (1876).

[24] These are respectively claims 1 and 3 of U.S. Patent no. 775,134, "Razor," issued to King Gillette, November 15, 1904.

Table 4.2 Claim characteristics of patents litigated in 1870, 1890, and 1910, by year of suit.

Year of suit	Average number of words in first claim	Average number of claims per patent	% of first claims incorporating the specification[a]
1870	32.8	2.1	91
1890	44.5	3.8	90
1910	60.8	9.0	35

[a] Claims expressly incorporating the specification are those that define the protected invention by reference to the longer written description, using phrases such as "arranged substantially as herein described."

Source: Decadal sample of patent cases, SDNY/EDPA.

Table 4.3 Claim characteristics of patents litigated in 1870, 1890, and 1910, by year of issue.

Year of issue	Average number of words in first claim	Average number of claims per patent	% of first claims incorporating the specification
1850–1859	45.2	1.9	84
1860–1869	30.1	2.0	93
1870–1879	35.3	3.7	88
1880–1889	48.5	5.0	85
1890–1899	65.6	7.8	62
1900–1910	59.0	9.6	25

Note: For patents reissued before litigation, the date of the litigated reissue patent is used instead of the original grant date.

Source: Decadal sample of patent cases, SDNY/EDPA.

litigated patent's first claim nearly doubled from 32.8 in 1870 to 60.8 in 1910.[25] Table 4.3 captures the same development by the issue year of the patent, rather

[25] I use the first claim of each patent as a metric of claim length because (a) all patents had at least one claim, and (b) the first is always an independent claim rather than "depending on" (that is, incorporating by reference) an earlier claim. However, the first claim may not always have been at issue in the case. Case files of the period are often silent as to which claim or claims of the patent were asserted. In counting the words of these claims, I excluded boilerplate wording such as "substantially as and for the purposes set forth," since these clauses varied widely in length and reflected only the writing style of the drafter, without affecting the content of the claim.

than the date of litigation.[26] The clear trend over time was toward more detailed claims, suggesting both that these claims were individually narrower and that they were playing a greater role in defining patent scope.

This is not to say that, at the level of the *patent*, protection necessarily became less broad. Even as patentees drafted longer claims, they added more of them. Adding claims to the patent may have the effect of broadening the scope of the patent as a whole. By writing more independent claims, the patentee may add coverage of different aspects of the invention or of a greater range of versions and embodiments. Tables 4.2 and 4.3 show that the average number of claims per patent rose from around two to around nine over the same period. Patent drafters were writing narrower claims but were also layering multiple claims on top of one another to create the overall scope of the patent.

In any case, the relevant change for our purposes may be less about breadth than about clarity. One other suggestive indicator of the growing role of the claim is stylistic. Claims that simply referred back to the written description of the invention—the classic central-claiming format—were associated with a very impressionistic test for infringement: courts essentially compared the defendant's device to the patentee's, with a greater or lesser degree of "liberality" (Lutz 1938, p. 472). These claims offered vaguer boundaries than a stand-alone claim that attempted to define the metes and bounds of protection within the text of the claim itself. To capture this distinction between claim types, Tables 4.2 and 4.3 both show the proportion of claims that expressly incorporated the contents of the specification—that is, they claimed the invention "substantially as herein described" in the longer written description (or words to that effect). This type fell from 90 percent of the patents litigated in 1870 to 40 percent of those litigated in 1910. Only a quarter of the sample patents issued after 1900 took this form.

The decline of referential claiming is not a perfect proxy for the shift from central to peripheral claim drafting: it likely understates the transition, since in the 1890s and 1900s some claims were clearly complete definitions of the invention that added the language "substantially as described" as boilerplate. Crucially, the stylistic change did not have independent legal force: judicial decisions as early as the 1870s held that the language "substantially as described" was implied in every claim whether stated or not (Walker 1883, pp. 129–30). But even if claims were still construed in light of the specification, they increasingly took center stage, moving adjudication away from the "gist" approach and toward a stricter theory of patent interpretation.

The effect of these trends in practice remains hard to gauge. Courts throughout the nineteenth century were persistently split over questions of broad and

[26] Where patents were reissued before litigation (generally with newly rewritten claims), the date of reissue was used.

narrow construction (Lutz 1938, pp. 470–71). The judicial shift to peripheral claim interpretation was gradual and partial, with countervailing doctrines surviving alongside it well into the twentieth century (Woodward 1948, pp. 760–64; Anderson and Menell 2014, pp. 13–18). But if the changing breadth of patents over time remains hard to measure, it is still possible that the clarity of patent boundaries improved. Longer claims, coupled with a trend toward a more metes-and-bounds claim-drafting style, at least in theory provided better notice of the scope of the patent right.

To sum up: changes in patents and patent practice in the later nineteenth century make very plausible contributors to the decreasing litigiousness of the system. Patents granted in the 1860s and 1870s were simply wilder and woollier creatures than their later counterparts: their scope was vaguer; reissues made them broader and more malleable still; the combination of reissues and term extensions enabled patentees to prolong their grants and enforce them against older, more widely adopted technologies. After the 1880s, reissue had become a liability rather than a strength—a generation of patents that had been broadened using reissues prior to the Supreme Court's hostile rulings now faced invalidation if brought into court—and extensions were a thing of the past. Meanwhile patent scope was now increasingly defined by claims, which were becoming individually narrower and more precise. All told, patents of this later era were less promising material for litigated disputes.

Multiple Litigation and Mass Enforcement

Changing patents made up one layer of the patent litigation system. Overlaid on these developments was another stratum: litigation strategy. It is clear that repeat suits by certain patent owners went a long way toward driving quantitative trends in nineteenth-century patent litigation. This was especially true in the early part of the period sampled here. In 1850, just 29 plaintiffs brought the 227 patent suits filed in the Southern District of New York and Eastern District of Pennsylvania. In later years the ratio was not as dramatic, but multiple litigation still accounted for a large share of all suits. Across the whole sample, nearly three-quarters of plaintiffs appearing brought only a single suit, while the 29 plaintiffs filing the most suits accounted for a third of all the litigation (Table 4.4). Litigants such as Oliver H. P. Parker (assignee of the Parker water wheel patent), the Goodyear Dental Vulcanite Company, Charles Goodyear, and American Bell were all engaged in national campaigns. These four plaintiffs collectively accounted for around 15 percent of all the suits in the SDNY/EDPA sample. Alongside them were a variety of other repeat plaintiffs across a wide range of industries, from lamps to candy-making. Multiple litigation was a broad-based pattern.

Table 4.4 Proportion of plaintiffs filing multiple suits in the SDNY and EDPA, sample years 1840–1910.

Number of plaintiffs filing	No. of plaintiffs	% of all plaintiffs	No. of suits	% of total suits
1 suit	618	71	618	30
2–4 suits	177	20	465	22
5–9 suits	46	5	301	14
10+ suits	29	3	697	33

Source: Decadal sample of patent cases, SDNY/EDPA.

Multiple enforcement connected with two other layers of the patent litigation system: the characteristics of patents (discussed in the previous section) and the organization of the economy (discussed in the next). First, the SDNY/EDPA sample includes further evidence of the role played by extensions and reissues. One way to examine the relationship between these practices and the quantity of litigation is to look at the characteristics of the most- and least-litigated patents. Table 4.5 describes two groups: "high-volume" patents, meaning those appearing in ten or more suits in the sample, and "single-suit" patents that were litigated only once in the sample years. The former group is relatively small, comprising just 39 patents, but accounts for a large share of the overall litigation in the sample.

High-volume litigation during the boom was closely associated with practices of patent stretching. For as long as term extensions were available, the patents in the high-volume category were much more likely to have been extended than were the single-suit patents. A significant fraction of the single-suit patents had been reissued before litigation—around 30–35 percent in the 1850–1880 samples—but again, the high-volume patents were generally more likely to have been reissued.

As Table 4.5 suggests, it was the high-volume group that primarily accounted for the pattern of older patents being asserted over established technologies. The average age of once-litigated grants generally remained in the five- to seven-year range throughout the sampled period. By contrast, the average age of the high-volume patents stood at over ten years through 1890, before converging with that of the single-suit population in 1900 and 1910.

A second dimension of multiple litigation relates to the parties involved. One dynamic that is clear from the peak of the litigation explosion—apparent in both the leading national mass-enforcement campaigns and in the SDNY/EDPA sample—is that patentees sued many small-scale defendants. In modern parlance, suits against large numbers of technology customers or users, as opposed to larger suppliers and intermediaries, are known as "end-user" suits (Bernstein 2014). The historical context fits the term somewhat awkwardly: widespread enforcement against individuals and small enterprises in the nineteenth century loomed large partly for the simple reason that most business operations consisted of individuals and small enterprises, and the option of suing large manufacturers, retailers, or intermediaries was far less available than it would be today. That said, it was not unknown for patent holders to target downstream customers even when a suit against the supplier was available. For example, as part of its strategy to dissuade people from signing up for rival telephone services, the American Bell Telephone Company periodically chose to sue en masse the individual subscribers to infringing exchanges (*New York Times*, 16 October 1887, p. 1).

As with the nationwide mass-enforcement campaigns, the SDNY/EDPA sample suggests a tendency toward end-user litigation by the most prolific plaintiffs. Litigation brought on high-volume patents was more likely than single-suit patent cases to name individuals as defendants in the title of the suit, rather than naming partnerships or corporations (Figure 4.4). Case titles are an imperfect measure of defendants' end-user or small-entity status—named individuals could be officers or agents of companies, for example—but the most active litigants in the sample are known to have sued small-scale users. The Goodyear Dental Vulcanite Company targeted dentists; American Bell sued customers of

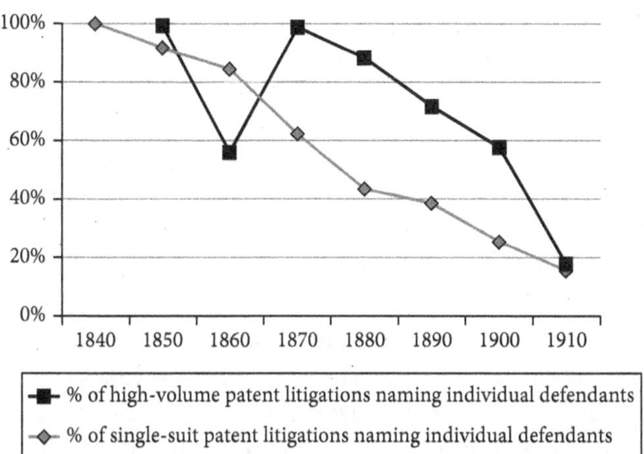

Figure 4.4 Percentage of patent litigations on high-volume and single-suit patents that named only individuals as defendants, SDNY and EDPA, sample years 1840–1910.

Source: Decadal sample of patent cases, SDNY/EDPA.

rival telephone companies and drugstore owners who provided pay-telephone services to the public. Further down the list of the most prolific plaintiffs in the sample were refrigerator-patent owner George C. Roberts, who sued butchers, and photography patentee Jehyleman Shaw, who sued individual photographers. With the exception of 1860—when two patent owners sued a slew of railroad companies in Philadelphia—high-volume litigation was consistently directed against individual non-company defendants at a higher rate than one-off suits were. That is, until 1910, at which point the two groups' respective rates of litigation against individuals were under 20 percent for the first time. End-user litigation had waned across the board by this point, and the most-litigated patents were now no more likely to target individuals than the least-litigated.

What caused the decline in end-user litigation? It is possible that political pressure played a role in bringing this type of litigation into disfavor. The 1870s and 1880s saw a political backlash against mass patent litigation, much of it driven by Western and Midwestern farmers who had been subjected to mass-enforcement campaigns by the driven well and barbed wire interests. Farmers and their political representatives in the 1870s and 1880s proposed a variety of statutory changes designed to eliminate small-value litigation against users, which they alleged amounted to "legalized blackmailing and robbery" (*Congressional Record* 1878, 8:303; Beauchamp 2016, p. 928). Several bills passed the House of Representatives between 1877 and 1884, some of them by wide margins, only to fail in the Senate (Hayter 1947, pp. 80–81).

With statutory reforms unable to break through, it is possible that judicial attitudes (at least in some courts) took up the cause. Among those engaged in nationwide patent litigation, judicial sensitivity to patent politics was a constant concern. *Scientific American*, a close watcher of all things patent law, detected in 1885 a "recent tendency of the courts to destroy patents" and in 1887 depicted a Supreme Court "much more vigorous in its treatment of patents than were the old school of judges" (*Scientific American*, 22 August 1885, p. 113; 5 February 1887, p. 80). In that same year, the Supreme Court invalidated the driven well patent it had previously upheld.[27] Henry Wallace, a leader of the farmers' movement against the barbed wire patent, opined in 1888 that "[t]wenty years ago almost any patent would be sustained and any kind of robbery could be practiced under the plea of a 'Patent;' now the courts discriminate and the people get their rights if they will but fight for them" (Kirkendall 2002, p. 55).

Notwithstanding such commentary, downstream enforcement strategies retained their appeal to patentees through the 1890s and into the first decade of the twentieth century. Individuals, retailers, and other small enterprises

[27] *Andrews v. Hovey*, 123 U.S. 267 (1887); *Beedle v. Bennett*, 122 U.S. 71 (1887); *Eames v. Andrews*, 122 U.S. 40 (1887).

continued to attract suits. Larger incumbent firms were also willing to target their competitors' clients with threatening circulars and litigation. Bell Telephone's suits against rival subscribers fit this category, as did the efforts of the National Harrow Company, a patent-holding trust company formed by the major harrow manufacturers, which filed suits against the customers and dealers of companies outside the trust (Rinehart 2018). A subgenre of litigation grew up around the propriety of targeting customers, with the affected manufacturers seeking injunctions against menacing circulars and—occasionally successfully—asking courts to prevent "harassing" customer suits.[28]

Ultimately, though, there is little sign that multiple litigation or end user suits were suppressed by policies directed against them. Absent clear changes in the legal viability of multiple enforcement, the most important influences on litigation strategy at the turn of the twentieth century may have been organizational.

From the Artisanal to the Corporate Economy

The next layer of the patent litigation system—economic organization—experienced tectonic shifts during the late nineteenth and early twentieth centuries. Broadly speaking, the sample of suits under discussion begins in an artisanal world of individual traders and small-scale business units and ends in an economy that, if not yet fully corporatized, was more organized, more consolidated, and featured a growing number of large firms (Chandler 1977; Lamoreaux 1985; Chandler 1990). The 1880s and 1890s were the "critical decades" during which leading firms made the investments in organization, production, and marketing that launched the era of managerial capitalism (Chandler 1990, pp. 62–63). An even more dramatic consolidation occurred at the turn of the century, in the form of the "great merger wave." More than 1,800 manufacturing enterprises merged in the decade after 1895 to form fewer than 150 industrial combinations, of which more than half controlled 40 percent or more of their respective markets and perhaps as many as a third controlled 70 percent (Lamoreaux 1985, p. 2).

These changes did not reach evenly across the economy, and indeed left many sectors largely untouched (Scranton 1997). But it would be surprising if crossing this threshold of industrial organization had no effect on the patent litigation system. One would expect the setting of small-scale proprietary capitalism to provide more opportunities for litigation: it featured more entities in the potentially infringing population, as well as greater information

[28] See, for example, *Adriance, Platt and Co. v. Nat'l Harrow Co.*, 111 F. 637, 638 (S.D.N.Y. 1901), *rev'd*, 121 F. 827, 829 (2d Cir. 1903); *Kessler v. Eldred*, 206 U.S. 285 (1907); Hilliard and Eble 1917, pp. 793–94; Vaughan 1925, pp. 147–48.

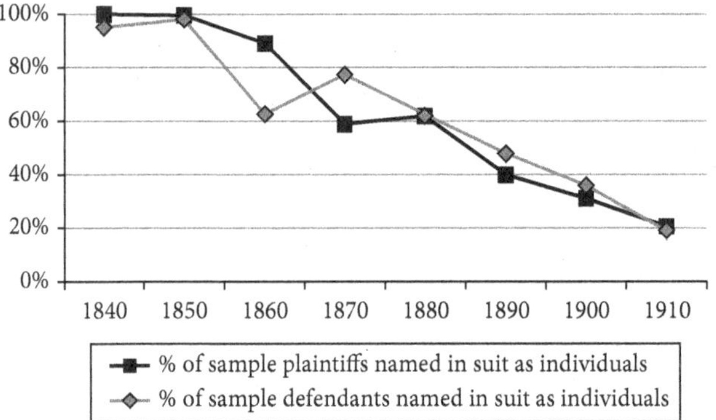

Figure 4.5 Percentage of plaintiffs and defendants named in suit as individuals, SDNY/EDPA, sample years 1840–1910.
Source: Decadal sample of patent cases, SDNY/EDPA.

asymmetries between parties. Independent inventors may have had a greater personal incentive (either economic or psychological) to enforce their own patents. Conversely, as industries become more concentrated and organized, having larger firms on both sides of a patent dispute should reduce the likelihood of litigation. Bigger enterprises would presumably be more evenly matched as parties, have better information about the patented invention and its market value, and might be in possession of conflicting patents or patent portfolios—all factors making successful bargaining and litigation avoidance more likely.

Several measures from the SDNY/EDPA sample illustrate the shift from an atomized to a more corporatized litigation environment. Figures 4.5 and 4.6 show the percentages of plaintiffs and defendants identified in the case title as individuals (Figure 4.5) and companies (Figure 4.6). Again, this is an imperfect proxy for the identity of the actual parties to the dispute: plaintiffs listed by their individual names may have been inventors who were also principals of their own companies, whereas individual defendants may in some cases have been officers or agents of companies that were not named in the complaint or docket.[29] Incorporated status also says nothing about the size of the business in question. Nevertheless, it is a suggestive indicator of the increasingly organized environment in which patent litigation operated. The percentages of suits brought by and against individuals fell steadily from nearly 100 percent to barely 20 percent,

[29] Where suit was brought by or against an individual and a company together, I categorized the party as a company.

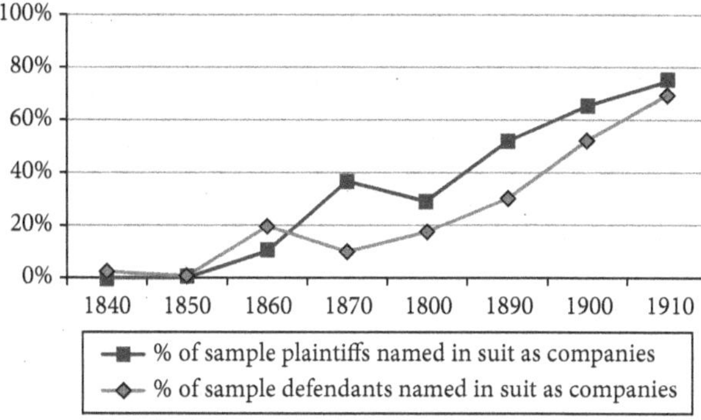

Figure 4.6 Percentage of plaintiffs and defendants named in suit as companies, SDNY/EDPA, sample years 1840–1910.
Source: Decadal sample of patent cases, SDNY/EDPA.

between 1850 and 1910 while the percentages naming companies as parties rose to 70–75 percent.[30]

The changing basis of the economy went hand-in-hand with changes in the context of invention and patent ownership. Inventive activity throughout the nineteenth century was dominated by what we would now think of as independent inventors: entrepreneurs, freelancers, or contractors who retained their patent rights or sold them on the open market, rather than employee-inventors inventing for hire and automatically assigning their patent rights to their employers (Fisk 2009; Lamoreaux and Sokoloff 1999). The market for patent rights was active from an early date (Khan 2005, p. 96). Those who received patents commonly obtained a return either by selling them outright or by using the grants to commercialize their inventions in a variety of ways. Some assigned territorial rights to producers in different geographic markets; others attracted capital by assigning partial shares to investors (Lamoreaux and Sokoloff 1999, pp. 27–29).

These arm's-length arrangements for marketing patents, especially territorially, were closely linked to particular types of enforcement. One reason that certain patents generated widespread litigation in the 1860s through 1880s may be that their assertion operated on a franchise model. To pick the largest example: royalty collection and litigation under the notorious driven well patent was often handled by local agents and attorneys working on commission (Smith 1891, p. 59; Hayter 1942, pp. 18–20). Similar arrangements appeared elsewhere. One of the high-volume patents litigated in the SDNY/EDPA sample belonged to Richard Imlay, a pioneering early railroad car designer. Imlay subcontracted

[30] Not every party was clearly an individual (or group of individuals) or a company. Some titles that suggested partnerships or involved government entities or charities were categorized separately.

enforcement of his most valuable car patent to a series of attorneys, who filed dozens of patent suits against railroad companies in their designated territories in return for 20–50 percent of gross receipts.[31] Sean O'Connor (2021) has described such arrangements of assignment, licensing, and subcontracted enforcement as "patent farming," capturing its resemblance to the delegated "tax farming" of early-modern states. Logistical details like this help to explain how patent owners in the mid-nineteenth century could mount litigation on such a sprawling scale, and also perhaps how the incentives of the agents handling enforcement pointed toward ready litigation.

In turn, the flow of patent business drew the rapidly expanding legal profession into the patent system. The number of trained lawyers grew dramatically in the United States after the Civil War—a rush of supply in legal services that has been associated with a surge of litigation in other areas, such as accident suits (Witt 2004 p. 59). The patent bar was one of the first areas of practice to begin to specialize within the profession and one of the first to involve a regional or national rather than purely local practice (Mason, Fenwick & Lawrence 1907; Swanson 2009). Many if not most lawyers involved in patent cases remained nonspecialists until the end of the nineteenth century. But the rise of a class of patent enforcement professionals was an important part of the institutional infrastructure for large-scale litigation.

Toward the end of the nineteenth century, invention began to occur more frequently under the sponsorship and direction of established firms. According to data gathered by Naomi Lamoreaux and Kenneth Sokoloff, the proportion of patents assigned on or before the date of issue—generally an indicator of a prepatenting financing or employment relationship between the inventor and the assignee—rose from 18 percent in 1870–71 to 29 percent in 1890–91 and 31 percent in 1910–11. Within that group, inventors became less likely to assign to entities in which they were themselves principals and more likely to assign all of their rights, rather than just a portion (Lamoreaux and Sokoloff 1999, p. 28).

The assignment profile of patents in litigation changed in keeping with these developments. Most patent suits in the SDNY/EDPA sample were not brought by the inventors themselves, or at least not by inventors acting alone. The proportion of litigated patents that had never been assigned before suit fell steadily from just over 60 percent in 1840 to under 20 percent in 1910 (Figure 4.7). To be sure, that means a fair amount of litigation by purely independent inventors was still occurring in the early twentieth century. But the overall decline is another data point suggesting that patent owners who litigated were tied into an increasingly

[31] Bill of Complaint and Report of Examiner, *Imlay v. Williams*, US Circuit Court for the Eastern District of Pennsylvania, Equity Case No. 10 (April Term 1860), National Archives at Philadelphia; Bill of Complaint, *Gregerson v. Imlay*, US Circuit Court for the Southern District of New York, Equity Case No. 2-97 (1860), National Archives at New York City.

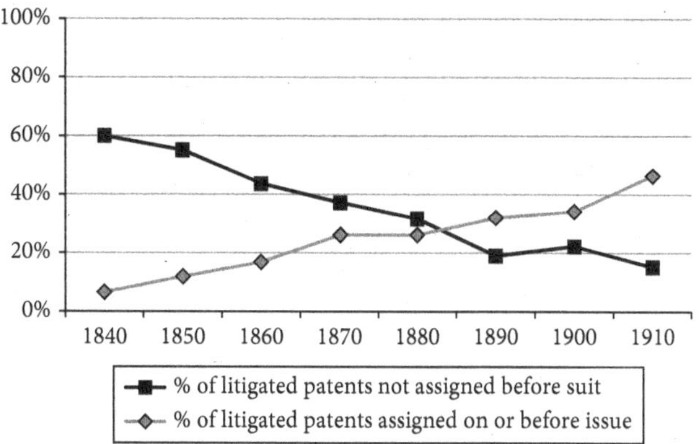

Figure 4.7 Percentages of litigated patents never assigned and assigned before issue, SDNY/EDPA, sample years 1840–1910.
Source: Decadal sample of patent cases, SDNY/EDPA.

organized financial or corporate setting as time went on. Likewise, the proportion of litigated patents assigned on or before issue rose to around 45 percent by 1910 (also Figure 4.7), a rate considerably higher than the 31 percent of all issued patents that Lamoreaux and Sokoloff found were assigned by the time of issue (Lamoreaux and Sokoloff 1999, p. 28).

It is unsurprising that patent litigation reflected the growing corporatization of the industrial economy over time. Without a control group of non-litigating patent owners, it is hard to gauge the extent to which either the type of entity or the relationship between inventor and assignee affected the propensity to litigate. But it remains likely that the drop-off in litigiousness in 1890, 1900, and 1910 resulted in part from the changing scale of business. At the very least, it is possible to trace the development of arrangements by which formerly litigious actors turned away from using the courts. Patent pools formed in a range of industries in the 1890s and 1900s, suppressing both competition and litigation among the participating firms (Vaughan 1925, pp. 36–52). Around the end of the century, the electrical manufacturing sector consolidated around a few corporate giants, whose size and dominance eventually made litigation among themselves undesirable and suits against smaller operators far less necessary (Passer 1975, p. 331). The Bell Telephone enterprise (later AT&T), prodigious enforcers of Alexander Graham Bell's controlling patents in the 1880s and early 1890s, held similarly fundamental patents on long-distance telephony in the 1900s—but almost never brought suit after 1908, preferring to seek market power by financial and organizational means (Federal Communications Commission 1939, pp. 213–14). Elsewhere—and to be sure, often after a burst of litigation—other industries began to form large-scale patent pooling arrangements: in automobiles, aviation, explosives, and film projection equipment, to name a few examples (Barnett 2015). As the twentieth century progressed, firms' ability to incorporate patents into broader schemes of industrial control pushed litigation to the margins.

Just as growing size reduced the demand for patent litigation *by* larger firms, it may also have reduced patentees' appetite for litigation *against* them. By the early twentieth century, observers were readily pointing out the ability of well-financed defendants to "drag out a patent suit indefinitely, until the weak opponent, unable to bear the ever-increasing expenses, collapses and withdraws" (US House Committee on Patents 1912, hearing no. 4, p. 24; Edelman 1915, p. 163). Leo Baekelund, the prominent chemist, inventor, and businessman, informed Congress in 1912 that "a well-organized patent department is a reliable machine, where money is the lubricant. This machine, in its slow but sure grinding way, can reduce to pulp any of the smaller competitors" (US House Committee on Patents 1912, hearing no. 4, p. 24). Louis Brandeis, the celebrated champion of small enterprise, added that litigation was "so expensive, and there are such delays attendant upon it, that it is not a question of being right; it is a question of having money enough to wear out the other man" (US House Committee on Patents 1912, hearing no. 18, p. 13).

Figure 4.8 attempts to capture the rising cost of patent litigation. Direct data on parties' costs is unavailable, but duration can serve as a very rough proxy for the expense and complexity of a suit. The vast majority of litigation expenses consisted of legal fees, which were in turn a function of the lawyers' time; and expert witness testimony, which took inordinately long to compile and may have

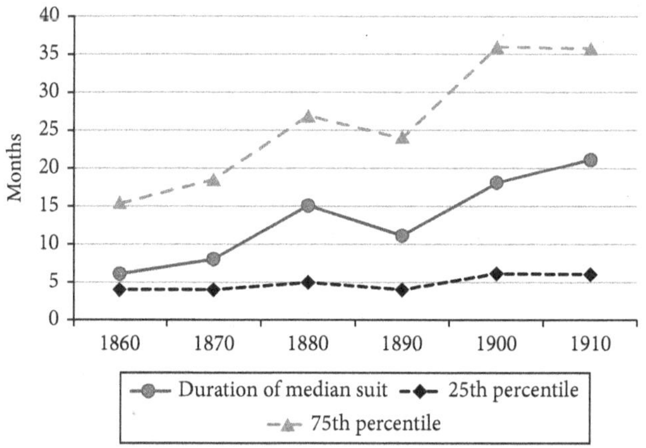

Figure 4.8 Duration of terminated suits, SDNY/EDPA, sample years 1840–1910.

Note: Chart includes only cases where a termination (of any kind, whether adjudicated or settled) was recorded in the docket.

Source: Decadal sample of patent cases, SDNY/EDPA.

been the primary contributor to the length of a suit. Figure 4.8 shows that case duration rose considerably over the years. Among cases that achieved some sort of recorded termination (of any kind, whether adjudicated or settled), the median suit lasted 8 months in 1870 and 21 months by 1910. There were always suits that settled or were decided quickly: 25th percentile duration remained at four to six months throughout the sample period. But at the other end, bigger cases ballooned, reaching three years at the 75th percentile.

This growing cost of litigation was associated with the greater resources that corporate litigants brought to the table. From 1870 through 1890, there was little difference in average duration between suits that pitted companies against companies and suits where both parties were named as individuals. In 1900 and 1910, however, a gulf opened up between the average length of company v. company suits (35–40 months) and individual v. individual suits (15–17 months). Suits between companies and individuals (in either direction) lay in between, with averages ranging from 24 to 30 months in those years. Whether this shows that corporate litigants were grinding independent inventors and little-guy defendants to a pulp is open to question—the "company" and "individual" categories are only crude indicators of resources, after all—but it does at least seem that such cases ran longer than in situations where both parties were individuals.

Technology

The final layer to the patent litigation system is the technology at issue. Having identified trends within the litigated patent population, such the transformation of claiming and the changing protagonists in suit, it is important to ask whether these were artefacts of some technological change—for example, a wholesale shift in patent litigation from mechanical devices to a new age of electrical and chemical inventions. Technological divergences are a feature of the recent patent landscape: highly litigious, non-practicing entities, for example, have been disproportionately concentrated in the computer and software field (Risch 2016a, pp. 1554–57). And famously, the late nineteenth and early twentieth centuries witnessed a "second industrial revolution," in which science-based inventions and new electrical, chemical, and automotive industries came to the fore (Mokyr 1999). It is natural to suspect that these developments would be reflected among patent contests.

Fortunately, the hard work of classifying patents by technology has been done. The US Patent and Trademark Office (PTO) assigns each patent to a technology class and has retrospectively classified all of its old grants on the same system. Based on these designations, the National Bureau of Economic Research (NBER) created a more compact system of classification, translating the 400 PTO classes into a shorter list of categories (Hall, Jaffe, and Trajtenberg 2001).[32] Historical data on the number of patents issued and in force by NBER category are available via the PTO (US Patent and Trademark Office. n.d.; Marco et al. 2015). It is important to note that these classifications are all based on technology type, which is not the same as industry or sector of use. For example, a machine for printing on yarn,[33] a new material for making phonograph cylinders,[34] and a device for covering candies with chocolate[35] all appear in NBER subcategory 12, "coatings," which in turn falls under the broad "chemical" category. One should be very cautious about assuming that these technology classes map onto particular industries.

Table 4.6 presents data on litigation propensity for a series of technology areas, each constructed by grouping together selected NBER subcategories. These areas are not the whole population of patents or suits—they constitute 65–70 percent of the total patents in force in any given year and 65–80 percent of the SDNY and EDPA litigation—but are meant to capture the major coherent fields of technology appearing in litigation.[36] Table 4.6 shows both the number of litigations[37] (column 6) and the number of patents litigated (column 9) in the SDNY and EDPA per 1,000 of that class in force.

There is much to say about each of these technology classes, but the central findings for our purposes are first, that patent litigation in these districts was technologically diverse and second, that the changes in patents and litigation strategies discussed elsewhere in this chapter were shared across technology types. It was rare—with a couple of exceptions discussed later—for a group's share of litigated patents (column 8) greatly to exceed its share of overall patents (column 2). Only in one instance did any of these groups account for as much as 20 percent of the patents litigated in a year. It was rather more common for the share of total litigation (column 5) to fall disproportionately in one technological area. Individual technology classes could account for a quarter or a third of all litigations in a year when one of the mass-enforcement or end-user campaigns

[32] The NBER scheme adopted six broad categories and thirty-seven subcategories. I have used the latter here.

[33] Charles L. Horack "Method of and Apparatus for Printing Yarns," U.S. Patent No. 603,992, May 10, 1898.

[34] Jonas W. Aylsworth, "Composition for Making Duplicate Phonograph Records," U.S. Patent No. 782,375, Feb. 14, 1905.

[35] Panayiotis Panoulias, "Candy-Coating Machine," U.S. Patent No. 685,790, Nov. 5, 1901.

[36] The rest of the litigation sample consists of smaller NBER technology classes (such as "amusement devices" and "receptacles") and two large residual NBER categories, "miscellaneous—mechanical" and "miscellaneous—other," which are capacious and unhelpful in thinking about how the technology in suit was changing.

[37] A "litigation" here counts every patent in every case—some cases involved more than one patent, so this number is higher than the number of suits filed.

was represented, such as Goodyear Dental Vulcanite in 1870 or Bell Telephone in 1890.

Where litigation propensity persistently differed from the overall average, several different things seemed to be going on. Agricultural inventions were underrepresented throughout, compared to their share of inventions. Given that agricultural machinery and tools were apparently widely litigated elsewhere in the country, this was probably an artefact of the two sampled courts' urban setting (Magliocca 2007). The most overrepresented field in 1870 and 1880 was apparel and textiles, and this too may have been a matter of economic geography. For a patentee in these fields, New York and Philadelphia represented an extremely target-rich environment: between retailers and manufactories, there were thousands of potential defendants in the two cities. Suits arising from this technology class included both patents for consumer products, such as hats, corsets, and hoop skirts, and for machinery, including a great variety of specialized sewing machines. In what was a mature technological sector by this period, the high level of litigation seems to have reflected energetic product competition in apparel and a disaggregated, specialized manufacturing base. By contrast, the overrepresented areas of the sample's later years were electrical and chemical classes. Here, the dynamics were different: in the electrical arts, new industries such as electric lighting and power attracted litigation as entrants jostled for position in manufacturing and service provision. In the chemical field, the biggest subclass of litigated patents by far was "miscellaneous—chemical," and covered a huge variety of different applications of chemistry: gramophone records, armor-piercing shells, dairy processing. This distribution hints that patent disputes reflected chemical sciences and scientific methods advancing across a broad front, rather than any particular industry driving patent litigation.

Trends observed in the overall sample were also common across the technology groups. High-volume patents (litigated more than ten times) were not limited to any particular category but were scattered across the technology fields. Changing patterns of claiming were also common across technologies: each of the groups and every NBER subclass with a significant number of litigated patents saw increases in the length and number of claims between 1870 and 1910. This reinforces the likelihood that changes in claiming were a product of their legal environment and drafting strategy. One alternative explanation for the growing length of claims might be that increasingly mature technological fields required narrower patents (and hence more detailed claims) necessary to avoid prior art. But there is no significant relationship between claim length and the number of existing patents in force in different technology classes, suggesting that this was not the case.[38]

[38] Such a relationship might be discernible using the more fine-grained PTO classifications rather than the composite NBER groups. But patent-in-force data is not available for the PTO classes.

It is hard to read through the list of patents litigated in this era without being struck by the incredible variety of inventions and activities at issue. Given the diversity of arts and industries they represented, it is perhaps surprising that their experiences of litigation did not diverge more than they did. But the business of these two courts seems to have reflected the endless novelty of the changing world around them.

Conclusion

This descriptive account has covered the ebbing of the nineteenth century's great patent litigation wave and the transition to a less contentious twentieth-century patent system. As befits one of the great periods of economic and technological upheaval in US history, the transformations involved are in some ways dramatic. But the conclusions of this study are modest. No one reform appears to account for litigation being reined in, although two legal changes of the period were particularly consequential. The first was a discrete intervention: the crackdown on reissues in the 1880s. The second was a more incremental shift: the steady migration of claim practice toward more clearly demarcated (and perhaps narrower) rights.

Other developments in the patent litigation system pull the spotlight away from public policy. Aspects of law and practice, especially the phenomenon of end-user litigation, certainly came under political pressure in the late nineteenth century, but the hoped-for procedural and substantive reforms did not come to pass. Patent law kept the character that has defined most of its history since 1836: adaptive but essentially stable in its framework (Reilly 2018). The contexts in which the law operated did change, however. Business and innovation passed into a new world of managerial capitalism, reconfiguring both the market for inventions and the markets in which patent-holding enterprises competed. Although many of these transformations would not be complete until later in the twentieth century, they were in full swing by the end of its first decade. The form and process of a lawsuit continued to look much as it had decades earlier, but it had a different role in a world of employee-inventors, patent pools, and corporate legal departments.

In any era, litigation is an outcome that nobody involved—with a few exceptions, most of them lawyers—really wants. The nineteenth-century United States moved beyond its wave of patent lawsuits, but not, as far as we can tell, by weakening the institutions of patent enforcement or by burdening certain categories of plaintiff. Instead, and in largely incremental fashion, the courts pushed to improve patents themselves, while the changing economy and private ordering began to erode the value of litigation as a tool. The mid-twentieth-century patent system may have replaced older crises of over-enforcement with new pathologies of under-enforcement. But that is another story.

References

Archival collections

Library of Congress, Manuscript Division. Charles Mason Remey Family Papers. Washington, D.C.

National Archives at Philadelphia. Philadelphia, PA.

National Archives at New York City. New York, NY.

References

Anderson, J. Jonas, and Peter S. Menell. "Informal Deference: A Historical, Empirical, and Normative Analysis of Patent Claim Construction." *Northwestern University Law Review* 108, no. 1 (2014): 1–84.

Barnett, Jonathan. "The Anticommons Revisited." *Harvard Journal of Law and Technology* 29, no. 1 (2015): 127–203.

Beauchamp, Christopher. *Invented by Law: Alexander Graham Bell and the Patent that Changed America*. Cambridge, MA: Harvard University Press, 2015.

_______. "The First Patent Litigation Explosion." *Yale Law Journal* 125, no. 4 (2016): 848–944.

Bernstein, Gaia. "The Rise of the End User in Patent Litigation." *Boston College Law Review* 55, no. 5 (2014): 1443–1500.

Bessen, James, and Michael J. Meurer. *Patent Failure: How Judges, Bureaucrats, and Lawyers Put Innovators at Risk*. Princeton, NJ: Princeton University Press, 2009.

________. "The Patent Litigation Explosion." *Loyola University Chicago Law Journal* 45, no. 2 (2013): 401–40.

Biagioli, Mario, Peter Jaszi, and Martha Woodmansee, eds. *Making and Unmaking Intellectual Property: Creative Production in Legal and Cultural Perspective*. Chicago, IL: University of Chicago Press, 2011.

Burk, Dan L., and Mark A. Lemley, *The Patent Crisis and How the Courts Can Solve It*. Chicago, IL: University of Chicago Press, 2009a.

________. "Fence Posts or Sign Posts? Rethinking Patent Claim Construction." University of Pennsylvania Law Review 157, no. 6 (2009b): 1743–99.

Byrd, Owen, and Brian Howard, eds. *Lex Machina 2013 Patent Litigation Year in Review*. Menlo Park, CA: Lex Machina, 2014.

Carlson, W. Bernard. *Innovation as a Social Process: Elihu Thomson and the Rise of General Electric, 1870–1900*. New York: Cambridge University Press, 1991.

Carter, Susan B. et al., eds. *Historical Statistics of the United States*. Vols. 1 and 3. New York: Cambridge University Press, 2006.

Chandler, Alfred D., Jr. *The Visible Hand: The Managerial Revolution in American Business*. Cambridge, MA: Harvard University Press, 1977.

_______. *Scale and Scope: The Dynamics of Industrial Capitalism*. Cambridge, MA: Harvard University Press, 1990.

Chien, Colleen V. "Of Trolls, Davids, Goliaths, and Kings: Narratives and Evidence in the Litigation of High-Tech Patents." *North Carolina Law Review* 87, no. 5 (2009): 1571–1616.

Congressional Record. 45th Cong., 2nd sess. Vol. 8. 1878.

Cotropia, Christopher A., Jay P. Kesan, and David L. Schwartz. "Unpacking Patent Assertion Entities (PAEs)." *Minnesota Law Review* 99, no. 2 (2014): 649–704.

Cox, Rowland. "Reissued Patents—The Position of the Supreme Court." *American Law Review* 15 (1881): 731–39.

Dood, Kendall J. "Pursuing the Essence of Inventions: Reissuing Patents in the 19th Century." Technology and Culture 32, no. 4 (1991): 999–1017.

Edelman, Philip E. *Inventions and Patents*. New York: D. Van Nostrand Company, 1915.

Federal Communications Commission. *Investigation of the Telephone Industry in the United States*. Washington, DC: GPO, 1939.

Fisk, Catherine. *Working Knowledge: Employee Innovation and the Rise of Corporate Intellectual Property*, 1800–1930. Chapel Hill: University of North Carolina Press, 2009.

Fromer, Jeanne C. "Claiming Intellectual Property." *University of Chicago Law Review* 76, no. 2 (2009): 719–96.

Gibson, Campbell. "Population of the 100 Largest Cities and Other Urban Places in the United States: 1790 to 1990." U.S. Census Bureau Population Division Working Paper No. 27, Washington, DC, 1998.

Grinvald, Leah Chan. "Policing the Cease-and-Desist Letter." *University of San Francisco Law Review* 49, no. 3 (2015): 409–63.

Gugliuzza, Paul R. "Patent Litigation Reform: The Courts, Congress, and the Federal Rules of Civil Procedure." *Boston University Law Review* 95, no. 1 (2015): 279–301.

Hall, B. H., A. B. Jaffe, and M. Trajtenberg. "The NBER Patent Citation Data File: Lessons, Insights and Methodological Tools." NBER Working Paper No. 8498, Cambridge, MA, Oct. 2001.

Hayter, Earl W. "The Western Farmers and the Drivewell Patent Controversy." *Agricultural History* 16, no. 1 (1942): 16–28.

_______. "The Patent System and Agrarian Discontent, 1875–1888." *Mississippi Valley Historical Review* 34, no. 1 (1947): 59–82.

Henry, Matthew, and John Turner. "Across Five Eras: Patent Validity and Infringement Rates in U.S. Courts, 1929–2006." *Journal of Empirical Legal Studies* 13, no. 3 (2016): 454–86.

Hilliard, John H., and Eugene Eble, eds. *Walker on Patents*. New York: Baker, Voorhis & Co, 1917.

Howson, Hubert. *Patents and the Useful Arts*. Philadelphia, PA: Times Printing House, 1878.

Katznelson, Ron D. "A Century of Patent Litigation in Perspective." SSRN, 17 November 2014. https://ssrn.com/abstract=2503140.

Khan, B. Zorina. *The Democratization of Invention: Patents and Copyrights in American Economic Development, 1790–1920*. New York: Cambridge University Press, 2005.

Kirkendall, Richard. *Uncle Henry: A Documentary Profile of the First Henry Wallace*. 2nd ed. Ames, IA: Iowa State University Press, 2002.

Lamoreaux, Naomi R. *The Great Merger Movement in American Business, 1895–1904*. New York: Cambridge University Press, 1985.

Lamoreaux, Naomi R., and Kenneth L. Sokoloff. "Inventors, Firms, and the Market for Technology: U.S. Manufacturing in the Late Nineteenth and Early Twentieth Centuries." In *Learning by Doing in Firms, Markets, and Countries*, edited by Naomi R. Lamoreaux, Daniel M. G. Raff, and Peter Temin, 19–60. Chicago: University of Chicago Press, 1999.

_______. "Intermediaries in the U.S. Market for Technology, 1870–1920." In *Finance, Intermediaries, and Economic Development*, edited by Stanley L. Engerman et al., 209–46. New York: Cambridge University Press, 2003.

Lemley, Mark A., and Carl Shapiro. "Probabilistic Patents." *Journal of Economic Perspectives* 19, no. 2 (2005): 75–98.
Lemley, Mark A., Kent Richardson, and Erik Oliver. "The Patent Enforcement Iceberg." *Texas Law Review* 97, no. 4 (2019): 801–33.
Lutz, Karl B. "Evolution of the Claims of U.S. Patents." *Journal of the Patent Office Society* 20, no. 2 (1938): 134–55.
Magliocca, Gerard N. "Blackberries and Barnyards: Patent Trolls and the Perils of Innovation." *Notre Dame Law Review* 82, no. 5 (2007): 1809–38.
Marco, Alan C. et al. "The USPTO Historical Patent Data Files: Two Centuries of Innovation." U.S. Patent and Trademark Office Economic Working Paper No. 2015-1, Alexandria, VA, 2015.
Mason, Fenwick and Lawrence. *Patents for Profit*. Washington, DC: privately printed, 1907.
McLaurin, John J. *Sketches in Crude Oil: Some Accidents and Incidents of the Petroleum Development in All Parts of the Globe*. 2nd ed. Harrisburg, PA: Published by the author, 1898.
Mokyr, Joel. "The Second Industrial Revolution, 1870–1914." In *Storia Dell'Economia Mondiale*, edited by V. Castronovo, 219–45. Rome: Laterza Publishing, 1999.
Mossoff, Adam. "The 'Patent Litigation Explosion' Canard." *Truth on the Market*, 18 October 2012. http://truthonthemarket.com/2012/10/18/the-patent-litigation-explosion-canard/ [http://perma.cc/EJK4-D36F].
Mulligan, Christina, and Timothy B. Lee. "Scaling the Patent System." *NYU Annual Survey of American Law* 68, no. 2 (2012): 289–318.
New York Times, various dates.
O'Connor, Sean M. "The Damaging Myth of Patent Exhaustion." *Texas Intellectual Property Law Journal*, (2021) forthcoming.
Passer, Harold C. *The Electrical Manufacturers, 1875–1900: A Study in Competition, Entrepreneurship, Technical Change, and Economic Growth*. New York: Arno Press, 1975.
Patent Act of 1836. U.S. Statutes at Large 5:117–125.
Patent Act of 1842, U.S. Statutes at Large 5:543–45.
Patent Act of 1848, U.S. Statutes at Large 9:231–32.
Patent Act of 1861, U.S. Statutes at Large 12:246–49.
Reilly, Gregory. "Our 19th Century Patent System." IP Theory 7, no. 2 (2018): 1–20.
Rifkind, Simon H. "The Romance Discoverable in Patent Cases." *Journal of the Patent Office Society* 37, no. 5 (1955): 319–30.
Rinehart, Amelia. "E. Bement and Sons v. National Harrow Company: The First Skirmish between Patent Law and the Sherman Act." *Syracuse Law Review* 68, no. 1 (2018): 81–115.
Risch, Michael. "The Layered Patent System." *Iowa Law Review* 101, no. 4 (2016a): 1535–79.
________. "(Un)Reasonable Royalties." *Boston University Law Review* 98, no. 1 (2016b): 187–261.
________. "Sue First, Negotiate Later." *Arizona Law Review* 61, no. 3 (2019): 561–604.
Scranton, Philip. *Endless Novelty: Specialty Production and American Industrialization, 1865–1925*. Princeton, NJ: Princeton University Press, 1997.
Smith, Chauncey. "A Century of Patent Law." *Quarterly Journal of Economics* 5, no. 1 (1891): 44–69.
Swanson, Kara W. "The Emergence of the Professional Patent Practitioner." *Technology and Culture* 50, no. 3 (2009): 519–48.

Usselman, Steven W. *Regulating Railroad Innovation: Business, Technology, and Politics in America, 1840–1920*. New York: Cambridge University Press, 2002.

US Bureau of the Census. *Thirteenth Census of the United States, Taken in the Year 1910*. Vol. 9. *Manufactures, 1909*. Washington, D.C.: GPO, 1912.

US House Committee on Patents. *Oldfield Revision and Codification of the Patent Statutes: Hearings on H.R. 23417*. 62nd Cong., 2nd sess., various dates. Washington, DC: GPO, 1912.

US Patent Office. *Annual Reports of the Commissioner of Patents*. Washington, DC: 1836–1910.

US Patent and Trademark Office. "Historical Patent Data Files." n.d. https://www.uspto.gov/learning-and-resources/electronic-data-products/historical-patent-data-files.

Vaughan, Floyd R. *Economics of Our Patent System*. New York: Macmillan Co., 1925.

Walker, Albert H. *Text-Book of the Patent Laws of the United States of America*. New York: L.K. Strouse & Company, 1883.

Witt, John F. *The Accidental Republic: Crippled Workingmen, Destitute Widows, and the Remaking of American Law*. Cambridge, MA: Harvard University Press, 2004.

Woodward, William Redin. "Definiteness and Particularity in Patent Claims." *Michigan Law Review* 46, no. 6 (1948): 755–86.

World Intellectual Property Organization. "2013 World Intellectual Property Indicators." WIPO Publication No. 941E/2013, Geneva, Switzerland, 2013.

Yeh, Brian T., and Emily M. Lanza. *Patent Litigation Reform Legislation in the 114th Congress*. Congressional Research Service Report R43979. Washington, DC, 2015.

5

Ninth Circuit Nursery

Patent Litigation and Industrial Development on the Pacific Coast, 1891–1925

Steven W. Usselman

In March 1891, during the final hours of one of the most tumultuous sessions in its history, the US Congress reformed the federal judiciary. In passing the Evarts Act, Congress created the modern appeals court system. Cases arising from the nine geographic federal circuits would henceforth flow on appeal from districts, generally corresponding to state boundaries, to a circuit-wide appeals court. There, panels of three judges would review actions taken at district. The Supreme Court would, for the most part, confine itself thereafter to reviewing a few select cases heard at the circuit courts of appeal.[1]

In restructuring the federal judiciary, the lame duck Republican Congress sought to address the most pressing issue of the day—the rise of big business and the political resistance it had spawned. Agitated rural Democrats and third-party agrarians, long at the vanguard of resistance to national corporations, were riding high. That November, they had routed the incumbent Republicans, sweeping into Congress in record numbers and securing gains in many state legislatures (Kazin 2006; McMath 1992). The agrarian reformers threatened national corporations with a thicket of state and municipal regulatory laws and antimonopoly statutes (McCurdy 1978; Novak 1996; Lamoreaux and Novak 2017). Large firms naturally would have preferred to operate free of any such constraints. When mounting pressure forced their hands, they and their Republican allies sought to redirect the reform impulse toward outcomes that privileged federal authorities and accentuated the role of the federal courts (Saunders 1999; Rauchway 2006; Balogh 2009; Sklar 1988; Livingston 1986). The Interstate Commerce Commission (ICC), created in 1887 after the Supreme Court curbed state railroad commissions, provided one example (Skowronek

[1] On the Evarts Act, see the website of the Federal Judicial Center (https://www.fjc.gov). According to that source, the backlog of cases before the Supreme Court fell from 1,199 in 1890 to 346 in 1900, while the number of cases the Court decided by written opinion fell from 291 in 1890 to 186 in 1910. A 1911 act implemented further reforms that drew sharper lines between the district courts and the appeals courts.

Steven W. Usselman, *Ninth Circuit Nursery* In: *The Battle over Patents.* Edited by: Stephen H. Haber and Naomi R. Lamoreaux, Oxford University Press. © Oxford University Press 2021. DOI: 10.1093/oso/9780197576151.003.0006

1982; Usselman 2002). The Sherman Antitrust Act, passed by Congress in 1890, appeared poised to exert a similar effect on antimonopoly law, which would now be subject to federal jurisdiction (McCurdy 1979; Lamoreaux 1985; Hovenkamp 2015; John 2010).

As the skeletal federal judiciary braced to assume these new burdens, it faced a pressing crisis arising from one of its existing responsibilities: patent law. A dramatic spike in patenting since the Civil War had produced an inevitable surge in litigation (Beauchamp 2015). The stakes involved in those actions had climbed markedly, moreover, as firms such as Singer, Pullman, Westinghouse, and Bell looked to leverage patent rights and build enterprises of national scope. Their efforts outraged agrarians in the South and West and put the Republican agenda at risk. Farmers and small proprietors in these regions decried a system under which a federal bureaucracy seemingly granted monopolies to firms, overwhelmingly located in the industrial north, which then used those rights to restrict competition and drive up prices of desirable technologies (Usselman 2002; Usselman and John 2006). Agrarians called for reforms that would protect consumers from patent infringement, while pressing Congress to fund agricultural research, the results of which would be made freely available to the public (Olmstead and Rhode 2008).

Of more concern to the federal courts, these patent-based firms became targets of extended lawsuits brought by deep-pocketed competitors and consumers. In March 1888, after months of labor, a sharply divided Supreme Court had narrowly ruled in favor of the reviled Bell Monopoly, in the first of several closely watched cases involving the telephone patents. The opinions filled an entire volume of federal proceedings, fully a fifth of the court's output that year (Beauchamp 2015).[2] An exhausted Chief Justice Waite retired to his bed and died a week later. The episode surely boosted the cause of judicial reform, at a time when numerous patent cases were still pending on the High Court's docket and patent rights grew ever more integral to the strategies of big business and the economic structure of the nation (Hovenkamp 2015; Fisk 2009; Lamoreaux and Sokoloff 2009; Lamoreaux, Sokoloff, and Sutthiphisal 2013; Mowery 1995; Reich 1985; 1992).

In contrast to regulation and antitrust, reforms aiming to centralize activity, the revised judicial structure worked in the opposite direction for patents, pushing patent law out to the regional circuits and their new appeals courts. With the patent system already administered by a federal bureaucracy and subject to review by the Supreme Court, one might presume that these circuit courts of appeal would simply defer to well-established centralized authorities.

[2] According to the Federal Judicial Center (FJC), the opinions filled one of five volumes that year. Another major patent case pertaining to the glycerin process was decided the same term.

In reality, however, patent doctrine was much more muddled. Cases hinged on the particulars of specific technologies. Seldom did they yield clear analogies and conform readily to generalized principles. As the exhausted justices of the Supreme Court well understood, judges had considerable room for interpretation. This was especially true because rulings at one circuit would not be binding upon others. While remaining cognizant of doctrines and principles articulated by the Supreme Court and the Patent Office in Washington, circuit appeals judges would review local disputes arising between parties who were often engaged with technologies and activities highly specific to their region. In these judicial forums, the nationalizing impulses of the age would meet local realities and regional priorities.

This chapter examines how this dynamic played out in one of those forums—the sprawling Ninth Circuit of the Far West. Then as now, the Ninth Circuit occupied a distinctive place in the nation and the federal judiciary. Much of this was a function of geography. Anchored in the three vibrant Pacific Coast states of California, Oregon, and Washington, the circuit also included the mining districts and range lands of Montana, Idaho, Nevada, and Arizona, plus the stunning and strategically vital territories of Alaska and Hawaii. Vast but still sparsely populated, with less than 3 percent of the nation's population in 1891, the region stood on the brink of spectacular economic development. By 1925, it contained nearly 8 percent of the US population and 3 of its 20 largest cities—Los Angeles, San Francisco, and Seattle. Their growth had spurred massive investments in infrastructure and housing (Nugent 1999). The intervening years had also featured the unprecedented development of a technologically sophisticated agricultural sector, producing high-value goods for national markets; the rise of the nation's most productive oil and minerals industries; and the emergence of a diverse manufacturing sector producing both intermediate goods and consumer products (Olmstead and Rhode 2008; Nugent 1999). The economy somehow blended the agrarian Plains and the industrial East, while remaining apart from both. This regional character was reflected in its patenting rates (Lamoreaux and Sokoloff 2009; Carlton and Coclanis 1995). It was captured as well in the region's agrarian reform movements, which exhibited little of the desperate passion of their Southern and Plains counterparts, while taking a decidedly business-like approach (Postel 2007; Woeste 1998; Deverell 1994; Blackford 1993).

Along with its distinctive economy, the Ninth Circuit was also distinguished by the extraordinary longevity and political diversity of its appeals judges. A trio of them—William Gilbert, William W. Morrow, and Erskine Ross—served together from the court's founding through 1925.[3] The group constituted by far

[3] Prior to 1897, Morrow was the district judge for the northern district of California, while Joseph McKenna held the appeals post. In practice, their roles were often reversed. Morrow formally assumed the appeals post when McKenna rose to the Supreme Court. He assumed senior status in

the most stable contingent of appeals judges on any circuit in US history. (A fourth appeals judge, William H. Hunt Jr., joined them in 1915 and soon exerted a strong influence.) Born in the mid-1840s, each had come west following the Civil War and cast his fortunes in one of the region's bourgeoning cities. All developed a fierce loyalty to the region and took pride in its material achievements (Frederick 1994).

While sharing many attributes, the three appeals judges brought distinctive judicial philosophies to the court, each of which aligned to considerable degree with a broad strand of national politics and undoubtedly shaded their rulings in patent cases. Gilbert was an old-guard Republican. Characterized by the court's historian as "thoroughly a nineteenth century man," he was the most inclined of the three to bestow strong patent rights upon inventors, but often held them to high standards (Frederick 1994). Morrow openly displayed his allegiances to the liberal or progressive wing of the Republican Party associated with Governor Hiram Johnson and ex-President Theodore Roosevelt.[4] He took many of the most difficult cases and was strongly inclined to weaken patent rights. Ross was a southern Democrat (and local citrus land developer) who adhered to the party's libertarian Jacksonian principles. Like his mentor, Justice Stephen J. Field, Ross looked dimly on government sponsored monopolies, especially when they worked against the interests of farmers and small proprietors. He tended to read patents very strictly and narrowly.

Over the course of some 35 years, these three judges, with occasional help from their district colleagues and from Hunt, heard appeals and issued final opinions in nearly 150 known patent cases. Drawing on those opinions and on transcripts and accompanying documents provided by the district courts, this chapter presents an overview of how Ninth Circuit patent litigation framed inventive enterprise on the Pacific Coast and shaped economic development during this formative period in the region and the nation (see Appendix for details on these sources).

These materials indicate that the appeals court exhibited a strong regional bias. Panels consistently favored local interests. Litigants from outside the Ninth Circuit prevailed just 20 times in 75 opportunities. Appeals panels, inclined to weaken patents in most circumstances, were particularly begrudging toward patent holders from outside the circuit. Only late in the period, after Chief Justice

1923 but remained very active in patent matters. Ross served several years as district judge for the Southern District of California before assuming the appeals post in 1895.

[4] Morrow, whose daughter married a Roosevelt, had intended to retire on his seventieth birthday, in June 1913, but changed course after Democrat Woodrow Wilson was elected president. "Circuit Judge Morrow Announces Retirement," *Marin County Tocsin*, 36, no. 24 (7 December 1912).

William Howard Taft and his colleagues issued strong rebukes, did the Ninth Circuit balance the scales of justice on a regional basis.

While insulating local interests from national competitors, Ninth Circuit judges diverged in their treatment of local patent holders. In some instances, particularly those involving established Bay Area manufacturers, judges were inclined to award strong patent rights that gave West Coast firms a foothold in national markets. In cases arising from other districts, where inventors often fared poorly, appeals judges were more likely to referee disputes in ways that promoted competition among West Coast suppliers. The approach helped nurture infant regional supply industries in pioneering fields such as oil drilling and refining, agricultural processing and irrigation, logging equipment, furniture manufacture, and building materials, while also insulating farmers, drillers, contractors, and other small proprietors from concerns about infringement.

While Ninth Circuit patent law exhibited a strong regional character, it reflected larger national attitudes and trends. Appeals panels in many respects mirrored debates occurring in Congress and on the Supreme Court. Decisions often betrayed widely held political opinions regarding the patent system and antitrust, which grew deeply intertwined. A split between the Northern and Southern Districts of California, for instance, largely played out along party lines.

Although those differences persisted to some degree throughout the period, Ninth Circuit judges eventually gravitated toward a less divisive administrative style favored by Taft. The transition accelerated after 1915, as the federal courts coped with a deluge of litigation generated by World War I and passage of new federal statutes (including the Clayton Antitrust Act, which sought to curb business practices that leveraged patent rights). Judgements in Ninth Circuit patent disputes were more likely to balance competing interests, often by relying upon court-appointed masters, rather than declaring clear winners and losers. West Coast judges also deferred more often to the DC Court of Appeals when considering matters of validity. Yet even then, Ninth Circuit judges retained considerable autonomy regarding matters of infringement and damages, which they continued to exercise when adjudicating disputes among regional suppliers. The administrative approach did not necessarily result in a strengthening of patent rights. More typically, it narrowed rights held by multiple competing interests.

The chapter proceeds in two distinct parts. The first offers a quantitative profile of patent litigation over the course of the entire period. From there the chapter develops a discursive chronological account, drawing upon the supporting case materials and opinions. Together, these elements trace how judges on the Ninth Circuit adapted national doctrines to meet local conditions and in the process shaped economic development in the region.

A Bird's Eye View

The appeals court issued opinions in 148 documented patent cases from 1891 through 1925, an average of four to five per year (see Table 5.1). The actual number of patent cases decided varied substantially from year to year and period to period. The court heard considerably more patent cases during the first and last decades of the study (see Table 5.2). In the opening years, this resulted in part from a pent-up demand prior to the moment of judicial reform. The surge in the last decade reflected national trends that saw an explosion of circuit appeals spanning all manner of subjects (including the notorious burdens imparted by the Volstead Act establishing Prohibition).

Both periods of intense activity corresponded with high numbers of patent litigants from outside the circuit. Over the course of the entire period, almost exactly half of the cases (75/148) included an outside litigant (see Table 5.5). During the 1890s, 32 of 48 involved such litigants. From 1916 through 1925, some 28 of 59 cases involved an outsider. Perhaps not surprisingly, these periods brought high levels of involvement from the Supreme Court. During the 1906–1915 decade, when only 10 of 37 cases involved an outsider, the High Court heard no patent appeals from the Ninth Circuit. Overall, about 15 percent of the

Table 5.1 Ninth Circuit patent appeals cases and outcomes, 1891–1925

	1891–1900	1901–1910	1911–1920	1921–1925	Total
Appeals Cases	43	26	50	29	148
District Court Action					
Patent Strengthened	27	13	26	10	76
Patent Weakened	16	13	24	19	72
Appeals Court Action					
Affirmed to Strengthen	15	7	14	3	39
Affirmed to Weaken	12	11	16	16	55
Reversed to Strengthen	4	2	8	3	17
Reversed to Weaken	12	6	12	7	37
Final Outcome					
Patent Strengthened	19	9	22	6	56
Patent Weakened	24	17	28	23	92

Table 5.2 Patent appeals cases per half decade, 1891–1925

Cases	1891–1895	1896–1900	1901–1905	1906–1910	1911–1915	1915–1920	1921–1925
40							
35							
						X	
30							
							X
25							
	X						
20					X		
		X		X			
15							
10			X				
5							
0							

patent appeal cases made it to the Supreme Court, which granted cert and issued opinions about half the time. This was about double the rate of review by the high court in all cases heard by the Ninth Circuit court of appeals (Frederick 1994). In the peak periods at the beginning and end of the study, appeals to the Supreme Court would have occurred at triple or more the ordinary rate.

Circuit court cases were not indexed by topic until 1931. Based on the limited information available regarding district and appeals court dockets, patent cases appear on average to have constituted about 5 percent of the overall appeals caseload (Frederick 1994). During periods of peak activity, however, they likely constituted something approaching 10 percent of opinions authored by particularly active judges. Raw case counts, moreover, almost certainly underestimate the amount of time and energy devoted to patents. By all accounts, patent cases were notorious time sinks. Many district judges on the Ninth Circuit ducked them entirely. Grounded in arcane technical details, patent cases often involved days or weeks of expert testimony and even field trips to observe machinery in action.

We can get a sense of the burden by counting the share of materials forwarded to the appeals court accounted for by patent cases (see Table 5.3). Over the course of the entire period, patent appeals generated about 10 percent of this material, well over double the average amount per appeals case. During the busy periods with large numbers of outside litigants, this volume rose even higher, accounting for in excess of 15 percent of the forwarded material (see Table 5.4).

Table 5.3 Appeals court documents devoted to patent cases, 1891–1925

Years	Total Volumes	Patent Volumes	%	Patent Cases	Volumes/ Patent Case
1891–1895	42 7	8	18.6	24	0.325
1896–1900	83	10.3	12.4	19	0.542
1901–1905	225	11.5	5.1	9	1.278
1906–1910	272	23.8	8.8	17	1.400
1911–1915	369	24.8	6.7	20	1.240
1916–1920	275	46.4	16.9	32	1.450
1921–1925	194	25.6	13.2	27	0.948
Total	1,460	150.2	10.3	148	1.105

Table 5.4 Share of case materials devoted to patents, 1891–1925

%	1891–1895	1896–1900	1901–1905	1906–1910	1911–1915	1921–1925	1921–1925
20							
	X						
18							
						X	
16							
14							
							X
12		X					
10							
				X			
8							
					X		
6							
			X				
4							
2							
0							

Table 5.5 Appeals Court outcomes of litigants from outside Ninth Circuit

Year	Cases	Outsider Wins	(On Appeal)	Local Wins	(On Appeal)
1896-1900	10	1	(0)	9	(2)
1901-1905	5	2	(1)	3	(0)
1906-1910	4	2	(0)	2	(0)
1911-1915	6	0	(0)	6	(1)
1916-1920	13	2	(1)	11	(2)
1921-1925	15	7	(1)	8	(2)
Total	75	20	(5)	55	(13)

Clearly, these were high-stakes cases that could bear extraordinary amounts of discovery costs. The biggest of them were, without question, among the most expensive trials ever conducted on the circuit. Even the most routine patent dispute could easily generate 1,000 pages of supporting documents. Those involving weightier matters, such as refining methods used in the Butte copper mining industry, Marconi radio, petroleum drilling, hydraulic engineering, and various agricultural processing industries, could generate ten times that amount.

No matter what the stakes, cases came to the appeals court through one of two channels. Either a patent holder who had sued another party for infringement and lost appealed to have the patent strengthened, or a convicted or enjoined infringer appealed to have the patent weakened. The 148 cases were split almost evenly between the two types: 76 times an infringer sought to have a patent weakened; 72 times patent holders sought to have their rights restored (see Table 5.1).

The two groups met with dramatically different outcomes. Alleged infringers who sought to weaken patents succeeded almost half the time (37 of 76). Essentially, an accused infringer had a fifty-fifty chance of prevailing upon appeal. Patent holders who had seen their patents weakened at the district court, by contrast, succeeded only one time in four (17 of 72). Over the course of the period, patent rights were thus significantly weakened by the appeals court. Patent holders came to the appeals court holding the advantage at district 76 times, infringers 72 times. By the time the appeals court was finished, the record favored patent holders just 56 times and alleged infringers 92 times.

These patterns prevailed, with some variation in strength, across the entire period. In every decade, reversals worked significantly to the advantage of alleged infringers, so that when the dust had settled, the number of patents weakened by the legal process outnumbered those strengthened. Even in the 1920s, the one decade in which patent holders entered appeals courtrooms already at a significant collective disadvantage, they emerged from the appeals process with their rights further diminished.

The tendency of the appeals court to weaken patents was, to considerable degree, intrinsic to the patent system. Because appeals judges were essentially free to reconsider the validity of the patent in question, based on their own reading of the facts (including, in many instances, evidence that had come to light since the district ruling), patent holders effectively faced double jeopardy. They could lose, moreover, without giving up their rights entirely. More typically, they would have their claims narrowed or limited in scope, or have an accounting of damage compensation due them reduced to their detriment. Alleged infringers thus had strong incentives to challenge the district court rulings. Patent holders who had lost at district, on the other hand, faced stiff odds of finding relief. They must defend or restore the validity of their patent, while also establishing infringement and specifying damages. Perhaps it is not surprising that they failed more than three-quarters of the time.

While these odds held quite steady across time, they varied considerably depending on whether the litigant resided within the Ninth Circuit or came from outside. (Typically, outside litigators at the appeals court were aggrieved patent holders, but in a few instances—such as a series of cases involving phonograph horns—they were alleged infringers doing business in the West.) *Of the 75 cases involving outsiders, the local parties prevailed 55 times (73 percent)* (see Table 5.5). In 42 of these 55 cases (77 percent), the appeals court affirmed the lower court. Thirteen times, an appeals panel worsened things for an outsider. *Only five times, in 47 opportunities, did the appeals court reverse a judgement to the benefit of an outsider who had lost at the district level.* The overall reverse rate of just 24 percent in cases involving outsiders lagged well behind the overall reverse rate of 37 percent in all patent cases. The appeals court essentially affirmed, and mildly accentuated, the harsh treatment of outsiders at the district level.

Isolating the 75 cases with outside litigants sheds further light on the 73 disputes between litigants residing within the Ninth Circuit (see Table 5.6). The most striking result is the overall balance. On 28 occasions the patent holder prevailed (including eight times through reversal on appeal); on 26 occasions the patent holder lost (including seven times on reversal on appeal); and on 19 occasions the appeals court modified a lower court ruling in what amounted to a split decision. The 15 clear reversals and 19 modifications, all of which can be classified as reversals to at least some degree, amount to a reverse rate of 47 percent (34 of 73). Appeals panels were thus much more likely to intervene in cases involving Ninth Circuit litigants exclusively than in those involving an outsider.

Table 5.6 Appeals Court outcomes in cases involving only local litigants

Year	Cases	Inventor Wins*	(On Appeal)	Inventor Loses	(On Appeal)	Split Decision**
1891–1895	2	0	(0)	1	(1)	1
1896–1900	9	3	(0)	3	(0)	3
1901–1905	4	1	(1)	2	(1)	1
1906–1910	13	6	(0)	4	(3)	3
1911–1915	14	8	(3)	6	(0)	0
1916–1920	19	9	(4)	6	(1)	4
Total	73	28	(8)	26	(7)	19

*Inventor = Patent Holder

**Split Decision = ruling with no clear winner

As discussed more fully in the sections to follow, this portrait by numbers is highly suggestive of a court that treated outsiders differently, but did so more starkly at various moments in time than others. The court was much more balanced in its treatment of cases involving internal disputes within the Ninth Circuit. To some extent, this balance reflected outcomes at the district courts, which did not dramatically favor inventors or infringers. Yet the high reverse rates also indicate that the appeals court was much more inclined to meddle in these local cases. This tendency increased over time, as the appeals court came to function as something like an arbitrator or administrator among competing interests. Its willingness to assume this role manifested itself initially in cases arising at the Southern District of California, which from 1906 onward became the primary source of patent appeals cases on the Ninth Circuit (see Table 5.7).

Table 5.7 District of Origin of Appeals Cases and Reverse Rates, 1891–1925

Years	Appeals	Northern CA	Southern CA	Other Districts	Reversals	Rate (%)
1891–1900	43	37	3	3	15	32.6
1901–1910	26	10	12	4	10	37.0
1911–1920	50	14	21	15	17	34.7
1921–1925	29	10	11	8	10	34.5
Total	148	71	47	30	52	34.4

Table 5.8 Appeals outcomes by district of origin, 1911–1925

		Affirmed		Reversed	
District	**Cases**	**Strengthened**	**Weakened**	**Strengthened**	**Weakened**
Northern CA	24	13	7	2	2
Southern CA	32	7	16	4	5
Non-CA	23	0	10	5	8
Total	79	20	33	11	15

A decade later, a stream of prominent appeals from outside California further complicated the role of the appeals court. Remarkably, the appeals court reversed over half the time in these disputes, compared to just one-sixth of the cases originating in Northern California and a third of the cases from Southern California (see Table 5.8). These disparities among districts, combined with those involving outside and local litigants, drew critical scrutiny from the Supreme Court and triggered significant adjustments in Ninth Circuit patent litigation during the early twenties.

Explaining these variations and developments requires taking a closer look at particular cases, including those involving Supreme Court review. It also requires examining the proclivities of judges, which differed quite markedly and exerted varied influences across time. Such nuances are best understood through a more narrative account.

1891–1900: Marking Territory

During its initial decade, the revamped appeals court was dominated by disputes brought by outside litigants seeking to enforce their old patent rights. Their targets were usually established Bay Area general-purpose machine shops that supplied equipment for farmers, agricultural processors, mining interests, and builders of infrastructure such as street railways and wharves. Judge Joseph McKenna, the senior appeals judge (appointed one day prior to William Gilbert), was eager to accommodate the outsiders. Gilbert and his colleagues at the district courts, who frequently filled out appeals panels, resisted him. Often sitting in review of opinions issued and trials conducted by the inexperienced McKenna at district, they reversed him frequently (see Table 5.9 and Table 5.1).

Table 5.9 Participation of judges on appeals panels and outcomes when reversing, 1891–1925

Judge*	Reversals			Reversals		
	Panels	Weakened	Strengthened	Opinions	Weakened	Strengthened
McKenna (1892–1897)	13	1	0	7	1	0
Hanford (1892–1895)	6	4	1	3	3	0
Hawley (1892–1906)	31	6	3	6	0	0
Gilbert (1892–1925)	132	26	16	52	13	8
Ross (1892–1925)	85	18	12	28	6	2
Morrow (1892–1925)	43	14	2	16	4	0
Hunt (1911–1925)	58	8	10	15	2	3
Wolverton (1906–1925)	19	1	3	6	0	0
Dietrich (1913–1922)	8	3	2	3	1	2
Rudkin (1923–1925)	23	3	2	7	1	1

* Hanford, Hawley, Wolverton, and Dietrich were district court judges. Totals for Ross, Morrow, Hunt, and Rudkin include a few panels while serving as district court judges, prior to their appointments to the appeals court. Ross served at district from 1892 to 1895; Hunt from 1904 to 1911; Rudkin from 1911 to 1923; and Morrow from 1892 to 1897. Morrow continued to hear many patent cases at district for another decade after his appointment to the appeals court.

McKenna aided them by making a hash of things. He confused assignees with licensees.[5] He botched the rules of compensation for damages.[6] He wrongly prevented an alleged infringer from presenting evidence regarding his own subsequent patent.[7] He misread an opinion regarding a patent for canning equipment, interpreting it as providing pioneer status to an inventor associated with the American Can Company, when in actuality the court had declared a local rival as non-infringing.[8] He allowed the Brush Electric Company of Cleveland to excuse itself from a suit, leaving its local licensee in the lurch[9] and permitted the giant Singer Sewing Machine Company—a firm notorious for its manipulation of the patent system—to hide its identity from a jury.[10]

In fairness McKenna, like many other federal judicial appointees, had virtually no experience with patent law. His primary legal experience was as a district attorney to a small rural county. From 1885 until 1892, when President Harrison nominated him to the appeals slot, he had served in the House of Representatives, where he was a loyal lieutenant to Harrison and future president William McKinley, who chaired the House Ways and Means Committee. In 1897, to the surprise of virtually everyone, McKinley would nominate McKenna to fill the seat on the US Supreme Court vacated by the famous California jurist Stephen J. Field. McKenna's fellow appeals court judges, Gilbert and Erskine Ross (who President Grover Cleveland had promoted from the Southern District of California to the appeals court in 1895), openly opposed the nomination on grounds of incompetence. Gilbert went so far as to circulate a petition, signed by more than one hundred members of the West Coast bar (Frederick 1994).

It did not help McKenna that during his time on the appeals court he was hearing arguments from attorneys whose knowledge of patent law drastically exceeded his own. Two of them, Milton A. Wheaton and John H. Miller, had argued patent cases at the Supreme Court. As recently as 1888, during the same session of the Bell case, they had faced off against one another there, when Wheaton defended the pioneering Bay Area machine builder Joshua Hendy from charges of infringement.[11] The stance was typical of Wheaton. During the 1870s and 1880s, he had won notable victories, legendary in the annals of the California bar for the volume of evidence and magnitude of their returns (Shuck 1889, pp. 229–39). One involved the California inventor Nathan Spaulding,

[5] *Chauche v. Pare* 75 F. 283 (1896).

[6] *City of Seattle v. James McNamara* 81 F. 863 (1897).

[7] *Ransome v. Hyatt* 69 F. 148 (1895).

[8] *Norton v. Jensen* 49 F. 859 (1892); *Wheaton v. Norton* 70 F. 833 (1895); and *Norton v. Wheaton* 165 U.S. 518 (1897).

[9] *Brush Electric Corp. v. California Electric Light Co., et.al.* (1892) 9CHRIS 8:7-408.

[10] *Herman Cramer v. Willis B. Fry* 59 F. 74 (1893); and *Herman Cramer v. Singer Manufacturing Company* 93 F. 636 (1899).

[11] *Hendy v. Golden States Miners' Iron Works, et.al.* 8 S. Ct. 1275 (1888).

who had developed a method for replacing saw teeth. A series of victories earned Spaulding and Wheaton a small fortune in royalty payments from saw mill operators around the country. Another case of note preserved the rights of San Francisco clothier Levi Strauss to make clothing from duck cloth bound by rivets. Wheaton's avid defense of Western interests frequently brought him headlong into conflict with an exasperated McKenna. A series of cases involving excavator patents sparked particularly vitriolic exchanges between them.[12]

When the federal courts were reorganized in 1891, Wheaton had several patent matters pending before the Supreme Court. Two especially prominent cases, resolved in 1895, dealt with leather belting and cast iron pulleys used to power machinery in factories. In addition to their economic significance, each case addressed issues of fundamental importance to patent law of the period. One clarified rules involving damage payments due to infringed patent holders who had failed to establish clear license fees.[13] The opinion limited their claims severely, and although that outcome worked to the detriment of his client, Wheaton wasted no time in exploiting it to his benefit in cases before the Ninth Circuit (where McKenna initially remained ignorant of the new rules).[14]

Wheaton secured a better outcome for his client in the second case, when he successfully defended a Bay Area machinery builder from charges of infringement brought by Philip Medart, a St. Louis inventor who claimed to have developed a new way of manufacturing strong, lightweight pulleys.[15] The highly cited case touched upon basic issues regarding the validity of patents and the scope of their claims. The High Court deprived Medart of his claims because he had failed to disclose details of a piece of machinery deployed in manufacturing the pulleys. Without those details, Medart was left trying to patent an unspecified process that no one could replicate. The court could only conclude that he had achieved the end—better pulleys—through superior workmanship, rather than through either a novel apparatus or a novel sequence of operations, or what courts termed a "combination of elements." To deserve a patent, the specification needed to convey how arrangements of mechanical components or steps in a process were more than a mere *aggregation* of elements. The patent must show how the components or steps interacted in a distinctive manner. The inventor must further disclose at least one particular way of implementing that effect. Inventors such as Medart wished to do this in a manner that gave them broad coverage over all manner of such combinations, under what courts referred to as

[12] *Bowers v. Von Schmidt* 63 F. 572 (1894); *Bowers v. San Francisco Bridge Co.* 69 F. 640(1895); and *Von Schmidt v. Bowers* 80 F. 121 (1897).

[13] *Coupe v. Royer* 155 U.S. 565 (1895).

[14] *City of Seattle v. James McNamara* 81 F. 863 (1897).

[15] *Risdon Iron and Locomotive Works v. Medart* 158 U.S. 68 (1895).

the "doctrine of equivalents." If interpreted broadly, these equivalents could constitute a "pioneer patent," such as that awarded to Bell in the recently completed telephone cases.

The issues raised by the *Medart* case, and others like it, persisted for a generation or more. They would be addressed and clarified by the Supreme Court in famous opinions such as *Morley v. Lancaster*[16] (a case cited frequently by attorney Miller on the Ninth Circuit) and the exhaustive 1898 case *Boyden v. Westinghouse*,[17] which ended three decades of dominance by famed railroad air brake inventor George Westinghouse. Decades later, Chief Justice Taft would return to these same issues in *Eibel* (1923), a case involving Fourdrinier papermaking machines.[18] The matter of combinations, aggregations, and equivalents, all of which were subject to broad interpretive latitude, came up time and again in cases involving finished goods (everything from horse carts to advertising envelopes, whose arrangement of three components was deemed a synergistic combination rather than a mere aggregation) and the processes used to produce them. In case after case, involving all sorts of technologies, attorneys and judges evoked these concepts.

The regular presence of such nationally prominent attorneys as Wheaton and Miller indicates that Ninth Circuit judges, while perhaps inexperienced in patent law, were brought up to speed with established and evolving doctrine. During this busy first decade, the two seasoned attorneys appeared before 34 of the 43 appeals panels in patent cases (79 percent), including 13 occasions in which they opposed one another. When facing other attorneys, they prevailed 18 of 21 times. By the time Wheaton died, in 1907, the tally stood at 44 of 60 cases, with the two combatants splitting 19 head-to-head confrontations and prevailing 20 of 25 times against other attorneys. Clearly, Wheaton and Miller had a large hand in implementing patent law on the Ninth Circuit.[19]

The extent of their influence is apparent in a pair of watershed cases that in many respects defined patent jurisprudence on the Ninth Circuit during this initial decade. Each case reached the Supreme Court in 1895, after being heard on appeal by a Ninth Circuit panel that reversed McKenna. In the first, Miller defended the Vulcan Iron Works, an esteemed Oakland manufacturer, against a prominent Cincinnati firm that built equipment used in large band saw mills.[20] Miller won on appeal, and the Cincinnatians appealed to the high court. Wheaton

[16] *Morley Sewing Machine v. Lancaster* 129 U.S. 263 (1889).

[17] *Boyden v. Westinghouse* 170 U.S. 537 (1898).

[18] *Eibel Process Co. v. Minnesota and Ontario Paper Co.* 261 U.S. 45 (1923).

[19] Miller, who was a generation younger than Wheaton, remained a prominent figure in patent cases throughout the period studied here. He was counsel in more than half the cases in the Northern District of California and appeared increasingly in the Southern District, where he often faced off against Raymond Ives Blakeslee and Frederick Lyon.

[20] *Vulcan Iron Works v. Smith, Myers, and Schnier* 62 F. 444 (1894).

faced a similar predicament in a case involving his own patents for canning equipment. (In addition to his legal skills, Wheaton was also an accomplished inventor.) The Norton brothers, holders of patents that formed the basis of giant American Can Company, sued for infringement.[21] Wheaton lost at district but eventually obtained a favorable reading from the newly promoted Erskine Ross, along with district judges William Morrow of Northern California and Thomas Hawley of Nevada, who sat on most patent case panels (see Table 5.9). Again the appeals court reversed McKenna, whose misinterpretation of an earlier canning case had formed the basis of the lower court decision. The error confounded appeals judges and delayed their ruling for two years. Norton's exasperated attorney, none other than John Miller, cried foul in his writ to the Supreme Court. In a clear knock at the recently appointed Ross, who wrote the opinion, Miller attributed the appeals outcome solely to a "change in personnel."

The Supreme Court sat on the two writs for over a year, until February 1897, when it issued a joint opinion favoring the two Bay Area firms and denying writ to the outside patent holders.[22] The ruling came down from the high court just as McKenna, whose judgements had been reversed, was about to depart for his new appointment in Washington. The ruling offered a vote of confidence to the appeals judges who McKenna left behind in California. In addition to Gilbert and Ross, their ranks now included Morrow, tapped by McKinley to replace McKenna and fill the post many thought he should have held all along. Although Morrow primarily heard patent cases at the district level until 1908, while Hawley and later Judge Charles Wolverton of the Oregon District filled out appeals panels, he, Ross, and Gilbert would impose their stamp on patent litigation on the Ninth Circuit for nearly three decades, until Ross retired in 1925 (see Table 5.9).

The 1897 rulings by the high court also went a long way toward discouraging appeals from outsiders, which fell precipitously over the next decade (see Table 5.5). Virtually all of the early cases, some 22 of 24 through 1895, had involved outside litigants. Had the appeals court affirmed every outcome from the districts, outsiders would have prevailed 10 times and lost 12. Once the appeals panels had finished their work, only 6 of the 22 outsiders had prevailed. Largely, this was the result of Gilbert and others reversing McKenna at district. During the next five years, with McKenna gone to Washington, outsiders lost nine of ten times. Seven times they lost at district, and twice the appeals court reversed district opinions that had gone in their favor. In no instance did the appeals court reverse on behalf of an outsider. These outcomes contrasted markedly with those in the nine cases involving only Ninth Circuit litigants. In these internal disputes,

[21] *Wheaton v. Norton* 70 F. 833 (1895); and *Jensen Can-Filling Machine Co. v. Norton* 67 F. 236 (1895).

[22] *Smith v. Vulcan Iron Works* and *Norton v. Wheaton* 165 U.S. 518 (1897).

inventors lost three times, won three times, and split the decision three times (see Table 5.6). The contrasting outcomes in the two types of cases marked Ninth Circuit patent litigation with a distinctive regional stamp, one which would persist and evolve over the decades to come.

1901–1917: Alternative Regimes

At the dawn of the new century, this West Coast patent regime appeared secure. The Supreme Court seemingly blessed the approach when it denied writ to outsiders Overweight Elevator[23] and American Sales Book,[24] national firms who had lost suits against alleged Ninth Circuit infringers. With few outsiders bringing suit, the number of patent cases heard on appeal dwindled to just nine in five years (see Table 5.2).

This was, however, the proverbial lull before the storm. In reality, the appeals court was passing into a new phase, as it wrestled with how patent law might shape competition in several of the Pacific Coast's emergent industries. The struggle, which resonated with an emergent discourse in national politics and at the Supreme Court, brought to light conflicting visions of innovation and markets. On the Ninth Circuit, these alternative approaches came to be embodied in differences between two strong-willed appeals judges, Republican William Gilbert of San Francisco and Democrat Erskine Ross of Los Angeles. As the flow of patent cases picked up in 1906, the two handled virtually all the work. They staked out alternatives that drew an increasingly sharp distinction between patent regimes in the Northern and Southern Districts of California.

As is often the case, the initial lull actually hinted at a new drift. As soon became clear, the Supreme Court had not fully embraced the Ninth Circuit's brusque handling of outsiders. The justices sent notice in 1904, when they reversed a 1901 judgement by Morrow at district holding Singer to be infringing a local inventor.[25] The following year, an appeals panel itself reversed Morrow's ruling at district and deemed local asparagus growers to be infringing American Can.[26] Miller had finally got the better of Wheaton in a canning case. More significantly, a national supplier had gained a foothold in one of California's lucrative agricultural processing industries.

[23] *Overweight Counterbalance Elevator Co. v. Improved Order of Red Men's Hall Ass'n* 94 F. 155 (1899). Denied cert. 19 S. Ct. 886 (1899).

[24] *American Sales Book v. Josephus Bullivant* 117 F. 255 (1902). Denied cert. 190 U.S. 560 (1903).

[25] *Singer v. Cramer* 192 U.S. 265 (1904), reversing *Singer v. Cramer* 109 F. 652 (1901), in which Gilbert, Ross, and Hawley had affirmed Morrow.

[26] *American Can Co. v. Hickmott Asparagus* 142 F. 73 (1905).

Several other cases from the period raised a similar prospect. Two years earlier, the Northern District had considered a patent suit brought by a small packer of dried fruit against the powerful United States Consolidated Seedless Raisin Company (USCSRCO). The large firm had licensed patents for raisin-seeding machines developed at a plant located in the Central Valley town of Fresno. Funded partly by local interests, but with support from New York affiliates who licensed machines and marketed raisins in the East, USCSRCO looked to leverage its patents by regulating entry into the booming new industry. The firm was quickly tagged the Raisin Trust by growers who felt dependent upon USCSRCO to reach markets outside the Golden State.[27] The firm also raised the hackles of independent fruit processors. Some challenged the legality of USCSRCO's contractual arrangements and patent licensing agreements, which they deemed in violation of antitrust laws because they effectively fixed prices.[28] The case arrived at the appeals court just after the Supreme Court had issued a fundamental ruling on this matter in the *Bement* case (Hovenkamp 2015).[29] The justices held that such contractual agreements did not violate the Sherman Act. Citing this precedent, Gilbert promptly reversed the district court and absolved USCSRCO.

The 1903 case, the first of several involving the Raisin Trust, pointed to a set of issues regarding the relationships among patents, contracts, and laws governing trade practices and commerce. These matters arose in another series of cases at the time involving suppliers of wooden pipe to Pacific Coast cities. The Supreme Court again had to clarify issues regarding contractual arrangements, this time between a licensee and a patentee who infringed the licensed patent and refused to enter suits, and determine whether the matter fell under contract or patent law. The lingering ambiguity regarding ownership of the rights left Ross free to circumvent both parties and grant the City of Seattle carte blanche to purchase pipe from any supplier.[30]

Similar issues arose in a prominent turn-of-the-century case involving makers of patent medicines based on extract of fig syrup. In the course of a dispute involving patent and trademark rights, attorney Miller discovered that the established supplier (the plaintiff) had in fact been perpetrating a fraud. His elixir contained no fig extract. Such fraud, argued Miller, deprived him of protection

[27] 9CHRIS 608:7-296 contains extensive documentation on the origins and explosive growth of the seedless raisin industry, including an affidavit from the founders of USCSRCO. Woeste (1998) offers an excellent treatment of the legal efforts by raisin growers to gain leverage against processors by forming cooperatives, but does not discuss the extensive patent fight, which was waged primarily by small independent processors who had supported the growers' cooperatives.

[28] *United States Consolidated Seedless Raisin Co. v. Griffin-Skelly Co.* 126 F. 364 (1903).

[29] *E. Bement & Sons v. Nat'l Harrow Co.* 186 U.S. 70, 91 (1902). See Hovenkamp (2015).

[30] *Excelsior Wooden Pipe Co. v. Allen* 104 F. 553 (1900); *v. Pacific Bridge Co.* 185 U.S. 282 (1902); and *v. City of Seattle* 117 F. 140 (1902). This was one of nearly a dozen infringement suits brought by a patent holder against a West Coast municipality between 1891 and 1925; the patent holder lost every time. In many instances, the inventor was from outside the Ninth Circuit.

under patent law. Morrow disagreed at district, as did Gilbert on appeal, but Ross issued a rare dissent supporting Miller. The Supreme Court took the case and agreed with Ross, while expressing its hope that the California assembly (and the US Congress) would join the parade of states passing legislation to this effect. Congress would heed the call in 1906, with passage of the Food and Drug Act.[31]

Each of these cases pointed to ways in which patent law was linked to other legal measures intended to shape markets and govern competition. These ties grew ever more apparent in the Ninth Circuit after 1906, as patent litigation again kicked into high gear. A surge of cases arising from the previously quiescent southern district of California prompted Ross to assert himself as never before. Over the course of the next five years, he sat on every panel and wrote half the opinions, with Gilbert handling the others (see Table 5.9). The cases from Southern California, where Democrat Olin Wellborn was the sole federal district judge, were largely concentrated on three areas: light manufactures; oil-well drilling supplies; and agricultural processing equipment. The latter two subjects were especially dear to Ross, a citrus grower and packer who in 1909 married the widow Ida Hancock, owner of some of the city's most productive oil fields.

Panels consisting of Gilbert, Ross, and often Morrow produced a series of opinions aimed at introducing an element of competition into these three sectors. The appeals court affirmed lower court rulings that narrowed claims of patent holders producing well equipment, including those of a pioneering firm that had participated in drilling some 500 wells.[32] The appeals court also cleared the way for several prominent West Coast machine builders (including Hendy, Vulcan, and Risdon) to manufacture ore tables, hundreds of which were deployed in mining districts of the West.[33] In an especially telling opinion, Ross (with support from Morrow) reversed the lower court and deprived the Llewellyn Iron Works, LA's most heralded general purpose manufacturer, of a patent for sewer pipe fixtures. Llewellyn's admirable record of commercial success in the fixture market, Ross suggested, resulted from its superior workmanship. It should compete on quality, without dependence on spurious claims of novelty backed by patent monopoly.[34]

This market-oriented approach, emphasizing process improvement among competitors rather than the pursuit of discrete patented innovations, was evident in the several cases involving agricultural processors. Major cases involving three regional agricultural products—walnuts, sugar beets, and raisins—came to the appeals court in successive years, 1908 through 1910. Ross issued another rare dissent

[31] *Clinton E. Worden & Co. v. California Fig Syrup Co.* 23 S. Ct. 161 (1903); 102 F. 334 (1900) at appeal; and 95 F. 132 (1898) at district.

[32] *Hardison v. Brinkman* 156 F. 962 (1907).

[33] *Wilfley v. New Standard Connector Co.* 164 F. 421 (1908).

[34] *F.E. Morton v. Llewellyn* 164 F. 693 (1908).

in the first of them, which involved methods for bleaching walnuts with acid to obtain uniform color. Anderson-Barngrover, a prominent San Jose agricultural supply company, had obtained a patent covering bleaching equipment utilizing a "weak acid" bath. The notion clearly offended Ross, who saw nothing novel in a process walnut growers had long practiced on their own. In a classic example of the sort of strict construction that characterized his jurisprudence, Ross noted that the patent specified a "weak" acid, when the proper term was "dilute." He further suggested that the Anderson-Barngrover technique still relied on the judgement of the growers, who must adjust the actual concentration and time of exposure to account for the particular quality of their nuts.[35]

The sugar beet case addressed an industry that had rapidly transformed tens of thousands of acres of Southern California, including a broad swath running from Long Beach to the southeast frontiers of Orange County.[36] The industry was a political lightning rod. The domestic beet industry took advantage of protection from large tariffs on imported cane sugar, used by the American Sugar trust centered in Philadelphia (the subject of the famous *E.C. Knight* antitrust case). The Southern California beet industry had been pioneered by the Los Alamitos Sugar Company, with funds provided by the controversial "Copper King" William A. Clark. Los Alamitos owned more than 10,000 acres, which it leased to tenant farmers, who brought their beets to a central refinery in horse-drawn carts. During the lengthy harvest season, a perpetual stream of carts arrived at the mill. An inventor, Timothy Carroll, had devised a mechanical means of unloading these carts directly into rail cars. Around 1908, several rival mills had sprung up to challenge Los Alamitos. At least one had paid for the vital innovation, a fact Ross emphasized when affirming Wellborn's judgement that the incumbent Los Alamitos had infringed and must compensate the inventor as had its rival processors.[37]

This blow to the incumbent sugar beet processor preceded a pair of opinions regarding USCSRCO, the raisin pioneer, which had now leveraged its patents into an empire. Disgruntled growers and independent processors sought to escape its reach, and USCSRCO responded with infringement suits. The trust scored a significant victory in 1910 in a suit against Kings County growers, when Gilbert (with assistance from district judge Charles Wolverton of Oregon) declared its seeding machine a pioneer invention.[38] A year earlier, however, independent processor E.L. Chaddock had scored a victory of its own, when its experiments with alternative seeding machines were deemed non-infringing

35 *Fullerton Walnut Growers Assn. v. Anderson-Barngrover Mfg. Co.* 166 F. 443, 452 (1908).

36 "Wealth in Sugar Beets," *Santa Ana Daily Register*, 9, no. 259 (1 October 1914): 7. historicsouthernsantaana.wordpress.com/businesses/farming-sugar-beets/.

37 *Los Alamitos Sugar Co. et.al. v. Timothy Carroll* 173 F. 280 (1909).

38 *Kings County Raisin & Fruit Co. v. U.S. Consolidated Seedless Raisin Co.* 182 F. 59 (1910).

and permissible under its contract with USCSRCO.[39] In 1912, the appeals court would deal the Raisin Trust another blow. Judge Morrow affirmed Wellborn's ruling denying USCSRCO's claims to possess controlling patents over the process for drying grapes as well as seeding them.[40] Together, these rulings trimmed USCSRCO's reach substantially.

While the appeals court inserted itself into matters of prime importance to Southern California agriculture, another set of cases arose from among machinery builders of the Bay Area. Three cases involved businesses of great significance in this "high tech" cluster of machine shops and foundries on the shores of San Francisco Bay. The first involved the Pelton Water Wheel Company, a venerable manufacturer of hydraulic equipment used in the mining and electric power industries. Marketing sophisticated machinery in mining districts around the globe, Pelton was arguably the preeminent industrial enterprise in the Golden State. A lower court decision by Judge Morrow had opened the firm to competition from local upstart Abner Doble, whose designs Morrow deemed not to have infringed Pelton patents covering so-called Hurdy-Gurdy water wheels. Gilbert, again with help from Wolverton, affirmed the characteristically stingy Morrow.[41]

The other two cases went quite differently at district. In each, newly appointed District Judge William Van Fleet had granted pioneer status to a firm engaged in fierce competition with another. The first case involved frequent litigator Risdon Iron and Locomotive Works. It had acquired rights to an Australian patent for dredges that reclaimed fine gold particles from river silt. The dredges, which pumped water actively through a set of fine filters, had sparked a boom by enabling dredging companies to offset the cost of dredging with revenue from the precious metals, whose price was rocketing. Dredging operators could reclaim land at virtually no expense. An appeals panel agreed that the admittedly inexperienced Van Fleet, confused by expert witnesses spinning tales about miraculous hydraulic flows, had erred in granting strong rights to Risdon. The appeals judges seized the opportunity to curtail them, although in characteristic fashion, Ross did so more severely through his narrow reading of the claims than did Gilbert (with Morrow), who issued a separate concurring opinion more generous to Risdon.[42]

39 *U.S. Consolidated Seedless Raisin Co. v. Chaddock* 173 F. 577 (1909). USCSRCO denied writ 215 U.S. 591 (1910).

40 *U.S. Consolidated Seedless Raisin Co. v. Selma Fruit Co.* 195 F. 264 (1912). Morrow's opinion leaned heavily upon *Risdon v. Medart*, the case successfully argued by Wheaton at the Supreme Court in 1895, as discussed earlier.

41 *Pelton v. Doble* 151 F. 29 (1907).

42 *Risdon v. Western Engineering* 174 F. 224 (1909). Also see 9CHRIS 538:7-460, which includes an amicus brief filed by attorney Miller and an extensive discussion of the "selective theory of hydraulic action" spun by expert witness William Smyth, as well as Van Fleet's blatant errors in instructing the jury.

The same trio also reversed Van Fleet in a case involving two pioneering manufacturers of steam tractors and other farm equipment. The two firms—Best Tractor Company of Oakland and Holt Manufacturing Company of Stockton—were frequent litigators of significant accomplishment and ambition. (Holt would soon be rechristened Caterpillar, after its famed tread design, and open a second factory in Peoria, Illinois.) The patents in question involved hydraulic systems utilizing steam, compressed air, or other pressurized fluids to power various components of combines. Again under heavy influence of expert witnesses, Van Fleet had granted Best pioneer rights covering all applications of hydraulic power and ordered a large damage payment from Holt. Ross reversed emphatically, declaring unequivocally that Van Fleet had erred by not instructing the jury that Best did not deserve pioneer status. The appeals court ordered a rehearing, before which the tractor companies settled their differences.[43]

The net effect of these rulings was clear. The appeals judges, led by Ross and Morrow, had looked to foster competition among the leading technological enterprises of Northern California, just as they had looked to promote competition among the emergent Southern California suppliers of equipment used in the oil and agricultural processing sectors. Yet one could also perceive in this flurry of important cases an emerging split between two visions of how that competition might occur. One would involve weak patent rights, with firms competing primarily on workmanship, service, and other qualities. The other would involve awards of strong patent rights, with firms seeking to win inventive contests and establish significant barriers to entry.

This contrast in visions (and patent regimes) came out in sharp relief in the years that followed. District Judge Van Fleet in San Francisco pursued a dramatically different path from the paths of Judge Olin Wellborn and his successor Oscar Trippet in Los Angeles. Patent cases from each venue percolated up regularly to the appeals judges for review (see Tables 5.7 and 5.8). Ross himself went silent, perhaps owing to the fatal illness of his new bride, who died in 1913. He sat on panels, especially those arising from the Southern District, but wrote no opinions. Without his resistance, Van Fleet generated an uninterrupted stream of opinions assigning strong rights to one party. Many of these were appealed by well-funded alleged infringers, often from outside the Ninth Circuit, who met with disappointment (see Table 5.5). In every instance, some dozen cases in all from 1911 through 1917, the appeals court (usually with Gilbert or Wolverton writing the opinion) affirmed Van Fleet's grant of strong patent rights.

These cases covered a wide range of products. A few still involved manufactured producers goods. Abner Doble received what many observers deemed a

[43] *Holt Manufacturing Co. v. Best Tractor Co.* 172 F. 409 (1909). See also secondary sources on Caterpillar, including Holt-Best patent battles leading to merger in 1925.

preposterously generous award in a suit against Pelton involving nozzles used to propel water wheels.[44] Later, Van Fleet assigned strong rights to West Coast manufacturers of digester doors,[45] refining filters,[46] and irrigation gates.[47] Two other rulings, granting strong rights to pump builder Byron Jackson, were settled just prior to appeal.[48] Other cases before Van Fleet reflected the emergence of consumer goods and associated commercial activities. They involved products ranging from decorative cornices[49] and folding Murphy beds[50] (an archetypal feature of West Coast residential architecture), to receipt books[51] and mailing envelopes,[52] to such consumer appliances as automobile windshields and phonograph horns.[53] Time and again, these opinions bestowed strong patent rights on a California firm, often at the expense of a national firm, including such giants as Heinz (who used the envelopes to promote its 57 varieties) and the phonograph makers Victor, Columbia, and American, East Coast suppliers of the most sensational home appliance of the day.

This run of strong rights awarded at the Northern District stood in sharp contrast to appeals cases arising from the Southern District and other states. During these same years, 1911 through 1917, eight of ten cases originating in the Southern District resulted in the weakening of a patent. In only one trivial instance did the appeals court affirm a Southern District opinion that had strengthened a patent. On the sole occasion that an appeals panel reversed a lower court and strengthened a patent, it almost immediately took steps to reverse course and limit those rights severely.

This instance involved the Stebler Sorter, a vibrating table with ridges and slots used by citrus packers to sort fruit by grade. Again the case brought a machine builder, allied with an association of fruit processors, into conflict with fruit growers and smaller independent packers. Ross, himself an unaligned citrus grower and packer, sat out the case, but Morrow stepped up to adjudicate a series of disputes that ultimately generated four distinct opinions. After a panel headed

[44] *The Pelton Water-Wheel Co. v. Abner Doble Co.* 190 F. 760 (1911). For comments deriding the opinion, see transcript of *Byron Jackson Iron Works v. United Iron Works* 197 F. 44 (1911), a district court case heard by Van Fleet regarding centrifugal pumps, available in 9CHRIS. See also *Byron Jackson v. Krogh* (1917), another district case available in 9CHRIS that apparently was settled before appeal.

[45] *Pederson v. Patrick F. Dundon* 220 F. 309 (1915).

[46] *Moore Filter Co. v. John L. Taugher* 239 F. 105 (1917).

[47] *Frank P. Snow v. Kellar-Thomason Co.* 241 F. 119 (1917).

[48] *Byron Jackson Iron Works v. United Iron Works* 197 F. 44 (1911) and *Byron Jackson v. Krogh* (1917), available via 9CHRIS.

[49] *Andrew Beyrle v. San Francisco Cornice Co.* 181 F. 692 (1912).

[50] *Marshall & Stearns & Co. v. Murphy* 199 F. 772 (1912).

[51] *John Kitchen, jr. Co. v. Alexander Levinson* 188 F. 658 (1911).

[52] *Heinz v. Cohn* 207 F. 547 (1913).

[53] *Sherman Clay v. Searchlight Horn* 214 F. 86, 99 (1914); *Pacific Phonograph v. Searchlight Horn* 214 F. 257 (1914); *Sherman Clay & Co. v. Searchlight Horn* 225 F. 497 (1915); *Columbia Gramophone Co. v. Searchlight Horn* 236 F. 135 (1916).

by Judge Frank Dietrich of Idaho affirmed a lower court ruling granting Stebler broad rights,[54] Morrow blocked the patent holder from pursuing infringement suits against growers who obtained sorters from a rival manufacturer.[55] The ruling effectively segmented markets, framing a competition among equipment suppliers, while leaving growers and packers free to obtain equipment without fear of infringement suits. Morrow and the appeals court later endorsed a court-appointed master's report awarding Stebler minimal damages, based solely on sales lost to the rival equipment manufacturer, without considering the benefits packers obtained from using the sorters.[56] When a defiant Stebler pressed suit against growers, an appeals panel delivered a swift and sharp rebuke that deemed him in contempt and directed him to repay growers all legal expenses, plus additional damages for their troubles.[57]

That chastening opinion was written by Appeals Judge William H. Hunt Jr., something of a new voice in patent matters. Promoted to the appeals post by President Taft in 1911, after seven years at the Montana district, Hunt had recently returned to the Ninth Circuit following several years of service on Taft's ill-fated Commerce Court. Taft had envisioned the Commerce Court as a place of legal refuge. It would provide business interests with a forum where they could have disputes involving complex matters refereed by a permanent panel of expert judges familiar with arcane elements of commercial law, such as finance, regulation, and (if Taft had his way) patents. The court had become a ready target for Democratic critics, who viewed it as having erected an improper barrier between business interests and those looking to exercise what they deemed the public interest. With passage of the Clayton Antitrust Act and creation of the politically appointed Federal Trade Commission eminent, Taft's Democratic successor Woodrow Wilson had eliminated the controversial Commerce Court (Skowronek 1982; Sklar 1988).[58]

Hunt's return to the West, and his bold intervention in the ongoing Stebler dispute, in many respects heralded a fundamental turn in patent litigation on the Ninth Circuit. Over the decade to come, Hunt would hear virtually every patent appeals case and issue opinions in many of the most important ones, especially those involving outside parties. To a considerable degree, he displaced Gilbert as the dominant influence upon Ninth Circuit patent law (see Table 5.9). In the process, he imposed a new, more administrative approach to the subject, characterized by the ongoing refereeing of disputes among competing parties, rather than the anointing of clear winners and losers. The approach was reminiscent of

[54] *Stebler v. Riverside Heights Orange Growers Assn.* 205 F. 735 (1913).
[55] *Stebler* v. *Riverside Heights Orange Growers Assn.* 214 F. 550 (1914).
[56] *Riverside Heights Orange Growers Assn. v. Stebler* 240 F. 714 (1917).
[57] *Pomona Fruit Growers Exch. v. Stebler* 241 F. 123 (1917).
[58] FJC for specifics.

what Taft had envisioned for the Commerce Court. Perhaps not coincidentally, Hunt's efforts would unfold with significant input from the Supreme Court, a body stacked with justices appointed by the former president, and over which Taft himself would preside as Chief Justice beginning in July 1921.

1916–1925: Administrative Patent Justice

While instrumental in this transformative decade, Hunt alone was not responsible for the emergence the new regime. The decade was marked above all by a surge in patent litigation, which taxed the entire Ninth Circuit to a degree not seen since the days of Joseph McKenna (see Table 5.1). The appeals court heard 32 patent cases from 1916 through 1920 and another 27 from 1921 through 1925. The surge was driven by the return of outside litigants, continued growth of activity in Los Angeles, and a sudden rise in cases coming from outside California.

The latter phenomenon, triggered by a spate of four significant appeals in 1914, exerted a disproportionate influence on Ninth Circuit patent jurisprudence. In contrast to what occurred in cases originating from California, appeals panels displayed a marked tendency to reverse rulings from these other districts. All told, they reversed 13 times in 23 opportunities between 1911 and 1925, as many times as they did in 56 cases originating from California (see Table 5.8). The 57 percent reversal rate was double that of the Southern District of California and more than triple that of the Northern District. These reversals, moreover, worked profoundly against the interests of patent holders. Astoundingly, all eight times a panel heard an appeal from an alleged infringer in a district outside California, the appeals judges reversed and weakened the patent. Appeals panels did restore rights five times (out of 15 opportunities) to patent holders whose rights were weakened at those districts, a rate in line with prevailing practice across the circuit. On the whole, however, the appeals court took a difficult environment for patent holders and made it even more daunting.

In many instances, these actions worked to insulate Northwest loggers and construction trades from concerns about patent infringement, while also protecting local equipment supply firms from incursions by patent holders from Wisconsin and other lumbering centers to the east.[59] Such outcomes resembled what had occurred in the oil and agricultural sectors of Southern California. On a few occasions, however, the strict regime drew Ninth Circuit judges into

[59] *Clayton T. Eaid v. Joseph A. McConnell* 230 F. 444 (1916); *Jerome F. Stafford v. Alber Bros. Milling Co.* 263 F. 86 (1920); *Overlin v. Dallas Machine and Locomotive Works* 297 F. 7 (1924); and *D.J. Murray Mfg. Co. v. Sumner Iron Works and Silverton Lumber Co.* 300 F. 911 (1924), which blocked a prominent Wisconsin firm.

high-stakes disputes with national suppliers engaged in less localized pursuits. Such cases in turn brought heightened scrutiny from the US Supreme Court.

One monumental conflict involved the froth process, a novel technique used to separate zinc and other valuable minerals from ore mined at Butte, Montana, and other Ninth Circuit locales. Developed and patented by British interests, the technique assumed heightened importance with the outbreak of World War I, as demand for zinc soared. The associated patent litigation began in 1913 and dragged on longer than the war itself. Over the course of seven years, it generated more than 10,000 pages of testimony at district and eventually elicited opinions from all four Ninth Circuit appeals judges. First Gilbert in 1914 and then Ross four years later reversed District Judge George Bourquin of Montana and weakened the patents, only to be reversed in turn by the Supreme Court.[60] Each had exhibited his characteristic traits, with Gilbert denying pioneer status to an outsider and the nitpicking Ross pointing out discrepancies in the patent specification that in his estimate rendered several claims invalid. Hunt and Morrow, recognizing that Ross's brazen opinion would surely spark further review from the Supreme Court, produced measured concurrences intended to steer the justices toward a compromise. Even under Ross's strict reading, they suggested, the patent holders actually retained strong rights, since mining companies could circumvent the patent only by using excessive amounts of costly oils in the frothing solution. The added expense for the extra oil effectively set a license fee for the patent. The opinion by the high court reversing Ross largely embraced this logic.

Morrow performed a similar function in a parallel case involving wireless telegraphy, another technology of military significance. The Marconi Company, the dominant East Coast supplier of radio equipment, brought suit against a Seattle radio manufacturer. The case generated unprecedented amounts of expert testimony. District Judge Joseph Neterer turned his courtroom over to demonstrations by the world's leading radio experts for several weeks in 1916 and made numerous sojourns to laboratories at the University of Washington, before rendering a judgement against Marconi. Three years later, Morrow devoted weeks to reviewing the materials, then issued a lengthy opinion affirming the lower court. His opinion withstood review and helped guide the Supreme Court in subsequent cases, as firms battled to exploit emerging opportunities for commercial radio.[61]

60 *Minerals Separation, Ltd. V. Hyde* 214 F. 100 (1914), reversed by 242 U.S. 261 (1916) after two years of preparation and four days of hearings; and *Butte and Superior Mining Co. v. Minerals Separation, Ltd.* 250 F. 241 (1918), reversed by 250 U.S. 336 (1919).

61 *Marconi Wireless Telegraph Co. v. Kilborne & Clarke Mfg. Co.* 265 F. 644 (1920). On evidence in the case, see 9CHRIS v. 1157-1162.

While these cases captured the public limelight and absorbed extraordinary amounts of time and energy, perhaps the most significant intervention by the Supreme Court was sparked by what looked to be a minor case from Oregon. The dispute involved patents held by a Boston confectioner for taffy-pulling machines. District Judge Wolverton, aware that the DC appeals court had blessed the patent as a pioneer invention, had quickly deemed a Portland storekeeper to be infringing. An unimpressed Gilbert reversed just as perfunctorily. Noting the simplicity of the device, Gilbert suggested that the interferences adjudicated before the DC appeals court demonstrated that many inventors had similar ideas.[62] Newly installed Chief Justice Taft, just months into his term, seized the opportunity to send an object lesson intended to emphasize the primacy of the DC appeals court in patent work. Interferences might well indicate that inventors had triumphed in a hotly contested field, Taft observed, and thus justify their receiving particularly strong patent protection.[63] Ironically, this was a sentiment Gilbert had himself embraced when affirming opinions from Van Fleet upholding patents granted to Northern Californians such as the hydraulic engineer Abner Doble. Now the logic had been turned back against him, and for a second time in five years, Gilbert found himself reversed by the high court when weakening a patent.

On both of these occasions, not surprisingly, the patents had been held by inventors from outside the Ninth Circuit. Three decades into his work on the appeals court, Gilbert remained strongly resistant to the patent claims of outsiders, while steadfastly defending those of native inventors. Between 1918 and 1920, Gilbert and his colleagues on the appeals bench intervened on multiple occasions to restore rights to West Coast inventors who had lost cases heard by more stringent visiting district judges such as Bourquin and Neterer.[64] The aging and overworked Van Fleet gradually relinquished more of his duties to these younger colleagues, especially in major cases. In 1917, after attorneys and appeals judges openly criticized Van Fleet's cavalier treatment of expert witnesses in one case,[65] the district court introduced new rules and procedures designed to funnel more patent cases into the hands of court-appointed masters. Frequent litigators Holt and Best, the tractor builders, jumped at the chance and promptly consolidated several patent disputes into a single case to be heard by a master.[66] Even at the Northern District, a more administrative approach to patent litigation was slowly taking hold.

62 *Mastoras v. Hildreth* 263 F. 571 (1920).

63 *Hildreth v. Mastoras* 257 U.S. 27 (1921).

64 *Simplex Window Co. v. Hauser Reversible Window Co.* 248 F. 919 (1918) and *Petroleum Rectifying Co. of California v. Reward Oil Co.* 260 F. 177 (1919) are two notable instances.

65 *Moore Filter Co. v. Taugher* 239 F. 105 (1917).

66 *Holt v. Best* 245 F. 354 (1917).

While monitoring events in the north, Hunt asserted himself more actively into appeals originating from the Southern District. There judges Oscar Trippet and Benjamin Bledsoe presided, with occasional assistance from outsiders such as Frank Rudkin and Edward Cushman of Washington. Each of them took part in a run of cases between 1915 and 1920 that ultimately elicited review by the Supreme Court. The patents in dispute covered various designs of under-reamers, a piece of drilling equipment that had proved essential for tapping oil resources in the challenging geology of the West. The suits brought into conflict Elihu "Clem" Wilson, an independent West Coast inventor who had founded his own oil supply business, and the Union Oil Tool Supply Company, a firm affiliated with California's large Union Oil Company, but with roots and alliances among the drilling equipment suppliers of Pennsylvania.[67] Between 1915 and 1918, Wilson prevailed in a complicated series of rulings that effectively gave him priority over Union in the market for under-reamers.[68] On this basis, he rapidly built a supply business that grew to employ several hundred people. Rudkin and Hunt wrote the key appeals opinions, which were upheld when the Supreme Court denied cert to Union.[69]

Hunt got involved again in 1920, when he was compelled to reverse opinions by Bledsoe. The inexperienced district judge, appointed by Woodrow Wilson in 1915 at the unusually young age of 40, had badly bungled the damage award to Clem Wilson and mistakenly allowed Union Tool to continue making spare parts for infringing under-reamers.[70] When Union appealed, Justice Louis Brandeis vigorously upheld Hunt.[71] The widely cited opinion humbled Bledsoe, who bitterly voiced his frustration with patent law in open court.[72] Two years later, he would resign his judgeship and run as the Democratic candidate for Mayor of Los Angeles, a hopeless venture in the solidly Republican city. It marked the first time that a Ninth Circuit judge had willingly resigned his post, knowing that his seat would pass into the hands of the opposing political party.

The series of disputes involving under-reamers highlighted several features of patent litigation on the Ninth Circuit at the dawn of the 1920s. The cases

[67] "Wilson Tool Co.," *A History of California and an Extended History of Los Angeles and Environs*, Vol. 3 (Los Angeles: Historic Record Co., 1915); "Wilson Underreamer Sustained by Supreme Court Decision," *The Oil Trade Journal* 9 (Dec. 1918): 101; and "The Wilson Bros.," *Oil Age*, February 1920, p. 14.

[68] *Wilson & Willard Mfg. Co. et.al. v. Robert E. Bole and Edward Double* 227 F. 607 (1915); *Wilson & Willard Mfg. Co. v. Union Tool Co.* 249 F. 729 (1918); *Union Tool Co. v. Wilson* 249 F. 736 (1918); and *Arthur G. Willard & William W. Wilson v. Union Tool Co.* 253 F. 48 (1918).

[69] 248 U.S. 559 (1918).

[70] *Union Tool Co. et.al. v. United States et.al.* 262 F. 431 (1920) and *Wilson v. Union Tool Co.* 265 F. 669 (1920).

[71] Writ granted 254 U.S. 624 (1920). Argued 3/1–2/1922. Brandeis opinion 259 U.S. 107 (5/15/1922).

[72] *Wilson v. Union Tool and Lucy Mfg. Co.* 275 F. 624 (1921).

demonstrated how judges such as Hunt could adjudicate ongoing conflicts among competing suppliers, even in a dynamic emerging sector such as drilling equipment. Hunt did not seek to drive Union Tool from the market through an unequivocal grant of strong rights to the entrepreneur Wilson. He examined claims in a manner that left room for both suppliers, while making sure that the incumbent Union Tool could not run roughshod over the upstart through trade practices that in Hunt's view had unduly leveraged its ties to a large oil company.

Within a few years, the Southern District and the appeals court would achieve similar outcomes in at least two other segments of the oil supply industry: Trumble Gas Traps, used to capture natural gas from petroleum wells, and Perkins oil well cementing technology, used to prevent water from seeping into the wells. In the former case, the court refereed a dispute between the inventor Trumble and an incumbent supplier, first trimming his claims and forcing him to make modifications in order to avoid infringement and then blocking the incumbent from overreaching by expanding its claims unduly through a reissued patent.[73] The Perkins case simply upheld the rights of a West Coast pioneer whom the court deemed deserving of compensation from large oil companies.[74]

In addition to showing how the court laid the foundation for a competitive regional oil supply industry, the Wilson cases further illustrate the glaring gap that had opened by 1920 between the approach of Hunt at the southern district and Gilbert to the north. Perhaps not surprisingly under these circumstances, patent holders with sufficiently deep pockets had begun to pursue parallel actions at both venues. Such instances placed extraordinary burdens upon the circuit court.

In one notorious example, Samuel Dunkley, a Michigan supplier of fruit processing equipment with backing from New York investors, pursued parallel suits involving its patent for a peach peeler that combined lye baths, hydraulic jets, and mechanical wire brushes. To no one's surprise, Trippet in Los Angeles and Van Fleet in San Francisco produced conflicting judgements, with the former narrowing Dunkley and Van Fleet bestowing his usual pioneer status upon him.[75] Appeals went directly to the Supreme Court, which already had a New York suit involving the same patents under review. After a long delay, the high court returned the matter without comment to the circuit courts. By then, both Trippet and Van Fleet were on death's door (they would both die in 1923). Judge Morrow stepped in and placed the matter in the hands of a master. His accounting severely squeezed Dunkley. It offered him a small pittance in compensation, when he had once dreamed of tens or even hundreds of thousands.

[73] *David G. Lorraine v. Townsend* 290 F. 54 (1923) and *Lorraine v. Townsend* 8 F.2d 673 (1925). Townsend is Trumble Gas Trap.

[74] *Owen v. Perkins Oil Well Cementing Co.* 2 F.2d 247 (1924).

[75] *Central California Canneries v. Dunkley* 247 F. 790 (1917) and *Dunkley v. Pasadena Canning Co. & George E. Greer* 261 F. 386 (1919).

The disappointed outside inventor brought the matter to appeals judges Hunt, Morrow, and Wallace McCamant, a Taft protégé who had temporarily filled the post vacated by the recently retired Ross. Clearly anxious to wash their hands of the matter, the trio conceded that the master may have been a tad stingy in determining an appropriate license fee, before accepting his report without modification.[76] Essentially, the court had affirmed Trippet's judgement of seven years earlier. It was the sort of outcome that invited cynicism from those outside the legal system and exasperated those within it—not least, the likes of Hunt, Taft, and McCamant.

A more telling and ultimately more significant instance of a case involving parallel suits at district pertained to deep well centrifugal pumps. These sophisticated machines, introduced around the turn of the century, had become essential components of Western irrigation, valued especially among foothill orchardists and others who lacked ready access to gravity-fed canals. Two pioneers laid claim to the initial breakthroughs (Lundy 1968). One was Byron Jackson, owner of a respected San Francisco iron works that had moved to Berkeley following the earthquake and fire of 1906. Jackson's original patent dated to 1890, but he had taken out subsequent patents emphasizing techniques for keeping the pumps in balance under various conditions. Van Fleet had blessed these patents in suits brought in 1911 and again in 1917, enabling Jackson to keep frustrated rivals and new entrants at bay and close them out of the booming Southern California market.[77]

The second pump pioneer, a Texan named Mahlon Layne, had come to Los Angeles in 1909 looking to make hay in that market (Green 1973). Layne's designs emphasized ways of stabilizing the pump and its rotating shaft underground, using bearings that could be lubricated from above. These methods did not conflict with Jackson's, but rather supplemented them. A balanced pump helped minimize the wear and tear on bearings, but did not eliminate the need for them entirely. The challenge of getting these components to work in sync, under difficult and highly variable field conditions, made deep well pumping an endeavor ripe for invention. New entrants, including several who had once worked for the curmudgeon Layne, stood ready to enter the field, as did more established Midwest firms such as American Well Works. Layne threatened them with lawsuits.

These disputes first reached the Supreme Court in 1916, when state courts in Texas and Arkansas posed a jurisdictional question regarding whether public threats of patent suit, such as those used by Layne to sow doubts in the mind

[76] *Dunkley Co. v. Central California Cannery Cos.* 7 F.2d 972 (1925).

[77] *Byron Jackson Iron Works v. United Iron Works* 197 F. 44 (1911) and *Byron Jackson v. Krogh* (1917), available via 9CHRIS.

of potential American Well customers, should be considered a matter of state libel proceedings or federal patent law. The question reflected the ongoing effort to clarify the relationship between patent law and state laws governing trade practices. Justice Holmes offered an unequivocal answer: until the parties actually entered into patent suits, the matter remained one of libel and trade, and should be handled by the state courts.[78]

Apparently stimulated by Holmes, Layne soon brought infringement suits in Los Angeles District Court against American Well Works and in San Francisco District Court against Western Well Works, a San Jose company founded by his former employee. Layne won a favorable ruling from Judge Trippet, who issued an injunction and sent the matter to a master for accounting in 1920. With Van Fleet no longer handling significant new patent cases, the suit in San Francisco was heard by Frank Dietrich of Idaho, a highly respected judge who often dealt with patent matters and would eventually be promoted to the appeals court. Generally an advocate of strong patent rights, Dietrich also found in favor of Layne.

Western Well promptly appealed, before a panel consisting of Gilbert, Morrow, and District Judge Wolverton of Oregon, who had sat on many such panels since 1906 and consistently followed Gilbert's lead. Everything pointed toward a quick affirmation in favor of Layne. Much to Gilbert's disgust, however, Wolverton joined Morrow's opinion reversing the district court and absolving the startup firm of infringement. A flabbergasted Gilbert issued a vehement dissent, accusing Western Well of perpetrating a virtual fraud by submitting drawings of its device that differed wildly from equipment it had actually installed in the field. The court, Gilbert complained, was rewarding Western Well for marketing an inferior version of Layne's device, which in Gilbert's view was universally recognized as one of the true pioneer inventions of the West.[79]

Gilbert's dissent marked a moment of passage in Ninth Circuit patent litigation. Remarkably, the dissent appeared in the same month—October 1921—that Taft issued his opinion making an object lesson of Gilbert in the candy-pulling case. The pump case would now also make its way to the chief justice. In March 1923, Taft took the highly unusual step of issuing an opinion while denying Layne cert.[80] Deftly dissecting the issues, the chief justice again sought to send an unambiguous message to circuit judges. Taft wanted them to stop approving petitions to the high court in patent cases, unless those cases involved clear conflicts between the circuits regarding questions of validity (rather than merely local disputes between self-interested parties over infringement) or were somehow vital to the national interest (as with the minerals separation cases). The Layne case, Taft drolly observed, met neither qualification.

[78] *Layne and Bowler v. American Well Works* 242 U.S. 261 (1916).
[79] *Western Well Works v. Layne and Bowler* 276 F. 465 (1921).
[80] *Layne and Bowler Corp. v. Western Well Works* 261 U.S. 387 (1922).

Taft intended his message for all federal judges. He was looking, as ever, for ways to streamline judicial processes and reduce the burdens of patent cases on the high court. He did so by establishing a clear division of labor. His approach embraced both a hierarchical division, which limited appeals, and a regional one, which left the circuits free to referee infringement suits within their own geographic jurisdictions. (His earlier object lesson, in the candy machine case, had created a further division of labor by instructing the circuits to lean upon the DC appeals court for assessments of validity.)

Taft's approach had immediate repercussions for the Ninth Circuit. One practical effect was that it opened the pump business to competition. With the denial of writ to Layne, the southern district reversed its previous judgement in his favor.[81] Almost immediately, several new firms entered the pump business, which grew rapidly and became a hotbed of competition among highly inventive enterprises who patented frequently but also competed on matters of sales and service. Byron Jackson remained the leader, and Layne a player, but no firm occupied the dominant position those founders had once held (Lundy 1968). The Ninth Circuit refereed disputes among them, without bestowing pioneer status upon any one of them, much as it had done under Hunt's influence in the oil supply business.

This outcome reflected broader changes affecting patent litigation in all fields of technical endeavor and in every district. From 1921 onward, and especially after a wholesale turnover of California's district judges in 1923, Hunt and Morrow steered the circuit toward the more administrative approach (see Table 5.9). Gilbert retreated, issuing just three opinions in patent appeals cases from 1921 through 1925, although still exhibiting his penchant for rewarding locals when given the chance. Hunt asserted himself, writing opinions in almost every case of significance involving outside inventors. And Morrow, who had always exhibited a strong inclination to weaken patent rights, issued a series of opinions that undid much of the earlier work of Van Fleet and Gilbert and opened West Coast pioneers such as Murphy to competition.[82] As these changes occurred, a new generation of district judges stepped to the fore, handling patent cases with a deftness seldom witnessed from their predecessors. Taft's influence was evident everywhere, and would endure for many years to come.

Conclusions

Assessing the full impact of patent litigation upon Pacific Coast industry and enterprise is a daunting task. Each case and each industry presents its own story.

[81] *Layne and Bowler Corp. v. American Well and Prospecting Co. et.al.* 300 F. 228 (1924).

[82] *Rip Van Winkle v. Murphy* 1 F.2d 673 (1924), essentially reversing *Perfection Disappearing Bed v. Murphy* 266 F. 698 (1920), in which Gilbert affirmed Van Fleet for Murphy.

The records sent from the district courts to the appeals court are rich with information. They are an invaluable source for historians seeking to trace the emergence and evolution of the region's firms and industries.

The overview presented here serves a different purpose. By offering a global view and tracing broad tendencies across time, it seeks to establish an overarching framework for understanding the legal context in which all enterprises operated. That context, as I have stressed, incorporated both local and national elements. At no point did the Ninth Circuit operate in isolation from that larger national context. The judges and attorneys of the circuit were engaged in an ongoing conversation taking place in legal quarters and in political and legislative arenas regarding the nature of patent rights and their relation to competition policy and the shifting context of the US economy and business system. Over time, that conversation, and with it the Ninth Circuit, came to embrace tendencies toward national standards and formal administrative procedures. Yet those trends did not obliterate the localism and regionalism that were in many respects inherent to the patent system and to the realities of the distribution of power in a federated, state-heavy political economy. Blatant favoritism toward West Coast litigants might diminish, but the issues coming before the court would still emerge from industries and economic activities often distinctive to the West Coast. To a greater degree than one might gather by focusing solely upon patent opinions and rulings issued by the US Supreme Court, the patent system and patent law persisted as a federalist system, capable of accommodating regional distinctiveness.

The decentralized approach worked to the advantage of West Coast innovators. In erecting a protective barrier against established eastern firms looking to exploit patent rights in national markets, Ninth Circuit judges buffered innovative local enterprises from the intense nationalizing impulses of the age. The federated court system muted what might have been a disruptive revolutionary experience, dominated by the abrupt intrusion of experienced outsiders, and transformed it into an evolutionary phenomenon, characterized by sustained learning and experiment with techniques suited to the Pacific Coast. All the while, the Ninth Circuit itself evolved. Through practical experience derived from frequent patent cases conducted in West Coast courtrooms, and in conversation with national authorities, the district and appeals courts gradually matured into forums capable of adjudicating disputes occurring among innovative enterprises, be they local or national in origin. Law and enterprise evolved together, nurturing institutions and technical capabilities that set the Pacific Coast apart and launched it on a distinctive trajectory within the emergent national economy.

Appendix. A Note on Sources

This study is built from printed materials that accompanied cases forwarded from district courts to the Ninth Circuit Court of Appeals. The materials include trial transcripts, legal briefs, petitions for appeal, and exhibits (including depositions and testimony of expert witnesses). They were printed, bound, and shelved in the San Francisco Law Library in the order received, without indexing by subject matter or litigant. Together they encompass nearly 1,500 volumes, running some 800 to 1,200 pages apiece, just for the years 1891–1925. Through a collaboration between the Internet Archive and the University of California's Hastings School of Law, these materials were scanned and made available for research. They are accessible online via 9CHRIS: 9th Circuit Historical Records Index System at www.9CHRIS.org. The unwieldy collection of materials has been rendered searchable, in some fashion, thanks to the extraordinary efforts of Professor Eric Nystrom of Arizona State University. I am deeply indebted to Professor Nystrom not only for creating this free, publicly accessible archive and finding aid, but also for conducting inquiries on my behalf using more advanced tools still under development.

By combing this unique online digital archive (unavailable for any other federal circuit) and searching the federal circuit court opinions available via Westlaw, I have constructed a database that includes what I believe to be essentially all patent cases (some 148 in all) in which the appeals court issued a formal opinion during these 35 years. (The database does not include mere rulings by appeals judges regarding routine procedural matters, such as the granting of rehearings.) The database contains information regarding the volume of cases, the nature of the litigants (such as whether they included a party from outside the Ninth Circuit), the area of technology under review, the judges who sat on the panel and wrote the opinion, the attorneys, and most importantly, the outcomes of the cases—in particular, whether the appeals court reversed or affirmed the lower court and, in the process, whether it served to strengthen the patent or weakened it. The database also includes information about whether the US Supreme Court considered the case on appeal and, if so, what happened there.

Unfortunately, the database does not include patent cases heard at the district court but not appealed. Since the cost of appeal was substantial and the reversal rate was just 36 percent, we can assume that many patent disputes went no further than the district. The appeals files contain occasional materials collected in anticipation of an appeal that did not come to pass, presumably because the parties settled. While the database of 148 appeals cases cannot, then, be said to encompass all of patent litigation on the Ninth Circuit, these cases most certainly include many of the most significant disputes. After the 1891 legal reforms, appeal to the circuit was the only path through which parties to a patent dispute could reach the US Supreme Court. Rulings on appeal, moreover, set guidelines that significantly shaped judicial actions at the district level.

References

Balogh, Brian. *A Government Out of Sight: The Mystery of National Authority in Nineteenth-Century America.* Cambridge, UK; New York: Cambridge University Press, 2009.

Beauchamp, Christopher. *Invented by Law: Alexander Graham Bell and the Patent That Changed America.* Cambridge, MA: Harvard University Press, 2015.

Blackford, Mansel G. *The Lost Dream: Businessmen and City Planning on the Pacific Coast, 1890–1920.* Columbus: Ohio State University Press, 1993.

Carlton, David, and Peter Coclanis, "The Uninventive South? A Quantitative Look at Region and American Inventiveness." *Technology and Culture* 36, no. 2 (1995): 302–26.

Deverell, William. *Railroad Crossing: Californians and the Railroad, 1850–1910.* Berkeley; Los Angeles: University of California Press, 1994.

Fisk, Catherine. *Working Knowledge: Employee Innovation and the Rise of Corporate Intellectual Property, 1800–1930.* Chapel Hill: University of North Carolina Press, 2009.

Frederick, David C. *Rugged Justice: The Ninth Circuit Court of Appeals and the American West, 1891–1941.* Berkeley; Los Angeles: University of California Press, 1994.

Green, Donald E. *Land of the Underground Rain: Irrigation on the Texas High Plains, 1910–1970.* Austin: University of Texas Press, 1973.

Hovenkamp, Herbert. "Antitrust and the Patent System: A Reexamination," *Ohio State Law Journal* 76 (2015): 467.

John, Richard R. *Network Nation: Inventing American Telecommunications.* Cambridge, MA: Harvard University Press, 2010.

Kazin, Michael. *A Godly Hero: The Life of William Jennings Bryan.* New York: Random House, 2006.

Lamoreaux, Naomi R. *The Great Merger Movement in American Business, 1895–1904.* Cambridge, UK; New York: Cambridge University Press, 1985.

Lamoreaux, Naomi R., and William J. Novak, eds. *Corporations and American Democracy.* Cambridge, MA: Harvard University Press, 2017.

Lamoreaux, Naomi R., and Kenneth L. Sokoloff, "The Rise and Decline of the Independent Inventor: A Schumpeterian Story." In *The Challenge of Remaining Innovative: Insights from Twentieth-Century American Business*, edited by Sally H. Clarke, Naomi R. Lamoreaux, and Steven W. Usselman, 43–78. Palo Alto, CA: Stanford University Press, 2009.

Lamoreaux, Naomi R., Kenneth L. Sokoloff, and Dhanoos Sutthiphisal. "Patent Alchemy: The Market for Technology in US History." *Business History Review* 87, no. 1 (2013): 3–38.

Livingston, James. *Origins of the Federal Reserve System: Money, Class, and Corporate Capitalism, 1890–1913.* Ithaca, NY: Cornell University Press, 1986.

Lundy, Everett W. "A History of the Deep Well Turbine Pump Industry." Unpublished Manuscript, Los Angeles, CA, January 1968.

McCurdy, Charles W. "American Law and the Marketing Structure of the Large Corporation, 1875–1890." *Journal of Economic History* 38, no. 3 (1978): 631–49.

———. ""The *Knight* Sugar Decision and the Modernization of American Corporation Law, 1869–1903." *Business History Review*. 53, no. 3 (1979): 304–42.

McMath, Robert C., Jr., *American Populism: A Social History, 1877–1898*. New York: Hill and Wang, 1992.

Mowery, David C. "The Boundaries of the U.S. Firm in R&D." In *Coordination and Information*, edited by Naomi R. Lamoreaux and Daniel M. G. Raff, 147–76. Chicago, IL: University of Chicago Press, 1995.

Novak, William. *The People's Welfare: Law and Regulation in Nineteenth Century America*. Chapel Hill: University of North Carolina Press, 1996.

Nugent, Walter T. K. *Into the West: The Story of Its People*. New York: Random House, 1999.

Olmstead, Alan L., and Paul W. Rhode. *Creating Abundance: Biological Innovation and American Agricultural Development*. Cambridge, UK; New York: Cambridge University Press, 2008.

Postel, Charles. *The Populist Vision*. New York: Oxford University Press, 2007.

Rauchway, Eric. *Blessed Among Nations: How the World Made America*. New York: Hill and Wang, 2006.

Reich, Leonard S. *The Making of American Industrial Research: Science and Business at GE and Bell, 1876–1926*. New York: Cambridge University Press, 1985.

———. "Lighting the Path to Profit: GE's Control of the Electric Lamp Industry, 1892–1941." *Business History Review* 66, no. 2 (1992): 305–34.

Saunders, Elizabeth. *Roots of Reform: Farmers, Workers, and the American State, 1877–1917*. Chicago, IL: University of Chicago Press, 1999.

Shuck, Oscar T. *Bench and Bar in California: History, Anecdotes, Reminiscences*. San Francisco, CA: The Occident Publishing House, 1889.

Sklar, Martin. *The Corporate Reconstruction of American Capitalism, 1890–1916* Cambridge, UK; New York: Cambridge University Press, 1988.

Skowronek, Stephen. *Building a New American State: The Expansion of National Administrative Capacities, 1877–1920*. Cambridge, UK; New York: Cambridge University Press, 1982.

Usselman, Steven W. *Regulating Railroad Innovation: Business, Technology, and Politics in America, 1840–1920*. Cambridge, UK; New York: Cambridge University Press, 2002.

Usselman, Steven W., and Richard R. John, "Patent Politics: Intellectual Property, the Railroad Industry, and the Problem of Monopoly." *Journal of Policy History* 18, no. 1 (2006): 96–125.

Woeste, Victoria Saker. *The Farmer's Benevolent Trust: Law and Agricultural Cooperation in Industrial America, 1865–1945*. Chapel Hill: University of North Carolina Press, 1998.

6
The Great Patent Grab

Jonathan M. Barnett

Economic historians have documented extensively the operation of the US patent system in the late nineteenth and early twentieth centuries (Khan 2005; Lamoreaux, Levenstein, and Sokoloff 2004; Lamoreaux and Sokoloff 2003). During that period, courts largely enforced patents rigorously and narrowly interpreted antitrust constraints on patent licensing. Markets in financing innovation and commercialization thrived, marrying risk capital supplied by investors with the R&D expertise of inventors. That innovation ecosystem bears a strong resemblance to the period inaugurated by the enactment of the Bayh-Dole Act in 1980 and the establishment of the Court of Appeals for the Federal Circuit in 1982. Until the policy shift toward patent skepticism that commenced in the mid-2000s, the current period had shared with the late nineteenth century a largely sympathetic judicial attitude toward patents and cautious application of antitrust constraints on patent licensing. As in the late nineteenth century, small R&D-specialist firms emerged in certain industries, venture capital and other transactional structures for financing innovation proliferated, and patent licensing activity expanded (Barnett 2021).

Between these two periods of strong patent protection lies an important period that has been largely unexplored by scholars from the perspective of patent and innovation policy.[1] From the late 1930s through the 1970s, the US innovation economy operated under a starkly different property rights regime. Courts and regulators were largely unsympathetic toward patents and expansively interpreted antitrust constraints on patent licensing. This patent-skeptical climate was illustrated by an extended sequence of antitrust enforcement actions that resulted in the compulsory licensing or forfeiture of patent portfolios held by some of the largest US firms. Concurrently, the federal government instituted an implicit compulsory licensing regime through the dramatic infusion of R&D funding into the private sector, accompanied by legal constraints on firms' control over technology developed using those funds. These three core elements—weak patent protection, strong antitrust enforcement, and contractually

[1] For prior relevant discussions of this period, see Hart (2001); Mowery (1995, pp. 162–69); Mowery and Rosenberg (1989, pp. 150–51, 156–58).

Jonathan M. Barnett, *The Great Patent Grab* In: *The Battle over Patents.* Edited by: Stephen H. Haber and Naomi R. Lamoreaux, Oxford University Press. © Oxford University Press 2021. DOI: 10.1093/oso/9780197576151.003.0007

constrained R&D funding—formed the property-rights infrastructure for the postwar innovation economy.

This weak-IP regime provides an imperfect natural experiment by which to assess recent policy actions and proposals that favor weakening patent protection. Contemporary advocates echo New Deal and postwar policymakers who argued that using antitrust law to unlock corporate patent portfolios would facilitate entry, reduce concentration, and promote follow-on innovation. The results were mixed at best. While R&D investment persisted robustly for a substantial part of this period, it was concentrated among a small group of large integrated firms that received extensive government funding and declined as government funding fell starting in the mid-1960s. These "innovation oligopolies" prospered under a weak-IP regime, which favors integrated firms that capture returns on R&D through non-patent assets, such as capital-intensive production and distribution infrastructure, economies of scale, and access to government funding. Although this period achieved important technological achievements, the postwar weak-IP regime relied on government transfers (and faltered once those transfers declined), preserved high levels of market concentration, and may have induced an organizational bias toward integrated structures for conducting innovation and commercialization activities.

The chapter is organized as follows. First, I describe the explicit compulsory licensing regime implemented by the antitrust agencies during the postwar period, situated against a broader patent-skeptical legal environment. Second, I describe the implicit compulsory licensing regime implemented by federal agencies through R&D funding and defense procurement. Third, I present evidence concerning the possible effects of the postwar weak-IP/strong-antitrust regime on concentration levels, patenting behavior, and innovation investment. Last, I present case studies of the innovation performance and organizational choices of two entities that were targeted by compulsory licensing during this period.

The Postwar Weak Patents Regime

The effective strength of patent protection—as set forth by statutory and case law and then implemented through actual and threatened enforcement—determines owners' expected ability to enforce a patent or license it to third parties. Antitrust laws also impact patent holders' enforcement and licensing capacities. Starting in the late New Deal, the effective strength of patent protection declined substantially, driven by weak patent and strong antitrust enforcement. This patent-hostile environment persisted for several decades, culminating in the antitrust litigation and compulsory licensing order against Xerox in 1975.

Patent Hostility

The late New Deal and postwar period was generally perceived to be inhospitable to patent enforcement. This was reflected especially by the infrequency with which courts upheld the validity of issued patents when contested by defendant-infringers. Supreme Court decisions during the 1930s elevated the standard for holding patents valid, leading a lower court judge to observe in a 1935 decision: "We should indeed have no question as to validity, were it not for the high standard demanded for invention by the decisions of the Supreme Court."[2] In 1941, this process culminated in the Court's statement that patents are reserved for exceptional inventions that represent a "flash of genius."[3] Although the Patent Act of 1952 arguably included language to attenuate the "flash of genius" test—a reading supported by legislative history ("Patent Law" 1955, pp. 147–48)—case outcomes show that the lower courts maintained a high bar for patent validity. Henry and Turner (2016) present data on validity determinations in all reported federal court decisions on patent infringement during 1929–2006. For district court decisions, they find a significant drop in the validity rate in 1939, which remains largely unchanged through the early 1980s, although its effects are somewhat attenuated by an increase in the rate at which patents are found to be infringed starting in 1951.[4] In some appellate circuits, courts were especially unsympathetic toward patentees. In the prominent Second Circuit, the rate at which a court upheld the validity of a patent (when contested) fell from 57 percent during 1921–1930 to 36 percent during 1931–1940 to 15 percent during 1941–1950 and remained at 18 percent through 1973 (Baum 1974, p. 782).

Antitrust Enthusiasm

Patent holders not only faced formidable obstacles to enforcing patents, but also significant uncertainty concerning the enforceability of patent licenses. In 1931, the Supreme Court adopted the patent misuse doctrine, which bars use of a patent beyond the "scope" of the patent grant.[5] This vaguely defined doctrine

[2] *Buono v. Yankee Maid Dress Corp.*, 77 F.2d 274, 276 (2d Cir. 1935).

[3] *Cuno Engineering v. Automatic Devices*, 314 U.S. 84, 91 (1941).

[4] The authors reach similar findings on trends in validity and infringement rates for appellate litigation and when integrating district and appellate court outcomes. The increase in infringement rates starting in 1951 may indicate a moderate improvement in the treatment of patentees (roughly concurrently with enactment of the 1952 Patent Act). However, the validity rate, which does not increase significantly until 1983, may be a more salient indicator of "patent strength" given that an invalidity determination not only terminates the particular litigation prior to a determination of infringement but prevents the patent owner from bringing future litigations on the basis of the invalidated patent against any party.

[5] *Carbice Corp. of America v. American Patents Development Corp.*, 283 U.S. 27, 31–32 (1931).

not only provides a defense to patent infringement but, as the Court indicated in a 1942 decision,[6] also provides the basis for an antitrust claim by the alleged *infringer* against the patent holder, triggering the possibility of monetary damages. That is: the patent misuse doctrine raises the possibility that the patent owner can be held liable to the alleged infringer, which obviously has a deterrent effect on patent enforcement actions. Subsequent applications of the patent misuse doctrine and antitrust doctrines relating to vertical restraints effectively put in place something close to per se prohibitions of a large menu of licensing terms, even without evidence of market power or anticompetitive effects (Hoerner 2002, pp. 671–72). This postwar trend culminated in the Department of Justice's "Nine No Nos," which targeted several commonly used licensing terms as potential triggers of antitrust liability (Wilson 1972).

Patent Expropriation

The erosion of patent rights during the postwar period is dramatically illustrated by the compulsory licensing remedies secured by federal antitrust agencies starting in 1941 and culminating in the order against Xerox in 1975.

Compulsory Licensing Proposals

The pursuit of compulsory licensing remedies by antitrust agencies starting in the late New Deal followed multiple prior efforts to institute compulsory licensing by legislation. At least 28 bills were introduced during 1877–1946, but principally since 1908, to provide for the compulsory licensing of patents in various circumstances (Compulsory Patent Licensing 1946, p. 116). During this time, two statutes with compulsory patent licensing provisions were enacted, both in connection with wartime activities: (i) the Act of 1910 (as amended in 1918), which immunized government contractors from an injunction in connection with a patent infringement suit while enabling patentees to seek monetary damages from the government;[7] and (ii) the Trading with the Enemy Act, enacted in 1917 and amended in 1941,[8] which authorized the government to seize patents owned by nationals of enemy-designated states. The latter statute resulted in considerable licensing of seized patents during World War I, primarily with respect to patents held by German firms (Moser and Voena 2009; White 2007).

[6] *Morton Salt Co. v. G.S. Suppiger Co.*, 314 U.S. 488 (1942).

[7] Act of 1910, Pub. L. No. 61-305, 36 Stat. 851, 851-52 (1910), amended by the Act of July 1, 1918, Pub. L. No. 65-182, ch. 114, 40 Stat. 704, 705 (1918).

[8] Trading with the Enemy Act, Pub. L. No. 65-91, § 10, 40 Stat. 411, 420–22 (1917), amended by the First War Powers Act, 55 Stat. 838 (1941), 50 U.S.C. App. §§ 611–22 (Supp. 1942).

During 1938–1941, the Temporary National Economic Committee (TNEC), a congressional committee formed to investigate economic concentration, conducted extensive hearings on the patent system. The TNEC extensively examined alleged cartels implemented through cross-licensing agreements and often involving German firms in defense-related industries. The TNEC ultimately adopted a proposal, promoted by President Roosevelt (US President 1938, p. 9), to mandate licensing of all patents at a "fair price" (Temporary National Economic Committee 1941, pp. 36–37). In testimony before a Senate committee in 1942, Thurman Arnold, the head of the Antitrust Division of the Department of Justice, proposed an amendment to the Sherman Act that would have prohibited the use of a patent "which has the effect of unreasonably limiting the supply of any article" and would have authorized cancellation of a patent that had been used in this manner (Patents: Hearings before the Committee on Patents 1942, Part 6, pp. 3281–82). In 1945, a government commission rejected these proposals ("Third Report of the National Patent Planning Commission" 1945, p. 603).

Compulsory Licensing Orders (1938–1975)

While neither the patent nor antitrust statutes were ever amended to provide for compulsory licensing, federal antitrust agencies effectively implemented this remedy on a significant scale through litigation and specifically, consent decrees[9] secured through litigation. In the first litigation to secure a compulsory licensing order, the defendant's counsel argued: "The provisions of this decree are a thinly disguised replica of the Department of Justice's recommendations to the TNEC, which in turn the TNEC recommended to Congress, and were rejected by Congress" (Petro 1944, p. 99). The attorney's observations were prescient. During 1938–1975, the agencies secured a total of 132 compulsory patent licensing orders in antitrust enforcement actions. Additionally, as part of a legal settlement with the government, Alcoa agreed in 1948 to license portions of its patent portfolio to two competitors[10] . That brings the total to 133 compulsory licensing orders, of which 89.5 percent were issued pursuant to a consent decree and (aside from the Alcoa settlement) the remainder were issued through a litigated judgment.

Use of compulsory licensing as an antitrust remedy initially encountered resistance from the courts. When a plaintiff sought this remedy in an antitrust case in 1934, a lower court summarily dismissed the proposition as

[9] An antitrust consent decree represents a negotiated settlement between the government and defendant, which must then be approved by a court. A consent decree can be mutually advantageous to both parties because (i) it saves on litigation costs and (ii) from the defendant's perspective, it cannot be used by third parties for purposes of pursuing a private antitrust action.

[10] *U.S. v. Aluminum Co. of America*, 91 F.Supp. 333, 402–410 [S.D.N.Y. 1950].

being inconsistent with the inventor's "absolute property in his invention."[11] Concurrently, commentators raised doubts concerning the constitutionality of compulsory licensing (Schechter 1935). In the *Hartford-Empire* and *National Lead* decisions, issued in 1945 and 1947 respectively,[12] the Supreme Court largely put these doubts to rest. In *Hartford-Empire*, the Court rejected the government's petition for patent "dedication" (equivalent to forfeiture), on the grounds that it may raise a constitutional issue, but granted a compulsory license remedy with a reasonable royalty.[13] In *National Lead*, the Court declined to revisit the constitutionality of a royalty-free license but suggested that it may be "reasonable" in certain circumstances.[14] In 1953, a federal district court specifically noted the Court's prevarications but nonetheless ordered the "dedication to the public" of General Electric's (GE) fundamental patents on incandescent lamps and lamp parts and required GE to provide a royalty-free license to its patents on lamp-making machinery, together with technical documentation.[15]

The Court's endorsement of compulsory licensing as an antitrust remedy, and some lower courts' expansive use of that remedy, provided the green light for the antitrust agencies' regular use of the remedy (both with and without a royalty) in the years that followed. The following discussion comprehensively documents the use of this remedy during the period starting in 1938, the year in which the Antitrust Division launched its enforcement program, and ending in 1975, the year in which the government secured a compulsory licensing order against Xerox. In a report prepared for a Senate committee, Hollabaugh and Wright (1960) estimated that compulsory licensing orders in antitrust enforcement actions during 1941–1959 had affected an estimated 40,000–50,000 patents, representing 8 percent of all unexpired patents at that time.[16] Scherer (1977) identified additional compulsory licensing orders for the period after 1959, as did Contreras (2015, App. B). I obtained and verified the relevance of the orders identified by those authors and identified additional orders through the BNA CCH Intelliconnect (now known as the Cheetah Antitrust and Competition Law) database. The search was limited to compulsory patent licensing or dedication orders issued as part of a consent decree or final order in a litigation brought

[11] *Radio Corp. of America v. Hygrade Sylvania Corp.*, 10 F.Supp. 879, 883 (D.N.J. 1934).

[12] *Hartford-Empire Co. v. U.S.*, 323 U.S. 386 (1945); *U.S. v. National Lead Co.*, 332 U.S. 319 (1947).

[13] *Hartford-Empire Co. v. U.S.*, 323 U.S. 386, 415 (1945).

[14] *U.S. v. National Lead Co.*, 332 U.S. 319, 338 (1947).

[15] *U.S. v. General Electric Co. et al.*, 115 F.Supp. 835, 843, 846–47 (D.N.J. 1953). While General Electric apparently contemplated appealing the court's decision ("GE May Appeal" 1953), this does not appear to have taken place. Not all district courts interpreted the Court's guidance so aggressively. In 1951, a district court rejected the government's petition for a royalty-free compulsory license in an antitrust prosecution of Du Pont and other firms in the nylon industry on the ground that it was not authorized by statute, see *U.S. v. Imperial Chem. Indus., Ltd.*, 100 F.Supp. 504 (S.D.N.Y. 1951), *opinion on relief*, 105 F.Supp. 215, 225 (S.D.N.Y. 1952).

[16] The authors' methodology for reaching this estimate is unclear.

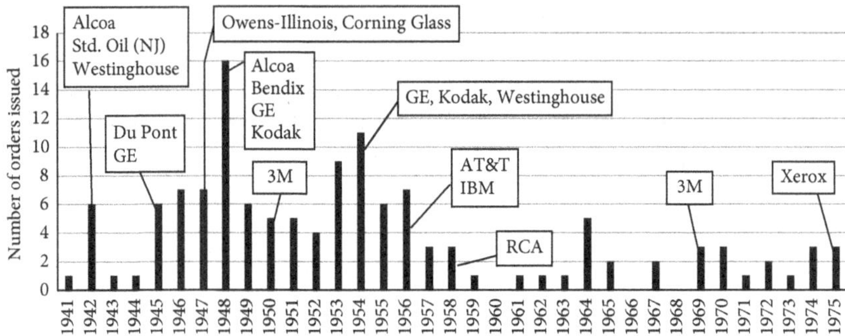

Figure 6.1 Compulsory licensing orders in antitrust enforcement actions, 1941–1975.

Note: Labels refer to selected, not all, firms subject to compulsory licensing orders in any particular year.

Source: Cheetah Antitrust & Competition Law database. Figure 6.1 originally appeared in Barnett (2021) and is reproduced with permission of Oxford University Press.

under the federal antitrust statutes. Additionally, as noted, I included Alcoa's 1948 patent licensing settlement as the equivalent of a compulsory licensing order. Appendix 6.A provides a list of all such compulsory patent licensing and dedication orders during 1938–1975.

Evidence: All Firms

Figure 6.1 shows the total number of compulsory licensing orders issued each year in antitrust enforcement actions between 1941 (the year in which the first order was issued) and 1975. Actions against some of the largest firms are indicated to provide context. The most intensive use of this remedy occurred during the immediate postwar years, 1945–1958, culminating in the orders issued against AT&T, IBM, and RCA.

It is important to note that compulsory licensing orders are not identical. Scherer (1977, p. 35) makes a useful distinction between "high-impact" and "low-impact" orders. The impact of any particular order depends on several factors, including: (i) whether the order provides for a positive "reasonable" royalty;[17] (ii) whether the order requires that licensees provide the patentee with a reciprocal license; (iii) whether the order applies to future patents for some period of time; (iv) whether the licensor must provide the licensee with technical

[17] Orders that provided for a "reasonable" royalty typically contemplated that the patentee and applicant-licensees would negotiate a rate and, in the event agreement could not be reached, the applicant could petition the court to determine the rate. The last step could involve nontrivial transaction costs that might dissuade certain applicants or could result in a royalty that did not differ substantially from prevailing market rates.

Table 6.1 Characteristics of compulsory patent licensing orders, 1941–1975

Characteristics	Incidence (% Total Orders)
Reasonable royalty license	82
Royalty-free license	33
Patent dedication	15.8
Applies to future patents	41.4
Requires reciprocal license	10.5
Must provide technical know-how	41.4

Notes: Percentages for royalty-free license, reasonable royalty license, and patent dedication may sum to greater than 100 percent because some orders prescribed different types of licenses for different portions of the defendant's patent portfolio. When orders apply to future patents, this is typically limited in time.

Source: Cheetah Antitrust & Competition Law database. Table 6.1 originally appeared in Barnett (2021) and is reproduced with permission of Oxford University Press.

know-how; and (v) the total number and commercial value of the patents to which the order applies. Table 6.1 provides information on the distribution of all but the last of these "impact" characteristics within the total population of compulsory licensing orders issued during 1938–1975. Note that different portions of a patent portfolio subject to a compulsory licensing order may be impacted differently. For example, in the compulsory licensing order issued against GE in 1945, the company's licensing obligation was subject to a reciprocity requirement on the part of licensees with respect to the company's future, but not then-owned, patents.[18] For purposes of Table 6.1, I considered each "impact" characteristic to be present in a particular order so long as it applied to at least some of the patents subject to that order. Note further that provisions relating to future patents, reciprocity and know-how can differ in severity (for example, orders applying to future patents were usually limited to varying periods of time). Subsequently I provide details on these provisions with respect to orders issued against particular firms (see Table 6.2).

The practical effect of any compulsory licensing order depends ultimately on the extent to which third parties actually exploit the opportunity to license the relevant patents at a reasonable or, when applicable, zero royalty rate. Information on this point is limited. As a general matter, it should be noted that, in the case of a zero-royalty license (which, as shown in Table 6.1, applied to some portion of the defendant's patents in almost 33 percent of the compulsory licensing orders), third parties may elect to use the patented technology without formally entering

[18] *U.S. v. General Electric Co., et al.*, 1946–1947 Trade Cas. (CCH) ¶57,448 (D.N.J. Mar. 7, 1945).

Table 6.2 Compulsory licensing orders against selected Fortune 100 firms, 1941–1975

Year(s)	Patentee	Fortune 100 Ranking	Remedies	Apply to Future Patents?	Reciprocity Required?	Require Technical Know-How?
1942	Standard Oil (N.J.)[a]	2	RFL, RRL	Y	N	Y
1942, 1948[b]	Alcoa	35	RFL, RRL	N	Y[c]	N
1942, 1949, 1953/54	Westinghouse Electric	13	RFL; RRL; PD	Y	Y	Y
1945, 1948–49, 1953/54	General Electric	4	RFL; RRL; PD	Y	Y	Y
1945, 1952	Du Pont	10	RRL	N	Y	Y
1946, 1948, 1953	Bendix Aviation	46	RFL; RRL	Y	N	Y
1946, 1947, 1949[d]	Owens-Illinois	89	RFL; RRL	Y	N	Y
1948, 1954	Eastman Kodak	43	RFL; RRL	Y	N	Y
1956	IBM	59	RFL; RRL	Y	N	Y
1956	AT&T	12	RFL; RRL	Y	Y	Y
1958	RCA	29	RFL; RRL	Y	Y	Y
1975	Xerox	41	RFL; RRL	Y	Y	Y

Legend: RFL: royalty-free license; RRL: reasonable royalty license; PD: patent dedication.

Notes: Fortune 100 ranking is as of the year of the first compulsory licensing order to which the patentee-firm was subject (or, if the first order was issued prior to 1955, then as of 1955, the year in which the rankings first appeared). Fortune 100 rankings are based on total annual revenue. Note Standard Oil (NJ) is listed in the Fortune rankings archive (http://archive.fortune.com/magazines/fortune/fortune500_archive/full/1955/401.html) as Exxon, and Westinghouse Electric is listed as CBS, due to subsequent acquisitions, other transactions or name changes.

Source: Cheetah Antitrust & Competition Law database.

[a] In 1943, Standard Oil voluntarily relinquished to a government entity, for the duration of the war, its patents relating to synthetic rubber production (Fleming 1943). Given that this was an ad hoc forfeiture limited to the duration of the war, I do not treat this event as an additional compulsory licensing order.

[b] In 1948, Alcoa agreed to license certain patents to competitors, in connection with the settlement of the remedies phase of the government's antitrust prosecution against it. For further details, see the section, "Alcoa: The Dangers of Going It Alone."

[c] In the case of the 1942 order, patents subject to a zero-royalty compulsory license converted to a positive "reasonable" royalty license in the event a licensee declined to grant the patentee a zero-royalty cross-license, and certain patents were subject to a reasonable royalty in all cases following termination of the war (*U.S. v. Aluminum Co. of America et al.*, S.D.N.Y., 1940–1943 Trade Cases ¶56,200 [Apr. 15, 1942]).

[d] The 1949 order applied principally to Owens Corning Fiberglas Corp., which appears to have been controlled by Owens-Illinois and Corning Glass (*U.S. v. Owens Corning Fiberglas Corp. et al.*, N.D. Ohio, 1948–49 Trade Cases ¶62,442, 460 F.Supp. 1094 [June 23, 1949]).

into a license, based on the expectation that a patent holder would have no rational incentive to incur the costs of an infringement suit. The best source of information is a report commissioned by a Senate subcommittee, which surveyed licensing behavior following selected compulsory licensing orders issued during 1941–1959. The key findings in the report were: (i) the number of licensees in any particular case was highly variable, ranging from zero to over 300; (ii) a significant portion of the orders was followed by infrequent or no licensing; but (iii) in the case of orders that resulted from a fully adjudicated proceeding, rather than a consent decree, licensing activity almost always took place (Hollabaugh and Wright 1960, pp. 5, 13, and 18, respectively).[19] Significantly, the latter category included orders affecting patent portfolios held by some of the largest firms subject to compulsory licensing, including GE, Du Pont, and Hartford-Empire (Hollabaugh and Wright 1960, pp. 19–20). In at least seven cases, the consent decree may have had limited incremental effect since the defendant had already adopted a zero or nominal royalty policy (Hollabaugh and Wright 1960, p. 15)—most notably, AT&T, which had already licensed its fundamental transistor technology and associated know-how at low royalty rates (Levin 1982, pp. 75–77; Tilton 1971, pp. 74–75).

Evidence: Selected Fortune 100 Firms

Table 6.2 provides more detailed information on the compulsory licensing orders issued against some of the largest US firms (all members of the "Fortune 100" list of the largest US companies as of 1955). The total impact of the order (as reflected in the factors identified in the four columns from the right) differs in particular cases and, for some firms, differs with respect to different portions of the firm's patent portfolio. Appendix 6.A provides the same details for all firms targeted by compulsory licensing orders during 1938–1975.

Compulsory Licensing as Market Re-Engineering

The practical effect of these antitrust remedies was a compulsory licensing program that "socialized" substantial portions of the patent portfolios of some of the country's leading companies, ranging from computing (IBM), to chemicals (Du Pont), to communications (AT&T). This use of antitrust law as a tool for market re-engineering in the postwar period was anchored in the landmark

[19] The report (Hollabaugh and Wright 1960) identified the following explanations for meager licensing activity in the case of some orders: (i) lack of awareness that the patents were available for licensing (pp. 39-41, 53); (ii) lack of economic value (pp. 23, 54); and (iii) transaction costs associated with determining a reasonable royalty (p. 53).

decision against Alcoa in 1945.[20] The *Alcoa* opinion subjected defendants with large market shares to almost certain antitrust liability in monopolization cases, stating that a firm found to possess market power could escape liability only if it showed that it fell within an exception for firms that "do not seek, but cannot avoid, the control of a market."[21] Effectively, this virtually equated large market share with a monopolization violation under Section 2 of the Sherman Act (a proposition that would be soundly rejected by antitrust law following the "Chicago revolution" several decades later).

In the influential *United Shoe* case[22] , which involved a portfolio of approximately 4,000 patents (*United Shoe*, p. 332), the *Alcoa* decision was interpreted as empowering a court to engage in market re-engineering, even if the defendant had secured its dominant position through legitimate business practices. Justifying its use of a compulsory patent licensing remedy, the court candidly stated: "Defendant is not being punished for abusive practices respecting patents *for it engaged in none* [my emphasis] . . . it is being required to reduce the monopoly power it has . . . compulsory licensing is in effect a partial dissolution on a non-confiscatory basis" (*United Shoe*, p. 351). The market engineering objectives behind the *United Shoe* decision are further illustrated by subsequent developments in this same litigation. In 1965, the court renewed the compulsory licensing order on grounds that industry concentration had not declined and, in 1968, the Supreme Court similarly found that United Shoe's market share had not fallen sufficiently and ordered a break-up of the company.[23] In that same year, the antitrust agencies adopted guidelines that instituted low market share thresholds for triggering a challenge to a merger, generally without the possibility for a defense on efficiency grounds (US Department of Justice 1968, pp. 5–8).

Set against the background of the *Alcoa* decision in 1945, the *United Shoe* decisions in 1953, 1965, and 1968, and adoption of the low "merger challenge" thresholds in 1968, the compulsory licensing remedies pursued by the antitrust agencies were part of a postwar policy of periodically intervening to reallocate market shares in order to institute an ideal of atomistic competition, sometimes to the detriment of firms that had made pioneering technological advancements in a particular market. The antitrust action against Xerox, which opened Xerox's patent portfolio to all interested parties (mostly on a royalty-free basis),[24] illustrates the motivations behind this policy. The legal bases for the Federal

[20] *U.S. v. Alcoa*, 148 F.2d 416 (2d Cir. 1945).

[21] *U.S. v. Alcoa*, 148 F.2d 416, 431 (2d Cir. 1945).

[22] United Shoe Machinery Corp. v. U.S., 110 F.Supp. 295 [1953].

[23] *U.S. v. United Shoe Machinery Corp.*, 331 U.S. 244 (1968); *United Shoe Machinery Corp. v. U.S.*, 266 F.Supp. 330, 334 (1965).

[24] Specifically, the decree provided that third parties could use (i) three patents on a royalty-free basis; (ii) an additional three patents at a 0.5% royalty each; and (iii) all remaining patents at a zero royalty (*In the Matter of Xerox Corp.*, 86 F.T.C. 364 (1975), 1975 WL 173245).

Trade Commision (FTC)'s enforcement action against Xerox, the acknowledged pioneer in photocopying technology, were contestable, given compelling efficiency explanations for most of Xerox's allegedly "exclusionary" price discrimination practices (Tom 2001). F. M. Scherer, who served as chief economist of the FTC during the Xerox litigation, even recognized this point in retrospect, stating that he viewed the use of compulsory licensing in the Xerox case as a form of market reconstruction undertaken without any substantive antitrust violation: "[T]he essence of the [Xerox] case was, frankly, social engineering. It was time to break open this monopoly and create competition. . . . The theory about acquisition and some of the price discrimination practices . . . was fluff. The center of the case was the extension over time of monopoly through patent accumulation" ("Roundtable Discussion" 1998, p. 449).[25]

The Implicit Compulsory Licensing Regime

Compulsory licensing through antitrust litigation was not the only policy instrument through which the federal government partially implemented the compulsory licensing proposals that had been unsuccessfully advanced by the Roosevelt administration in the late 1930s. This explicit compulsory licensing regime was accompanied by a shadow compulsory licensing regime implemented through a flood of federal funding for industry R&D, and related defense procurement expenditures, commencing in the early 1940s. This generous flow of dollars came with strings attached: recipient firms were typically subject to some limitation on the ability to patent, or exclusively license from the government, technologies developed using federal funds. Through this mechanism, direct and indirect government funding for R&D instituted an undeclared compulsory licensing regime that permeated the postwar US economy.

Public R&D Funding: A Gift with Strings Attached

Starting during World War II and extending into the postwar period, the federal government dramatically increased the infusion of funds to academic and business entities for R&D purposes. These funds were encumbered with contractual and other legal constraints that limited significantly recipients' ability

[25] Elsewhere F. M. Scherer has described the Xerox case as advising "greater caution in future cases to ensure that opening up patent portfolios does not cause a loss of US firms' advantages vis-à-vis overseas rivals" (Scherer 1992, p.187). The statement refers to the fact that, in part due to the compulsory licensing order against Xerox, Japanese firms captured a substantial portion of the US photocopying equipment market.

to apply for patents, or otherwise assert legal exclusivity over, innovations developed using those funds. Given the volume of federal R&D expenditures, which constituted a clear majority of total national R&D expenditures throughout this period, these limitations effectively displaced significantly the role of the patent system in the US innovation ecosystem.

Wartime Patent Policy

The economics of war at least partially motivated both the explicit and implicit compulsory licensing regime and its World War I-era precursors (namely, the 1918 amendment to the Act of 1910, which clarified that government contractors were immune from injunctive relief or damages for patent infringement, and the Trading with the Enemy Act, enacted in 1917 to authorize the confiscation of "enemy-owned" patents). Both as president and, previously, as assistant secretary of the navy during World War I, Roosevelt advocated for both policies.[26] With the dramatic increase in military production accompanying US entry into World War II, the federal government had a powerful incentive to dilute patent holders' rights and, as a principal customer with coercive powers, the ability to do so. To illustrate the government's predicament, consider that, in 1943, data based solely on a selected set of aircraft-related items shows that the War and Navy Departments incurred an estimated $27 million in patent royalties, as compared to an estimated $178,000 in patent royalties for those same items in 1938.[27]

The government took three actions to reduce its input costs. First, in 1942, Congress enacted the Royalty Adjustment Act,[28] which enabled military procurement agents to compel contractors to enter into "renegotiations" to adjust patent royalty rates (and other contract terms). During the period from 31 October 1942 to 30 June 30 1945, the military renegotiated royalties in 541 agreements, at an estimated savings of $500 million (Chappell and Kenyon 1947, p. 712). Second, as part of the Manhattan Project, the government extensively patented inventions relating to atomic energy, with the intent of foreclosing private firms and inventors from doing so (Wellerstein 2013, pp. 140, 147–48, 160–61). Third, government agencies (most notably, the Office of Scientific Research and Development (OSRD), which coordinated government R&D funding during World War II) sometimes disbursed R&D funding subject to a "government

[26] In 1918, Roosevelt, as assistant secretary of the navy, had lobbied for the 1918 amendment to the 1910 Act in response to a court decision that had raised concerns about government contractors' exposure to patent infringement claims (*Decisions of the Comptroller General*, Decision B-159356, pp. 231–32). In 1917, Roosevelt, in the same position, had advocated for the formation of an aircraft patent pool, apparently in an effort to reduce the government's expected royalty burden in connection with aircraft procurement (Katznelson and Howells 2015, pp. 21–22). As noted earlier in the chapter, President Roosevelt had advocated amending the patent statute to provide for blanket compulsory licensing (US President 1938, p. 9).

[27] Author's calculations, based on data reported in Chappell and Kenyon (1947, p. 703, table I).

[28] Royalty Adjustment Act of 1942, 56 Stat. 1013, 35 U.S.C.A. §§ 89–96 (Supp. 1946).

title" policy under which the government retained title to any resulting patents, with the discretion to grant a license to (or waive title in favor of) the contractor. One of the architects of postwar innovation policy, Vannevar Bush, implemented a government title policy in connection with the Manhattan Project and recollected: "I suppose that in the process . . . I personally destroyed more property in the form of patents than any other man living" (Wellerstein 2013, pp. 148–49).[29] An exception to the government title policy was the War Department (the precursor to today's Department of Defense), which typically permitted the contractor to apply for a patent but retained a non-exclusive, royalty-free license (Wellerstein 2013, pp. 143–45; Kreeger 1947, p. 742).

Postwar Patent Policy

After the war, the federal government sought to extend both the substantial flow of federal R&D funding and the associated weak property-rights regime across military and non-military related R&D activities. This took place through several steps. In 1944, President Roosevelt urged the preservation of OSRD in some form after the war as a public source of R&D funding (Roosevelt 1944). In 1945, President Truman advocated requiring that all recipients of federal R&D funds make the results of that research freely available (Kreeger 1947, p. 728). In 1947, a government commission issued a report endorsing a compulsory licensing policy for federally funded research, with minor qualifications (US Department of Justice 1947, pp. 6–7). In 1950, Congress acted in the spirit of Roosevelt's 1944 proposal by establishing the National Science Foundation to allocate funds for industry and academic research.[30] Most importantly, during the postwar period, the federal government effectively reduced the reach of the patent system through the systematic disbursement of R&D funds—for defense-related and other purposes—accompanied by policies that limited recipients' ability to assert exclusivity over inventions developed using those funds. Put differently: public R&D funding with exclusivity constraints on R&D outputs crowded out private R&D funding without such constraints.

The Gift: Federal R&D Funding

The infusion of federal R&D dollars into the wartime and postwar economies was massive and rapidly overtook private R&D funding. Total federal funds allocated for R&D expenditures increased from $370 million in 1941 ($6.38 billion

[29] Bush apparently made this statement regretfully. He later criticized courts' postwar hostility toward the patent system (Bush 1970, pp. 196–97, 200).

[30] National Science Foundation Act, P.L. 507 (81st Cong.), codified at 42 U.S.C. §§ 1861-75.

in 2020 dollars) to $1.61 billion in 1950 ($17.17 billion in 2020 dollars) to $8 billion in 1960 ($70.35 billion in 2020 dollars) to $13.5 billion in 1970 ($89.64 billion in 2020 dollars).[31] While industry remained the primary *performer* of R&D, government R&D funding as a share of total R&D funding surpassed industry R&D funding as of 1942 and the private sector only started to recover "market share" starting in the mid-1960s, nearly reaching parity as of 1975. At its peak, federal R&D funding accounted for 65 percent of all national R&D expenditures in 1963, in contrast to estimated percentages of 12–20 percent in the 1930s (Mowery 1981, p. 132; Markham 1962).

The Strings: Contractual Restrictions on Recipients of Federal R&D Funding

Federal R&D funding streams were accompanied by ownership and licensing policies that varied across agencies. During the postwar period, Congress instituted various types of compulsory licensing requirements in connection with R&D funding by various federal agencies, which then implemented those policies by administrative action. For a reasonably comprehensive list, see Appendix 6.B. I will focus on patent ownership and licensing policies at NASA, the Atomic Energy Commission (AEC) and the Department of Defense (DOD)[32] because these entities accounted for the overwhelming majority (approximately 90 percent[33]) of all federal R&D funds disbursed to the private sector during this period.

NASA and AEC

Both NASA and the AEC operated under statutes that presumptively precluded recipients of agency R&D funding from owning patents arising out of research using that funding.

NASA typically retained patent ownership and then granted an exclusive or non-exclusive license to the contractor, although it sometimes waived its ownership rights for purposes of promoting commercialization, allowing the

[31] For sources, see caption under Figure 6.2. All 2020 equivalent values calculated using "CPI Inflation Calculator" provided by the U.S. Bureau of Labor Statistics, https://www.bls.gov/data/inflation_calculator.htm.

[32] For simplicity, I use "DOD" to refer to all military services, even though the Department of Defense was not formally established until 1949.

[33] Author's calculations, based on data in Harbridge House 1968, I-3.

contractor to seek a patent independently (Harbridge House 1968, I-43, III-24, Exh. 1; Dobkin 1967, pp. 574–76).

The AEC followed a more tailored policy consisting of three elements. First, the AEC operated under a statute that prohibited patents for inventions relating to atomic energy and "useful *solely*" (my emphasis) for military purposes.[34] Second, with respect to other inventions relating to atomic energy, the AEC retained title to patents but granted contractors non-exclusive or (less commonly) exclusive rights (Harbridge House 1968, III-20, III-21). As of November 1965, the AEC had been issued 3,667 patents, of which 368 patents had been licensed to contractors on an exclusive basis (Harbridge House 1968, III-24, Exh. 1). Third, with respect to inventions not relating to atomic energy, the AEC retained broader discretion and sometimes waived its right to take title, thereby allowing the contractor to seek a patent (Harbridge House 1968, III-21, III-24, Exh. 1). As of November 1965, AEC contractors had been issued (and retained title to) 405 patents arising out of research funded by the AEC (Harbridge House 1968, III-24, Exh. 1).

Department of Defense

The DOD, the largest source of federal R&D funding during the postwar period (Mowery 2010, p. 1229), followed a less aggressive policy, typically allowing contractors to take title to the patent while retaining a royalty-free, non-exclusive license (Statement of Elmer B. Staats 1968, p. 103; Dobkin 1967, p. 587; Olson 1959, p. 722). If the contractor elected not to apply for a patent on an invention resulting from a procurement contract, the government had the option to do so (Olson 1959, p. 722). As of 1962, out of 1,722 patents arising out of DOD-funded research projects, title had vested in the contractor (which then granted a license to the government) 81 percent of the time (Harbridge House 1968, table 1, I-3). Even if the contractor took title to the invention, multiple factors limited its practical exclusivity. First, as noted, the government typically retained a royalty-free license. Second, by statute, the contractor was limited to monetary remedies against the government in the case of infringing use by other government contractors.[35] In 1958, the Office of the Comptroller General even held that military procurement officers *must* award contracts to the lowest bidder irrespective of the possibility of patent infringement, on the ground that patent holders could then seek compensation by bringing suit against the government.[36] Third, the DOD's license sometimes extended to a contractor's

[34] Atomic Energy Act of 1954 (P.L. 83-703) § 151, 42 USC § 2181.
[35] See note 7 and accompanying text.
[36] Herbert Cooper Co., 38 Comp. Gen. 276, 277 (1958).

"background patents" (that is, patents embodying a contractor's pre-existing technical knowledge) or unpatented technical data (Olson 1959, pp. 737–38; Scherer et al. 1959, p. 129). This policy was unpopular with contractors, who expressed dissatisfaction concerning the sharing of technical data and potential trade secrets with suppliers and bidders on subsequent projects (Olson 1959, pp. 737–38; Scherer et al. 1959, p. 129).[37] Finally, a contractor's exclusivity was sometimes limited by contractual provisions that imposed a "second-sourcing" obligation, especially in the semiconductor industry, which compelled a contractor to share know-how with other suppliers (Mowery and Rosenberg 2000, pp. 884–85; Mowery and Steinmuller 1994, p. 211; Levin 1982, pp. 64–65; Webbink 1977, p. 97).

The Private Beneficiaries of Public R&D Funding

The implicit compulsory licensing regime, implemented through public R&D funding and defense procurement contracts, often targeted the same firms that were concurrently or subsequently targeted by the explicit compulsory licensing regime, implemented through antitrust enforcement actions. Table 6.3 lists eight firms that were leading contractors with the OSRD (the entity that coordinated defense-related R&D during World War II), leading defense contractors during World War II, the Korean War, and the Cold War, and subjected to compulsory licensing orders during or after World War II.

The wartime skew in R&D funding toward large firms persisted in the postwar period. Reflecting the national security concerns that drove government R&D funding (at least through its peak in the mid-1960s (Levin 1982, p. 66)), the recipients of federal largesse were mostly larger enterprises in the aerospace, computing and communications industries (Mowery 1981, pp. 138–39, 145, 175, 304–05). During 1946–1962, twenty large corporations were the recipients of two-thirds of all federal R&D funds (Watson and Holman 1967, p. 380). Given the fact that government R&D funding represented the majority of all R&D funding during this time (see Figure 6.2), this promoted the concentration of R&D activity in general. In 1964, a report prepared for a congressional committee found that the "top 300 manufacturing companies

[37] Contractors' concerns apparently led to a change in policy during the 1960s. Olson (1959, pp. 736–37) notes that, starting in 1955, DOD licenses in favor of the government generally did not extend to background patents, and Dobkin (1967, pp. 589–91) states that the DOD only enjoyed a license to a contractor's background patents in the case of procurement contracts that followed an initial R&D contract with same contractor. As of the late 1960s, Hall and Johnson (1968, pp. 55–59) observed that the government sought to secure technical data to enable multi-firm procurement but sometimes struggled to do so due to contractor resistance.

Table 6.3 Leading R&D/defense contractors and compulsory license orders

Firm	OSRD Contractor Ranking	Defense Contractor Ranking (1940–1944)	Defense Contractor Ranking (1951–1953)	Defense Contractor Ranking (1958–1960)	Years of Compulsory License Orders
AT&T	1[a]	13	13	7	1956
GE	3	9	3	4	1945, 1948/49, 1953/54
RCA	4	43	22	14	1958
Du Pont	5	15	26	86	1945, 1947, 1952
Westinghouse	6	21	14	19	1942, 1949, 1953/54
Eastman Kodak	8	62	36	–	1948, 1954
Standard Oil (NJ)	11	31	49	24	1942
Bendix Aviation	–	17	17	17	1946, 1948, 1953
IBM	–	–	44	15	1956

Note: All rankings are based on the dollar value of funds contracted during the relevant period. OSRD contractor rankings are limited to the top 25 firms. If a firm does not have a ranking for defense contractor in any particular period, then the firm was not among the top 100 defense contractors for that period.

Sources: For OSRD contractor rankings, Baxter (1946, pp. 456–47, App. C); for defense contractor rankings, Peck and Scherer (1962, pp. 613-621, tables 5A.2, 5A.4).

[a]Ranking attributed in source to Western Electric, the manufacturing division of AT&T.

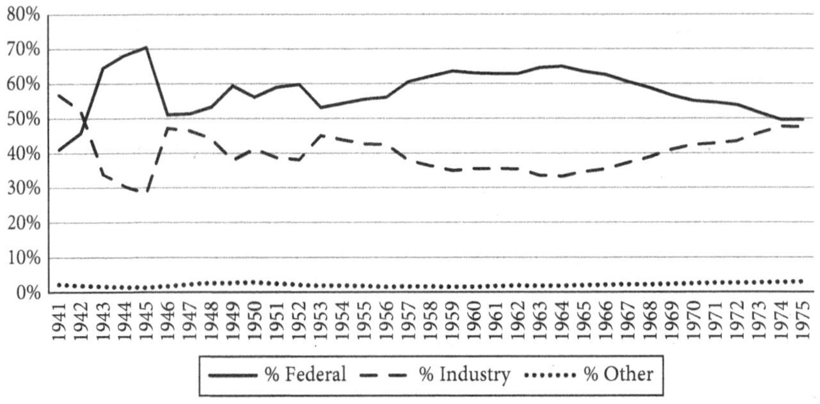

Figure 6.2 Sources of funding for R&D, 1941–1975.

Note: "Other" refers to non-federal governmental and nonprofit entities.

Sources: Author's calculations, based on: for 1953–1975, National Science Foundation, National Center for Science and Engineering Statistics, National Patterns of R&D Resources (annual series); for 1941–1952, US Department of Commerce (1953). Data collection and analysis may differ to some extent between these sources. Figure 6.2 originally appeared in Barnett (2021) and is reproduced with permission of Oxford University Press.

which perform 97% of all [f]ederally financed research and development in industry, also perform 91% of *all* research and development in industry, regardless of the source of funds . . . [and] 82% of industrial research and development, paid for by their own and other non-Federal funds" ("Impact of Federal Research" 1964, p. 59). In 1967, a Department of Commerce report noted that small firms faced obstacles in accessing federal R&D funding, and DOD funding trends had increasingly favored large-firm recipients (US Department of Commerce 1967).

Large firms similarly dominated military procurement expenditures, which indirectly supported private R&D: as of 1960, large firms accounted for more than 96 percent of all military equipment procurement expenditures (Peck and Scherer 1962, p. 139).[38] Mowery (1981, p. 137) and Levin (1982, p. 65) observe that military procurement in the 1950s and 1960s favored new, smaller firms in the nascent semiconductor market, some of which (most notably, Motorola, Texas Instruments, and Control Data) later grew into large dominant players (Schnee 1978, pp. 11–13). However, the military located early semiconductor production projects at large integrated firms (specifically, Western Electric, GE, Raytheon, RCA, and Sylvania) (Schnee 1978, p. 4), and a large share of the industry's

[38] Small firms did account for substantially higher and, in some categories, even majority percentages of non-equipment purchases (e.g., textiles, food, see data in Peck and Scherer 1962, p. 139, table 5.12); however, this is unlikely to have had a follow-on effect on R&D activity.

fundamental product and process innovations emerged from incumbents' corporate laboratories, in particular AT&T's Bell Labs (Malerba 1985, pp. 86, 90 n.10; Schnee 1978, p. 19; Tilton 1971, pp. 60–63). Additionally, Tilton (1971, pp. 94–95) argues that government R&D funding (as distinguished from military procurement contracts) relating to semiconductors primarily flowed to larger, older firms and, as a result, "impeded entry." Data covering 1958–1972 show that, while there was continuous entry into certain segments of the US semiconductor market, concentration levels remained at high or slightly increasing levels (Webbink 1977, pp. 18–39, esp. table II-6), suggesting a trend toward consolidation. More generally, military procurement in the broader category of electronics and communications systems strongly favored large firms, which represented over 92 percent of total defense expenditures for that procurement category during 1955–1960 (Peck and Scherer 1962, pp. 140–41, table 5.13).

It might nonetheless be thought that the government's ownership of patents relating to inventions arising out of government-funded R&D, which were then typically made available on a royalty-free, non-exclusive basis to all interested parties, would have attenuated the concentration effects of federal R&D funding. With a limited exception to be noted shortly, available evidence suggests a contrary result. That is: the *absence* of exclusivity—whether by license or title—impeded the commercialization of government-funded R&D. A 1968 government-commissioned report found that, despite marketing efforts by NASA and the AEC (Harbridge House 1968, III-7–15, III-20–23), the rate of commercialization of patented government-funded inventions was "very low" in general (Harbridge House 1968, I-6). Critically, the rate of commercialization was substantially lower for patents to which the contractor lacked title (and therefore only had a non-exclusive license from the government) (Harbridge House 1968, I-vi, I-vii, I-ix, IV-4, IV-16, IV-18). Interview evidence suggested that this link between non-commercialization and non-exclusivity was strongest in the case of contractors that were small or in the case of technologies that demanded significant additional development costs (Harbridge House 1968, IV-1–IV-33). This finding may explain why government commercialization did achieve success in the case of licenses to inventions sponsored by the Department of Agriculture and the Tennessee Valley Authority, which largely performed the necessary R&D close to the point of commercialization and, as a result, firms that adopted the technology did not have to make significant additional expenditures for purposes of commercial release (Harbridge House 1968, IV-57–IV-60).

This low level of market interest in commercializing government-sponsored inventions led some agencies to exercise discretion and sometimes grant title to the contractor, qualified by a license in favor of the government (Harbridge House 1968, I-43 [concerning NASA]; Dobkin 1967, pp. 582–83 [concerning the Department of Health, Education, and Welfare]) or, in the case of the DOD, grant title to the contractor even without a license in favor of the government (Dobkin 1967, pp. 588–89). Ultimately, the White House took steps to alleviate commercialization roadblocks posed by inflexible "government title" policies. President Kennedy, in 1963, and President Nixon, in 1971, issued policies enabling (in Kennedy's case) or encouraging (in Nixon's case) agencies to vest patent ownership in, or provide exclusive licenses to, contractors (Nixon 1971; Presidential Memorandum 1963). By 1974, the Federal Non-Nuclear Energy and Research Development Act, which allocated funds for research into alternative energy technologies, reflected a nuanced "title-with-waiver" policy that presumptively provided that all funded research would be freely available but empowered administrators to waive the government's ownership rights or provide contractors with exclusive licenses.[39]

A change in policy at the National Institutes of Health (NIH) illustrates why the government's royalty-free licensing approach may have suppressed market interest in commercializing federally funded R&D. In 1962, the NIH announced that any pharmaceutical firm that made use of a compound developed by academic researchers using NIH funds would be required to seek government consent in order to patent new products based on the compound (Harbridge House 1968, II-12). Prior to this change, industry and academia had regularly exchanged information and cooperated through long-standing relationships in which firms had screened compounds for academic investigators—a costly process necessary to determine therapeutic potential—free of charge, subject to informal agreements that conferred exclusivity on the screening firm with respect to products subsequently developed based on the compounds (Harbridge House 1968, II-19–II-22, II-40–II-46). As a result of the NIH's policy change, pharmaceutical firms that partnered with academic institutions lost assurance that they would enjoy exclusivity over products resulting from the testing process. Industry reaction was decisive. Thereafter almost no pharmaceutical firm agreed to screen compounds developed by academic researchers using NIH funds (Harbridge House 1968, II-12, II-14), resulting in the "nearly complete blockage of testing" and an "insurmountable obstacle to the ultimate utilization" of any compounds with therapeutic potential (Harbridge House 1968, II-29).

Assessing the Welfare Effects of Generalized Compulsory Licensing

We now have a substantially complete picture of the postwar innovation regime: explicit and implicit forms of compulsory licensing, implemented through

[39] Federal Non-Nuclear Energy and Research Development Act of 1974, Pub. L. 93-577, 88 Stat. 1887-91, 42 USC §§ 5908 (see especially §§ 5908(c), (g)(2)).

antitrust enforcement actions, government R&D funding, and defense procurement, set against a background of substantial constraints on patent enforcement and licensing. It now remains to consider whether this regime secured the policy objectives that motivated it. The launch of the antitrust enforcement campaign in the late 1930s, and the concurrent TNEC hearings, reflected prevalent views concerning the relationship between patents, concentration, and innovation that were endorsed both in popular debate and by much of the economics profession (Hart 2001, p. 928). Specifically, it was widely argued that incumbents accumulated patent portfolios to erect barriers to entry, which in turn suppressed incumbents' incentives to innovate (Hart 2001, pp. 927–28; Hart 1998, pp. 92–93). These views pointed toward a simple policy conclusion: opening up the patent portfolios held by the country's largest incumbents would reduce entry barriers, which would in turn lower entry costs and increase innovation by both small firms (due to lower entry costs) and large firms (due to greater competitive discipline).

The postwar innovation economy largely did not conform to these expectations. Market concentration levels in general did not fall and, while robust investment in innovation persisted for some time, it started to decline by the mid-1960s. To be sure, the large corporate laboratories of the postwar period achieved and implemented fundamental innovations in computing, electronics, and telecommunications that translated into important military and civilian applications. However, it is precisely the fact that these innovations originated primarily in large-firm laboratories that raises concern. Specifically, postwar innovation activity was heavily concentrated among large firms that maintained integrated R&D, production, and distribution infrastructures and enjoyed established channels to federal funding. Rather than expanding access, it appears that the postwar weak-IP regime mostly sustained state-subsidized "innovation oligopolies"—that is, large integrated firms that captured returns from innovation through non-patent assets and capacities and were therefore well-suited to a weak property-rights environment.

Compulsory Licensing Optimists

F. M. Scherer, the author or co-author of the most extensive studies of the compulsory licensing orders during the late New Deal and postwar period, has concluded that these policy actions most likely had a net favorable welfare effect. This view relies on three key observations. First, and most generally, the postwar period appears to be a period of robust innovation, as indicated by the technological advancements that emerged from the corporate research laboratories maintained by the period's incumbents. Second, Scherer and co-authors found in survey studies that large firms (outside pharmaceuticals) indicated that they would not expect to reduce R&D expenditures in response to compulsory licensing orders (Scherer 1977, pp. 59–60, 62–64; Scherer et al. 1959, pp. 123–25). Third, Scherer (1977, pp. 67–75) found that, based on data for 1975, the compulsory licensing orders had not induced targeted firms to reduce R&D intensity (R&D as a percentage of sales).[40] Given these observations, Scherer concluded that the postwar compulsory licensing regime most likely constituted a welfare-improving intervention that reduced the social costs inherent to the patent system—in particular, the use of patents for monopolization purposes—without materially offsetting losses in the form of reduced innovation. However, he recognized that compulsory licensing likely encourages secrecy (Scherer et al. 1959, pp. 154–55) and, more tentatively, may disadvantage smaller firms and discourage pharmaceutical R&D (Scherer 1977, pp. 63–64, 85–86).

Recent empirical studies relating to the Trading with the Enemy Act, a forerunner to the compulsory licensing orders subsequently pursued by the antitrust agencies, similarly express mostly sanguine views concerning compulsory licensing, with varying levels of qualification. Using data on citations to confiscated patents as a proxy for follow-on innovation, Moser and Voena (2009) present evidence suggesting that the confiscation of German-owned patents on chemical inventions during World War I increased domestic US invention in the chemical industry during the interwar period. Baten, Bianchi, and Moser (2017) present evidence suggesting positive effects on invention (as measured by interwar patenting at the German patent office) by the German holders of US patents that had been confiscated under the Trading with the Enemy Act. Moser (2015) and Moser and Voena (2009) conclude that compulsory licensing can have favorable effects on innovation, while Baten, Bianchi, and Moser (2017) take the more nuanced view that this may be the case but only if used exceptionally so as to avoid undermining first-mover innovation incentives. Also using citation data as a proxy for follow-on innovation, Watzinger et al. (2020) observe that compulsory royalty-free licensing of Bell Labs' patent portfolio in the 1956 consent decree (i) induced follow-on innovation among smaller firms in markets outside the telecommunications sector (markets into which AT&T could not enter under the consent decree) but (ii) had no comparable effect in the telecommunications market in which AT&T retained its government-granted monopoly over telephone service and, effectively, telephone equipment.[41]

[40] Additionally, Scherer (1977, pp. 67–75) finds that firms targeted by compulsory licensing orders exhibited, as of 1975, higher R&D expenditures as compared to firms that were not so targeted (adjusting for firm size and industry segment).

[41] It is not clear that the increase in patenting (and, by implication, innovation) outside the telecommunications sector would have been substantially foreclosed but for the 1956 compulsory licensing order. Bell may have agreed to license to more efficient follow-on innovators, especially

As the work of Scherer and these later contributors sometimes acknowledges, any net welfare analysis of compulsory licensing must weigh expected short-run positive effects on follow-on, incremental, and lower-cost invention against longer-run adverse effects on first-mover, fundamental, and higher-cost invention. Any such analytical exercise is likely to yield mixed results in varying degrees. In a study of a large sample of decisions by the Court of Appeals for the Federal Circuit during 1982–2008, Galasso and Schankerman (2014) find that judicial invalidation of patents only yields positive incremental effects on follow-on innovation in the case of patents that (i) are more likely to survive a validity challenge, (ii) are held by large firms, and (iii) relate to certain complex technology environments. They further caution that even these modest context-specific positive effects may not represent net long-term welfare gains, given the likely disincentive effects of compulsory licensing on smaller firms that are often reliant on patents and other potential disincentive effects on first-mover innovation. As will be discussed, the experience of the postwar period supports these types of concerns.

Reasons for Caution: Revisiting Compulsory Licensing

In this section, I discuss quantitative and qualitative evidence relating to the possible aggregate effects of the postwar weak-IP/strong-antitrust regime (including explicit and implicit forms of compulsory licensing) on innovation activity. While the evidence is not definitive and I do not make any causal claims, a critical examination of available evidence tends to support three observations that cast doubt on the view that the postwar weak-IP regime (including but not limited to compulsory licensing) had net positive welfare effects, especially over a medium to long time period. First, while innovation investment (by various measures) was robust for a substantial portion of the postwar years, this period was limited and innovation activity started to decline in the mid-1960s. Second, the postwar innovation economy relied heavily on federal R&D funding, which necessarily gives rise to the distortions inherent to any resource-allocation system that relies

in the case of markets which it did not intend to enter or complementary-goods markets that would promote demand for AT&T's telecommunications services and equipment. If that is the case, then compulsory licensing mostly induces a redistributive (as distinguished from an efficiency) effect in favor of follow-on innovators by eliminating the original innovator's bargaining leverage (while depressing its incentives to undertake future innovation or to provide know-how and other support to licensees). The possibility that AT&T would have voluntarily licensed follow-on innovators is not mere speculation. Prior to the consent decree, Bell had already licensed patents relating to the transistor, its landmark invention, to all interested parties at what was widely perceived to be a below-market royalty rate (Levin 1982, pp. 75–77; Tilton 1971, pp. 74–75). On the redistributive and efficiency effects of patents in sequential innovation contexts, see Green and Scotchmer (1995).

on political rather than market mechanisms. Third, innovation activity was concentrated among large integrated firms that maintained a capital-intensive R&D, production, and distribution infrastructure. These observations suggest that the postwar regime provided at best a workable mechanism for supporting innovation by a relatively small group of larger and more integrated firms, which in turn relied on a steady stream of government funding. More generally, this implies that (i) a weak-IP system does not constitute a model for a self-sustaining innovation economy over a substantial time horizon, especially in industries characterized by high capital requirements, and (ii) insecure IP rights may distort the market's selection of organizational forms for executing the innovation and commercialization process, favoring larger and more integrated entities. The latter effect in turn potentially distorts the allocation of innovation resources toward the type of R&D projects that large firms tend to favor.

The Rise-and-Decline Pattern

I use three principal measures to indirectly (and imperfectly) assess innovation activity during the postwar period: (i) patenting intensity; (ii) R&D intensity; and (iii) R&D employment intensity. These measures (each of which is defined precisely in the subsequent discussion) provide complementary perspectives on the postwar innovation environment: R&D intensity and R&D employment intensity reflect R&D inputs while patenting intensity reflects R&D outputs.[42] Remarkably, these measures exhibit a similar "rise-and-decline" pattern in which innovation activity intensified during the 1950s and early to mid-1960s and declined thereafter. Critically, the same rise-and-decline pattern appears in the flow of federal R&D funding into the private sector during this time, strongly suggesting an innovation environment in which innovation was governed by governmental largesse rather than the judgment of the market.

[42] An alternative measure of R&D outputs is total factor productivity (TFP). This attempts to measure the residual portion of economic growth that is not attributable to capital or labor inputs (and is therefore often presumed to reflect technological advancement). While TFP is widely used as a measure of the impact of innovation on economic growth, it is also widely acknowledged that TFP at least partially reflects factors unrelated to innovation and TFP methodologies face measurement challenges with respect to quality improvements (because these may not be reflected in increased output) and service industries (due to the lack of a clearly defined unit of output). For detailed discussion of these issues, see Hulten (2001, p. 40), who concludes that "[t]he [TFP] residual should *not* be equated with technical change, although it often is" (emphasis in original). Despite these limitations, TFP nonetheless can provide some insight into an economy's innovation performance. Subsequently (see note 47), I discuss historical movements in TFP during the postwar period, which largely track the rise-and-decline pattern exhibited by the other measures of innovation inputs and outputs, including patenting intensity, R&D intensity and R&D employment intensity.

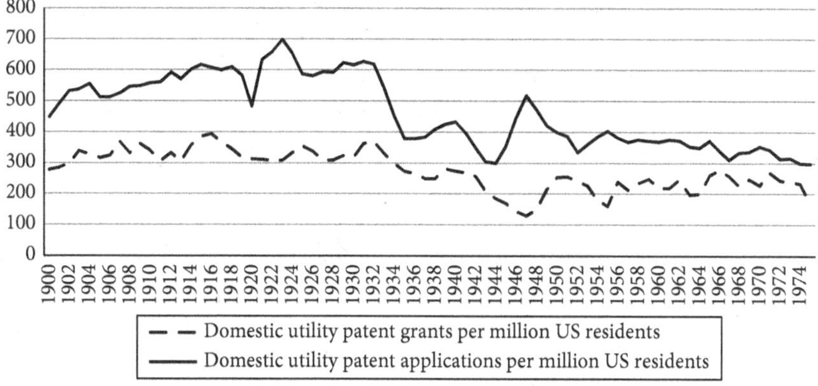

Figure 6.3 Domestic utility patent applications and grants per capita, 1900–1975.
Sources: For patent data, US Patent and Trademark Office, "U.S. Patent Statistics Chart, Calendar Years 1963–2015" and "U.S. Patent Activity, Calendar Years 1790 to Present." For population data, US Census Bureau, Historical National Population Estimates: 1 July 1900 to 1 July 1999, https://www.census.gov/population/estimates/nation/popclockest.txt, and U.S. Census Bureau, National Intercensal Tables: 2000-2010, https://www.census.gov/data/tables/time-series/demo/popest/intercensal-2000-2010-national.html. Population data were extracted at 10-year intervals. Figures for intervening years are estimates. Figure 6.3 originally appeared in Barnett (2021) and is reproduced with permission of Oxford University Press.

Patenting Intensity

Innovation activity is often measured indirectly by patent applications and grants. While this is an inherently incomplete measure since not all inventions are patented, it provides some indication of innovation activity and, with appropriate qualification, is therefore widely used in the innovation economics literature. As measured on a per capita basis, patent applications by, and patent grants to, US resident inventors declined markedly starting in the early 1930s (possibly reflecting court decisions that had indicated the onset of a patent-skeptical legal climate, see the section, Patent Hostility), spiked immediately after World II, and, concurrently with the regular use of compulsory patent licensing orders, exhibited intermittent stasis and moderate decline through 1975. Similar trends are observed if patenting rates are normalized on a per GDP basis.[43]

Figure 6.3 depicts per capita domestic patent application and issuance rates for US resident inventors during 1900–1975, providing a longer timeline in order to

[43] In 1938, when the Department of Justice's Antitrust Division commenced the pursuit of compulsory licensing remedies through antitrust enforcement, there were approximately 58 utility patent applications by, and almost 30 patents issued to, US inventors per $1 billion GDP (in 2009 dollars); in 1975, less than 7 patents were issued and less than 19 patent applications were filed per $1 billion GDP (in 2009 dollars). Source: Author's calculations based on patenting data from US Patent Office and GDP data from US Bureau of Economic Analysis.

place in historical context the long-lived patent drought that started in the early 1930s, except for a brief recovery shortly after the war.

It is important not to conflate patenting rates with innovation rates. Especially in this historical context, patenting activity may understate innovation activity to the extent that any decline in patenting rates is attributable in part to the reduction in patent values as a result of legal "shocks" to patent strength starting in the 1930s. In response, firms may have sustained R&D investment but shifted to secrecy and other non-patent mechanisms by which to extract returns from those investments (Scherer 1977, pp. 64, 67; Scherer et al. 1959, pp. 153–55). Relatedly, Scherer (1977, pp. 66–67) and Scherer et al. (1959, pp. 137–45) find that the reduction in patenting activity was more significant among firms targeted by compulsory licensing orders (in particular, firms targeted by orders that covered future patents) as compared to comparably sized firms that were not so targeted. Even subject to this qualification, however, the decline in per GDP and per capita patenting rates by US inventors is so substantial that it may indicate a longer-term decline in innovation activity or at least a distortion in the types of firms that conduct innovation and, consequently, the types of innovation projects that are undertaken.

R&D Intensity

The possibility that firms adopted trade secrecy or other non-patent monetization strategies (and therefore, did not necessarily reduce R&D investment) in response to the weakening of patent protection finds some support by measuring innovation activity through total R&D intensity (total R&D expenditures as a percentage of GDP) or business R&D intensity (business R&D expenditures as a percentage of GDP). (For the purposes of these measures, R&D expenditures are attributed to the source of R&D funding, rather than the entities that perform R&D.) In contrast to the per capita and per GDP patenting measures, both R&D intensity measures rose during the postwar period through the mid-1960s, although business R&D grew at a significantly lower rate as compared to total R&D intensity, reflecting the preponderant role of federal R&D funding during this time. However, as shown in Figure 6.4, total R&D intensity exhibited a significant decline starting in the mid-1960s, while business R&D intensity exhibited steady if modest growth. Data on R&D expenditures as a percentage of net sales of manufacturing companies shows a more uniform rise-and-decline pattern: as documented by Richard Caves (1980, pp. 533–35), manufacturing firms' R&D intensity increased during the 1950s and 1960s, reaching 4.3 percent in 1965, and then declined through 1976, falling to 3 percent. Caves further notes that the post-1965 decline in R&D spending was sharpest among chemicals, electrical equipment, communications equipment, and aircraft, the latter three of which were the primary industry recipients of federal R&D funding

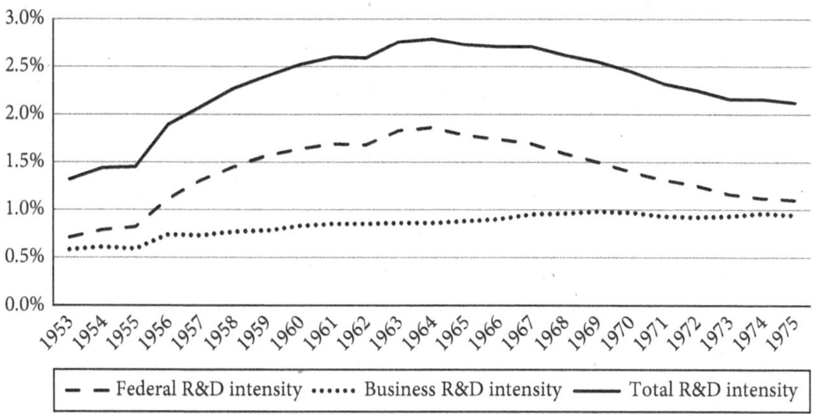

Figure 6.4 National US R&D intensities, 1953–1975.

Notes: "R&D intensity" is defined as R&D expenditures as a percentage of total US GDP. "R&D expenditures" are attributed to the sources of R&D funding, not entities that perform R&D.

Source: National Science Foundation, National Center for Science and Engineering Statistics 2019. National Patterns of R&D Resources: 2017/18 Data Update. Figure 6.4 originally appeared in Barnett (2021) and is reproduced with permission of Oxford University Press.

and defense procurement expenditures. This common rise-and-decline pattern in R&D expenditures during the postwar period closely tracks trends in federal R&D funding (see Figure 6.2), which increased as a share of total R&D funding starting in the early 1940s, peaked in 1964, and then declined thereafter. This observation provides further evidence of the substantial extent to which R&D activity under the postwar period's weak-patent regime had become dependent on public funding.

R&D Employment Intensity

Firms' R&D employment intensity (defined as the percentage of firms' labor force involved in R&D) provides an indirect measure of R&D activity.[44] Consistent with the rise-and-decline pattern, National Science Foundation (NSF) data on all companies that perform R&D show that the number of R&D personnel per 1,000 employees ranged from 20 in 1958 to 30 in 1965 and then declined to approximately 25 for the period through 1975.[45] To achieve more granular insights,

[44] I do not measure R&D activity by firm-specific R&D expenditures because these are typically unavailable for this period. Public firms were only required to disclose R&D expenditures starting in 1972 (Nix and Nix 1992).

[45] Author's calculations, based on NSF data.

I collected data on total and R&D employment at firms that were (i) ranked in the Fortune 100 (based on revenues) as of 1955, and (ii) reported R&D employment in the Industrial Research Laboratories (IRL) reports published by the National Research Council.[46] I then distinguished between firms that were and were not targeted by compulsory licensing orders prior to 1970.[47] The targeted group includes all 24 firms that were subject to compulsory licensing orders prior to 1970 and ranked in the Fortune 100 as of 1955. The non-targeted group includes 65 out of 75 firms that appeared in the Fortune 100 as of 1955 but were not subject to compulsory licensing orders prior to 1970.[48] The omitted firms did not report R&D employment data for purposes of the IRL reports.

Figure 6.5 shows these two firm populations' median R&D employment intensity (the percentage that R&D personnel constituted out of a firm's total personnel). The data conforms to the rise-and-decline pattern observed previously for national R&D intensities. Firms exhibited increasing R&D employment intensity through 1965 (the year in which federal R&D intensity peaked), after which the trend reverts to approximately the 1955 rates and by 1975 drops below them. That is: by 1975, the median large US firm was less R&D intensive (as measured by R&D employment intensity) than it had been as of 1955. As shown in Figure 6.5, firms targeted by compulsory licensing orders exhibited higher rates of median R&D employment intensity than non-targeted firms, although the two populations exhibit similar relative increases and decreases in R&D employment intensity.

Figure 6.6 provides more granular data, showing R&D employment intensity at five-year intervals for selected Fortune 100 firms targeted by compulsory licensing orders. Two points are most salient. First, during 1955–1965, there are substantial increases in R&D employment intensity in the case of most firms, but especially firms such as AT&T, Bendix, Dow, Du Pont, and RCA, all of which exhibited intensity rates by 1965 or earlier in excess of 8 percent. Second, starting in 1965, there are moderate to significant declines in R&D employment intensity in the case of most firms. Both trends are consistent with the familiar rise-and-decline pattern in the postwar innovation economy (with more moderate declines in the case of AT&T and Bendix).

[46] For further information on data sources, see note to Figure 6.5.

[47] For this purpose, "targeted" firms did not include Fortune 100 firms that were subject to compulsory licensing orders during 1970–1975 on the rationale that these firms' actions with respect to the hiring of R&D personnel did not operate under the "shadow" of a compulsory licensing decree for the largest portion of the period starting in 1956. These firms (five total) were treated as non-targeted firms.

[48] Careful readers will note that the total number of targeted and non-targeted firms that were ranked in the Fortune 100 as of 1955, mentioned in this and the preceding sentence, only sum to 99. This is attributable to the fact that Nabisco is listed as both Nabisco Group Holdings and Nabisco Brands in the Fortune rankings but, for purposes of tracking R&D employment, I treat these firms as a single entity (following the treatment in the IRL reports).

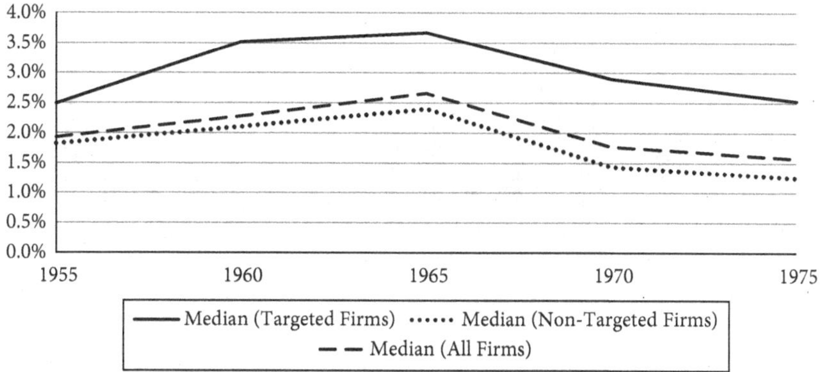

Figure 6.5 Median R&D employment intensity of Fortune 100 firms, 1955–1975.

Notes: R&D employment intensity refers to the percentage that R&D personnel constitutes out of a firm's total personnel. "Targeted" firms are firms that were subject to a compulsory patent licensing order during 1941–1969. The graph is based on data extracted at five-year intervals starting in 1955. Intervening values are estimates. In the case of an acquisition involving entities that were both members of the Fortune 500 at the time of the acquisition, *Fortune* uses the name of the surviving entity even in years preceding the acquisition. In those cases (and in the case of any other changes in a firm's name), I used information from the company website and other sources to reasonably ascertain the predecessor entities for purposes of extracting employment data for the relevant years from the IRL reports. In some years (almost entirely, 1970 and 1975), some companies only listed senior research personnel in the IRL reports, rather than all R&D personnel. Those firms' data were disregarded for those years. Finally, the 1960 edition of the IRL relies on data collected during November 1959 through March 1960; hence, the data may apply to either year. This is unlikely to have a material effect.

Sources: Data on total employment obtained from the Fortune 500 digital archives http://archive.fortune.com/magazines/fortune/fortune500_archive/full/1955/401.html. Data on the number of R&D personnel (including technical and non-technical personnel) for each firm and its subsidiaries was obtained from Industrial Research Laboratories (1956, 1960, 1965, 1970, 1975), which reflect questionnaires sent to reporting companies (or, if a response was not received, public sources in some cases).

Trends in reported R&D employment intensity among the largest postwar firms (whether or not targeted by compulsory licensing orders) track closely (i) trends in total and business R&D intensity (see Figure 6.4) and (ii) trends in federal R&D funding as a share of total R&D funding (see Figure 6.2). The confluence of these measures strongly suggests the extent to which the postwar innovation economy relied on infusions of government funding and faltered once that funding was not as abundant. The postwar period does not convincingly demonstrate that innovation can thrive without secure IP rights; more precisely, it suggests that innovation can persist for a limited period if there is substantial supplemental government support to cover any funding shortfalls. As is sometimes overlooked in innovation policy discussions, governmental support necessarily imposes distortionary social costs insofar as it relies on funds sourced from taxes or government borrowing. Tellingly, leading innovations attributed to the

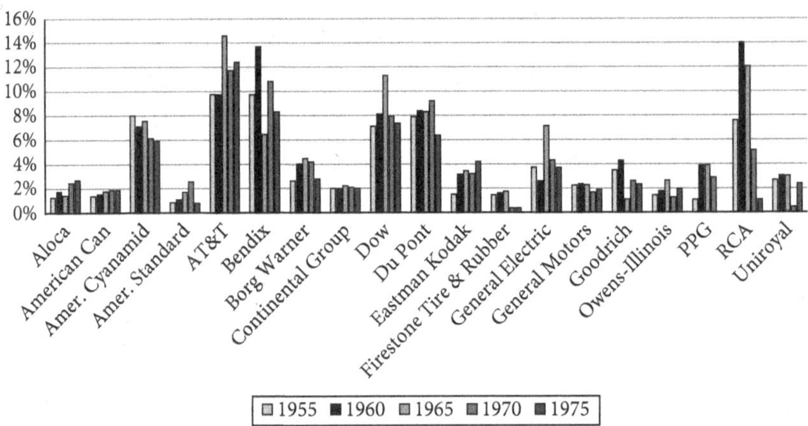

Figure 6.6 R&D employment intensity of selected targeted Fortune 100 firms, 1955–1975.

Notes: Firms are listed using the name of the firm or predecessor entity as of 1955. IBM and Westinghouse were omitted because they failed to report, or grossly underreported, information on R&D personnel in 1970 and/or 1975. See also Notes under Figure 6.5.

Sources: See Figure 6.5.

postwar period typically arose out of government-funded defense and space related R&D at large corporate laboratories: radar for purposes of detecting enemy aircraft; computing for purposes of calculating missile trajectories; the laser for purposes of a tank range finder; and semiconductors and related advances in digital communications and graphics for purposes of the space program and "SAGE" air defense system (Chiang 1995; Levin 1982, p. 58). Once government funding fell in the mid-1960s, there was a decline in all three measures of innovation activity (patenting intensity, R&D intensity, and R&D employment intensity),[49] which suggests that firms may have had difficulty securing private funding to substitute for withdrawn government funding in an institutional environment characterized by weak IP rights that limited investors' expected profits in the case of an innovation project's technical and commercial success.

While further empirical inquiry is warranted, this possibility is consistent with widespread observations that the US economy suffered from an innovation slowdown during the 1970s. These observations are supported by the

[49] The same is true of TFP, which, as discussed earlier (see note 40), is often used as a measure of innovative activity (or more precisely, the impact of innovative activity on economic growth). After an extended period of growth that started in the late 1920s and peaked in the mid-1960s, TFP started declining, especially during the 1970s. For discussion, see Field (2007); Shackleton (2013). This movement in postwar TFP trends largely coincides with movements in the other measures of innovative activity discussed earlier in the chapter.

aforementioned declines in patenting rates (see Figure 6.3), total R&D and business R&D intensity (see Figure 6.4), and R&D employment intensity (see Figure 6.5), each of which commenced starting in the mid to late 1960s coincident with the reduction in federal R&D funding. Commentators often have made qualitative observations of a national decline in technological leadership (Scherer 1992, pp. 1–3; Crawford and Tellis 1981; Schlesinger 1980, p. 552; Rabinow 1976), yet rarely has this been attributed to the contemporary weakness in the force of patent protections. Two extensive corporate histories document notable project failures during the later years of the postwar period at RCA (Graham 1986 and Alcoa (Graham and Pruitt 1990), both of which had formerly been viewed as innovation leaders. While certain factors associated with the more general and much-discussed "productivity slowdown" in the 1970s certainly contributed to this quantitative and qualitative decline in innovation intensity, it may at least partly reflect the fact that, as is widely asserted in the innovation literature on both theoretical and empirical grounds, large firms are inclined to focus R&D efforts on incremental "improvement" innovation, rather than fundamental "radical" innovation (for theoretical arguments, see McAfee and McMillan 1995, Arrow 1993; for empirical evidence, see Cohen 2010, pp. 137–39). In a prescient contribution, Hamberg (1963) anticipated this risk when he cautioned that the then-thriving innovation environment led by large corporate research laboratories may yield a distorted selection of innovation projects.

Innovation Oligopolies

For a limited but substantial part of the weak-IP period, there is little doubt that innovation persisted at robust levels. Firms targeted by compulsory licensing orders were apparently undeterred from expending substantial amounts on breakthrough R&D projects that led to notable innovation successes, such as color television, introduced by RCA in 1951 (Scherer et al. 1959, pp. 26–27), and the System/360 mainframe computer system, released by IBM in 1964 after reportedly spending $5 billion (equivalent to almost $42 billion in 2020 dollars)[50] on the project (Wise 1966). The fact that firms undertook these high-cost R&D projects under a weak-IP regime appears to challenge the view that patents are a precondition for substantial innovation. Relatedly, some scholars portray the period from 1948 through 1973 as an historically unique "golden age" of

[50] Amount updated using "CPI Inflation Calculator" provided by the US Bureau of Labor Statistics, https://www.bls.gov/data/inflation_calculator.htm.

technological advancement, based in large part on the significant growth in total factor productivity (TFP) during this period.[51]

Any such conclusion, however, must address three complications. First, as Field (2007) observes, the growth in TFP commenced in the late 1920s and may have reflected in part the deployment of technological innovations during the 1920s and 1930s (which were therefore initially developed under historically robust levels of patent protection).[52] Second, as discussed previously (see the section, Public R&D Funding: A Gift with Strings Attached), the postwar innovation economy relied substantially on government funding. As such, it does not provide a generalizable model of a stand-alone innovation system or, taking into account the exceptionally large expenditures made by the US government in connection with the Space Race, an economically sustainable model of even a publicly supported innovation system over a longer term. Third, the postwar period's apparent innovative vigor under a weak-IP regime may have come at a substantial social price: namely, an innovation economy that advantaged larger and more integrated firms over smaller and less integrated firms. That in turn may have distorted the mix of innovation projects financed and undertaken by firms in the postwar innovation economy.

Concentration in the Postwar Innovation Economy

When ordering a dissolution remedy in the *United Shoe* case, the Supreme Court observed that, after a decade, the compulsory licensing order had apparently done little to erode the firm's dominant position in the shoe manufacturing equipment market.[53] With the exception of the photocopying machine market,[54] the judge's frustration with the apparent ineffectiveness of the compulsory licensing order generalizes to virtually every US market in which these orders were issued. This is consistent with the well-established finding that, under various measures, concentration trends increased or held constant throughout the postwar period. For the period 1947–1958, Shephard reported that overall concentration ratios

[51] For the leading proponent of this view, see Gordon (2016, pp. 319–20, 537–38, 543–44). For some of the limitations of relying on TFP as a measure of innovation, see the discussion in note 40.

[52] On the US patent regime (including patent-related antitrust law) that prevailed during the 1920s and 1930s, see Barnett (2021).

[53] 391 U.S. 244, 252 [1968].

[54] In the photocopying market, there was substantial entry by Japanese manufacturers after issuance of the compulsory licensing order against Xerox in 1975 (Scherer 1982, p. 187). Another possible exception is the color television market. A 1958 consent decree required RCA to license its color television patents to domestic licensees at no charge. Chandler (2011, pp. 34–35) states that this induced RCA to more aggressively license its technology to foreign competitors (principally, Phillips and Japanese firms) in order to sustain its licensing income. Hence, the consent decree may have played a role in the entry (after some time lag) by Japanese electronics manufacturers into the US market, formerly dominated by RCA and other US firms.

in large samples of firms had increased since the end of World War II, while intra-industry concentration ratios had held approximately constant (Shephard 1964, p. 212). For 1947–1970, Mueller and Hamm (1974) report that four-firm concentration ratios in a sample of 166 manufacturing industries had increased moderately, while Scherer (1980, table 4.8) finds, using the same measure for 154 industries, that concentration increased during approximately the same period in consumer goods industries but declined slightly in producer goods industries. Based on shares of total value added among the top 200 manufacturing firms, as measured at periodic intervals, Caves (1980, p. 511, table 7.6) identifies a significant increase in concentration in 1954 as compared to 1947, which then grows incrementally at periodical intervals through 1972. Other concentration measures based on shares of assets and sales show a similar trend of incrementally increasing concentration among the 200 largest non-financial firms during 1956–1977 (Caves 1980, p. 512, table 7.7). Using four-firm concentration ratios, Scherer (1977, pp. 75–78) finds that compulsory licensing orders had no statistically significant effect on concentration levels in affected industries.

These tendencies toward high and stable levels of concentration reappear in data on R&D spending and activity during the postwar period. During this time, R&D spending was concentrated among a small number of large firms in a few industries (Nelson et al. 1967, p. 56). For example, a 1964 Senate committee report stated that the top 300 manufacturing firms performed 82 percent of all industrial R&D ("Impact of Federal Research" 1964, p. 59). Over a broader time period, NSF data shows that this skewed concentration persisted: R&D expenditures by large firms (as defined by number of employees)[55] consistently represented in excess of 90 percent of total industry R&D expenditures during 1957–1975.[56] This extreme skew is not inherent to innovation markets: as of 2006, NSF data shows that large firms represented only 76 percent of total industry R&D expenditures[57] and prior research has shown that small R&D-intensive firms played a prominent role in US innovation markets from the mid-nineteenth century through the early twentieth century (Lamoreaux, Levenstein, and Sokoloff 2004; Lamoreaux and Sokoloff 2003). The lack of NSF data prior to 1957 raises the possibility that high concentration levels during the postwar period may have represented a continuation of existing high R&D concentration levels during the interwar period; however, at a minimum, it is apparent that R&D concentration did not decline during this time.

[55] NSF data defines "large firms" as firms having more than 1,000 employees.

[56] National Science Foundation, "Company and other (except Federal) funds for R&D, by industry and by size of company: 1957–98."

[57] National Science Foundation, Division of Science Resource Statistics, Industrial Research and Development (Annual Reports, 1999-2007). For further discussion of this point, see Barnett (2021, pp. 100, 109).

Contrary to the expectations that drove the New Deal and postwar antitrust campaign against large patent holders, the socialization of innovation, implemented through explicit and implicit forms of compulsory licensing, did not democratize innovation or generate an entrepreneurial economy of small innovator-firms. To the contrary, it mostly supported (or, at a minimum, did not challenge) a big-firm innovation economy in which industry R&D took place primarily in the large university-like research laboratories of dominant incumbents with integrated production and distribution capacities (Mowery and Rosenberg 2000, pp. 809–10; Hart 2001, p. 929; Galambos 2000, p. 951), substantially supported by defense-related government funding. As David Mowery has documented, large corporate laboratories had already expanded during the interwar period, although in part to monitor and purchase technologies developed by outside inventors (Mowery 1981, pp. 37–42, 48–59; see also Lamoreaux, Levenstein, and Sokoloff 2011). The concentration of R&D activity among large firms continued and strengthened during the postwar decades (Mowery 1981, pp. 131–32, 145, 151–52, 174, 216–17, 224–34). While smaller firms may have played an important role in the early development of semiconductors (Levin 1982, p. 65; Mowery 1981, p. 137), this is not the principal environment in which innovation and commercialization activities took place generally during this period. That environment was comprised by the large research laboratories of firms such as AT&T, Du Pont, GE, IBM, and RCA. As will be discussed shortly, the postwar organization of innovation activity may be in part attributable to an insecure property-rights environment. A weak-IP/strong antitrust regime advantaged large integrated firms that could capture returns on innovation through non-patent assets, such as internal capital markets, economies of scale and scope, and channels to government funding.[58] If that is the case, then it is no surprise that public and private capital to fund innovation flowed disproportionately to these firms.

Interpreting Innovation "Success" in the Postwar Economy

Contemporary commentators had observed, but mostly triumphantly, the apparent connection between innovation and size during the postwar

[58] Other scholars have observed that strong antitrust enforcement during the postwar period induced firms to pursue innovation and commercialization internally, rather than acquiring innovations through licensing or acquisition transactions involving other firms (Hart 2001, p. 929; Mowery and Rosenberg 2000, pp. 809–10, 826; Hart 1998, p. 96; Mowery 1995, pp. 148, 162–63; Mowery and Nelson 1994, p. 205; Mowery and Rosenberg 1989, pp. 15–51, 156-58; Mowery 1981, p. 129). My inquiry focuses more broadly on the effects of both strong antitrust and weak patent enforcement in (i) inducing large firms to substitute toward non-patent complementary assets (including but not limited to secrecy) and (ii) discouraging entry or growth by smaller R&D-specialist firms that lacked a comparable suite of non-patent assets.

period, tending to view it as a general characteristic of well-functioning R&D markets. This interpretation was advocated most prominently by Galbraith (1952, p. 91), relying ultimately on the views of Schumpeter (1942), who had asserted that imperfectly competitive markets populated by large dominant firms provide the best environment for innovation. Economic historians widely adopted a narrative according to which US capitalism had optimized the innovation process by locating it in the large corporation, complemented by long-standing relationships with the military (Graham 2007, p. 346, who describes, rather than adopts, this view). Given the disaggregated structures in many current technology markets (especially, the biotechnology market and the "fabless" semiconductor market (Barnett 2021; 2011), this view now seems like an artifact of a particular historical period, rather than a generally valid proposition.

More precisely, this view is likely an artifact of a weak property-rights regime. The shift of innovation activities during the postwar period toward large-firm modes of organization—essentially, the substitution of internal for external markets in intellectual assets—may have reflected in part the organizational bias that is inherent to a weak-IP environment. Teece (1986) observed that a firm can secure returns on innovation through two types of strategies: (i) it can block imitation of the product directly through use of an effective IP right; or (ii) even in the absence of IP protection, it can embed the product within a difficult-to-replicate suite of complementary assets. In an environment in which strategy (i) is not feasible, then, everything else being equal, firms that can most efficiently execute strategy (ii) operate at a competitive advantage. Hence, a large firm that has access to substantial complementary assets may even welcome weakened patent protection to the extent it blocks a path by which a smaller but more innovative entrant could challenge incumbents without incurring the costs of acquiring a comparable stock of non-patent assets. Firms such as AT&T, GE, IBM, and Du Pont enjoyed a rich stock of complementary assets, including economies of scale, distribution networks, internal capital resources, and reputational capital. Hence, even when compelled to license out some of their patented technologies at a zero or nominal royalty, these firms' competitive position may have remained largely unchanged or even enhanced, especially if the legal climate was generally hostile to patent owners.

Elsewhere I have argued that insecure IP rights remove analytical confidence that the observed mix of organizational structures for undertaking innovation and commercialization activities represents the *efficient* mix of such structures. In a weak-IP environment, the market may maintain robust levels of R&D investment but only by shifting to integrated structures in which scale, secrecy, and other complementary assets can substitute for "missing" property rights coverage (Barnett 2011). This implicit bias toward locating innovation in large-firm organizations may give rise to efficiency losses, even if robust innovation activity persists.

There are two possible losses. First, a weak patent regime may suppress entry by smaller-firm innovators, who lack the complementary assets required to capture value on R&D investments in markets dominated by vertically integrated incumbents with existing production and distribution capacities. Suggestive evidence for this counterfactual scenario is supplied by the fact that, as described in Barnett (2011), small-firm innovation has flowered in R&D and patent-intensive markets following the strengthening of patent protection starting in the early 1980s. Second, a weak patent regime may inefficiently shift innovation toward large firms that are not always the preferred setting for certain types of innovation—especially, breakthrough innovations that challenge dominant technologies as distinguished from incremental innovations that merely refine or improve upon existing technologies. Consistent with this view, Graham (2017, 2010) has lamented the lack of entrepreneurship in the period's large corporate research laboratories, as illustrated by several missed opportunities at RCA, Xerox, and other large corporate laboratories to translate research breakthroughs into commercially viable products.

Case Studies: The Subtle Costs of Weak IP Protection

This chapter is intended as the start of an inquiry into the relationship between IP protections, antitrust enforcement and innovation behavior during the postwar period. To reach more confident conclusions, it will be necessary to examine in "micro-level" detail specific firms' or specific industries' innovation behavior during this time. In this section, I provide two "mini" case studies for this purpose.

Hartford-Empire: Coerced Integration

As described earlier (see the section, Compulsory Licensing Orders [1938–1975]), the *Hartford-Empire* case[59] established the legality of compulsory licensing (at least with a reasonable royalty) as an antitrust remedy in 1945. For our purposes, however, the pre- and post-litigation history of the Hartford-Empire entity provides insight into the structural distortions that may have been

[59] *Hartford-Empire Co. v. U.S.*, 323 U.S. 386 (1945). Unless otherwise noted, this paragraph draws on *U.S. v. Hartford-Empire Co., et al.*, Civil No. 4426 (N.D. Ohio May 23, 1947); *Hartford-Empire Co. v. U.S.*, 323 U.S. 386 (1945); *U.S. v. Hartford-Empire*, 46 F.Supp. 541 (N.D. Ohio 1942); Engelbourg (1966, 60-62); and "Compulsory Patent Licensing" (1946).

induced by the regular use of compulsory licensing orders and associated weak-IP regime during the postwar period.

The Hartford-Empire entity (Hartford) was formed in 1922 (together with Corning, which held a substantial ownership interest) and subsequently assembled a patent pool through a series of cross-licensing agreements with other glass-machinery manufacturers (most notably, Owens-Illinois, the inventor of the leading alternative manufacturing process) (*Investigation of Concentration of Economic Power* 1939, p. 769). Hartford then entered into licensing agreements with virtually all downstream glassware manufacturers (accounting for 96 percent of the glassware manufacturing market by the late 1930s, *Investigation of Concentration of Economic Power* 1939, p. 763). Additionally, as evidenced by its patenting activity and sizable research staff (see Figure 6.7; "Compulsory Patent Licensing" 1946, p. 104; *Investigation of Concentration of Economic Power* 1939, p. 770), Hartford carried out significant R&D activities resulting in a steady flow of technological improvements to its licensees. Hartford contracted out production of its glass-making machinery, which it then distributed through royalty-based leasing, support, and repair services contracts, sometimes accompanied by field-of-use and output limitations (the provisions that drew the closest antitrust scrutiny). During this time (specifically, 1925–1937), evidence presented to

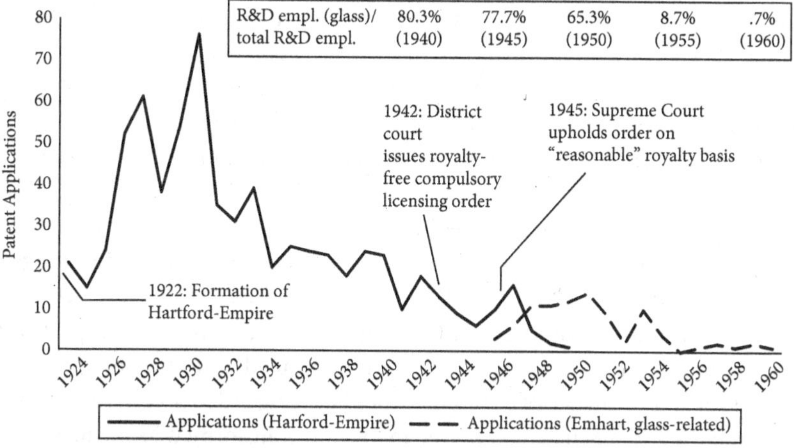

Figure 6.7 Hartford/Emhart patenting activity, 1922–1960.

Notes: Figure shows patent applications that (i) matured into patent grants and (ii) name "Hartford-Empire" or "Emhart" as the first-named assignee. With respect to patent applications by Emhart, the graph only shows patent applications that relate to glass or glass-making technology. Overlap in applications among Hartford-Empire and Emhart (successor entity to Hartford-Empire following name change in 1951) is most likely due to either (i) time lag between application date and grant date or (ii) retroactive name changes of assignee by Emhart management.

Sources: R&D personnel data gathered from Industrial Research Laboratories (1938–1960). Patent applications identified through Google Patents, Advanced Search.

the TNEC by the glass container industry association showed a steady *decline* in the average price of glass containers (*Investigation of Concentration of Economic Power* 1939, p. 823).

The courts in the *Hartford-Empire* litigation effectively treated these licensing arrangements as "per se" violations under Sections 1 and 2 of the Sherman Act. Therefore the courts apparently did not consider evidence brought by defendants (and, as just noted, previously collected by the TNEC) that output had increased and prices had declined in the glass-making markets during the period in question ("Compulsory Patent Licensing" 1946, p. 98 n.55). While the district court issued a "patent dedication" order in 1942 (after rejecting the government's demand to dissolve Hartford), the final decree as modified by the Supreme Court in 1945 removed this royalty-free licensing requirement but still ordered Hartford to enter into licensing and lease agreements at a uniform "reasonable" royalty and without the offending use limitations.[60]

This was still an especially "high-impact" order for two reasons. First, with respect to certain product categories, it applied to future patents without a time limitation (contrasting with the time limitations that typically applied to compulsory licensing orders with prospective effect) and without a cross-licensing requirement being imposed on licensees. Second, while it required Hartford to grant licenses at uniform "reasonable" rates, it provided that any dissatisfied licensee could petition the court to review Hartford's proposed rate and, with respect to certain licensing scenarios, specified formulas by which to determine the royalty.[61] This quasi-administrative mechanism contrasted with other decrees that typically provided in general terms for a "reasonable" royalty standard, designated private negotiations as the principal mechanism by which to determine "reasonable" terms, and contemplated judicial intervention only as a last resort in case of dispute.

Hartford responded to the order in two ways. First, the number of Hartford's patent applications declined and the company never returned to active usage of the patent system (see Figure 6.7). While this decline had commenced before the filing of the antitrust suit (which may have reflected the onset of a legal climate of patent-skepticism in the mid-1930s), it continued and was never reversed during and after issuance of the compulsory licensing order. Second, as the company reported to a Senate committee in 1960, it transformed its business from primarily a licensing and leasing operation to primarily a manufacturing and sales-based enterprise. As of 1954, Hartford's licensing revenues had fallen to zero (Hollabaugh and Wright 1960, pp. 19–20). Unable to monetize its R&D

[60] *Hartford-Empire Co. v. U.S.*, 323 U.S. 386, 417, 419 (1945).

[61] *Hartford-Empire Co. v. U.S.*, 323 U.S. 386, 424 (1945); "Compulsory Patent Licensing" (1946, 91–96).

assets through patent licensing and equipment leasing, it appears that Hartford had vertically integrated forward into production and distribution. This was even reflected in a name change in 1951, after which it operated as Emhart Manufacturing.[62]

There is no reason to believe that Hartford suffered economically as a result of the compulsory licensing order. As of 1946 (four years after the district court's patent dedication order and one year after the Supreme Court's compulsory licensing order subject to a reasonable royalty), Hartford's stock price had largely recovered, and it reportedly enjoyed strong revenues from the sale of glass-making machinery ("Compulsory Patent Licensing" 1946, pp. 97–98). Fifteen years after entry of the compulsory licensing decree, Hartford (as a division of Emhart) remained one of the two leading manufacturers of glass-making machinery for use by glassware manufacturers (Frost et al. 1957, p. 140). Subject to further inquiry, Hartford's organizational response to the compulsory licensing orders and ensuing commercial fortunes can be reasonably interpreted as either a workable adaptation to a weak property-rights regime or a cautionary tale of an organizational "design-around" with potentially adverse efficiency consequences.

Hartford's choice to vertically integrate following judicial devaluation of its patent portfolio conforms to theoretical expectations. As discussed earlier (see the section, Interpreting Innovation "Success" in the Postwar Economy), firms are expected to respond to a weak property-rights environment by shifting to integrated structures in which scale, secrecy, and other complementary assets can at least partially substitute for "missing" property rights coverage. But this is not merely an aesthetic change. Integration compelled by a change in the surrounding property-rights environment can have adverse consequences for both large-firm and small-firm innovation. First, if integrated structures inflate total innovation and commercialization costs beyond levels that could be achieved through alternative (but now infeasible) transactional structures, then expected net returns will fall and, everything else being equal, firms will invest fewer resources in innovation activities. Second, if integrated structures inflate the capital requirements for market entry, then smaller firms will face higher entry costs and (assuming some level of imperfection in the capital markets for financing innovation) incumbents will face weaker competitive threats.

There is some indication, however, that the limitations imposed on Hartford's patenting and licensing incentives may have indirectly harmed smaller downstream glass-manufacturers—ironically, the very population

[62] See EmhartGlass, http://old.emhartglass.com/history.

that the regulators and courts had purported to protect.[63] In the *Hartford-Empire* litigation, medium-sized glass manufacturers who were licensees of Hartford filed an amicus brief *against* finding antitrust liability as well as the royalty-free provisions in the proposed compulsory licensing order. The stated grounds were two-fold: (i) Hartford had licensed its technology broadly, thereby promoting entry into the industry by smaller bottle manufacturers, and (ii) a royalty-free compulsory licensing remedy would undermine Hartford's ability to continue supplying smaller manufacturers with the fruits of its R&D efforts (Brief on Behalf of Certain Medium Sized Glass Manufacturing Companies 1943).[64] Without the capital or scale to support an independent R&D operation that could rival larger manufacturers, the smaller licensees expected that they would operate at a competitive disadvantage.

On this last point, it appears that the manufacturers' concerns turned out to be at least partly well founded. As of 1960, Hartford reported that it had been compelled to reduce its R&D activities (which were substantial at the time of the consent decree, see "Compulsory Patent Licensing" 1946, p. 103) due to the drop in royalty income (Hollabaugh and Wright 1960, p. 20) and, presumably, due to the unattractiveness of licensing patented technology following the 1945 decision. Data on Hartford's (and its successor entity, Emhart's) R&D employment are consistent with this assertion with respect to the glass-making field. As shown in Figure 6.7, while Emhart's total R&D personnel remained stable in the years following the decision, the portion of R&D personnel that appear to be dedicated to glass-making technology steadily fell, from 80 out of 130 total (approximately 80 percent) at the time of the order to 29 out of 140 (approximately 9 percent) by 1960.[65] Rather than promoting the production and dissemination of technological knowledge, the compulsory licensing order against Hartford may have discouraged it.

[63] The *Hartford-Empire* decision had another potentially adverse effect on industrial organization. Following the decision, US firms virtually ceased to make use of patent pools until changes in antitrust enforcement policies in the mid-1990s (Barnett 2015, pp. 149–50). This de facto prohibition on patent pools may have provided a further inducement to expand firm size and internal markets in order to avoid the transaction costs inherent to aggregating patented technology inputs from multiple sources.

[64] Another group of licensees recommended a royalty schedule but nonetheless similarly emphasized the importance of preserving a sufficient royalty system so that Hartford could continue to invest in R&D ("Compulsory Patent Licensing" 1946, p. 103).

[65] The attribution of the firm's R&D employees to glass-related or other areas was based on the description of research activities in the IRL reports. Other significant areas of R&D activity to which the firm devoted personnel related to plastics and, starting in 1955, machines for food manufacturing and packaging (Industrial Research Laboratories 1945–1960).

Alcoa: The Dangers of Going It Alone

The case of Alcoa, the first major firm targeted successfully by a compulsory licensing order, illustrates both the military origins of the postwar weak-IP/strong-antitrust regime and the distortions that this regime may have had on the manner in which targeted firms conducted innovation.

In 1938, the federal government commenced an antitrust prosecution against Alcoa, then the only domestic producer of aluminum (although it faced competition from European firms, mitigated to some extent by tariffs) and the acknowledged technological pioneer in the field. During the war, the litigation was delayed and Alcoa entered into agreements with the military to construct and operate aluminum production plants, which were especially critical for aircraft manufacture (Stein 1952, 318). In 1942, the government and Alcoa entered into a consent decree providing for royalty-free licensing of certain patents held by Alcoa.[66] Following the war, the government actively resumed the antitrust litigation and pressured Alcoa to license additional patents, together with technical know-how, to two competitors in the aluminum market that had been effectively organized by the government (and to whom the government had transferred some of the wartime plants constructed by Alcoa) (Graham and Pruitt 1990, pp. 243–44). Alcoa's resistance proved futile. In 1945, the government prevailed on liability in the antitrust case, which then entered the remedies phase in which the government sought dissolution. In 1948, Alcoa avoided break-up by reaching a settlement that involved agreeing to license certain patents to the two entrants (Graham and Pruitt 1990, p. 249; Smith 1988, pp. 233–42; Stein 1952, p. 351). In short, Alcoa had been compelled by its chief buyer, the US government, to finance the entry of, and transfer intellectual assets to, two competitors into the industry.

Starting around the time of the TNEC hearings and persisting through the 1950s, the company reduced its patenting activity, as measured both by the number of patent applications filed annually and its "patent productivity." Figure 6.8 shows: (i) the number of patent applications filed annually by Alcoa that resulted in an issued patent; and (ii) at the top of the graph, the firm's patent productivity. The latter indicator is measured by (i) the number of such patent applications in each five-year period divided by (ii) the number of R&D personnel at the start of that period.[67] Both indicators of R&D output (or more precisely, patented R&D output) declined sharply from the late 1930s through

[66] *U.S. v. Aluminum Co. of America, et al.*, 1940-1943 Trade Cas. (CCH) ¶56,200 (S.D.N.Y. Apr. 15, 1942)

[67] A five-year prospective measure of patent issuance was adopted in order to avoid using a single, potentially idiosyncratic year and to reflect the fact that R&D personnel require time in order to develop patentable research. Note that the patent applications are restricted to patent applications that ultimately yielded an issued patent.

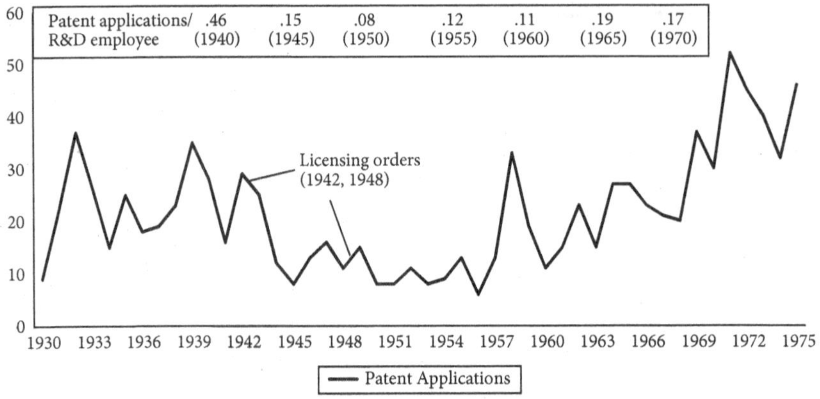

Figure 6.8 Alcoa patenting activity, 1930–1975.

Notes: Figure shows patent applications filed annually that (i) resulted in patent grants and (ii) name "Alcoa" or "Aluminum Co. of America" as the first-named assignee. "Patent applications/R&D employee" is calculated by dividing (i) the number of such Alcoa patent applications filed during a five-year period by (ii) the number of Alcoa R&D employees as of the first year in that period.

Sources: For data on number of R&D personnel, Industrial Research Laboratories (1940–1970). Patent applications identified through Google Patents, Advanced Search.

the late 1950s. Thereafter, Alcoa's patent applications increased but patent productivity only rose moderately and never approached the levels that the company had exhibited as of 1940. A more complex picture emerges if we take into account R&D employment intensity, as measured by the number of R&D personnel (including technical and non-technical personnel) divided by the total number of firm personnel. From the mid-1950s through the mid-1970s, Alcoa's R&D employment intensity held constant or moderately increased, ranging from 1.19 percent in 1956 to 1.42 percent in 1965 and 2.67 percent in 1975.[68]

This continued investment in R&D (as measured indirectly by R&D employment intensity), coupled with declining and then mostly constant patent productivity, conforms to theoretical expectations. In a weak-IP environment, a large integrated incumbent will rely more heavily on its non-patent complementary assets, such as scale economies, internal financing, tacit knowledge, and production and distribution infrastructure, in order to secure returns on its R&D investment. To the extent those non-patent assets can secure returns on a cost-comparable basis, the firm's incentive to invest in innovation should be unaffected. These non-patent assets were available to Alcoa and were most likely

[68] Author's calculations, based on: (i) R&D personnel data extracted from Industrial Research Laboratories (1956–1975); and (ii) total personnel data extracted from Fortune 500 digital archives at http://archive.fortune.com/magazines/fortune/fortune500_archive/full/1955/401.html.

especially potent given the substantial capital requirements in the aluminum industry (as of 1958, the total investment required to construct an aluminum plant approached $800 million, see Smith 1988, 368[69]), which implied high minimum efficient economies of scale that apparently dissuaded all potential entrants into the industry without substantial government assistance (including coerced technology transfers from the incumbent).

While Alcoa did not appear to reduce its R&D activities in response to the compulsory licensing orders, it modified in two respects how it conducted, and extracted returns on, those activities. Both of these modifications suggest that, even though Alcoa adapted to the postwar weak-IP regime, those adaptations may have constituted distortions away from first-best efficient structures for organizing the innovation and commercialization process.

First, Alcoa appeared to employ secrecy, rather than patents, as the principal tool by which to safeguard its R&D investments (Graham and Pruitt 1990, p. 270). This is suggested by the fact that, as noted, Alcoa maintained or moderately increased its R&D employment intensity even while its patenting volume and patent productivity fell or approximately held constant. Even when Alcoa increased the number of patent applications starting in the late 1950s, its patent productivity increased only moderately despite a concurrent substantial increase in R&D employment intensity. Relatedly, Alcoa adopted a "closed-door" policy focused on blocking leakage of its technical knowledge (Graham and Pruitt 1990, pp. 318, 391–92; Smith 1988, p. 388).[70] Second, Alcoa reallocated R&D resources toward process innovations that lowered production costs, rather than product innovations (Smith 1988, pp. 288–89; Graham and Pruitt 1990, p. 291), which may have reflected the fact that process innovations are generally more amenable than product innovations to protection through secrecy.

These adaptations to a weak-IP environment apparently came at a price. The emphasis on secrecy and related limitations on academic publication (Smith 1988, p. 262) constrained Alcoa's ability to attract the highest-quality researchers, which limited access to the scientific community and ultimately, combined with the focus on incremental process innovation, adversely affected the firm (Mowery 1995, p. 163; Graham and Pruitt 1990, p. 326; Smith 1988, pp. 401–06). By the 1970s, Alcoa was regarded as an innovation laggard.

[69] This is equivalent to approximately $7.2 billion in 2020 dollars, as updated through the "CPI Inflation Calculator" provided by the US Bureau of Labor Statistics, https://www.bls.gov/data/inflation_calculator.htm.

[70] Alcoa management reconsidered this strategy in the early 1970s, when it renewed its technology transfer activities (Smith 1988, pp. 388–89), which is consistent with the increase in patenting activity at approximately the same time.

Conclusion

Academic and other policy commentators have widely advocated weakening patent protection and, since the mid-2000s, the US Congress, federal courts, and antitrust agencies have taken significant steps consistent with this view. It is therefore valuable to learn more about a prolonged period in which patent and antitrust law placed substantial limitations on patent holders' enforcement and licensing capacities. While changes in technology, economic environment, and other factors do not permit a perfect natural experiment, and therefore caution against drawing any definitive conclusions, the weak property-rights regime implemented during this four-decade period provides cautionary lessons for commentators who advocate weakening patents to facilitate entry and promote innovation. While the latter objective may have been achieved (albeit with extensive public funding that may be unsustainable over an extended time) for a limited period, the former was not. The postwar years exhibited robust innovation for a substantial but constrained period, followed by a noticeable slowdown commencing in the mid-1960s. Innovation mostly took place in the R&D laboratories of large firms that relied on government transfers, economies of scale, and large market share to secure the funding streams required to support R&D activities. The mixed performance of the postwar innovation economy suggests that significantly weakening patent protection may skew the market selection of organizational structures for undertaking innovation and commercialization activities, necessitates substantial public funding, and does not provide a self-sustaining model for a market-based innovation economy.

Acknowledgments

I am grateful for comments from an anonymous referee, Stephen Haber, Naomi Lamoreaux, and participants at the 2018 conference of the Hoover Institution Working Group on Intellectual Property, Innovation, and Prosperity, the annual conference of the American Law & Economics Association, the annual conference of the Society for Institutional and Organizational Economics, and workshops at the University of Southern California (USC) Gould School of Law, Bar-Ilan University Faculty of Law, Hebrew University Faculty of Law, and Tel Aviv University Faculty of Law. I thank Natalie Amsellem, Kate Lee, Mingmei Zhu, and the library staff of the USC Gould School of Law for invaluable research assistance. This project has been supported by the Hoover Institution at Stanford University.

References

Arrow, Kenneth J. "Innovation in Large and Small Firms." *Journal of Small Business Finance*, 2, no. 2 (1993): 111–24.

Barnett, Jonathan M. "Intellectual Property as a Law of Organization." *Southern California Law Review* 84, no. 4 (2011): 785–858.

———. "The Anti-Commons Revisited." *Harvard Journal of Law & Technology* 29, no. 1 (2015): 127–203.

———. *Innovators, Firms, and Markets: The Organizational Logic of Intellectual Property*. New York: Oxford University Press, (2021).

Baten, Joerg, Nicola Bianchi and Petra Moser. "Compulsory Licensing and Innovation—Historical Evidence from German Patents after World War I." *Journal of Development Economics* 126 (2017): 231–42.

Baum, Lawrence. "The Federal Courts and Patent Validity: An Analysis of the Record." *Journal of the Patent Office Society* 56, no. 12 (1974): 758–87.

Baxter, James P. *Scientists Against Time*. New York: Little, Brown & Co., 1946.

Brief on Behalf of Certain Medium Sized Glass Manufacturing Companies with Respect to the Remedy, Appearing by Counsel as Amicus Curiae. *Hartford-Empire Co. et al. v. United States*. Supreme Court of the United States. 7 October 1943.

Bush, Vannevar. *Pieces of the Action*. New York: William Morrow & Co., 1970.

Caves, Richard E. "The Structure of Industry." In *The American Economy in Transition*, edited by Martin Feldstein, 501–45. Chicago, IL: University of Chicago Press, 1980.

Chandler, Alfred D. Jr. *Inventing the Electronic Century: The Epic Story of the Consumer Electronics and Computer Industries*. New York: The Free Press, 2011.

Chappell, Ralph L., and W. Houston Kenyon Jr. "Patent Costs of Military Procurement in Wartime." *Law & Contemporary Problems* 2 (1947): 695–713.

Chiang, T.J. "Technology Policy Paradigms and Intellectual Property Strategies: Three National Models." *Technological Forecasting and Social Change* 49, no. 1 (1995): 35-49.

Cohen, Wesley. "Fifty Years of Empirical Research of Innovative Activity and Performance." In *Handbook of Economics of Innovation*, edited by Bronwyn Hall and Nathan Rosenberg, Vol. I, 129–213. Amsterdam: North-Holland, 2010.

"Compulsory Patent Licensing by Antitrust Decree." *Yale Law Journal* 56, no. 1 (1946): 77–126.

Contreras, Jorge L. "A Brief History of FRAND: Analyzing Current Debates in Standard Setting and Antitrust Through a Historical Lens." *Antitrust Law Journal* 80 (2015-16): 39–120.

Crawford, C. Merle, and Gerard Tellis. "The Technological Innovation Controversy." *Business Horizons* 24, no. 4 (1981): 76–88.

Decisions of the Comptroller General of the United States. Vol. 46. Washington, DC: GPO, 20 September 1966.

Dobkin, James A. "Patent Policy in Government Research and Development Contracts." *Virginia Law Review* 53, no. 3 (1967): 564–653.

Engelbourg, Saul. "Some Consequences of the Leasing of Industrial Machinery." *Journal of Business* 39, no. 1 (1966): 52–66.

Field, Alexander J. "The Origins of U.S. Total Factor Productivity Growth in the Golden Age." *Cliometrica* 1 (2007): 63–90.

Fleming, Harold. "Standard Oil Seen Smart in Giving Away Buna-S Patents." *Christian Science Monitor*, 23 April 1943.

Frost, George E., S. Chesterfield Oppenheim and Neil F. Twomey. 1957. "Compulsory and Patent Dedication Provisions of Anti-Trust Decrees - A Foundation of Detailed Factual Case Studies", *Patent Trademark & Copyright Journal Research & Education* 1, no. 1 (1957): 127–44.

Galambos, Louis. "The U.S. Corporate Economy in the Twentieth Century." In *The Cambridge Economic History of the United States*, edited by Stanley L. Engerman and Robert E. Gallman, Vol. III, 927–68. Cambridge, UK: Cambridge University Press, 2000.

Galasso, Alberto, and Mark Schankerman. "Patents and Cumulative Innovation: Causal Evidence from the Courts." *The Quarterly Journal of Economics* 130, no. 1 (2014): 317–69.

Galbraith, John Kenneth. *American Capitalism: The Concept of Countervailing Power.* New York: Houghton Mifflin, 1952.

"GE May Appeal Order to Turn Over Patents on Incandescent Lamps." *Wall Street Journal*, 5 October 1953.

Gordon, Robert J. *The Rise and Fall of American Growth: The U.S. Standard of Living since the Civil War.* Princeton, NJ: Princeton University Press, 2016.

Graham, Margaret B.W. *The Business of Research: RCA and the Videodisc.* Cambridge, UK: University of Cambridge Press, 1986.

———. "Technology and Innovation." In *The Oxford Handbook of Business History*, edited by Geoffrey Jones and Jonathan Zeitlin, 347–73. Oxford: Oxford University Press, 2007.

———. "Entrepreneurship in the United States." In *The Invention of Enterprise: Entrepreneurship from Ancient Mesopotamia to Modern Times*, edited by David S. Landes, Joel Mokyr, and William J. Baumol, 401–42. Princeton, NJ: Princeton University Press, 2010.

———. "When the Corporation Almost Displaced the Entrepreneur: Rethinking the Political Economy of Research and Development." *Enterprise and Society* 18, no. 2 (2017): 245–81.

Graham, Margaret B.W., and Bettye H. Pruitt. *R&D for Industry: A Century of Technical Innovation at Alcoa.* Cambridge: Cambridge University Press, 1990.

Green, Jerry R., and Suzanne Scotchmer. "On the Division of Profit in Sequential Innovation." *RAND Journal of Economics* 26, no. 1 (1995): 20–33.

Hall, G. R., and R. E. Johnson. Competition in the Procurement of Military Hard Goods. Prepared statement submitted in *Hearings Before the Subcommittee on Antitrust and Monopoly of the Committee on the Judiciary*. U.S. Senate, 49–81. 90th Cong., 2nd sess. Washington, DC: GPO, 17 June 1968.

Hamberg, D. "Invention in the Industrial Research Laboratory." *Journal of Political Economy* 71 (1963): 95–115.

Harbridge House, Inc. *Government Patent Policy Study: Final Report.* Prepared for the Federal Council for Science and Technology. Washington, DC: GPO, 1968.

Hart, David M. *Forged Consensus: Science, Technology and Economic Policy in the United States, 1921–1953.* Princeton, NJ: Princeton University Press, 1998.

———. "Antitrust and Technological Innovation in the United States: Ideas, Institutions, Decisions and Impacts, 1890–2000." *Research Policy* 30, no. 6 (2001): 923–36.

Henry, Matthew D., and John L. Turner. "Across Five Eras: Patent Enforcement in the United States 1929–2006." *Journal of Empirical Legal Studies* 13, no. 3 (2016): 454–86.

Hoerner, Robert J. "The Decline (and Fall?) of the Patent Misuse Doctrine in the Federal Circuit." *Antitrust Law Journal* 69, no. 3 (2002): 669–85.

Hollabaugh, Marcus A. and Robert Wright. "Compulsory Patent Licensing under Antitrust Judgments." *Staff Report of the Subcommittee on Patents, Trademarks and Copyrights, Senate Committee on the Judiciary*. 86th Cong., 2nd sess. Washington, DC: GPO, 1960.

Hulten, Charles R. "Total Factor Productivity: A Short Biography." NBER Working Paper No. 7471, Cambridge, MA, January 2001.

"Impact of Federal Research and Development Programs, Study Number VI." *Report of the Select Committee on Government Research of the House of Representatives*. 88th Cong., 2nd sess. December 1964.

Industrial Research Laboratories of the United States. Washington, DC: National Research Council, 1938, 1940, 1946, 1950, 1956, 1960.

Industrial Research Laboratories of the United States. New York: R.R. Bowker Company, 1965, 1970, 1975.

Investigation of Concentration of Economic Power. "Part 2. Patents—Automobile Industry, Glass Container Industry." *Hearings before the Temporary National Economic Committee, pursuant to Public Resolution No. 113*. 75th Cong., 3rd sess. December 5, 6, 12, 13, 14, 15 and 16, 1938. Washington, DC: GPO, 1939.

Katznelson, Ron D., and John Howells. "The Myth of the Early Aviation Patent Hold-Up: How a U.S. Government Monopsony Commandeered Pioneer Airplane Patents." *Industrial & Corporate Change* 24, no. 1 (2015): 1–64.

Khan, Zorina. *The Democratization of Invention: Patents and Copyrights in American Economic Development, 1790–1920*. New York: Cambridge University Press, 2005.

Kreeger, David Lloyd. "The Control of Patent Rights Resulting from Federal Research." *Law & Contemporary Problems* 12 (1947): 714–45.

Lamoreaux, Naomi R., Margaret Levenstein, and Kenneth L. Sokoloff. "Financing Invention During the Second Industrial Revolution: Cleveland, Ohio 1870–1920." NBER Working Paper No. 10923. Cambridge, MA, November 2004.

Lamoreaux, Naomi R., and Kenneth L. Sokoloff. "Intermediaries in the U.S. Market for Technology, 1870–1920." In *Finance, Intermediaries and Economic Development*, edited by Stanley L. Engerman, Philip T. Hoffman, Jean-Laurent Rosenthal, and Kenneth L. Sokoloff, 209–46. Cambridge: Cambridge University Press, 2003.

Lamoreaux, Naomi R., Kenneth L. Sokoloff, and Dhanoos Sutthiphisal. "The Reorganization of Inventive Activity in the United States During the Early Twentieth Century." In *Understanding Long-Run Economic Growth*, edited by Dora L. Costa and Naomi R. Lamoreaux, 235–74. Chicago: University of Chicago Press, 2011.

Levin, Richard C. "The Semiconductor Industry." In *Government and Technical Progress: A Cross-Industry Analysis*, edited by Richard R. Nelson, pp. 9–100. New York: Pergamon Press, 1982.

Malerba, Franco. *The Semiconductor Business: Economics of Rapid Growth and Decline*. Madison: University of Wisconsin Press, 1985.

Markham, Jesse. "Inventive Activity: Government Controls and the Legal Environment." *The Rate and Direction of Inventive Activity: Economic and Social Factors*. NBER Special Conference Series. Vol. 13. Princeton: Princeton University Press, 1962.

McAfee, Preston R., and John McMillan. "Organizational Diseconomies of Scale." *Journal of Economic and Management Strategy* 4, no. 3 (1995): 399–426.

Moser, Petra. "Determinants of Creativity and Innovation—Evidence from Economic History," *NBER Reporter* no. 3 (2015): 23–26.

Moser, Petra and Alessandra Voena. "Compulsory Licensing—Evidence from the Trading with the Enemy Act." NBER Working Paper No. 15598. Cambridge, MA, December 2009.

Mowery, David C. "The Emergence and Growth of Industrial Research in American Manufacturing, 1899–1945." Ph.D. diss. Stanford University, 1981.

———. "The Boundaries of the U.S. Firm in R&D." In *Coordination and Information: Historical Perspectives on the Organization of Enterprise*, edited by Naomi R. Lamoreaux and Daniel M. G. Raff, 147–76. Chicago, IL: University of Chicago Press, 1995.

———. "Military R&D and Innovation." In *Handbook of the Economics of Innovation*, vol. 2, edited by Bronwyn H. Hall and Nathan Rosenberg, 1220–56. Amsterdam: Elsevier, 2010.

Mowery, David C., and Richard R. Nelson. *The U.S. Corporation and Technical Progress*. Berkeley: University of California at Berkeley, Center for Research in Management, 1994.

Mowery, David C., and Nathan Rosenberg. *Technology and the Pursuit of Economic Growth*. Cambridge, UK: Cambridge University Press, 1989.

Mowery, David C., and Nathan Rosenberg. "Twentieth Century Technological Change." In *The Cambridge Economic History of the United States*, vol. III, edited by Stanley L. Engerman and Robert E. Gallman, 803–926. Cambridge: Cambridge University Press, 2000.

Mowery, David C., and W. Edward Steinmuller. "Prospects for Entry by Developing Countries into the Global Integrated Circuit Industry: Lessons from the United States, Japan, and the NIEs, 1955–1990." In *Science and Technology Policy in Interdependent Economies*, edited by David C. Mowery, 199–254. New York: Springer Science and Business Media, 1994.

Mueller, William F., and Larry G. Hamm. "Trends in Industrial Market Concentration: 1947 to 1970." *Review of Economics & Statistics* 56, no. 4 (1974): 511–20.

National Science Foundation, "Company and Other (Except Federal) Funds for R&D, by Industry and Size of Company, 1957–98."

National Science Foundation, Division of Science Resource Statistics, Industrial Research and Development (Annual Reports, 1999–2007).

Nelson, Richard R., Merton J. Peck, and Edward D. Kalachek. *Technology, Economic Growth, and Public Policy: A RAND Corporation and Brookings Institution Study*. Washington, DC: Brookings Institution, 1967.

Nix, Paul E., and David E. Nix. "A Historical Review of the Accounting Treatment of Research and Development Costs." *Accounting Historians Journal* 19, no. 1 (1992): 51–78.

Nixon, Richard. "Memorandum About Government Patent Policy". 23 August 1971. http://www.presidency.ucsb.edu/ws/?pid=3130.

Olson, Thomas F. "Patent Rights in Department of Defense Research and Development Contracts." *California Law Review* 47 (1959): 721–39.

"Patent Law: 'Flash of Genius' Test for Invention Rejected." *DePaul Law Review* 5 (1955): 144–49.

Patents: Hearings before the Committee on Patents, U.S. Senate, on S. 2303, a Bill to Provide for the Use of Patents in the Interest of National Defense or the Prosecution of the War, and for Other Purposes. 77th Cong., 2nd sess. Part 6. May 20, 21 and 22, 1942. Washington, DC: GPO, 1942.

Peck, Merton J., and Frederic M. Scherer. *The Weapons Acquisition Process: An Economic Analysis*. Boston: Harvard University, 1962.

Petro, Sylvester. "Patents: Judicial Developments and Legislative Proposals." *University of Chicago Law Review* 12 (1944): 80–103.

Presidential Memorandum and Statement of Government Policy. *Federal Register* 28, no. 200 (1963).

Rabinow, Jacob. "Are Patents Needed?" *P.T.C. Journal of Research & Education* 18 (1976): 19–35.

Roosevelt, President Franklin D. Letter to Dr. Vannevar Bush, Office of Scientific Research and Development. 17 November 1944. https://www.nsf.gov/about/history/nsf50/vbush1945_roosevelt_letter.jsp.

"Roundtable Discussion on Competition Policy, Intellectual Property and Innovation Markets." In *Competition Policy and Intellectual Property Rights in the Knowledge-Based Economy,* edited by Robert D. Anderson and Nancy T. Gallini, pp. 448–49. Calgary: Calgary University Press, 1998.

Shackleton, Robert. "Total Factor Productivity Growth in Historical Perspective." Congressional Budget Office Working Paper Series, No. 2013-01, 2013.

Schechter, Frank. "Would Compulsory Licensing of Patents Be Unconstitutional?" *Virginia Law Review* 22 (1935): 287–314.

Scherer, Frederic M. *The Economic Effects of Compulsory Licensing.* Monograph Series in Finance and Economics, Center for the Study of Financial Institutions. New York: NYU Graduate School of Business Administration, 1977.

———. *Industrial Market Structure and Economic Performance.* 2nd. ed. Boston: Houghton Mifflin Co., 1980.

———. *International High-Technology Competition.* Boston: Harvard University Press, 1992.

Scherer, Frederic M. et al. *Patents and the Corporation: A Report on Industrial Technology under Changing Public Policy.* 2nd ed. Boston: Harvard University, Graduate School of Business Administration, 1959.

Schlesinger, James R. "Whither American Industry." In *The American Economy in Transition,* edited by Martin Feldstein, 551–60. Chicago, IL: University of Chicago Press, 1980.

Schnee, Jerome E. "Government Programs and the Growth of High-Technology Industries." *Research Policy* 7, no. 1 (1978): 3–24.

Schumpeter, F. M. *Capitalism, Socialism and Democracy.* New York: Harper & Row, 1942.

Shephard, William G. "Trends of Concentration in American Manufacturing Industries." *Review of Economics and Statistics* 46, no. 2 (1964): 200–12.

Smith, George David. *From Monopoly to Competition: The Transformations of Alcoa, 1888–1986.* Cambridge, UK: Cambridge University Press, 1988.

Statement of Elmer B. Staats, Comptroller General of the United States. *Hearings Before the Subcommittee on Antitrust and Monopoly of the Committee on the Judiciary, U.S. Senate*, 88–188. 90th Cong., 2nd sess. Washington, DC: GPO. 21 June 1968.

Stein, Harold. *The Disposal of the Aluminum Plants.* Tuscaloosa, Alabama: University of Alabama Press, 1952.

Teece, David. "Profiting from Technological Innovation: Implications for Integration, Collaboration, Licensing and Public Policy." *Research Policy* 15 (1986): 285–305.

Temporary National Economic Committee. *Final Report of the Executive Secretary to the Temporary National Economic Committee on the Concentration of Economic Power in the United States, pursuant to Public Resolution No. 113.* 77th Cong., 1st sess. Washington, DC: GPO, 1941.

"Third Report of the National Patent Planning Commission." *American Bar Associations Journal* 31 (1945): 602–03, 607.

Tilton, John E. *International Diffusion of Technology: The Case of Semiconductors.* Washington, DC: The Brookings Institution, 1971.

Tom, Willard K. "The 1975 Xerox Consent Decree: Ancient Artifacts and Current Tensions." *Antitrust Law Journal* 68, no. 3 (2001): 967–90.

US Department of Commerce. *Statistical Abstract of the United States.* Washington, DC: GPO, 1953.

US Department of Commerce. *Technological Innovation: Its Environment and Management.* Washington, DC: GPO, 1967.

US Department of Justice. *1968 Merger Guidelines.* https://www.justice.gov/sites/default/files/atr/legacy/2007/07/11/11247.pdf.

US Department of Justice. *Report and Recommendations of the Attorney General to the President, Investigation of Government Patent Practices and Policies.* Washington, DC: GPO, 1947.

US President. "Strengthening and Enforcement of Antitrust Laws: Message from the President of the United States Transmitting Recommendations Relative to the Strengthening and Enforcement of Antitrust Laws." Washington, DC: GPO, April 20, 1938.

Watson, Donald Stevenson and Mary A. Holman. "Concentration of Patents from Government Financed Research in Industry." *Review of Economics and Statistics* 49, no. 3 (1967): 375–81.

Watzinger, Martin, Thomas A. Fackler, Markus Nagler, and Monika Schnitzer. "How Antitrust Enforcement Can Spur Innovation: Bell Labs and the 1956 Consent Decree." *American Economic Journal: Economic Policy* 12 (2020): 1–32.

Webbink, Douglas W. *The Semiconductor Industry: A Survey of Structure, Conduct and Performance.* Staff Report to the Federal Trade Commission. Washington, DC: Federal Trade Commission, Bureau of Economics, 1977.

Wellerstein, Alex. "Patenting the Bomb: Nuclear Weapons, Intellectual Property and Technological Control." In *Science and the American Century: Readings from Isis*, edited by Sally Gregory Kohlstedt and David Kaiser, 139–69. Chicago, IL: University of Chicago Press, 2013.

White, Michael J. "U.S. Alien Property Custodian Patent Documents: A Legacy Prior Art Collection from World War II." *World Patent Information* 29, no. 4 (2007): 339–45.

Wilson, Bruce B. "Remarks before Annual Joint Meeting of Michigan State Bar Antitrust Law Section and Patent, Trademark and Copyright Section," reprinted in 4 Trade Reg. Rep. (CCH) ¶ 13,126. September 21, 1972.

Wise, T.A. "IBM's $5,000,000,000 Gamble." *Fortune.* September 1966.

Appendix 6.A Compulsory patent licensing orders, 1938–1975

Year	First-Named Defendant	Affected Product	RRL (Y/N)	RFL (Y/N)	PD (Y/N)	Future Patents (Y/N)	Cross-License Condition (Y/N)	Provide Know-how (Y/N)
1941	Kearney & Trecker Corp.[a]	Milling machines	N	N	Y	N	N	N
1942	Whitehead Brothers Co.[b]	Bentonite	Y	N	N	N	N	N
1942	Standard Oil Co.[c]	Petroleum	Y	Y	N	Y	N	Y
1942	General Electric Co.[d]	Lamps, lamp parts	Y	Y	N	N	Y	N
1942	Aluminum Co. of Am.[e]	Magnesium	Y	Y	N	N	Y	N
1942	Aqua Systems, Inc.[f]	Hydraulic gasoline storage system	N	Y	Y	Y	N	N
1942	American Bosch Corp.[g]	Diesel fuel injection equipment	Y	N	N	N	Y	N
1943	Aerofin Corp.[h]	Encased/un-encased coils	N	Y	N	N	N	N
1944	Rail Joint Co.[i]	Rail joint bars	N	N	Y	N	N	N
1945	Crosby, Steam & Valve Co.[j]	Valves	Y	Y	N	N	N	N
1945	General Electric Co.[k]	Glass bulbs, tubing, machinery	N	Y	N	Y	Y	Y
1945	Vehicular Parking, Ltd.[l]	Parking meters	Y	N	N	N	N	N
1945	Merck & Co.[m]	Pharmaceutical chemicals	N	Y	N	N	N	N

Continued

Appendix 6.A *Continued*

Year	First-Named Defendant	Affected Product	RRL (Y/N)	RFL (Y/N)	PD (Y/N)	Future Patents (Y/N)	Cross-License Condition (Y/N)	Provide Know-how (Y/N)
1945	National Lead Co.[n]	Titanium pigments	Y	N	N	N	Y	N
1945	Auditorium Condition Corp.[o]	Air conditioning equipment	N	N	Y	N	N	N
1946	Wisconsin Alumni Research Foundation[p]	Vitamin D products	N	N	Y	N	N	N
1946	Bendix Aviation Corp.[q]	Aircraft accessories and instruments	Y	Y	N	N	N	N
1946	Diamond Match Co.[r]	Matches, match machinery and chemicals	Y	Y	N	N	N	N
1946	Western Precipitation Corp.[s]	Electrical precipitation	N	N	Y[t]	N	N	Y
1946	Libbey-Owens Ford Glass Co.[u]	Types of glass	Y	N	N	N	N	N
1946	American Air Filter Co. Inc.[v]	Air filters and filter apparatus	Y	N	Y	N	N	N
1946	Owens-Illinois Glass Co.[w]	Glass containers and vacuum packing machinery	Y	N	N	N	N	N
1947	National Cash Register[x]	Cash registers	N	N	Y	Y	N	N
1947	American Lecithin Co.[y]	Lecithin	Y	Y	N	N	N	N

1947	Hartford-Empire Co.[z]	Glass containers, forming machines	Y	N	N[aa]	Y	N	N
1947	Patent Button Co.[bb]	Fasteners, fastening machines	Y	N	N	N	N	N
1947	Timken-Detroit Axle Co.[cc]	Multiwheel units	Y	N	N	N	N	N
1947	American Locomotive Co.[dd]	Spring plates	Y	N	N	Y	N	N
1947	The Electric Storage Battery Co.[ee]	Electric storage batteries	Y	N	N	N	N	N
1948	Scovill Manufacturing Co.[ff]	Button-fastening machinery	Y	N	N	N	N	N
1948	Automatic Sprinkler Co. of Am.[gg]	Rate-of-rise devices	Y	N	N	Y	N	Y
1948	Gamewell Co.[hh]	Fire alarm systems	Y	N	N	N	N	N
1948	A.B. Dick Co.[ii]	Stencil duplicating machines	N	N	Y	Y	N	Y
1948	Universal Button[jj]	Fastening machinery	Y	N	N	N	N	N
1948	American Bosch Corp.[kk]	Diesel fuel injection equipment	Y	N	N	N	N	N
1948	White Cap Co.[ll]	Closure and sealing machinery	Y	N	N	N	N	N
1948	US Pipe & Foundry Co.[mm]	Cast-iron pressure pipes	Y	N	Y	N	N	N

Continued

Appendix 6.A *Continued*

Year	First-Named Defendant	Affected Product	RRL (Y/N)	RFL (Y/N)	PD (Y/N)	Future Patents (Y/N)	Cross-License Condition (Y/N)	Provide Know-how (Y/N)
1948	General Cable Corp.[nn]	Fluid-filled cables	Y	N	N	Y	N	N
1948	American Optical Co.[oo]	Ophthalmic goods	Y	N	N	Y	N	N
1948	Allegheny Ludlum Steel Corp.[pp]	Stainless steel	Y	N	N	N	N	N
1948	Aluminum Co. of Amer.[qq]	Aluminum production processes	Y	Y	N	N	N	N
1948	Libbey-Owens-Ford Glass Co.[rr]	Flat glass	Y	Y	Y	Y	N	N
1948	Rohm & Haas Co.[ss]	Acrylic products	N	Y	N	N	N	Y
1948	Technicolor, Inc.[tt]	Color motion picture prints	Y	Y	N	Y	N	Y
1948	Bendix Aviation Corp.[uu]	Braking systems	Y	Y	N	Y	N	N
1949	Scophony Corp. of Am.[vv]	Television installation apparatus	Y	N	N	N	N	N
1949	Phillips Screw Co.[ww]	Cross-recessed head screws and screwdrivers	Y	N	N	Y	N	Y
1949	Owens-Corning Fiberglas Corp.[xx]	Glass fibers and fiber products	Y	Y	N	N	N	Y

1949	Sand Spun Patents Corp.[yy]	Cast iron pressure pipe	N	N	Y	N	N	N
1949	General Electric Co.[zz]	Disconnecting switches and ground switches	Y	N	N	Y	N	N
1949	Standard Register Co.[aaa]	Platens and auxiliary equipment	Y	N	N	N	N	N
1950	Technicolor, Inc.[bbb]	Color film technology	Y	Y	N	Y	N	Y
1950	American Can Co.[ccc]	Container closing machines	Y	Y	N	Y	N	Y
1950	Continental Can Co., Inc.[ddd]	Container closing machines	Y	Y	N	Y	N	Y
1950	Textile Machine Works[eee]	Hosiery	Y	Y	N	Y	N	Y
1950	Minnesota Mining & Manufacturing Co.[fff]	Coated abrasive products	Y	N	N	Y	N	Y
1951	US Gypsum Co.[ggg]	Gypsum boards	Y	N	N	Y	N	N
1951	Liquidometer Corp.[hhh]	Measurement gages	Y	N	N	N	N	N
1951	Austenal Laboratories[iii]	Vitallium dentures	Y	N	Y	N	N	Y
1951	Permutit Co.[jjj]	Water conditioning equipment	Y	N	N	N	N	N
1951	Parke, Davis & Co.[kkk]	Hard gelatin capsules	Y	Y	N	Y	N	Y
1952	Mager & Gougelman, Inc.[lll]	Plastic artificial eyes	Y	Y	N	N	N	N

Continued

Appendix 6.A *Continued*

Year	First-Named Defendant	Affected Product	RRL (Y/N)	RFL (Y/N)	PD (Y/N)	Future Patents (Y/N)	Cross-License Condition (Y/N)	Provide Know-how (Y/N)
1952	Liquid Carbonic Corp.[mmm]	Dry ice	Y	N	N	Y	N	Y
1952	Imperial Chemical Industries, Ltd.[nnn]	Chemical products	Y	N	N	N	N	Y
1952	Davis Co.[ooo]	Elastic top hosiery	Y	N	N	N	N	N
1953	United Shoe Machinery Co.[ppp]	Shoemaking machinery	Y	N	N	N	N	N
1953	Westinghouse Electric & Manufacturing Co.[qqq]	Electrical equipment	Y	N	Y	N	N	Y
1953	General Instrument Corp.[rrr]	Variable condenser	Y	N	N	Y	N	N
1953	General Electric Co.[sss]	Electrical equipment	Y	N	Y	N	N	N
1953	Bendix Aviation Corp.[ttt]	Hydraulic braking systems	Y	Y	N	Y	N	Y
1953	General Electric Co.[uuu]	Incandescent lamps	Y	N	Y	Y	Y	Y
1953	Switzer Brothers, Inc.[vvv]	Daylight fluorescent materials	Y	Y	N	N	N	N
1953	Bearing Distributors Co.[www]	Tractor cabs	Y	N	N	Y	N	N
1953	Telescope Carts, Inc.[xxx]	Telescope carts	Y	N	N	Y	N	N
1954	Servel, Inc.[yyy]	Absorption refrigerating units	Y	N	N	Y	N	Y

1954	General Electric Co.[zzz]	Fluorescent lamps	N	Y	N	N	Y	N
1954	Cincinnati Milling Machine[aaaa] Co.	Milling machines	Y	N	N	N	N	Y
1954	US Rubber Co.[bbbb]	Natural latex	Y	Y	N	N	N	Y
1954	General Electric Co.[cccc]	Lamps, lamp parts	N	Y	N	N	Y	N
1954	Hunter Douglas Corp.[dddd]	Aluminum slats for venetian blinds	Y	N	N	N	N	N
1954	Wallace & Tiernan Co., Inc.[eeee]	Chlorinating equipment	N	Y	N	N	N	N
1954	Food Machinery & Chemical Corp.[ffff]	Peach pitting machinery	Y	N	N	N	N	Y
1954	Besser Manufacturing Co.[gggg]	Concrete block machines	Y	N	N	N	N	N
1954	Pittsburgh Crushed Steel Co.[hhhh]	Metal abrasives	Y	N	N	N	N	Y
1954	Eastman Kodak Co.[iiii]	Color film	Y	N	N	Y	N	N
1955	General Railway Signal Co.[jjjj]	Crossing gates, gate-activating mechanisms	Y	N	N	Y	N	N
1955	Magcobar, Inc.[kkkk]	Hydraulic oilwell pumps	Y	N	N	N	N	N

Continued

Appendix 6.A *Continued*

Year	First-Named Defendant	Affected Product	RRL (Y/N)	RFL (Y/N)	PD (Y/N)	Future Patents (Y/N)	Cross-License Condition (Y/N)	Provide Know-how (Y/N)
1955	Kelsey-Hayes Wheel Co.[llll]	Metal wheels	Y	N	N	Y	N	Y
1955	New Wrinkle, Inc.[mmmm]	Wrinkle finish enamels, varnishes	Y	N	N	N	N	N
1955	American Steel Foundries[nnnn]	Side frames, bolsters	Y	Y	N	N	N	Y
1955	New Wrinkle, Inc.[oooo]	Wrinkle finish enamels, varnishes	Y	N	N	N	N	N
1956	Western Electric Co.[pppp]	Communication services & equipment	Y	Y	N	Y	Y	Y
1956	IBM Corp.[qqqq]	Data-processing systems	Y	Y	N	Y	N	Y
1956	General Shoe Corp.[rrrr]	Shoe manufacturing	Y	N	N	Y	N	Y
1956	Michigan Tool Co.[ssss]	Gear finishing & cutting machines	Y	N	N	Y	N	Y
1956	Logan Co.[tttt]	Sheet chargers	Y	N	N	Y	N	N
1956	Int'l Cigar Machinery Corp.[uuuu]	Cigarmaking machinery	Y	N	N	N	Y	Y
1956	Crown Zellerback Corp.[vvvv]	Linen & paper towel cabinets	Y	N	N	Y	N	N

1957	Robertshaw-Fulton Controls Co.[wwww]	Temperature controls	Y	N	N	Y	N	N
1957	Magnaflux Corp.[xxxx]	Magnetic testing	N	N	Y	N	N	N
1957	Greyhound Corp.[yyyy]	Buses	N	N	N	Y	N	N
1958	B.F. Goodrich Co.[zzzz]	Sponge rubber	Y	N	N	N	N	N
1958	Radio Corp. of America[aaaaa]	Radio television apparatus	Y	Y	N	Y	Y	Y
1958	Chemical Specialties Co.[bbbbb]	Barbasco root and synthetic steroid hormones	Y	N	N	N	N	N
1959	Pitney-Bowes, Inc.[ccccc]	Postage meters	Y	Y	N	Y	N	Y
1961	Driver-Harris Co.[ddddd]	Electrical alloy resistance product	Y	Y	Y	Y	N	Y
1962	Borg-Warner Corp.[eeeee]	Oil well servicing	Y	N	N	Y	N	N
1963	A.C. Nielsen Co.[fffff]	Market research	Y	Y	N	Y	N	N
1964	Singer Mfg[ggggg]	Household sewing	Y	N	N	N	N	N
1964	Becton, Dickinson, & Co.[hhhhh]	Hypodermic sponges	Y	N	N	Y	N	Y
1964	American Cynamid Co.[iiiii]	Melamine products	Y	Y	N	Y	N	Y
1964	Alloy Metal Wire Co.[jjjjj]	Electrical resistance products	Y	N	N	Y	N	Y

Continued

Appendix 6.A *Continued*

Year	First-Named Defendant	Affected Product	RRL (Y/N)	RFL (Y/N)	PD (Y/N)	Future Patents (Y/N)	Cross-License Condition (Y/N)	Provide Know-how (Y/N)
1964	General Railway Signal Co.[kkkkk]	Railroad signaling, control equipment	Y	Y	N	N	N	Y
1965	Driver-Harris Co.[lllll]	Electrical resistance products	Y	N	N	Y	N	Y
1965	General Motors Corp.[mmmmm]	Buses	Y	Y	N	Y	Y[nnnnn]	N
1967	Dymo Industries, Inc.[ooooo]	Plastic tape and embossing tools	Y	N	N	N	N	N
1967	American Cyanamid Co.[ppppp]	Antibiotics (tetracycline)	Y	N	N	N	N	Y
1969	Union Camp Corp.[qqqqq]	Mesh-covered window bags	N	N	Y	N	N	N
1969	Minnesota Mining & Mfg. Co.[rrrrr]	Pressure-sensitive tape	Y	N	N	Y	Y	Y
1969	Scott Paper Co.[sssss]	Polyurethane foam	Y	N	N	N	N	Y
1970	Sonoco Products Co.[ttttt]	Paper cones	N	Y	N	N	N	Y
1970	Wisconsin Alumni Research Foundation[uuuuu]	Technology licensing	N	N	Y	N	N	N
1970	CIBA Corp.[vvvvv]	Dyestuffs	Y	N	N	N	N	Y
1971	Koppers Co.[wwwww]	Resorcinol	Y	N	N	N	N	Y

1972	Fisons Ltd.[xxxxx]	Drugs	Y	N	N	Y	N	Y
1972	General Telephone & Electronics Corp.[yyyyy]	Telephone manufacturing	Y	N	N	N	Y	Y
1973	United Aircraft Corp.[zzzzz]	Fuel cells	N	N	Y	N	N	N
1974	Glaxo Group Ltd.[aaaaaa]	Griseofulvin	Y	Y	N	Y	N	Y
1974	Glaxo Group Ltd.[bbbbbb]	Griseofulvin	Y	Y	N	N	N	N
1974	American Technical Industries[cccccc]	Artificial Christmas trees	N	Y	N	N	N	Y
1975	Xerox Corp.[dddddd]	Office copiers	Y	Y	N	Y	Y	Y
1975	Copper Development Ass'n[eeeeee]	Cooper fabrication	Y	N	N	Y	N	Y
1975	Mfrs. Aircraft Ass'n[ffffff]	Aircraft	Y	N	N	N	N	Y

Legend: RRL: reasonable royalty license; RFL: royalty-free license; PD: patent dedication.

Notes: Provisions in consent decrees or court orders relating to "future patents," "cross-license condition" and "provide know-how" differ in severity. For purposes of this table, I entered a "Y" for any of these items so long as this type of provision is included in at least some form in the consent decree or court order, even if it only applies to certain patents subject to the decree or order. For the sake of brevity, only the first-named defendant is listed in each enforcement action.

Sources: All information gathered through examination of consent decrees and judicial orders as found in Cheetah Antitrust and Competition Law Database (formerly known as BNA CCH Intelliconnect). Orders also identified through Contreras (2015, App. B); Scherer (1977); Hollabaugh and Wright (1960).

[a] *U.S. v. Kearney & Trecker Corp. et al.*, 1940–1943 Trade Cas. (CCH) ¶56,147 (N.D. Ill. Aug. 22, 1941).

[b] *U.S. v. Whitehead Bros. Co.*, 1940–1943 Trade Cas. (CCH) ¶56,182 (S.D.N.Y. Jan. 7, 1942).

[c] *U.S. v. Standard Oil Co., et al.*, 1940–1943 Trade Cas. (CCH) ¶56,198 (D.N.J. Mar. 25, 1942).

[d] *U.S. v. General Electric Co., et al.*, 1940–1943 Trade Cas. (CCH) ¶56,201 (D.N.J. Apr. 10, 1942).

[e] *U.S. v. Aluminum Co. of America, et al.*, 1940–1943 Trade Cas. (CCH) ¶56,200 (S.D.N.Y. Apr. 15, 1942).

Continued

Appendix 6.A *Continued*

[f] *U.S. v. Aqua Systems, Inc., et al.*, 1940–1943 Trade Cas. (CCH) ¶56,248 (S.D.N.Y. Nov. 10, 1942).

[g] *U.S. v. American Bosch Corp. et al.*, 1940–1943 Trade Cas. (CCH) ¶56,147 (S.D.N.Y. Dec. 29, 1942).

[h] *U.S. v. Aerofin Corp., et al.*, 1940–1943 Trade Cas. (CCH) ¶56,264 (S.D.N.Y. Mar. 5, 1943).

[I] *U.S. v. Rail Joint Co., et al.*, 1944–1945 Trade Cas. (CCH) ¶57,287 (N.D. Ill. Sept. 20, 1944).

[j] *Crosby Steam, Gage & Valve Co. v. Manning, Maxwell & Moore, Inc.*, 1944–1945 Trade Cas. (CCH) ¶57,336 (D. Mass, Feb. 1, 1945). Crosby was the plaintiff-patentee in this litigation, which it filed concerning alleged patent infringement by Manning, the defendant-licensee. The United States filed a motion in this case as "intervenor" seeking a compulsory licensing remedy.

[k] *U.S. v. General Electric Co., et al.*, 1946–1947 Trade Cas. (CCH) ¶57,448 (D.N.J. Mar. 7, 1945).

[l] *U.S. v. Vehicular Parking, Ltd. et al.*, 1944–1945 Trade Cas. (CCH) ¶57,404 (D. Del. Aug. 8, 1945).

[m] *U.S. v. Merck & Co.*, 1944–1945 Trade Cas. (CCH) ¶57,416 (D.N.J. Oct. 6, 1945).

[n] *U.S. v. National Lead Co., et al.*, 65 F.Supp. 513 (S.D.N.Y. 1945), *aff'd* 332 U.S. 319 (1947).

[o] *U.S. v. Auditorium Conditioning Corp., et al.*, 1944–1945 Trade Cas. (CCH) ¶57,428 (S.D.N.Y. Dec. 28, 1945).

[p] *Wisconsin Alumni Research Foundation v. Rene Douglas*, 1946–1947 Trade Cas. (CCH) ¶57,433 (N.D. Ill. 1946). Wisconsin was the plaintiff-patentee in this litigation, which it filed concerning alleged patent infringement by Douglas. The United States filed a motion in this case as "intervenor" seeking a compulsory licensing remedy.

[q] *U.S. v. Bendix Aviation Corp.*, 1946–1947 Trade Cas. (CCH) ¶57,444 (D.N.J. Feb. 13, 1946).

[r] *U.S. v. Diamond Match Co., et al.*, 1946–1947 Trade Cas. (CCH) ¶57,456 (S.D.N.Y. Apr. 9, 1946).

[s] *U.S. v. Western Precipitation Corp., et al.*, 1946–1947 Trade Cas. (CCH) ¶57,458 (S.D. Cal. Apr. 11, 1946).

[t] Defendants enjoined from enforcing patents, which is functionally equivalent to a patent dedication remedy.

[u] *U.S. v. Libbey-Owens-Ford Glass Co. et al.*, 1946–1947 Trade Cas. (CCH) ¶57,489 (N.D. Ohio Sept. 5, 1946).

[v] *U.S. v. American Air Filter Corp, Inc. et al.*, 1946–1947 Trade Cas. (CCH) ¶57,492 (W.D. Ky. Sept. 10, 1946).

[w] *U.S. v. Owens-Illinois Glass Co.*, 1946–1947 Trade Cas. (CCH) ¶57,498 (N.D. Cal. Sept. 18, 1946).

[x] *U.S. v. National Cash Register et al.*, Criminal Action No. 7092 (S.D. Ohio Jan. 8, 1947).

[y] *U.S. v. American Lecithin Co., et al.*, 1946–1947 Trade Cas. (CCH) ¶57,542 (N.D. Ohio Feb. 17, 1947).

[z] *U.S. v. Hartford-Empire Co., et al.*, 1946–1947 Trade Cas. (CCH) ¶57,571 (N.D. Ohio May 23, 1947), *modified*, Hartford-Empire Co. v. U.S., 323 U.S. 386 (1945).

[aa] The district court awarded a patent dedication remedy. However, the Supreme Court rejected this element of the remedy. See *Hartford-Empire Co. v. U.S.*, 323 U.S. 386 (1945).

[bb] *U.S. v. Patent Button Co.*, 1946–1947 Trade Cas. (CCH) ¶57,579 (D. Conn. Jun. 27, 1947).

[cc] *U.S. v. Timken-Detroit Axle Co.*, 1946–1947 Trade Cas. (CCH) ¶57,603 (E.D. Mich. Aug. 14, 1947).

[dd] *U.S. v. American Locomotive Co., et al.*, 1946–1947 Trade Cas. (CCH) ¶57,621 (N.D. Ind. Oct. 4, 1947).

[ee] *U.S. v. Electric Storage Battery Co. et al.*, 1946–1947 Trade Cas. (CCH) ¶57,645 (S.D.N.Y. Nov. 24, 1947).

[ff] *U.S. v. Scovill Manufacturing Co.*, 1948–1949 Trade Cas. (CCH) ¶62,223 (D. Conn. Feb. 17, 1948).

[gg] *U.S. v. Automatic Sprinkler Co. of America, et al.*, 1948–1949 Trade Cas. (CCH) ¶62,230 (N.D. Ill. Mar. 22, 1948).

[hh] *U.S. v. Gamewell Co., et al.*, 1948–1949 Trade Cas. (CCH) ¶62,236 (D. Mass. Mar. 22, 1948).

[ii] *U.S. v. A. B. Dick Co., et al.*, 1948–1949 Trade Cas. (CCH) ¶62,233 (N.D. Ohio Mar. 25, 1948).

[jj] *U.S. v. Universal Button Fastening and Buttons Co.*, 1948–1949 Trade Cas. (CCH) ¶62,255 (N.D. Mich. May 7, 1948).

[kk] *U.S. v. American Bosch Corp.*, 1948–1949 Trade Cas. (CCH) ¶62,284 (S.D.N.Y. Jun. 4, 1948)

[ll] *U.S. v. White Cap Co.*, 1948–1949 Trade Cas. (CCH) ¶62,268 (N.D. Ill. Jun. 17, 1948)..

[mm] *U.S. v. U.S. Pipe and Foundry Co., et al.*, 1948–1949 Trade Cas. (CCH) ¶62,285 (D.N.J. Jul. 21, 1948).

[nn] *U.S. v. General Cable Corp., et al.*, 1948–1949 Trade Cas. (CCH) ¶62,300 (S.D.N.Y. Aug. 25, 1948).

[oo] *U.S. v. American Optical Co., et al.*, 1948–1949 Trade Cas. (CCH) ¶62,308 (S.D.N.Y. Sep. 17, 1948).

[pp] *U.S. v. Allegheny Ludlum Steel Corp., et al.*, 1948–1949 Trade Cas. (CCH) ¶62,330 (D.N.J. Oct. 25, 1948).

[qq] This entry reflects the patent licensing terms that were agreed upon by Alcoa and the government on 29 October 1948, in connection with the disposal of certain war plants operated by Alcoa and the entry of a new firm (*U.S. v. Aluminum Co. of Amer. (Alcoa) et al.*, 91 F.Supp. 333, 405–411 (S.D.N.Y. 1950). The licensing terms as agreed upon with the entrant were judicially approved, except for invalidation of a grant-back clause in Alcoa's favor (*U.S. v. Alcoa*, pp. 409–10).

[rr] *U.S. v. Libbey-Owens-Ford Glass Co., et al.*, 1948–1949 Trade Cas. (CCH) ¶62,323 (N.D. Ohio Oct. 30, 1948).

[ss] *U.S. v. Rohm & Haas Co.*, 1948–1949 Trade Cas. (CCH) ¶62,334 (E.D. Pa. Nov. 18, 1948).

[tt] *U.S. v. Technicolor, Inc., et al.*, 1948–1949 Trade Cas. (CCH) ¶62,338 (S.D. Cal. Nov. 24, 1948).

[uu] *U.S. v. Bendix Aviation Corp., et al.*, 1948–1949 Trade Cas. (CCH) ¶62,349 (S.D.N.Y. Dec. 22, 1948).

[vv] *U.S. v. Scophony Corp. of America*, 1948–1949 Trade Cas. (CCH) ¶62,356 (S.D.N.Y. Jan. 12, 1949).

[ww] *U.S. v. Phillips Screw Co.*, 1948–1949 Trade Cas. (CCH) ¶62,394 (N.D. Ill. Mar. 28, 1949).

[xx] *U.S. v. Owens-Corning Fiberglass Corp.*, 1948–1949 Trade Cas. (CCH) ¶62,442 (N.D. Ohio Jun. 23, 1949).

[yy] *U.S. v. Sand Spun Patents Corp, et al.*, 1948–1949 Trade Cas. (CCH) ¶62,462 (D.N.J. Jul. 22, 1949).

[zz] *U.S. v. General Electric Co.*, 1948–1949 Trade Cas. (CCH) ¶62,518 (S.D. Cal. Nov. 4, 1949).

[aaa] *U.S. v. Standard Register Co.*, 1950–1951 Trade Cas. (CCH) ¶62,533 (D.D.C. Dec. 13, 1949).

Continued

Appendix 6.A *Continued*

[bbb] *U.S. v. Technicolor, Inc.*, 1950–1951 Trade Cas. (CCH) ¶62,586 (S.D. Cal. Feb. 28, 1950).

[ccc] *U.S. v. American Can Co.*, 1950–1951 Trade Cas. (CCH) ¶62,679 (N.D. Cal. Jun. 22, 1950).

[ddd] *U.S. v. Continental Can Co.*, Inc., 1950–1951 Trade Cas. (CCH) ¶62,680 (N.D. Cal. Jun. 26, 1950).

[eee] *U.S. v. Textile Machine Works, et al.*, 1950–1951 Trade Cas. (CCH) ¶62,709 (S.D.N.Y. Oct. 9, 1950).

[fff] *U.S. v. Minnesota Mining and Manufacturing Co., et al.*, 1950–1951 Trade Cas. (CCH) ¶62,724 (D. Mass. Nov. 6, 1950).

[ggg] *U.S. v. U.S. Gypsum Co., et al.*, 1950–1951 Trade Cas. (CCH) ¶62,853 (D.C. May 15, 1951).

[hhh] *U.S. v. Liquidometer Corp.*, 1950–1951 Trade Cas. (CCH) ¶62,867 (S.D.N.Y. Jun. 15, 1951).

[iii] *U.S. v. Austenal Laboratories, Inc.*, 1950–1951 Trade Cas. (CCH) ¶62,880 (S.D.N.Y. Jun. 29, 1951).

[jjj] *U.S. v. Permutit Co. et al.*, 1950–1951 Trade Cas. (CCH) ¶62,888 (S.D.N.Y. Jun. 29, 1951).

[kkk] *U.S. v. Parke, Davis & Co. et al.*, 1950–1951 Trade Cas. (CCH) ¶62,914 (E.D. Mich. Sep. 6, 1951).

[lll] *U.S. v. Mager and Gougelman, Inc. et al.*, 1952–1953 Trade Cas. (CCH) ¶67,233 (N.D. Ill. Feb. 15, 1952).

[mmm] *U.S. v. Liquid Carbonic Corp., et al.*, 1952–1953 Trade Cas. (CCH) ¶67,248 (E.D.N.Y. Mar. 7, 1952).

[nnn] *U.S. v. Imperial Chemical Industries Ltd.*, 1952–1953 Trade Cas. (CCH) ¶67,282 (S.D.N.Y. May 16, 1952).

[ooo] *U.S. v. Davis Co., et al.*, 1952–1953 Trade Cas. (CCH) ¶67,403 (S.D.N.Y. Dec. 24, 1952).

[ppp] *U.S. v. United Shoe Machinery Corp.*, 1952–1953 Trade Cas. (CCH) ¶67,436 (D. Mass. Feb. 18, 1953).

[qqq] *U.S. v. Westinghouse Electric & Mfg. Co., et al.*, 1952–1953 Trade Cas. (CCH) ¶67,501 (D.N.J. Jun. 1, 1953).

[rrr] *U.S. v. General Instrument Corp., et al.*, 1952–1953 Trade Cas. (CCH) ¶67,574 (D.N.J. Aug. 11, 1953).

[sss] *U.S. v. General Electric Co., et al.*, 1952–1953 Trade Cas. (CCH) ¶67,585 (D.N.J. Oct. 6, 1953).

[ttt] *U.S. v. Bendix Aviation Corp.*, 1952–1953 Trade Cas. (CCH) ¶67,583 (S.D.N.Y. Oct. 7, 1953).

[uuu] *U.S. v. General Electric Co., et al.*, 1952–1953 Trade Cas. (CCH) ¶67,576 (D.N.J. Oct. 2, 1953).

[vvv] *U.S. v. Switzer Bros., Inc.*, 1952–1953 Trade Cas. (CCH) ¶67,598 (N.D. Cal. Oct. 22, 1953).

[www] *U.S. v. Bearing Distributors Co., et al.*, 1952–1953 Trade Cas. (CCH) ¶67,595 (W.D. Mo. Oct. 27, 1953).

[xxx] *U.S. of America v. Telescope Carts, Inc. et al.*, 1952–1953 Trade Cas. (CCH) ¶67,573 (W.D. Mo. Dec. 24, 1953).

[yyy] *U.S. v. Servel, Inc.*, 1954 Trade Cas. (CCH) ¶67,665 (E.D. Pa. Jan. 18, 1954).

[zzz] *U.S. v. General Electric Co., et al.*, 1954 Trade Cas. (CCH) ¶67,714 (D.N.J. Mar. 26, 1954).

[aaaa] *U.S. v. Cincinnati Milling Machine Co., et al.*, 1954 Trade Cas. (CCH) ¶67,733 (E.D. Mich. Apr. 19, 1954).

[bbbb] *U.S. v. U.S. Rubber Co., et al.*, 1954 Trade Cas. (CCH) ¶67,771 (S.D.N.Y. May 28, 1954).

[cccc] *U.S. v. General Electric Co., et al.*, 1954 Trade Cas. (CCH) ¶67,794 (D.N.J. Jun. 30, 1954)

[dddd] *U.S. v. Hunter Douglas Corp.*, 1954 Trade Cas. (CCH) ¶67,802 (S.D. Cal. Jun. 30, 1954).

[eeee] *U.S. v. Wallace & Tiernan Co., Inc.*, 1954 Trade Cas. (CCH) ¶67,828 (D.R.I. Jul. 26, 1954).

[ffff] *U.S. v. Food Machinery & Chemical Corp., et al.*, 1954 Trade Cas. (CCH) ¶67,829 (N.D. Cal. Aug. 9, 1954).

[gggg] *U.S. v. Besser Manufacturing Co., et al.*, 1955 Trade Cas. (CCH) ¶67,977 (E.D. Mich. Nov. 8, 1954).

[hhhh] *U.S. v. Pittsburgh Crushed Steel Co., et al.*, 1954 Trade Cas. (CCH) ¶67,892 (N.D. Ohio Nov. 13, 1954).

[iiii] *U.S. v. Eastman Kodak Co.*, 1954 Trade Cas. (CCH) ¶67,920 (W.D.N.Y. Dec. 21, 1954).

[jjjj] *U.S. v. General Railway Signal Co.*, 1955 Trade Cas. (CCH) ¶67,992 (W.D.N.Y. Mar. 15, 1955).

[kkkk] *U.S. v. Magcobar, Inc.*, 1955 Trade Cas. (CCH) ¶68,023 (S.D. Cal. Apr. 6, 1955).

[llll] *U.S. v. Kelsey-Hayes Wheel Co.*, 1955 Trade Cas. (CCH) ¶68,093 (E.D. Mich. Jul. 1, 1955)

[mmmm] *U.S. v. New Wrinkle, Inc.*, 1955 Trade Cas. (CCH) ¶68,161 (S.D. Ohio Sep. 27, 1955)

[nnnn] *U.S. v. American Steel Foundries*, 1955 Trade Cas. (CCH) ¶68,156 (N.D. Ohio Sep. 30, 1955).

[oooo] *U.S. v. New Wrinkle, Inc.*, 1955 Trade Cas. (CCH) ¶68,203 (S.D. Ohio Oct. 27, 1955).

[pppp] *U.S. v. Western Electric Co., Inc., and American Telephone & Telegraph Co.*, 1956 Trade Cas. (CCH) ¶68,246 (D.N.J. Jan. 24, 1956).

[qqqq] *U.S. v. IBM Corp.*, 1956 Trade Cas. (CCH) ¶68,245 (S.D.N.Y. Jan. 25, 1956).

[rrrr] *U.S. v. General Shoe Corp.*, 1956 Trade Cas. (CCH) ¶68,271 (M.D. Tenn. Feb. 17, 1956).

[ssss] *U.S. v. Michigan Tool Co.*, 1956 Trade Cas. (CCH) ¶68,290 (E.D. Mich. Feb. 28, 1956).

[tttt] *U.S. v. Logan Co. et al.*, 1956 Trade Cas. (CCH) ¶68,375 (W.D. Pa. Jun. 7, 1956).

[uuuu] *U.S. v. International Cigar Machinery Corp.*, 1956 Trade Cas. (CCH) ¶68,426 (S.D.N.Y. Jul. 25, 1956).

[vvvv] *U.S. v. Crown Zellerback Corp.*, 1956 Trade Cas. (CCH) ¶68,544 (N.D. Ill. Nov. 19, 1956).

[wwww] *U.S. v. Robertshaw-Fulton Controls Co.*, 1957 Trade Cas. (CCH) ¶68,592 (W.D. Pa. Jan. 8, 1957).

[xxxx] *U.S. v. Magnaflux Corp.*, 1957 Trade Cas. (CCH) ¶68,707 (N.D. Ill. May 6, 1957).

[yyyy] *U.S. v. Greyhound Corp.*, 1957 Trade Cas. (CCH) ¶68,756 (N.D. Ill. Jun. 27, 1957).

[zzzz] *U.S. v. B.F. Goodrich Co.*, 1958 Trade Cas. (CCH) ¶68,994 (S.D.N.Y. Mar. 31, 1958).

Continued

Appendix 6.A *Continued*

[aaaaa] *U.S. v. Radio Corp. of Am.*, 1958 Trade Cas. (CCH) ¶69,164 (S.D.N.Y. Oct. 28, 1958).

[bbbbb] *U.S. v. Chemical Specialties Co. Inc. et al.*, 1958 Trade Cas. (CCH) ¶69,186 (S.D.N.Y. Nov. 5, 1958).

[ccccc] *U.S. v. Pitney-Bowes, Inc.*, 1959 Trade Cas. (CCH) ¶69,235 (D. Conn. Jan. 9, 1959).

[ddddd] *U.S. v. Driver-Harris Co. et al.*, 1961 Trade Cas. (CCH) ¶70,031 (D.N.J. May 25, 1961).

[eeeee] *U.S. v. Borg-Warner Corp. et al.*, 1962 Trade Cas. (CCH) ¶70,461 (S.D. Texas Oct. 22, 1962).

[fffff] *In re A.C. Nielsen Co.*, 63 F.T.C. 1082 (1963).

[ggggg] *U.S. v. Singer Manufacturing Co.*, 231 F.Supp. 240 (S.D.N.Y. June 1, 1964). The order directs the parties to submit a consent decree providing for reasonable royalty licensing.

[hhhhh] *U.S. v. Becton, Dickinson and Co.*, 1964 Trade Cas. (CCH) ¶71,144 (D.N.J. Jul. 20, 1964).

[iiiii] *U.S. v. American Cyanamid Co.*, 1964 Trade Cas. (CCH) ¶71,166 (Aug. 4, 1964).

[jjjjj] *U.S. v. Alloy Metal Wire Co. et al.*, 1964 Trade Cas. (CCH) ¶71,170 (D.N.J. Aug. 13, 1964).

[kkkkk] *In re General Railway Signal Co. et al.*, 66 F.T.C. 882 (1964).

[lllll] *U.S. v. Driver-Harris Co. et al.*, 1966 Trade Cas. (CCH) ¶71,658 (D.N.J. Dec. 7, 1965).

[mmmmm] *U.S. v. General Motors Corp.*, 1965 Trade Cas. (CCH) ¶71,624 (E.D. Mich. Dec. 31, 1965).

[nnnnn] Only applies if licensee is not a bus manufacturer.

[ooooo] *U.S. v. Dymo Industries, Inc.*, 1967 Trade Cas. (CCH) ¶72,102 (N.D. Cal. Jun. 15, 1967)

[ppppp] *In re American Cyanamid Co. et al.*, 72 F.T.C. 623 (1967).

[qqqqq] *U.S. v. Union Camp Corp. and Bemis Co., In.*, 1969 Trade Cas. (CCH) ¶72,689 (E.D. Va. Feb. 24, 1969).

[rrrrr] *U.S. v. Minnesota Mining and Mfg Co., et al.*, 1969 Trade Cas. (CCH) ¶72,865 (N.D. Ill. Sep. 2, 1969).

[sssss] *U.S. v. Scott Paper Co. & Chemotronics, Inc.*, 1969 Trade Cas. (CCH) ¶72,919 (E.D. Mich. Oct. 24, 1969).

[ttttt] *U.S. v. Sonoco Products Co.*, 1970 Trade Cas. (CCH) ¶73,008 (E.D.S.C. Jan. 22, 1970).

[uuuuu] *U.S. v. Wisconsin Alumni Research Foundation*, 1970 Trade Cas. (CCH) ¶73,015 (W.D. Wis. Jan. 30, 1970).

[vvvvv] *U.S. v. CIBA Corp. et al.*, 1970 Trade Cas. (CCH) ¶73,269 (S.D.N.Y. Sep. 8, 1970).

[wwwww] *In re Koppers Co., Inc.*, 79 F.T.C. 837 (1971).

[xxxxx] *U.S. v. Fisons Ltd., et al.*, 1972 Trade Cas. (CCH) ¶73,794 (N.D. Ill. Feb. 18, 1972).

[yyyyy] *International Telephone and Telegraph Corp. v. General Telephone and Electronics Corp. et al.*, 1973-1 Trade Cas. (CCH) ¶74,270 (D. Haw. Dec. 13, 1972).

[zzzzz] *U.S. v. United Aircraft Corp.*, 1973-1 Trade Cas. (CCH) ¶74,467 (D. Conn. Jun. 11, 1973).

[aaaaaa] *U.S. v. Glaxo Group Ltd. & Imperial Chemical Industries, Ltd.*, 1974-1 Trade Cas. (CCH) ¶74,883 (D.D.C. Mar. 1, 1974). This decision imposes a licensing obligation on Imperial Chemical Industries.

[bbbbbb] *U.S. v. Glaxo Group Ltd. & Imperial Chemical Industries, Ltd.*, 1974-1 Trade Cas. (CCH) ¶75,000 (D.D.C. May 10, 1974). This decision imposes a licensing obligation on Glaxo Group.

[cccccc] *U.S. v. American Technical Industries, Inc.*, 1974-2 Trade Cas. (CCH) ¶75,376 (M.D. Penn. Dec. 3, 1974).

[dddddd] *In re Xerox Corp.*, 86 F.T.C. 364 (1975).

[eeeeee] *U.S. v. Copper Dev. Ass'n et al.*, 1975-2 Trade Cas. (CCH) ¶60,535 (S.D.N.Y. Oct. 2, 1975).

[ffffff] *U.S. v. Manufacturers Aircraft Ass'n, Inc., et al.*, Civil No. 1976-1 Trade Cas. (CCH) ¶60,810 (S.D.N.Y. Nov. 12, 1975).

Appendix 6.B Compulsory patent licensing statutes, 1946–1975

Date	Act	Citation	Coverage
1946	Atomic Energy Act	Pub. L. 79-585, § 11, 60 Stat. 755, 768–70 (1946), *amended by* Pub. L. 83–703, §§ 68, 151-160, 68 Stat. 919, 934–935, 943–48 (1954).	AEC-funded research relating to atomic energy and weapons; patents relating to atomic weapons.
1946	Synthetic Liquid Fuel Act	30 U.S.C. § 323, Pub. L. 290, 58 Stat. 191, amended by Pub. L. 247, 65 Stat. 709).	Government-funded research relating to synthetic liquid fuels.
1946	Research and Marketing Act	7 U.S.C. § 427i(a), Pub. L. 79-733.	Government-funded research relating to agricultural commodities.
1950	National Science Foundation Act	42 U.S.C. § 1871(a), Pub. L. No. 507–81, 82 Stat. 360.	NSF-funded scientific research.[a]
1958	National Aeronautics and Space Act	Pub. L. 85–568, §§ 203(b)(3), 305(a), 72 Stat. 426, 430, 435–37 (1958).	NASA-funded research relating aeronautical and space technologies.
1960	Coal Research Act	Pub. L. 86–599, § 6, 74 Stat. 336, 337 (1960).	Government-funded research coal-related research.
1960	Helium Act (amendments)	50 U.S.C. § 176(b); Pub. L. 86–777, § 4, 74 Stat. 918, 920 (1960).	Government-funded research relating to helium production and purification.
1961[b]	Saline Water Conversion Act (amendments)	42 U.S.C. § 1959, Pub. L. 87–295, §§ 3–4, 75 Stat. 628–29 (1961).	Government-funded research relating to desalination processes.
1961	Arms Control and Disarmament Act	22 U.S.C. § 2572, Pub. L. 87–297, 75 Stat. 634.	Government-funded research relating to arms-control.
1964	Water Resources Research Act	42 U.S.C. § 1961 c-3	Government-funded research relating to water conservation.
1965	Appalachian Regional Development Act	40 U.S.C. App. 302(e); 79 Stat. 5.	Government-funded research relating to Appalachian regional development.

Appendix 6.B *Continued*

Date	Act	Citation	Coverage
1966	National Traffic and Motor Vehicle Safety Act	15 U.S.C. § 1395(c), Pub. L. 89-563, 80 Stat. 721	Government-funded research relating to motor vehicle safety.
Date	Act	Citation	Coverage
1969	Coal Mine Health and Safety Act	30 U.S.C. § 951(c), Pub. L. 91-193, 83 Stat. 799.	Government-funded research relating to coal mine health and safety.
1970	Clean Air Act	Pub. L. 91-604, § 308, 48 Stat. 1676, 1708–1709 (1970).	Government-funded research relating to pollution abatement.
1970	Solid Waste Disposal Act (amendments)	42 U.S.C. §3253(c), 79 Stat. 992; Pub. L. 89–272, as amended Pub. L. 91–512, 84 Stat. 1227 (1970).	Government-funded research relating to solid waste disposal.
1972	Consumer Product Safety Act	15 U.S.C. § 2054(d); 86 Stat. 1211.	Government-funded research relating to product safety.
1974	Federal Fire Prevention and Control Act[c]	15 U.S.C. § 2218(d); 88 Stat. 1548; Pub. L. 93–498.	Government-funded research relating to fire prevention.
1974	Federal Non-Nuclear Energy and Research Development Act[d]	42 U.S.C. § 5901; Pub. L. 93-577, § 9, 88 Stat. 1878, 1887–91 (1974).	Government-funded research relating to non-nuclear energy technologies.

Note: This list is intended to provide a reasonably but not fully comprehensive list of federal statutes enacted during 1946–1975 that implicate ownership, or other interests in, inventions developed in connection with federal R&D grants or contracts. Provisions in other statutes likely implicate or otherwise affect these matters. Unless otherwise noted, the date refers to the year in which the statute was originally enacted, irrespective of subsequent amendments or repeal. Unless otherwise noted, citations are to the compulsory licensing provisions in the original statute only, except in the case of amendments that are materially relevant to compulsory licensing.

[a] The act does not specifically provide for compulsory patent licensing; rather, it broadly empowers the NSF to address patent ownership and licensing issues, without specifically excluding the possibility of compulsory licensing.

[b] The statute was enacted in 1952; however, the provisions relating to compulsory patent licensing were included in amendments enacted in 1961.

[c] This statute provides for the possibility of compulsory licensing but is designed to confer substantial discretion on agency administrators to waive title in favor of, or grant exclusive licenses to, recipients of R&D funding from the agency.

[d] See note 3.

7

The Long History of Software Patenting in the United States*

Gerardo Con Díaz

For nearly 50 years, the computing industry has embraced an origin story about the birth of software patenting.[1] Prominent industry periodicals and biographical accounts have posited a narrative that begins in 1968, when a firm called Applied Data Research (ADR) obtained Sorting System, a patent issued for a program of the same name.[2] At a time when software firms were struggling to carve out a market for their programs, the story usually goes, this patent ran against established legal wisdom and caused a sudden and unexpected expansion of the categories of invention eligible for patent protection. For the first time ever, patents could be used to protect computer programs.[3]

This account has likely stood the test of time in part because the chronology it implies is compatible with our understanding of the history of computing.[4] The 1960s were a period of extraordinary growth in the US computing industry.[5] Hardware manufacturers, IBM chief among them, had normally distributed their computer programs through so-called bundles (free of charge with the purchase or lease of their hardware). Several smaller firms made their profits by developing custom software on a contract-by-contract basis, but the manufacturers' bundles were by far the most popular way of acquiring computer

* This essay is drawn partly from Con Diaz (2019).

1 See, for instance, "First Patent Is Issued for Software, Full Implications Are Not Yet Known," "Unprecedented Patent," Goetz (2002; 2011).

2 Goetz, Patent 3,380,029 (1968). See also "First Patent Is Issued for Software, Full Implications Are Not Yet Known"; "Unprecedented Patent"; Goetz (2002; 2011).

3 Patent eligibility is codified in 17 USC 101, which reads, "Whoever invents or discovers any new and useful process, machine, manufacture, or composition of matter, or any new and useful improvement thereof, may obtain a patent therefor, subject to the conditions and requirements of this title."

4 This is also why this narrative has been much more widely adopted than a later one identifying the origins of software patenting in the early 1980s. The first patent according to this more recent narrative is Asija, Patent 4,270,182 (1981). See "First Patentee Writes 'How to Patent Programs'"; "May 26, 1981: Programmer-Attorney Wins First US Software Patent"; Asija (1983).

5 The standard historical surveys of the American computing industry are Campbell-Kelly (2003), Campbell-Kelly et al. (2013), Ceruzzi (2003). See also Usselman, (2009).

Gerardo Con Díaz, *The Long History of Software Patenting in the United States* In: The Battle over Patents.* Edited by: Stephen H. Haber and Naomi R. Lamoreaux, Oxford University Press.
DOI: 10.1093/oso/9780197576151.003.0008

programs. The origin story suggests plausibly that when IBM started to consider selling its programs in the late 1960s, programmers turned to patent law for the first time to compete in what would soon become the modern software products industry—that is, the business of offering software for sale, as opposed to free of charge.

However, this narrative overlooks the rich history of patent drafting that has accompanied the history of programming since the end of World War II. This chapter shows how the patent protection of computer programs originated not in the late 1960s at software firms but in the early 1950s as industrial research laboratories started to patent their newest sources of automation and data processing: computers and their programming. Well before the word "software" had even come into being, programmers, engineers, and lawyers at places such as Mobil Oil and Bell Telephone Laboratories (Bell Labs) were obtaining patent protection for the programs developed by their researchers and engineers. These patents employed a patent-drafting technique that lawyers in the late 1960s would retroactively call "embodying software." It consisted of securing patent protection for a program indirectly, by patenting instead a computing system that worked in accordance with it.

Software patenting emerged organically from traditions of patent drafting almost as old as the modern electronic computer. In the late 1940s and early 1950s, when a computer's programming was as tangible as the circuits that the machine comprised, there was nothing unusual about the idea that a patent could protect a program. After all, programming a computer could involve, literally, its manual rewiring. During the next decade, programs grew in complexity and programming languages enabled their creation through textual means. Inventors and their lawyers then relied on the means-plus claim structure—a claim that discloses a machine as the means to perform a given collection of functions—as a shorthand to disclose the kinds of physicality that their predecessors would have spelled out. This often brought them into conflict with patent examiners, who required them to revise their claims' phrasing to identify the tangible components of the computing system that would carry out the functions at stake. The resulting patents combined means-plus language with very specific descriptions of interconnected electronic components to secure patent protections for the computer programs at their core.

In this revised account, Sorting System stands out as the start of the US software industry's embrace of the patent-drafting techniques that hardware manufacturers and industrial research laboratories had been honing for nearly two decades. A series of court opinions that the now-defunct Court of Customs of Patent Appeals (CCPA) handed down in the 1950s and 1960s created the legal precedents necessary for judges and examiners to accept these patents. Thus, by the time the modern software industry started to develop in the late 1960s, the idea that firms could obtain protection for their programs in one way or another was well established in the industry.

This chapter is divided into three parts. The first shows how Bell Labs secured patent protection for an error correcting code developed in the late 1940s.[6] The ensuing patent, *Error Detecting and Correcting System*, issued in 1951, is the earliest known example of how a firm secured protection for a computer's programming by patenting a machine that works in accordance with it.[7] The second analyzes how firms in the 1950s followed Bell Labs' lead by protecting their computer programs using patents for machines and methods of operating them.[8] The third shows how the CCPA validated software embodiment as a patent-drafting technique soon after the issuance of Sorting System.

These three sections draw on the methods for the history of patenting that historians of business, law, and technology have developed in recent years. These scholars have shown that the act of drafting a patent is, in effect, an exercise in the discursive construction of technology.[9] Since the professionalization of patent drafting in the late nineteenth century, patent applications have been byproducts of human networks—fruits of the collaboration among people intimately familiar with an invention and others fluent in the standard discourse and format required to bring the invention into the Patent Office.[10] A patent's history can therefore reveal not just the invention at its core, but also the negotiations that preceded it, the conventions with which its drafters grappled, and even its assignors' standing in their industry's patenting landscape.[11]

Applied to software patenting, these insights encourage a shift away from discussing whether software is patent-eligible and toward analyzing how firms have sought patent protection for their programs.[12] This shift requires two

[6] Other scholars have hinted that the history of software patenting begins in the nineteenth century, either with the patenting of looms controlled by patterned cards or with Samuel Morse's 1840 patent over Morse Code, which the US Supreme Court partially invalidated in 1854. These earlier precedents are best understood not as the first software patents—software did not exist at the time, and modern electronic computing would not develop for almost another century—but as evidence that some of the thorny legal problems surrounding software patents have been present in US patent law for more than a century (Risch 2012; Mossoff 2014; Stobbs 2012).

[7] Legal scholars before me have identified this patent as an important precursor to modern software patenting, but their work generally does little more than acknowledge its existence as a potential starting point. My aim is, instead, to show how and why this patent came into being and how its issuance shaped patent-drafting practice for decades to come. See, for instance, Allison, Dunn, and Mann (2007), Stobbs (2012).

[8] In this sense, I aim to redirect the line of inquiry away from debating whether or not Hamming and Holbrook's patent was truly the first patent of its kind to be issued and to focus instead on the fact that the patent-drafting techniques that enabled it to be issued spread quickly across several industries.

[9] Lamoreaux, Sokoloff, and Sutthiphisal (2013), Pottage and Sherman (2010), Biagioli (2006).

[10] Beauchamp (2015), Biagioli (2012), Swanson (2009), Rankin (2011).

[11] Swanson (2007), Kevles (1994), Kevles and Berkowitz (2002).

[12] A focus on the patent-eligibility of software has characterized work by legal scholars and historians of technology alike (Con Diaz 2015a; Con Diaz 2015b; Samuelson 2006; Campbell-Kelly 2005).

methodological imperatives. First is the need to analyze the technical content and discursive patterns of individual patents—how the inventions at stake work and how the patents disclose this work—in their original legal and technological contexts. The printed patents themselves rarely reveal much more about these contexts than the prior art in their citations, so it is helpful also to consider the inventors' patent applications and any documents they submitted to appeal the Patent Office's rejections.[13] The second imperative is to disassociate the analysis from any preconceptions of what the words "software" and "program" may mean today. Back in the 1950s, programs were not something that could be bought or sold, and the word "software" could refer to anything other than a computer's hardware, including the maintenance services that manufacturers provided.[14] In short, the burden of identifying patents that protect computer programs falls not on our contemporary technological sensibilities but on our understanding of the historical interface between computing and the law.

Patents for Code

In 1946, a mathematician named Richard Hamming arrived for his first day of work at Bell Labs.[15] World War II had given Bell Labs an opportunity to demonstrate that their computers were reliable and useful.[16] Chief among them was a series of computers, the Model I through Model V, which the laboratory had in operation from 1940 to 1965. Unlike cutting-edge all-electronic machines, which had no moving parts, these used telephone relays that physically switched on and off. The Model V (shown in Figure 7.1) had 2 separate processors and about 9,000 relays.[17] It was so versatile and powerful that both the national Advisory Committee on Aeronautics and the Ballistics Research Laboratory at Aberdeen eventually purchased one machine each.[18]

Hamming used the Model V while working at the Labs' Mathematics Research Group.[19] However, this computer was in such demand that he only had access to it during the weekends. This meant that Hamming had exactly two days to test out the programs he had produced during the week. With so many hours of work

[13] These patent applications and appeals documents are housed at the National Archives in Kansas City.

[14] For more on the multiple historical meanings of the word "software," see Con Diaz (2019), Con Diaz (2016), Haigh (2002), Ensmenger (2010).

[15] Morgan (1998).

[16] Millman (1984, p. 354).

[17] Andrews (1963).

[18] The Model V was patented in 1954, after an examination procedure that lasted nearly ten years. Stibitz Patent 2,666,579, 1954.

[19] This paragraph is based on Thompson (1984), Morgan (1998), Lee (2017).

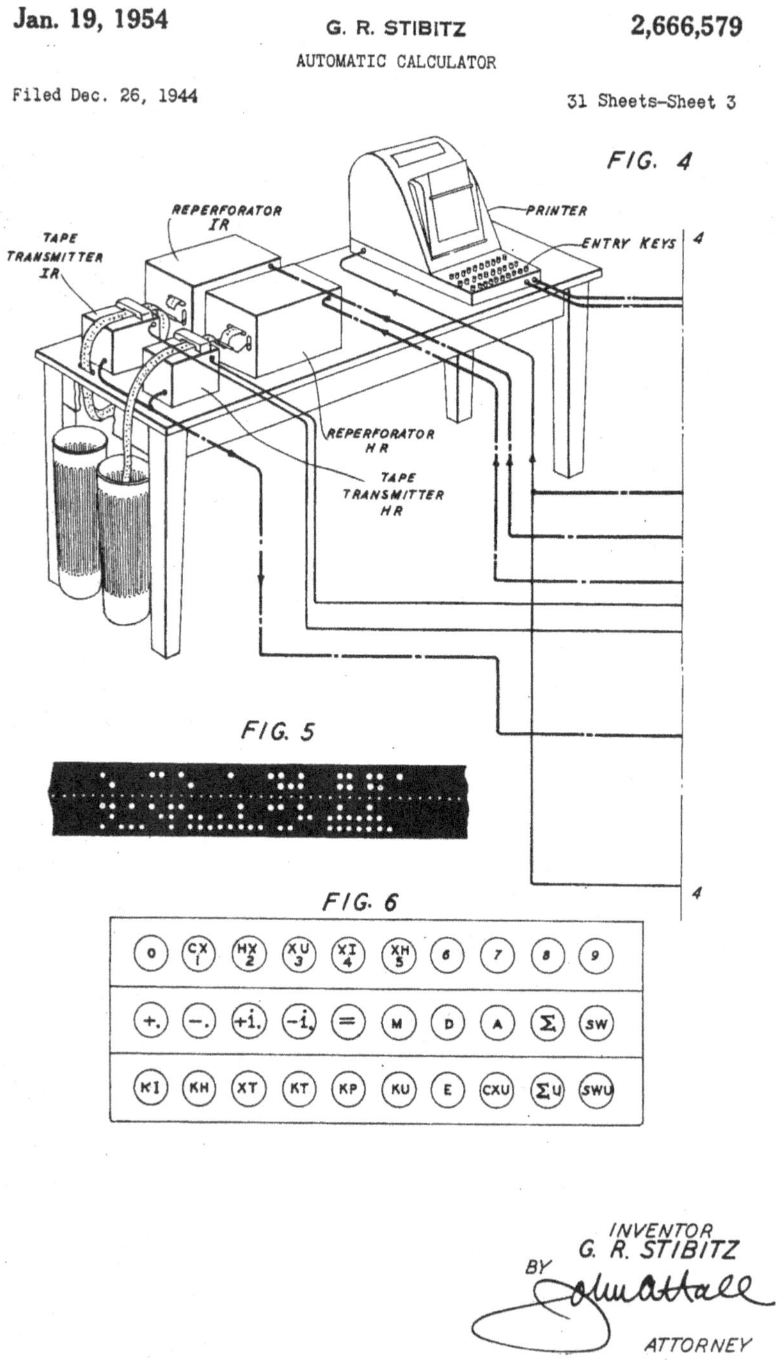

Jan. 19, 1954 G. R. STIBITZ 2,666,579

AUTOMATIC CALCULATOR

Filed Dec. 26, 1944 31 Sheets-Sheet 3

FIG. 4

REPERFORATOR IR

TAPE TRANSMITTER IR

PRINTER

ENTRY KEYS

REPERFORATOR HR

TAPE TRANSMITTER HR

FIG. 5

FIG. 6

0	CX 1	HX 2	XU 3	XI 4	XH 5	6	7	8	9
+.	−.	+i.	−i.	=	M	D	A	Σ	SW
KI	KH	XT	KT	KP	KU	E	CXU	ΣU	SWU

INVENTOR
G. R. STIBITZ
BY

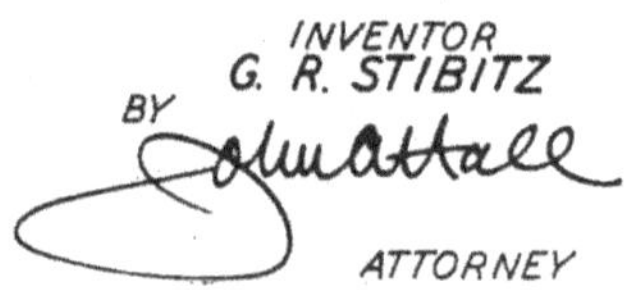

ATTORNEY

Figure 7.1 The first page of the patent for the Model V.

Source: George Stibitz. Automatic Calculator. US Patent 2,666,579 filed December 26, 1944 and issued January 19, 1954.

at stake, he became frustrated with the computer's habit of aborting its programs as soon as it encountered a processing error. These errors could be caused by common physical problems such as faulty relay contacts, open circuitry, or even outside disturbances.[20] To correct this, he devised an error correcting code—a series of instructions loaded onto the Model V with the use of punched tape—that would enable the computer to correct certain processing errors in order to avoid a complete stop.[21]

In 1948, Hamming shared a draft of a paper on these codes, "Error Detecting and Error Correcting Codes," as an interdepartmental memorandum. He was eager to publish it in the *Bell System Technical Journal*, but the lawyers at the Legal and Patent Division explained to him that they would not allow the paper to be published until Hamming obtained a patent for his error correcting codes.[22] The mathematician did not know much about patent law, but he suspected that he couldn't patent what he considered to be a "bunch of mathematical formulas." Dismissing his concern, the lawyers told him, "Watch us."

To secure Hamming's patent, the lawyers would need to bypass the mental steps doctrine, which at the time dictated that steps that a human being with proper training could perform are ineligible for patent protection.[23] This doctrine was grounded on court opinions that date back to the nineteenth century. Central to it was *Cochrane v. Deener* (1876), in which the Supreme Court had written that a process is "a mode of treatment of certain materials to produce a given result. It is an act, or a series of acts, performed upon the subject-matter to be transformed and reduced to a different state or thing."[24] In practice, this meant that the patent-eligibility of a process hinged on whether or not it caused a transformation in something tangible.

An earlier opinion, *O'Reilly v. Morse* (1854), implicitly offered a somewhat different reading of patent-eligibility. There, the US Supreme Court had upheld

20 "Hamming's Technique of Error Correction Marks 30th Birthday," 1980.

21 Thompson (1984).

22 This paragraph is based on Thompson (1984, p. 27).

23 The definition of the mental steps doctrine has changed over time. This particular definition applies to the doctrine as the Patent Office understood it in the early 1950s. The earliest articulation of this idea in this form occurs in a 1943 decision by the Patent Office Board of Patent Appeals, *Ex Parte Read*, which rejected a claim for a method to determine a vehicle's speed that required the user to correlate his or her speed measurements using two different scales on the ground that it was a "purely mental act." 123 USPQ 446 (Board of Appeals, 1943). Of course, this was not the first time that a process had been rejected because a human being could perform it, but it was the first time such a process was labelled as a mental act in the modern sense. For instance, in Don Lee v. Walker 61 F.2d 58 (9th Circuit, 1932), the court had rejected a method of calculating the position of weights on an engine that relied on the usage of a mathematical formula. Its rationale was that such a patent would grant a monopoly on the formula itself. Moreover, the Board had based the *Read* rationale on its reading of *Ex Parte Meinhardt*, Decisions of the Commissioner of Patents, 1907, 237. Here the Commission had rejected a claim for a process that could be performed entirely by a human being using a paper and pencil, but it did not label the process as a mental act or mental step.

24 *Cochrane v. Deener*.

most of Samuel Morse's 1848 patent for Morse code.[25] The patent was aimed at an "apparatus for and a system of transmitting intelligence between distant points by means of electro-magnetism."[26] Its fifth claim, which the Court had upheld without comment, read "The system of signs consisting of dots and spaces, and of dots, spaces, and horizontal lines, for numerals, letters, words, or sentences, substantially as herein set forth and illustrated, for telegraphic purposes."[27] This was not necessarily incompatible with the ruling in *Cochrane*, as Morse's patent explained that these signs were transmitted by electro-magnetism "which puts in motion machinery," but it did suggest that patents for code, albeit not computer code, were not entirely out of the question.[28]

Despite the prominence of *O'Reilly v. Morse* in the canon of patent law, the mental steps doctrine in the late 1940s was grounded mostly on *Cochrane*.[29] The primary precedent for it was *Halliburton v. Walker* (1944).[30] This decision involved the patent-eligibility of a method to detect obstructions in oil pipes using the automatic detection of sound waves. In agreement with the Halliburton Corporation's arguments, the Court of Appeals of the Ninth Circuit had ruled as unacceptable a method claim wherein a user was required to perform actions such as measuring times and calculating velocities. Based on *Cochrane v. Deener*, it had placed special emphasis on the words of the claims themselves, and it found that steps described with words such as "determining," "registering," "counting," and "computing" were ineligible for patent protection.[31]

The *Halliburton* rationale was, of course, not an absolute rule. After all, the telecommunications industry routinely patented technology that enabled the transmission, processing, and manipulation of electrical or radio signals. In the late 1940s and early 1950s, Bell Labs' lawyers obtained patents for signal receivers and decoders, air traffic control systems, encrypting devices, telephone pagers, and even electric wave transmission systems.[32] In fact, telecommunications

[25] The rest of this paragraph is based on Mossoff (2014).

[26] As noted by Mossoff (2014), the original patent was Morse, US Patent 1,647 (1840): 1. However, the suit focused instead on a revised and reissued patent, Morse, Patent RE117 (1848).

[27] Morse, Patent RE117 (1848): 3.

[28] Michael Risch has demonstrated that the history of nineteenth-century weaving offers patenting precedent for the idea that the control of a machine (a loom) by using a coded medium (punched cards) can be patented, but no evidence suggests that Bell Labs' lawyers were aware of this precedent. Bigelow Patent 546 (1838), cited in Risch (2012). The history of weaving provided important metaphors for the justification of software patenting. See Con Diaz (2015a).

[29] As Mossoff (2014) points out, this likely occurred because *O'Reilly v. Morse* focused primarily on invalidating claim 8 of the Morse patent, wherein Morse tried to assert broad ownership over the use of electric or galvanic currents. As a result, the case was read primarily as an affirmation of the limited scope of patent rights and the exclusion of natural phenomena from patent protection. This validated the existence of the mental steps doctrine, but the CCPA did not interpret it as the primary source of guidance to deal with the patents in *Halliburton v. Walker*.

[30] Halliburton Oil Well Cementing Co. v. Walker.

[31] Halliburton Oil Well Cementing Co. v. Walker, 821.

[32] Rack Patent 2,514,671 (1950); Saint Patent 2,495,139 (1950), Bacon Patent 2,504,621 (1950), Laberty Patent 2,496,629 (1950).

firms routinely secured patents that involved data processing in one way or another.[33] There was even precedent at AT&T for patents in error detection; in 1950, a subsidiary called the Teletype Corporation had submitted a patent application titled Error Detecting Code System, for a telegraph system that detected transmission systems automatically.[34] These patents were aimed at systems and devices. They rarely, if ever, raised any red flags in patent-eligibility under the *Halliburton* rationale, most likely because they disclosed signal processing in terms of the movement of electrical pulses and radio waves through circuits, air, relays, antennas, and so on.

All this is to say that Bell Labs' lawyers could draw on their firm's extraordinary patenting tradition to protect Hamming's codes despite recent doctrinal developments. Their plan was to bypass the *Halliburton* rationale by drafting a patent for a machine. First, they would obtain diagrams showing the arrangement of relays that characterized a computer onto which Hamming codes had been loaded. In charge of producing them was Bernard Holbrook, a staff engineer who was especially well acquainted with Bell's patents. He worked at the Switching Department designing and patenting computing equipment; in 1945 alone, he had submitted two patent applications for naval artillery computers.[35] Second, the lawyers would draft a patent for a relay computer designed with Holbrook's circuits at its core. This machine would function in accordance with Hamming's program, and the patent application would disclose it in terms specific enough to describe an actual functioning computer but broad enough to cover any relay computer in which Hamming's code was installed.

It took two years for Holbrook and Bell's legal staff to complete this work, but their drafting technique was so successful that it only took a year for the patent, Error Detecting and Correcting System, to be issued, in 1951.[36] The application's surviving documentation in the Patent Office's archives suggests that no examiners expressed concerns with the invention or the patent itself. On the contrary, the only revisions that Bell performed on the application were punctuation changes and small improvements to the phrasing of the specification.[37] Hamming's concern—that his invention comprised a collection of formulae—was meaningless at the Patent Office because the application disclosed a machine in lieu of his code.

[33] The author has performed several patent searches to confirm this assertion.

[34] Potts Patent 2,512,038, 1950.

[35] Holbrook Patent 2,317,191 (1943), Holbrook et al. Patent 2,405,214 (1946), Holbrook et al. Patent 2,658,680 (1953), Holbrook et al. Patent 2,658,678 (1953).

[36] Hamming et al. Patent 2,552,629 (1951).

[37] Letter from Richard Hamming and Bernard Holbrook to the Commissioner of Patents, January 10, 1951. File Wrapper for US Patent 2,552,629.

The notion that a computer's programming was something tangible was not an artifice. On the contrary, programming a digital electronic computer in the 1940s and 1950s could be a distinctly physical task. In charge of programming the most widely celebrated computer at the time, ENIAC, were a group of women who rewired the machine manually before every task.[38] In their hands, programming was equivalent to creating new circuitry arrangements inside the machine. Using switches like vacuum tubes, numbers could be represented as sequences of on and off states. Performing basic arithmetic operations therefore amounted to manipulating the on and off states of a computer's switches—a task that Bell Labs mathematician George Stibitz had studied and formalized in the 1930s using relay computers.[39]

The physicality of programming was a central feature of Hamming and Holbrook's patent application, which was aimed at an "apparatus for and a method of detecting and correcting errors which impair the accuracy of the output" of a machine.[40] Like other patents that would gain notoriety in the history of software patenting, theirs contained a series of mathematical formulas and tables, and it made several references to computer code, but it was not directed at the code itself. Instead, it claimed as the invention a specific "digital information system" disclosed in terms of its internal circuitry, and a way of using it that would enable the machine to detect its own processing errors.[41] Even Holbrook's illustrations (one of which is shown in Figure 7.2) disclosed a circuit arrangement, not the internal logic of the program that Hamming had developed.

The story of Hamming and Holbrook's patent demonstrates that patent protections have been available for computer code since the mid-twentieth century. Unlike Hamming, Holbrook and the lawyers perceived an equivalence (or at least an exchangeability) between code and circuitry that they could use to their legal benefit. The resulting patent protection was indirect—aimed at machines, not the code itself—but it was nevertheless designed to cover the computerization of a mathematical algorithm. This reveals that the content and word choices in the patents can be meant to mask the programs that they protect.

It is worth noting that patents modeled after Hamming and Holbrook's blend into the broader computer patenting landscape of the 1950s. The patents themselves did not use keywords such as "software" (which had not yet become a standard term), nor did they announce that a computer's programming stood at their cores. As a result, modern discourse-based search methods fail to generate lists of these patents without also listing scores of others aimed at electronic components and equipment. This is true even for the Bessen-Hunt technique,

[38] Haigh, Priestley, and Rope (2016), Light (1999).
[39] Con Diaz, (2019).
[40] "Patent Application," 1. File Wrapper for US Patent 2,552,629.
[41] "Patent Application," 1. File Wrapper for US Patent 2,552,629, 45.

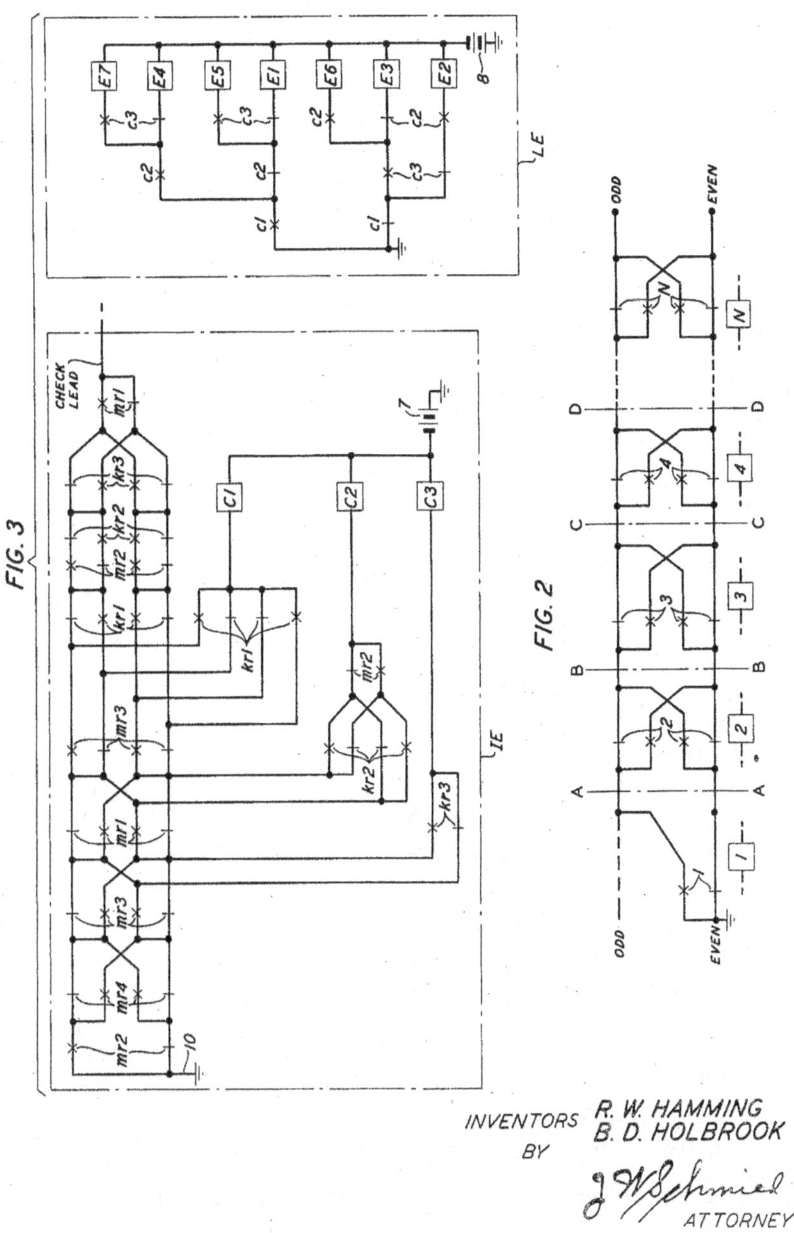

Figure 7.2 One of Bernard Holbrook's circuit designs.

Source: Richard Hamming and Bernard Holbrook. Error Detecting and Correcting System. US Patent 2,552,629, filed January 11, 1950 and issued May 15, 1951.

the keyword-based Boolean search method for the Patent and Trademark Office's patent database with which the technique's developers identified software patents from the 1970s onward.[42] For these reasons, the sections that follow advance not quantitative analyses of patenting trends but instead historical examinations of patents, applications, and court opinions.[43]

Machines and Methods

In 1951, two opinions from the CCPA gave patent examiners the responsibility of being especially vigilant regarding the mental steps doctrine. The first one concerned a patent application titled Improvements in Petroleum Prospecting Method, submitted in 1944 by Armand J. Abrams.[44] Abrams was the director of the laboratory at the Magnolia Petroleum Company, a subsidiary of the Socony-Vacuum Oil Company in Dallas, Texas.[45] His invention was a method to identify underground deposits of hydrocarbons such as natural gas or petroleum by analyzing the flow rates of gaseous emanations from the ground.[46] Users would first drill holes in the ground and seal them in a way that enabled underground gases to diffuse into the hole. They would then measure the flowrate of gases into the hole and perform computations such as "determining the rate of pressure rise" and "comparing the rates" at different boreholes.[47]

The examiner at the Patent Office rejected the application. He explained that the claims were improper because they were directed at "a process that predominantly involves merely a mental process in obtaining such result."[48] The evidence that these processes were mental was in the claims' phrasing; words such as "calculating," "comparing," "converting," and "determining" all referred to processes carried out by the human mind. Abrams's attorney, Sidney A. Johnson, appealed to the Patent Office's Board of Appeals, which agreed with the examiner's reasoning and decision, adding that the mental steps were "of the essence of the procedure claimed" and that the claims themselves would "lose their meaning if these steps are omitted."

[42] For more on the Bessen-Hunt technique, see Bessen and Hunt (2007), Bessen and Meurer (2009).

[43] I found the patents mentioned later by searching the Patent and Trademark Office database firm by firm, covering first firms in the computing industry and, later, firms in telecommunications and oil.

[44] "Appeal from the Board of Appeals," 1. In the Matter of the Application of Armand J. Abrams. Appeal 5726.

[45] National Research Council (1940, p. 179).

[46] "Appeal from the Board of Appeals," Appeal 5726, 4–5.

[47] "Examiner's Statement," in "Appeal from the Board of Appeals," Appeal 5726.

[48] This paragraph is based on "Appeal from the Board of Appeals," Appeal 5726, 34-35.

Johnson construed the Board's rejection as an opportunity to ask the CCPA for guidance on what constituted the mental steps doctrine. Based on his own survey of the case law, he proposed that this doctrine boiled down to three rules of law. First, if all the steps listed in a method claim "are purely mental in character," then the subject matter of the claim is not patent-eligible. Second, if a method claim involves both mental and physical steps, and if the method's novelty lies only in the former, then the claim is not patent-eligible. Third, if the novelty of a method claim that comprises both kinds of steps lies in the physical steps, and if the mental ones are "incidental parts of the process which are essential to define, qualify or limit its scope," then the claim is patent-eligible. Taken together, these rules meant that a method claim would be patent-eligible if, and only if, its novelty lies in its physical steps.[49]

Ironically, the CCPA adopted Johnson's doctrine, but Abrams lost his patent because the court found that the invention fell under the lawyer's second category of invention. One month later, the court refined this reasoning in a similar opinion, *In re Yuan*.[50] The inventor, Shao Wen Yuan from the Glenn L. Martin Company, had designed and produced a new kind of airplane wing that was well adapted for high speed aircrafts.[51] Like Abrams, Yuan had included in his application claims wherein mathematical computations were central. For example, Claim 9 listed a method to determine the optimal shape of a plane's wing for a given performance goal. It comprised steps such as "computing the pressure distribution," "determining the airfoil altitude," and "determining values" for certain parameters following a simple trigonometric function.[52]

Yuan's experience at the Patent Office was very similar to that of Abrams: both inventors faced examiners who scrutinized the verbs used in their claims; they faced a Board of Patent Appeals that stood by the examiners; and they took their cases to the CCPA, which made the rejections final. The rationales that the CCPA advanced in these cases resembled one another, although the *Yuan* court emphasized that the first rule that Abrams' attorney had proposed was, indeed, valid. It explained that Yuan's claim comprised no more than purely mental steps meant to be performed by human beings using paper and pencil. These humans would need no subjectivity; they were simply performing prescribed computations. This situation was unacceptable under the reasoning advanced in *Cochrane*, wherein processes are only patent-eligible if they act upon physical materials and effect a change in their condition.[53]

49 *In re Abrams* (1951, p. 166).
50 *In re Yuan* (1951).
51 "Brief for Appellant," in the Matter of the Application of Shao Wen Yuan. Appeal 5776: 3.
52 "Application of Shao Wen Yuan," in *Transcript of Record*, 49. the Matter of the Application of Shao Wen Yuan. Appeal 5776.
53 *In re Yuan* (1951).

These two opinions remained very influential even after Congress passed a new Patent Act in 1952. Behind them was the assumption, grounded on *Halliburton v. Walker*, that actions such as calculating, measuring, determining, and comparing did not constitute patent-eligible subject matter because they could also be performed by human beings. Their joint wisdom provided a two-step procedure for the assessment of the patent-eligibility of a claim involving physical and mental steps. First, examiners should study the relationships between both kinds of steps to determine if the physical steps are essential to the claim. Second, they should decide if the claim's novelty resided entirely in the mental steps. The invention would be patent-eligible only if its physical steps were essential and carried some novelty.

This legal environment pushed firms at home and abroad to rely on Bell Labs' patent-drafting techniques to secure US patents for their programs, such as the British Tabulating Machine Company (BTM), a prominent British firm that started adding electromechanical computers to its line of products during World War II.[54] Many of BTM's US patents were aimed at components such as special relays, contact devices, or impulse generators.[55] However, the firm started following Bell's patenting footsteps when it secured protection for the work of Raymond Bird, a pioneering electronics engineer best known for having developed Britain's first mass-produced business computer.[56]

Two of Bird's patents disclosed machines that performed basic data processing tasks such as adding quantities or translating a number from one number system to another.[57] Like Hamming and Holbrook's patent, these were directed at machines that processed and transmitted electricity. As a result, BTM used its patent applications to transform mathematical algorithms that would normally qualify as mental steps (including arithmetic operations) into statements about specific ways of storing and transmitting electrical pulses among tangible components such as shift registers and memory units. This was, of course, made possible by the fact that the ones and zeroes of a computer's binary notation could be registered electronically as the on and off states of electronic switches such as vacuum tubes.

In 1953, BTM submitted a patent titled Data Translating Apparatus aimed at an "electronic apparatus for data translation," namely a device that could translate numbers from the binary system to standard decimal notation. [58] The translation of a number from one system to another at the patent's core involved little

[54] Heide (2009).

[55] See, for instance, Keen US Patent 2,694,758 (1954), Ivor Patent 2,688,665 (1954), Hill Patent 2,782,304 (1957).

[56] For Bird's work on commercial computers, see Campbell-Kelly (1989) and Bird (1989).

[57] Bird US Patent 2,861,741 (1958), Bird US Patent 2,970,765 (1961).

[58] Bird, Data Translating Apparatus.

more than the algorithmic application of the four basic arithmetic operations, and in fact the patent notes that the "translation may be effected by a computer itself under control of an appropriate programme."[59] However, the patent also discloses a computer specifically designed to perform only Bird's translation algorithm, and it uses its figures to disclose the computer's architecture and even the internal circuitry of some of its components (Figure 7.3).

While applying for this patent, the firm had responded to the examiner's complaints about the application's lack of specificity by incorporating tangible components into its claims.[60] Its first claim is reproduced on the left-hand side of Table 7.1. BTM's revisions to this claim transformed statements about the machine's ability to process numbers into descriptions of how electricity moved from one electronic component to the next. Chief among the changes were the firm's modifications to items [3] and [4] , wherein the italicized phrases above stand in for something that enables the claimed apparatus to perform the actual translation algorithm—an "analyzing means" that the claim describes as something that acts upon values and numbers. In the published claim, this analyzing means became the control system for a tangible circuit that processed electricity, a "control means" that moves electrical signals between objects such as memory units and arithmetic circuits. Table 7.1 shows the revised claim on the right-hand side.

Like BTM, IBM and the other hardware manufacturers (especially RCA and Honeywell) embraced the notion that electricity is an allowable substance on which a process can act without losing its patent-eligibility. Patent applications for data translating programs, which allowed for greater compatibility across different storage media, show that this notion would allow patent drafters to follow data from one component of the computer to the next. Patents in this vein include RCA's Data Translating System (submitted in 1953) and IBM's Data Transfer and Translating System (1953) and Decimal to Binary Translator (1959).[61] RCA's patent even described the invention as one with the ability to "sense data encoded on perforated cards, supplement and arrange that data, verify the data, convert it to a code suitable for magnetic tape, and record the data on magnetic tape."[62]

In contrast, industrial research laboratories appeared more likely to foreground the same mental steps that IBM and its competitors would conceal behind electronic components, even when dealing with data translation. Throughout the 1950s, Bell Labs developed several error detection and data translation

59 Bird, Data Translating Apparatus, 1.

60 Examiner's Letter from L.M. Andrews to Frederick Hane, September 22, 1954. File Wrapper for Patent 2,970,765.

61 Brustman Patent 2,702,380 (1955); Greenhalgh Patent 2,872,666 (1959); Reynolds Patent 3,021,065 (1962).

62 Brustman Patent 2,702,380 (1955): 2.

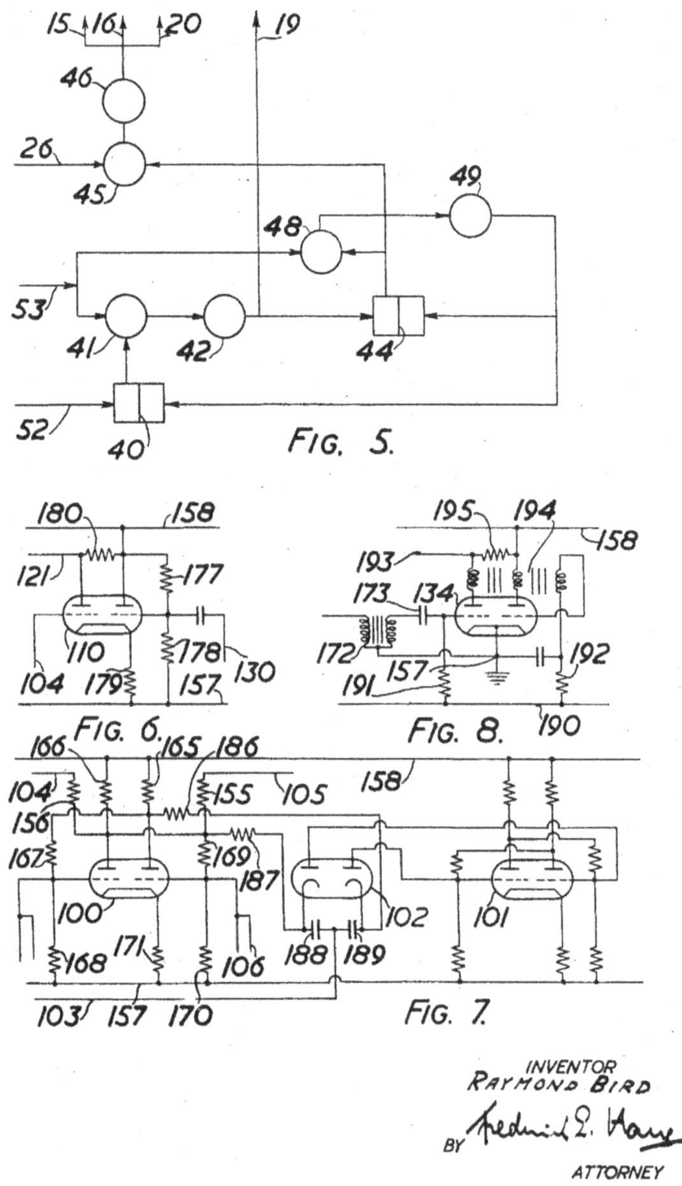

Figure 7.3 One of the circuits for the electronic components in Raymond Bird's patent.

Source: Raymond Bird, Data Translating Apparatus. US Patent 2,970,765 filed November 4, 1952 and issued February 7, 1961.

inventions, most likely for use with its increasingly computerized telephony systems.[63] Among them was Binary Decoder, a patent filed in 1956 for a binary-to-decimal translator similar in aims to BTM's Data Translating Apparatus.[64] This application faced no pushback at the Patent Office; it was issued about a year after its submission, and the examiner requested no changes other than the correction of a few typos. The first page of the application notes that the translation process at hand is "an arithmetic operation which a computer can be programmed to do" and explains that the invention is not the program itself but a component that performs the same function.[65] The application's claims underscore this materiality by disclosing a device called a "translator"; its specification outlines in detail the means that allow this translator to process bits and digits—a combination of specific circuits and pre-programmed components.

The contrasts between both families of data translation patents illustrate how the Patent Office has not been a unified entity that applies patent drafting standards uniformly across its art units and how the standards on which examiners made assessments of patent-eligibility could vary from one unit to the next. Bell's patent applications were read by examiners in communications and not by those specializing in registers and electrical engineering (as applications from IBM, RCA, and other hardware manufacturers normally were). The discursive variations that this generates precludes industry-wide analyses into whether firms tended to do any examiner shopping—that is, whether they selected the department to which they would apply based on the department's likelihood of issuing their patent.[66] However, it does appear that firms submitting their applications to classes other than electrical engineering in the mid-1950s did not need to disclose circuitry and electronic components in as much detail as hardware manufacturers did.

In other fields, the disclosure of electronic components was entirely unnecessary if there was an uncontrovertibly tangible substance involved in the inventive process. This was especially clear for firms in the geological sciences, which sometimes disclosed the earth itself in lieu of a machine that could generate electrical impulses. Consider Correlation of Seismic Signals, which was filed by Dallas firm Geotechnical Corporation (GC) in 1954 and issued in 1959. It was classified as an invention in Class 367, "Communications, Electrical: Acoustic Wave Systems," subclass 40 (Received correlation). The inventor, Thomas Swafford, had developed a new way of processing seismic information. His

[63] See, for instance, Motte Patent 2,856,597 (1958); Hagelbarger Patent 2,956,124 (1960); Taylor et al. Patent 3,140,463 (1960).

[64] Woodbury Patent 2,814,437 (1957).

[65] "Patent Application," 1. File Wrapper for Patent 2,814,437.

[66] For more on examiner shopping, see Lemley and Moore (2004) and *Dayco Products v. Total Containment*.

Table 7.1 BTM's patent application, Data Translating Apparatus.

The application's first claim is on the left-hand side. The right-hand side shows the first claim in the issued patent, a revision of the original claim intended to specify the electronic components that carry out the operations at hand and the relationships among those components. This revision transformed the patent claim into an outline of the specific electronic arrangement that carried out the data translation at hand.[a]

1. Apparatus for translating a number from a first to a second radix of notation having	1. Apparatus for translating a number from a first radix to a second radix of notation, said apparatus comprising
[1] *means for storing* a limited number of equivalent values of one of the radices expressed in the other of the radices,	a first store for registering signals representing a number in the first radix;
[2] *means for reading* out the stored values sequentially,	a cyclically operable, serial mode second store for storing a plurality of groups of signals representing said first radix the equivalents of predetermined values in said second radix, said predetermined values being such that any desired number in the second radix may be expressed as combinations of such values;
[3] *analyzing means* for determining which of the equivalent values is contained in said number and	a subtracting circuit having a first and a second input and one output responsive to serial-mode signals respecting members in the first radix applied to the inputs thereof to form difference representing signals at the output thereof;
[4] *means controlled by the analyzing means* for selecting and summing those read out values which are contained in said number.	means to apply signals read during successive cycles from said second store to the first input of said subtracting circuit;
	a third store to register successive difference signals during successive cycles of operation;
	control means to apply signals read-out from said third store to the second input of said subtracting circuit and to said first store when said third store contains a positive number, and to apply signals read-out from said first store to the second input of said subtracting circuit and to said first store when said third store contains a negative number;
	and a fourth store to store a record of the sequence of operation of said control means.

[a] In this and all other quotations of patent claims, any spacing, emphasis, and numbering were added by the author for ease of reading. Application of Raymond Bird. File Wrapper for Patent 2,970,765

invention allowed for the reduction of noise in seismic data, and his patent claimed a method and an apparatus. The patent's first claim read,

> The method of detecting and presenting seismic signals including
> [1] the steps of creating a local disturbance in the earth,
> [2] translating vibrations therefrom into an electrical signal,
> [3] *dividing* said signal into two components,
> [4] *multiplying* one component by a time function and the other by a related time function but delayed in time,
> [5] *squaring* the resulting products, and
> [6] *summing* and continuously integrating the products to
> [7] provide a composite correlogram wherein the said time functions have cancelled out.[67]

This claim comprises manipulations of tangible substances such as causing vibrations on the surface of the earth ([1] and [2]) and intangible ones such performing arithmetic operations ([3]–[6]). It presents these manipulations as part of a single process and specifies a tangible output, namely the printout of an image (the correlogram [7]). This strategy is likely to have made the claim less liable to facing rejection on the grounds that it covers mathematical computations and causes no transformations on tangible substances.

This method amounts to using a computer to perform correlations based on seismic data. Figure 7.4 shows a schematic representation of an analog computer that carries out GC's method. The patent calls this machine a "function correlator"—a device that allows for the statistical correlation between two functions—and specifies the mathematical formulae that it applies to the data.[68] Some of the machine's internal components were also covered by the patent, but nothing in the claims or specification restricted the scope of protection to a specific device; any computer that carried out GC's correlations could potentially be construed as infringing on this patent.

These broad claims started to become more prevalent among computing firms in the late 1950s, as hardware manufacturers became interested in developing computers that were faster, smaller, and more powerful than their predecessors.[69] Enabled by developments in magnetic drum memory technology and, more important, the invention of transistors earlier in the decade, these firms filed patent applications using both the method-oriented drafting techniques that GC and Bell Labs had been employing and the machine-oriented ones that they had

67 Swafford Patent 2,907,400 (1959), 6.
68 Swafford Patent 2,907,400 (1959), 3.
69 Campbell-Kelly (2003), Campbell-Kelly et al. (2013).

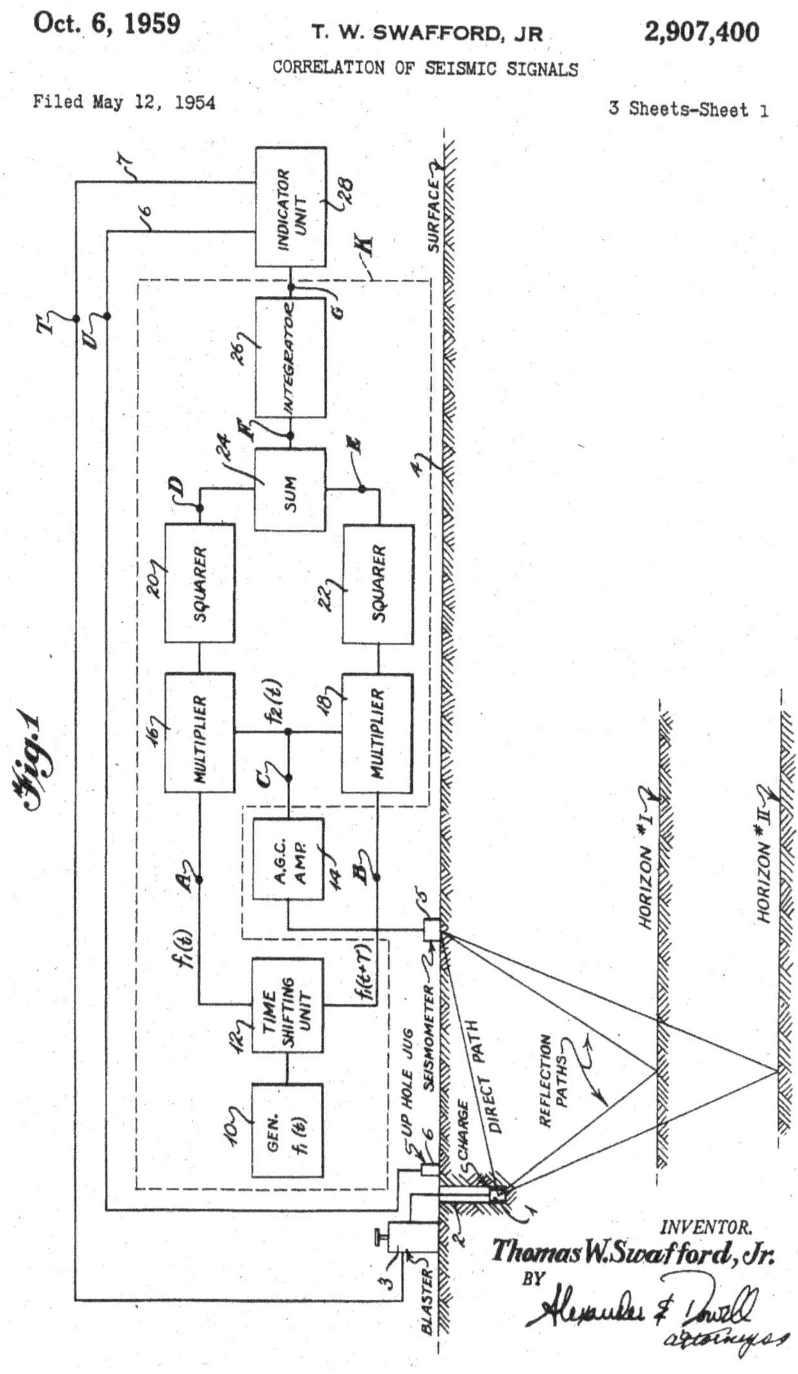

Oct. 6, 1959 T. W. SWAFFORD, JR 2,907,400

CORRELATION OF SEISMIC SIGNALS

Filed May 12, 1954 3 Sheets-Sheet 1

INVENTOR.
Thomas W. Swafford, Jr.
BY

Figure 7.4 The analog computer disclosed in Thomas Swafford's patent, shown schematically in relation to its surroundings.

Source: Thomas Swafford, Correlation of Seismic Signals. US Patent 2,907,400 filed May 12, 1954 and issued October 6, 1959.

known for a few years. This was true at IBM, which by the end of the decade had filed several patents for error correction and automatic program management.[70] One of the resulting patents, Program Interrupt System (filed in 1957 and issued in 1962), even noted in its very first paragraph that the invention "relates to a program controlled data processing machine."[71]

Over the course of the 1950s, programming lost a lot of the physicality that once characterized it.[72] The development of discursive programming languages in the mid-1950s made it easier than ever for users of all skill levels to learn how to write basic programs. In lieu of having to write a program in esoteric machine-specific languages or rewiring computers one at a time, users could use very intuitive languages to write machine-independent programs. It was certainly still possible to program things by rewiring them, but this practice was significantly more difficult, time consuming, and expensive than simply typing out lines of code. Still, for the next decade, the two practices would coexist—both in programmers' day-to-day work and in the patent applications that they submitted to the Patent Office.

By the 1960s, IBM was routinely rephrasing patent applications to bypass *Halliburton*-style rejections using disclosures of tangible electronic components. One of the most striking examples was Unambiguous Identification Systems, issued in 1963.[73] The invention in this patent corrected the so-called "ambiguity of output" that occurred when imperfections in the scrutinized object made it difficult for the computer to determine what the object is. This problem was especially common in processes such as the computer recognition of printed characters, wherein printing imperfections could make one letter appear to be another one. For instance, in Figure 7.5, the machine could interpret each of the imperfectly printed characters as an A, an R, or a P.

The invention provided a method of removing this ambiguity by having the computer transform a given input (the printed letters) into a collection of numbers. The computer would first create a grid over the input and translate the input's placement on the grid into a collection of numbers in accordance with a series of predetermined rules. It would then compare this collection of numbers to a stored collection of numbers corresponding to ideal types of the input. To understand this process, imagine a computer trying to determine what letter corresponds to an imperfectly printed letter A as in Figure 7.5. Stored in the computer's memory were the number collections generated by perfectly printed letters. Once the printed letter A was scanned, the computer would generate a

[70] See, for instance, Reynolds Patent 3,024,992 (1962), McDonnell Patent 2,968,027 (1961), Melas Patent 3,213,426 (1965).

[71] Brooks and Sweeney Patent 3,048,332 (1962).

[72] This paragraph is based on Nofre, Priestley, and Alberts (2014) and Ensmenger (2010).

[73] McDermid, Petersen, and Glenmore Patent 3,167,743 (1965).

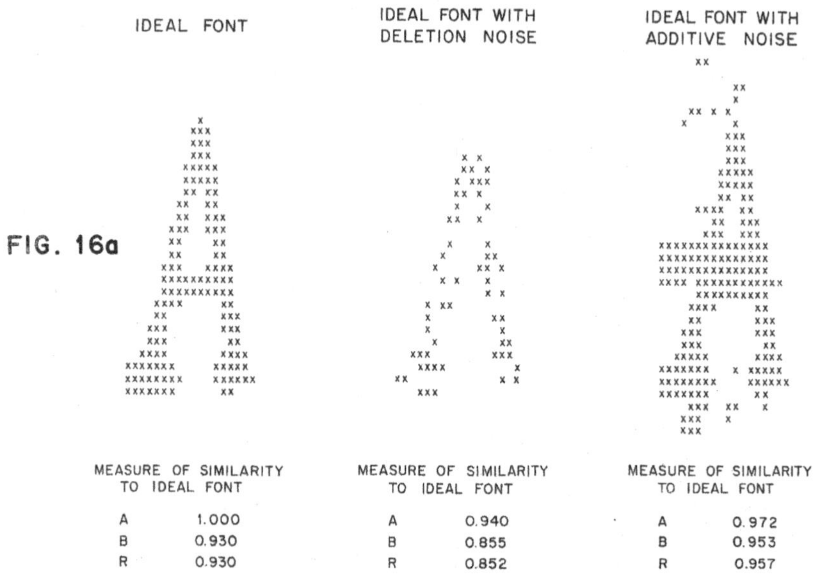

FIG. 16a

IDEAL FONT		IDEAL FONT WITH DELETION NOISE		IDEAL FONT WITH ADDITIVE NOISE	
MEASURE OF SIMILARITY TO IDEAL FONT		MEASURE OF SIMILARITY TO IDEAL FONT		MEASURE OF SIMILARITY TO IDEAL FONT	
A	1.000	A	0.940	A	0.972
B	0.930	B	0.855	B	0.953
R	0.930	R	0.852	R	0.957

Figure 7.5 Identifying the letter A.
From left to right, a perfectly printed letter "A" as stored in a computer's memory, an imperfectly printed one that the computer may recognize as an "R," and another that may be recognized as a "P."
Source: William McDermid, Harold Petersen, and Shelton Glenmore. Unambiguous Identification Systems. US Patent 3,167,743 filed December 19, 1960 and issued January 26, 1965.

collection of numbers and compare it with each of the collections corresponding to perfectly printed letters stored in its memory. To determine its output, namely the character corresponding to the scanned letter, the computer would choose the preloaded number collection that most resembled the one it had generated for the printed character.

The patent application claimed a method and an apparatus to perform these functions. Table 7.2 shows the original text of Claim 1 on the left-hand side. The examiner rejected it and others like it because they were either "merely mental in character" or "merely drawn to the inherent function of the apparatus."[74] His rejection hinged on what he viewed as improper relationships between methods and machines in a patent application. On the one hand, if a machine is necessary to perform a given method, then claiming the method amounted to claiming any machine that could perform the method. On the other hand, if the method could be carried out without use of the claimed machine, then the method

[74] The rest of this paragraph is based on "Responsive to the amendment filed February 9, 1962," January 30, 1962. File Wrapper for Patent 3,167,743.

Table 7.2 Unambiguous Identification Systems claim, as transformed by IBM's lawyers.

The application's method claim, on the left-hand side, became the apparatus claim on the right-hand side. This is an example of how firms could use "means plus" claims—claiming a machine as a means to accomplish a given task—to secure indirect protections for mathematical algorithms. This method of claiming, which dates back to the nineteenth century, is currently enabled by 35 USC, 112(f).[a]

1. The method of generating an unambiguous output in a system that generates an ambiguous output function as a function of unambiguous intermediary functions of the applied input function comprising the steps of:	1. An apparatus for generating an unambiguous outcome in a system that generates an ambiguous output function as a function of unambiguous intermediary functions of the applied input function comprising in combination:
generating the unambiguous intermediary functions of the input function,	means for generating the unambiguous intermediary functions of the input function;
generating a control function dependent upon an unambiguous characteristic of an intermediary function,	means for generating a control function which function is dependent upon an unambiguous characteristic of an intermediary function;
generating the ambiguous output function from the intermediary functions and	means for generating the ambiguous output function from the intermediary functions; and
generating an unambiguous output from the output function and the control function.	means responsive to the output function and the control function for generating am unambiguous output.

[a] File Wrapper for Patent 3,167,743.

claims are "recitations of a mental exercise." In either case, the method claim was unallowable.

In response to the examiner's complaints, IBM's attorneys cancelled the method claim and replaced it with one for a machine.[75] Different only in a few words, this revised claim became better aligned with the claim formats that the firm had used the decade prior. It was directed at a device, not a method.[76] Subtle changes throughout the text allowed IBM to bypass Morrison's rejection: the phrase "a method of generating an unambiguous output in a system" became "an apparatus for generating an unambiguous outcome in a system;" and clause [1] changed from "generating the unambiguous intermediary functions of the input

[75] "Amendment, March 24, 1964" File Wrapper for Patent 3,167,743.

[76] The rest of this paragraph is based on "Amendment, March 24, 1964" File Wrapper for Patent 3,167,743.

function" to "means for generating the unambiguous intermediary functions of the input function." These changes made the invention described in the claim tangible: a method became an apparatus, and the creation of mathematical functions became a means to create them.

The Patent Office issued this patent in 1965, and for the next few years IBM continued to obtain patents of this kind. Some of them belonged to the same family of error correcting codes to which Richard Hamming and Bernard Holbrook's patent belonged. These include Detection and Correction of Transposition Errors, for a computer system that corrected errors in data in high-stakes contexts wherein errors such as a misplaced digit could have catastrophic effects.[77] Others were directed at processes that performed mathematical computations. For instance, a patent called Optimum Result Computer covered a computer system that performed a series of arithmetic operations to determine the optimum way of cutting a stock of paper to optimize the return from its sale.[78]

It is important to note that IBM was not securing these patents with the aim of blocking other firms out of specific areas of technological development.[79] In 1956, the firm and the Department of Justice's Antitrust Division had negotiated a consent decree designed to curb the firm's dominance in the computing industry. A key provision of the decree required IBM to grant reasonably priced licenses to almost anyone who asked. If IBM failed to propose a price that the potential licensee deemed satisfactory, the District Court for the Southern District of New York would determine the appropriate pricing scheme. This made patents at IBM primarily defensive tools. As a result, IBM's managers considered patents to be an extremely dangerous matter, and in fact throughout the 1960s and 1970s the firm was the country's most vocal opponent of software patenting despite its growing portfolio of patents aimed at its computers' programming.[80] The firm's managers reasoned that it was preferable to lose any patents in the firm's portfolio than to risk being locked out of a crucial software technology by a smaller and highly litigious competitor.

Patents aimed at computer programs proliferated in the industry despite IBM's protests. Many of them spelled out a mathematical algorithm through detailed formulae or flowcharts and suggested (or at least implied) that the algorithm could be programmed on the computer. Texas Instruments' Multi-Point, Multi-Channel Linear Processing of Seismic Data (filed in 1962) noted that "a digital technique" to perform one of the invention's processes was to load a

[77] Hamburger Patent 3,333,243 (1967).
[78] Horwitz Patent 3,339,182 (1967).
[79] This paragraph is based on Con Diaz (2019, ch. 2).
[80] IBM's opposition to software patenting in the late 1960s is documented by Con Diaz (2015a).

series of formulae "on magnetic tape and program a digital computer" to process them.[81] Issued in Class 340 (Communications: Electrical), the patent comprised both apparatus and method claims. Its first claim used means plus language to disclose the special purpose device at the patent's core:

> A linear processor for seismological and seismic prospecting data comprising
> [1] a plurality of seismic traces,
> [2] *summation means*, and
> [3] *means for coupling* said traces to said summation means, said last means including
> [4] *means for applying* to at least two of said traces different weighting and time delay factors as a function of desired signal frequency and which are dependent upon the noise character in at least one of said traces not included in said two of said traces, whereby said processor synthesizes a velocity filter.[82]

A similar claim structure occurs in Fire Control Systems (Class 89: Ordnance), filed in 1964 and assigned to a Swiss patent-holding company called Brevets Aero-Mechaniques. Aimed at antiaircraft guns (Figure 7.6a) , this patent includes several pages of what it calls a "flow sheet for the digital computer."[83] Shown in Figure 7.6b, this diagram outlines the mathematical algorithm that the computer controlling the system would carry out.[84] This patent's fourth claim is reproduced below in abridged form.,

> A fire control system for directing a gun toward a target which comprises . . .
> *a computer* including,
> [1] *a bearing coder* arranged to receive at its input, from said bearing determining means, said target bearing and to deliver, at its output, the values of the cosine and the sine of said target bearing,
> [2] *a site coder* arranged to receive at its input, from said site determining means, said target site and to deliver at its output the values of the cosine and the sine of said target site,
> . . .
> [3] *generator means*, arranged to receive at the input there of from said distance determining means through said squaring means the square of the distance of the target from the gun, for delivering the value of the time of flight of the projectile from the gun,

[81] Burg Patent 3,284,763 (1966), 8.
[82] Burg Patent 3,284,763 (1966), 13.
[83] Pun Patent 3,339,457 (1967).
[84] Pun Patent 3,339,457 (1967), 20.

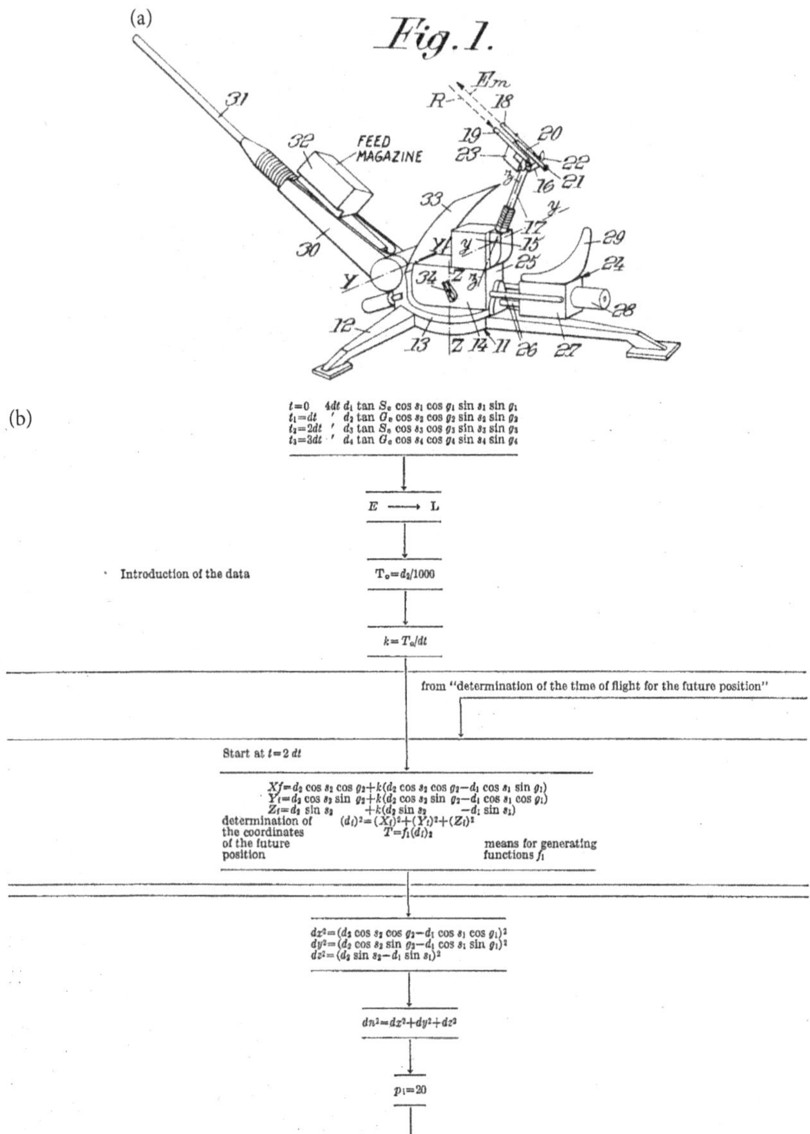

Figure 7.6 (a) Lucas Pun's weapon system; (b) part of the computer program's flowsheet.

Source: Lucas Pun. Fire Control Systems. US Patent 3,339,457 filed August 18, 1964 and issued September 5, 1967.

[3] *computer unit means* through said squaring means responsive to said respective delivered values for delivering the tangents of the horizontal angle and of the vertical angle of the gun from reference planes, and

[4] *means responsive to the outputs of said computer* unit means for aiming said gun barrel in accordance with the values of said last mentioned tangents, so that a projectile fired from said gun normally reaches said target. 5. A system according to claim 4 wherein said computer is a digital computer.[85]

This claim used means plus language to claim some of the special purpose computer that carried out the program: The fifth claim simply read, "A system according to claim 4 wherein said computer is a digital computer."[86]

Disclosures of special purpose computers could include snippets of computer code. This was the case in Processing of Geophysical Data, a patent filed in 1964 in Class 340: Communications: Electrical.[87] Assigned to Mobil Oil, this patent is directed at both a device and a method, and it explicitly claims a "digital computing apparatus for processing seismograms."[88] The patent provides two ways of representing the algorithms at its core. It characterizes Figure 7.7 as a schematic representation of the data processing system. At the same time, it explains that the functions that the diagram represents can be "implemented with either digital or analog techniques" because the items in the diagram's blocks correspond either to "well known analog circuits" or to ones that the patent itself discloses.[89] The patent's specification offers the source code necessary to perform this operation, mentions that "a number of suitable digital processing systems" can carry it out, and notes that the inventors had already programmed a CDC 1604 computer in accordance with it.[90] Its claims cover primarily the data processing methods at hand, though a handful of machine claims use means-plus function to cover the "digital computing apparatus for processing seismograms" that carries them out.[91]

New Legal Precedent

A series of lawsuits over the course of the 1960s steadily increased the legal grounding on which firms could rely to justify the validity of these patent-drafting techniques. These lawsuits generally revolved around two key distinctions in the

[85] Pun Patent 3,339,457 (1967), 30.
[86] Pun Patent 3,339,457 (1967), 30.
[87] Foster, Kerns, and Sengbush Patent 3,689,874 (1972).
[88] Foster, Kerns, and Sengbush Patent 3,689,874 (1972), 1
[89] Foster, Kerns, and Sengbush Patent 3,689,874 (1972), 7.
[90] Foster, Kerns, and Sengbush Patent 3,689,874 (1972), 7–8.
[91] Foster, Kerns, and Sengbush Patent 3,689,874 (1972), 22.

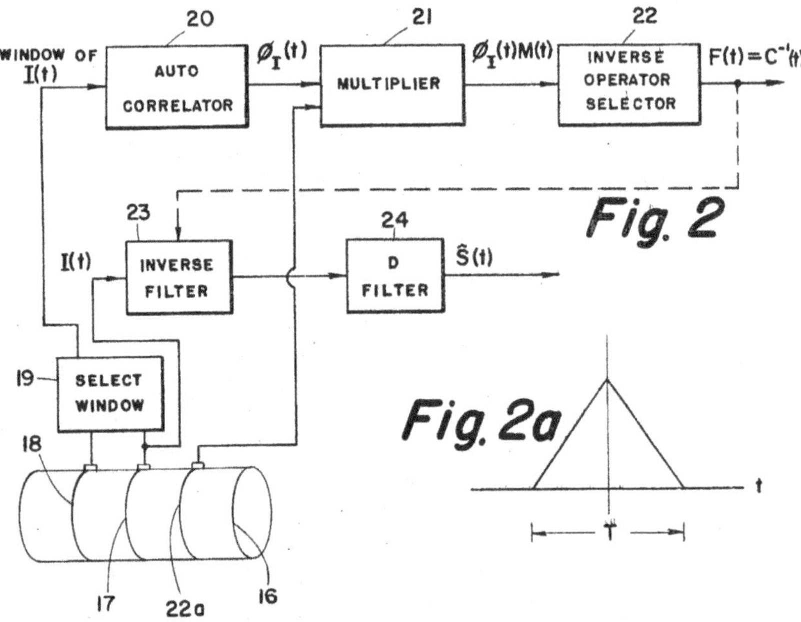

Figure 7.7 A schematic representation of Manus Foster, Clyde Kerns, and Raymond Sengbush's data processing system.

Source: Manus Foster, Clyde Kerns, and Raymond Sengbush. Processing of Geophysical Data. US Patent 3,689,874 filed in 1964 and issued in 1972.

history of computing.[92] The first one concerns a computer's ability to be reprogrammed. On the one hand there were special purpose computers, namely devices designed to perform only a single function such as the solution of a specific kind of equation or the correction of certain kinds of errors. Special purpose computers had been especially important in the 1950s; the patents described in the previous section were aimed at computers of this kind. On the other hand, there were general purpose computers, which could be programmed to meet a wide range of needs. Some of the best-known electronic computers in history, including the ENIAC, were of this variety, as were the computer that Richard Hamming used at Bell Labs and the smaller commercial devices that started to infiltrate office buildings and laboratories in the late 1950s.

The other key distinction concerns the kinds of work that programs performed. By 1960, hardware manufacturers generally classified their computer programs into one of two categories.[93] First were systems programs, which

[92] This paragraph is based on Campbell-Kelly (2003), Campbell-Kelly et al. (2013), and Ceruzzi (2003).

[93] This paragraph is based on Campbell-Kelly (2003), Campbell-Kelly et al. (2013), and Ceruzzi (2003).

controlled a computer's basic operations and which all users would need regardless of their specific computational needs. These programs performed functions such as reading the computer's memory or writing onto it; enabling communication among different components; or allocating processing time when several terminals were connected to the same mainframe. Second were application programs, which a user would choose depending on the needs of the organization that had purchased or leased the machine. They performed very specific computational requirements such as processing payrolls, generating flowcharts, or sorting data into a fixed set of categories.

Hardware manufacturers protected their systems programs by patenting both a machine and a method of operating it. For instance, in 1962 Morton Lewin, an employee at RCA, applied for a patent called Ordered Retrieval of Information Stored in a Tag-Addressed Memory.[94] The Patent Office allowed the application's machine claims, which were directed at a computer designed to use special digital tags to retrieve data from its memory storage. Figure 7.8 shows two flowcharts of the program at the core of this computer, which the patent describes respectively as the "operation of the memory system" and "how any content-addressed memory may be interrogated according to the method of the present invention."[95] The patent claims this computer as a "combination comprising a content-addressed memory which stores words in random order in different rows; and means responsive to a tag word applied to the memory."[96]

Even if the special purpose computer that Lewin had invented was patent-eligible, the examiner rejected the method of operating that Lewin claimed on the grounds that it was the computer's inherent function.[97] This rejection was grounded on the examiner's assumption that a patent over the special purpose machine that functioned in accordance with the program would preclude other machines from running the program. In other words, the issue at stake was whether a computer different from the one that Lewin had claimed would be able to perform the same functions without committing infringement. To reverse the examiner's rejection, it would be necessary to show that computers other than Lewin's could perform the same process.

Lewin's appeal hinged on demonstrating that a special purpose computer designed to carry out a given program was materially different from a general purpose computer programmed to run it.[98] At the Patent Office Board of Appeals, his lawyer argued that "a programmer of ordinary skill could program a general purpose computer to practice the invention" if he or she was supplied with his

[94] Lewin Patent 3,329,937 (1967).
[95] Lewin Patent 3,329,937 (1967), 1.
[96] Lewin Patent 3,329,937 (1967), 17.
[97] Ex Parte Lewin.
[98] Graham (1968).

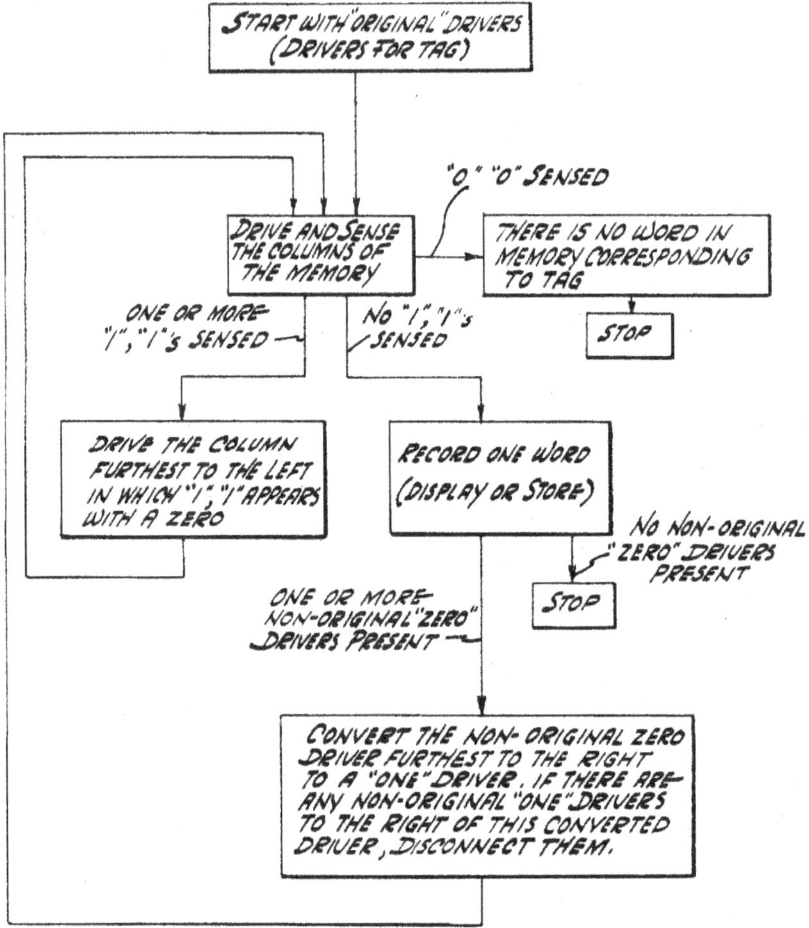

Figure 7.8 Flowchart in Morton Lewin's patent.

Source: Morton Lewin. Ordered Retrieval of Information Stored in a Tag-Addressed Memory. US Patent 3,329,937 filed March 28, 1962 and issued July 4, 1967.

patent application's disclosure. In opposition, the patent examiner argued that a properly programmed general purpose computer "would not be a materially different apparatus" from the one that Lewin had disclosed.[99] In other words, the examiner complained that any general purpose computer programmed to run in accordance with the program in Figure 7.8 would be equivalent to the special purpose machine that Lewin claimed. In 1966, the Board ruled in Lewin's

[99] Graham (1968).

favor and noted that "a general purpose computer is [a] materially different apparatus from the special purpose computer" that he had disclosed. The Board grounded this assertion primarily on an earlier decision, Ex Parte King (1964), that affirmed the patent-eligibility of a special purpose computer even though it performed the same function as a general purpose computer programmed to carry out the same task.[100] Lewin obtained his patent, though it is unlikely that this reasoning would have worked in his favor if he had ever filed a patent infringement suit, since the Board seemed to suggest that his patent was narrowly aimed at a very specific special purpose computer.

The ultimate endorsement of all the patent-drafting techniques discussed so far was In re Prater and Wei (1968/9), which resulted from an eight-year-long legal battle led by Mobil Oil.[101] This opinion concerned the work of two scientists, Charles Prater and James Wei, who worked on a technique to determine the constituents of a gaseous mixture called spectrographic analysis.[102] Their invention allowed for the analysis of a kind of inscription called a spectrogram (a graph with several peaks produced during the spectrographic analysis). It involved the use of a computer to automate a series of computations that a human being would probably need several days to perform.

The mathematical method that interested Prater and Wei allowed users to determine the concentrations of a mixture's constituents based on a spectrogram's peaks.[103] Linked to each peak was a linear equation relating its height to the concentrations under question, so any given spectrogram would generate a system of linear equations. However, the number of peaks in a spectrogram was usually higher than the number of constituents in the mixture, so there were often many more equations than there were constituents. The mathematics of linear equations made it impossible to solve all these equations at once, so the first step to determine the concentrations was to determine which equations should be solved. Choosing this collection could be very labor intensive. For instance, if 30 peaks formed in the spectrogram for a mixture with 10 components, the number of possible collections surpassed 30 million.

Prater and Wei's patent application identified as the invention a process and machine that would select the best collection of equations.[104] Given a spectrogram, this invention would simply output the collection of equations that the user would need to solve. The identification of these equations involved

[100] Ex Parte King and Barton.

[101] This is based on Con Diaz (2019, ch. 3).

[102] "Application of Charles D. Prater and James Wei," November 20, 1961. In the Matter of the Application of Charles D. Prater and James Wei. Appeal 7987.

[103] This paragraph is based on "Application of Charles D. Prater and James Wei," November 20, 1961. In the Matter of the Application of Charles D. Prater and James Wei. Appeal 7987.

[104] This paragraph is based on "Application of Charles D. Prater and James Wei," November 20, 1961. In the Matter of the Application of Charles D. Prater and James Wei. Appeal 7987.

generating all the possible equations connected with the spectrogram and then testing every sub-collection of equations possible to determine if they were suited to providing the most accurate approximation of the concentrations possible. This testing involved hundreds of thousands, if not millions, of calculations using only addition, subtraction, multiplication, and division. Performing these operations required a simple program that could easily be loaded onto a general purpose computer, though Mobil's application claimed instead a special purpose one.

Back in October 1961, Mobil had filed an application entitled Multicomponent Reaction Analysis and Control, claiming a computer and a method of operating it to select these equations. The Patent Office rejected the application partly because the mathematical algorithms at the core of the process that Prater and Wei had invented were ineligible for protection, but in 1968 the CCPA reversed the rejection. The court considered that the presence of a digital computer in Prater and Wei's claims granted them their patent-eligibility. This computer distinguished this process from the one in Abrams, wherein the patent application disclosed no means of performing calculations aside from a user's mind.[105] The CCPA added that it would be "an anomaly" not to allow the machine claims if the process at the patent's core was found to be patent-eligible.[106]

In 1969, a legal technicality and the death of one of the CCPA judges enabled the Patent Office to petition for a rehearing of the *Prater and Wei* decision. The court's new decision affirmed its previous opinion and added that a step is considered "purely mental" if it "may only be performed in, or with the aid of, the human mind."[107] These steps stood in contrast to "purely physical steps," which can only be performed "by physical means, machinery, or apparatus." These two kinds of steps thus formed the ends of a spectrum and in between them was "an infinite variety of steps that may be either machine-implemented or performed in, or with the aid of, the human mind." In order to determine whether a step is mental or physical, it was necessary to consider the entire application in determining which end of the spectrum is closest to the step under review.

The court explained that the "disclosure of apparatus for performing the process without human intervention" could constitute prime evidence of the fact that "the disclosed process is not mental and is, therefore, statutory." This meant that there was no reason to believe that claims encompassing the operation of a general-purpose digital computer are necessarily ineligible for a patent. Such a computer may constitute nothing more than "a storeroom of parts and/or electrical components," but introducing a program into it made it into something

[105] Application of Charles D. Prater and James Wei.
[106] Application of Charles D. Prater and James Wei, 1389.
[107] This paragraph is based on Application of Charles D. Prater and James Wei, 1402.

else—a special purpose digital computer, namely a "specific electrical circuit" which may be eligible for patent protection.[108]

This is all to say that patent-drafting strategies for computer programs were well-established and widely used by the late 1960s, and that they were starting to gain traction at the CCPA well before ADR obtained Sorting System in 1968.[109] In this sense, Sorting System stands out not as the first software ever to protect a computer program, but as evidence that the patent-drafting techniques that hardware manufacturers and industrial research laboratories had been using since the 1950s were starting to arrive at the nascent software industry. The patent disclosed "an embodiment" of the program—a machine "in which a plurality of tape memory units are utilized for serially storing data records."[110] There was certainly a program at this patent's core, but the patent presented it as something that was built into the system and which, as far as its text was concerned, was as central to the functioning of the machine as a memory unit or electrical circuitry. The patent images, shown in Figure 7.9, include both a schematic representation of a "data processing system" that worked in accordance with the program and a flowchart of the program that controls it.[111]

Since then, Sorting System has become a landmark patent in the history of computing, but it would be a mistake to think of it as the beginning of the history of modern software patenting. Even its inventor, Martin Goetz, eventually explained that ADR had sought to "patent a machine process and not a program," and that the processes at the patent's core could "implemented in software or hardware."[112] In other words, Sorting System had done something that inventors and their lawyers had been doing for decades: securing patent protection for a computer program indirectly, aiming the claims at a collection of electrical and mechanical components that worked in accordance with the program.

Conclusion and Epilogue

Modern software patents are rooted on the patent-drafting practices that industrial research laboratories and hardware manufacturers have employed since the late 1940s. For the next decade, firms secured patent protection for their programs indirectly by patenting machines that worked in accordance with the programs they developed. Their patent drafting strategies enabled them to bypass the mental steps doctrine, and they were grounded on the fact that any

[108] This paragraph is based on Application of Charles D. Prater and James Wei, 1402, 1404 n.29
[109] Goetz Patent 3,380,039 (1968).
[110] Goetz Patent 3,380,039 (1968), 2.
[111] Goetz Patent 3,380,039 (1968), 2.
[112] Goetz (1973).

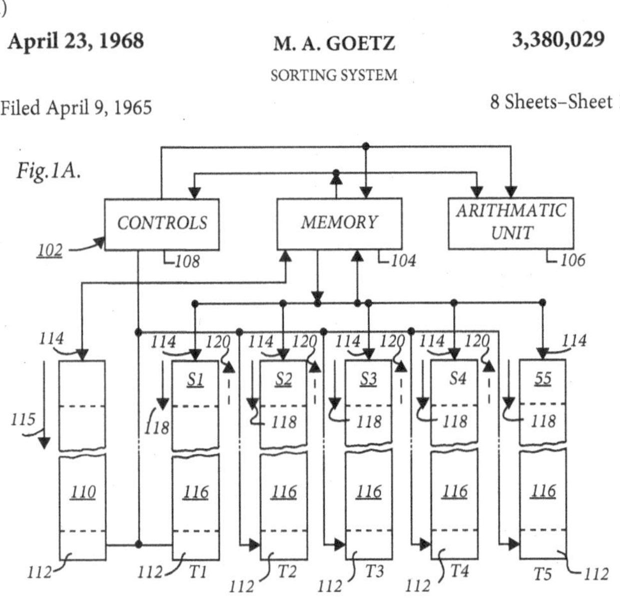

Figure 7.9 Application for Sorting System: (a) a schematic representation; (b) a flowchart for the program.
Source: Martin Goetz. Sorting System. US Patent 3,380,029 filed April 9, 1965 and issued April 23, 1968.

program could be disclosed as a special purpose computer and a means of operating it. Their patents gave legal weight to the physicality that had characterized computer programming since the ENIAC years, when programming a machine meant manually rewiring its circuits.

Assessments of the patent-eligibility for inventions involving computer programs and mathematical algorithms have led courts and patent examiners to blend novelty (35 USC 102) and disclosure (35 USC 112) with patent-eligibility (35 USC 101). The geological invention at stake in *In re Abrams* led the CCPA to develop a test of eligibility that required examiners to determine whether novelty resides on mental and physical steps. The resulting test bears a striking resemblance to the machine-or-transformation test that the Court of Appeals for the Federal Circuit would develop two decades later, which specified that a process is patent-eligible if it is implemented in a non-trivial manner by a machine, or if it causes the transformation of an article from one state to another.[113] In the aftermath of *Abrams*, means-plus claim structures served as shortcuts to craft discursive embodiments in patent applications, though examiners sometimes insisted that the specific means needed to be spelled out in the patent application.

[113] Con Diaz (2019).

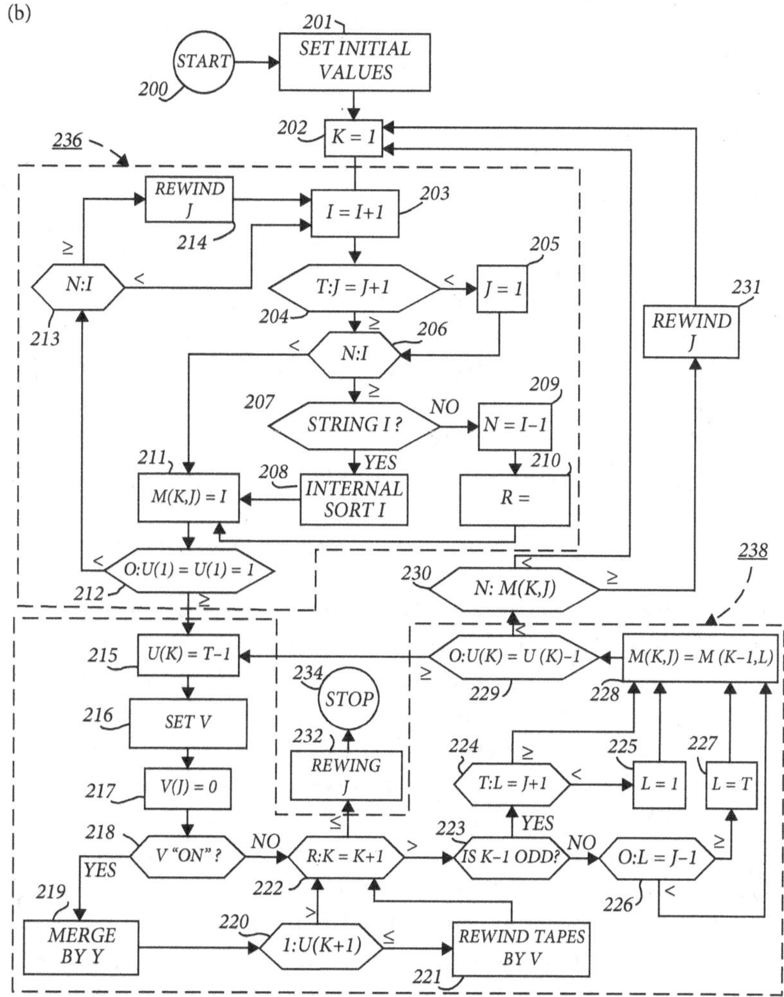

Figure 7.9 Continued

Legal doctrine alone is insufficient to understand how and why the patent protection of computer programs has been possible in the United States. Well before courts started to hand down landmark opinions on the matter, the Patent Office was already handling the classificatory and bureaucratic problems surrounding the patent protection of computer programs. By carefully drafting patent applications to disclose programming as circuitry and the operation of computer systems, inventors and their lawyers were able to bypass even strict tests for patent-eligibility such as the one delivered in *Halliburton*. The same is true today, as several prominent patent law firms recommend inventors to disclose as many tangible components as they can in their patent applications to bypass the doctrinal restrictions generated by *Alice v. CLS*.[114]

The patent protection of computer programs is not a byproduct of the software industry's birth, nor is it a legal artifice that courts have invented and imposed upon the computing industry. Instead, these protections emerged organically from the early cultures of electronic computing. They spread among hardware makers and industrial research laboratories in the 1950s, and they are nearly as old as the practice of programming digital electronic computers. In the 1960s, the main issue surrounding the patent protection of software was not whether software was eligible for patent protection but instead how patents could be drafted to present it as something that was unproblematically so. This involved disclosing algorithms as circuitry arrangements; data manipulations as the movement of electrical impulses; and the running of a program as the use of a device. Made tangible by patent applications, programs became much more than code.

The computing industry's major transformations starting in the late 1960s made this rich history of patent-drafting strategically challenging to hardware manufacturers. In 1969, IBM implemented its so-called "unbundling" decision: it started charging a separate price for its application programs instead of offering them free of charge with the purchase or lease of its hardware.[115] Software firms such as ADR and Informatics had been selling their software for nearly half a decade, but hardware manufacturers had not done so because IBM was powerful enough to make bundled sales the industry norm.[116] By the late 1960s, software firms' growing sales had shown computer users that bundling was not necessarily the only way in which computing systems could be monetized. Users in all sectors wherein computing was prominent—government agencies, banks, insurance companies, and so on—started to express their dissatisfaction with IBM's bundles. If the price of a computing system included all programs in IBM's software library, they reasoned, then users are likely paying for programs that they would never use. After all, it would be unlikely that an accounting firm would need to use high-level scientific applications. This widespread dissatisfaction, along with the launch of an investigation from the Department of Justice's Antitrust Division, ultimately encouraged IBM's managers to unbundle the firm's hardware, software, and services.

IBM's unbundling was what one scholar has called an "inflection point" in the computing industry's history.[117] Able to sell their application programs without

114 This claim is grounded on my examination of firms' publicly available online tips and guidelines. I have not quoted any of them in order to avoid disseminating what they may consider to be proprietary advice.

115 Usselman (2009).

116 The rest of this paragraph is based on Con Diaz (2019).

117 Yates (1995).

the fear that hardware manufacturers would release free alternatives to them, software firms started to grow at an unprecedented rate, and the dynamics of the modern software industry started to crystallize.[118] Leading these firms was ADR, which for the next decade grounded its legal arguments in favor of software patenting on the notion at Sorting System's core: programs, as far as patent law was concerned, are machines. The firm's chief patent lawyer would eventually argue that the word software was not as well-suited for patenting debates as "softwiring," by which he meant the use of a computer program to achieve in a computer the effect that would result from manually wiring it.[119] He construed decisions such as *In re Prater and Wei* as the CCPA's implicit embrace of softwiring as patent-eligible inventions—a recognition that "computers are built by software."[120]

IBM emerged from this history as the country's leading opponent of software patenting.[121] For many years, it led hardware manufacturers' efforts to establish computer programs as ineligible for patent protection and to have courts reject patent-drafting techniques such as ADR's as unallowable (and even disingenuous) efforts to establish exclusivity rights over mathematical algorithms. Should the patent protection of computer programs flourish, IBM's managers reasoned during the 1970s, then small software firms would be able to create high barriers to entry into the nascent industry for software products. This, in turn, could cause R&D costs to skyrocket, and it could deteriorate hardware firms' dominance over the computing industry. The rise of the minicomputer and PC industries in the late 1970s and early 1980s would eventually change the hardware manufacturers' views on software patenting, but by then courts and industry commentators had forgotten a crucial historical fact: that the patent protection of computer programs was as old and well established as the computing industry itself.

References

Court Opinions and Archival Documents

Application of Charles D. Prater and James Wei, 415 F.2d 1393 (CCPA 1979).
Cochrane v. Deener, 94 U.S. 780 (1876).
Dayco Products v. Total Containment, 329 F.3d 1358 (Federal Circuit, 2003).
Ex Parte King and Barton, 146 USPQ 590 (CCPA, 1965).
Ex Parte Lewin, 154 USPQ 487 (CCPA 1966).
File Wrapper for Patent 2,814,437. Records of the Patent and Trademark Office, RG 241. National Archives, Kansas City.

[118] Campbell-Kelly (2003).
[119] Jacobs (1973).
[120] Jacobs (1973, p. 134).
[121] Con Diaz (2019).

File Wrapper for Patent 2,970,765. Records of the Patent and Trademark Office, RG 241. National Archives, Kansas City.

File Wrapper for Patent 3,167,743. Records of the Patent and Trademark Office, RG 241. National Archives, Kansas City.

File Wrapper for US Patent 2,552,629. Records of the Patent and Trademark Office, RG 241. National Archives, Kansas City.

Halliburton Oil Well Cementing Co. v. Walker, 146 F.2d 817 (Circuit Court of Appeals, Ninth Circuit, 1944).

In re Abrams, 188 F.2d 165 (CCPA 1951).

In re Yuan, 188 F.2d 377 (CCPA 1951).

In the Matter of the Application of Armand J. Abrams. Appeal 5726, Records of the U.S. Court of Customs and Patent Appeals, Patent Appeal Case Files, 1910–82. National Archives, Kansas City.

In the Matter of the Application of Charles D. Prater and James Wei. Appeal 7987, Records of the U.S. Court of Customs and Patent Appeals, Patent Appeals Cases, 1927–1973. National Archives, Kansas City.

In the Matter of the Application of Shao Wen Yuan. Appeal 5776, Records of the U.S. Court of Customs and Patent Appeals, Patent Appeal Case Files, 1910–82. National Archives, Kansas City.

Patents

Asija, Satya. Automated Information Input, Storage, and Retrieval System. US Patent 4,270,182 filed 30 December 1974 and issued 26 May 1981.

Bacon, Walter. Enciphering and Deciphering Device for Secret Telegraph Systems, US Patent 2,504,621 filed 3 December 1946 and issued 18 April 1950.

Bigelow, E.B., Loom, US Patent 546 issued 6 January 1838.

Bird, Raymond. Binary Adder. US Patent 2,861,741 filed 8 October 1953 and issued 25 November 1958.

———. Data Translating Apparatus. US Patent 2,970,765 filed 4 November 1952 and issued 7 February 1961.

Brooks, Frederick, and Dura Sweeney, Program Interrupt System. US Patent 3,048,332 filed 9 December 1957 and issued 7 August 1962.

Brustman, Joseph. Data Translating System. US Patent 2,702,380 filed 24 December 1953 and issued 15 February 1955.

Burg, John, and William Schneider. Multi-Point, Multi-Channel Linear Processing of Seismic Data. US Patent 3,284,763 filed 30 October 1962 and issued 8 November 1966.

Foster, Manus, Clyde Kerns, and Raymond Sengbush. Processing of Geophysical Data. US Patent 3,689,874 filed in 1964 and issued in 1972.

Goetz, Martin. Sorting System. US Patent 3,380,029 filed 9 April 1965 and issued 23 April 1968.

Greenhalgh, Roger. Data Transfer and Translating System. US Patent 2,872,666 filed 21 December 1955 and issued 3 February 1959.

Hagelbarger, David. Continuous Digital Error Correcting System. US Patent 2,956,124 filed 1 May 1958 and issued 11 October 1960.

Hamburger, Arthur. Detection and Correction of Transposition Error. US Patent 3,333,243 filed 16 September 1963 and issued 25 July 1967.

Hamming, Richard, and Bernard Holbrook. Error Detecting and Correcting System. US Patent 2,552,629, filed 11 January 1950 and issued 15 May 1951.

Hill, William. Electrical Impulse Generator. US Patent 2,782,304 filed 13 January 1953 and issued 19 February 1957.

Holbrook, Bernard. Telephone System. US Patent 2,317,191 filed 24 January 1941 and issued 20 April 1943.

Holbrook, Bernard, and Alexis Lundstrom. Sight Order Computer. US Patent 2,658,678 filed 13 February 1945 and issued 10 November 1953.

Holbrook, Bernard, Alexis Lundstrom, and William Malthaner. US Patent 2,658,680 filed 13 February 1945 and issued 10 November 1953;

Holbrook, Bernard, and Logan Mason. Call Distributing System. US Patent 2,405,214 filed 10 April 1945 and issued 6 August 1946;

Horwitz, Lawrence, and Richard Karp. Optimum Result Computer. US Patent 3,339,182 filed 30 June 1964 and issued 29 August 1967.

Ivor, Vivian. Electrical Contact Device. US Patent 2,688,665 filed 21 February, 1952 and issued 7 September, 1954.

Keen, Harold. Interlocking Electromagnetic Relay. US Paten 2,694,758 filed 29 March 1951 and issued 16 November 1954.

Laberty, Frederick. Combined Telephone and Paging System. US Patent 2,496,629 filed 16 December 1947 and issued 7 February 1950.

Lewin, Morton. Ordered Retrieval of Information Stored in a Tag-Addressed Memory. US Patent 3,329,937 filed 28 March 1962 and issued 4 July 1967.

McDermid, William, Harold Petersen, and Shelton Glenmore. Unambiguous Identification Systems. US Patent 3,167,743 filed 19 December 1960 and issued 26 January 1965.

McDonnell, James. Data Processing System Memory Controls. US Patent 2,968,027, filed 29 August 1958 and issued 10 January 1961.

Melas, Constantin. Error Correcting System. US Patent 3,213,426 filed 25 September 1959 and issued 19 October 1965.

Morse, Samuel. Improvement in Electro-Magnetic Telegraphs, US Patent RE117, issued 13 June 1848.

———. Telegraph Signs, US Patent 1,647 issued 29 June1840

Motte, Frank. Matrix Translator. US Patent 2,856,597, filed 26 July 1956 and issued 14 October 1958.

Potts, Louis. Error Detecting Code System. US Patent 2,512,038 filed 7 June 1947 and issued 20 June 1950.

Pun, Lucas. Fire Control Systems. US Patent 3,339,457 filed 18 August 1964 and issued 5 September 1967.

Rack, Alois. Decoder for Pulse Code Modulation. US Patent 2,514,671 filed 23 September 1947 and issued 11 July 1950.

Reynolds, Andrew. Decimal to Binary Translators. US Patent 3,021,065 filed 16 March 1959 and issued 13 February 1962.

———. Error Detection and Correction System. US Patent 3,024,992 filed 16 March 1959 and issued 13 March 1962.

Saint, Samuel. Means for Airplane Approach Control," US Patent 2,495,139 filed 22 December 1944 and issued 17 January 1950.

Stibitz, George. Automatic Calculator. US Patent 2,666,579, filed 26 December 1944 and issued 19 January 1954.

Swafford, Thomas. Correlation of Seismic Signals. US Patent 2,907,400 filed 12 May 1954 and issued 6 October 1959.

Taylor, Robert. and James Volgenson, Error-Checking Circuit for Data Transmission System, US Patent 3,140,463 filed 22 November 1960 and July 7 issued 1960.

Woodbury, James. Binary Decoder. US Patent 2,814,437 filed 30 July 1956 and issued 26 November 1957.

Published Sources

Andrews, E. G. "Telephone Switching and the Early Bell Laboratories Computers," *Bell Systems Technical Journal* 42:2 (1963): 341–53.

Allison, John, Abe Dunn, and Ronald Mann, "Software Patents, Incumbents, and Entry," *Texas Law Review* 85, no. 7 (June 2007): 1579–1625.

Asija, Satya. *How to Protect Computer Programs: A Case History of the First Pure Software Patent.* Allahabad: Law Publishers, 1983.

Beauchamp, Christopher. *Invented by Law: Alexander Graham Bell and the Patent that Changed America.* Cambridge: Harvard University Press, 2015.

Bessen, James, and Robert Hunt, "An Empirical Look at Software Patents," *Journal of Economics and Management Strategy* 16, no. 1 (Spring 2007): 157–89.

Bessen, James, and Michael Meurer. *Patent Failure: How Judges, Bureaucrats, and Lawyers Put Innovators at Risk.* Princeton, NJ: Princeton University Press, 2009.

Biagioli, Mario. "Patent Republic: Representing Inventions, Constructing Rights and Authors," *Social Research* 73, no. 4 (Winter 2006): 1129–72.

———. "Between Knowledge and Technology: Patenting Methods, Rethinking Materiality", *Anthropological Forum* 22 (2012): 285–300.

Bird, Raymond. "BTM's First Steps Into Computing," *Resurrection: The Bulletin of the Computer Conservation Society* 22 (Summer 1999). http://www.computerconservationsociety.org/resurrection/res22.htm#c.

Campbell-Kelly, Martin. *ICL: A Business and Technical History.* New York: Oxford University Press, 1989.

———. *From Airline Reservations to Sonic the Hedgehog: A History of the Software Industry.* Cambridge, MA: MIT Press, 2003.

———. "Not All Bad: An Historical Perspective on Software Patents," *Michigan Telecommunications and Technology Law Review* 11 (2005): 191–249.

Campbell-Kelly, Martin, William Aspray, Nathan Ensmenger, and Jeffrey R. Yost, eds. *Computer: A History of the Information Machine.* Boulder, CO: Westview Press, 2013.

Ceruzzi, Paul. *A History of Modern Computing.* Cambridge, MA: MIT Press, 2003.

Con Diaz, Gerardo. "Contested Ontologies of Software: The Story of Gottschalk v. Benson, 1963-1972," *IEEE Annals of the History of Computing*, 37, no. 3 (2015a): 8–19.

———. "Embodied Software: Patents and the History of Software Development, 1946–1970, 1945–1970," *IEEE Annals of the History of Computing* 37, no. 3 (July–September 2015b): 2–14.

———. "The Text in the Machine: American Copyright Law and the Many Natures of Software, 1974–1978," *Technology & Culture* 57:4 (October 2016): 753–79.

———. *Software Rights: How Patent Law Trasnformed Software Development in America.* New Haven, CT: Yale University Press, 2019.

Ensmenger, Nathan. *The Computer Boys Take Over: Computers, Programmers, and the Politics of Technical Expertise.* Cambridge, MA: MIT Press, 2010.

"First Patentee Writes 'How to Patent Programs,'" *Infoworld*, 22 February 1982, 1.

"First Patent Is Issued for Software, Full Implications Are Not Yet Known," *Computerworld*, 19 June 1968: 1.

Goetz, Martin. "A Different Viewpoint on the Benson-Tabbot Decision." *Communications of the ACM* 16, no. 5 (1973): 334.

———. "Memoirs of a Software Pioneer, Part 1," *IEEE Annals of the History of Computing* (January–March 2002): 43.

———. "Should Software be Patentable? That's the Wrong Question to Ask," 29 October 2011. https://www.zdnet.com/article/should-software-be-patentable-thats-the-wrong-question-to-ask/.

Graham, Max. "Process Patents for Computer Programs." *California Law Review* 56, no. 2 (April 1968): 466–96.

"Hamming's Technique of Error Correction Marks 30th Birthday," *Computerworld*, September 8, 1980.

Haigh, Thomas. "Software in the 1960s as a Concept, Service, and Product," *IEEE Annals of the History of Computing* 24, no. 1 (January–March 2002): 5–13.

Haigh, Thomas, Mark Priestley, and Crispin Rope. *ENIAC in Action: Making and Remaking the Modern Computer*. Cambridge, MA: MIT Press, 2016.

Heide, Lars. *Punched Card Systems and the Early Information Explosion, 1880–1945*. Baltimore, MD: Johns Hopkins University Press, 2009.

Jacobs, Morton. "Patents for Software Inventions in the Supreme Court's Decision." *Jurimetrics* Journal 13, no. 3 (Spring 1973): 133.

Kevles, Daniel. "Ananda Chakrabarty Wins a Patent: Biotechnology, Law and Society," *Historical Studies of the Physical and Biological Sciences* 25:1 (1994): 111–35.

Kevles, Daniel, and Ari Berkowitz. "The Gene Patenting Controversy: A Convergence of Law, Economic Interests, and Ethics," *Brooklyn Law Review* 67 (2002): 233–48.

Lamoreaux, Naomi, Kenneth Sokoloff, and Dhanoos Sutthiphisal, "Patent Alchemy: The Market for Technology in US History," *Business History Review* 87, no. 1 (Spring 2013): 3–38.

Lee, J. A. N., "Richard Wesley Hamming," *Computer Pioneers*, https://history.computer.org/pioneers/hamming.html, accessed September 14, 2017.

Lemley, Mark, and Kimberly Moore, "Ending Abuse of Patent Continuations." *Boston Law Review* 84 (2004): 63–124.

Light, Jennifer. "When Computers Were Women." *Technology & Culture* 40, no. 3 (July 1999): 455–83.

"May 26, 1981: Programmer-Attorney Wins First US Software Patent," *Wired* 26 May 2009. https://www.wired.com/2009/05/dayintech-0526/.

Millman, S., ed. A History of Engineering and Science in the Bell System: Communications Sciences (1925–1980). New Jersey: AT&T Bell Laboratories, 1984.

Morgan, Samuel. "Richard Wesley Hamming (1915–1998)," *Notices of the AMS* 45, no. 8 (September 1998): 972–77.

Mossoff, Adam. "O'Reilly v. Morse," Hoover IP2 Working Paper 14010, May 2014.

National Research Council. *Industrial Research Laboratories of the United States Including Consulting Research Laboratories*. Washington, D.C: The National Academies Press, 1946.

Nofre, David, Mark Priestley, and Gerard Alberts. "When Technology became Language: The Origins of the Linguistic Conception of Computer Programming, 1950–1960." *Technology & Culture* 55, no. 1 (January 2014): 40–75.

Pottage, Alain, and Brad Sherman, *Figures of Invention: A History of Modern Patent Law*. New York: Oxford University Press, 2010.

Rankin, William. "The Person Skilled in the Art is Really Quite Conventional: US Patent Drawings and the Persona of the Inventor." In *Making and Unmaking Intellectual*

Property: Creative Production in Legal and Cultural Perspective, edited by Mario Biagioli et al, 55–78. Chicago, IL: University of Chicago Press, 2011.

"Richard W. Hamming," *Association for Computing Machinery*. http://amturing.acm.org/award_winners/hamming_1000652.cfm.

Risch, Michael. "America's First Patents," *Florida Law Review* 64, no. 5 (2012): 1279–1336.

Samuelson, Pamela. "The Strange Odyssey of Software Interfaces as Intellectual Property;" Maureen O'Rourke, "The Story of Diamond v. Diehr: Toward Patenting Software." In *Intellectual Property Stories*, edited by Jane Ginsburg and Rochelle Dreyfuss, 194–219. New York: Foundation Press, 2006.

Stobbs, Gregory. *Software Patents*. Frederick, MD: Wolters Kluwer Law & Business, 2012.

Swanson, Kara. "Biotech in Court: A Legal Lesson on the Unity of Science," *Social Studies of Science* 37, no. 3 (June 2007): 357–84.

———. "The Emergence of the Professional Patent Practitioner," *Technology & Culture* 50 (July 2009): 519–48.

Thompson, *Thomas. From Error-Correcting Codes through Sphere Packings to Simple Groups*. New York: Carus, 1984.

"Unprecedented Patent," *Fortune*, August 1968, 34.

Usselman, Steven. "Unbundling IBM: Antitrust and Incentives to Innovation in American Computing." In *The Challenge of Remaining Innovative: Insights from the Twentieth-Century American Business*, edited by Sally Clarke, Naomi Lamoreaux, and Steven Usselman, 249–80. Stanford, CA: Stanford University Press, 2009.

Yates, JoAnne. "Application Software for Insurance in the 1960s and Early 1970s." *Business and Economic History* 24, no. 1 (Fall 1995): 123–34.

8

History Matters

National Innovation Systems and Innovation Policies in Nations

B. Zorina Khan

The province of reward is the last asylum of arbitrary power.
—Jeremy Bentham (1824)[1]

Introduction

The contrast between the state and the market is persistent and pervasive in both theory and empirical studies. Few would contest the view that a centralized government can provide vital support for markets and private enterprise through enforcement of private property rights, measures to reduce transactions costs, and provisions to prevent or resolve market failure. In recent years, however, there has been a resurgence of scholarship alleging that direct government involvement in technology markets and innovation strategies has led to, and is even necessary for, economic progress. According to these authors, the historical evidence demonstrates the effectiveness of interventions by an activist "entrepreneurial state." Ha-Joon Chang, for instance, appeals to a selection of the secondary literature to support the hypothesis that institutions like private property and free markets were less important than state initiatives in funding, direct investment, and regulation.[2] Studies in this vein even claim that the "courageous State" has led a timid private sector and has "been behind most technological revolutions and periods of long-run growth."[3]

Numerous studies that promote the role of the state in technological change employ variants of the concept of national innovation systems (NIS).[4] NIS

[1] Bentham (1824).
[2] Chang (2003).
[3] Mazzucato (2015, pp. 22–23).
[4] Freeman (1995), Nelson (1993), Lundvall (1992).

B. Zorina Khan, *History Matters* In: *The Battle over Patents*. Edited by: Stephen H. Haber and Naomi R. Lamoreaux, Oxford University Press. © Oxford University Press 2021. DOI: 10.1093/oso/9780197576151.003.0009

research identifies explicit structures and purposeful linkages among technological activities and federal government organizations and agencies, corporations, universities, and state-funded research.[5] The general assumption is that markets fail in the realm of knowledge and technology, so technical progress and success in commercialization can best be achieved through non-market mechanisms established by enlightened government actions. Like the advocates of the "entrepreneurial state," NIS proponents highlight the advantages that accrue from statist direction and participation in entrepreneurship and innovation. This research cadre is persuaded that history reveals the "vast innovation potential that can be unleashed with adequate government policies."[6]

Empirical studies about the efficacy of the "entrepreneurial state" tend to be limited to generalizations from the experience of the late twentieth century. The methodology is typically based on verification, in which authors cite allegedly successful examples of government support for innovation, without equal attention to failures, crowding out, unintended consequences, or foregone alternatives.[7] However, variation over time and place is required to shed light on the extent to which explicit linkages between administrators, innovators, and universities are generally relevant for understanding long-run economic development. Thus, the discussion in this chapter considers policies in Britain, France, and the United States during the first and second industrial revolutions. The assessment of key innovation institutions is not based on potentially unrepresentative case studies, but draws on "hyperlinked" research analyses of large samples of panel data providing information on approximately one hundred thousand inventors and inventions over the course of two centuries, in Europe and the United States.[8]

This analysis of technological innovation across time and place distinguishes between markets in ideas and administered systems. *Administered systems* refer to arrangements where economic decisions about rewards, prices, values, and the allocation of resources are made by administrators or panels. Administered systems range along a spectrum that includes centralized state agencies and NIS to decentralized prize-granting bodies. Decision-making in such institutions lacks transparency, their internal control mechanisms are weak, and they tend to lack feedback mechanisms or incentives for adjustments in response to incorrect

[5] Another perspective on state measures to promote technological change and growth involves the notion of "national innovative capacity," which includes institutions, the ecosystem affecting industrial clusters, and linkages across these broad categories. Furman, Porter, and Stern (2002) conducted country-level analysis, which suggested that variation in total factor productivity was due to policies such as the strength of intellectual property protection, the share of academic research that was funded by private enterprise, technological specialization, and the stock of knowledge.

[6] Perez (2013).

[7] Breznitz (2007).

[8] The empirical data are discussed in Khan (2020a).

choices or external changes. Principals in most administered systems are not subject to a right of appeal from their judgements and typically do not directly bear the consequences of their choices. Stakeholders in such organizations have an interest in projecting overly optimistic assessments of their activities, without adequately acknowledging failures and inefficiencies. I propose to show that decentralized administered institutions are empirically tractable, and their analysis helps to shed light on more centralized institutions such as the "entrepreneurial state." This approach offers the reader an objective quantitative context for assessing qualitative accounts and case studies.

Market efficiency is enhanced when property rights are well-defined, when transactions costs are minimized, and exchange is depersonalized. Scholars such as Friedrich Hayek point to the benefits of markets for the determination of prices and for effectively incorporating decentralized knowledge.[9] American innovation institutions were more market-oriented, because the US patent system defined property rights in inventions and reduced transactions costs through mechanisms such as disclosure, patent officials and the judiciary did not attempt to determine economic value. Patent rules facilitated decentralized markets in ideas, and economic outcomes were determined by the productivity of the invention rather than the identity of the inventor. This distinction between markets in ideas and administered processes arguably allows us to better understand the rate and direction of innovation and industry during the past two centuries.

Innovation Policies in Britain

Administered Innovation Systems

Scholars of European economic development have celebrated the claim that elites played a central role in the process of technological innovation. In France, for instance, some studies contend that elites (proxied by subscribers to the French *Enclyopédie*) or "upper-tail knowledge" generated French industrialization and growth.[10] Another thesis correlates the location of membership in scientific societies with exhibits at the Crystal Palace Exhibition and argues that such elites should be credited with the advances in technological innovation during the Industrial Revolution.[11] Joel Mokyr highlights the role of elite

[9] "This raises for a competitive society the question, not how we can 'find' the people who know best, but rather what institutional arrangements are necessary in order that the unknown persons who have knowledge specially suited to a particular task are most likely to be attracted to that task" (Hayek 1948, p. 95).

[10] Squicciarini and Voigtländer (2015).

[11] Dowey (2014).

"cultural entrepreneurs" who freely circulated knowledge and ideas in a Republic of Letters prior to the era of modern economic growth.[12]

Societies that regarded knowledge as the province of a special class, and as a means of social control, were unlikely to create open institutions that would offer equal opportunity for all ideas or all groups in society. Scientists in England or France or Italy certainly shared their ideas with others whom they regarded as their peers. At the same time, the so-called Republic of Letters was something of a misnomer for an exclusive Aristocracy of Letters. As Oliver Goldsmith noted: "The Republic of Letters, is a very common expression among the Europeans and yet, when applied to the learned of Europe, is the most absurd that can be imagined, since nothing is more unlike a republic than the society which goes by that name."[13] European knowledge-elites treated the less eminent with disdain and despised practitioners who were merely versed in applied knowledge and practical pursuits. According to this group of alleged republicans, "the mysteries of the universe were beyond the capacities of the vulgar."[14] Throughout the first industrial era in Britain, the state and other non-market institutions were involved in various pursuits that influenced inventors and inventions, but these initiatives were largely lacking in "connexity" and included few positive feedback mechanisms to ensure productive adjustments to changes. Subsequent economic growth was unbalanced, productivity gains were largely concentrated in a few capital-intensive industries, and Britain's early industrial leadership was soon eroded and ultimately lost.[15]

The specific way in which elite administered systems functioned can be detected from a closer examination of the experience of prize-granting innovation institutions. Numerous societies for the promotion of science and useful knowledge were founded after the middle of the eighteenth century throughout Britain and other European countries. Early antecedents included the Royal Society, which coalesced in the 1660s as an "invisible college" for the improvement of "natural knowledge" through observation and experimentation.[16] Such communities of intellectuals and entrepreneurs as the Birmingham Lunar

[12] These arguments appear in a plethora of papers and books, including Mokyr (2016).

[13] Goldsmith (1837, p. 269).

[14] Eamon (2006, p. 223).

[15] Davis and Huttenback (1986), in a careful quantitative analysis, show how inefficient outcomes could be sustained because of skewed political economic institutions. Colonial ventures created a net social loss but were nevertheless maintained, because they redistributed income from consumers and domestic enterprise to the influential financiers and gentry who were disproportionately represented in Parliament. Reform efforts were stymied by the privileged groups who disproportionately benefited from the inefficiencies and operation of the standing rules, regulations, and institutions.

[16] In Scotland and Ireland, individuals with more specific applied interests in agriculture and industry formed such associations as the Scottish Society of Improvers (1723). The Dublin Society for Improving Husbandry, Manufactures and other Useful Arts (1731) was in part funded by the government, and gave out £42,000 in awards between 1761 and 1767 (Wood 1913, p. 3).

Society, the Dublin Society, and the Society for the Encouragement of National Industry in France, typify the incentives and institutions that have been credited with generating cultural and industrial progress in eighteenth-century Europe.

The London Society for the Encouragement of Arts, Manufactures, and Commerce, most often known as the Royal Society of Arts (RSA) engaged in prize-granting policies for over a century, and thus offers a valuable opportunity to go beyond limited case studies and systematically investigate the costs and benefits of administered systems. Moreover, other assessments of innovation prizes fail to accurately estimate their independent effects because inventors could also obtain patents for the same idea, and this complementarity meant that patents were positively correlated with prizes. The RSA, however, prohibited the award of prizes for patented inventions, so inventors had to choose whether to apply for a patent or to pursue the prize. The example of the RSA is therefore especially useful for the empirical analysis of such institutions, because their data allow us to uniquely identify the effects of different incentives for innovation.

The RSA certainly embodied the improving spirit of the age. This organization was established in 1754, and became a model for other institutions subsequently founded for the promotion of technological progress in Europe and beyond. The RSA bestowed many thousands of cash and honorary prizes on applicants, and this case study is frequently offered as proof of the success of innovation prize systems and of substitutes for patent institutions.[17] The RSA initially was convinced that its efforts were central to the process of industrial and cultural development: "Whoever attentively considers the benefits which have arisen to the Publick since the institution of this Society . . . will readily allow, no money was ever more usefully expended; nor has any nation received more real advantage from any public body whatever than has been derived to this country from the rewards bestowed by this Society."[18] Many observers, then and now, uncritically accepted this self-promoting assessment. Similarly, the correlation between the operation of the RSA and the "take off" of industrialization in Britain has led scholars to make a causal inference between its administered policy of granting prizes and the pace of technological innovation.

My research project on the RSA examined several thousand of these inducement prizes, matched with patent records and biographical information about the applicants for awards. The analysis of these data indicates that the RSA failed to induce useful inventions. Scholars typically gauge the activities of the society

[17] For instance, Stiglitz (2006, p. 21) proclaims that, instead of patents, "the alternative of awarding prizes would be more efficient and more equitable. It would provide strong incentives for research but without the inefficiencies associated with monopolisation. This is not a new idea—in the UK for instance, the Royal Society of Arts has long advocated the use of prizes. But it is, perhaps, an idea whose time has come."

[18] Cited in *The Gentleman's Magazine* (London, England), Volume 83, 1798, p. 333.

Table 8.1 Patentability of prize-winning submissions by industry, 1754–1840

		18th Century	19th Century	Total
		% Patentable	**% Patentable**	**% Patentable**
Agriculture	row %	4.5	9.7	5.4
	% all	0.9	0.8	0.9
Chemistry	row %	14.3	10	12.5
	% all	0.4	0.3	0.4
Colonies	row %	21.6	0	16.9
	% all	0.7	0	0.4
Manufactures	row %	40.2	30.6	37.3
	% all	2.8	1.7	2.4
Mechanics	row %	78.6	72.6	75.1
	% all	7.2	16.9	10.6
Polite Arts	row %	0.1	0.2	0.1
	% all	0.1	0.1	0.1
TOTAL				
	%	12.1	19.9	14.8
	N	1592	874	2466

Notes: The industrial categories were assigned by the names of the committees that adjudicated the applications and bestowed the awards. Patentability was determined by whether the item fell under subject matter that could be eligible for a patent and by searches of patent records during the entire period. The row percentage indicates the proportion of all awards in that sector that was patentable, while "% all" indicates the percentage of all awards in that period that were patentable.

Source: Archival data from RSA.

in terms of the total number of premiums that were offered, without engaging in further assessment of the relevant details. Closer examination reveals that the majority of the proposed prizes were never claimed and failed to attract any attention from inventors. Table 8.1 categorizes some 2,500 RSA awards in terms of whether or not they were eligible for patent protection.[19] Patentable inventions were more likely to be commercially and technically valuable, but only 14.8 percent of the awards over the entire period were patentable.

[19] Patentability of exhibits was determined by subject-matter, conformity with the patent laws, and by searches in the patent records to establish whether a patent had ever been granted for that type of invention.

The RSA awards were arbitrary, and the prizes for inventions proved to be unrelated to economically important technologies. This lack of systematic variation owed in part to the inherently idiosyncratic nature of decision-making in such administered systems. The overall explanatory power of regressions that assess variation in gold and silver medals and other prizes was quite low.[20] Decisions were based on the views of what judges considered to be a valuable or worthy contribution, which often diverged from the factors that would prove to be successful in the marketplace. Elite members of RSA committees instead considered that one of its missions was to decry the "vulgar and gaudy" tastes of the masses and to educate consumers by example so that "no manufacturer will have to complain that his best productions are left on his hands, and his worst preferred."[21]

Inventors had to choose whether to obtain rewards in the marketplace or by appealing to the RSA administrators. We observe a process of adverse selection in which inventors of valuable discoveries obtained patent protection, whereas "lemons" were submitted for prize awards. The binomial regressions in Table 8.2 consider the consequences of such policies in terms of the relationship between awards and the course of technological progress. The dependent variable comprises the cumulative stock of patented inventions that had been filed in the specific technology field of the prize award through 1890. Thus, a positive coefficient would be expected if the prize were given for an influential area of technological discovery. Instead, one finds that both gold and silver medals are negatively and significantly related to the cumulative stock of future innovations, consistent with the notion of adverse selection. Indeed, several of the RSA leadership obtained patents for their commercially valuable discoveries and only applied for prizes for minor unmarketable innovations.

The RSA members themselves ultimately became disillusioned with their prize system, which they acknowledged had done little to promote technological progress and industrialization. Elite members of the society were initially able to block reforms that the more pragmatic advocated, including the abandonment of the premium-granting system. However, by the turn of the nineteenth century the society faced bankruptcy and irrelevance and was forced to change or become extinct.[22] The RSA then openly conceded the inability of committees to predict the course of technology and to calibrate rewards to inventive value. The administrators recognized that their efforts had been "futile" because of their hostility to patents and switched from offering inducement prizes toward

[20] Khan (2017a).

[21] The International Exhibition of 1862, Vol. 1, p. 10 (no author).

[22] "Of the petty premiums presented by the Societies for the Encouragement of Arts and Manufactures, supported by popular subscription, I shall say but little, as indeed but little is to be said. Instituted on public-spirited principles, but perverted by private cabals, the laudable purposes of their institution have been seldom attained" (Kenrick 1774, pp. 27–28).

Table 8.2 Relationship between prizes and technologically significant innovations, RSA, 1750–1850

Dependent Variable: Cumulative stock of future inventions						
	Coefficient	Chi-Sq.	Coefficient	Chi-Sq.	Coefficient	Chi-Sq.
Intercept	−11.55	9.1***	−14.82	17.8***	−0.35	0.02
Gold medal	−1.15	109.0***	–	–	–	–
Silver Medal	−0.90	76.4***	–	–	–	–
Patentability	-	–	–	–	4.59	2430.1***
Honorary awards	-	-	-1.01	130.1***	-0.08	1.1
Frequent winner	−0.15	82.8***	−0.15	82.2***	0.00	0
Female	−0.25	5.0*	−0.24	4.5*	0.04	0.2
London	−0.02	0.1	−0.05	0.3	0.20	7.0***
Prior patents	0.10	148.2***	0.11	156.9***	0.04	95.1***
Textiles	1.69	142.3***	1.68	140.6***	0.04	0.1
Agriculture	0.77	63.7***	0.73	59.6***	0.05	0.5
Chemistry	2.87	288.9***	2.87	287.2***	0.49	13.0***
Mechanics	3.07	989.1***	3.03	1011.7***	0.07	0.5
Colonies	3.08	345.8***	3.05	341.9***	0.48	12.8***
Year	0.01	10.9***	0.01	20.5***	0.00	0.01
Log Likelihood	−6237.5		−6239.6		−4973.9	

Notes: Binomial regressions of RSA cash prizes and medals. *Frequent winner* indicates the total number of awards received by each person over the entire period. *Patentable invention* is a dummy variable that indicates whether the RSA award comprised patentable subject matter. *Honorary awards* is a dummy variable with a value of 1 for medals and honorary prizes, and 0 for financial awards. The industry dummies are defined relative to the excluded variable of the Polite Arts. Statistical significance:*=.05 level;**=.01;***=<.01.

lobbying for reforms to strengthen the patent system. These findings suggest some skepticism is warranted about claims regarding the role that elites and non-market-oriented institutions played in generating technological innovation and long-term economic development.

Similar conclusions are evident in the more centralized provision of funding for technology by the state. The British government expended large sums to promote inventive activity throughout the early industrial period, but in a largely idiosyncratic and unsystematic fashion. The ability of inventors to attract state payouts and prizes was related to their social status and the influence of patrons, rather than to the inherent economic or technical value of the contribution.[23] Decisions made by the state and by similar administered systems could not be appealed, increasing the potential for misallocation of resources. Numerous examples indicate that awards did not have the force of contracts that could be prosecuted if the authorities failed to deliver on their promises. George Murray (1761–1803), an inventor of the telegraph, whose innovations contributed in part to the development of the Internet, was promised £16,500 but only received £2,000 and as a result died deeply in debt.

When the Fourdrinier brothers claimed compensation for improvements in papermaking machines, the recommendations in the parliamentary debates in 1840 ranged from £20,000 to nothing, but Parliament finally settled on £7,000 as a compromise.[24] Some felt "surprised at the smallness" of the accorded sum, while others such as the Chancellor of the Exchequer thought this payout would be a "very serious evil" that would encourage rent-seeking. Another Member of Parliament wished to increase the award to cover the £3,000 that Fourdrinier's son had spent on lobbying expenses. In a similarly arbitrary decision, Sir Humphry Davy received £2,000 for his invention of a safety lamp in 1816, whereas the uneducated artisan George Stephenson, who had resolved the same problem using more practical methods, was given just 100 guineas. Stephenson's supporters were so outraged at this blatant unfairness on the part of the government authorities that they raised a private subscription of £1,000, which they presented to him at a celebratory dinner.

As Adam Smith had cautioned, administrative decisions about who should be rewarded and how much should be given to them were often capricious and unpredictable from an economic perspective.[25] The allocation of public awards was often explicitly and demonstrably influenced by questions of social status.[26]

[23] Khan (2011). As William Kenrick warned (1774, p. 27), "There is indeed no little danger that both the quantum and the facility of obtaining of parliamentary premiums, may depend as well on personal interest as on particular ingenuity, or public utility . . . this method, of giving public encouragement to the authors of new inventions, is so liable to be perverted by partiality or prejudice, that it can, by no means, be consistent with sound policy to permit the indiscriminate application of individuals to be indulged in the use of it."

[24] Great Britain (1840, pp. 1328–30).

[25] "For if the legislature should appoint pecuniary rewards for the inventors of new machines, etc., they would hardly ever be so precisely proportional to the merit of the invention as this is. For here, if the invention be good and such as is profitable to mankind, he will probably make a fortune by it; but if it be of no value he will also reap no benefit" (Smith 1982, p. 103).

[26] "It is obvious that rewards of this nature were unequally distributed, and were apt to be the result not of merit but of influence. An inventor without merit might secure recognition through political agencies, and a man deserving recognition but lacking connection with parliamentary and ministerial forces was likely to be neglected. Minor improvements and devices or processes of dubious merit were at times the subjects of prolonged discussion, while many of the most important inventions were entirely unnoticed" (Bowden 1919, p. 12).

Parliament discussed at the same sitting awards to Edward Jenner for his work on vaccines and to Henry Greathead for his improvement in lifeboats. Greathead was a boatbuilder and thus belonged to a lower class than either Jenner or the members of Parliament who debated his merits. "Mr. Freere thought that in fixing rewards, the rank of the persons to whom they were to be given ought to be considered, and he could not but think that the sum of £1000 a proper remuneration to one in Mr. Greathead's circumstances." The Chancellor of the Exchequer agreed that "reference should be had to the condition in life of the person to be rewarded, and it would probably be felt, that in £1000 was a larger sum to Mr. Greathead, than £10,000 to Dr. Jenner."[27] Nevertheless, although Jenner was deemed superior to a boatbuilder, he was still not of the highest standing, and Parliamentarians objected that it would "pollute and desecrate the ground" if a statue to honor him were placed in Trafalgar Square.[28]

Scholars of NIS cite the successes of state intervention, largely drawn from military initiatives in the twentieth century. Government support of inventors and scientific research in Britain, however, was longstanding, and the lessons from this history are somewhat different from the claims of statists. The rosters of awards by administrators and government actors highlight the frequent lack of specialized knowledge among decision-makers, incorrect prices, unreliable promises, cognitive dissonance, and outright corruption, as well as high costs of lobbying and incentives for rent-seeking. Instead, the majority of a sample of eminent inventors in Britain who achieved financial and technical success did so in the marketplace, either by directly commercializing products or through their patents and intellectual property rights.

British Patents and Government Oversight

The early British patent system operated as a form of taxation by the government, rather than as a means of providing incentives for technological creativity. The system was an outgrowth of a classical regime of privileges, whereby the English Crown bestowed vast numbers of heritable monopoly rights to raise revenues and to reward favourites.[29] In 1624, the Statute of Monopolies codified existing

27 Mr. Grey and Sir M. W. Ridley "denied that Mr. Greathead was a man at all apt to be injured by £2000 or a much larger sum. He was a very intelligent and ingenious man, and had been long a respectable boat-builder." However, Greathead was awarded £1,000 and £200 to reimburse his stay in London, since the Chancellor had long delayed bringing the question of his compensation before Parliament (Woodfall 1802, pp. 421–22).

28 T. Duncombe, reported in British Medical Journal: BMJ Assoc, 1858, p. 398.

29 Members of the royal court and petty officers were not interested in offering incentives for riskier new inventions, they were primarily attracted by the more secure returns from monopoly rights to existing goods and markets. Hyde (1920, p. 17), notes that "The system of monopolies, designed originally to foster new arts, became degraded into a system of plunder."

common law policies by authorizing patent grants for 14 years as long as they were not "mischievous to the state."[30] Patentees paid extremely high fees that benefited the Crown and its administrators. Despite the statutory phrasing that implied patents were to be limited to actual inventors, exclusive rights could be obtained by the importers or introducers of inventions from overseas. Moreover, no examination was required to filter out invalid applications, and this registration system ensured that property rights were bestowed on the wealthy and well-connected who were able to pay the significant patent fees. Administrators who benefited from accrued payments constituted an interest group with strong incentives to block any policy reforms that would reduce their revenue stream.

Patent grants themselves were viewed as de facto monopolies. As such, judges construed patent rights narrowly and limited the options that patentees could exercise. Patent rules were enforced in the context of English common laws that prohibited contracts in restraint of trade, general agreements to refrain from competition, collusion between rivals to fix prices or to restrict output, and other anticompetitive practices that were likely to result in public harm. These limits to property were later formalized as working requirements, and licenses of right or compulsory licenses. The practice of using patents and associated joint-stock companies to engross existing industries continued, with the approbation of a Parliament that wished to ensure the continuity of businesses with connections to influential individuals and families. British industrial policy generally followed the principle of favoring specific businesses and interest groups, rather than promoting innovation and competition for the benefit of the general public.

Administrators of the patent system explicitly wished to limit the sorts of inventors that would be granted monopoly rights. Part of the advantage of costly patent fees was that the expense served to deter working class inventors from obtaining property rights in invention, and the stated assumption was that only elites were capable of making valuable contributions.[31] Moreover, the number of outside investors in patent rights was restricted, which limited the ability of impecunious inventors to mobilize funding in venture capital markets. As a result of the costly fees and limitations on inventive capital markets, patented inventions in Britain tended to be highly capital intensive, and many patentees belonged to the class of elite or well-connected inventors. These features served to inhibit the efforts of relatively disadvantaged groups such as working-class inventors and women. For instance, as Table 8.3 shows, British women in general were less likely to obtain patents than female inventors in the United States, and over 35 percent of female British patentees were drawn from the professional and elite classes.[32]

[30] The Statute of Monopolies, 1623–24, 21 Jac. c. 3, § 6 (Eng.).
[31] Khan (2005).
[32] For more details, see Khan (2017a).

Table 8.3 Occupations of women inventors in Britain, France, and the United States, 1790–1920

	United States		Britain	France	
Occupations	Patents (%)	Exhibits (%)	Patents (%)	Patents (%)	Exhibits (%)
Artisan/worker	26.9	11.7	8.8	10.6	8.8
Artist/designer	6.4	32.9	7	0	5.7
Businesswoman	18.4	2.5	5.3	9	7.6
Corsetmaker	9.7	3.2	7	9.8	5
Manufacturer	19.3	28.6	24.6	47.4	62.6
Mechanical	3.5	3.9	5.3	0	4.1
Professional/elite	11.1	7.8	35.1	17.9	6
Teacher	4.7	9.5	7	5.3	0.3
Percentage who did not work outside the home	33.7	41.1	45.7	38.0	50.5

Notes: The percentages for jobs outside the home are based on all women with listed occupations, exclusive of those who did not work outside the home (keeping house, at home, none).

Sources: Occupations in the United States were obtained from city directories, and from the manuscript federal population census. British occupations were included in patent documents and in the population census. French occupations were drawn from the patent documents and from the reports of industrial exhibitions.

Patents comprised a royally bestowed privilege, which meant that "Crown use" enabled the British government to expropriate or use any patented invention without making payments or even acknowledging the rights of the inventor.[33] In 1872, the case of *Dixon v. The London Small Arms Company* raised the question of whether the Crown could delegate the right to infringe without legal repercussions. The War Department had been acting on the assumption that, as the Queen's agents, they could enter into agreements with rifle manufacturers who would inherit this immunity and be indemnified against patentees' claims, and could therefore infringe on patented inventions as freely as the Crown. The War Department issued a memorandum noting that "the companies should be protected by the department against the patentees in the manufacture of the

[33] Terrell (1895, p. 150). See *Feather v. Regina*, 6 B. & S. 257.

arms to be contracted for." The judicial ruling held that employees of the Crown did indeed have the right to expropriate patented inventions.[34]

Royal Commissions on Awards to Inventors (RCAI) were convened to consider remuneration to patentees and inventors for government usage of their inventions during wartime. These commissions included government officials and technical experts, as well as consultants, whose deliberations illustrate the difficulties that arise when administrators supplant the price system. The first commission paid out some £1.5 million for a few hundred cases from a total of over 1,800 claims that were submitted after World War I, in hearings that dragged on for many years.[35] Their deliberations about key inventions such as the development of the tank revealed the extent to which status and connections influenced administered military technological decisions and outcomes. For instance, in 1912 the British War Office received a design for a tank which the RCAI admitted was a "very brilliant invention which anticipated and in some respects surpassed that actually put into use in the year 1916." This invention was submitted (twice) by an unknown Australian, Lancelot de Mole, but the War Office completely ignored his proposals, so he received no compensation from the RCAI. Whereas, a British Colonel, who merely declared that a large share of the credit for the tank belonged to him, was awarded £1,000.[36]

Surprisingly, World War II led to smaller total payments. But there was much larger variance in the individual awards, to patentees primarily in telecommunications and wireless technologies, armaments, and aeronautics. The work of this second committee was even slower and largely ineffective, and after an entire decade they had paid out total compensation of just £600,000. Of this amount, Sir Frank Whittle, the engineer who helped to invent the turbojet engine and gas turbines, received £100,000, in part because the Ministry of Supply lobbied the committee on his behalf.[37] The RCAI also allocated £50,000 to Sir Watson-Watt, one of a large team of contributors to the development of radar. In short, fully 25 percent of the payments over a period of ten years went to just two prominent inventors.

The Earl of Denbigh had earlier on highlighted the deficiencies and conflicts of interest arising from public rewards for inventors, especially in the context

[34] The Justice of the Peace, Volume 39, London: Henry Shaw, 1875, pp. 86–87. The statutory reforms of 1883 required the Crown to offer compensation for patentees whose rights were overturned.

[35] The United States had been informed that the total liability for usage of patented inventions would amount to $50.7 million and that the United States would be responsible for covering 4 percent of this total payment. Based on this estimate, the United States appropriated $40,000 to cover the expenses of envoys who participated in the deliberations of the committee.

[36] For further details, see Smithers (1986).

[37] Giffard (2016). Whittle accumulated numerous prizes and honors, including the Draper Prize award of $185,000, and his estate was valued at £673,000.

of inventions that the War Office had administered.[38] Denbigh pointed to the enormous waste in resources, noting that "where one invention had succeeded and been adopted into the service, many had failed and been found wanting." These government bodies frequently made mistakes or showed inconsistencies in their decisions, such as when the Admiralty offered £15,000 for the rights to an untested fish torpedo, while another such device by a different inventor, that had been successfully commercialized, was rejected. Some officials had exploited their positions to profit from the ideas submitted by inventors, who were "brought into collision with the officials of the Government, who from interested reasons or professional jealousy might be disposed to throw obstacles in the way of a fair estimate of the inventor's claims to recompense."

Representatives of the artisanal working class similarly objected to the inefficiencies of the administered systems that prevailed in Britain. They noted that non-market institutions of this nature "give more power to Government . . . It would tax the whole nation for the benefit of a few. Only a small portion of the nation derives any immediate advantage from an invention. No competent judge or tribunal could be found for carrying such a scheme into effect. No plan upon this basis would work satisfactorily, and the whole odium of maladministration would be cast upon the men who directed the machinery, instead of, as at present, upon a system or upon the laws of human progress. It is not the business of Government or any of its agents to bestow rewards, or to stimulate invention."[39]

French National Innovation System

Administered Systems in France

France provides the closest historical analogue to a "national innovation system" that has continuously operated in dirigiste mode for three centuries through to the modern period. A number of observers point to the French experience as a successful example of how governments and elites can promote positive outcomes. However, France was an early leader in scientific achievements and technological discoveries, but rapidly lost its initial advantage. It is therefore worth considering whether this decline in comparative advantage in part owed to the net costs of administration relative to markets.

[38] Great Britain (1871). Lord Northbrook bridled at the suggestion that any impropriety had occurred, since "on that Council there were the Surveyor General of Ordnance, the Financial Secretary, the Adjutant General, the Inspector General of Artillery, the Inspector General of Fortifications, and other high officials," indicating that the administration "afforded no ground for the imputation of prejudice."

[39] Mechanics' Magazine, 1861, p. 163.

The French experience indeed offers insight into the operation of an extensive national innovation system, that spanned the entire portfolio of government incentives and institutions that could be directed to influence industrial change and innovation. This comprehensive array of publicly administered rewards and incentives was part of an import substitution strategy, designed to increase the nation's standing relative to England and other industrial competitors.[40] Inventors and importers or introducers of inventions could profit from appointment to the nobility, lifetime pensions, assistance to spouses and offspring, interest-free loans, lump-sum grants, bounties or subsidies, tax exemptions, gifts of land and other assets, royal employment, as well as a host of other pecuniary and nonmonetary benefits. Large numbers of exclusive privileges were allocated to applicants, especially those who were well-connected and could find favor with members of the court or influential statesmen.[41]

Numerous panels of administrators were marshalled in Paris and around the country to assess thousands of petitions for awards from hopeful parties, in an ever-changing institutional context.[42] For instance, in 1791 the state-appointed members of the Bureau of Consultation of Arts and the Trades included 30 appointees, and only six years later this Bureau was replaced by the National Institute of the Sciences and Arts. Members of these boards deliberated about the submitted inventions, recommended whether or not rewards should be bestowed on the petitioners, the amount that should be given, and the terms of the grant. National institutions were replicated by, and overlapped with, regional and local analogues; and often it was necessary for a petitioner to negotiate with several different organizations with evolving rules in order to achieve a single objective. These procedures created a class of professional supplicants, many of whom had no intention of commercializing their products and instead directed their efforts to arbitrage among the many potential administrative channels for state compensation.

[40] See, for instance, Hilaire-Pérez (2000).

[41] As one study notes: "The government was eager to develop the nation's economic life, and to this end made heavy subsidies . . . Unfortunately the government had no uniform policy for all inventors. Some it aided financially; others it did not. More flagrantly inconsistent was its policy of granting monopolistic rights in many lines to court favorites, so that the greater number enjoying exclusive privileges were not inventors" (McCloy 2015, p. 171).

[42] The French state and key ministries such as the Conseil d'Etat and the Conseil d'Administration du Commerce et des Manufacturers actively engaged in economic and innovation policies. A central hub in this nexus was the powerful Ministry of the Interior, which supervised the Conseil General du Commerce and the Conseil General des Manufactures. The second tier of the ministry's portfolio included the Bureau d'Agriculture, Bureau de Commerce (overseeing the Chambres de Commerce), Bureau de la Balance du Commerce, Bureau des Arts et Manufactures (overseeing the Chambres consultatives des Arts et Manufactures, the Bureau consultative des Arts et Manufactures, and the Conseils de Prud'hommes), Bureau de Statistique, and the Bureau des Subsistances. Similar institutions operated at the provincial level and among the municipalities, adding another layer of complexity and potential inconsistency.

French innovation policies thus transmuted a potential market for inventions into a political market for favors to special interests. In an administered system of pleas and negotiations, returns were not simply based on the underlying technical or economic value of the discovery. For innovators, outcomes were decidedly probabilistic since, even when assured of assistance, they could not rely on politically motivated promises. Mechanisms to enforce such contracts were limited, and participants did not have the right of appeal to legal rules based on a stock of analogous precedents. Obviously, the risk of hold up or outright expropriation was heightened if the inventor had already made large fixed investments with low resale value. Other things being equal, expected rewards were positively associated with influential patrons who could convince committee members that it would be worthwhile to accept a particular project, and also signal that it would be costly for the decision-makers if the petition were rejected or if bargains were not honored. As Liliane Hilaire-Perez aptly noted, in France "to invent meant to go into politics."[43]

The Société d'encouragement pour l'industrie nationale (SENI) provides a canonical example of the French network of administered innovation. This national institution was founded in 1801 to provide state sponsorship of technological and industrial developments throughout France.[44] The objectives of the society included the assessment of new inventions, support for inventors, the publication of a bulletin, and other means to disseminate information about discoveries. The initial focus was on employing honorary and pecuniary awards as the central policy instrument for encouraging technological innovations. However, as the inefficiency of this prize system was increasingly evident, the institution became more involved in providing support and funding for laboratories and R&D.

As in other French institutions, individual administrators wielded a marked degree of personal patronage and influence within the ostensibly rational bureaucratic structure. The formidable Jean-Antoine Chaptal, Comte de Chanteloup, chemist and minister of interior, cofounded and served as the first president of SENI. Chaptal was inspired by the popular myth of the central contributions that the RSA in London had made to British industrial progress, and SENI's own "founding myth" claimed that the institution was organized purely through private initiatives.[45] Throughout its first century most of the administrators, committees, and members were drawn from the elite circles of aristocrats, scientists, politicians, professors, bankers, and wealthy manufacturers; while

[43] Hilaire-Pérez (2000).

[44] This section is largely based on my own perusal of several thousand pages of handwritten committee reports, stored in the attic of the society's headquarters in Saint-Germain des Prés, Paris.

[45] Butrica (1998).

artisans, machinists and technicians, and ordinary businessmen were poorly represented.

In accordance with its charter, the society's primary objective was to promote economic development by furthering technological innovation and manufacturing, and the award of prizes to induce inventiveness was considered to be a central part of achieving this mission. SENI published an annual list of proposed areas where it sought to attract applicants for cash prizes, medals, and "encouragements" or other support for projects. The list identified the problem, in specific terms in some cases and quite broad, vague phrases in others, along with the monetary value of the award at stake. Foreigners, as well as French inventors, were allowed to apply for benefits, although the former were required to cede the property rights to their ideas to SENI.

The society was able to point to a number of achievements. In particular, it offered valuable support for heavy industry and metals, including forges, locomotives, machine tools, and steam engines, and at times sponsored systematic research and development initiatives among multiple award winners. Marguerite-Marie Degrand, an entrepreneur who made remarkable contributions to scientific and industrial advances in France, became one of its rare female members. In 1819, the society awarded her an honorable mention, reporting in its Bulletin that "Mme Degrand knows how to make a type of Damascus steel which the Turks might take for a product made in their own country. It is a veritable conquest over the East which enriches our industry." SENI later bestowed its Grand Medal on Degrand for her contributions to French industry and innovation, and this likely enhanced her already lofty standing and reputation.

A more representative perspective on the work of the society can be obtained from archival data on the subject matter for the total amount of prizes granted during the first half century of SENI's existence (Table 8.4). The percentage distribution by value indicates the relative importance of the awards during this critical period, suggesting the prizes were not aligned with the economic value of innovations for the individual industry. Awards for the domestic cultivation of sugar beets and sugar production accounted for 9.3 percent of prizes, compared to a mere 1.2 percent for locomotives, and it is not clear why sugar should have been viewed as more meritorious than transportation. The ceramics industry obtained a surprising 12.7 percent of funding, while fine arts and music received 11 percent of the prizes and encouragements. The criteria for some grants were associated with inventive novelty and higher productivity, but others were less related to technological excellence and included justifications that ranged from close imitation of foreign goods, to good workmanship and the beauty of an item, and even references to the moral character of the applicants and their relatives.

Table 8.4 Awards of the French Society for the Encouragement of National Industry, 1802–1851 (French Francs)

Category	Prizes	%	Medals and Other	%	Total	%
Agriculture	28,600	12.3	21,980	8.3	50,580	10.1
Beaux-Arts	16,100	6.9	32,040	12.1	48,140	9.7
Boats	11,000	4.7	8,935	3.4	19,935	4.0
Ceramics	34,700	14.9	28,810	10.8	63,510	12.7
Chemical products	6,600	2.8	2,480	0.9	9,080	1.8
Clocks and opticals	0	0.0	8,575	3.2	8,575	1.7
Domestic economy	1,200	0.5	1,000	0.4	2,200	0.4
Dyes	0	0.0	3,990	1.5	3,990	0.8
Foods	8,500	3.6	9,150	3.4	17,650	3.5
Forges	0	0.0	11,050	4.2	11,050	2.2
Hats and shoes	4,000	1.7	3,930	1.5	7,930	1.6
Heat and light	9,000	3.9	9,670	3.6	18,670	3.7
Legacies	0	0.0	16,613	6.3	16,613	3.3
Locomotives	0	0.0	6,185	2.3	6,185	1.2
Machine tools	8,500	3.6	23,350	8.8	31,850	6.4
Metals	22,000	9.4	11,180	4.2	33,180	6.7
Music	2,000	0.9	4,495	1.7	6,495	1.3
Orthopedics	1,000	0.4	5,315	2.0	6,315	1.3
Paper	5,000	2.1	3,030	1.1	8,030	1.6
Political economy	0	0.0	1,500	0.6	1,500	0.3
Prize Argenteuil	24,000	10.3	0	0.0	24,000	4.8
Steam engines	17,500	7.5	15,900	6.0	33,400	6.7
Sugar	21,700	9.3	6,620	2.5	28,320	5.7
Weapons	0	0.0	795	0.3	795	0.2
Weaving	11,800	5.1	27,665	10.4	39,465	7.9
Wines	0	0.0	1,280	0.5	1,280	0.3
Total	233,200	100	265,538	100	498,738	100

Source: *Annuaire de la Société d'Encouragement pour L'industrie Nationale* (Paris, 1852).

Part of the disconnect between the decisions of the society and practical artisans or manufacturing enterprises lay in the tendency for the elaborate or complicated to attract favorable notice, even if a simple outcome might be more feasible or profitable. An example is the prize of 3,000 francs the society offered in 1818 for the best means of producing artesian wells. Just three entries were received and the winner, M. Garnier, an engineer at the elite Royal Corps of Mines, provided detailed specifications of his proposed solution. Numerous copies of Garnier's report were printed up and distributed to various government officials, at the expense of the state. The *American Quarterly Review* declared that Garnier's work was impressive in offering extremely convoluted propositions for achieving the desired end, but "whether all the minutiae that he has laid down in his work be essential to the boring of these Artesian wells, is left for the consideration of the French." The US reviewer added blandly that in America "the case is different; we adopt a more simple process."[46]

Jury members were generally appointed as a means of honoring the individual in question, rather than because they were technically qualified to make such determinations. Juries made awards that were often based on questionable judgements about the marketability of the inventions that were presented. They selected uneconomical devices because they were substitutes for foreign imports, or were overly optimistic about the extent to which the submissions for prizes were likely to succeed as commercial products. The Franklin Institute of Philadelphia reported an award that the Society for the Encouragement of National Industry had offered for improvements in the art of lithographic printing.[47] M. Tudot had submitted a plan to use rollers made with costly, soft calf skin that distributed ink evenly over paper. His rollers were far more expensive than the existing seamed models, but he received the prize because the judges "confidently" expected that once it went into manufacture, the high price of the rollers would eventually fall to a more economical level.

As the RSA had shown, accounts of such institutions typically emphasize successes but omit consideration of failures or nonresponses. The SENI report for 1820 declared that 184,000 francs had been offered as prizes since the founding of the institution, whereas only 41.6 percent of this sum was actually granted. In some instances, the prize was withdrawn because the problem had already been resolved elsewhere, or because no applicants were deemed worthy. Such decisions provide positive indications that attention was being paid to the progress of the specific technology and that standards were being maintained.

[46] American Quarterly Review, Volume 22, 1837, p. 331.
[47] Anon (1832, p. 284).

However, in many other areas, the award remained unclaimed throughout its history because nobody had been "induced" by the offer: because the award was too low or the problem was insoluble or uninteresting. In general, the lack of productive and disinterested results from the state-sponsored, administered system led to the formation of private substitutes, such as the Société générale de contrôle et de garantie alimentaires, which hired its own chemists to verify the safety of foods.[48] The overall patterns for encouragement societies in France thus mirror similar administered innovation systems in England.

French Patents and Government Oversight

French innovation institutions, despite the democratic rhetoric, functioned in a manner that reflected the elitist biases in Britain. Patents were similarly granted through a registration system, where the sole filter was the ability to pay costly fees. After 1844, the fees amounted to 500 francs (approximately one year's average income) for a 5-year patent, 1,000 francs for a 10-year patent, and 1,500 for a patent of 15 years.[49] Figure 8.1 reports the occupational distribution of patentees in general and, as the data on women inventors similarly showed, members of the nobility and manufacturers obtained a disproportionate number of patents in the nineteenth century. Key contributory factors for the bias against the poor included the high price of patent protection, the ability to obtain property rights without necessarily being the original creator, the lack of government assurance regarding the validity of the grant, and the uncertainty of enforcement at law. Working requirements further necessitated setting up a manufacturing establishment, which could be avoided with the exercise of legal ingenuity, but the need to justify a "non-practicing" strategy comprised an added transaction and monetary cost that disadvantaged unconnected inventors. The underlying uncertainty of the property right in patents increased the difficulties for impecunious inventors who wished to mobilize venture capital through the marketplace.

Legal statutes included further provisions that encouraged rent-seeking rather than commercialization through individual initiative. The patent decree of 1790 allowed that "when the inventor prefers to deal directly with the government, he is free to petition either the administrative assemblies or the legislature, if appropriate, to turn over his discovery, after demonstrating its merits and soliciting a reward." In other words, the inventor of a discovery of proven utility could

48 Fressoz (2007).

49 See Morrisson and Snyder (2000), who estimate that average annual income in 1831 was 573 francs.

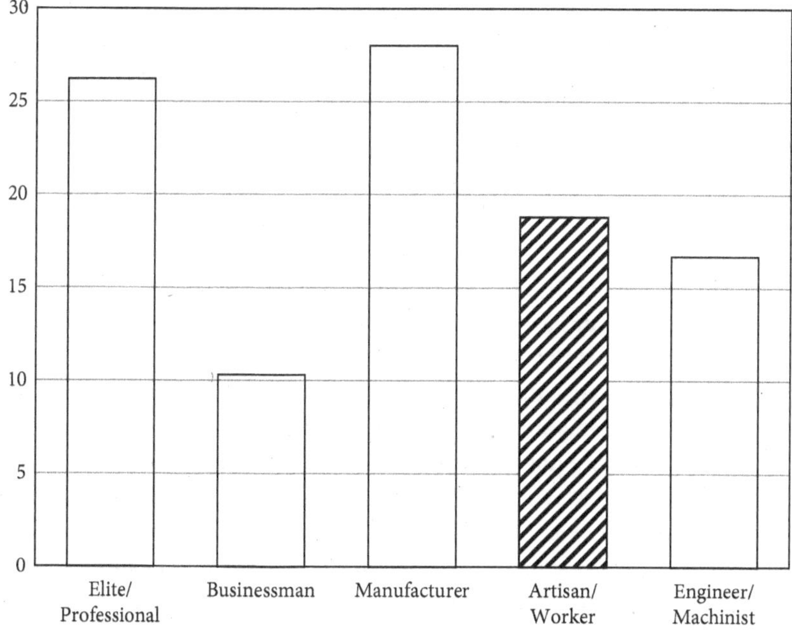

Figure 8.1 Occupations of patent inventors in France, 1791–1855.
Source: Sample of patents from Ministère de l'agriculture, *Catalogue des brevets d'invention d'importation et de perfectionnement*, various years, categorized into the industry of final use.

choose between a patent or making a gift of the invention to the nation in exchange for an award from funds that were set aside for the encouragement of industry. Instead of efforts to engage in private enterprise, patentees and inventors had an incentive to lobby the state for upfront benefits for their discoveries which (they assured) were guaranteed to assure the French of world leadership in that particular industry.

Adjacent Institutions in France

Protectionist agendas on the part of the state melded well with the interests of domestic innovators who were not necessarily competitive in the market place. According to David Landes, the French entrepreneurial state unsuccessfully attempted to force "hothouse growth" and transformed individual innovators into dependent "functionaries" of the state.[50] The French approach to technology

50 Landes (1949).

policy certainly illustrates the analogues between the eighteenth-century world of privileges and the allegedly more rational and objective administered approach to innovation. In both cases, these arrangements can be regarded as an exchange between a largely closed group of statist technocrats, who allocated compensation and resources, and a broader class of demanders, who were well aware of the idiosyncratic nature of the transactions that would determine their fortunes and attempted to reduce the resulting uncertainty through investments in rent-seeking.

Scholars of mobility in France are struck by the strong degree of continuity in socioeconomic status across generations and by the extent to which class and power were replicated through the educational hierarchy.[51] The overall philosophy of the French educational system was based on "an ingrained belief that manual work was undignified, the province of the lower classes, whereas intellectual work was more noble, and suited uniquely for the upper class."[52] These class-oriented biases were replicated in the pedagogical approach to science, engineering, and technology. The elite state professional schools such as the École Polytechnique, the École des Mines, and the École des Ponts et Chaussées ("the grandest of the grandes écoles") gave preferment to the upper classes who could satisfy the preparation, admissions process, and expenses that were required for entry. Most of the students at the École Polytechnique in the first half of the nineteenth century were the sons of prominent men from the military, state administrators, and wealthy professionals; by design, few were from the business or manufacturing sector and almost none from the working class.[53] In contrast, the disdained Écoles d'Arts et Metiers primarily offered manual training in jobs with few prospects of socioeconomic advancement. It might be argued that the curriculum of the top schools provided valuable human capital that explains the relationship with income and employment. However, this was hardly the case, since their classes emphasized rote learning in pure theory, classical studies in Greek and Latin, and abstract mathematics, with little attention to critical reasoning, original research or practical applications.

Engineers and graduates of the grandes écoles obtained favored positions through the interlocking relationship of these institutions with the state bureaucracy. The state reserved its most powerful and highly paid positions for elite engineers from the upper social classes in the Ponts et Chaussées, Mines, Génie Maritime, Génie Militaire, Artilleries, Manufactures de l'État, Hydrographie, Poudres et Saltpêtres, and Télégraphes. Civil engineering jobs were regarded as less important, and these employees typically belonged to the middle classes,

51 Anderson (1982).
52 Kranakis (1989).
53 See Daumard (1958, p. 12).

whereas the practical jobs for machinists and other skilled artisans were left to the lower classes. The elitist structure of education and employment had negative implications for the allocation of talent and for technological progress.

In short, the welter of administered policies toward innovation in France provide an excellent model of a national innovation system in historical perspective. Conscious linkages between the state, industry, and higher education resulted in uncoordinated and often conflicting initiatives that encouraged inventors to engage in rent-seeking and to arbitrage multiple awards across disparate agencies. When combined with a bias toward elites, both in the centers of decision-making and in the recipients of favors, this top-down dominance of relevant institutions by bureaucrats and elites contributed to an ossified economic and social structure. In an era of industrialization that required the capacity to initiate and respond to rapid changes in the marketplace, the French national innovation system and its adjacent institutions created inhibitions for private entrepreneurship and initiative whose repercussions are still evident today.

Inventing the US Knowledge Economy

Early Innovation Policies

The "founding" of American institutions is often presented as an epiphany experienced by a cadre of extraordinary individuals. The intellectual property clause of the Constitution especially might project this aura of inevitability because it was passed unanimously and without debate, with the intent to "promote the Progress of Science and useful Arts, by securing for limited Times to Authors and Inventors the exclusive Right to their respective Writings and Discoveries." Instead, it is worth noting that the Founders' choices were initially expansive and fluid, before crystallizing into an innovation system that was unique in its objective and structure relative to any other in the world.

Many of the European innovation policies were prevalent in the early American colonies. Americans recognized the importance of technological innovation, implemented a wide range of policy instruments to further manufactures and inventions, and engaged in close government regulation of business.[54] Strategies included monopoly privileges in the form of patents of introduction, bounties, grants, and other encouragements for infant enterprises and imported discoveries. Typically, patent grants were conditioned on compliance with strict conditions, such as maximum prices, minimum quantities

[54] For further details, see Khan (2010).

produced and marketed, compulsory licensing, and working requirements. Innovation prizes, or premiums, were regarded as a particularly desirable instrument for the inducement or reward of inventions. In 1775 the Continental Congress "recommended to the several Provincial Conventions, to grant such premiums, . . . as may be judged proper." The influential Alexander Hamilton was also a strong supporter of the use of premiums as an integral element of a national innovation policy.[55]

In the early Republic, the legislature's deliberate and conscious process of selection from among existing alternatives resulted in innovation policies that provided a marked contrast to historical precedent in the American colonies and in other countries. The Commerce Clause of the US Constitution notably authorized federal oversight of interstate economic activity.[56] Since transactions across state lines were strongly affected by technologies that facilitated connections between places and people, it is not surprising that federal policies were typically directed toward innovations in transportation and communications. Many of these technologies were associated with economies of scale and industrial concentration, which raised questions about how to supervise and order business conduct to best promote efficient outcomes. These debates often addressed whether it was advisable for the government to acquire controlling interests in businesses, with advocates of nationalization invoking European precedents favoring government ownership.

According to some researchers, "state capacity" was a primary factor in explaining the progress of American technology, and they test this hypothesis by using the extent of postal services as a proxy for state capacity.[57] The Post Office was an anomalous institution, however.[58] The Postal Service monopoly is a rare and unrepresentative example where the advocates of nationalization prevailed,

[55] See, for instance, the Report on Manufactures (1791), recommending a fund: "to induce the prosecution and introduction of useful discoveries, inventions and improvements, by proportionate rewards, judiciously held out and applied—to encourage by premiums both honorable and lucrative the exertions of individuals . . . It may confidently be affirmed that there is scarcely any thing, which has been devised, better calculated to excite a general spirit of improvement than the institutions of this nature. They are truly invaluable."

[56] U.S. CONST. art I., § 8, cl. 3. The landmark Supreme Court decision in *Gibbons v. Ogden*, 22 U.S. (9 Wheat.) 1 (1824) affirmed that the Constitution granted Congress the right to regulate interstate commerce. As with many antitrust cases since, Gibbons decided the scope of monopoly rights over a new technology; in this instance, the steamboat. Gibbons provided the legal foundation for federal regulation of American enterprise, both through the regulation of natural monopolies and the Sherman Act.

[57] Acemoglu, Moscona, and Robinson (2016).

[58] Direct employment in the United States federal government in the early nineteenth century was primarily in the postal and military services. In 1900, total government expenditures accounted for approximately 7 percent of gross national output. That pattern changed dramatically over the twentieth century, but the expansion in scale did not result in a fundamental change in scope, until after the "defining moment" of the Great Depression. Sunstein (1987) discusses the way in which the regulatory administration of the New Deal has failed to incorporate the checks and balances embodied in the Constitution.

resulting in the oldest government-owned enterprise in the United States. The Constitution gave Congress the right to establish postal roads and post offices, and was held to authorize the federal government to retain a monopoly over the industry.[59]

Joseph Nock's dealings with the Post Office provide an early example indicating that government affiliates would be subject to the same laws as other participants in the market place and held especially accountable in their interactions with inventors and "meritorious patentees."[60] Nock was an award-winning lock and key maker from Philadelphia, who had obtained two patents in 1838 and 1839 for a new means of manufacturing locks, which together were valued at $80,000. He entered into an agreement whereby his patent rights were partially assigned to the Post Office; to fulfill the contract he moved his business and family to Washington, DC, to manufacture locks for the postal service. The Post Office reneged on the contract, leading to his bankruptcy and loss of patent rights.[61] He appealed to the Senate, which repudiated the Post Office's allegations, and awarded him damages of approximately $22,000 plus interest.

Complaints against the Postal Service were continually voiced about poor service, oppressive prices, lack of innovation, and even corruption. Private providers such as Lysander Spooner's American Letter Mail Company began service in contravention of the ban on private delivery, and the emergence of such private competition led to steep declines in postal rates and revenues.[62] In response, postal officials harassed private carriers with lawsuits, and many were arrested. Transportation firms were held vicariously liable for the conveyance of private letters in violation of the Postal Service exclusive franchise. Congress enacted legislation in 1845 to reinforce government control of the industry, and significant fines were levied against private firms that attempted to make incursions into the monopoly. Regardless of the attempts to shore up its market power, the Postal Service provided a cautionary tale that ultimately *reduced* public support for government entry into business and innovation.

The Louisville and Portland Canal provides another perspective on federal policies toward monopoly and the public interest, as it was possibly the first

[59] See the 1825 "Act to reduce into one the several acts establishing and regulating the post-office department," United States Official Postal Guide 35 (1859).

[60] Report to accompany bill S. No. 625, 32nd Congress, 2d. Session, 1853.

[61] The case was prolonged on technical issues, and Nock was finally awarded approximately $27,500 (see *Nock v. the United States*, 1866, Court of Claims).

[62] Lysander Spooner deliberately set out to break the Postal Service monopoly, offering competing services at prices significantly below the official rates. Many newspapers reported on his conflict with the Post Office, observing that "the persons engaged in this enterprise contend that the laws of Congress prohibiting private mails are unconstitutional, and they are anxious to have them tested on this point as speedily as possible," Philadelphia Inquirer, 18 January 1844, 2. Spooner and several private letter carriers were arrested.

private enterprise to be transformed into a US government-owned corporation.[63] In this case, the government was backed into ownership: the canal's private investors were anxious to divest themselves of a losing proposition and engineered a gradual buyout by withholding dividend payments to the government. However, the Post Office and the Louisville and Portland Canal proved to be anomalies; unlike most other countries, in the United States the response to monopoly concerns was not national ownership of enterprise, but arms-length regulation by legislative and legal institutions.

Congress occasionally ceded to requests for funding to support business interests that were deemed to be in the national interest. Lobbyists pointed to the example of Europe, where the French state offered large sums to support transatlantic shipping services, as did England and several other seafaring European nations. Despite strong opposition, and a very narrow majority vote in the Senate on the measure, Congress likewise appropriated annual subsidies for the operation of ocean-going steam liners. The rationale was that the subsidy was necessary to match the French and British policies, and to ensure US competitiveness in the international market. As a result, the Edward K. Collins steamship line was established to transport mail between New York and Liverpool 20 times each year.[64] The initial contract in 1847 promised government outlays of $19,250 for each roundtrip, but the venture proved unprofitable. Collins requested further aid, leading to a net government expenditure of approximately $800,000 each year between 1853 and 1855.

Subsidies toward any particular endeavor essentially functioned as a relative tax on alternatives that were not similarly supported. Cornelius Vanderbilt protested that "it is utterly impossible for a private individual to stand in competition with a line drawing nearly $1 million per annum from the national treasury, without serious sacrifice."[65] Vanderbilt was probably not averse to receiving a share of government funding as well, but he nevertheless launched his own steamship line in 1855 as a wholly private enterprise. Other competitors, such as the Inman line and the American line, also plied the transatlantic trade without any help from the government. Despite the federal payout, the Collins corporation struggled to survive in the international market, and its shareholders never received any dividends. The federal subsidy was withdrawn, and bankruptcy was declared in 1858. Further attempts to revive the policies of offering large public grants for transatlantic shipping projects achieved little success, meeting with

[63] See Trescott (1958). The waterway was critical to Western commerce; it bypassed the Ohio Falls, the only significant obstacle along the well-traveled Ohio River.

[64] Fowler (2017). I am grateful to Michael Andrews for pointing out this example of government policy.

[65] Barney (1856, p. 5).

the caustic rejoinder that the example of France and its national imitators in state activism could "hardly be appealed to as successful."[66]

France had a longstanding interest in military aeronautics, dating back to its employment of hot-air balloons and dirigibles early in the nineteenth century and, on the eve of World War I, led the world in government support for the aviation industry. By contrast, any US government support for new technologies was sporadic and transient, as the aeronautical industry further illustrates.[67] In 1898, President McKinley authorized an appropriation to aid scientist Samuel Langley in developing aircraft, as part of a military strategy. Langley, Secretary of the Smithsonian, quickly spent down some $50,000 in government funding, as well as a further sum of $20,000 from the Smithsonian Institution. The Board of Ordnance and Fortification, which administered the support to Langley, rejected competing designs from other aircraft inventors because they regarded them as less applicable for the military sector. Langley's scientific approach to manned flight failed and led to widespread censure in Congress (one member scathingly stated that "the only thing [Langley] made fly was Government money"). As a result, board policy in 1904 stipulated that aeronautic devices "must have been brought to the stage of practical operation without expense to the government." That was the response they offered when rejecting the application of the Wright Brothers the following year.

The greatest test of the American belief in decentralized enterprise occurred in markets for information technology and telecommunications that have since been deemed "natural monopolies." Technological innovations such as the telegraph and more efficient transatlantic shipping expanded the size and complexity of national and international markets. Many of the "great inventions" of the era were associated with enormous economies of scale and industrial concentration, which raised questions about how to supervise and order business conduct to assure socially efficient outcomes. These debates often addressed whether it was advisable for the government to acquire controlling interests in businesses, with advocates of nationalization invoking European precedents favoring government ownership and administered systems.

The telegraph emerged in the 1840s as the first commercially viable means of interstate electronic communication and raised questions about the role of the government in confronting natural monopolies or instances where economies of scale were so prevalent that only a few firms could survive in the market.[68] In most European countries, the telegraph was regarded as essential for the military and national security and was either owned or operated by the state. The French

66 Lalor (1884, p. 821).
67 Parkinson (1963).
68 Standage (1998).

government constructed an early telegraph system in 1845 and monopolized its use until 1850, arguing that "the telegraph must be a political, and not a commercial, instrument."[69] In England, private enterprise introduced the telegraph, but the government nationalized the industry in 1870 and turned its control over to the state-owned Post Office.[70]

Similar arguments for government ownership were put before Congress, but lobbyists for the Postal Service, who wished to acquire the telegraph operations, were soundly defeated. Although the US Congress funded the first telegraph line between Baltimore and Washington, government oversight of the developing telecommunications sector was minimal, and the industry was soon dominated by the Western Union Corporation.[71] Western Union was the object of extensive legislative efforts to restrain its monopoly power but, despite widespread concerns, the telegraph remained a private enterprise in the United States. The decision not to nationalize the telegraph was due to a realization that the buyout and operation would be an unprofitable drain on the exchequer and the unpopularity of such measures among the US electorate.

Public aversion to government control over key innovations was temporarily defeated during public crises such as during the Great War, but (apart from the government monopoly on postal service) the United States generally avoided public ownership and instead opted for regulation of varying degrees. In particular, judicial intervention had important implications for the oversight of railroad, telegraph, and telephone enterprises. The telephone industry, like the telegraph, reflected a distinctly American approach to addressing natural monopolies in new technologies and raised similar issues regarding the limits of the legitimate exercise of monopoly power in an emerging technology. In Britain, the telephone system was nationalized in 1912 as an extension of the state's post office monopoly, but this option was rejected in the United States.

Alexander Graham Bell received the key patents for the electric speaking telephone and assigned the patent rights to the American Bell Telephone Company, a Massachusetts corporation that was ultimately reorganized as American Telephone & Telegraph, one of the most dominant firms in US history.[72] After Congress rejected yet another bill seeking to regulate the prices charged for telephony, Bell executives observed that the measure was defeated largely because

[69] Kieve (1973).

[70] Holcombe (1906).

[71] See Postmaster General (1914). Telegraphy diffused so rapidly that, by 1851, 75 companies with over 20,000 miles of wire were in operation. Western Union came from a consolidation of regional telegraph companies in 1851 and by 1866 accounted for more than 90 percent of the market. The company was the target of almost 100 legislative initiatives that proposed to limit its reach and constrain its "monopoly of knowledge."

[72] "The Telephone Monopoly: Annual Meeting of the American Bell Company," *New York Times*, 28 March 1888, 3. In 1887, American Bell reported total revenues of $3.45 million relative to expenditures of $1.24 million and had 6,000 employees on its roster.

legislators were persuaded by the firm's claim that rapid innovation in the industry required constant updates and investment costs, which public enterprise was ill-suited to administer.

Patents and the Market for Inventions

The first article of the US Constitution reflected the national commitment to promoting technological progress through a market-based patent system. Contemporary observers attributed an important role to the US patent system in influencing the rate of industrialization and economic growth. The United States deliberately introduced novel patent policies that were designed to stimulate individual initiative, independently of the identity of the inventor, rather than to confer special benefits for special classes. The patent applicant was not a petitioner for a privilege; instead, all true inventors had an affirmative default right to the property rights in their ideas, which could only be overturned if there were evidence of fraud. The Patent Office fulfilled the Coasian mandate for market efficiency by securing property rights for the first and true inventor, facilitating trade in ideas, and ensuring the early dissemination of information to potential patentees and to the public.

Once the patent was granted, it was up to the inventor to secure returns from his ideas, through commercialization of ideas and innovations that were of value in the marketplace. A flourishing market in patent rights and inventions quickly developed, facilitated by an extensive cadre of specialized intermediaries who helped to minimize transactions costs for buyers and sellers of patented ideas and innovations.[73] Both the transparency of the patent application process, and the effective national and international market in ideas disproportionately benefited inventors from relatively disadvantaged backgrounds. These individuals were able to use their patent rights to secure venture capital and to obtain advance funding for potential research and development. Some chose to completely specialize in inventive activity, appropriating returns by transferring their rights to others who were more adept at commercialization. As a result, as I have shown elsewhere, the distribution of both inventions and inventors in the United States was more "democratic" than in Europe.[74]

A central feature of administered systems is that deliberations of decision-makers and the rationale for outcomes tend to lack transparency. Rules are little more than suggestions, no mechanisms are in place to ensure that they are implemented consistently, and there is no mechanism to ensure that unfair

[73] Lamoreaux and Sokoloff (2001).
[74] Khan (2005).

outcomes are scrutinized and overturned. By contrast, legal procedures were designed to ensure the right of appeal against allegedly arbitrary decisions by officials in the Patent Office, and contested or conflicting decisions could be appealed all the way to the US Supreme Court. Patents were granted as a constitutional right (the only time that the word "right" appears in the Constitution), which meant that the claims of true inventors were to be liberally interpreted. Legislators and courts alike emphatically rejected such restrictions as working requirements and compulsory licenses, which were regarded as unwarranted infringements of the rights of "meritorious inventors." Key decisions at law affirmed that property rights in ideas represented the "sacred rights of genius," which created benefits not just for their inventors but also for society in general.[75]

This is not to say that the early patent rules were entirely bereft of non-market features, and some might consider extensions of the term of qualified patents to be somewhat subject to discretion or political connections. Patents in the antebellum era were granted for 14 years with the prospect of an increase in the term, in order to allow the inventors of demonstrably important discoveries to extract higher potential income.[76] In the period through to 1865, terms were extended in some 1,150 cases (fewer than 2 percent of total grants), and these extensions generated a great deal of public controversy precisely because the inventions were socially valuable. For the most part, however, the extension process was systematic and transparent, with rules and procedures that were predictable and established at law.[77] Unlike the initial grant of the patent, the presumption was against the petition, and the patentee was required to provide, under oath, documented proof of the estimated value of the invention, receipts of expenses and receipts,

[75] According to *Ex Parte Wood and Brundage*, 22 U.S. (9 Wheat.) 603, 608 (1824), the patentee has "a property . . . of which the law intended to give him the absolute enjoyment and possession." "In the courts of the United States, a more just view had been taken of the rights of inventors . . . the construction of the British statute had been exceedingly straight and narrow, and different from the more liberal interpretation of our laws," *Pennock v. Dialogue*, 27 U.S. (2 Pet.) 1, 10 (1829). "And when we consider the priceless blessings which have accrued to our land, by the intellect and ingenuity of the country in this department, we feel almost lost in wonder at the vastness of the interests which have been created by the ingenuity of the country, and the immense amount now invested, in this department of property," *Singer v. Walmsley*, 22 F. Cas. 207, 208-09 (C.C. Md. 1860).

[76] Khan (2005). The Patent Act of 1836 noted that the public interest should be considered before granting extensions, but "it is just and proper that the term of the patent should be extended, by reason of the patentee, without neglect or fault on his part, having failed to obtain, from the use and sale of his invention, a reasonable remuneration for the time, ingenuity and expense bestowed upon the same, and the introduction thereof into use." Similar policies exist at present, such as extensions in the patent term for new chemical entities that have been subjected to regulatory delays in the FDA approval process.

[77] Moore (1860). Some inventors submitted petitions to Congress, but these authorities deferred to the Patent Office. See for instance, the Senate Committee on Patents response of June 1854, regarding Cyrus McCormick's claims: "Every inventor of a valuable article adds so much to the wealth of the world, and it is but just that the law should secure to him a fair reward. The committee, therefore, recommend a reference of the question to the Commissioner of Patents, to be by him tried and determined upon its merits, and *according to the settled principles of the patent laws*." (My emphasis).

and proof of due diligence in commercialization. The Commissioner of Patents gave notice to the public of the application and moderated formal hearings that included the depositions of all interested parties, with all evidence entered into the legal record. The transaction costs of these proceedings were high, so the 1861 revision of the statutes increased all patent terms to 17 years without the possibility of further extension.

In the British system, all patents were held to be monopolies; whereas, US legal traditions distinguished between dominance resulting from patented innovation and unlawful practices that lead to monopoly power. Courts applied a rule of reason, even concluding that Western Union was justified in price discrimination, because this allowed the firm to reduce the problem of an undue burden of liability owing to asymmetric information.[78] Patentees were able to establish exclusive territories, to include non-compete clauses, participate in patent pools, and to enforce vertical restraints; and courts held that state antitrust laws were not applicable to the federal property rights vested in patents.

At the same time, populist protesters throughout the nation lobbied against monopolistic dominance of innovative enterprises, and the 1884 platform of the Greenback and Antimonopoly parties declared their intention to regulate patent-based monopolies. Still, legislators were aware that patents incentivized substitutes that could actually serve to promote competition: "But for the patent laws there would, probably, be but one printing-press company, but one typewriter company, but one electric company, but one adding-machine company, but one of many now listed in the thousands."[79] Even on the eve of the passage of the federal antitrust statute in 1890, patentees were given wide latitude in the strategies they adopted. Indeed, antitrust authorities would not achieve significant success in prosecuting claims about patent-based business practices until well into the twentieth century.[80]

Adjacent Institutions in the United States

The proponents of NIS emphasize the importance of explicit linkages between innovation and educational institutions. From the founding of the early

[78] *Camp v. W. Union Tel. Co.*, 58 Ky. (1 Met,) 164, 168 (1858): "it does not exempt the company from responsibility, but only fixes the price of that responsibility, and allows the person who sends the message either to transmit it at his own risk at the usual price, or by paying in addition thereto half the usual price to have it repeated, and thus render the company liable for any mistake that may occur." This was simply the standard of limiting liability to the level of foreseeable reliance, as in the classic 1854 case of *Hadley v. Baxendale*, (1854) 156 Eng. Rep. 145 (Ct. of Exchequer), but its application to the telegraph industry was delayed because of the common carrier analogy inherited from the railroads.

[79] Hearing on H.R. 23417, before the House Committee on Patents, 62nd Cong. 10 (1912).

[80] Khan (1999).

Republic, Americans recognized that, as the Northwest Ordinance of 1787 expressed it, "Knowledge, being necessary to good government and the happiness of mankind, schools and the means of education shall forever be encouraged." Copyrights were protected primarily as a means to promote learning and education. By the end of the nineteenth century, the number of colleges and universities in the United States exceeded those in Europe. The states adopted various and disparate efforts to promote specialized knowledge in science and engineering in higher education. Rensselaer Polytechnic Institute was established in 1824 and was the precursor of numerous other specialized institutions that were founded after the Civil War. The US Military Academy at West Point, as well as the Army Corps of Engineering, engaged in pragmatic training and operations that had a significant effect on both infrastructure and human capital.

The federal government occasionally bestowed land for schools in the antebellum period, including institutions with special purposes, such as education for the physically disabled. Justin Butterfield, the Land Office Commissioner, further proposed in 1849: "With an industrious population possessing extraordinary ingenuity our country, it is believed, would soon stand foremost among the nations of the earth, if suitable rewards were held out by the government for important improvement in agriculture and the arts and sciences. This could be done by the appropriation, for the purpose, of a small portion of the proceeds of the public lands." The landmark Morrill Act of 1862 was the first federal initiative to underwrite higher education throughout the United States, through the allotment of over 11 million acres in land grants to the states. Within the space of a decade, this policy had led to the endowment of some 32 industrial colleges and universities, with a special emphasis on agriculture and mechanical training.[81] Many of the top universities in the nation today, such as the University of California, the University of Michigan, the University of Minnesota, and Cornell University, were the beneficiaries of this transfer from the federal government.

At the centennial celebrations of the Morrill Act, President John F. Kennedy characterized this policy as the "most ambitious and fruitful system of higher education in the history of the world." However, most scholars in this area warn against such overly optimistic assessments.[82] Private institutions and their students vastly outnumbered the land grant institutions, and the course

[81] Subsequent laws in 1890 and the Nelson Amendment of 1908 allocated annual endowments of $25,000 and $50,000 respectively to these institutions. Federal appropriations (in nominal dollars) increased over time, from $404,000 in 1875, to $1,303,000 in 1890, $3,462,000 in 1920, and $3,677,000 in 1930.

[82] Geiger and Sorber (2013). According to the Office of Education, in 1915–1917 there were 68 land grant colleges, 17 of which were "historically black" institutions, with student enrollments of approximately 121,000 white individuals and just under 11,000 black scholars. During the same period, 662 institutions of higher learning existed in the United States, with total enrollments of approximately 330,000 students and over $110 million in expenditures.

of higher education was influenced by many other factors besides this legislation. The impact of the measure was uneven and questionable in scope, as its aims were rejected by populists in the South and in the West, and the policy was largely ineffective in a number of key states like Texas. Many of the most successful initiatives were not in agriculture but in engineering studies, which became more prominent toward the end of the nineteenth century. Still, the land grant institutions and agricultural research and extension services enhanced the ability of disadvantaged individuals ("the sons of toil") to invest in human capital and to achieve higher incomes and social mobility.

The strength of the US university network undoubtedly depended in part on such government investments. However, it owed even more to the proliferation of differentiated and decentralized institutions that competed to meet the needs of a diverse array of professions, interests, and populations. Most notably, unlike British and French institutions, elite universities in the United States like Yale and Columbia responded quickly to changing demands of industry, introducing courses and departments in applied science and engineering. As such, any linkages between university and industry in the United States emerged spontaneously through a market process, long before the advent of government initiatives. In the 1930s, federal funding barely covered a quarter of academic research spending, and this appropriation overwhelmingly financed work that was directly related to the specific procurement needs of national defense and the military.[83]

The NIS approach assumes that innovation depends on "upper tail knowledge" such as highly specialized research science, university-trained professionals, and spillovers from academic ideas in the public domain. The claim that highly specialized knowledge and capital were fundamental for growth seems inconsistent with much of the twentieth-century experience. When Claudia Goldin and Larry Katz characterized the twentieth century as the "human capital century," and pointed to the central role that human capital played in the rise of the US economy, they were mainly referring to US leadership in improving literacy and broad-based skills through decentralized investments in primary and secondary education.[84] Leading European countries funneled resources to tertiary education, but lagged in economic achievements owing to their elitist orientation and a "closed, unforgiving" system of learning that undervalued basic literacy and mass education.

Studies that investigate the specific mechanisms through which universities might have generated higher productivity and technological progress typically

[83] Mowery et al. (2015).

[84] Examples of this extensive literature include Goldin and Katz (2008), Goldin (2001), and Engerman and Sokoloff (2012).

fail to robustly identify causal linkages. For instance, a study of patenting between 1839 and 1954 finds that only a minor fraction of total patents were derived from university faculty and alumni and concludes that inventive activity was boosted by migration of creative individuals to counties in which colleges were located.[85] The majority of great inventors who were active well into the twentieth century were not college educated and many acquired their expertise through apprenticeships.[86] In sum, centralized linkages between higher education, industry, and innovation were neither necessary nor typical of the sorts of creativity that generated the most significant spurt of productivity and technological growth.

Governing Inventions

The United States attained global leadership in technological change and innovation mainly through its market-oriented innovation polices. The notion of a national innovation system draws heavily on the experience of the period after the outbreak of World War II, which was obviously skewed owing to the military need to mobilize resources for national security and defense. Such patterns were hardly typical of the development of US technology during peace-time, nor were they representative of the activities during prior conflicts such as the Civil War era and World War I. The government in the nineteenth century, acting as the representative of the public interest, was hesitant to substitute its powers of making awards for compensation that could be allocated through the market mechanism. In the United States, although William T. G. Morton repeatedly appealed to Congress for a similar reward as Jenner's in England, he failed to obtain any payment.[87] When the National Academy of Sciences was founded, its objective was not to lobby the state to fund the sciences, but rather for scientists to offer the government the benefits of their specialized knowledge.[88]

The most common suspension of the American belief in the limited role of government in the realm of innovative activities has allegedly occurred in the context of the military and during wartime. Vernon Ruttan, for example, proposed that government actions during military conflict have promoted crucial technological advances, leading to general purpose technologies that have revolutionized entire industries and dramatically transformed economic prospects.[89] Like many other scholars, he cites the Springfield Armory and the development

[85] Andrews (2018).
[86] Khan (2020b).
[87] Report No. 114, 30 Cong. 2nd Sess. HR, Feb 23, 1849. Morton (1853).
[88] Proceedings of the National Academy of Sciences: 1863–94, Washington, DC, 1895.
[89] Ruttan (2006).

of interchangeable gun parts, which have been touted as a pioneering example of an active role for the government in technologies that had larger consequences and spillover benefits beyond the initial investments.[90] The conventional accounts credit the dissemination of these techniques through the establishment and employment of government contractors like Simeon North and Asa Waters, which allegedly created efficiency gains that spread through time and place, to the sewing machine and automobile industries, and to broader economic activities in the modern economy.

These Panglossian narratives have been challenged by scholars who have engaged in closer examination of the historical evidence. Government-sponsored efforts sporadically occurred during wartime appropriations and waned in the aftermath; whereas the private sector independently and continuously developed and commercialized key inventions and production processes throughout the past three centuries. The French had introduced the method of interchangeable parts by 1785, but the process floundered owing, ironically, to its character as a failed "engineering project driven by state bureaucrats following their own operational logic."[91] Other American patentees had invented devices capable of uniform production, which were applied in sectors independently of the armories, ranging from axes, clocks, and watches, to woodwork.[92] Productivity in industries such as harvesters and agricultural machines advanced without reference to interchangeability; and the Singer Sewing Machine Company grew to become a global multinational not because of engineering best practice, but because of its innovative marketing and sales techniques. As such, it is not at all clear whether manufacturing would have been retarded had the armories never existed.

The Civil War had a negative effect on aggregate patenting in the United States, and this was also true of the Confederacy which had set up a shadow Patent Office. According to Stanley Engerman and Matthew Gallman, "the wartime procurement system left the Northern economy largely in the hands of small entrepreneurs who responded to market incentives rather than to government incentives."[93] My own studies of several thousand inventors during the Civil War point to the significant diversion of efforts from private sector inventive activity to war-time technologies that is evident in Figure 8.2.[94] The market in patent rights flourished during this period, and a number of inventors prospered from their engagement with provisioning for the military and the war effort through

[90] Smith (1985).

[91] Alder (2010, p. 6).

[92] Hoke (1990, p. 12) shows that "the American System is primarily a private sector phenomenon," independent of any public sector initiatives. He points out that technological change stagnated in the federal armories where market prices and costs were secondary or even ignored.

[93] Engerman and Gallman (1997).

[94] Khan (2015).

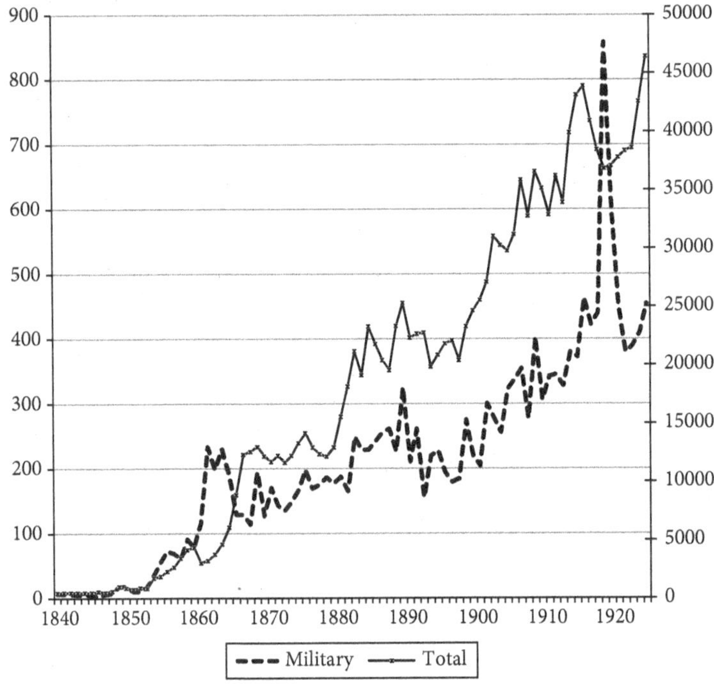

Figure 8.2 US patents for weapons and total patents granted, 1840–1925.
Note: The left axis refers to the number of military inventions, and the right axis shows total patents.
Source: US Patent Office *Annual Reports*.

these markets.[95] However, the majority of these military-oriented inventors failed to earn significant profits, and their wealth fell relative to their peers.[96]

The case-study approach tends to focus on claims of successes that were fostered by the government, ranging from innovations in weaponry to the atomic bomb, the space program, and the contributions of the defense agencies to the development of the computer and Internet. Other lessons, however, can be drawn from less well-examined facets of these administered innovation systems. For instance, in both Europe and the United States, government efforts during wars were directed to expropriating patent rights rather than to promoting inventive activity and innovation. The Secretary of War in 1869 was so incensed by

[95] Wartime demand for Smith & Wesson revolvers far exceeded the firm's ability to supply them, and the firm had over $1 million in gross income between 1862 and 1868 (see Bill S. No. 273, January 11, 1870, Senate Ex. Doc. 23, 41st Congress, 2d Session). The Smith and Wesson factory in Springfield grew rapidly from an establishment with 700 employees in June 1861 to 2,600 employees by January 1865.

[96] Khan (2009).

the need to negotiate with patentees and their "improper claims," he proposed a statute that would, as in England, allow for the use of eminent domain against patents.[97] His proposal failed to pass Congress, but similar measures succeeded during World War I. The government also allowed patented inventions to be held secret during wartime, if deemed to pose a risk to safety or to the war effort.[98] Against these actions by the War Department in the United States, foreign and domestic patentees had the right to appeal to the Court of Claims, the Supreme Court and to Congress; and the government could not avoid liability by seeking to undermine the validity of the patent right or by delegating responsibility to agents such as contractors.

Even enemy aliens who owned US patents were compensated by the federal government for property seized during the two world wars. After World War I, compensation was made for 1,069 claims by inventors from formerly hostile nations, and over $13 million was paid out to inventors from Germany, Austria, and Hungary.[99] American concern about the German monopoly in chemicals and dyes peaked during the outbreak of hostilities in World War I, and an Amendment of the Trading with the Enemy Act of 1917 authorized the confiscation of German intellectual property.[100] The Chemical Foundation, Inc., was formed two years later to manage several thousand expropriated patents, trademarks, and copyrights on behalf of the US chemical industry. This windfall stock of intellectual property revealed the extent to which effective transfer of technology also requires tacit and explicit knowledge and experience since, after the end of the war, the German firms were able to leverage their expertise and know-how to retain their competitive edge in dyes and chemicals.

These non-market policies were aberrations, however. In general, when the government became involved in the market for inventions, it was typically as a consumer of patented innovations that paid inventors the competitive price or a fair and reasonable royalty rate. This form of participation involved different considerations from monopsonistic rewards or prize systems, since the government was simply one demander among many others in the deep and efficient market for patented inventions. The famous inventor Thomas Blanchard, for instance, received almost $19,000 in government royalties for the right to use his

[97] "These [patent] difficulties have continued to embarrass this Department, and to affect injuriously the interests of the Government; and it is respectfully suggested whether a law may not be devised, which, while affording protection to all inventors in the rights secured to them by patents, will enable the Government to use unrestrictedly any improvement which it may be desirable for it to use. . . . Such a law would relieve this Department of much annoyance and embarrassment, and would tend, in my opinion, to increase to a considerable degree the efficiency of the public service." United States (1871, p. 251).

[98] Act Oct. 6, 1917, c. 95.

[99] Anon (1941). The Tennessee Valley Authority was allowed to use patents without prior permission of the patentee, but with just compensation (48 St. 68 (1933), 16 U. S. C. 831r (1934).)

[100] Steen (2001).

patent for turning irregular lathes to fashion gunstocks. Government payments for J. H. Hall's patent rights and machinery to make breech-loading rifles and carbines amounted to over $37,500. The Navy similarly expended millions of dollars on royalties and patent rights for inventions, such as George Taylor's "marine camel," Frederick Sickel's cut-off engines, and Worthington and Baker's steam pumps and percussion water-gauges. The Departments of War and the Navy accounted for 90 percent of the federal government usage of patented inventions during World War I, and they received a Congressional appropriation of $1 million to acquire basic patents relating to aircraft manufacturing.[101]

The development of the computer is often cited as an example of government incubation of an important technology. However, as in the case of the military, the initial role of these agencies was predominantly as a customer procuring needed supplies, rather than as a promoter of innovative activities. This was certainly the case with Hollerith's tabulating system, which created the data processing industry and was the first significant practical step toward the electronic computer.[102] The director of the US Census Office wished to speed up the processing of the 1890 decennial census, and Hollerith was selected based on the patent applications he had submitted in 1884.[103] Clearly, the business of the decennial census could hardly sustain a profitable venture, and Hollerith's start-up (the Tabulating Machine Company of 1896) did not attain a stable financial basis until after the firm entered into deals with private corporations like the railroads.

On the expiration of Hollerith's original patents in 1906, the government bureau decided to develop its own tabulating system, in order to "emancipate the Census Office from outside dictation."[104] Hollerith's company had already received almost $750,000 in revenues, and the Census Office was loath to continue to pay prices based on his other unexpired patents that covered improvements on the original machine. The Bureau of Standards appropriated $40,000 in federal funds to experiment in its own machine shop, employing former workers of Hollerith in the attempt to circumvent, and potentially infringing on, his existing patents. According to Hollerith's counsel, "this purpose is simply to put the Government with all its power and resources in competition with this sole inventor in respect of this matter of tabulating machines," and this would allow "the greatest competitor in the world, the United States government, [to] undertake, if successful, to destroy the inventor's property." Although Hollerith obtained a temporary injunction, his legal dispute with the federal government

[101] War Expenditures: Aviation. pts. 1–44 in 4 vols, United States (1919).

[102] United States Congress (1906).

[103] Hollerith's patent applications included an "Apparatus for Compiling Statistics" and the "Art of Compiling Statistics," filed on September 23, 1884.

[104] The quotes and details in this paragraph are drawn from the Hearings before the Subcommittee of House Committee on Appropriations, U.S. Congress (1906).

was unsuccessful; he opted not to pursue the matter before the Court of Claims and instead negotiated a buyout of his company. The bureau's project to build its own tabulators ultimately failed, and they instead retained the services of IBM, the successor to Hollerith's firm.[105]

Conclusion

Although few would contest that technological innovation is a major determinant of social welfare, the sources of inventive progress are still under debate. At present, intermediaries and markets in invention are deprecated, innovation prizes are being promoted in government and private sectors, and scholars as well as policymakers are touting the benefits of protectionism and widespread state intervention. Advocates of centralized NIS appeal to unique case studies that shed little light on the general relationship between technology policy and the rise and fall of industrial nations. As such, the need to assess systematic evidence regarding the sources of technological progress has become all the more important.

France, Britain, and the United States have sequentially dominated the records of technological achievements over the past three centuries. In Europe, administered systems were prevalent during industrialization, in the selection of favored parties who would benefit from subsidies, in mercantilist policies to influence the course of technology and commerce, in the selection of winners and the determination of financial returns for inventive ideas, by parliaments, bureaucrats, elites, and influential members of private and public committees. Americans deliberately rejected such administered systems, as inherently political means of allocating inventive talent and resources, in favor of market-oriented incentives and institutions. Rather than depending on the rents that could be gained from a diverse array of administered schemes, creative individuals were encouraged to appeal to market demand and to bear the consequences of success or failure themselves. This approach offered effective encouragement for the creation of new and useful ideas, and adjacent institutions such as educational institutions accommodated the rapid transformations that characterize the knowledge economy then and now.

Unlike administered innovation prizes, patents fulfilled the economic function of securing property rights, but delegated the prospect of returns to the market. As the *Westminster Review* noted, "Give a man a sum of money for his invention, and you run the risk of paying him either too much or too little. Give him a patent, and you secure the invention for the public, while his remuneration

[105] Heide (2009).

in money is absolutely determined according to its value. If the invention enrich him, it must also have benefited the nation. If the invention be a delusion, the public suffers no loss and the patentee reaps no gain. As a means for providing that the reward shall be fairly apportioned to the service rendered, and shall be paid by those who profit by it, the grant of letters-patent takes precedence of any arrangement hitherto made, and of every proposition yet advanced."[106] These sentiments were echoed by the US federal judiciary: "But if the invention . . . be more or less useful is a circumstance very material to the interest of the patentee, but of no importance to the public. If it be not extensively useful, it will silently sink into contempt and disregard."[107]

During eras of national crises and military control of key sectors, US policies became skewed toward the European model, and these episodes created residual effects that survived the advent of peace. The operation of administered innovation systems in the United States indicates that no jurisdiction is immune to the drawbacks associated with top-down initiatives regarding technological advances. At the same time, such effects were moderated by productive adjacent institutions. Endogenous institutional adjustments occurred in response to specific changes in costs and benefits, as illustrated by the way in which legal innovations accommodated the advent of disruptive technologies. In short, it is worth reminding ourselves that the attempts by the state, military-industrial measures, and administered systems to allocate rewards and resources have been historical aberrations in US innovation policies, suggesting that they are neither sufficient nor necessary for technological progress. Flexible and market-oriented institutions, rather than an "entrepreneurial state" or administered systems, propelled the rise and global dominance of US industry and innovation for more than a century.

Recent research, including the aptly-titled "Boulevard of Broken Dreams," highlights the successes of administrators in a number of key technological areas but also offers a balanced assessment of the manifold deficiencies and failures of government attempts to manage technological progress.[108] Econometric studies of the effects of federal research and development investments find rates of return that do not exceed returns on private expenditures. Innovations and commercialization in the development of the Internet economy succeeded because a lack of centralized authority enabled a diversity of viewpoints "from the edges," and permitted risk-taking that generated both useful contributions and failures. A scholar of current information technology further reaches the "surprising conclusion" that the ability of governments to significantly shape outcomes has been

[106] *Westminster Review*, Volumes 91–92, London: J.M. Mason, 1869, p 64.
[107] *Lowell v. Lewis*, 15 F. Cas. 1018, 1019 (1817).
[108] Lerner (2009).

limited and that technological change occurred through the combined—often unpredicted and sporadic—effects of numerous uncoordinated institutions.[109] The evidence from two centuries of technological history in Europe and the United States suggests that such a conclusion is hardly surprising.

Bibliography

Acemoglu, D., J. Robinson, and T. Verdier. "Asymmetric Growth and Institutions in an Interdependent World." *Journal of Political Economy* 125:5 (2017): 1245–1305.

Acemoglu, Daron, Jacob Moscona, and James A. Robinson. "State Capacity and American Technology: Evidence from the Nineteenth Century." *The American Economic Review* 106, no. 5 (2016): 61–67.

Acemoglu, Daron, and James Robinson. *Why Nations Fail: The Origins of Power, Prosperity, and Poverty*. New York: Crown Business, 2012.

Aghion, Philippe, et al. *Endogenous Growth Theory*. Cambridge, MA: MIT press, 1998.

Alder, Ken. *Engineering the Revolution: Arms and Enlightenment in France, 1763–1815*. Chicago, IL: University of Chicago Press, 2010.

Allen, Robert C. *The British Industrial Revolution in Global Perspective*. Cambridge; New York: Cambridge University Press, 2009.

Alter, Peter. *The Reluctant Patron: Science and the State in Britain,1850–1920*. New York: Berg, 1987.

Anderson, R. D. "New Light on French Secondary Education in the Nineteenth Century." *Social History* 7, no. 2 (1982): 147–65.

Andrews, Michael. "The Role of Universities in Local Invention: Evidence from the Establishment of U.S. Colleges." Unpublished Manuscript, 2018.

Anon. "Government Use of Patented Inventions." *Harvard Law Review* 54, no. 6 (April 1941): 1051–60.

Anon. *Journal of the Franklin Institute* 10, no. 4 (October, 1832): 284.

Babbage, Charles. *Reflections on the Decline of Science in England, and on Some of Its Causes*. London: B. Fellowes, 1830.

Barnes, Sarah V. "England's Civic Universities and the Triumph of the Oxbridge Ideal," *History of Education Quarterly* 36, no. 3 (1996): 271–305.

Barney, William C. *The Ocean Monopoly and Commercial Suicide*. New York: Private Publication, 1856.

Beauchamp, Christopher. *Invented by Law: Alexander Graham Bell and the Patent that Changed America*. Cambridge, MA: Harvard University Press, 2015.

Bentham, Jeremy. *The Rationale of Reward*. London: John Hunt, 1824.

Bottomley, Sean. "Patenting in England, Scotland and Ireland during the Industrial Revolution, 1700–1852." *Explorations in Economic History* 54 (2014): 48–63.

Bourdieu, Pierre. *The State Nobility: Elite Schools in the Field of Power*. Palo Alto, CA: Stanford University Press, 1998.

Bowden, Witt. *The Rise of the Great Manufacturers in England, 1760–1790*. London: H.R. Haas, 1919.

[109] Greenstein (2015).

Bret, Patrice. "L'État, l'armée, la science. L'invention de la recherche publique en France (1763-1830)." In *Annales historiques de la Révolution française* 328, no. 1 (2002): 278, Paris: Armand Colin.

Breznitz, Dan. *Innovation and the State: Political Choice and Strategies for Growth in Israel, Taiwan, and Ireland*. New Haven, CT: Yale University Press, 2007.

Broadberry, Stephen, et al. *British Economic Growth 1270–1870*. Cambridge; New York: Cambridge University Press, 2015.

Buchanan, R. A. "Institutional Proliferation in the British Engineering Profession, 1847–1914," *Economic History Review, New Series* 38 no. 1 (1985): 42–60.

Butrica, Andrew J. "Creating a Past: The Founding of the Société d'encouragement pour l'industrie nationale Yesterday and Today." *The Public Historian* 20 no. 4 (1998): 21–42.

Chang, Ha-Joon. *Globalization, Economic Development and the Role of the State*. Brooklyn, NY: Zed Books, 2003.

Chesnais, François. "The French National System of Innovation." In *National Innovation Systems: A Comparative Analysis*, edited by Richard R. Nelson, 192–229. New York: Oxford University Press, 1993.

Cronin, Bernard. *Technology, Industrial Conflict and the Development of Technical Education in 19th-Century England*. Aldershot, UK: Ashgate, 2001.

Dowey, J. "Mind over Matter: Access to Knowledge and the British Industrial Revolution." PhD diss. London School of Economics, 2014.

Daumard, Adeline. "Les élèves de l'École polytechnique de 1815 à 1848." Revue d'histoire moderne et contemporaine V (1958): 226–34.

Davis, Lance Edwin, and Robert A. Huttenback. *Mammon and the Pursuit of Empire: The Political Economy of British Imperialism, 1860–1912*. New York: Cambridge University Press, 1986.

Duckett, Jane. *The Entrepreneurial State in China: Real Estate and Commerce Departments in Reform Era Tianjin*. London: Routledge, 2006.

Eamon, William. "Markets, Piazzas, and Villages." In *The Cambridge History of Science*, Vol. 3, edited by Katharine Park and Lorraine Daston, 206–223. New York: Cambridge University Press, 2006.

Engerman, Stanley, and Matthew Gallman. "The Civil War Economy: A Modern View." In *On the Road to Total War: the American Civil War and the German Wars of Unification, 1861–1871*, edited by Stig Förster and Jörg Nagler, pp. 217–48. Washington, DC: German Historical Institute, 1997.

Engerman, Stanley L., and Kenneth L. Sokoloff. *Economic Development in the Americas since 1500: Endowments and Institutions*. New York: Cambridge University Press, 2012.

Epstein, Stephan R., and Maarten Prak, eds. *Guilds, Innovation and the European Economy, 1400–1800*. Cambridge, UK: Cambridge University Press, 2008.

Fox, Robert, and Anna Guagnini, eds. *Education, Technology and Industrial Performance in Europe, 1850–1939*. Cambridge, UK: Cambridge University Press, 1993.

Freeman, C. "The National System of Innovation in Historical Perspective." *Cambridge Journal of Economics* 19 (1995): 5–24.

Fressoz, Jean-Baptiste. "Beck Back in the 19th Century: Towards a Genealogy of Risk Society." *History and Technology* 23, no. 4 (2007): 333–50.

Fowler, William M., Jr. *Steam Titans: Cunard, Collins, and the Epic Battle for Commerce on the North Atlantic*. New York: Bloomsbury Publishing USA, 2017.

Furman, Jeffrey L., Michael E. Porter, and Scott Stern. "The Determinants of National Innovative Capacity." *Research Policy* 31, no. 6 (2002): 899–933.

Galvez-Behar, Gabriel. *La République des inventeurs: Propriété et organisation de l'innovation en France (1791–1922)*. Rennes: University of Rennes, 2008.

Geiger, Roger L., and Nathan M. Sorber, eds. *The Land-Grant Colleges and the Reshaping of American Higher Education*. Vol. 1. Piscataway, NJ: Transaction Publishers, 2013.

Giffard, Hermione. *Making Jet Engines in World War II: Britain, Germany, and the United States*. Chicago, IL: University of Chicago Press, 2016.

Goldin, Claudia. "The Human-Capital Century and American Leadership: Virtues of the Past." *The Journal of Economic History* 61, no. 2 (2001): 263–92.

Goldin, Claudia, and Lawrence F. Katz. *The Race between Education and Technology*. Cambridge, MA: Harvard University Press, 2008.

Goldsmith, Oliver. The Miscellaneous Works. Philadelphia, PA: J. Crissy, 1837.

González, J. Patricio Sáiz. Legislación histórica sobre propiedad industrial: España (1759–1929). Madrid: Oficina Española Patentes, 1996.

Gowing, Margaret. "Science, Technology and Education: England in 1870." *Oxford Review of Education* 4 no. 1 (1978): 3–17.

Great Britain. Hansard's Parliamentary Debates, 3rd Series. Vol. LXXX. 1840.

Great Britain, Hansard's Parliamentary Papers. "War Office, Rewards to Inventors." 10 July 1871.

Greenstein, Shane. *How the Internet Became Commercial: Innovation, Privatization, and the Birth of a New Network*. Princeton, NJ: Princeton University Press, 2015.

Haber, Stephen, ed. *Crony Capitalism and Economic Growth in Latin America: Theory and Evidence*. Palo Alto, CA: Hoover Institution Press, 2013.

Haber, Stephen H., F. Scott Kieff, and Troy A. Paredes. "On the Importance to Economic Success of Property Rights in Finance and Innovation." *Washington University Journal of Law and Policy* 26 (2008): 215.

Hanushek, Eric A., and Ludger Woessmann. *The Knowledge Capital of Nations: Education and the Economics of Growth*. Cambridge, MA: MIT University Press, 2015.

Hayek, F. A. *Individualism and Economic Order*. Chicago, IL: University of Chicago Press, 1948.

Heide, Lars. *Punched-Card Systems and the Early Information Explosion, 1880–1945*. Baltimore, MD: Johns Hopkins University Press, 2009.

Hilaire-Pérez, Liliane. "Invention and the State in 18th-Century France." *Technology and Culture* 32, no. 4 (1991): 911–31.

———. *L'invention technique au siècle des Lumières*. Paris: Albin Michel, 2000.

Hirsch, Jean-Pierre. *Les deux rêves du commerce: entreprise et institution dans la région lilloise (1780-1860)*. Paris: EHESS, 1991.

Hoke, Donald. *Ingenious Yankees: The Rise of the American System of Manufactures in the Private Sector*. New York: Columbia University Press, 1990.

Holcombe, A.N. "The Telephone in Great Britain." *The Quarterly Journal of Economics* 21 no. 1 (1906): 96–135.

Horn, Jeff. *Economic Development in Early Modern France: The Privilege of Liberty, 1650–1820*. New York: Cambridge University Press, 2015.

Howarth, Janet. "Science Education in Late-Victorian Oxford: A Curious Case of Failure?" *The English Historical Review* 102, no. 403 (1987): 334–71.

Hu, Albert G. Z., and Gary H. Jefferson. "A Great Wall of Patents: What is Behind China's Recent Patent Explosion?" Journal of Development Economics 90, no. 1 (2009): 57–68.

Hunter, Michael. *The Royal Society and its Fellows, 1669–1700, the Morphology of an Early Scientific Institution*. Oxford: British Society for the History of Science, 1994.

Hyde, William. *The English Patents of Monopoly.* Vol. 1. Cambridge, MA: Harvard University Press, 1920.

Kenrick, William. *An Address to the Artists and Manufacturers of Great Britain Respecting an Application to Parliament for the farther Encouragement of New Discoveries and Inventions in the Useful Arts.* London: Domville, 1774.

Khan, B. Zorina. "Federal Antitrust Agencies and Public Policy toward Patents and Innovation." *Cornell Journal of Law and Public Policy*, 9 (1999):133–69.

———. *The Democratization of Invention: Patents and Copyrights in American Economic Development.* New York: Cambridge University Press, 2005.

———. "War and the Returns to Entrepreneurial Innovation among U.S. Patentees, 1790–1870." *Special Issue on the Cliometrics of Patents. Brussels Economic Review* 52, no. 3/4 (2009): 239–74.

———. "Looking Backward: Founding Choices in Innovation and Intellectual Property Protection." In *Founding Choices: American Economic Policy in the 1790s*, edited by Douglas Irwin and Richard Sylla, 315–342. NBER and University of Chicago, 2010.

_______. "Antitrust and Innovation Before the Sherman Act." *Special Issue on Antitrust and Innovation. Antitrust Law Journal* 77, no. 3 (2011): 1001–29.

———. "Premium Inventions: Patents and Prizes as Incentive Mechanisms in Britain and the United States, 1750–1930." In *Understanding Long-Run Economic Growth: Geography, Institutions, and the Knowledge Economy*, edited by Dora L. Costa and Naomi R. Lamoreaux, 205–34. NBER and University of Chicago, 2011.

______. "Trolls and Other Patent Inventions: Economic History and the Patent Controversy in the Twenty-First Century." *George Mason Law Review* 21 (2014): 825–63.

———. "The Impact of War on Resource Allocation: 'Creative Destruction,' Patenting, and the American Civil War." *Journal of Interdisciplinary History* 46, no. 3 (2015): 315–53.

———. "Designing Women: Technological Innovation and Creativity in Britain, France and the United States, 1750–1900." NBER Working Paper No. 23086, January 2017a.

———. "Prestige and Profit: The RSA and Incentives for Innovation, 1750–1850." NBER Working Paper No. 23042, January 2017b.

_______. "Human Capital, Knowledge and Economic Development: Evidence from the British Industrial Revolution, 1750–1930." *Cliometrica* 12, no. 2 (2018): 313–41.

———. *Inventing Ideas: Patents, Prizes, and the Knowledge Economy.* New York: Oxford University Press, 2020a.

_______. "One for All? Intellectual Property Laws and Developing Countries in Historical Perspective." In Patent Cultures: Global Diversity and Harmonization in Historical Perspective, edited by Graeme Gooday and Steven Wilf, 69–88. New York: Cambridge University Press, 2020b.

Kieve, Jeffrey L. *The Electric Telegraph: A Social and Economic History.* Newton Abbott, UK: David and Charles, 1973.

Kranakis, Eda. "Social Determinants of Engineering Practice: A Comparative View of France and America in the Nineteenth Century." *Social Studies of Science* 19, no. 1 (1989): 5–70.

Lalor, John J. *Cyclopaedia of Political Science, Political Economy, and of the Political History of the United States.* Vol. 3. Chicago: Rand McNally, 1884.

Lamoreaux, Naomi R., and Kenneth L. Sokoloff. "Long-Term Change in the Organization of Inventive Activity." *Proceedings of the National Academy of Sciences* 93, no. 23 (1996): 12686–92.

———. "Inventors, Firms, and the Market for Technology in the Late Nineteenth and Early Twentieth Centuries." In *Learning by Doing in Markets, Firms, and Countries*, pp. 19–60. Chicago, IL: University of Chicago Press, 1999.

———. "Market Trade in Patents and the Rise of a Class of Specialized Inventors in the 19th-Century United States." *The American Economic Review* 91, no. 2 (2001): 39–44.

Lamoreaux, Naomi R., Kenneth L. Sokoloff, and Dhanoos Sutthiphisal. "Patent Alchemy: The Market for Technology in US history." *Business History Review* 87, no. 1 (2013): 3–38.

Landes, David S. "French Entrepreneurship and Industrial Growth in the Nineteenth Century." *The Journal of Economic History* 9 no. 1 (1949): 45–61.

Lemercier, Claire. "La chambre de commerce de Paris, acteur indispensable de la construction des normes economiques (premiere moitie du XIXE siècle)." Genèses 1 (2003): 50–70.

Lerner, Josh. *Boulevard of Broken Dreams: Why Public Efforts to Boost Entrepreneurship and Venture Capital Have Failed—and What to Do about It*. Princeton, NJ: Princeton University Press, 2009.

Lundvall, B-Å., ed. *National Innovation Systems: Toward a Theory of Innovation and Interactive Learning*. London: Pinter, 1992.

MacLeod, Roy M., and Russell Moseley. "The 'Naturals' and Victorian Cambridge: Reflections on the Anatomy of an Elite, 1851–1914." *Oxford Review of Education* 6, no. 2 (1980): 177–95.

Mazzucato, Mariana. *The Entrepreneurial State: Debunking Public vs. Private Sector Myths*. Vol. 1. New York: Anthem Press, 2015.

McCloy, Shelby T. *French Inventions of the Eighteenth Century*. Lexington: University Press of Kentucky, 2015.

Minard, Philippe. *La Fortune du colbertisme. État et industrie dans la France des Lumières*. Paris: Fayard, 1998.

Mokyr, Joel. *A Culture of Growth: The Origins of the Modern Economy*. Princeton, NJ: Princeton University Press, 2016.

Moore, J. G. *Patent Office and Patent Laws*. Philadelphia, PA: H.C. Baird, 1860.

Morrisson, Christian, and Wayne Snyder. "The Income Inequality of France in Historical Perspective." *European Review of Economic History* 4, no. 1 (2000): 59–83.

Morton, G., M. D. On His Claim to the Discovery of the Anaesthetic Properties of Ether, Submitted to the Select Committee Appointed by the Senate of the United States. 32d Congress, 2d Session, January 21, 1853.

Mowery, David C., Richard R. Nelson, Bhaven N. Sampat, and Arvids A. Ziedonis. *Ivory Tower and Industrial Innovation: University-Industry Technology Transfer before and after the Bayh-Dole Act*. Palo Alto, CA: Stanford University Press, 2015.

Musselin, Christine. *The Long March of French Universities*. London: Routledge, 2013.

Mustar, Philippe, and Philippe Larédo. "Innovation and Research Policy in France (1980–2000) or the Disappearance of the Colbertist State." *Research Policy* 31, no. 1 (2002): 55–72.

Nelson, R., ed. *National Innovation Systems. A Comparative Analysis*. New York; Oxford: Oxford University Press, 1993.

O Grada, Cormac. "Did Science Cause the Industrial Revolution?" *Journal of Economic Literature* 54, no. 1 (2016): 224–39.

Parkinson, Russell J. "Politics, Patents and Planes: Military Aeronautics in the United States, 1863–1907." PhD diss. Duke University, 1963.

Romer, Paul M. "Endogenous Technological Change." *Journal of Political Economy* 98, no. 5, Part 2 (1990): S71–S102.

Rosanvallon, Pierre. *Le Modèle politique français. La société civile contre le jacobinisme de 1789 à nos jours*. Paris: Seuil, 2004.

Ruttan, Vernon. *Is War Necessary for Economic Growth: Military Procurement and Technology Development*. New York: Oxford University Press, 2006.

Perez, Carlota. "Unleashing a Golden Age after the Financial Collapse: Drawing Lessons from History." *Environmental Innovation and Societal Transitions* 6 (2013): 9–23.

Postmaster General. "Government Ownership of Electrical Means of Communication." S. Doc. No. 63-399. 2d Sess. 1914.

Sanderson, Michael. *Education and Economic Decline in Britain, 1870 to the 1990s*. New York: Cambridge University Press, 1999.

Smith, Adam. Lectures on Jurisprudence. Edited by R. L. Meek, D. D. Raphael, and P. G. Stein. Indianapolis, IN: Liberty Fund, 1982.

Smith, Merritt Roe. "Army Ordnance and the 'American system' of Manufacturing, 1815–1861." In *Military Enterprise and Technological Change*, edited by Merritt Roe Smith, 39–86. Cambridge, MA: MIT Press, 1985.

Smithers, A. J. *A New Excalibur: The Development of the Tank 1909–1939*. Barnsley, UK: Pen and Sword, 1986.

Squicciarini, Mara P., and Nico Voigtländer. "Human Capital and Industrialization: Evidence from the Age of Enlightenment." *Quarterly Journal of Economics* 130, no. 4 (2015): 1825–83.

Standage, Tom. *The Victorian Internet: The Remarkable Story of the Telegraph and the Nineteenth Century's Online Pioneers*. London: Phoenix, 1998.

Steen, Kathryn. "Patents, Patriotism, and Skilled in the Art: USA v. The Chemical Foundation, Inc., 1923–1926." Isis 92 (March 2001): 91–122.

Stiglitz, Joseph. "Give Prizes not Patents." *New Scientist*, 16 September 2006.

Stimson, Dorothy. *Scientists and Amateurs: A History of the Royal Society*, New York: H. Schuman, 1948.

Sunstein, Cass R. "Constitutionalism after the New Deal." *Harvard Law Review* Vol. 101, No. 2 (Dec., 1987): 421–510.

Terrell, Thomas. *The Law and Practice Relating to Letters Patent for Inventions*. London: Sweet and Maxwell, 1895.

Tiberghien, Yves. *Entrepreneurial States: Reforming Corporate Governance in France, Japan, and Korea*. Ithaca, NY: Cornell University Press, 2007.

Trescott, Paul B. "The Louisville and Portland Canal Company, 1825–1874." *Mississippi Valley Historical Review* 44, no. 4 (1958): 686.

United States. Annual Reports of the Secretary of War. Vol. 1, Washington, DC: Government Printing Office, 1871.

United States Congress, Hearings before Subcommittee of House Committee on Appropriations. Washington, DC: Government Printing Office, 1906.

United States Congress. Select Committee on Expenditures in the War Department. Washington, DC: Government Printing Office, 1919.

Wood, Henry Trueman. *A History of the RSA*. London: J. Murray, 1913.

Woodfall, W. *The Parliamentary Register: Or, an Impartial Report of the Debates that Have Occurred in the Two Houses of Parliament in the Course of the Second Session of the First Parliament*. Vol. 3, June 1802.

Index

For the benefit of digital users, indexed terms that span two pages (e.g., 52–53) may, on occasion, appear on only one of those pages.